S0-AIA-315

In this table we see historical data for the various components of nominal GDP. These are given in the first four columns. We then show the rest of the national income accounts going from GDP to NDP to NI to PI to DPI. The last column gives real GDP.

	The Sum of These Expenditures				Equals	Less	Equals	Plus	Less	Equals	Less			Plus	Equals	Less	Equals	
Year	Personal Consumption Expenditures	Gross Private Domestic Investment	Government Purchases of Goods and Services	Net Exports	Gross Domestic Product	Depreciation	Net Domestic Product	Net U.S. Income Earned Abroad	Indirect Business Taxes, Transfers, Adjustments	National Income	Undistributed Corporate Profits	Social Security Taxes	Corporate Income Taxes	Transfer Payments and Net Interest Earnings	Personal Income	Personal Income Taxes and Nontax Payments	Disposable Personal Income	Real GDP (2005 dollars)
1984	2503.3	735.6	797.0	-102.7	3933.2	472.6	3460.6	36.3	14.6	3482.3	130.3	257.5	97.5	292.5	3289.5	377.5	2912.0	6568.5
1985	2720.3	736.2	879.0	-115.2	4220.3	506.7	3713.6	26.5	16.7	3723.4	133.4	281.4	99.4	317.5	3526.7	417.4	3109.3	6839.7
1986	2899.7	746.5	949.3	-132.7	4462.8	531.1	3931.7	17.8	47.2	3902.3	103.7	303.4	109.7	336.9	3722.4	437.3	3285.1	7076.0
1987	3100.2	785.0	999.5	-145.2	4739.5	561.9	4177.6	17.9	21.8	4173.7	126.1	323.1	130.4	353.3	3947.4	489.1	3458.3	7316.0
1988	3353.6	821.6	1039.0	-110.4	5103.8	597.6	4506.2	23.6	-19.6	4549.4	161.1	361.5	141.6	368.5	4253.7	505.0	3748.7	7618.0
1989	3598.5	874.9	1099.1	-88.2	5484.4	644.3	4840.1	26.2	39.7	4826.6	122.6	385.2	146.1	415.1	4587.8	566.1	4021.7	7887.8
1990	3839.9	861.0	1180.2	-78.0	5803.1	682.5	5120.6	34.8	66.3	5089.1	123.3	410.1	145.4	468.3	4878.6	592.8	4285.8	8034.8
1991	3986.1	802.9	1234.4	-27.5	5995.9	725.9	5270.0	30.4	72.5	5227.9	131.9	430.2	138.6	523.8	5051.0	586.7	4464.3	8022.3
1992	4235.3	864.8	1271.0	-33.2	6337.9	751.9	5586.0	29.7	102.9	5512.8	142.7	455.0	148.7	595.6	5362.0	610.6	4751.4	8288.7
1993	4477.9	953.4	1291.2	-65.0	6657.5	776.4	5881.1	31.9	139.6	5773.4	168.1	477.7	171.0	601.9	5558.5	646.6	4911.9	8511.0
1994	4743.3	1097.1	1325.5	-93.6	7072.3	833.7	6238.6	26.2	142.5	6122.3	171.8	508.2	193.7	593.9	5842.5	690.7	5151.8	8853.5
1995	4975.8	1144.0	1369.2	-91.4	7397.6	878.4	6519.2	35.8	101.1	6453.9	223.8	532.8	218.7	673.7	6152.3	744.1	5408.2	9075.0
1996	5256.8	1240.3	1416.0	-96.2	7816.9	918.1	6898.8	35.0	93.7	6840.1	256.9	555.2	231.7	724.3	6520.6	832.1	5688.5	9411.0
1997	5547.4	1389.8	1468.7	-101.6	8304.3	974.4	7329.9	33.0	70.7	7292.2	287.9	587.2	246.1	744.1	6915.1	926.3	5988.8	9834.9
1998	5879.5	1509.1	1518.3	-159.9	8747.0	1030.2	7716.8	21.3	-14.7	7752.8	201.7	624.2	248.3	744.4	7423.0	1027.1	6395.9	10245.6
1999	6282.5	1625.7	1620.8	-260.5	9268.5	1101.3	8167.2	33.8	-35.7	8236.7	255.3	661.4	258.6	741.0	7802.4	1107.4	6695.0	10701.5
2000	6739.4	1735.5	1721.6	-379.5	9817.0	1187.8	8629.2	39.0	-127.0	8795.2	174.8	691.7	265.2	766.2	8429.7	1235.7	7194.0	11093.2
2001	7055.0	1614.3	1825.7	-367.0	10128.0	1281.5	8846.5	43.6	-89.7	8979.8	192.3	717.5	204.1	858.2	8724.1	1237.3	7486.8	11176.5
2002	7350.7	1582.1	1961.2	-424.4	10469.6	1292.0	9177.6	30.7	-21.0	9229.3	294.5	734.3	192.6	874.0	8881.9	1051.8	7830.1	11355.2
2003	7703.6	1664.1	2092.5	-499.4	10960.8	1336.5	9624.3	68.1	60.1	9632.3	325.1	758.9	243.3	858.6	9163.6	1001.1	8162.5	11640.3
2004	8195.9	1888.6	2216.8	-615.4	11685.9	1436.1	10249.8	53.7	-3.3	10306.8	384.4	805.2	307.4	917.4	9727.2	1046.3	8680.9	12063.6
2005	8694.1	2086.1	2367.3	-713.6	12433.9	1609.5	10824.4	68.5	-81.1	10974.0	378.6	849.3	392.9	916.6	10269.8	1207.8	9062.0	12433.9
2006	9207.2	2220.4	2524.4	-757.3	13194.7	1615.2	11579.5	58.0	-158.2	11795.7	400.9	901.6	453.9	954.6	10993.9	1353.2	9640.7	12790.9
2007	9710.2	2130.4	2708.5	-707.8	13841.3	1692.3	12149.0	64.4	-57.5	12270.9	349.5	920.6	470.7	1133.1	11663.2	1193.0	10470.2	13070.5
2008[a]	10148.6	2136.7	2868.5	-732.8	14421.0	2026.7	12394.3	67.7	-54.7	12516.7	382.4	924.8	440.6	1108.8	11877.8	1222.2	10655.6	13194.6
2009[a]	10618.6	2149.6	3037.4	-760.1	15045.5	2367.3	12678.2	71.2	-52.0	12801.4	390.6	942.1	449.2	1072.8	12092.3	1152.5	10939.8	13338.7

[a] author's estimates

*Note: Some rows may not add up due to rounding errors.

Economics Today

The Macro View

Economics Today

THE MACRO VIEW

Fifteenth Edition

Roger LeRoy Miller

Institute for University Studies, Arlington, Texas

Addison-Wesley

Boston San Francisco New York
London Toronto Sydney Tokyo Singapore Madrid
Mexico City Munich Paris Cape Town Hong Kong Montreal

Dedication

To Mac Williams,

Thanks for continuing to guide me through the changes in the macro world and for keeping my theoretical analyses always on point. — R. L. M.

Editor in Chief: Donna Battista
Acquisitions Editor: Noel Kamm Seibert
Development Editor: Julie Z. Lindstrom
Assistant Editor: Courtney E. Schinke
Editorial Assistant: Carolyn Terbush
Managing Editor: Nancy H. Fenton
Senior Production Supervisor: Kathryn Dinovo
Digital Assets Manager: Marianne Groth
Supplements Production Coordinator: Alison Eusden
Senior Author Support/Technology Specialist: Joe Vetere
Rights and Permissions Advisor: Shannon Barbe

Director of Media: Susan Schoenberg
Senior Media Producer: Melissa Honig
Content Lead, MyEconLab: Douglas Ruby
Executive Marketing Manager: Roxanne McCarley
Marketing Assistant: Kendra Bassi
Senior Manufacturing Buyer: Carol Melville
Senior Media Buyer: Ginny Michaud
Senior Cover Designer: Beth Paquin
Text Designer: Geri Davis, The Davis Group, Inc.
Production Coordinator: Orr Book Services
Compositor: Nesbitt Graphics, Inc.
Art Studio: ElectraGraphics, Inc.

Photo credits appear on page C-1, which constitutes a continuation of the copyright page.

Copyright © 2010 Pearson Education, Inc. All rights reserved. No part of this publication may be reproduced, stored in a retrieval system, or transmitted, in any form or by any means, electronic, mechanical, photocopying, recording, or otherwise, without the prior written permission of the publisher. Printed in the United States of America. For information on obtaining permission for use of material in this work, please submit a written request to Pearson Education, Inc., Rights and Contracts Department, 501 Boylston Street, Suite 900, Boston, MA 02116, fax your request to 617-671-3447, or e-mail at http://www.pearsoned.com/legal/permissions.htm.

Many of the designations used by manufacturers and sellers to distinguish their products are claimed as trademarks. Where those designations appear in this book, and Addison-Wesley was aware of a trademark claim, the designations have been printed in initial caps or all caps.

Library of Congress Cataloging-in-Publication Data
Miller, Roger LeRoy.
  Economics today / Roger LeRoy Miller. -- 15th ed.
     p. cm. -- (The Addison-Wesley series in economics)
  Includes index.
  ISBN 978-0-321-57131-1 (main volume; chapters 1-34) -- ISBN 978-0-321-59453-2
     (macro view; chapters 1-19 and 33-34) -- ISBN 978-0-321-59452-5 (micro view;
     chapters 1-6 and 20-34)
  1. Economics. 2. Microeconomics. 3. Macroeconomics. I. Title.

HB171.5.M642 2010
330--dc22

                                            2008049775

1 2 3 4 5 6 7 8 9 10—CRK—12 11 10 09 08

Addison-Wesley
is an imprint of

www.pearsonhighered.com

ISBN-10: 0-321-59453-3
ISBN-13: 978-0-321-59453-2

The Addison-Wesley Series in Economics

Abel/Bernanke/Croushore
Macroeconomics*

Bade/Parkin
Foundations of Economics*

Bierman/Fernandez
Game Theory with Economic Applications

Binger/Hoffman
Microeconomics with Calculus

Boyer
Principles of Transportation Economics

Branson
Macroeconomic Theory and Policy

Bruce
Public Finance and the American Economy

Byrns/Stone
Economics

Carlton/Perloff
Modern Industrial Organization

Caves/Frankel/Jones
World Trade and Payments: An Introduction

Chapman
Environmental Economics: Theory, Application, and Policy

Cooter/Ulen
Law & Economics

Downs
An Economic Theory of Democracy

Ehrenberg/Smith
Modern Labor Economics

Ekelund/Ressler/Tollison
Economics*

Fusfeld
The Age of the Economist

Gerber
International Economics

Ghiara
Learning Economics

Gordon
Macroeconomics

Gregory
Essentials of Economics

Gregory/Stuart
Russian and Soviet Economic Performance and Structure

Hartwick/Olewiler
The Economics of Natural Resource Use

Hoffman/Averett
Women and the Economy: Family, Work, and Pay

Holt
Markets, Games and Strategic Behavior

Hubbard
Money, the Financial System, and the Economy

Hughes/Cain
American Economic History

Husted/Melvin
International Economics

Jehle/Reny
Advanced Microeconomic Theory

Johnson-Lans
A Health Economics Primer

Klein
Mathematical Methods for Economics

Krugman/Obstfeld
International Economics: Theory & Policy*

Laidler
The Demand for Money

Leeds/von Allmen
The Economics of Sports

Leeds/von Allmen/Schiming
Economics*

Lipsey/Ragan/Storer
Economics*

Melvin
International Money and Finance

Miller
Economics Today*

Miller
Understanding Modern Economics

Miller/Benjamin
The Economics of Macro Issues

Miller/Benjamin/North
The Economics of Public Issues

Mills/Hamilton
Urban Economics

Mishkin
The Economics of Money, Banking, and Financial Markets*

Mishkin
The Economics of Money, Banking, and Financial Markets, Business School Edition*

Murray
Econometrics: A Modern Introduction

Parkin
Economics*

Perloff
Microeconomics*

Perloff
Microeconomics: Theory and Applications with Calculus

Perman/Common/McGilvray/Ma
Natural Resources and Environmental Economics

Phelps
Health Economics

Riddell/Shackelford/Stamos/Schneider
Economics: A Tool for Critically Understanding Society

Ritter/Silber/Udell
Principles of Money, Banking & Financial Markets*

Rohlf
Introduction to Economic Reasoning

Ruffin/Gregory
Principles of Economics

Sargent
Rational Expectations and Inflation

Scherer
Industry Structure, Strategy, and Public Policy

Sherman
Market Regulation

Stock/Watson
Introduction to Econometrics

Stock/Watson
Introduction to Econometrics, Brief Edition

Studenmund
Using Econometrics: A Practical Guide

Tietenberg/Lewis
Environmental and Natural Resource Economics

Tietenberg
Environmental Economics and Policy

Todaro/Smith
Economic Development

Waldman
Microeconomics

Waldman/Jensen
Industrial Organization: Theory and Practice

Weil
Economic Growth

Williamson
Macroeconomics

---

* denotes 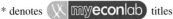 titles   Log onto www.myeconlab.com to learn more

Brief Contents

Contents

34 Exchange Rates and the Balance of Payments

Preface

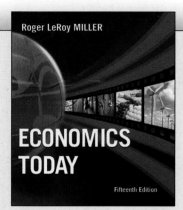

Generating the Motivation to Learn with Current News and Applications

We as professional economists find so much of what is happening around us exciting because we use the tools of economic analysis to analyze and investigate issues. As educators, we have the ability to persuade our students that economics is relevant, that it is a powerful tool for analysis, and that it represents a tool for managing one's life.

Throughout the years, I have found that the single most effective way to motivate students to learn more about economics is to present them with current and relevant examples. The new edition has a wide range of student-oriented examples—domestic, global, policy, and e-commerce—that demonstrate how relevant our discipline is in everyday life.

You will notice a new feature in every chapter called *You Are There*. These new features are all drawn from real-world experiences of real people making real policy and business decisions. Students can thereby see the importance and application of some of the theory that they have learned in each chapter.

Students learn most effectively when they can apply the concepts to their everyday lives.

As with each new edition, I have revised significant sections of this text. For instance, you will find that the content of Chapters 15 through 17 has been restructured and updated to provide more details about policymaking by today's Federal Reserve System. Elasticity and consumer choice (Chapters 20 and 21) have been reversed to better present these topics to students. Chapter 27 applies game theory to the issue of product compatibility, and Chapter 32 examines the European Union's system of emissions caps and tradable permits. Of course, all chapters have also been thoroughly updated to incorporate the latest developments, data, and policy debates.

The latest developments, data, and policy debates allow students to be on the cutting edge of economic theory and research.

Assessment has become an important topic on many campuses, and I aim to foster that type of learning. Students can continue to utilize the *Quick Quizzes* throughout each chapter, and Clicker/Personal Response Systems questions banks are available to instructors. Addison-Wesley and I continue to expand the assessment aspect of *MyEconLab*, our online course management and tutorial system. Now 100 percent of the end-of-chapter exercises are assignable in *MyEconLab* for greater flexibility in assessing students. We also strive to continue to provide students with current events coverage and analysis through weekly news and ABC News clips.

My goal in the Fifteenth Edition of *Economics Today* is to empower students to be able to analyze the way economics is involved in every aspect of their lives. Once they arrive at this realization, they can appreciate the relevance of economic principles.

— Roger LeRoy Miller

New to This Edition

This new edition of *Economics Today* tackles the most recent issues while keeping in mind key hurdles to student learning. The primary objectives, as ever, are to show students how economics is relevant to *them* and to give them many opportunities in each chapter to verify their understanding of fundamental concepts.

Cutting-edge developments have been incorporated throughout this new edition. These include:

- *Federal Reserve Interest-Rate-Based Policymaking and Assistance to Banks During the **Subprime Crisis**:* Chapters 15 through 17 have been restructured to include expanded discussions of the monetary policy procedure the Fed utilizes in determining and adhering to an **interest rate target.** Chapter 17 includes a clear explanation of the temporary assistance program that the Fed implemented beginning in 2007 and 2008 to cushion the impact of the subprime-mortgage "mess" on the U.S. banking industry.

- *Developments in **New Keynesian Macroeconomics**:* In addition to enhanced discussion of the sticky-price theory and policy analysis, Chapter 18 evaluates policy implications of the New Keynesian theory of the Phillips curve.

- *Application of **Game Theory**:* Chapter 27 applies game theory to the issue of product compatibility for those firms utilizing electronic technologies.

- *Containing **Greenhouse Gas Emissions** via Caps and Permit Trading:* Chapter 32 explains how Europe's program operates and evaluates the experience to date.

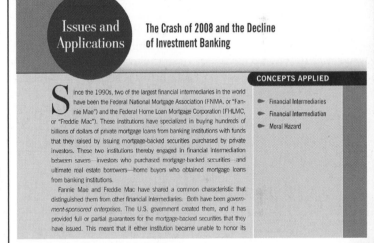

An all new Issues and Applications in Chapter 15 examines the Wall Street and investment banking crisis.

In the macro portion of the text, I've added analyses of the following:

- Chapter 7 delves into causes of a recent drop-off in U.S. labor force participation.
- Chapter 11 discusses the surprisingly muted economic impacts of **jumps in oil prices** during the 2000s.
- In Chapter 13, potential crowding-out effects of growing government **health care spending** are explored.
- In Chapter 14, the relationship between the **growing federal budget deficit** and expanding U.S. trade deficits is scrutinized.

In the micro portion, I've included the following:

- Chapters 20 and 21 have been reversed so that elasticity is now covered before consumer choice, a sequence that helps students better understand these important concepts.
- Chapter 21 examines efforts by **behavioral economists** to compare levels of satisfaction across individuals and groups.
- Chapter 26 describes the important role of product differentiation and trademarks in today's **auto industry**.
- Chapter 29 seeks to explain the difference in **earnings of male and female workers** in the United States.

Making the Connection— from the Classroom to the Real World

Today's students need to connect and apply economic theory to their diverse interests and lives. *Economics Today* speaks to students of all backgrounds, providing relentlessly current examples that effectively demonstrate economic principles. For this edition, **95 percent** of the examples are new.

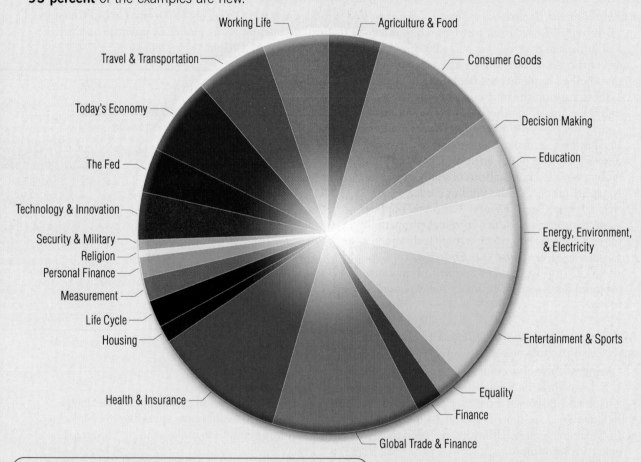

Domestic topics and events are presented through thought-provoking discussions, such as:

- Why Women Are Confronting Higher Inflation Than Men
- Zero-Priced Seats at Graduation Ceremonies Become Hot Items
- Explaining the Low U.S. "Saving Rate"

EXAMPLE
The Rising Price of Using Old Songs as Video Background Music

As video content pours onto televisions, cellphones, and computers, producers of videos are scrambling for background music. Indeed, an increasing number of video creators are producing videos carefully synchronized with music, in some cases with videos scripted to fit storylines in song lyrics. The result has been a significant increase in the demand for background music, often purchased for these specific uses from catalogs of long-retired or deceased songwriters. As more producers seek to include hit songs from the past in their video productions, the prices of the rights to use the songs have increased, too. Nearly forgotten songs once available for a few hundred dollars now cost as much as $50,000.

FOR CRITICAL ANALYSIS
What do you suppose has happened to the market clearing price of copyrighted songs newly written for use as background music for video productions?

Important policy questions help students see how they can evaluate public debates, such as:

- Incentives Coax Senior Citizens from Behind the Wheel
- The U.S. Military Confronts a Trade-Off
- Why It Can Pay to Form a Partnership Instead of a Corporation

POLICY EXAMPLE
How Empirical Evidence Aids in Thwarting Terrorism

Since 1968, there have been more than 13,000 incidents of "transnational" terrorism, or violent attacks in nations where the attackers do not reside. These data suggest predictable cycles in terrorist attacks. When terrorists launch a complex large-scale operation, such as an attack aimed at the destruction of high-rise buildings, public pressure to thwart such attacks remains high for a long time afterwards. Consequently, government countermeasures also remain in place for a lengthy period. Knowing this, terrorists lie low and begin long-term planning for a future large-scale attack. Thus, there are predictably long lulls between large-scale attacks. In contrast, public pressure to prevent simple small-scale attacks, such as bus bombings, wanes more

quickly. Government prevention efforts also dissipate more rapidly, thereby tempting terrorists to launch more small-scale attacks. Thus, there tend to be predictably short pauses between smaller-scale attacks.

Recognition of empirical regularities in terrorism has assisted governments in predicting terrorism upsurges. Governments can utilize these predictions to determine how to allocate their antiterrorism resources more effectively.

FOR CRITICAL ANALYSIS
Why do you suppose that when making predictions to help thwart terrorism, economists typically assume that terrorists behave rationally?

Global and international policy examples emphasize the continued importance of international perspectives and policy decisions, including:

- In a Global Economy, World Saving Equals World Investment
- A French Handbag Manufacturer Opts for Multitasking
- Struggling to Boost Government Spending in Peru
- EU Governments Get Serious About Emissions —Or Do They?

INTERNATIONAL EXAMPLE
For Greenland, a Warming Climate Is Good Economic News

Greenland is the world's largest island by surface area, but its population is only about 60,000. The island nation is located at the meeting point of the Atlantic and Arctic oceans. Greenland owes its name to the fact that when it was discovered [ ] Medieval Warm Period wa [ ] and willows lined its sho [ ] slightly in later centuries, [ ] the country is covered w [ ] however, the nation's ave [ ] degrees Fahrenheit. Some [ ] land's average temperatur [ ]

tional degrees by the end of this century. Warmer days allow farmers to take advantage of the extended sunlight and raise more crops and animals, and fishermen have begun catching large numbers of warm-water cod that previously had been

INTERNATIONAL POLICY EXAMPLE
Greece Pays a Price for Broadening Its GDP Definition

The government of Greece recently announced that its official tabulation of GDP would now include the total estimated value of production in black market industries, such as illegal gambling and prostitution. Consequently, the Greek government revised upward by about 25 percent its official GDP figures for every year since 2000. This change in GDP measurement came at a price, however. The European Union (EU), of which Greece is a member nation, makes regular payments to governments of the lowest-income EU mem-

bers. As a result of the big jump in its annual GDP figures, Greece was no longer officially as "poor" in the eyes of the EU, which reduced its annual payments to the Greek government by almost $600 million.

FOR CRITICAL ANALYSIS
Why do you suppose that economists now have a harder time comparing Greek GDP to the levels of GDP in other nations, such as the United States?

Information technology is presented in relevant e-commerce examples, such as:

- The New Online Dating Incentive: Health Insurance
- Digital Imaging Boosts the Supply of Dentistry Services
- Help, I'm Shopping, and I Can't Stop!

E-COMMERCE EXAMPLE
Moviemakers Try to Avoid Projecting Negative Marginal Utility

In an average week during 1948, when the U.S. population was less than half its present level, 90 million people paid to view a motion picture at a movie theater. Today, the average weekly number of moviegoers is only 30 million. Since the late 1940s, a steady wave of close substitutes—television, videocassettes, DVDs, digital movie downloads—has reduced the number of movies that people choose to see at theaters. One way that moviemakers hope to lure people back to theaters is by producing more movies in digital three-dimensional (3D) formats. More than 2,000 U.S. theaters are now equipped with 3D digital projection systems, and some directors have indicated that they plan to make only digital 3D movies.

Hollywood's newfound fascination with digital 3D has one drawback, however: viewing digital 3D movies for much longer than 90 minutes causes some viewers to experience headaches, dizziness, or even nausea. Thus, a key objective of today's designers of digital 3D projection systems is to minimize the potential for some moviegoers to derive negative marginal utility from viewing 3D motion pictures.

FOR CRITICAL ANALYSIS
Why do you suppose that some in Hollywood are predicting that initially most digital 3D movies will be action packed and relatively short?

Helping Students Focus and Think Critically

New and revised pedagogical tools in each chapter engage students and help them focus on the central ideas in economics today.

Demand and Supply

3

Three decades ago, about 45 percent of U.S. residents were classified as "overweight." Today, estimates indicate that as many as 67 percent of U.S. residents fall into this category. About 31 percent of the U.S. population is classified as extremely overweight, or obese, which is more than double the percentage of 30 years ago. One explanation for higher body weights is that people are exercising less, and thus the calories they consume are being transformed into body mass instead of energy. Another is that people are simply choosing to consume more food than in years past. Determining why individuals are opting to eat more requires an understanding, which you will develop by reading this chapter, of how two key factors—price and income—influence desired consumption of an item such as food.

LEARNING OBJECTIVES

After reading this chapter, you should be able to:

➤ Explain the law of demand

➤ Discuss the difference between money prices and relative prices

➤ Distinguish between changes in demand and changes in quantity demanded

➤ Explain the law of supply

➤ Distinguish between changes in supply and changes in quantity supplied

➤ Understand how the interaction of the demand for and supply of a commodity determines the market price of the commodity and the equilibrium quantity of the commodity that is produced and consumed

51

Chapter Openers tie to the **Issues and Applications** feature at the end of each chapter.

The current applications in the book—all new to this edition—get students' attention right at the beginning of the chapter, then follow through at the end of the chapter with an Issues and Applications feature that presents a more in-depth discussion of the issue.

Issues and Applications

Why Are People Eating More?

Being overweight or obese predisposes an individual to ailments such as arthritis, diabetes, heart disease, high blood pressure, respiratory problems, and strokes. Nevertheless, about two-thirds of the U.S. population is overweight. Nearly half of these people are classified as obese.

CONCEPTS APPLIED

➤ Relative Price
➤ Law of Demand
➤ Normal Good

Each **Issues and Applications** concludes by encouraging students to visit **MyEconLab** for additional news coverage of this topic. Critical Analysis questions, Web Resources, and a Suggested Research Project give students opportunities for in-depth discussion and exploration of the application. Suggested answers to critical analysis questions appear in the *Instructor's Manual*.

Some food items, such as canned beans and packaged macaroni and cheese, are inferior goods, so higher incomes have reduced consumption of these and similar foods. The vast majority of food items, however, are normal goods. Hence, the substantial rise in individual incomes has tended to raise the demand for foods as well as for other normal goods, such as personal computers and video games.

A Double-Whammy Effect on Food Consumption

Thus, two key factors have contributed to greater food consumption: the lower relative price of food and higher incomes. Increases in incomes have boosted demands for most food items, and declines in the relative prices have induced people to buy even more foods. Hence, people have been consuming more food and, with it, more calories. Without additional exercise, they have also been gaining more weight.

myeconlab

Test your understanding of this chapter by going online to MyEconLab. In the Study Plan for this chapter, select Section N: News.

For Critical Analysis

1. If the demands for most food items have been rising as incomes have increased, what must have happened to the supplies of most food items to account for the declining relative price of food?

2. What factors might have accounted for the changes in food supplies discussed in Question 1? (Hint: What *ceteris paribus* conditions affect the position of a supply curve?)

Web Resources

1. For a review of the worldwide trend toward higher body masses, go to www.econtoday.com/chapter03.

2. To learn about various ways states and the federal government are trying to combat childhood obesity,

click on the link to the National Center for Chronic Disease Prevention and Health Promotion, available at www.econtoday.com/chapter03.

Research Project

One way that the federal government seeks to assist low-income people is by issuing them food stamps, which they can use to purchase food items. Some observers have suggested that the government's food stamp program contributes to the higher obesity rates observed among low-income people as compared with rates observed among middle- and high-income individuals. Evaluate this argument. (Hint: Many of the least-expensive food items are often the highest-fat foods containing the most calories per unit of food.)

Quick Quizzes encourage students' interaction with the text, providing them the opportunity to quickly judge their understanding of a section through fill-in-the-blank concept checks. Answers to Quick Quizzes at the end of each chapter provide immediate feedback. To further test their understanding of the concepts covered, students are encouraged to go to **MyEconLab.**

QUICK QUIZ See page 50 for the answers. Review concepts from this section in MyEconLab.

_____ is the situation in which human wants always exceed what can be produced with the limited resources and time that nature makes available.

We use scarce resources, such as _____, _____, _____ and _____ capital, and _____, to produce economic goods—goods that are desired but are not directly obtainable from nature to the extent demanded or desired at a zero price.

_____ are unlimited; they include all material desires and all nonmaterial desires, such as love, affection, power, and prestige.

The concept of _____ is difficult to define objectively for every person; consequently, we simply consider every person's wants to be unlimited. In a world of **scarcity,** satisfaction of one want necessarily means non-satisfaction of one or more other wants.

Critical Thinking Captions
New to this edition, margin photos illustrate key concepts underlying current issues. Captions pose critical thinking questions to engage students' analyses of the topic. Suggested answers to all captions appear on the Companion Web site at www.econtoday.com.

How does marginal utility derived from a music download influence the quantity of music downloads consumed?

INTERNATIONAL EXAMPLE
Evidence of a More Unequal Distribution of Income in China

In addition to using Lorenz curves to measure the degree of income inequality, economists sometimes calculate an index measure of inequality known as the Gini coefficient, which has a value varying between 0 and 1. A Gini-coefficient value of 0 represents complete equality of income, and a value of 1 represents complete income inequality in which one person receives all income. In the late 1970s, the value of the Gini coefficient for China was 0.15,

indicating considerable income equality. Today, it is estimated to be closer to 0.60, indicating that income in China has become much more unequal during the past three decades.

FOR CRITICAL ANALYSIS
Based on the change in value of the Gini coefficient since the late 1970s, has the Lorenz curve for China likely become more or less outward bowed?

For Critical Analysis questions
At the end of each boxed example, students are asked to "think like economists" as they answer For Critical Analysis questions. These probing questions are effective tools for sharpening students' analytical skills. Suggested answers to all questions are found in the *Instructor's Manual.*

ECONOMICS ON THE NET

Looking at the Unemployment and Inflation Data This chapter reviewed key concepts relating to unemployment and inflation. In this application, you get a chance to examine U.S. unemployment and inflation data on your own.

Title: Bureau of Labor Statistics: Employment and Unemployment

Navigation: Use the link at www.econtoday.com/chapter07 to visit the "Employment & Unemployment" page of the Bureau of Labor Statistics (BLS). Click on *Labor Force Statistics from the Current Population Survey.*

Application Perform the indicated operations, and answer the following questions.

1. Click checkmarks in the boxes for Civilian Labor Force Level, Employment Level, and Unemployment Level. Retrieve the data, and click a checkmark next to "include graphs." Can you identify periods of sharp cyclical swings? Do they show up in data for the labor force, employment, or unemployment?

2. Are cyclical factors important?

For Group Study and Analysis Divide the class into groups, and assign a price index to each group. Ask each group to take a look at the index for All Years at the link to the BLS statistics on inflation at www.econtoday.com/chapter07. Have each group identify periods during which their index accelerated or decelerated (or even fell). Do the indexes ever provide opposing implications about inflation and deflation?

Economics on the Net activities are designed to build student research skills and reinforce key concepts. The activities guide students to a Web site and provide structured assignments for both individual and group work.

The **end-of-chapter summary** makes *Economics Today* an efficient study tool by integrating chapter contents with online learning resources available in **MyEconLab.** A thorough summary of the key concepts—What You Should Know—is directly linked with the text and online resources—Where to Go to Practice.

A variety of end-of-chapter problems offer students opportunities to test their knowledge and review chapter concepts. These problem sets have been heavily revised for this edition. Answers for all odd-numbered questions are provided in the back of the text, and **all** questions are assignable in **MyEconLab.**

---

myeconlab (continued)

WHAT YOU SHOULD KNOW		WHERE TO GO TO PRACTICE
Relative Prices versus Money Prices When determining the quantity of a good to purchase, people respond to changes in an relative price, which is the price of the good in terms of other goods. If the price of a unit of health care services rises by 50 percent next year while at the same time all other prices, including your wages, also increase by 50 percent, then the relative price of the good that affect the amount demanded are tive price of the health care services has not changed. Thus, in a world of generally rising prices, you have to compare the price of one good with the general level of prices of other goods in order to decide whether the relative price of that one good has gone up, gone down, or stayed the same.	relative price, 53 money price, 53	• **MyEconLab** Study Plan 3.1 • Video: The Difference Between Relative and Absolute Prices and the Importance of Looking at Only Relative Prices
A Change in Quantity Demanded versus a Change in Demand The demand schedule shows the relationship between various possible prices and respective quantities purchased per unit of time. Graphically, the demand schedule is a downward-sloping demand curve. A change in the price of this good generates a change in the quantity demanded, which is a movement along the demand curve. Factors other than the price of the good that affect the amount demanded are (1) income, (2) tastes and preferences, (3) the prices of related goods, (4) expectations, and (5) market size (the number of potential buyers). Whenever any of these *ceteris paribus* conditions of demand changes, there is a change in the demand for the good, and the demand curve shifts to a new position.	demand curve, 56 market demand, 56 *ceteris paribus* conditions, 59 normal goods, 59 inferior goods, 59 substitutes, 60 complements, 60 KEY FIGURE Figure 3-2, 56 Figure 3-4, 58 Figure 3-5, 62	• **MyEconLab** Study Plans 3.2, 3.3 • Video: The Importance of Distinguishing Between a Shift in a Demand Curve and a Move Along the Demand Curve • Animated Figures 3-2, 3-4, 3-5 • ABC News Video: What Drives the Market: Supply and Demand
The Law of Supply According to the law of supply, sellers will produce and offer for sale more units of a good at a higher price, and they will produce and offer for sale fewer units of the good at a lower price.	supply, 62 law of supply, 63	• **MyEconLab** Study Plan 3.4
A Change in Quantity Supplied versus a Change in Supply The supply schedule shows the relationship between various possible prices and respective quantities produced and sold per unit of time. On a graph, the supply schedule is a supply curve that slopes upward. A change in the price of the good generates a change in the quantity supplied, which is a movement along the supply curve. Factors other than the price of the good that affect the amount supplied are (1) input prices, (2) technology and productivity, (3) taxes and subsidies, (4) price expectations, and (5) the number of sellers. Whenever any of these *ceteris paribus* conditions changes, there is a change in the supply of the good, and the supply curve shifts to a new position.	supply curve, 64 subsidy, 68 KEY FIGURES Figure 3-6, 64 Figure 3-7, 65 Figure 3-9, 67	• **MyEconLab** Study Plans 3.5, 3.6 • Video: The Importance of Distinguishing Between a Change in Supply versus a Change in Quantity Supplied • Animated Figures 3-6, 3-7, 3-9

Economic Concepts in Today's News

Economics Today strives to bring the latest news and current events into the classroom, keeping students engaged and interested.

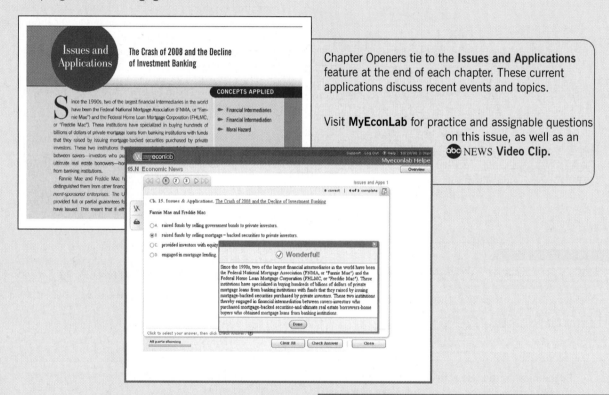

Chapter Openers tie to the **Issues and Applications** feature at the end of each chapter. These current applications discuss recent events and topics.

Visit **MyEconLab** for practice and assignable questions on this issue, as well as an abc NEWS **Video Clip.**

Each week, new microeconomic and macroeconomic current events are updated in **MyEconLab**'s **Weekly News** feature. Discussion questions, also posted weekly, test students' knowledge of the issues and ask them to apply the economic concepts.

You Are There

New to this edition, margin notes lead students to the You Are There feature at the conclusion of the text of each chapter. This feature, which depicts events involving **actual people confronting specific concepts** covered in the text, helps students see the relevance of those concepts in daily life. Topics include:

- An Invention Becomes a Market Innovation—By Accident
- In a Cold Twist, a Millionaire Bequeaths His Wealth to Himself
- Why Pouring Vegetable Oil into a Car Is Illegal in Illinois

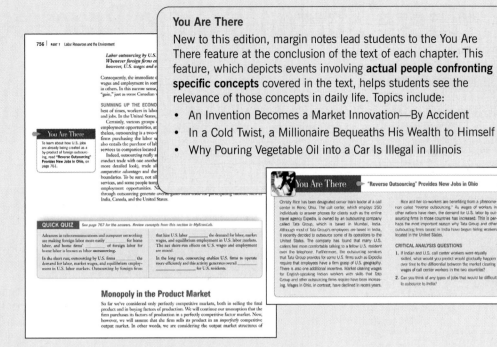

Economics Videos featuring abc NEWS

A series of videos covering core economic concepts including ABC News footage and commentary by economists can be found in **MyEconLab.** New **assessment questions** have been added for optional instructor assignment.

Videos in this series include:

- *Coca Cola in India,* which examines international trade, incentives, causation, and externalities.
- *The Ripple Effects of Oil Prices,* which discusses equilibrium and inflation.
- *Big Government: Who Is Going to Pay the Bill?* which discusses concepts such as taxes, budget, GDP, and fiscal policy.

MyEconLab now offers RSS feed for up-to-the-minute coverage of economic news. Please see page **xxxi** for additional news and issues options.

Where Students Go to Practice

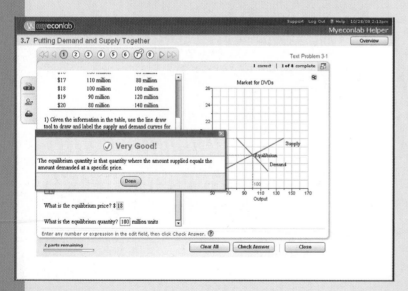 is the premier student and instructor tool, integrating lessons from the text into a powerful online learning and teaching resource.

New in MyEconLab for *Economics Today*

3-1. Suppose that in a recent market period, the following relationship existed between the price of prerecorded movie DVDs and the quantity supplied and quantity demanded.

Price	Quantity Demanded	Quantity Supplied
$19	100 million	40 million
$20	90 million	60 million
$21	80 million	80 million
$22	70 million	100 million
$23	60 million	120 million

Graph the supply and demand curves for movie DVDs given the information in the table. What are the equilibrium price and quantity? If the industry price is $20, is there a shortage or surplus of DVDs? How much is the shortage or surplus?

- **100% of all end-of-chapter problems** are now assignable.

- For most chapters, **additional, instructor-only questions** are available to provide a larger pool of assignable options. A selection of these questions is algorithmic for additional learning opportunity. Instructors can also always choose from end-of-chapter problems, select test bank problems, or create their own exercises.

- Each chapter includes **questions for the Issues and Applications feature** found in the text, along with a related abc NEWS **Video Clip** and critical thinking questions. All questions in this section are paired, so half are visible for student practice and half are instructor-only for assignable options.

Students control their learning through a variety of features unique to MyEconLab.

- **Sample Tests,** two for every chapter, ask students to test their understanding of the concepts. The powerful graphing application allows students to draw graphs themselves, and **MyEconLab** evaluates and grades them automatically.

- **Personalized Study Plans** analyze students' performance on Sample Tests, identify areas where they need further study, and offer additional exercises to reinforce learning. Tutorial instruction provides targeted learning aids and step-by-step explanations.

- **An integrated eText** allows access to the textbook on any computer.

- **Learning aids** such as animated graphs with audio explanations for each step, video clips of author Roger LeRoy Miller reviewing key points in every chapter, and glossary flashcards allow review of important terms.

Students can get additional help and resources.

- **Weekly News updates** feature new micro and macro current events. Discussion questions posted online each week by Andrew J. Dane of Angelo State University test students' knowledge of relevant issues and their ability to apply economic concepts. Instructor answer keys are available. The Weekly News is now **archived for easy searching and reference.**

- A subscription to **MyEconLab** includes complimentary access to a tutoring service provided by **Pearson Tutor Services**, powered by SMARTHINKING, Inc. Highly qualified tutors use whiteboard technology and feedback tools to help students understand and master the major concepts of economics. Students can receive real-time, one-on-one instruction, submit questions for response within 24 hours, and view archives of past sessions.

- **Economic Videos featuring ABC News** provide students with a glimpse of economics behind the news. Each video presents an issue using ABC News footage and includes commentary by economists.

- **Research Navigator** develops students' research skills by offering exclusive access to databases of *The New York Times*, the *Financial Times*, and peer-reviewed journals. This is available with **MyEconLab in CourseCompass.**

Instructors save time and gain flexibility.

- Instructors can design their own quizzes, tests, or homework assignments from the significant bank of questions or assign pre-loaded Sample Tests. All problems in **MyEconLab** are directly correlated to the text.

- **MyEconLab** automatically grades tests, quizzes, or homework—including graphing questions—and tracks the results in an online gradebook.

- For more information about **MyEconLab,** or to request an Instructor Access code, visit www.myeconlab.com.

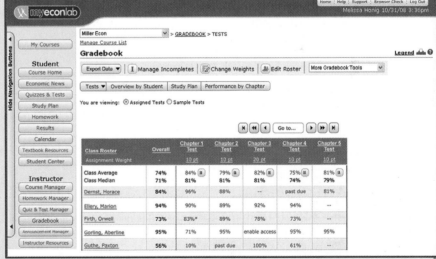

Supplemental Resources

Student and instructor materials provide tools for success.

Meticulously Revised and Updated! Test Banks 1, 2, and 3 offer over 10,000 multiple choice and short answer questions, all of which are available in computerized format in the TestGen software. A selection of questions is also in **MyEconLab**. The significant revision process by authors David Findlay of Colby College and Jim Lee of Texas A&M–Corpus Christi and reviewer David VanHoose of Baylor University ensures the accuracy of problems and solutions in these heavily revised and updated test banks.

The Instructor's Manual, prepared by Andrew J. Dane of Angelo State University and reviewed by Victoria L. Figiel of Troy University, offers instructors materials to make the course successful. Features include lecture-ready examples; chapter overviews, objectives, and outlines; points to emphasize; answers to all critical analysis questions; answers to end-of-chapter problems; suggested answers to *You Are There* questions; and selected references.

The Instructor's Resource Disk offers instructors electronic supplements conveniently packaged on a CD-ROM. **PowerPoint lecture presentations** for each chapter, revised by Dennis Kovach of the Community College of Allegheny County and reviewed by Pete Mavrokordatos of Tarrant County College, include graphs from the text and outline key terms, concepts, and figures from the text. The entire **Instructor's Manual** is included as Microsoft Word files, and all three **Computerized Test Banks** are offered with TestGen software for simple test preparation.

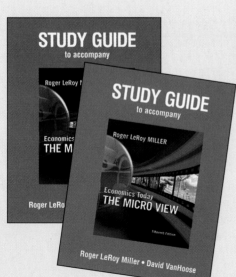

Clicker PowerPoint Slides allow professors to instantly quiz students in class and receive immediate feedback through Clicker Response System technology.

The Instructor Resource Center puts supplements right at instructors' fingertips. By registering for the Instructor Resource Center, instructors can download supplements directly from the Internet. Visit www.pearsonhighered.com/irc to register.

The Study Guide offers the practice and review students need to excel. Written by Roger LeRoy Miller and updated by David VanHoose, the study guide has been thoroughly revised to take into account changes to the Fifteenth Edition.

PearsonChoices

A variety of options for students and instructors provide convenience and flexibility.

Books à la Carte Plus Edition is created for the student who wants a more flexible portable text. Students who use this three-hole punched version of *Economics Today* can take only what they need to class, incorporate their own notes, and save money. This version is packaged with a laminated study card and comes with access to MyEconLab.

CourseSmart improves teaching and learning through the availability of a lower-cost fully electronic alternative to the traditional textbook, in a reliable Web application. For additional information, log on to www.coursesmart.com.

Standalone Access to MyEconLab and the Complete eText may be purchased online at www.myeconlab.com or through the campus bookstore. This access to MyEconLab includes online access to the complete, searchable eText.

MyEconLab access may be purchased online at www.myeconlab.com. Students gain full access to MyEconLab's assessment and learning resources. Partial access to the eText is included, which links practice problems to relevant sections of the text.

Print Upgrade to the à la Carte Edition from within MyEconLab may be purchased at any point following students' online purchase of MyEconLab.

Pearson Custom Business Resourcees offers instructors the option of building their own book by selecting just the chapters they want and ordering them to fit their syllabus. Professors can also select chapters of the accompanying Study Guide as well as readings from Miller/Benjamin/North's *The Economics of Public Issues* and Miller/Benjamin's *The Economics of Macro Issues.* For more information, please contact your local Pearson sales representative.

Economist.com provides your students with the premier online source of news analysis, insight, and opinion on current economic events. When packaged with the text, students receive a low-cost subscription to Economist.com for three months, including the complete text of the current issue and access to searchable archives. Professors receive a complimentary one-year subscription to Economist.com.

The *Wall Street Journal* can be packaged with the text, and a 15-week subscription to the print and interactive editions of the *Wall Street Journal* is available at a reduced cost to students. Professors receive a complimentary one-year subscription to the print and interactive editions.

The *Financial Times* features international news and analysis from journalists in more than 50 countries. For a small charge, a 15-week student subscription to the *Financial Times* can be included with the text. Professors will receive a complimentary one-year print subscription, as well as access to the online edition at FT.com.

Acknowledgments

I am the most fortunate of economics textbook writers, for I receive the benefit of literally hundreds of suggestions from those of you who use *Economics Today*. I continue to be fully appreciative of the constructive criticisms that you offer. There are some professors who have been asked by my publisher to participate in a more detailed reviewing process of this edition. I list them below. I hope that each one of you so listed accepts my sincere appreciation for the fine work that you have done.

Ali A. Ataiifar, *Delaware County Community College*
Emil Berendt, *Siena Heights University*
John Bockino, *Suffolk County Community College*
Patrick M. Crowley, *Texas A&M University–Corpus Christi*
Diana Denison, *Red Rocks Community College*
Victoria L. Figiel, *Troy University*
Timothy S. Fuerst, *Bowling Green State University*
Peter A. Groothuis, *Appalachian State University*
Michael J. Haupert, *University of Wisconsin–La Crosse*
George Hughes, *University of Hartford*
Nancy Jianakoplos, *Colorado State University*
Brian Kench, *University of Tampa*

Dennis Lee Kovach, *Community College of Allegheny County–North Campus*
Dan Marburger, *Arkansas State University*
Pete Mavrokordatos, *Tarrant County College*
William H. Moon, *Georgia Perimeter College–Lawrenceville*
Ronald M. Nate, *Brigham Young University–Idaho*
Joan Osborne, *Palo Alto College*
Leila J. Pratt, *University of Tennessee at Chattanooga*
Basel Saleh, *Radford University*
Phil Smith, *Georgia Perimeter College*
Sharmila Vishwasrao, *Florida Atlantic University*
Ethel Weeks, *Nassau Community College*
George K. Zestos, *Christopher Newport University*

I also thank the reviewers of previous editions:

Rebecca Abraham
Cinda J. Adams
Esmond Adams
John Adams
Bill Adamson
Carlos Aguilar
John R. Aidem
John W. Allen
Mohammed Akacem
E. G. Aksoy
M. C. Alderfer
John Allen
Ann Al-Yasiri
Charles Anderson
Leslie J. Anderson
Fatma W. Antar
Rebecca Arnold,
Mohammad Ashraf
Aliakbar Ataiifar
Leonard Atencio
John M. Atkins
Glen W. Atkinson
Thomas R. Atkinson
James Q. Aylesworth
John Baffoe-Bonnie
Kevin Baird
Charley Ballard
Maurice B. Ballabon
G. Jeffrey Barbour
Daniel Barszcz
Robin L. Bartlett
Kari Battaglia
Robert Becker
Charles Beem
Glen Beeson
Bruce W. Bellner
Daniel K. Benjamin
Charles Berry
Abraham Bertisch
John Bethune

R.A. Blewett
Scott Bloom
M. L. Bodnar
Mary Bone
Karl Bonnhi
Thomas W. Bonsor
John M. Booth
Wesley F. Booth
Thomas Borcherding
Melvin Borland
Tom Boston
Barry Boyer
Maryanna Boynton
Ronald Brandolini
Fenton L. Broadhead
Elba Brown
William Brown
Michael Bull
Maureen Burton
Conrad P. Caligaris
Kevin Carey
James Carlson
Robert Carlsson
Dancy R. Carr
Scott Carson
Doris Cash
Thomas H. Cate
Richard J. Cebula
Catherine Chanbers
K. Merry Chambers
Richard Chapman
Ronald Cherry
Young Back Choi
Marc Chopin
Carol Cies
Joy L. Clark
Curtis Clarke
Gary Clayton
Marsha Clayton
Dale O. Cloninger

Warren L. Coats
Ed Coen
Pat Conroy
James Cox
Stephen R. Cox
Eleanor D. Craig
Peggy Crane
Jerry Crawford
Joanna Cruse
John P. Cullity
Will Cummings
Thomas Curtis
Margaret M. Dalton
Andrew J. Dane
Mahmoud Davoudi
Diana Denison
Edward Dennis
Julia G. Derrick
Carol Dimamro
William Dougherty
Barry Duman
Diane Dumont
Floyd Durham
G. B. Duwaji
James A. Dyal
Ishita Edwards
Robert P. Edwards
Alan E. Ellis
Mike Ellis
Steffany Ellis
Frank Emerson
Carl Enomoto
Zaki Eusufzai
Sandy Evans
John L. Ewing-Smith
Frank Falero
Frank Fato
Abdollah Ferdowsi
Grant Ferguson
Mitchell Fisher

David Fletcher
James Foley
John Foreman
Diana Fortier
Ralph G. Fowler
Arthur Friedberg
Peter Frost
Tom Fullerton
E. Gabriel
James Gale
Byron Gangnes
Steve Gardner
Peter C. Garlick
Neil Garston
Alexander Garvin
Joe Garwood
Doug Gehrke
J. P. Gilbert
Otis Gilley
Frank Glesber
Jack Goddard
Michael G. Goode
Allen C. Goodman
Richard J. Gosselin
Paul Graf
Anthony J. Greco
Edward Greenberg
Gary Greene
Philip J. Grossman
Nicholas Grunt
William Gunther
Kwabena Gyimah-
  Brempong
Demos Hadjiyanis
Martin D. Haney
Mehdi Haririan
Ray Harvey
E. L. Hazlett
Sanford B. Helman
William Henderson

John Hensel
Robert Herman
Gus W. Herring
Charles Hill
John M. Hill
Morton Hirsch
Benjamin Hitchner
Charles W. Hockert
R. Bradley Hoppes
James Horner
Grover Howard
Nancy Howe-Ford
Yu-Mong Hsiao
Yu Hsing
James Hubert
Joseph W. Hunt Jr.
Scott Hunt
John Ifediora
R. Jack Inch
Christopher Inya
Tomotaka Ishimine
E. E. Jarvis
Parvis Jenab
Allan Jenkins
Mark Jensen
S. D. Jevremovic
J. Paul Jewell
Frederick Johnson
David Jones
Lamar B. Jones
Paul A. Joray
Daniel A. Joseph
Craig Justice
M. James Kahiga
Septimus Kai Kai
Devajyoti Kataky
Timothy R. Keely
Ziad Keilany
Norman F. Keiser
Randall G. Kesselring

Alan Kessler
E. D. Key
Saleem Khan
M. Barbara Killen
Bruce Kimzey
Philip G. King
Terrence Kinal
E. R. Kittrell
David Klingman
Charles Knapp
Jerry Knarr
Faik Koray
Janet Koscianski
Marie Kratochvil
Peter Kressler
Paul J. Kubik
Michael Kupilik
Larry Landrum
Margaret Landman
Richard LaNear
Keith Langford
Theresa Laughlin
Anthony T. Lee
Loren Lee
Bozena Leven
Donald Lien
George Lieu
Stephen E. Lile
Lawrence W. Lovick
Marty Ludlum
G. Dirk Mateer
Robert McAuliffe
James C. McBrearty
Howard J. McBride
Bruce McClung
John McDowell
E. S. McKuskey
James J. McLain
John L. Madden
Mary Lou Madden

John Marangos
Glen Marston
John M. Martin
Paul J. Mascotti
James D. Mason
Paul M. Mason
Tom Mathew
Warren Matthews
Warren T. Matthews
Akbar Marvasti
G. Hartley Mellish
Mike Melvin
Diego Mendez-Carbajo
Dan C. Messerschmidt
Michael Metzger
Herbert C. Milikien
Joel C. Millonzi
Glenn Milner
Daniel Mizak
Khan Mohabbat
Thomas Molloy
Margaret D. Moore
William E. Morgan
Stephen Morrell
Irving Morrissett
James W. Moser
Thaddeaus Mounkurai
Martin F. Murray
Densel L. Myers
George L. Nagy
Solomon Namala

Jerome Neadly
James E. Needham
Claron Nelson
Douglas Nettleton
William Nook
Gerald T. O'Boyle
Greg Okoro
Richard E. O'Neill
Lucian T. Orlowski
Diane S. Osborne
Melissa A. Osborne
James O'Toole
Jan Palmer
Zuohong Pan
Gerald Parker
Ginger Parker
Randall E. Parker
Kenneth Parzych
Norm Paul
Wesley Payne
Raymond A. Pepin
Martin M. Perline
Timothy Perri
Jerry Petr
Bruce Pietrykowski
Maurice Pfannesteil
James Phillips
Raymond J. Phillips
I. James Pickl
Dennis Placone
Mannie Poen

William L. Polvent
Robert Posatko
Greg Pratt
Reneé Prim
Robert W. Pulsinelli
Rod D. Raehsler
Kambriz Raffiee
Sandra Rahman
Jaishankar Raman
John Rapp
Richard Rawlins
Gautam Raychaudhuri
Ron Reddall
Mitchell Redlo
Charles Reichhelu
Robert S. Rippey
Charles Roberts
Ray C. Roberts
Richard Romano
Judy Roobian-Mohr
Duane Rosa
Richard Rosenberg
Larry Ross
Barbara Ross-Pfeiffer
Philip Rothman
John Roufagalas
Stephen Rubb
Henry Ryder
Patricia Sanderson
Thomas N. Schaap
William A. Schaeffer

William Schaniel
David Schauer
A. C. Schlenker
David Schlow
Scott J. Schroeder
William Scott
Dan Segebarth
Paul Seidenstat
Swapan Sen
Augustus Shackelford
Richard Sherman Jr.
Liang-rong Shiau
David Shorow
Vishwa Shukla
R. J. Sidwell
David E. Sisk
Alden Smith
Garvin Smith
Howard F. Smith
Lynn A. Smith
Phil Smith
Steve Smith
William Doyle Smith
Lee Spector
George Spiva
Richard L. Sprinkle
Alan Stafford
Amanda Stallings-Wood
Herbert F. Steeper
Diane L. Stehman
Columbus Stephens

William Stine
Allen D. Stone
Osman Suliman
J. M. Sullivan
Rebecca Summary
Joseph L. Swaffar
Thomas Swanke
Frank D. Taylor
Daniel Teferra
Lea Templer
Gary Theige
Dave Thiessen
Robert P. Thomas
Deborah Thorsen
Richard Trieff
George Troxler
William T. Trulove
William N. Trumbull
Arianne K. Turner
Kay Unger
Anthony Uremovic
John Vahaly
Jim Van Beek
David VanHoose
Lee J. Van Scyoc
Roy Van Til
Craig Walker
Robert F. Wallace
Henry C. Wallich
Milledge Weathers
Roger E. Wehr

Robert G. Welch
Terence West
James Wetzel
Wylie Whalthall
James H. Wheeler
Everett E. White
Michael D. White
Mark A. Wilkening
Raburn M. Williams
James Willis
George Wilson
Travis Wilson
Mark Wohar
Ken Woodward
Tim Wulf
Peter R. Wyman
Whitney Yamamura
Donald Yankovic
Alex Yguado
Paul Young
Shik Young
Mohammed Zaheer
Ed Zajicek
Sourushe Zandvakili
Paul Zarembka
William J. Zimmer Jr.

Revising *Economics Today* this time around was one of the biggest challenges I've faced with this textbook, given that changes in the economy within the United States and the world were so rapid. I believe that I was up to the task, but only because I had help along the way from not only the reviewers mentioned above, but my fantastic editorial team at Addison-Wesley. I was pushed hard by two unrelenting members of that team: Noel Seibert, my editor, and Julie Lindstrom, my developmental editor. In addition to managing this major project, they came up with numerous ideas "on the fly," which they suggested I incorporate into this new edition. Furthermore, all of us were dependent on Courtney Schinke, the assistant editor on this project. Courtney was great at coordination and making sure all aspects of the project moved along quickly.

On the production side of this revision, I was again fortunate enough to have as my production supervisor Kathryn Dinovo at Addison-Wesley. The designer, Geri Davis, succeeded in creating a new look that still kept the traditional feel of this text. As always, I benefited from the years of experience of John Orr of Orr Book Services. He has always faced the daunting task of putting this book together in a minimum amount of time—and he does it extremely well. I appreciate the fabulous copyediting and proofing services that Pat Lewis again provided. For this edition on the print supplements side, Marianne Groth and Alison Eusden did the job in a singularly professional matter, guaranteeing revised error-free ancillaries. I would also like to thank Roxanne McCarley for continued marketing and promotional efforts.

As you can imagine, more emphasis for each edition has been placed on online and other media materials. Melissa Honig and Susan Schoenberg worked overtime to make sure that MyEconLab was fully functional and without bugs. I also was lucky to have the services of Douglas Ruby who helped develop new content for MyEconLab.

This time around, I had some extremely talented colleagues who created a fully revised supplements package. Jim Lee of Texas A&M–Corpus Christi and David Findlay of Colby College authored the three test banks, and David VanHoose of Baylor University ensured they were error-free. He also continued to create not only accurate, but useful study guides. Similarly, Andrew J. Dane of Angelo State University has kept the *Instructor's Manual* in sync with the latest revisions, while Dennis Kovach of the Community College of Allegheny County provided the PowerPoint presentations. I would also like to thank the superb eagle-eyed professors who reviewed the text for accuracy: Victoria L. Figiel from Troy University, Ethel Weeks from Nassau Community College, Pete Mavrokordatos from Tarrant County College, and Leila J. Pratt from the University of Tennessee at Chattanooga.

Finally, there are two individuals I must thank for their work above and beyond the call of duty. The first is Professor Dan Benjamin of Clemson University, who continues to act as my "super reviewer" and "super proofreader." He again helped make this edition the best ever. Finally, Sue Jasin, my long-time assistant, could probably teach a course in economics after all of the typing and retyping of various drafts of this revision.

I welcome comments and ideas from professors and students alike and hope you enjoy the new edition of *Economics Today*.

R. L. M.

The Nature of Economics

1

Just a few years ago, a passenger on a commuter train in Mumbai, India (formerly known as Bombay), rarely had difficulty finding an empty seat even during peak commuting hours. Today, a Mumbai commuter train's passenger car built to hold a maximum of 200 people often carries as many as 550 passengers—some of whom hang out of the doors of the car or even cling to its exterior. Falls from train cars and other accidents are common events. As a consequence, at least 3,000 people are killed each year in the Mumbai commuter-rail system, and many more experience injuries. Why is Mumbai's rail system so overloaded? Why do people risk life and limb to ride the city's overcrowded trains? This chapter will equip you to contemplate the answers to these questions.

LEARNING OBJECTIVES

After reading this chapter, you should be able to:

➤ Discuss the difference between microeconomics and macroeconomics

➤ Evaluate the role that rational self-interest plays in economic analysis

➤ Explain why economics is a science

➤ Distinguish between positive and normative economics

 myeconlab

MyEconLab helps you master each objective and study more efficiently. See end of chapter for details.

? Did you know that economics is one of the fastest-growing college majors? During the past 10 years, the number of students majoring in economics at U.S. colleges and universities has increased by nearly 40 percent. Certainly, a key factor motivating many students to opt for extensive study of economics is that they find the subject fascinating. Nevertheless, another important factor is self-interest. The fact that economics majors typically land higher-paying jobs than other majors—for instance, at least 10 percent more than business management majors and 75 percent more than psychology majors—provides a strong incentive to consider majoring in economics.

In this chapter, you will learn why contemplating the nature of self-interested responses to **incentives** is the starting point for analyzing choices people make in all walks of life. After all, how much time you devote to studying economics in this introductory course depends in part on the incentives established by your instructor's grading system. As you will see, self-interest and incentives are the underpinnings for all the decisions you and others around you make each day.

Incentives
Rewards for engaging in a particular activity.

The Power of Economic Analysis

Simply knowing that self-interest and incentives are central to any decision-making process is not sufficient for predicting the choices that people will actually make. You also have to develop a framework that will allow you to analyze solutions to each economic problem—whether you are trying to decide how much to study, which courses to take, whether to finish school, or whether the U.S. government should provide more grants to universities or raise taxes. The framework that you will learn in this text is the *economic way of thinking.*

This framework gives you power—the power to reach informed judgments about what is happening in the world. You can, of course, live your life without the power of economic analysis as part of your analytical framework. Indeed, most people do. But economists believe that economic analysis can help you make better decisions concerning your career, your education, financing your home, and other important matters. In the business world, the power of economic analysis can help you increase your competitive edge as an employee or as the owner of a business. As a voter, for the rest of your life you will be asked to make judgments about policies that are advocated by political parties. Many of these policies will deal with questions related to international economics, such as whether the U.S. government should encourage or discourage immigration, prevent foreign residents and firms from investing in port facilities or domestic banks, or restrict other countries from selling their goods here.

Finally, just as taking an art, music, or literature appreciation class increases the pleasure you receive when you view paintings, listen to concerts, or read novels, taking an economics course will increase your understanding and pleasure when watching the news on TV or reading articles in the newspaper or on the Internet.

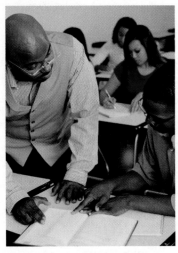

What determines how much time you decide to devote to studying one particular subject?

Defining Economics

Economics
The study of how people allocate their limited resources to satisfy their unlimited wants.

Economics is part of the social sciences and as such seeks explanations of real events. All social sciences analyze human behavior, as opposed to the physical sciences, which generally analyze the behavior of electrons, atoms, and other nonhuman phenomena.

> *Economics is the study of how people allocate their limited resources in an attempt to satisfy their unlimited wants. As such, economics is the study of how people make choices.*

To understand this definition fully, two other words need explaining: *resources* and *wants*. **Resources** are things that have value and, more specifically, are used to produce goods and services that satisfy people's wants. **Wants** are all of the items that people would purchase if they had unlimited income.

Whenever an individual, a business, or a nation faces alternatives, a choice must be made, and economics helps us study how those choices are made. For example, you have to choose how to spend your limited income. You also have to choose how to spend your limited time. You may have to choose how much of your company's limited funds to spend on advertising and how much to spend on new-product research. In economics, we examine situations in which individuals choose how to do things, when to do things, and with whom to do them. Ultimately, the purpose of economics is to explain choices.

Resources
Things used to produce goods and services to satisfy people's wants.

Wants
What people would buy if their incomes were unlimited.

Microeconomics versus Macroeconomics

Economics is typically divided into two types of analysis: **microeconomics** and **macroeconomics.**

Microeconomics is the part of economic analysis that studies decision making undertaken by individuals (or households) and by firms. It is like looking through a microscope to focus on the small parts of our economy.

Macroeconomics is the part of economic analysis that studies the behavior of the economy as a whole. It deals with economywide phenomena such as changes in unemployment, in the general price level, and in national income.

Microeconomics
The study of decision making undertaken by individuals (or households) and by firms.

Macroeconomics
The study of the behavior of the economy as a whole, including such economywide phenomena as changes in unemployment, the general price level, and national income.

Microeconomic analysis, for example, is concerned with the effects of changes in the price of gasoline relative to that of other energy sources. It examines the effects of new taxes on a specific product or industry. If price controls were reinstituted in the United States, how individual firms and consumers would react to them would be in the realm of microeconomics. The effects of higher wages brought about by an effective union strike would also be analyzed using the tools of microeconomics.

In contrast, issues such as the rate of inflation, the amount of economywide unemployment, and the yearly growth in the output of goods and services in the nation all fall into the realm of macroeconomic analysis. In other words, macroeconomics deals with **aggregates,** or totals—such as total output in an economy.

Be aware, however, of the blending of microeconomics and macroeconomics in modern economic theory. Modern economists are increasingly using microeconomic analysis—the study of decision making by individuals and by firms—as the basis of macroeconomic analysis. They do this because even though macroeconomic analysis focuses on aggregates, those aggregates are the result of choices made by individuals and firms.

Aggregates
Total amounts or quantities; aggregate demand, for example, is total planned expenditures throughout a nation.

The Economic Person: Rational Self-Interest

Economists assume that individuals act *as if* motivated by self-interest and respond predictably to opportunities for gain. This central insight of economics was first clearly articulated by Adam Smith in 1776. Smith wrote in his most famous book, *An Inquiry into the Nature and Causes of the Wealth of Nations,* that "it is not from the benevolence of the butcher, the brewer, or the baker that we expect our dinner, but from their regard to their own interest." Thus, the typical person about whom economists make behavioral predictions is assumed to act *as though* motivated by self-interest. Because monetary benefits and costs of actions are often the most easily measured, economists make behavioral predictions about individuals' responses to opportunities to increase their wealth, measured in money terms.

Is it possible to apply the theory of rational self-interest to help in explaining regular church attendance?

EXAMPLE
Earthly Rewards of Religiosity

Undoubtedly, most people who attend church regularly do so because they feel an innate desire to participate actively in their chosen religious faith. Nevertheless, habitual church attendance has concrete rewards as well, in the form of more education, a lower chance of divorce, and even higher income. A 10 percent increase in church attendance boosts a typical individual's income by nearly 1 percent.

Why might churchgoing lead to higher income? One possible explanation is that attending church helps people establish trust within a social network and find more business opportunities. Another is that church membership provides a type of insurance that helps people recover emotionally and even financially following life setbacks such as illnesses or job losses. Finally, religious faith may reduce personal stresses, thereby making churchgoers more productive and employable. Thus, there are several channels by which greater church involvement can contribute to higher incomes.

FOR CRITICAL ANALYSIS
How might the fact that many churches sponsor schools help to boost incomes of families that maintain their church memberships over a generation or more? (Hint: People who are better educated possess more skills and hence are more employable.)

The Rationality Assumption

Rationality assumption
The assumption that people do not intentionally make decisions that would leave them worse off.

The **rationality assumption** of economics, simply stated, is as follows:

We assume that individuals do not intentionally make decisions that would leave them worse off.

The distinction here is between what people may think—the realm of psychology and psychiatry and perhaps sociology—and what they do. Economics does *not* involve itself in analyzing individual or group thought processes. Economics looks at what people actually do in life with their limited resources. It does little good to criticize the rationality assumption by stating, "Nobody thinks that way" or "I never think that way" or "How unrealistic! That's as irrational as anyone can get!"

Take the example of driving. When you consider passing another car on a two-lane highway with oncoming traffic, you have to make very quick decisions: You must estimate the speed of the car that you are going to pass, the speed of the oncoming cars, the distance between your car and the oncoming cars, and your car's potential rate of acceleration. If we were to apply a model to your behavior, we would use the rules of calculus. In actual fact, you and most other drivers in such a situation do not actually think of using the rules of calculus, but to predict your behavior, we could make the prediction *as if* you understood those rules.

How might regular church attendance lead to higher income?

How can magnetic resonance imaging (MRI) scans aid in assessing the rationality assumption?

EXAMPLE
"Neuroeconomics" Evaluates Rational Choice

Neuroeconomics is a field of study aimed at determining how the human brain makes choices. Researchers in neuroeconomics have found that three parts of the brain typically interact in decision making. The *nucleus accumbens* processes emotions regarding the desirability of an item, and the *insular cortex* responds to the potential for a monetary loss associated with paying for the item. The *prefrontal cortex* handles rational calculation.

MRI scans reveal that when a person's brain is evaluating a purchase, the prefrontal cortex synthesizes conflicting positive feelings in the nucleus accumbens and negative emotions associated with payment in the insular cortex. Thus, there is evidence that the human brain naturally attempts to factor in reasoned calculations aimed at making a choice consistent with the "best" overall outcome. This conclusion, of course, supports the rationality assumption.

FOR CRITICAL ANALYSIS
Why might a person rationally pass up a choice that would yield a significant immediate gain in favor of a choice that would yield a series of smaller future gains? (Hint: The sum of many small numbers can exceed a single large number.)

Responding to Incentives

If it can be assumed that individuals never intentionally make decisions that would leave them worse off, then almost by definition they will respond to changes in incentives. Indeed, much of human behavior can be explained in terms of how individuals respond to changing incentives over time.

Schoolchildren are motivated to do better by a variety of incentive systems, ranging from gold stars and certificates of achievement when they are young, to better grades with accompanying promises of a "better life" as they get older. Of course, negative incentives affect our behavior, too. Penalties, punishments, and other forms of negative incentives can raise the cost of engaging in various activities.

What do you suppose is now a commonplace incentive at online dating sites?

You Are There

To contemplate how tax changes can provide incentives for people to alter their choices, consider **Herding Alpacas Toward a Tax Break,** on pages 11 and 12.

E-COMMERCE EXAMPLE
The New Online Dating Incentive: Health Insurance

"I'm looking for a woman who knows what she wants and isn't afraid to ask for it—one with a nice smile and a healthy attitude who is open and honest . . . and health insurance wouldn't hurt, either." So reads an ad at an online dating site. Another ad states: "Are you strong, smart and sophisticated, confident and kind, without being too uppity and conceited? Do you make at least $75,000 a year and have health insurance?" One ad is particularly straightforward: "My ideal man will have health insurance."

These ads reflect a growing trend at online dating sites. Alongside a winning personality, good looks, and other traditional attributes, another incentive that may induce an individual to agree to a date is a potential dating partner's access to health insurance.

FOR CRITICAL ANALYSIS
How might efforts by many U.S. companies to drastically reduce health insurance benefits influence the incentive effects of health insurance at online dating services?

Defining Self-Interest

Self-interest does not always mean increasing one's wealth measured in dollars and cents. We assume that individuals seek many goals, not just increased wealth measured in monetary terms. Thus, the self-interest part of our economic-person assumption includes goals relating to prestige, friendship, love, power, helping others, creating works of art, and many other matters. We can also think in terms of enlightened self-interest, whereby individuals, in the pursuit of what makes them better off, also achieve the betterment of others around them. In brief, individuals are assumed to want the ability to further their goals by making decisions about how things around them are used. The head of a charitable organization usually will not turn down an additional contribution, because accepting the funds yields control over how they are used, even though it is for other people's benefit.

Thus, self-interest does not rule out doing charitable acts. Giving gifts to relatives can be considered a form of charity that is nonetheless in the self-interest of the giver. But how efficient is such gift giving?

EXAMPLE
The Perceived Value of Gifts

Every holiday season, aunts, uncles, grandparents, mothers, and fathers give gifts to their college-aged loved ones. Joel Waldfogel, an economist at Yale University, surveyed several thousand college students after Christmas to find out the value of holiday gifts. He found that recorded music and outerwear (coats and jackets) had a perceived intrinsic value about equal to their actual cash equivalent. By the time he got down the list to socks, underwear, and cosmetics, the students' valuation was only about 85 percent of the cash value of the gift. He found out that aunts, uncles, and grandparents gave the "worst" gifts and friends, siblings, and parents gave the "best."

FOR CRITICAL ANALYSIS
What argument could you use against the idea of substituting cash or gift cards for physical gifts?

QUICK QUIZ　*See page 17 for the answers. Review concepts from this section in MyEconLab.*

Economics is a social science that involves the study of how individuals choose among alternatives to satisfy their _wants_, which are what people would buy if their incomes were _unlimited_.

micro, the study of the decision-making processes of individuals (or households) and firms, and _macro_, the study of the performance of the economy as a whole, are the two main branches into which the study of economics is divided.

In economics, we assume that people do not intentionally make decisions that will leave them worse off. This is known as the _rationality_ assumption.

Self interest is not confined to material well-being but also involves any action that makes a person feel better off, such as having more friends, love, power, or affection or providing more help to others.

Economics as a Science

Economics is a social science that employs the same kinds of methods used in other sciences, such as biology, physics, and chemistry. Like these other sciences, economics uses models, or theories. Economic **models,** or **theories,** are simplified representations of the real world that we use to help us understand, explain, and predict economic phenomena in the real world. There are, of course, differences between sciences. The social sciences—especially economics—make little use of laboratory experiments in which changes in variables are studied under controlled conditions. Rather, social scientists, and especially economists, usually have to test their models, or theories, by examining what has already happened in the real world.

Models, or **theories**
Simplified representations of the real world used as the basis for predictions or explanations.

Models and Realism

At the outset it must be emphasized that no model in *any* science, and therefore no economic model, is complete in the sense that it captures *every* detail or interrelationship that exists. Indeed, a model, by definition, is an abstraction from reality. It is conceptually impossible to construct a perfectly complete realistic model. For example, in physics we cannot account for every molecule and its position and certainly not for every atom and subatomic particle. Not only is such a model impossibly expensive to build, but working with it would be impossibly complex.

The nature of scientific model building is that the model should capture only the *essential* relationships that are sufficient to analyze the particular problem or answer the particular question with which we are concerned. *An economic model cannot be faulted as unrealistic simply because it does not represent every detail of the real world.* A map of a city that shows only major streets is not faulty if, in fact, all you need to know is how to pass through the city using major streets. As long as a model is able to shed light on the *central* issue at hand or forces at work, it may be useful.

A map is the quintessential model. It is always a simplified representation. It is always unrealistic. But it is also useful in making predictions about the world. If the model—the map—predicts that when you take Campus Avenue to the north, you always run into the campus, that is a prediction. If a simple model can explain observed behavior in repeated settings just as well as a complex model, the simple model has some value and is probably easier to use.

Assumptions

Every model, or theory, must be based on a set of assumptions. Assumptions define the array of circumstances in which our model is most likely to be applicable. When some people predicted that sailing ships would fall off the edge of the earth, they used the *assumption* that the earth was flat. Columbus did not accept the implications of such a model because he did not accept its assumptions. He assumed that the world was round. The real-world test of his own model refuted the flat-earth model. Indirectly, then, it was a test of the assumption of the flat-earth model.

Is it possible to use our knowledge about assumptions to understand why driving directions sometimes contain very few details?

EXAMPLE
Getting Directions

Assumptions are a shorthand for reality. Imagine that you have decided to drive from your home in San Diego to downtown San Francisco. Because you have never driven this route, you decide to use a travel-planner device such as global-positioning-system equipment.

When you ask for directions, the electronic travel planner could give you a set of detailed maps that shows each city through which you will travel—Oceanside, San Clemente, Irvine, Anaheim, Los Angeles, Bakersfield, Modesto, and so on—and then, opening each map, show you exactly how the freeway threads through each of these cities. You would get a nearly complete description of reality because the AAA travel planner will not have used many simplifying assumptions. It is more likely, however, that the travel planner will simply say, "Get on Interstate 5 going north. Stay on it for about 500 miles. Follow the signs for San Francisco. After crossing the toll bridge, take any exit marked 'Downtown.'" By omitting all of the trivial details, the travel planner has told you all that you really need and want to know. The models you will be using in this text are similar to the simplified directions on how to drive from San Diego to San Francisco—they focus on what is relevant to the problem at hand and omit what is not.

FOR CRITICAL ANALYSIS
In what way do small talk and gossip represent the use of simplifying assumptions?

THE *CERERIS PARIBUS* ASSUMPTION: ALL OTHER THINGS BEING EQUAL
Everything in the world seems to relate in some way to everything else in the world. It would be impossible to isolate the effects of changes in one variable on another variable if we always had to worry about the many other variables that might also enter the analysis. Similar to other sciences, economics uses the *ceteris paribus* **assumption.** *Ceteris paribus* means "other things constant" or "other things equal."

Consider an example taken from economics. One of the most important determinants of how much of a particular product a family buys is how expensive that product is relative to other products. We know that in addition to relative prices, other factors influence decisions about making purchases. Some of them have to do with income, others with tastes, and yet others with custom and religious beliefs. Whatever these other factors are, we hold them constant when we look at the relationship between changes in prices and changes in how much of a given product people will purchase.

Ceteris paribus [KAY-ter-us PEAR-uh-bus] assumption
The assumption that nothing changes except the factor or factors being studied.

Deciding on the Usefulness of a Model

We generally do not attempt to determine the usefulness, or "goodness," of a model merely by evaluating how realistic its assumptions are. Rather, we consider a model "good" if it yields usable predictions that are supported by real-world observations. In other words, can we use the model to predict what will happen in the world around us? Does the model provide useful implications about how things happen in our world?

Once we have determined that the model does predict real-world phenomena, the scientific approach to the analysis of the world around us requires that we consider evidence. Evidence is used to test the usefulness of a model. This is why we call economics an **empirical** science. *Empirical* means that evidence (data) is looked at to see whether we are right. Economists are often engaged in empirically testing their models.

How can empirical data help in combating terrorism?

Empirical
Relying on real-world data in evaluating the usefulness of a model.

POLICY EXAMPLE
How Empirical Evidence Aids in Thwarting Terrorism

Since 1968, there have been more than 13,000 incidents of "transnational" terrorism, or violent attacks in nations where the attackers do not reside. These data suggest predictable cycles in terrorist attacks. When terrorists launch a complex large-scale operation, such as an attack aimed at the destruction of high-rise buildings, public pressure to thwart such attacks remains high for a long time afterwards. Consequently, government countermeasures also remain in place for a lengthy period. Knowing this, terrorists lie low and begin long-term planning for a future large-scale attack. Thus, there are predictably long lulls between large-scale attacks. In contrast, public pressure to prevent simple small-scale attacks, such as bus bombings, wanes more quickly. Government prevention efforts also dissipate more rapidly, thereby tempting terrorists to launch more small-scale attacks. Thus, there tend to be predictably short pauses between smaller-scale attacks.

Recognition of empirical regularities in terrorism has assisted governments in predicting terrorism upsurges. Governments can utilize these predictions to determine how to allocate their antiterrorism resources more effectively.

FOR CRITICAL ANALYSIS
Why do you suppose that when making predictions to help thwart terrorism, economists typically assume that terrorists behave rationally?

Models of Behavior, Not Thought Processes

Take special note of the fact that economists' models do not relate to the way people *think*; they relate to the way people *act*, to what they do in life with their limited resources. Normally, the economist does not attempt to predict how people will think about a particular topic, such as a higher price of oil products, accelerated inflation, or higher taxes. Rather, the task at hand is to predict how people will behave, which may be quite different from what they *say* they will do (much to the consternation of poll takers and market researchers). The people involved in examining thought processes are psychologists and psychiatrists, not typically economists.

Behavioral Economics and Bounded Rationality

In recent years, some economists have proposed paying more attention to psychologists and psychiatrists. They have suggested an alternative approach to economic analysis. Their approach, which is known as **behavioral economics,** examines consumer behavior in the face of psychological limitations and complications that may interfere with rational decision making.

Behavioral economics
An approach to the study of consumer behavior that emphasizes psychological limitations and complications that potentially interfere with rational decision making.

BOUNDED RATIONALITY   Proponents of behavioral economics suggest that traditional economic models assume that people exhibit three "unrealistic" characteristics:

1. *Unbounded selfishness.* People are interested only in their own satisfaction.
2. *Unbounded willpower.* Their choices are always consistent with their long-term goals.
3. *Unbounded rationality.* They are able to consider every relevant choice.

Instead, advocates of behavioral economics have proposed replacing the rationality assumption with the assumption of **bounded rationality,** which assumes that people cannot examine and think through every possible choice they confront. As a consequence, behavioral economists suggest, people cannot always pursue their long-term

Bounded rationality
The hypothesis that people are *nearly,* but not fully, rational, so that they cannot examine every possible choice available to them but instead use simple rules of thumb to sort among the alternatives that happen to occur to them.

personal interests. From time to time, they must also rely on other people and take into account other people's interests as well as their own.

RULES OF THUMB A key behavioral implication of the bounded rationality assumption is that people should use so-called *rules of thumb*: Because every possible choice cannot be considered, an individual will tend to fall back on methods of making decisions that are simpler than trying to sort through every possibility.

A problem confronting advocates of behavioral economics is that people who *appear* to use rules of thumb may in fact behave *as if* they are fully rational. For instance, if a person faces persistently predictable ranges of choices for a time, the individual may rationally settle into repetitive behaviors that an outside observer might conclude to be consistent with a rule of thumb. The bounded rationality assumption indicates that the person should continue to rely on a rule of thumb even if there is a major change in the environment that the individual faces. Time and time again, however, economists find that people respond to altered circumstances by fundamentally changing their behaviors. Economists also generally observe that people make decisions that are consistent with their own self-interest and long-term objectives.

BEHAVIORAL ECONOMICS: A WORK IN PROGRESS It remains to be seen whether the application of the assumption of bounded rationality proposed by behavioral economists will truly alter the manner in which economists construct models intended to better predict human decision making. So far, proponents of behavioral economics have not conclusively demonstrated that paying closer attention to psychological thought processes can improve economic predictions.

As a consequence, the bulk of economic analysis continues to rely on the rationality assumption as the basis for constructing economic models. As you will learn in Chapter 20, advocates of behavioral economics continue to explore ways in which psychological elements might improve analysis of decision making by individual consumers.

Positive versus Normative Economics

Economics uses *positive analysis*, a value-free approach to inquiry. No subjective or moral judgments enter into the analysis. Positive analysis relates to statements such as "If A, then B." For example, "If the price of gasoline goes up relative to all other prices, then the amount of it that people buy will fall." That is a positive economic statement. It is a statement of *what is*. It is not a statement of anyone's value judgment or subjective feelings.

Distinguishing Between Positive and Normative Economics

Positive economics
Analysis that is *strictly* limited to making either purely descriptive statements or scientific predictions; for example, "If A, then B." A statement of *what is*.

Normative economics
Analysis involving value judgments about economic policies; relates to whether things are good or bad. A statement of *what ought to be*.

For many problems analyzed in the "hard" sciences such as physics and chemistry, the analyses are considered to be virtually value-free. After all, how can someone's values enter into a theory of molecular behavior? But economists face a different problem. They deal with the behavior of individuals, not molecules. That makes it more difficult to stick to what we consider to be value-free or **positive economics** without reference to our feelings.

When our values are interjected into the analysis, we enter the realm of **normative economics,** involving *normative analysis*. A positive economic statement is "If the price of gas rises, people will buy less." If we add to that analysis the statement "so we should not allow the price to go up," we have entered the realm of normative economics—we have expressed a value judgment. In fact, any time you see the word *should*, you will know that values are entering into the discussion. Just remember that positive statements are concerned with *what is*, whereas normative statements are concerned with *what ought to be*.

Each of us has a desire for different things. That means that we have different values. When we express a value judgment, we are simply saying what we prefer, like, or desire. Because individual values are diverse, we expect—and indeed observe—people expressing widely varying value judgments about how the world ought to be.

A Warning: Recognize Normative Analysis

It is easy to define positive economics. It is quite another matter to catch all unlabeled normative statements in a textbook, even though an author goes over the manuscript many times before it is printed. Therefore, do not get the impression that a textbook author will be able to keep all personal values out of the book. They will slip through. In fact, the very choice of which topics to include in an introductory textbook involves normative economics. There is no value-free way to decide which topics to use in a textbook. The author's values ultimately make a difference when choices have to be made. But from your own standpoint, you might want to be able to recognize when you are engaging in normative as opposed to positive economic analysis. Reading this text will help equip you for that task.

What might motivate U.S. residents to breed more llamas?

QUICK QUIZ   *See page 17 for the answers. Review concepts from this section in MyEconLab.*

A ~~models~~ , or ~~theories~~ , uses assumptions and is by nature a simplification of the real world. The usefulness of a _____ can be evaluated by bringing empirical evidence to bear on its predictions.

Most models use the ~~cpi~~ _____ _____ assumption that all other things are held constant, or equal.

_____ economics emphasizes psychological constraints and complexities that potentially interfere with rational decision making. This approach utilizes the _____ _____ hypothesis that people are not quite rational, because they cannot study every possible alternative but instead use simple rules of thumb to decide among choices.

_____ economics is value-free and relates to statements that can be refuted, such as "If A, then B."

_____ economics involves people's values and typically uses the word *should*.

You Are There ▶ Herding Alpacas Toward a Tax Break

Recently, Claudia Weiner, a teacher in Ventura, California, was looking for a way to shelter a portion of household income from federal taxation. She found that in 2003, Congress passed the Jobs and Growth Tax Relief Reconciliation Act, which authorizes a 100 percent tax deduction for an asset purchased by a small business. One asset that qualifies

under the law is an alpaca, a small, long-necked South American llama that yields fleece prized by some clothing designers.

Weiner learned that raising several alpacas requires only about an acre of land and a direct annual expense of about $300. On any property designated as an "alpaca farm,"

You Are There (cont.)

tax-deductible expenses include purchases of food, water, fences, land upkeep, and under some circumstances even additions to homes.

Weiner and her husband ultimately decided to reclassify their home as an alpaca farm, which they call "As You Like It Alpacas." By responding in this way to the tax incentive Congress created, she and her husband joined nearly 2,500 new entrants into the U.S. alpaca-farming industry, which increased to about 4,500 farms. Few of these alpaca farmers have earned significant profits from selling alpaca fleece. Many of them, however, have succeeded in reducing the

total taxes they must pay to the federal government each year.

CRITICAL ANALYSIS QUESTIONS

1. *How would a steep decline in the price of alpaca fleece, the main product of alpaca farmers, likely affect the incentive to raise alpacas?*

2. *Unless Congress takes action to renew the 2003 legislation, it will no longer be in force beginning in 2010. How might this affect the incentive to be an alpaca farmer?*

Risking Life and Limb on Mumbai Commuter Trains

Issues and Applications

CONCEPTS APPLIED

- Incentives
- Self-Interest
- Rationality Assumption

Every day, the commuter-rail network in Mumbai, India, carries more than 32,000 passengers per mile, a passenger rate 175 percent greater than the rail system was originally designed to transport. During peak hours, Mumbai rail commuters push their way across platforms and pack themselves into what they call the "super-dense crush load" of a typical passenger car—about 350 more passengers than the intended capacity of 200.

On a typical day, two or three people are killed when the surging crowd causes them to lose their footing on the platform and tumble onto the tracks. Two or three others die when they lose their grips on exterior handholds of passenger cars and fall from moving trains. Occasionally, someone is killed when he sticks his head out an open window or door to gasp for fresh air at an inopportune time, such as when the train is passing a pole near the tracks. Others die when they rush to catch a train and dart across the tracks in front of a locomotive. All told, 13 people on average are killed each working day in what media commentators have called the world's most dangerous train commute.

Incentives to Cram onto Mumbai Commuter Trains

Why do 6 million people per day wish to travel via Mumbai's commuter-rail system? To answer this question, we must consider the incentives faced by the 18 million residents of the Mumbai metropolitan area.

India's economy is growing rapidly. Most of the nation's highest-paying jobs are within its cities. Large numbers of people seeking to fill these positions are relocating from rural areas to the outskirts of metropolitan areas such as Mumbai. The government does not permit private autos to enter Mumbai's downtown interior, and taxi service into that area is sparse and relatively expensive. Reaching the central city from the city's outer edges by bus can take several hours, whereas commuter trains transit the same distance in 60 minutes or less. Furthermore, India's government, which operates the nation's rail systems, sets fares—typically little more than 25 cents for a one-hour ride—well below the levels that private operators would charge.

Self-Interest, Rationality, and Super-Dense Crush Loads

Clearly, higher-paying employment inside the city, lack of substitute transportation of equal quality, and low ticket prices are all strong positive incentives for the residents of Mumbai to choose rail transport. These incentives help to explain why so many self-interested people continue to brave the Mumbai rail commute.

At the same time, though, the discomfort of being packed into passenger cars or perhaps even having to hang to the outside of the cars is certainly a negative incentive to train travel in Mumbai. So is the average daily toll of 13 people killed in accidents. This overall death toll, however, implies an average daily death *rate* of about 2 per million passengers. The injury rate in the Mumbai commuter-rail system is somewhat higher than the death rate. Nevertheless, the overall chance of experiencing an injury to life or limb on a given day is still less than 1 out of 200,000.

Under the rationality assumption, people do not intentionally make decisions that make themselves worse off. Someone who resides on the outskirts of Mumbai typically can double her annual income by commuting into the city. In most cases, taking a commuter train to her place of employment is her only reasonable option, and the price of this mode of transport is very low. She must weigh these positive incentives against the disincentives of a cramped commute and a relatively low individual likelihood of injury or death. On net, a resident on the outer edge of Mumbai is unlikely to perceive the decision to make the "world's most dangerous commute" as inconsistent with her own self-interest. Thus, each working day she and 6 million others are likely to continue to traverse Mumbai's 813-mile commuter-rail system.

Test your understanding of this chapter by going online to **MyEconLab**. In the Study Plan for this chapter, select Section N: News.

For Critical Analysis

1. Under Indian law, the family of a commuter killed in an accident is entitled to a government death benefit. Why do you suppose that India's government imposes fines on people caught crossing tracks or riding on top of trains?

2. What do you think would happen to Mumbai's average daily rail passenger totals if a private company were to manage the system and charge higher fares?

Web Resources

1. For a description of the Mumbai passenger rail system, go to www.econtoday.com/chapter01.
2. Read an Indian court's directions for trying to reduce Mumbai's rail death toll at www.econtoday.com/chapter01.

Research Project

Suppose that you have been appointed to a commission that the Indian government has charged with making recommendations about how to reduce the death toll on Mumbai's commuter-rail system. The Indian government states that it already plans to lay 113 miles of new track, thereby extending the Mumbai rail network by 13 percent. It also plans to add 147 more trains, which will increase the number of passenger cars by more than 70 percent. Based on what you have learned about incentives, self-interest, and rational behavior, what other recommendations do you have for the Indian government?

Here is what you should know after reading this chapter. **MyEconLab** will help you identify what you know, and where to go when you need to practice.

WHAT YOU SHOULD KNOW		WHERE TO GO TO PRACTICE
Microeconomics versus Macroeconomics In general, economics is the study of how individuals make choices to satisfy wants. Economics is usually divided into microeconomics, which is the study of decision making by individual households and individual firms, and macroeconomics, which is the study of nationwide phenomena, such as inflation and unemployment.	incentives, 2 economics, 2 resources, 3 wants, 3 microeconomics, 3 macroeconomics, 3 aggregates, 3	• **MyEconLab** Study Plans 1.1, 1.2, 1.3 • Audio introduction to Chapter 1 • Video: The Difference Between Microeconomics and Macroeconomics
Self-Interest in Economic Analysis Rational self-interest is the assumption that people never intentionally make decisions that would leave them worse off. Instead, they are motivated mainly by their self-interest, which can relate to monetary and nonmonetary goals, such as love, prestige, and helping others.	rationality assumption, 4	• **MyEconLab** Study Plan 1.4 • Video: The Economic Person: Rational Self-Interest
Economics as a Science Economic models, or theories, are simplified representations of the real world. Economic models are never completely realistic because by definition they are simplifications using assumptions that are not directly testable. Nevertheless, economists can subject the predictions of economic theories to empirical tests in which real-world data are used to decide whether or not to reject the predictions.	models, or theories, 7 *ceteris paribus* assumption, 8 empirical, 8 behavioral economics, 9 bounded rationality, 9	• **MyEconLab** Study Plan 1.5 • ABC News Video: Coca-Cola in India

(continued)

 (continued)

WHAT YOU SHOULD KNOW		WHERE TO GO TO PRACTICE
Positive and Normative Economics Positive economics deals with *what is*, whereas normative economics deals with *what ought to be*. Positive economic statements are of the "if . . . then" variety; they are descriptive and predictive. In contrast, statements embodying values are within the realm of normative economics, or how people think things ought to be.	positive economics, 10 normative economics, 10	• **MyEconLab** Study Plan 1.6 • Video: Difference Between Normative and Positive Economics

Log in to MyEconLab, take a chapter test, and get a personalized Study Plan that tells you which concepts you understand and which ones you need to review. From there, MyEconLab will give you further practice, tutorials, animations, videos, and guided solutions.
Log in to www.myeconlab.com

PROBLEMS

All problems are assignable in  *. Answers to odd-numbered problems appear at the back of the book.*

1-1. Define economics. Explain briefly how the economic way of thinking—in terms of rational, self-interested people responding to incentives—relates to each of the following situations.

    a. A student deciding whether to purchase a textbook for a particular class

    b. Government officials seeking more funding for mass transit through higher taxes

    c. A municipality taxing hotel guests to obtain funding for a new sports stadium

1-2. Some people claim that the "economic way of thinking" does not apply to issues such as health care. Explain how economics does apply to this issue by developing a "model" of an individual's choices.

1-3. Does the phrase "unlimited wants and limited resources" apply to both a low-income household and a middle-income household? Can the same phrase be applied to a very high-income household?

1-4. In a single sentence, contrast microeconomics and macroeconomics. Next, categorize each of the following issues as either a microeconomic issue, a macroeconomic issue, or not an economic issue.

    a. The national unemployment rate

    b. The decision of a worker to work overtime or not

    c. A family's choice to have a baby

    d. The rate of growth of the money supply

    e. The national government's budget deficit

    f. A student's allocation of study time across two subjects

1-5. One of your classmates, Sally, is a hardworking student, serious about her classes, and conscientious about her grades. Sally is also involved, however, in volunteer activities and an extracurricular sport. Is Sally displaying rational behavior? Based on what you read in this chapter, construct an argument supporting the conclusion that she is.

1-6. Recently, a bank was trying to decide what fee to charge for "expedited payments"—payments that the bank would transmit extra speedily to enable customers to avoid late fees on cable TV bills, electric bills, and the like. To try to determine what fee customers were willing to pay for expedited payments, the bank conducted a survey. It was able to determine that many of the people surveyed already paid fees for expedited payment services that *exceeded* the maximum fees that they said they were willing to pay. How does the bank's finding relate to economists' traditional focus on what people do, rather than what they *say* they will do?

1-7. Explain, in your own words, the rationality assumption, and contrast it with the assumption of bounded rationality proposed by adherents of behavioral economics.

1-8. Why does the assumption of bounded rationality suggest that people might use rules of thumb to guide their decision making instead of considering every possible choice available to them?

1-9. Under what circumstances might people appear to use rules of thumb, as suggested by the assumption of bounded rationality, even though they really were behaving in a manner suggested by the rationality assumption?

1-10. Which of the following predictions appears to follow from a model based on the assumption that rational, self-interested individuals respond to incentives?

 a. For every 10 exam points Myrna must earn in order to pass her economics course and meet her graduation requirements, she will study one additional hour for her economics test next week.

 b. A coin toss will best predict Leonardo's decision about whether to purchase an expensive business suit or an inexpensive casual outfit to wear next week when he interviews for a high-paying job he is seeking.

 c. Celeste, who uses earnings from her regularly scheduled hours of part-time work to pay for her room and board at college, will decide to buy a newly released DVD this week only if she is able to work two additional hours.

1-11. Consider two models for estimating, in advance of an election, the shares of votes that will go to rival candidates. According to one model, pollsters' surveys of a randomly chosen set of registered voters before an election can be used to forecast the percentage of votes that each candidate will receive. This first model relies on the assumption that unpaid survey respondents will give truthful responses about how they will vote and that they will actually cast a ballot in the

election. The other model uses prices of financial assets (legally binding IOUs) issued by the Iowa Electronic Markets, operated by the University of Iowa, to predict electoral outcomes. The final payments received by owners of these assets, which can be bought or sold during the weeks and days preceding an election, depend on the shares of votes the candidates actually end up receiving. This second model assumes that owners of these assets wish to earn the highest possible returns, and it indicates that the market prices of these assets provide an indication of the percentage of votes that each candidate will actually receive on the day of the election.

 a. Which of these two models for forecasting electoral results is more firmly based on the rationality assumption of economics?

 b. How would an economist evaluate which is the better model for forecasting electoral outcomes?

1-12. Write a sentence contrasting positive and normative economic analysis.

1-13. Based on your answer to Problem 1–12, categorize each of the following conclusions as being the result of positive analysis or normative analysis.

 a. A higher minimum wage will reduce employment opportunities for minimum wage workers.

 b. Increasing the earnings of minimum wage employees is desirable, and raising the minimum wage is the best way to accomplish this.

 c. Everyone should enjoy open access to health care.

 d. Heath care subsidies will increase the consumption of health care.

1-14. Consider the following statements, based on a positive economic analysis that assumes that all other things remain constant. For each, list one other thing that might change and thus offset the outcome stated.

 a. Increased demand for laptop computers will drive up their price.

 b. Falling gasoline prices will result in additional vacation travel.

 c. A reduction of income tax rates will result in more people working.

ECONOMICS ON THE NET

The Usefulness of Studying Economics This application helps you see how accomplished people benefited from their study of economics. It also explores ways in which these people feel others of all walks of life can gain from learning more about the economics field.

Title: How Taking an Economics Course Can Lead to Becoming an Economist

Navigation: Go to **www.econtoday.com/chapter01** to visit the Federal Reserve Bank of Minneapolis publication, *The Region*. Select the last article of the issue, "Economists in *The Region* on Their Student Experiences and the Need for Economic Literacy."

Application Read the interviews of the six economists, and answer the following questions.

1. Based on your reading, which economists do you think other economists regard as influential? What educational institutions do you think are the most influential in economics?

2. Which economists do you think were attracted to microeconomics and which to macroeconomics?

For Group Study and Analysis Divide the class into three groups, and assign the groups the Blinder, Yellen, and Rivlin interviews. Have each group use the content of its assigned interview to develop a statement explaining why the study of economics is important, regardless of a student's chosen major.

ANSWERS TO QUICK QUIZZES

p. 6: (i) wants . . . unlimited; (ii) Microeconomics . . . macroeconomics; (iii) rationality; (iv) Self-interest

p. 11: (i) model . . . theory . . . model; (ii) *ceteris paribus*; (iii) Behavioral . . . bounded rationality; (iv) Positive . . . Normative

Reading and Working with Graphs

Independent variable
A variable whose value is determined independently of, or outside, the equation under study.

Dependent variable
A variable whose value changes according to changes in the value of one or more independent variables.

TABLE A-1

Gas Mileage as a Function of Driving Speed

Miles per Hour	Miles per Gallon
45	25
50	24
55	23
60	21
65	19
70	16
75	13

Direct relationship
A relationship between two variables that is positive, meaning that an increase in one variable is associated with an increase in the other and a decrease in one variable is associated with a decrease in the other.

A graph is a visual representation of the relationship between variables. In this appendix, we'll deal with just two variables: an **independent variable,** which can change in value freely, and a **dependent variable,** which changes only as a result of changes in the value of the independent variable. For example, even if nothing else is changing in your life, your weight depends on your intake of calories. The independent variable is caloric intake, and the dependent variable is weight.

A table is a list of numerical values showing the relationship between two (or more) variables. Any table can be converted into a graph, which is a visual representation of that list. Once you understand how a table can be converted to a graph, you will understand what graphs are and how to construct and use them.

Consider a practical example. A conservationist may try to convince you that driving at lower highway speeds will help you conserve gas. Table A-1 shows the relationship between speed—the independent variable—and the distance you can go on a gallon of gas at that speed—the dependent variable. This table does show a pattern. As the data in the first column get larger in value, the data in the second column get smaller.

Now let's take a look at the different ways in which variables can be related.

Direct and Inverse Relationships

Two variables can be related in different ways, some simple, others more complex. For example, a person's weight and height are often related. If we measured the height and weight of thousands of people, we would surely find that taller people tend to weigh more than shorter people. That is, we would discover that there is a **direct relationship** between height and weight. By this we simply mean that an *increase* in one variable is usually associated with an *increase* in the related variable. This can easily be seen in panel (a) of Figure A-1.

FIGURE A-1

Direct and Inverse Relationships

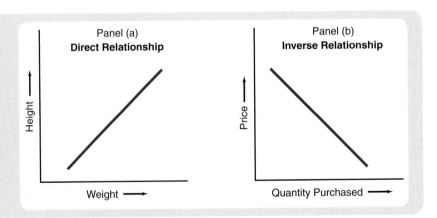

Let's look at another simple way in which two variables can be related. Much evidence indicates that as the price of a specific commodity rises, the amount purchased decreases—there is an **inverse relationship** between the variable's price per unit and quantity purchased. Such a relationship indicates that for higher and higher prices, smaller and smaller quantities will be purchased. We see this relationship in panel (b) of Figure A-1.

Inverse relationship
A relationship between two variables that is negative, meaning that an increase in one variable is associated with a decrease in the other and a decrease in one variable is associated with an increase in the other.

Constructing a Graph

Let us now examine how to construct a graph to illustrate a relationship between two variables.

A Number Line

The first step is to become familiar with what is called a **number line.** One is shown in Figure A-2. You should know two things about it:

Number line
A line that can be divided into segments of equal length, each associated with a number.

1. The points on the line divide the line into equal segments.
2. The numbers associated with the points on the line increase in value from left to right; saying it the other way around, the numbers decrease in value from right to left. However you say it, what you're describing is formally called an *ordered set of points.*

On the number line, we have shown the line segments—that is, the distance from 0 to 10 or the distance between 30 and 40. They all appear to be equal and, indeed, are each equal to $\frac{1}{2}$ inch. When we use a distance to represent a quantity, such as barrels of oil, graphically, we are *scaling* the number line. In the example shown, the distance between 0 and 10 might represent 10 barrels of oil, or the distance from 0 to 40 might represent 40 barrels. Of course, the scale may differ on different number lines. For example, a distance of 1 inch could represent 10 units on one number line but 5,000 units on another. Notice that on our number line, points to the left of 0 correspond to negative numbers and points to the right of 0 correspond to positive numbers.

Of course, we can also construct a vertical number line. Consider the one in Figure A-3 on the next page. As we move up this vertical number line, the numbers increase in value; conversely, as we descend, they decrease in value. Below 0 the numbers are negative, and above 0 the numbers are positive. And as on the horizontal number line, all the line segments are equal. This line is divided into segments such that the distance between −2 and −1 is the same as the distance between 0 and 1.

Combining Vertical and Horizontal Number Lines

By drawing the horizontal and vertical lines on the same sheet of paper, we are able to express the relationships between variables graphically. We do this in Figure A-4 on the next page. We draw them (1) so that they intersect at each other's 0 point and (2) so that they are perpendicular to each other. The result is a set of coordinate axes, where each line is called an *axis.* When we have two axes, they span a *plane.*

FIGURE A-2

Horizontal Number Line

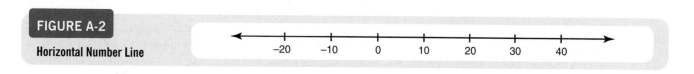

FIGURE A-3

Vertical Number Line

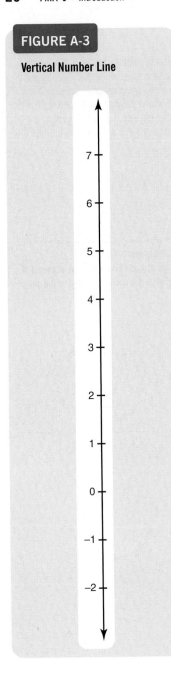

FIGURE A-4

A Set of Coordinate Axes

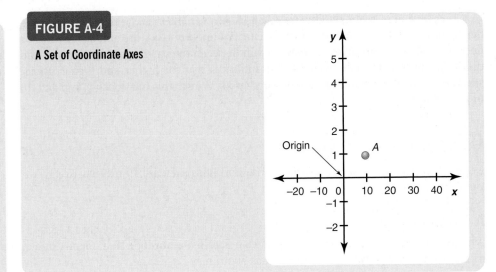

For one number line, you need only one number to specify any point on the line; equivalently, when you see a point on the line, you know that it represents one number or one value. With a coordinate value system, you need two numbers to specify a single point in the plane; when you see a single point on a graph, you know that it represents two numbers or two values.

The basic things that you should know about a coordinate number system are that the vertical number line is referred to as the **y axis,** the horizontal number line is referred to as the **x axis,** and the point of intersection of the two lines is referred to as the **origin.**

Any point such as A in Figure A-4 represents two numbers—a value of x and a value of y. But we know more than that: We also know that point A represents a positive value of y because it is above the x axis, and we know that it represents a positive value of x because it is to the right of the y axis.

Point A represents a "paired observation" of the variables x and y; in particular, in Figure A-4, A represents an observation of the pair of values $x = 10$ and $y = 1$. Every point in the coordinate system corresponds to a paired observation of x and y, which can be simply written (x, y)—the x value is always specified first and then the y value. When we give the values associated with the position of point A in the coordinate number system, we are in effect giving the coordinates of that point. A's coordinates are $x = 10$, $y = 1$, or $(10, 1)$.

Graphing Numbers in a Table

Consider Table A-2. Column 1 shows different prices for T-shirts, and column 2 gives the number of T-shirts purchased per week at these prices. Notice the pattern of these numbers. As the price of T-shirts falls, the number of T-shirts purchased per week increases. Therefore, an inverse relationship exists between these two variables, and as soon as we represent it on a graph, you will be able to see the relationship. We can graph this relationship using a coordinate number system—a vertical and horizontal number line for each of these two variables. Such a graph is shown in panel (b) of Figure A-5.

y axis
The vertical axis in a graph.

x axis
The horizontal axis in a graph.

Origin
The intersection of the y axis and the x axis in a graph.

In economics, it is conventional to put dollar values on the y axis and quantities on the horizontal axis. We therefore construct a vertical number line for price and a horizontal number line, the x axis, for quantity of T-shirts purchased per week. The resulting coordinate system allows the plotting of each of the paired observation points; in panel (a), we repeat Table A-2, with a column added expressing these points in paired-data (x, y) form. For example, point J is the paired observation $(30, 9)$. It indicates that when the price of a T-shirt is $9, 30 will be purchased per week.

If it were possible to sell parts of a T-shirt ($\frac{1}{2}$ or $\frac{1}{20}$ of a shirt), we would have observations at every possible price. That is, we would be able to connect our paired observations, represented as lettered points. Let's assume that we can make T-shirts perfectly divisible so that the linear relationship shown in Figure A-5 also holds for fractions of dollars and T-shirts. We would then have a line that connects these points, as shown in the graph in Figure A-6 on the following page.

In short, we have now represented the data from the table in the form of a graph. Note that an inverse relationship between two variables shows up on a graph as a line or curve that slopes *downward* from left to right. (You might as well get used to the idea that economists call a straight line a "curve" even though it may not curve at all. Economists' data frequently turn out to be curves, so they refer to everything represented graphically, even straight lines, as curves.)

The Slope of a Line (A Linear Curve)

An important property of a curve represented on a graph is its *slope*. Consider Figure A-7 on page 22, which represents the quantities of shoes per week that a seller is willing to offer at different prices. Note that in panel (a) of Figure A-7, as in Figure A-5, we have expressed the coordinates of the points in parentheses in paired-data form.

TABLE A-2

T-Shirts Purchased

(1) Price of T-Shirts	(2) Number of T-Shirts Purchased per Week
$10	20
9	30
8	40
7	50
6	60
5	70

FIGURE A-5

Graphing the Relationship Between T-Shirts Purchased and Price

Panel (a)

Price per T-Shirt	T-Shirts Purchased per Week	Point on Graph
$10	20	I (20, 10)
9	30	J (30, 9)
8	40	K (40, 8)
7	50	L (50, 7)
6	60	M (60, 6)
5	70	N (70, 5)

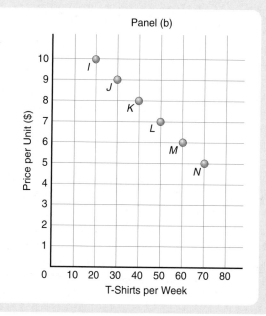

Panel (b)

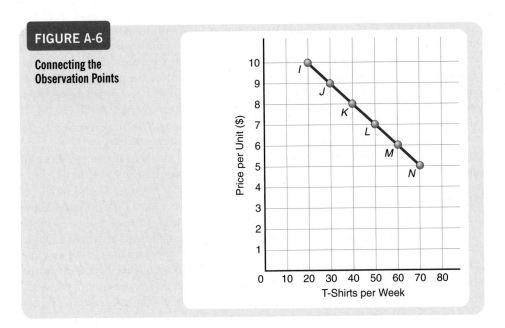

FIGURE A-6

Connecting the Observation Points

Slope
The change in the *y* value divided by the corresponding change in the *x* value of a curve; the "incline" of the curve.

The **slope** of a line is defined as the change in the *y* values divided by the corresponding change in the *x* values as we move along the line. Let's move from point *E* to point *D* in panel (b) of Figure A-7. As we move, we note that the change in the *y* values, which is the change in price, is +$20, because we have moved from a price of $20 to a price of $40 per pair. As we move from *E* to *D*, the change in the *x* values is +80; the number of pairs of shoes willingly offered per week rises from 80 to 160 pairs.

FIGURE A-7

A Positively Sloped Curve

Panel (a)

Price per Pair	Pairs of Shoes Offered per Week	Point on Graph
$100	400	A (400,100)
80	320	B (320, 80)
60	240	C (240, 60)
40	160	D (160, 40)
20	80	E (80, 20)

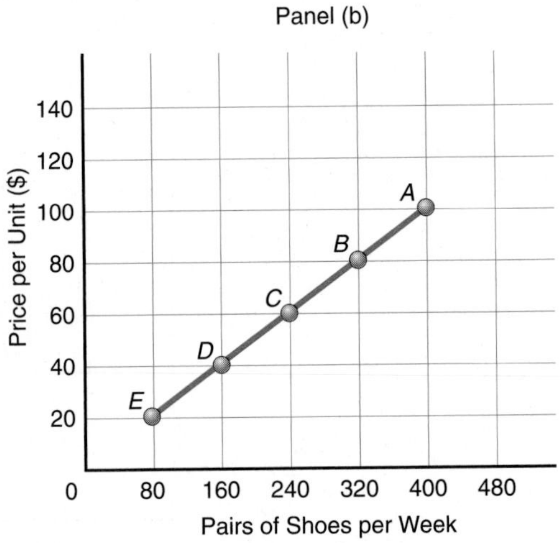

Panel (b)

[Graph: Price per Unit ($) vs. Pairs of Shoes per Week, showing points A, B, C, D, E along a positively sloped line]

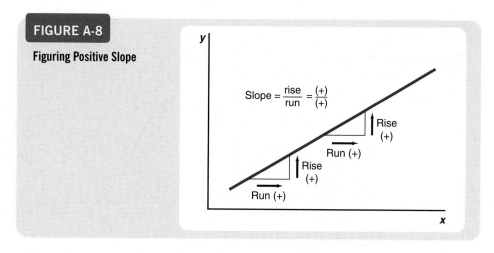

FIGURE A-8

Figuring Positive Slope

The slope, calculated as a change in the *y* values divided by the change in the *x* values, is therefore

$$\frac{20}{80} = \frac{1}{4}$$

It may be helpful for you to think of slope as a "rise" (movement in the vertical direction) over a "run" (movement in the horizontal direction). We show this abstractly in Figure A-8. The slope is the amount of rise divided by the amount of run. In the example in Figure A-8, and of course in Figure A-7, the amount of rise is positive and so is the amount of run. That's because it's a direct relationship. We show an inverse relationship in Figure A-9. The slope is still equal to the rise divided by the run, but in this case the rise and the run have opposite signs because the curve slopes downward. That means that the slope is negative and that we are dealing with an inverse relationship.

Now let's calculate the slope for a different part of the curve in panel (b) of Figure A-7. We will find the slope as we move from point *B* to point *A*. Again, we note that the slope, or rise over run, from *B* to *A* equals

$$\frac{20}{80} = \frac{1}{4}$$

A specific property of a straight line is that its slope is the same between any two points; in other words, the slope is constant at all points on a straight line in a graph.

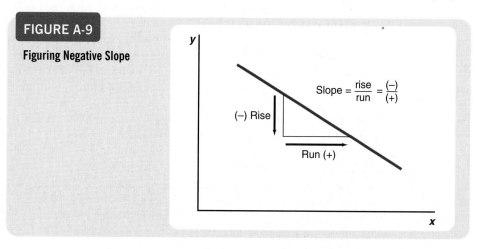

FIGURE A-9

Figuring Negative Slope

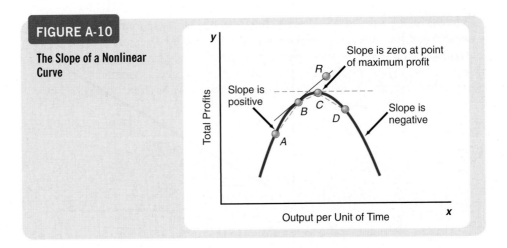

FIGURE A-10

The Slope of a Nonlinear Curve

We conclude that for our example in Figure A-7 on page 22, the relationship between the price of a pair of shoes and the number of pairs of shoes willingly offered per week is *linear*, which simply means "in a straight line," and our calculations indicate a constant slope. Moreover, we calculate a direct relationship between these two variables, which turns out to be an upward-sloping (from left to right) curve. Upward-sloping curves have positive slopes—in this case, the slope is $+\frac{1}{4}$.

We know that an inverse relationship between two variables shows up as a downward-sloping curve—rise over run will be negative because the rise and run have opposite signs, as shown in Figure A-9 on the previous page. When we see a negative slope, we know that increases in one variable are associated with decreases in the other. Therefore, we say that downward-sloping curves have negative slopes. Can you verify that the slope of the graph representing the relationship between T-shirt prices and the quantity of T-shirts purchased per week in Figure A-6 on page 22 is $-\frac{1}{10}$?

Slopes of Nonlinear Curves

The graph presented in Figure A-10 indicates a *nonlinear* relationship between two variables, total profits and output per unit of time. Inspection of this graph indicates that at first, increases in output lead to increases in total profits; that is, total profits rise as output increases. But beyond some output level, further increases in output cause decreases in total profits.

Can you see how this curve rises at first, reaches a peak at point *C*, and then falls? This curve relating total profits to output levels appears mountain-shaped.

Considering that this curve is nonlinear (it is obviously not a straight line), should we expect a constant slope when we compute changes in *y* divided by corresponding changes in *x* in moving from one point to another? A quick inspection, even without specific numbers, should lead us to conclude that the slopes of lines joining different points in this curve, such as between *A* and *B*, *B* and *C*, or *C* and *D*, will *not* be the same. The curve slopes upward (in a positive direction) for some values and downward (in a negative direction) for other values. In fact, the slope of the line between any two points on this curve will be different from the slope of the line between any two other points. Each slope will be different as we move along the curve.

Instead of using a line between two points to discuss slope, mathematicians and economists prefer to discuss the slope *at a particular point*. The slope at a point on the curve, such as point *B* in the graph in Figure A-10, is the slope of a line tangent to that point. A tangent line is a straight line that touches a curve at only one point. For example, it might be helpful to think of the tangent at *B* as the straight line that just "kisses" the curve at point *B*.

To calculate the slope of a tangent line, you need to have some additional information besides the two values of the point of tangency. For example, in Figure A-10, if we knew that the point R also lay on the tangent line and we knew the two values of that point, we could calculate the slope of the tangent line. We could calculate rise over run between points B and R, and the result would be the slope of the line tangent to the one point B on the curve.

myeconlab

Here is what you should know after reading this appendix. **MyEconLab** will help you identify what you know, and where to go when you need to practice.

WHAT YOU SHOULD KNOW

WHERE TO GO TO PRACTICE

Direct and Inverse Relationships In a direct relationship, a dependent variable changes in the same direction as the change in the independent variable. In an inverse relationship, the dependent variable changes in the opposite direction of the change in the independent variable.

independent variable, 18
dependent variable, 18
direct relationship, 18
inverse relationship, 19

• **MyEconLab** Study Plan 1.7

Constructing a Graph When we draw a graph showing the relationship between two economic variables, we are holding all other things constant (the Latin term for which is *ceteris paribus*).

number line, 19
y axis, 20
x axis, 20
origin, 20

• **MyEconLab** Study Plan 1.8

Graphing Numbers We obtain a set of coordinates by putting vertical and horizontal number lines together. The vertical line is called the *y* axis; the horizontal line, the *x* axis.

• **MyEconLab** Study Plan 1.9

The Slope of a Linear Curve The slope of any linear (straight-line) curve is the change in the *y* values divided by the corresponding change in the *x* values as we move along the line. Otherwise stated, the slope is calculated as the amount of rise over the amount of run, where rise is movement in the vertical direction and run is movement in the horizontal direction.

slope, 22

KEY FIGURES
Figure A-8, 23
Figure A-9, 23

• **MyEconLab** Study Plan 1.10
• Animated Figures A-8, A-9

The Slope of a Nonlinear Curve The slope of a nonlinear curve changes; it is positive when the curve is rising and negative when the curve is falling. At a maximum or minimum point, the slope of the nonlinear curve is zero.

KEY FIGURE
Figure A-10, 24

• **MyEconLab** Study Plan 1.10
• Animated Figure A-10

Log in to MyEconLab, take an appendix test, and get a personalized Study Plan that tells you which concepts you understand and which ones you need to review. From there, MyEconLab will give you further practice, tutorials, animations, videos, and guided solutions.
Log in to www.myeconlab.com

PROBLEMS

All problems are assignable in [X myeconlab] *. Answers to odd-numbered problems appear at the back of the book.*

A-1. Explain which is the independent variable and which is the dependent variable for each of the following examples.

   a. Once you determine the price of a notebook at the college bookstore, you will decide how many notebooks to buy.

   b. You will decide how many credit hours to register for this semester once the university tells you how many work-study hours you will be assigned.

   c. You anticipate earning a higher grade on your next economics exam because you studied more hours in the weeks preceding the exam.

A-2. For each of the following items, state whether a direct or an inverse relationship is likely to exist.

   a. The number of hours you study for an exam and your exam score

   b. The price of pizza and the quantity purchased

   c. The number of games the university basketball team won last year and the number of season tickets sold this year

A-3. Review Figure A-4 on page 20, and then state whether each of the following paired observations is on, above, or below the x axis and on, to the left of, or to the right of the y axis.

   a. $(-10, 4)$

   b. $(20, -2)$

   c. $(10, 0)$

A-4. State whether each of the following functions specifies a direct or an inverse relationship.

   a. $y = 5x$

   b. $y = 10 - 2x$

   c. $y = 3 + x$

   d. $y = -3x$

A-5. Given the function $y = 5x$, complete the following schedule and plot the curve.

y	x
	-4
	-2
	0
	2
	4

A-6. Given the function $y = 8 - 2x$, complete the following schedule and plot the curve.

y	x
	-4
	-2
	0
	2
	4

A-7. Calculate the slope of the function you graphed in Problem A-5.

A-8. Calculate the slope of the function you graphed in Problem A-6.

Scarcity and the World of Trade-Offs

2

The employer of seven former college athletes requires them to practice five days per week. Each day, they lift weights to maintain their muscle strength, and they sprint through obstacle courses to reduce their reaction time. To improve their footwork and hand speed, they watch videos of previous performances. They consider themselves to be professional athletes, but thousands of people with the opportunity to observe them at work pay little heed to their exertions. These seven individuals constitute a pit crew at a motor speedway. Each crew member performs a very specific task, and the crew's tasks are organized so as to attain maximum output from their combined resources. These aspects of the activities of a speedway pit crew conform to key economic concepts that are the subject of this chapter.

LEARNING OBJECTIVES

MyEconLab helps you master each objective and study more efficiently. See end of chapter for details.

After reading this chapter, you should be able to:

- Evaluate whether even affluent people face the problem of scarcity
- Understand why economics considers individuals' "wants" but not their "needs"
- Explain why the scarcity problem induces individuals to consider opportunity costs
- Discuss why obtaining increasing increments of any particular good typically entails giving up more and more units of other goods
- Explain why society faces a trade-off between consumption goods and capital goods
- Distinguish between absolute and comparative advantage

? Did you know that there are more than 105 million parking spaces in the United States? Although parking spaces vary in size, the typical space is about 19 feet long and 8 feet wide and takes up an area of about 152 square feet. Consequently, U.S. parking spaces occupy almost 16 billion square feet of space, or almost 575 square miles.

All of this land devoted to parking spaces could, of course, be allocated to numerous alternative uses, such as housing developments, office buildings, city parks, and green spaces. These alternative uses of land now occupied by parking spaces could yield benefits to numerous members of society. Because this land does not yield these benefits, the allocation of land to parking spaces entails costs. Land, like all other resources, is scarce.

Scarcity

Scarcity
A situation in which the ingredients for producing the things that people desire are insufficient to satisfy all wants at a zero price.

Whenever individuals or communities cannot obtain everything they desire simultaneously, they must make choices. Choices occur because of *scarcity*. **Scarcity** is the most basic concept in all of economics. Scarcity means that we do not ever have enough of everything, including time, to satisfy our *every* desire. Scarcity exists because human wants always exceed what can be produced with the limited resources and time that nature makes available.

What Scarcity Is Not

Scarcity is not a shortage. After a hurricane hits and cuts off supplies to a community, TV newscasts often show people standing in line to get minimum amounts of cooking fuel and food. A news commentator might say that the line is caused by the "scarcity" of these products. But cooking fuel and food are always scarce—we cannot obtain all that we want at a zero price. Therefore, do not confuse the concept of scarcity, which is general and all-encompassing, with the concept of shortages as evidenced by people waiting in line to obtain a particular product.

What underlying fact about parking spaces would motivate someone to buy a small car?

Scarcity is not the same thing as poverty. Scarcity occurs among the poor and among the rich. Even the richest person on earth faces scarcity. For instance, even the world's richest person has only limited time available. Low income levels do not create more scarcity. High income levels do not create less scarcity.

Scarcity is a fact of life, like gravity. And just as physicists did not invent gravity, economists did not invent scarcity—it existed well before the first economist ever lived. It has existed at all times in the past and will exist at all times in the future.

Scarcity and Resources

Production
Any activity that results in the conversion of resources into products that can be used in consumption.

Scarcity exists because resources are insufficient to satisfy our every desire. Resources are the inputs used in the production of the things that we want. **Production** can be defined as virtually any activity that results in the conversion of resources into products that can be used in consumption. Production includes delivering things from one part of the country to another. It includes taking ice from an ice tray to put it in your soft-drink glass. The resources used in production are called *factors of production*, and some economists use the terms *resources* and *factors of production* interchangeably. The total quantity of all resources that an economy has at any one time determines what that economy can produce.

Factors of production can be classified in many ways. Here is one such classification:

Land
The natural resources that are available from nature. Land as a resource includes location, original fertility and mineral deposits, topography, climate, water, and vegetation.

1. *Land.* **Land** encompasses all the nonhuman gifts of nature, including timber, water, fish, minerals, and the original fertility of land. It is often called the *natural resource*.

2. *Labor.* **Labor** is the *human resource*, which includes productive contributions made by individuals who work, such as Web page designers, ballet dancers, and professional football players.

3. *Physical capital.* **Physical capital** consists of the factories and equipment used in production. It also includes improvements to natural resources, such as irrigation ditches.

4. *Human capital.* **Human capital** is the economic characterization of the education and training of workers. How much the nation produces depends not only on how many hours people work but also on how productive they are, and that in turn depends in part on education and training. To become more educated, individuals have to devote time and resources, just as a business has to devote resources if it wants to increase its physical capital. Whenever a worker's skills increase, human capital has been improved.

5. *Entrepreneurship.* **Entrepreneurship** (actually a subdivision of labor) is the component of human resources that performs the functions of organizing, managing, and assembling the other factors of production to create and operate business ventures. Entrepreneurship also encompasses taking risks that involve the possibility of losing large sums of wealth on new ventures. It includes new methods of doing common things and generally experimenting with any type of new thinking that could lead to making more income. Without entrepreneurship, virtually no business organization could operate.

Why do you suppose that the U.S. Navy wants its top officers to develop entrepreneurial skills?

Labor
Productive contributions of humans who work.

Physical capital
All manufactured resources, including buildings, equipment, machines, and improvements to land that are used for production.

Human capital
The accumulated training and education of workers.

Entrepreneurship
The component of human resources that performs the functions of raising capital, organizing, managing, and assembling other factors of production, making basic business policy decisions, and taking risks.

POLICY EXAMPLE
Schooling Admirals in Entrepreneurship

The U.S. Navy regularly sends officers back to school for graduate courses in areas such as nuclear engineering and foreign policy analysis. In recent years, however, admirals are as likely to find themselves enrolling in graduate business courses with titles such as "Using Effects-Based Thinking" and "Organizational Innovation." The Secretary of the Navy has decided that top officers should know as much about supply-chain management, management delegation,

and organizational behavior as they know about seaborne aviation and submarine technology. Acquainting admirals with entrepreneurial skills, those heading the Navy have concluded, will lead to wiser allocation and utilization of military resources.

FOR CRITICAL ANALYSIS
In what ways is a military organization such as the U.S. Navy like a business?

Goods versus Economic Goods

Goods are defined as all things from which individuals derive satisfaction or happiness. Goods therefore include air to breathe and the beauty of a sunset as well as food, cars, and iPods.

Economic goods are a subset of all goods—they are scarce goods, about which we must constantly make decisions regarding their best use. By definition, the desired quantity of an economic good exceeds the amount that is available at a zero price. Virtually every example we use in economics concerns economic goods—cars, DVD players,

Goods
All things from which individuals derive satisfaction or happiness.

Economic goods
Goods that are scarce, for which the quantity demanded exceeds the quantity supplied at a zero price.

Services
Mental or physical labor or help purchased by consumers. Examples are the assistance of physicians, lawyers, dentists, repair personnel, housecleaners, educators, retailers, and wholesalers; items purchased or used by consumers that do not have physical characteristics.

computers, socks, baseball bats, and corn. Weeds are a good example of *bads*—goods for which the desired quantity is much *less* than what nature provides at a zero price.

Sometimes you will see references to "goods and services." **Services** are tasks that are performed for someone else, such as laundry, Internet access, hospital care, restaurant meal preparation, car polishing, psychological counseling, and teaching. One way of looking at services is to think of them as *intangible goods*.

Wants and Needs

Wants are not the same as needs. Indeed, from the economist's point of view, the term *needs* is objectively undefinable. When someone says, "I need some new clothes," there is no way to know whether that person is stating a vague wish, a want, or a life-saving requirement. If the individual making the statement were dying of exposure in a northern country during the winter, we might argue that indeed the person does need clothes—perhaps not new ones, but at least some articles of warm clothing. Typically, however, the term *need* is used very casually in conversation. What people mean, usually, is that they desire something that they do not currently have.

Humans have unlimited wants. Just imagine that every single material want that you might have was satisfied. You could have all of the clothes, cars, houses, DVDs, yachts, and other items that you want. Does that mean that nothing else could add to your total level of happiness? Undoubtedly, you might continue to think of new goods and services that you could obtain, particularly as they came to market. You would also still be lacking in fulfilling all of your wants for compassion, friendship, love, affection, prestige, musical abilities, sports abilities, and so on.

In reality, every individual has competing wants but cannot satisfy all of them, given limited resources. This is the reality of scarcity. Each person must therefore make choices. Whenever a choice is made to produce or buy something, something else that is also desired is not produced or not purchased. In other words, in a world of scarcity, every want that ends up being satisfied causes one or more other wants to remain unsatisfied or to be forfeited.

Would you classify a flat-screen TV as a want or a need? What is the difference?

QUICK QUIZ   *See page 50 for the answers. Review concepts from this section in MyEconLab.*

Scarcity is the situation in which human wants always exceed what can be produced with the limited resources and time that nature makes available.

We use scarce resources, such as _____, _____, _____ and _____ capital, and _____, to produce economic goods—goods that are desired but are not directly obtainable from nature to the extent demanded or desired at a zero price.

_____ are unlimited; they include all material desires and all nonmaterial desires, such as love, affection, power, and prestige.

The concept of _____ is difficult to define objectively for every person; consequently, we simply consider every person's wants to be unlimited. In a world of **scarcity,** satisfaction of one want necessarily means nonsatisfaction of one or more other wants.

Scarcity, Choice, and Opportunity Cost

The natural fact of scarcity implies that we must make choices. One of the most important results of this fact is that every choice made means that some opportunity must be sacrificed. Every choice involves giving up an opportunity to produce or consume something else.

Valuing Forgone Alternatives

Consider a practical example. Every choice you make to study economics for one more hour requires that you give up the opportunity to engage in any of the following activities: study more of another subject, listen to music, sleep, browse at a local store, read a novel, or work out at the gym. The most highly valued of these opportunities is forgone if you choose to study economics an additional hour.

Because there were so many alternatives from which to choose, how could you determine the value of what you gave up to engage in that extra hour of studying economics? First of all, no one else can tell you the answer because only *you* can put a value on the alternatives forgone. Only you know the value of another hour of sleep or of an hour looking for the latest digital music downloads—whatever one activity *you* would have chosen if you had not opted to study economics for that hour. That means that only you can determine the highest-valued, next-best alternative that you had to sacrifice in order to study economics one more hour. Only you can determine the value of the next-best alternative.

What is your next-highest alternative when you study an extra hour?

Opportunity Cost

The value of the next-best alternative is called **opportunity cost.** The opportunity cost of any action is the value of what is given up—the next-highest-ranked alternative—because a choice was made. When you study one more hour, there may be many alternatives available for the use of that hour, but assume that you can do only one other thing in that hour—your next-highest-ranked alternative. What is important is the choice that you would have made if you hadn't studied one more hour. Your opportunity cost is the *next-highest-ranked* alternative, not *all* alternatives.

Opportunity cost
The highest-valued, next-best alternative that must be sacrificed to obtain something or to satisfy a want.

In economics, cost is always a forgone opportunity.

One way to think about opportunity cost is to understand that when you choose to do something, you lose something else. What you lose is being able to engage in your next-highest-valued alternative. The cost of your chosen alternative is what you lose, which is by definition your next-highest-valued alternative. This is your opportunity cost.

What is the opportunity cost of precisely synchronizing the world's clocks?

INTERNATIONAL EXAMPLE
The Significant Opportunity Cost of a Second of Time

The tug of the moon's gravity slows the earth's rotation, so the length of a day on earth is always increasing a tiny bit. At intervals averaging about 18 months, astronomers notify a United Nations group charged with regulating global timekeeping that the world's day has gained another second. Telecommunications companies, satellite operators, and governments then add an extra, "leap" second to the planet's atomic clocks.

Many computers, however, are not equipped with software that can handle the 61-second minute that results when a leap second is added. Particularly vulnerable are programs that manage the global positioning systems (GPS) utilized by surveyors, engineers, surgeons, and navigators, among others. The last time a leap second was added, GPS breakdowns created snafus that temporarily idled equipment and workers on every continent.

The U.S. government has proposed adding a "leap minute" every century instead of leap seconds every 18 months. In this way, the world's economies might avoid a significant opportunity cost—that is, forgoing productive activities—in order to keep the earth's time precisely synchronized with its rotation.

FOR CRITICAL ANALYSIS

If leap seconds are not added, astronomical observatories would have to devote some of their budgets to paying $10,000 to $500,000 per facility for telescope realignments to take into account the extra seconds not appearing on clocks. Why do astronomers argue that they would bear opportunity costs if the U.S. government's "leap minute" proposal is adopted?

The World of Trade-Offs

Whenever you engage in any activity using any resource, even time, you are *trading off* the use of that resource for one or more alternative uses. The extent of the trade-off is represented by the opportunity cost. The opportunity cost of studying economics has already been mentioned—it is the value of the next-best alternative. When you think of any alternative, you are thinking of trade-offs.

Let's consider a hypothetical example of a trade-off between the results of spending time studying economics and mathematics. For the sake of this argument, we will assume that additional time studying either economics or mathematics will lead to a higher grade in the subject to which additional study time is allocated. One of the best ways to examine this trade-off is with a graph. (If you would like a refresher on graphical techniques, study Appendix A at the end of Chapter 1 before going on.)

Graphical Analysis

In Figure 2-1, the expected grade in mathematics is measured on the vertical axis of the graph, and the expected grade in economics is measured on the horizontal axis. We simplify the world and assume that you have a maximum of 12 hours per week to spend studying these two subjects and that if you spend all 12 hours on economics, you will get an A in the course. You will, however, fail mathematics. Conversely, if you spend all of your 12 hours studying mathematics, you will get an A in that subject, but you will flunk economics. Here the trade-off is a special case: one to one. A one-to-one trade-off means that the opportunity cost of receiving one grade higher in economics (for example, improving from a C to a B) is one grade lower in mathematics (falling from a C to a D).

The Production Possibilities Curve (PPC)

The graph in Figure 2-1 illustrates the relationship between the possible results that can be produced in each of two activities, depending on how much time you choose to devote to each activity. This graph shows a representation of a **production possibilities curve (PPC).**

Production possibilities curve (PPC)
A curve representing all possible combinations of maximum outputs that could be produced assuming a fixed amount of productive resources of a given quality.

Consider that you are producing a grade in economics when you study economics and a grade in mathematics when you study mathematics. Then the line that goes from A on one axis to A on the other axis therefore becomes a production possibilities curve. It is defined as the maximum quantity of one good or service that can be produced, given that a specific quantity of another is produced. It is a curve that shows the possibilities available for increasing the output of one good or service by reducing the amount of another. In the example in Figure 2-1, your time for studying was limited to 12 hours per week. The two possible outputs were your grade in mathematics and your grade in economics. The particular production possibilities curve presented in Figure 2-1 is a graphical representation of the opportunity cost of studying one more hour in one subject. It is a *straight-line production possibilities curve*, which is a spe-

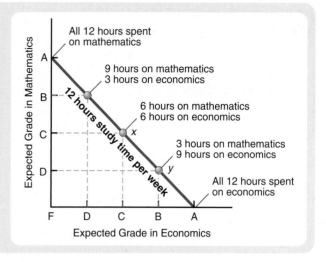

FIGURE 2-1

Production Possibilities Curve for Grades in Mathematics and Economics (Trade-Offs)

We assume that only 12 hours can be spent per week on studying. If the student is at point *x*, equal time (6 hours a week) is spent on both courses, and equal grades of C will be received. If a higher grade in economics is desired, the student may go to point *y*, thereby receiving a B in economics but a D in mathematics. At point *y*, 3 hours are spent on mathematics and 9 hours on economics.

cial case. (The more general case will be discussed next.) If you decide to be at point *x* in Figure 2-1, you will devote 6 hours of study time to mathematics and 6 hours to economics. The expected grade in each course will be a C. If you are more interested in getting a B in economics, you will go to point *y* on the production possibilities curve, spending only 3 hours on mathematics but 9 hours on economics. Your expected grade in mathematics will then drop from a C to a D.

Note that these trade-offs between expected grades in mathematics and economics are the result of *holding constant* total study time as well as all other factors that might influence your ability to learn, such as computerized study aids. Quite clearly, if you were able to spend more total time studying, it would be possible to have higher grades in both economics and mathematics. In that case, however, we would no longer be on the specific production possibilities curve illustrated in Figure 2-1. We would have to draw a new curve, farther to the right, to show the greater total study time and a different set of possible trade-offs.

What trade-off have the U.S. armed forces recently confronted as a result of the continuing military operations in Iraq and Afghanistan?

POLICY EXAMPLE
The U.S. Military Confronts a Trade-Off

Recently, U.S. military leaders decided to allocate an extra $1 billion in resources to expanding ground operations by troops in Iraq and Afghanistan. Given their available resources, the U.S. armed forces could undertake this expansion of troop operations only by forgoing the allocation of $1 billion in resources to a program known as Transformational Satellite Communications, or TSAT. The TSAT program would have involved development of space-based lasers and satellite-based Internet connections to facilitate ultrafast and highly secure data and video transmissions among military planes, ships, and troops. Thus, for the U.S. armed forces, the opportunity cost of maintaining troop levels in Iraq and Afghanistan was the forgone production of better military communications networks.

FOR CRITICAL ANALYSIS
How could Congress and taxpayers have made it possible for the U.S. armed forces to maintain their Iraq and Afghanistan operations without forgoing the allocation of resources to the TSAT program?

| QUICK QUIZ | See page 50 for the answers. Review concepts from this section in MyEconLab. |

Scarcity requires us to choose. Whenever we choose, we lose the _____-_____-valued alternative.

Cost is always a forgone _____.

Another way to look at **opportunity cost** is the trade-off that occurs when one activity is undertaken rather than the _____-_____ alternative activity.

A _____ _____ curve graphically shows the trade-off that occurs when more of one output is obtained at the sacrifice of another. This curve is a graphical representation of, among other things, opportunity cost.

The Choices Society Faces

The straight-line production possibilities curve presented in Figure 2-1 can be generalized to demonstrate the related concepts of scarcity, choice, and trade-offs that our entire nation faces. As you will see, the production possibilities curve is a simple but powerful economic model because it can demonstrate these related concepts.

A Two-Good Example

The example we will use is the choice between the production of computer servers and high-definition televisions (HDTVs). We assume for the moment that these are the only two goods that can be produced in the nation.

Panel (a) of Figure 2-2 gives the various combinations of servers and HDTVs that are possible. If all resources are devoted to server production, 50 million per year can be produced. If all resources are devoted to production of HDTVs, 60 million per year can be produced. In between are various possible combinations.

Production Trade-Offs

The nation's production combinations are plotted as points *A, B, C, D, E, F,* and *G* in panel (b) of Figure 2-2. If these points are connected with a smooth curve, the nation's production possibilities curve (PPC) is shown, demonstrating the trade-off between the production of servers and HDTVs. These trade-offs occur *on* the PPC.

Notice the major difference in the shape of the production possibilities curves in Figure 2-1 on the previous page and Figure 2-2 on the facing page. In Figure 2-1, there is a constant trade-off between grades in economics and in mathematics. In Figure 2-2, the trade-off between production of computer servers and HDTV production is not constant, and therefore the PPC is a *bowed* curve. To understand why the production possibilities curve for a society is typically bowed outward, you must understand the assumptions underlying the PPC.

Go to www.econtoday.com/chapter02 for one perspective, offered by the National Center for Policy Analysis, on whether society's production decisions should be publicly or privately coordinated.

Assumptions Underlying the Production Possibilities Curve

When we draw the curve that is shown in Figure 2-2, we make the following assumptions:

1. Resources are fully employed.
2. Production takes place over a specific time period—for example, one year.
3. The resource inputs, in both quantity and quality, used to produce computer servers or HDTVs are fixed over this time period.
4. Technology does not change over this time period.

FIGURE 2-2

Society's Trade-Off Between Computer Servers and HDTVs

The production of computer servers and HDTVs is measured in millions of units per year. The various combinations are given in panel (a) and plotted in panel (b). Connecting the points A–G with a relatively smooth line gives society's production possibilities curve for servers and HDTVs. Point R lies outside the production possibilities curve and is therefore unattainable at the point in time for which the graph is drawn. Point S lies inside the production possibilities curve and therefore entails unemployed or underemployed resources.

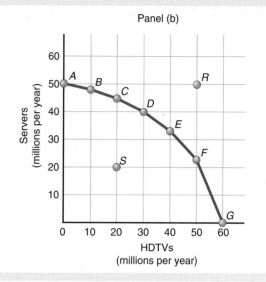

Panel (a)

Combination	Servers (millions per year)	HDTVs (millions per year)
A	50.0	0
B	48.0	10
C	45.0	20
D	40.0	30
E	33.0	40
F	22.5	50
G	0.0	60

Technology is defined as society's pool of applied knowledge concerning how goods and services can be produced by managers, workers, engineers, scientists, and artisans, using land, physical and human capital, and entrepreneurship. You can think of technology as the formula or recipe used to combine factors of production. (When better formulas are developed, more production can be obtained from the same amount of resources.) The level of technology sets the limit on the amount and types of goods and services that we can derive from any given amount of resources. The production possibilities curve is drawn under the assumption that we use the best technology that we currently have available and that this technology doesn't change over the time period under study.

The land available to a town with established borders is an example of a fixed resource that is fully employed and used with available technology along a production possibilities curve. Why do you suppose that deciding how to allocate a fixed amount of land recently posed "grave" problems for a town in France?

Technology
Society's pool of applied knowledge concerning how goods and services can be produced.

INTERNATIONAL EXAMPLE
Making Death Illegal—At Least, Inside City Limits

Le Lavandou, France, a Riviera community known for breathtaking views of a rocky coastline along a clear-blue section of the Mediterranean Sea, recently drew international ridicule when it passed a law that appeared aimed at regulating death. Specifically, the law stated, "It is forbidden without a cemetery plot to die on the territory of the commune."

Of course, it is not possible for a law to prevent someone from dying inside a town. The purpose of the law was to indicate a permissible choice along a production possibilities curve. Land is a scarce resource with many alternative uses, so trade-offs involving different productive uses of land arise everywhere on the planet where people establish communities. Le Lavandou is no exception. The town's cemetery filled up, and the townspeople had to decide whether to allocate more land to cemetery plots, thereby providing a service for deceased individuals and for their family and friends, or to continue allocating remaining land resources to the production of other goods and services. The point of the legal requirement was to emphasize that the town had decided not to incur an opportunity cost by allocating more space to cemetery plots.

Nonetheless, it was still true that someone who happened to die in Le Lavandou without first buying an existing cemetery plot was technically breaking the law.

FOR CRITICAL ANALYSIS
What is likely to happen to the opportunity cost of cemetery space as the world's population continues to increase and spread over available land resources?

Being off the Production Possibilities Curve

Look again at panel (b) of Figure 2-2 on the previous page. Point R lies *outside* the production possibilities curve and is *impossible* to achieve during the time period assumed. By definition, the PPC indicates the *maximum* quantity of one good, given the quantity produced of the other good.

It is possible, however, to be at point S in Figure 2-2. That point lies beneath the production possibilities curve. If the nation is at point S, it means that its resources are not being fully utilized. This occurs, for example, during periods of relatively high unemployment. Point S and all such points inside the PPC are always attainable but imply unemployed or underemployed resources.

Efficiency

The production possibilities curve can be used to define the notion of efficiency. Whenever the economy is operating on the PPC, at points such as A, B, C, or D, we say that its production is efficient. Points such as S in Figure 2-2, which lie beneath the PPC, are said to represent production situations that are not efficient.

Efficiency can mean many things to many people. Even in economics, there are different types of efficiency. Here we are discussing *productive efficiency*. An economy is productively efficient whenever it is producing the maximum output with given technology and resources.

A simple commonsense definition of efficiency is getting the most out of what we have. Clearly, we are not getting the most out of what we have if we are at point S in panel (b) of Figure 2-2. We can move from point S to, say, point C, thereby increasing the total quantity of servers produced without any decrease in the total quantity of HDTVs produced. Alternatively, we can move from point S to point E, for example, and have both more servers and more HDTVs. Point S is called an **inefficient point**, which is defined as any point below the production possibilities curve.

The Law of Increasing Relative Cost

In the example in Figure 2-1 on page 33, the trade-off between a grade in mathematics and a grade in economics was one to one. The trade-off ratio was constant. That is, the production possibilities curve was a straight line. The curve in Figure 2-2 is a more general case. We have re-created the curve in Figure 2-2 as Figure 2-3. Each combination, A through G, of computer servers and HDTVs is represented on the production

Efficiency
The case in which a given level of inputs is used to produce the maximum output possible. Alternatively, the situation in which a given output is produced at minimum cost.

Inefficient point
Any point below the production possibilities curve, at which the use of resources is not generating the maximum possible output.

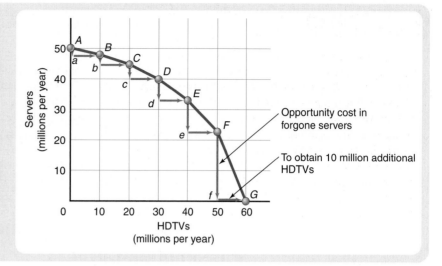

FIGURE 2-3

The Law of Increasing Relative Cost

Consider equal increments of production of HDTVs, as measured on the horizontal axis. All of the horizontal arrows—*aB, bC,* and so on—are of equal length (10 million). In contrast, the length of each vertical arrow—*Aa, Bb,* and so on—increases as we move down the production possibilities curve. Hence, the opportunity cost of going from 50 million HDTVs per year to 60 million (*Ff*) is much greater than going from zero units to 10 million (*Aa*). The opportunity cost of each additional equal increase in production of HDTVs rises.

possibilities curve. Starting with the production of zero HDTVs, the nation can produce 50 million servers with its available resources and technology.

INCREASING RELATIVE COSTS   When we increase production of HDTVs from zero to 10 million per year, the nation has to give up in servers an amount shown by that first vertical arrow, *Aa*. From panel (a) of Figure 2-2 on page 35 you can see that this is 2 million per year (50 million minus 48 million). Again, if we increase production of HDTVs by another 10 million units per year, we go from *B* to *C*. In order to do so, the nation has to give up the vertical distance *Bb*, or 3 million servers per year. By the time we go from 50 million to 60 million HDTVs, to obtain that 10 million increase, we have to forgo the vertical distance *Ff*, or 22.5 million servers. In other words, we see that the opportunity cost of the last 10 million HDTVs has increased to 22.5 million servers, compared to 2 million servers for the same increase in HDTVs when we started with none at all being produced.

What we are observing is called the **law of increasing relative cost.** When society takes more resources and applies them to the production of any specific good, the opportunity cost increases for each additional unit produced.

EXPLAINING THE LAW OF INCREASING RELATIVE COST   The reason that as a nation we face the law of increasing relative cost (shown as a production possibilities curve that is bowed outward) is that certain resources are better suited for producing some goods than they are for other goods. Generally, resources are not *perfectly* adaptable for alternative uses. When increasing the output of a particular good, producers must use less suitable resources than those already used in order to produce the additional output. Hence, the cost of producing the additional units increases.

With respect to our hypothetical example here, at first the computing specialists at server firms would shift over to producing HDTVs. After a while, though, networking technicians, workers who normally design servers, and others would be asked to help design and manufacture HDTV components. Clearly, they would be less effective at making HDTVs than the people who previously specialized in this task.

In general, *the more specialized the resources, the more bowed the production possibilities curve.* At the other extreme, if all resources are equally suitable for server production or production of HDTVs, the curves in Figures 2-2 and 2-3 would approach the straight line shown in our first example in Figure 2-1 on page 33.

Law of increasing relative cost
The fact that the opportunity cost of additional units of a good generally increases as society attempts to produce more of that good. This accounts for the bowed-out shape of the production possibilities curve.

QUICK QUIZ   *See page 50 for the answers. Review concepts from this section in MyEconLab.*

Trade-offs are represented graphically by a _____ _____ curve showing the maximum quantity of one good or service that can be produced, given a specific quantity of another, from a given set of resources over a specified period of time—for example, one year.

A **production possibilities curve** is drawn holding the quantity and quality of all resources _____ over the time period under study.

Points _____ the **production possibilities curve** are unattainable; points _____ are attainable but represent an inefficient use or underuse of available resources.

Because many resources are better suited for certain productive tasks than for others, society's production possibilities curve is bowed _____, reflecting the law of increasing relative cost.

Economic Growth and the Production Possibilities Curve

At any particular point in time, a society cannot be outside the production possibilities curve. *Over time*, however, it is possible to have more of everything. This occurs through economic growth. (An important reason for economic growth, capital accumulation, is discussed next. A more complete discussion of why economic growth occurs appears in Chapter 9.) Figure 2-4 shows the production possibilities curve for computer servers and HDTVs shifting outward. The two additional curves shown represent new choices open to an economy that has experienced economic growth. Such economic growth occurs because of many things, including increases in the number of workers and productive investment in equipment.

Scarcity still exists, however, no matter how much economic growth there is. At any point in time, we will always be on some production possibilities curve; thus, we will always face trade-offs. The more we have of one thing, the less we can have of others.

If a nation experiences economic growth, the production possibilities curve between servers and HDTVs will move outward, as shown in Figure 2-4. This takes time and does not occur automatically. One reason it will occur involves the choice about how much to consume today.

FIGURE 2-4

Economic Growth Allows for More of Everything

If the nation experiences economic growth, the production possibilities curve between computer servers and HDTVs will move out as shown. This takes time, however, and it does not occur automatically. This means, therefore, that we can have more of both computer servers and HDTVs only after a period of time during which we have experienced economic growth.

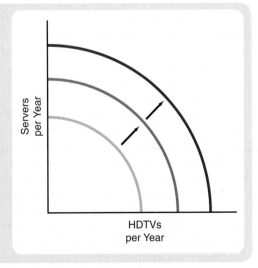

The Trade-Off Between the Present and the Future

The production possibilities curve and economic growth can be combined to examine the trade-off between present **consumption** and future consumption. When we consume today, we are using up what we call consumption or consumer goods—food and clothes, for example.

Consumption
The use of goods and services for personal satisfaction.

Why We Make Capital Goods

Why would we be willing to use productive resources to make things—capital goods—that we cannot consume directly? For one thing, capital goods enable us to produce larger quantities of consumer goods or to produce them less expensively than we otherwise could. Before fish are "produced" for the market, equipment such as fishing boats, nets, and poles is produced first. Imagine how expensive it would be to obtain fish for market without using these capital goods. Catching fish with one's hands is not an easy task. The cost per fish would be very high if capital goods weren't used.

Forgoing Current Consumption

Whenever we use productive resources to make capital goods, we are implicitly forgoing current consumption. We are waiting for some time in the future to consume the rewards that will be reaped from the use of capital goods. In effect, when we forgo current consumption to invest in capital goods, we are engaging in an economic activity that is forward-looking—we do not get instant utility or satisfaction from our activity.

The Trade-Off Between Consumption Goods and Capital Goods

To have more consumer goods in the future, we must accept fewer consumer goods today, because resources must be used in producing capital goods instead of consumer goods. In other words, an opportunity cost is involved. Every time we make a choice of more goods today, we incur an opportunity cost of fewer goods tomorrow, and every time we make a choice of more goods in the future, we incur an opportunity cost of fewer goods today. With the resources that we don't use to produce consumer goods for today, we invest in capital goods that will produce more consumer goods for us later. The trade-off is shown in Figure 2-5 on the following page. On the left in panel (a), you can see this trade-off depicted as a production possibilities curve between capital goods and consumption goods.

Assume that we are willing to give up $1 trillion worth of consumption today. We will be at point *A* in the left-hand diagram of panel (a). This will allow the economy to grow. We will have more future consumption because we invested in more capital goods today. In the right-hand diagram of panel (a), we see two goods represented, food and entertainment. The production possibilities curve will move outward if we collectively decide to restrict consumption now and invest in capital goods.

In panel (b), we show the results of our willingness to forgo even more current consumption. We move to point *C* in the left-hand side, where we have many fewer consumer goods today but produce many more capital goods. This leads to more future growth in this simplified model, and thus the production possibilities curve in the right-hand side of panel (b) shifts outward more than it did in the right-hand side of panel (a). In other words, the more we give up today, the more we can have tomorrow, provided, of course, that the capital goods are productive in future periods.

FIGURE 2-5

Capital Goods and Growth

In panel (a), the nation chooses not to consume $1 trillion, so it invests that amount in capital goods. As a result, more of all goods may be produced in the future, as shown in the right-hand diagram in panel (a). In panel (b), society chooses even more capital goods (point *C*). The result is that the production possibilities curve (PPC) moves even more to the right on the right-hand diagram in panel (b).

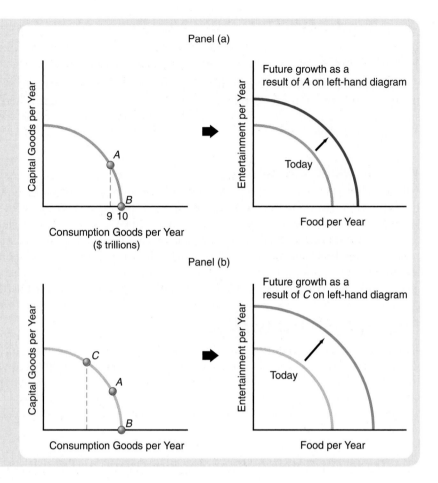

Panel (a)

Future growth as a result of *A* on left-hand diagram

Today

Panel (b)

Future growth as a result of *C* on left-hand diagram

Today

QUICK QUIZ See page 50 for the answers. Review concepts from this section in MyEconLab.

_____ goods are goods that will later be used to produce consumer goods.

A trade-off is involved between current consumption and capital goods or, alternatively, between current consumption and future consumption. The _____ we invest in capital goods today, the greater the amount of consumer goods we can produce in the future and the _____ the amount of consumer goods we can produce today.

Specialization and Greater Productivity

Specialization
The organization of economic activity so that what each person (or region) consumes is not identical to what that person (or region) produces. An individual may specialize, for example, in law or medicine. A nation may specialize in the production of coffee, computers, or digital cameras.

Specialization involves working at a relatively well-defined, limited endeavor, such as accounting or teaching. It involves the organization of economic activity among different individuals and regions. Most individuals do specialize. For example, you could change the oil in your car if you wanted to. Typically, though, you take your car to a garage and let the mechanic change the oil. You benefit by letting the garage mechanic specialize in changing the oil and in doing other repairs on your car. The specialist normally will get the job finished sooner than you could and has the proper equipment to make the job go more smoothly. Specialization usually leads to greater productivity, not only for each individual but also for the nation.

Comparative Advantage

Specialization occurs because different individuals experience different costs when they engage in the same activities. Some individuals can accurately solve mathematical problems at lower cost than others who might try to solve the same problems. Thus, those who solve math problems at lower cost sacrifice production of fewer alternative items. Some people can develop more high-quality computer programs than others while giving up less production of other items, such as clean houses and neatly manicured yards.

Comparative advantage is the ability to perform an activity *at a lower opportunity cost*. You have a comparative advantage in one activity whenever you have a lower opportunity cost of performing that activity. Comparative advantage is always a *relative* concept. You may be able to change the oil in your car; you might even be able to change it faster than the local mechanic. But if the opportunity cost you face by changing the oil exceeds the mechanic's opportunity cost, the mechanic has a comparative advantage in changing the oil. The mechanic faces a lower opportunity cost for that activity.

You may be convinced that everybody can do more of everything than you can during the same period of time and using the same resources. In this extreme situation, do you still have a comparative advantage? The answer is yes. You do not have to be a mathematical genius to figure this out. The market tells you so very clearly by offering you the highest income for the job for which you have a comparative advantage. Stated differently, to find your comparative advantage, simply find the job that maximizes your income.

Comparative advantage
The ability to produce a good or service at a lower opportunity cost compared to other producers.

Absolute Advantage

Suppose that, conversely, you have a job at a firm and are convinced that you have the ability to do every job in that company at a lower cost than everyone else who works there. You might be able to keyboard documents into a computer faster than any of the other employees, file documents in order in a file cabinet faster than any of the file clerks, and wash windows faster than any of the window washers. Indeed, you might even be able to manage the firm in less time just as effectively as the current company president—and in less time than you would have to spend in any alternative function.

If all of these self-perceptions were really true, then you would have an **absolute advantage** in all of these endeavors. In other words, if you were to spend a given amount of time in any one of them, you could produce more than anyone else in the company. Nonetheless, you would not spend your time doing these other activities. Why not? Because your advantage in undertaking the president's managerial duties is even greater. Therefore, you would find yourself specializing in that particular task even though you have an *absolute* advantage in all these other tasks. Indeed, absolute advantage is irrelevant in predicting how you will allocate your time. Only *comparative advantage* matters in determining how you will allocate your time.

Absolute advantage
The ability to produce more units of a good or service using a given quantity of labor or resource inputs. Equivalently, the ability to produce the same quantity of a good or service using fewer units of labor or resource inputs.

The coaches of sports teams often have to determine the comparative advantage of an individual player who has an absolute advantage in every aspect of the sport in question. Babe Ruth, who could hit more home runs and pitch more strikeouts per game than other players on the Boston Red Sox, was a pitcher on that professional baseball team. After he was traded to the New York Yankees, the owner and the manager decided to make him an outfielder, even though he could also hurl more strikeouts per game than other Yankees. They wanted "The Babe" to concentrate on his hitting because a home-run king would bring in more fans than a good pitcher would. Babe Ruth had an absolute advantage in both aspects of the game of baseball, but his comparative advantage was clearly in hitting homers rather than in practicing and developing his pitching game.

The opportunity cost of buying groceries is higher for some people than for others. How has this given entrepreneurs an opportunity to profit from taking grocery orders online?

E-COMMERCE EXAMPLE
A Comparative Advantage in Grocery Shopping

Traveling to a grocery store, grabbing a shopping cart, and searching through the store's aisles for items are time-consuming activities. Individuals who want a very particular grocery item, such as steak or salmon marinated with specific spices or herbs, may have to devote considerable time going to several grocery stores.

Increasingly, people are concluding that grocery shopping is a next-best alternative. These individuals allocate their time to other activities, such as earning more income, and pay others to shop for items on their grocery lists. FreshDirect is a company that takes online grocery orders from finicky eaters in

New York City. Each year FreshDirect's trucks fulfill 2 million grocery orders for $200 million worth of food by transporting 60 million items packed into 8 million boxes. The Web-based company has a comparative advantage in tracking down gourmet steaks, salmon, and a wide variety of other grocery items, so it specializes in this activity.

FOR CRITICAL ANALYSIS

Why do you suppose that people who frequently consume hard-to-find gourmet foods are among FreshDirect's most regular customers?

Scarcity, Self-Interest, and Specialization

In Chapter 1, you learned about the assumption of rational self-interest. To repeat, for the purposes of our analyses we assume that individuals are rational in that they will do what is in their own self-interest. They will not consciously carry out actions that will make them worse off. In this chapter, you learned that scarcity requires people to make choices. We *assume* that they make choices based on their self-interest. When they make these choices, they attempt to maximize benefits net of opportunity cost. In so doing, individuals choose their comparative advantage and end up specializing.

You Are There

For an example of how the concepts of comparative advantage and specialization can matter in a realistic business context, read **Specializing in Providing Baggage-Free Business Trips,** on page 44.

Division of labor
The segregation of resources into different specific tasks; for example, one automobile worker puts on bumpers, another doors, and so on.

The Division of Labor

In any firm that includes specialized human and nonhuman resources, there is a **division of labor** among those resources. The best-known example comes from Adam Smith, who in *The Wealth of Nations* illustrated the benefits of a division of labor in the making of pins, as depicted in the following example:

> One man draws out the wire, another straightens it, a third cuts it, a fourth points it, a fifth grinds it at the top for receiving the head; to make the head requires two or three distinct operations; to put it on is a peculiar business, to whiten the pins is another; it is even a trade by itself to put them into the paper.

Making pins this way allowed 10 workers without very much skill to make almost 48,000 pins "of a middling size" in a day. One worker, toiling alone, could have made perhaps 20 pins a day; therefore, 10 workers could have produced 200. Division of labor allowed for an increase in the daily output of the pin factory from 200 to 48,000! (Smith did not attribute all of the gain to the division of labor but credited also the use of machinery and the fact that less time was spent shifting from task to task.)

What we are discussing here involves a division of the resource called labor into different uses of labor. The different uses of labor are organized in such a way as to increase the amount of output possible from the fixed resources available. We can therefore talk about an organized division of labor within a firm leading to increased output.

This automobile assembly line is a good example of what concept in economics?

Comparative Advantage and Trade Among Nations

Most of our analysis of absolute advantage, comparative advantage, and specialization has dealt with individuals. Nevertheless, it is equally applicable to nations.

Trade Among Regions

Consider the United States. The Plains states have a comparative advantage in the production of grains and other agricultural goods. Relative to the Plains states, the states to the east tend to specialize in industrialized production, such as automobiles. Not surprisingly, grains are shipped from the Plains states to the eastern states, and automobiles are shipped in the reverse direction. Such specialization and trade allow for higher incomes and standards of living.

If both the Plains states and the eastern states were separate nations, the same analysis would still hold, but we would call it international trade. Indeed, the European Union (EU) is comparable to the United States in area and population, but instead of one nation, the EU has 27. What U.S. residents call *interstate* trade, Europeans call *international* trade. There is no difference, however, in the economic results—both yield greater economic efficiency and higher average incomes.

International Aspects of Trade

Political problems that normally do not occur within a particular nation often arise between nations. For example, if California avocado growers develop a cheaper method of producing a tastier avocado than growers in southern Florida use, the Florida growers will lose out. They cannot do much about the situation except try to lower their own costs of production or improve their product.

If avocado growers in Mexico, however, develop a cheaper method of producing better-tasting avocados, both California and Florida growers can (and likely will) try to raise political barriers that will prevent Mexican avocado growers from freely selling their product in the United States. U.S. avocado growers will use such arguments as "unfair" competition and loss of U.S. jobs. Certainly, avocado-growing jobs may decline in the United States, but there is no reason to believe that U.S. jobs will decline overall. Instead, former U.S. avocado workers will move into alternative employment—something that 1 million people do every *week* in the United States. If the argument of U.S. avocado growers had any validity, every time a region in the United States developed a better way to produce a product manufactured somewhere else in the country, U.S. employment would decline. That has never happened and never will.

When nations specialize where they have a comparative advantage and then trade with the rest of the world, the average standard of living in the world rises. In effect, international trade allows the world to move from inside the global production possibilities curve toward the curve itself, thereby improving worldwide economic efficiency. Thus, all countries that engage in trade can benefit from comparative advantage, just as regions in the United States benefit from interregional trade.

Go to www.econtoday.com/chapter02 to find out from the World Trade Organization how much international trade takes place. Under "Resources," click on "Trade statistics" and then click on "International Trade Statistics" for the most recent year.

QUICK QUIZ See page 50 for the answers. Review concepts from this section in MyEconLab.

With a given set of resources, specialization results in _____ output; in other words, there are gains to specilization in terms of greater material well-being.

Individuals and nations specialize in their areas of _____ advantage in order to reap the gains of specialization.

Comparative advantages are found by determining which activities have the _____ opportunity cost—that is,

which activities yield the highest return for the time and resources used.

A _____ of labor occurs when different workers are assigned different tasks. Together, the workers produce a desired product.

You Are There Specializing in Providing Baggage-Free Business Trips

When Steve Zilinek was working as an investment adviser, he noticed something about traveling businesspeople. Although many of these individuals possess considerable financial resources, they must expend another key resource when they travel—namely, time that they could otherwise devote to other activities. Zilinek estimated that packing bags, waiting at airport check-in, security, and baggage stations, and laundering clothing takes about three hours per trip—time that otherwise could be devoted to alternative pursuits.

Zilinek decided that he might have a comparative advantage in providing baggage services to frequent travelers. He founded FlyLite, a company that specializes in storing, caring for, and shipping all the items that individuals desire to have with them on business trips, such as clothing and toiletries. FlyLite's customers send the items they regularly take on business trips to the company, which places them in storage. Before a trip, a client fills out and submits a Web

form indicating which items she will require at her destination. FlyLite then arranges for the items to be shipped to her hotel. When her business trip concludes, the customer sends the items back to FlyLite, which dry cleans the clothing and then re-stores all items until her next trip. For FlyLite's clients, paying about $100 per trip for its services is the next-best alternative to devoting three hours to handling baggage on their own.

CRITICAL ANALYSIS QUESTIONS

1. *What is the approximate minimum opportunity cost of three hours of time per trip for the typical FlyLite customer?*

2. *How do you suppose that an increase in the average amount of time that people must spend dealing with baggage at airports affects the number of people utilizing FlyLite's services?*

Issues and Applications

Specialization and Division of Labor at the Speedway

CONCEPTS APPLIED

➤ Production
➤ Specialization
➤ Division of Labor

The driver wheels his high-performance racecar around the track at speeds up to 200 miles per hour. After the next turn, he decelerates down a side track to a pre-assigned location. As soon as his car comes to a halt, seven individuals rapidly converge around it: front- and rear-tire carriers, front- and rear-tire changers, an individual who jacks up the car, and two others carrying 11-gallon cans of fuel. These seven people together produce a combined service without which no auto race could long continue: the motor speedway "pit stop."

Achieving Speedy Production of Auto Services

Racing a car around an oval track at high speeds for a few hours consumes two key resources. The most obvious resource is the high-performance fuel required to keep racecar engine components spinning at thousands of revolutions per second. Another resource is tire tread, which must remain above a minimum threshold if the driver is to be able to safely accelerate, decelerate, and round turns.

Thus, the purpose of a pit stop is to refuel and change tires. From the moment that auto racing was born, racecar drivers began wrestling with how best to perform and organize these services. Obviously, at various points during a race, one person could perform the required tasks of pouring fuel, jacking up the racecar, and changing its four tires. Using a single person would never do, however, because in an auto race, speed is truly the name of the game. Racers recognized that several people could refuel a car and change its tires much faster than one person, and the idea of the speedway pit crew was born.

Division of Labor in the Pit

In gauging the production of pit services at a motor speedway, the fundamental unit of measurement is the rate at which refueling and tire-changing services are performed per unit of time. The involvement of several people is required to perform these services most rapidly. Hence, motor speedway pit crews have a natural division of labor: refueling, jacking up the car, carrying and changing front and rear tires.

After years of trial and error, racecar drivers settled on pit crews of seven members each. They found that given the technology involved in the provision of pit services, this division of labor yields the fastest rate of production.

Specialization Breeds Production Improvements in the Pits

Attaining the speediest possible pit stop requires each pit crew member's function to be highly specialized. Today, the person who jacks up a racecar aims to haul a 25-pound aluminum jack from the car's right side to the left within 3.8 seconds. Tire changers do their best to get five lug nuts off a car's wheel within 1.2 seconds. Tire carriers aim to raise 60-pound tires from the pavement to mounted positions on the car within 0.7 second. While five crew members carry out these activities with the car's body and wheels, the two crew members responsible for refueling are punching the necks of fuel cans into tank openings.

Twenty years ago, pit crews were doing well to complete a pit stop in fewer than 30 seconds. Today, a pit crew that takes more than 16 seconds to complete a stop is regarded as having failed to deliver a timely service to the driver. Thus, two decades of careful attention to division of labor and specialization have reduced by nearly 50 percent the time that a racecar driver typically spends obtaining pit services instead of racing in pursuit of prize money.

Test your understanding of this chapter by going online to **MyEconLab**.
In the Study Plan for this chapter, select Section N: News.

For Critical Analysis

1. Why do you suppose that having more than seven members tends to reduce a pit crew's service output per unit of time? (Hint: In a service pit area at a racetrack, there is limited physical space beside or beneath a racecar.)

2. Why do you suppose that there is a school, called 5 Off 5 On, that trains individuals in the fine art of rapidly removing and replacing the five lug nuts that attach tires to the wheels of racecars?

Web Resources

1. For information about a pit crew training program provided by the National Association for Stock Car Auto Racing (NASCAR), go to www.econtoday.com/chapter02.

2. To learn more about characteristics that NASCAR teams desire in their pit crew members, go to www.econtoday.com/chapter02.

Research Project

Compare the above description of the activities of a speedway pit crew with those of pin makers as described by Adam Smith (see page 42). In addition, compare the division of labor in the provision of pit services and eighteenth-century pin making to the division of labor in the production of educational services at your college or university (or, if you prefer, another production process with which you are familiar). Is the division of labor a fundamental aspect of production of goods and services?

 Here is what you should know after reading this chapter. **MyEconLab** will help you identify what you know, and where to go when you need to practice.

WHAT YOU SHOULD KNOW		WHERE TO GO TO PRACTICE
The Problem of Scarcity, Even for the Affluent Scarcity is very different from poverty. No one can obtain all one desires from nature without sacrifice. Thus, even the richest people face scarcity because they have to make choices among alternatives. Despite their high levels of income or wealth, affluent people, like everyone else, want more than they can have (in terms of goods, power, prestige, and so on).	scarcity, 28 production, 28 land, 28 labor, 29 physical capital, 29 human capital, 29 entrepreneurship, 29 goods, 29 economic goods, 29 services, 30	• **MyEconLab** Study Plan 2.1 • Audio introduction to Chapter 2 • Video: Scarcity, Resources, and Production

(continued)

 *(continued)*

WHAT YOU SHOULD KNOW		WHERE TO GO TO PRACTICE
Why Economists Consider Individuals' Wants but Not Their "Needs" Goods are all things from which individuals derive satisfaction. Economic goods are those for which the desired quantity exceeds the amount that is directly available from nature at a zero price. To economists, the term *need* is undefinable, whereas humans have unlimited *wants*, which are defined as the goods and services on which we place a positive value.		• **MyEconLab** Study Plan 2.2
Why Scarcity Leads People to Evaluate Opportunity Costs Opportunity cost is the highest-valued alternative that one must give up to obtain an item. The trade-offs that we face as individuals and as a society can be represented by a production possibilities curve (PPC), and moving from one point on a PPC to another entails incurring an opportunity cost. Along a PPC, all currently available resources and technology are being used, so obtaining more of one good requires shifting resources to production of that good and away from production of another. That is, there is an opportunity cost of allocating scarce resources toward producing one good instead of another good.	opportunity cost, 31 production possibilities curve (PPC), 32 KEY FIGURE Figure 2-1, 33	• **MyEconLab** Study Plans 2.3, 2.4 • Animated Figure 2-1 • ABC News Video: Incentives for Perfect Attendance
Why Obtaining Increasing Increments of a Good Requires Giving Up More and More Units of Other Goods Typically, resources are specialized. Thus, when society allocates additional resources to producing more units of a good, it must increasingly employ resources that would be better suited for producing other goods. As a result, the law of increasing relative cost holds. Each additional unit of a good can be obtained only by giving up more and more of other goods, which means that the production possibilities curve is bowed outward.	technology, 35 efficiency, 36 inefficient point, 36 law of increasing relative cost, 37 KEY FIGURES Figure 2-3, 37 Figure 2-4, 38	• **MyEconLab** Study Plan 2.5 • Animated Figures 2-3, 2-4
The Trade-Off Between Consumption Goods and Capital Goods If we allocate more resources to producing capital goods today, then, other things being equal, the economy will grow faster than it would have otherwise. Thus, the production possibilities curve will shift outward by a larger amount in the future, which means that we can have more consumption goods in the future. The trade-off, however, is that producing more capital goods today entails giving up consumption goods today.	consumption, 39	• **MyEconLab** Study Plans 2.6, 2.7

(continued)

 (continued)

WHAT YOU SHOULD KNOW

WHERE TO GO TO PRACTICE

Absolute Advantage versus Comparative Advantage A person has an absolute advantage if she can produce more of a good than someone else who uses the same amount of resources. An individual can gain from specializing in producing a good if she has a comparative advantage in producing that good, meaning that she can produce the good at a lower opportunity cost than someone else. By specializing in producing the good for which she has a comparative advantage, she assures herself of reaping gains from specialization in the form of a higher income.

specialization, 40
comparative
   advantage, 41
absolute advantage, 41
division of labor, 42

• **MyEconLab** Study Plans 2.8, 2.9
• Video: Absolute versus Comparative Advantage

Log in to MyEconLab, take a chapter test, and get a personalized Study Plan that tells you which concepts you understand and which ones you need to review. From there, MyEconLab will give you further practice, tutorials, animations, videos, and guided solutions.
Log in to www.myeconlab.com

PROBLEMS

All problems are assignable in myeconlab. *Answers to odd-numbered problems appear at the back of the book.*

2-1. Define opportunity cost. What is your opportunity cost of attending a class at 11:00 A.M.? How does it differ from your opportunity cost of attending a class at 8:00 A.M.?

2-2. If you receive a ticket to a concert at no charge, what, if anything, is your opportunity cost of attending the concert? How does your opportunity cost change if miserable weather on the night of the concert requires you to leave much earlier for the concert hall and greatly extends the time it takes to get home afterward?

2-3. Recently, a woman named Mary Krawiec attended an auction in Troy, New York. At the auction, a bank was seeking to sell a foreclosed property: a large Victorian house suffering from years of neglect in a neighborhood in which many properties had been on the market for years yet remained unsold. Her $10 offer was the highest bid in the auction, and she handed over a $10 bill for a title to ownership. Once she acquired the house, however, she became responsible for all taxes on the property and for an overdue water bill of $2,000. In addition, to make the house habitable, she and her husband devoted months of time and unpaid labor to renovating the property. In the process, they incurred explicit expenses totaling $65,000.

Why do you suppose that the bank was willing to sell the house to Ms. Krawiec for only $10? (Hint: Contemplate the bank's expected gain, net of all explicit and opportunity costs, if it had attempted to make the house habitable.)

2-4. The following table illustrates the points a student can earn on examinations in economics and biology if the student uses all available hours for study.

Economics	Biology
100	40
90	50
80	60
70	70
60	80
50	90
40	100

Plot this student's production possibilities curve. Does the PPC illustrate the law of increasing relative cost?

2-5. Based on the information provided in Problem 2-4, what is the opportunity cost to this student of allocating enough additional study time on economics to move her grade up from a 90 to a 100?

2-6. Consider a change in the table in Problem 2-4. The student's set of opportunities is now as follows:

Economics	Biology
100	40
90	60
80	75
70	85
60	93
50	98
40	100

Does the PPC illustrate the law of increasing relative cost? What is the opportunity cost to this student for the additional amount of study time on economics required to move her grade from 60 to 70? From 90 to 100?

2-7. Construct a production possibilities curve for a nation facing increasing opportunity costs for producing food and video games. Show how the PPC changes given the following events.

   a. A new and better fertilizer is invented.

   b. Immigration occurs, and immigrants' labor can be employed in both the agricultural sector and the video game sector.

   c. A new programming language is invented that is less costly to code and is more memory-efficient, enabling the use of smaller game cartridges.

   d. A heat wave and drought result in a 10 percent decrease in usable farmland.

Consider the following diagram when answering Problems 2-8, 2-9, and 2-10.

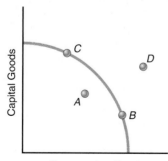

2-8. During a debate on the floor of the U.S. Senate, Senator Creighton states, "Our nation should not devote so many of its fully employed resources to producing capital goods because we already are not producing enough consumption goods for our citizens." Compared with the other labeled points on the diagram, which one could be con-

sistent with the *current* production combination choice that Senator Creighton believes the nation has made?

2-9. In response to Senator Creighton's statement reported in Problem 2-8, Senator Long replies, "We must remain at our current production combination if we want to be able to produce more consumption goods in the future." Of the labeled points on the diagram, which one could depict the *future* production combination Senator Long has in mind?

2-10. Senator Borman interjects the following comment after the statements by Senators Creighton and Long reported in Problems 2-8 and 2-9: "In fact, both of my esteemed colleagues are wrong, because an unacceptably large portion of our nation's resources is currently unemployed." Of the labeled points on the diagram, which one is consistent with Senator Borman's position?

2-11. A nation's residents can allocate their scarce resources either to producing consumption goods or to producing human capital—that is, providing themselves with training and education. The following table displays the production possibilities for this nation:

Production Combination	Units of Consumption Goods	Units of Human Capital
A	0	100
B	10	97
C	20	90
D	30	75
E	40	55
F	50	30
G	60	0

   a. Suppose that the nation's residents currently produce combination A. What is the opportunity cost of increasing production of consumption goods by 10 units? By 60 units?

   b. Does the law of increasing relative cost hold true for this nation? Why or why not?

2-12. Like physical capital, human capital produced in the present can be applied to the production of future goods and services. Consider the table in Problem 2-11, and suppose that the nation's residents are trying to choose between combination C and combination F. Other things being equal, will the future production possibilities curve for this nation be located farther outward if the nation chooses combination F instead of combination C? Explain.

2-13. You can wash, fold, and iron a basket of laundry in two hours and prepare a meal in one hour. Your roommate can wash, fold, and iron a basket of laundry in three hours and prepare a meal in one hour. Who has the absolute advantage in laundry, and who has an absolute advantage in meal preparation? Who has the comparative advantage in laundry, and who has a comparative advantage in meal preparation?

2-14. Based on the information in Problem 2-13, should you and your roommate specialize in a particular task? Why? And if so, who should specialize in which task? Show how much labor time you save if you choose to "trade" an appropriate task with your roommate as opposed to doing it yourself.

2-15. Using only the concept of comparative advantage, evaluate this statement: "A professor with a Ph.D. in physics should never mow his or her own lawn, because this would fail to take into account the professor's comparative advantage."

2-16. Country A and country B produce the same consumption goods and capital goods and currently have *identical* production possibilities curves. They also have the same resources at present, and they have access to the same technology.

　a. At present, does either country have a comparative advantage in producing capital goods? Consumption goods?

　b. Currently, country A has chosen to produce more consumption goods, compared with country B. Other things being equal, which country will experience the larger outward shift of its PPC during the next year?

ECONOMICS ON THE NET

Opportunity Cost and Labor Force Participation　Many students choose to forgo full-time employment to concentrate on their studies, thereby incurring a sizable opportunity cost. This application explores the nature of this opportunity cost.

Title: College Enrollment and Work Activity of High School Graduates

Navigation: Go to www.econtoday.com/chapter02 to visit the Bureau of Labor Statistics (BLS) home page. Select A–Z Index and then click on *Educational attainment (Statistics)*. Finally, under the heading "Economic News Releases," click on "Annual," and then click on *College Enrollment and Work Activity of High School Graduates*.

Application　Read the abbreviated report on college enrollment and work activity of high school graduates. Then answer the following questions.

1. Based on the article, explain who the BLS considers to be in the labor force and who it does not view as part of the labor force.

2. What is the difference in labor force participation rates between high school students entering four-year universities and those entering two-year universities? Using the concept of opportunity cost, explain the difference.

3. What is the difference in labor force participation rates between part-time college students and full-time college students? Using the concept of opportunity cost, explain the difference.

For Group Study and Analysis　Read the last paragraph of the article. Then divide the class into two groups. The first group should explain, based on the concept of opportunity cost, the difference in labor force participation rates between youths not in school but with a high school diploma and youths not in school and without a high school diploma. The second group should explain, based on opportunity cost, the difference in labor force participation rates between men and women not in school but with a high school diploma and men and women not in school and without a high school diploma.

ANSWERS TO QUICK QUIZZES

p. 30: (i) Scarcity; (ii) land . . . labor . . . physical . . . human . . . entrepreneurship; (iii) Wants; (iv) need

p. 34: (i) next-highest; (ii) opportunity; (iii) next-best; (iv) production possibilities

p. 38: (i) production possibilities; (ii) fixed; (iii) outside . . . inside; (iv) outward

p. 40: (i) Capital; (ii) more . . . smaller

p. 44: (i) higher; (ii) comparative; (iii) lowest; (iv) division

Demand and Supply

3

Three decades ago, about 45 percent of U.S. residents were classified as "overweight." Today, estimates indicate that as many as 67 percent of U.S. residents fall into this category. About 31 percent of the U.S. population is classified as extremely overweight, or obese, which is more than double the percentage of 30 years ago. One explanation for higher body weights is that people are exercising less, and thus the calories they consume are being transformed into body mass instead of energy. Another is that people are simply choosing to consume more food than in years past. Determining why individuals are opting to eat more requires an understanding, which you will develop by reading this chapter, of how two key factors—price and income—influence desired consumption of an item such as food.

LEARNING OBJECTIVES

MyEconLab helps you master each objective and study more efficiently. See end of chapter for details.

After reading this chapter, you should be able to:

➤ Explain the law of demand

➤ Discuss the difference between money prices and relative prices

➤ Distinguish between changes in demand and changes in quantity demanded

➤ Explain the law of supply

➤ Distinguish between changes in supply and changes in quantity supplied

➤ Understand how the interaction of the demand for and supply of a commodity determines the market price of the commodity and the equilibrium quantity of the commodity that is produced and consumed

? **DID YOU KNOW THAT** no new oil refineries—facilities that refine crude oil into transportation fuels such as gasoline—have been built in the United States since 1976? Recently, however, Hyperion, a Dallas-based company, announced its intention to build a new refinery at Elk Point, South Dakota, which would refine about 400,000 barrels of heavy Canadian crude oil per day. Hyperion indicated that the key factor motivating its decision was a significant, sustained increase in the U.S. price of gasoline during the preceding years.

If we use the economist's primary set of tools, *demand* and *supply,* we can develop a better understanding of why we sometimes observe relatively large increases in the price of gasoline. We can also better understand why a persistent increase in the price of gasoline ultimately induces an increase in gasoline production. Demand and supply are two ways of categorizing the influences on the prices of goods that you buy and the quantities available. Indeed, demand and supply characterize much economic analysis of the world around us.

As you will see throughout this text, the operation of the forces of demand and supply takes place in *markets*. A **market** is an abstract concept summarizing all of the arrangements individuals have for exchanging with one another. Goods and services are sold in markets, such as the automobile market, the health care market, and the market for Internet DSL services. Workers offer their services in the labor market. Companies, or firms, buy workers' labor services in the labor market. Firms also buy other inputs in order to produce the goods and services that you buy as a consumer. Firms purchase machines, buildings, and land. These markets are in operation at all times. One of the most important activities in these markets is the determination of the prices of all of the inputs and outputs that are bought and sold in our complicated economy. To understand the determination of prices, you first need to look at the law of demand.

Market
All of the arrangements that individuals have for exchanging with one another. Thus, for example, we can speak of the labor market, the automobile market, and the credit market.

Demand
A schedule showing how much of a good or service people will purchase at any price during a specified time period, other things being constant.

Law of demand
The observation that there is a negative, or inverse, relationship between the price of any good or service and the quantity demanded, holding other factors constant.

Demand

Demand has a special meaning in economics. It refers to the quantities of specific goods or services that individuals, taken singly or as a group, will purchase at various possible prices, other things being constant. We can therefore talk about the demand for microprocessor chips, french fries, multifunction printer-copiers, children, and criminal activities.

The Law of Demand

Associated with the concept of demand is the **law of demand,** which can be stated as follows:

> *When the price of a good goes up, people buy less of it, other things being equal. When the price of a good goes down, people buy more of it, other things being equal.*

The law of demand tells us that the quantity demanded of any commodity is inversely related to its price, other things being equal. In an inverse relationship, one variable moves up in value when the other moves down. The law of demand states that a change in price causes a change in the quantity demanded in the *opposite* direction.

Notice that we tacked on to the end of the law of demand the statement "other things being equal." We referred to this in Chapter 1 as the *ceteris paribus* assumption. It means, for example, that when we predict that people will buy fewer DVD players if their price goes up, we are holding constant the price of all other goods in the economy as well as people's incomes. Implicitly, therefore, if we are assuming that no other

How does the law of demand affect how much gas people buy?

prices change when we examine the price behavior of DVD players, we are looking at the *relative* price of DVD players.

The law of demand is supported by millions of observations of people's behavior in the marketplace. Theoretically, it can be derived from an economic model based on rational behavior, as was discussed in Chapter 1. Basically, if nothing else changes and the price of a good falls, the lower price induces us to buy more over a certain period of time because we can enjoy additional net gains that were unavailable at the higher price. If you examine your own behavior, you will see that it generally follows the law of demand.

Relative Prices versus Money Prices

The **relative price** of any commodity is its price in terms of another commodity. The price that you pay in dollars and cents for any good or service at any point in time is called its **money price.** You might hear from your grandparents, "My first new car cost only fifteen hundred dollars." The implication, of course, is that the price of cars today is outrageously high because the average new car may cost $32,000. But that is not an accurate comparison. What was the price of the average house during that same year? Perhaps it was only $12,000. By comparison, then, given that the average price of houses today is close to $270,000, the price of a new car today doesn't sound so far out of line, does it?

How much have both the price of attending college and the relative price of textbooks increased in recent years?

Relative price
The money price of one commodity divided by the money price of another commodity; the number of units of one commodity that must be sacrificed to purchase one unit of another commodity.

Money price
The price that we observe today, expressed in today's dollars; also called the *absolute* or *nominal price*.

EXAMPLE
College Students Face Higher Relative Prices

If you feel that you are paying relatively high prices for your college training, you are correct. During the past 20 years, average tuition and fees at U.S. colleges and universities have increased by 67 percent more than the average prices of other goods and services. The price of an average college textbook has risen about 60 percent compared with the average prices of other items. Thus, the relative prices of college enrollment and reading materials have increased substantially.

FOR CRITICAL ANALYSIS
In the past two decades, has the average price of attending college increased or decreased relative to the average price of a textbook?

The point is that money prices during different time periods don't tell you much. You have to calculate relative prices. Consider an example of the price of 4-gigabyte flash memory drives versus the price of 4 gigabytes of rewritable DVDs from last year and this year. In Table 3-1 on page 54, we show the money prices of flash memory drives and rewritable DVDs for two years during which they have both gone down. That means that in today's dollars we have to pay out less for both flash memory drives and rewritable DVDs. If we look, though, at the relative prices of flash memory drives and rewritable DVDs, we find that last year, 4-gigabyte flash memory drives were four times as expensive as 4-gigabytes of rewritable DVDs, whereas this year they are only three and a half times as expensive. Conversely, if we compare rewritable DVDs to flash memory drives, last year the price of rewritable DVDs was 25 percent of the price of flash memory drives, but today the price of flash memory drives is about

TABLE 3-1

Money Price versus Relative Price

The money prices of both 4-gigabyte flash memory drives and 4 gigabytes of rewritable DVDs have fallen. But the relative price of rewritable DVDs has risen (or conversely, the relative price of flash memory drives has fallen).

	Money Price		Relative Price	
	Price Last Year	Price This Year	Price Last Year	Price This Year
4-Gigabyte flash memory drives	$20	$14	$\dfrac{\$20}{\$5} = 4.0$	$\dfrac{\$14}{\$4} = 3.50$
4 Gigabytes of rewritable DVDs	$5	$4	$\dfrac{\$5}{\$20} = 0.25$	$\dfrac{\$4}{\$14} = 0.29$

29 percent of the price of flash memory drives. In the one-year period, although both prices have declined in money terms, the relative price of rewritable DVDs has risen relative to that of flash memory drives.

Sometimes relative price changes occur because the quality of a product improves, thereby bringing about a decrease in the item's effective *price per constant-quality unit*. The price of an item may decrease simply because producers have reduced the item's quality. Thus, when evaluating the effects of price changes, we must always compare *price per constant-quality unit*.

For many Web surfers, speed defines quality. What difference does it make when the speed of Internet access is taken into account in comparisons of monthly prices for Internet broadband access?

E-COMMERCE EXAMPLE
Adjusting the Price of Broadband Service for Quality

In most U.S. locales, basic broadband Internet service is priced at about $15 per month. This appears to compare favorably with most locations in France, where the price of basic broadband Internet access is about $36 per month.

U.S. providers, however, typically offer broadband speeds of less than 0.77 megabit per second, implying a speed-adjusted price as high as $20 per megabit in most U.S. locales. In contrast, French service providers offer speeds as high as 20 megabits per second, yielding a speed-adjusted price as low as $1.80 per megabit. Thus, the U.S. speed-adjusted price is nearly 10 times higher than the French price.

FOR CRITICAL ANALYSIS
In some U.S. locales, broadband access service with a speed of 20 megabits per second is now available at a price of about $50 per month. How does this price compare with the speed-adjusted price in France?

QUICK QUIZ   *See page 81 for the answers. Review concepts from this section in MyEconLab.*

The **law of demand** posits a(n) _____ relationship between the quantity demanded of a good and its price, other things being equal.

The law of _____ applies when other things, such as income and the prices of all other goods and services, are held constant.

The Demand Schedule

Let's take a hypothetical demand situation to see how the inverse relationship between the price and the quantity demanded looks (holding other things equal). We will consider the quantity of 256-megabyte secure digital cards (also known as "SD cards," used in cameras and other digital devices) demanded *per year*. Without stating the *time dimension*, we could not make sense out of this demand relationship because the numbers would be different if we were talking about the quantity demanded per month or the quantity demanded per decade.

In addition to implicitly or explicitly stating a time dimension for a demand relationship, we are also implicitly referring to *constant-quality units* of the good or service in question. Prices are always expressed in constant-quality units in order to avoid the problem of comparing commodities that are in fact not truly comparable.

In panel (a) of Figure 3-1, we see that if the price is $1 apiece, 50 secure digital (SD) cards will be bought each year by our representative individual, but if the price is $5 apiece, only 10 SD cards will be bought each year. This reflects the law of demand. Panel (a) is also called simply demand, or a *demand schedule*, because it gives a schedule of alternative quantities demanded per year at different possible prices.

The Demand Curve

Tables expressing relationships between two variables can be represented in graphical terms. To do this, we need only construct a graph that has the price per constant-quality secure digital card on the vertical axis and the quantity measured in constant-quality SD

FIGURE 3-1

The Individual Demand Schedule and the Individual Demand Curve

In panel (a), we show combinations *A* through *E* of the quantities of secure digital (SD) cards demanded, measured in constant-quality units at prices ranging from $5 down to $1 apiece. These combinations are points on the demand schedule. In panel (b), we plot combinations *A* through *E* on a grid. The result is the individual demand curve for SD cards.

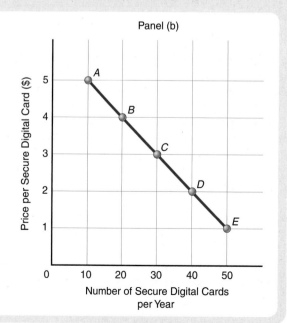

Panel (a)

Combination	Price per Constant-Quality Secure Digital Card	Quantity of Constant-Quality Secure Digital Cards per Year
A	$5	10
B	4	20
C	3	30
D	2	40
E	1	50

Panel (b)

Demand curve

A graphical representation of the demand schedule; a negatively sloped line showing the inverse relationship between the price and the quantity demanded (other things being equal).

Market demand

The demand of all consumers in the marketplace for a particular good or service. The summation at each price of the quantity demanded by each individual.

cards per year on the horizontal axis. All we have to do is take combinations *A* through *E* from panel (a) of Figure 3-1 and plot those points in panel (b). Now we connect the points with a smooth line, and *voilà*, we have a **demand curve.** It is downward sloping (from left to right) to indicate the inverse relationship between the price of SD cards and the quantity demanded per year. Our presentation of demand schedules and curves applies equally well to all commodities, including dental floss, bagels, textbooks, credit, and labor. Remember, the demand curve is simply a graphical representation of the law of demand.

Individual versus Market Demand Curves

The demand schedule shown in panel (a) of Figure 3-1 on the previous page and the resulting demand curve shown in panel (b) are both given for an individual. As we shall see, the determination of price in the marketplace depends on, among other things, the

---

FIGURE 3-2

The Horizontal Summation of Two Demand Curves

Panel (a) shows how to sum the demand schedule for one buyer with that of another buyer. In column 2 is the quantity demanded by buyer 1, taken from panel (a) of Figure 3-1 on page 55. Column 4 is the sum of columns 2 and 3.

We plot the demand curve for buyer 1 in panel (b) and the demand curve for buyer 2 in panel (c). When we add those two demand curves horizontally, we get the market demand curve for two buyers, shown in panel (d).

Panel (a)

(1) Price per Secure Digital Card	(2) Buyer 1's Quantity Demanded	(3) Buyer 2's Quantity Demanded	(4) = (2) + (3) Combined Quantity Demanded per Year
$5	10	10	20
4	20	20	40
3	30	40	70
2	40	50	90
1	50	60	110

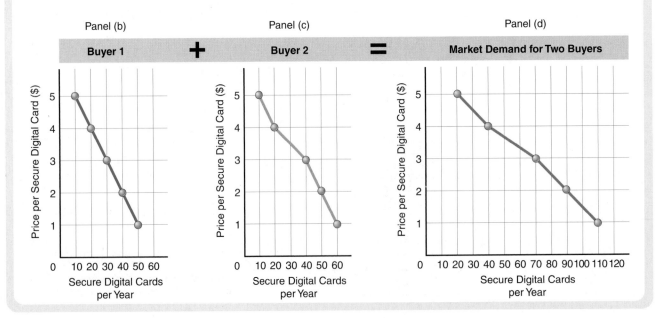

market demand for a particular commodity. The way in which we measure a market demand schedule and derive a market demand curve for secure digital cards or any other good or service is by summing (at each price) the individual quantities demanded by all buyers in the market. Suppose that the market demand for SD cards consists of only two buyers: buyer 1, for whom we've already shown the demand schedule, and buyer 2, whose demand schedule is displayed in column 3 of panel (a) of Figure 3-2 on the facing page. Column 1 shows the price, and column 2 shows the quantity demanded by buyer 1 at each price. These data are taken directly from Figure 3-1 on page 55. In column 3, we show the quantity demanded by buyer 2. Column 4 shows the total quantity demanded at each price, which is obtained by simply adding columns 2 and 3. Graphically, in panel (d) of Figure 3-2, we add the demand curves of buyer 1 [panel (b)] and buyer 2 [panel (c)] to derive the market demand curve.

There are, of course, numerous potential consumers of SD cards. We'll simply assume that the summation of all of the consumers in the market results in a demand schedule, given in panel (a) of Figure 3-3, and a demand curve, given in panel (b). The quantity demanded is now measured in millions of units per year. Remember, panel (b) in Figure 3-3 shows the market demand curve for the millions of users of SD cards. The "market" demand curve that we derived in Figure 3-2 was undertaken assuming that there were only two buyers in the entire market. That's why we assume that the "market" demand curve for two buyers in panel (d) of Figure 3-2 is not a smooth line, whereas the true market demand curve in panel (b) of Figure 3-3 is a smooth line with no kinks.

FIGURE 3-3

The Market Demand Schedule for Secure Digital Cards

In panel (a), we add up the existing demand schedules for secure digital cards. In panel (b), we plot the quantities from panel (a) on a grid; connecting them produces the market demand curve for secure digital cards.

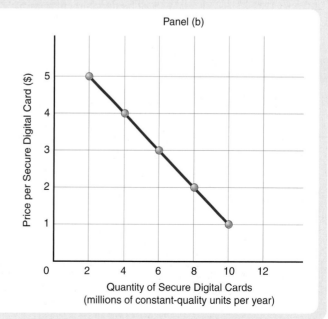

Panel (a)

Price per Constant-Quality Secure Digital Card	Total Quantity Demanded of Constant-Quality Secure Digital Cards per Year (millions)
$5	2
4	4
3	6
2	8
1	10

QUICK QUIZ *See page 81 for the answers. Review concepts from this section in MyEconLab.*

We measure the **demand schedule** in terms of a time dimension and in _____-quality units.

The _____ _____ curve is derived by summing the quantity demanded by individuals at each price. Graphically, we add the individual demand curves horizontally to derive the total, or market, demand curve.

Shifts in Demand

Assume that the federal government gives every student registered in a college, university, or technical school in the United States a laptop computer with a slot for secure digital cards. The demand curve presented in panel (b) of Figure 3-3 on the preceding page would no longer be an accurate representation of total market demand for SD cards. What we have to do is shift the curve outward, or to the right, to represent the rise in demand that would result from this program. There will now be an increase in the number of SD cards demanded at *each and every possible price*. The demand curve shown in Figure 3-4 will shift from D_1 to D_2. Take any price, say, $3 per SD card. Originally, before the federal government giveaway of laptop computers, the amount demanded at $3 was 6 million SD cards per year. After the government giveaway of laptop computers, however, the new amount demanded at the $3 price is 10 million SD cards per year. What we have seen is a shift in the demand for SD cards.

Under different circumstances, the shift can also go in the opposite direction. What if colleges uniformly prohibited the use of laptop computers by any of their students? Such a regulation would cause a shift inward—to the left—of the demand curve for SD cards. In Figure 3-4, the demand curve would shift to D_3; the number demanded would now be less at each and every possible price.

The Other Determinants of Demand

The demand curve in panel (b) of Figure 3-3 is drawn with other things held constant, specifically all of the other factors that determine how many SD cards will be bought.

FIGURE 3-4

A Shift in the Demand Curve

If some factor other than price changes, we can show its effect by moving the entire demand curve, say, from D_1 to D_2. We have assumed in our example that this move was precipitated by the government's giving a laptop computer to every registered college student in the United States. Thus, at *all* prices, a larger number of secure digital cards would be demanded than before. Curve D_3 represents reduced demand compared to curve D_1, caused by a prohibition of laptop computers on campus.

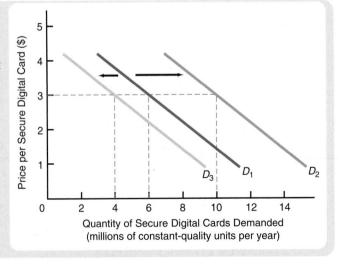

There are many such determinants. We refer to these determinants as ***ceteris paribus* conditions,** and they include consumers' income; tastes and preferences; the prices of related goods; expectations regarding future prices and future incomes; and market size (number of potential buyers). Let's examine each of these determinants more closely.

INCOME   For most goods, an increase in income will lead to an increase in demand. That is, an increase in income will lead to a rightward shift in the position of the demand curve from, say, D_1 to D_2 in Figure 3-4. You can avoid confusion about shifts in curves by always relating a rise in demand to a rightward shift in the demand curve and a fall in demand to a leftward shift in the demand curve. Goods for which the demand rises when consumer income rises are called **normal goods.** Most goods, such as shoes, computers, and flash memory drives, are "normal goods." For some goods, however, demand *falls* as income rises. These are called **inferior goods.** Beans might be an example. As households get richer, they tend to purchase fewer and fewer beans and purchase more and more meat. (The terms *normal* and *inferior* are merely part of the economist's lexicon; no value judgments are associated with them.)

Remember, a shift to the left in the demand curve represents a decrease in demand, and a shift to the right represents an increase in demand.

TASTES AND PREFERENCES   A change in consumer tastes in favor of a good can shift its demand curve outward to the right. When Pokémon trading cards became the rage, the demand curve for them shifted outward to the right; when the rage died out, the demand curve shifted inward to the left. Fashions depend to a large extent on people's tastes and preferences. Economists have little to say about the determination of tastes; that is, they don't have any "good" theories of taste determination or why people buy one brand of product rather than others. Advertisers, however, have various theories that they use to try to make consumers prefer their products over those of competitors.

How has "Web buzz" influenced preferences regarding remote-controlled toy helicopters and hence the demand for these items?

Ceteris paribus conditions
Determinants of the relationship between price and quantity that are unchanged along a curve; changes in these factors cause the curve to shift.

Normal goods
Goods for which demand rises as income rises. Most goods are normal goods.

Inferior goods
Goods for which demand falls as income rises.

E-COMMERCE EXAMPLE
Video Bloggers Generate a Takeoff in Toy Helicopter Demand

During the past couple of years, video bloggers on YouTube and Internet viral-network participants have directed Web viewers to creative videos of remote-controlled toy helicopters in action. Kids of all ages, including adults rediscovering the "child within," have been captivated by videos of toy helicopters rumbling above rough terrain, gliding over lakes, and being chased by housecats. Many have decided that they wish to have one of the toys to control on their own. As a consequence, the number of toy helicopters demanded at prevailing prices has risen by hundreds of thousands of units per year. The demand curve for remote-controlled toy helicopters has shifted outward and to the right.

FOR CRITICAL ANALYSIS
What do you suppose has happened in recent years to the demand for toy helicopters that are incapable of flying under their own power via remote control?

PRICES OF RELATED GOODS: SUBSTITUTES AND COMPLEMENTS   Demand schedules are always drawn with the prices of all other commodities held constant. That is to say, when deriving a given demand curve, we assume that only the price of the good under study changes. For example, when we draw the demand curve for butter, we assume that the price of margarine is held constant. When we draw the demand curve for home cinema speakers, we assume that the price of surround-sound amplifiers is held constant. When we refer to *related goods*, we are talking about goods for which demand is interdependent. If a change in the price of one good shifts the demand for another good, those two goods have interdependent demands. There are two types of demand interdependencies: those in which goods are *substitutes* and those in which goods are *complements*. We can define and distinguish between substitutes and complements in terms of how the change in price of one commodity affects the demand for its related commodity.

Substitutes

Two goods are substitutes when a change in the price of one causes a shift in demand for the other in the same direction as the price change.

Butter and margarine are **substitutes.** Either can be consumed to satisfy the same basic want. Let's assume that both products originally cost $2 per pound. If the price of butter remains the same and the price of margarine falls from $2 per pound to $1 per pound, people will buy more margarine and less butter. The demand curve for butter shifts inward to the left. If, conversely, the price of margarine rises from $2 per pound to $3 per pound, people will buy more butter and less margarine. The demand curve for butter shifts outward to the right. In other words, an increase in the price of margarine will lead to an increase in the demand for butter, and an increase in the price of butter will lead to an increase in the demand for margarine. For substitutes, a change in the price of a substitute will cause a change in demand *in the same direction*.

How do you suppose that laboratory techniques that replicate natural geologic processes are contributing to a decrease in the demand for diamonds extracted from the earth's interior?

EXAMPLE
Diamonds May Not Really Be Forever

The day that sellers of diamonds have long dreaded has arrived. Several professionals who have each spent more than 700 hours in classrooms to become certified experts on precious stones examine three gems. The first gem is a real diamond, created by natural geologic processes beneath the earth's surface. The second is cubic zirconia, a fake diamond commonly used in costume jewelry. The third is something new—a "synthetic" diamond. It is a gem-quality diamond produced in a laboratory by machines that exert pressures 58,000 times that of the earth's at temperatures exceeding 2,300 degrees Fahrenheit. The jewelry experts readily distinguish cubic zirconia from the true diamond. But when they view the synthetic diamond, they cannot tell that it is not a real

diamond until they examine it under a microscope and spot its inscribed serial number. Yet the experts have already pronounced the synthetic gem the highest quality of the three.

A number of U.S. jewelry retailers are utilizing synthetic diamonds, which are available at lower prices than real diamonds. At the same time, they are purchasing fewer real diamonds. Thus, the availability of the lower-priced substitute gems is reducing the demand for true gems.

FOR CRITICAL ANALYSIS

In what direction has the demand curve for real diamonds shifted as lower-priced synthetic diamonds have become available?

Complements

Two goods are complements when a change in the price of one causes an opposite shift in the demand for the other.

For **complements,** goods typically consumed together, the situation is reversed. Consider desktop computers and printers. We draw the demand curve for printers with the price of desktop computers held constant. If the price per constant-quality unit of computers decreases from, say, $700 to $500, that will encourage more people to purchase computer peripheral devices. They will now buy more printers, at any given printer price, than before. The demand curve for printers will shift outward to the right. If, by contrast, the price of desktop computers increases from $550 to $750, fewer people will purchase computer peripheral devices. The demand curve for printers will shift inward to the left. To summarize, a decrease in the price of computers leads to an increase in the demand for printers. An increase in the price of computers leads to a decrease in the demand for printers. Thus, for complements, a change in the price of a product will cause a change in demand *in the opposite direction* for the other good.

EXPECTATIONS Consumers' expectations regarding future prices and future incomes will prompt them to buy more or less of a particular good without a change in its current money price. For example, consumers getting wind of a scheduled 100 percent increase in the price of secure digital cards next month will buy more of them today at today's prices. Today's demand curve for SD cards will shift from D_1 to D_2 in Figure 3-4 on page 58. The opposite would occur if a decrease in the price of SD cards were scheduled for next month (from D_1 to D_3).

Expectations of a rise in income may cause consumers to want to purchase more of everything today at today's prices. Again, such a change in expectations of higher future income will cause a shift in the demand curve from D_1 to D_2 in Figure 3-4.

Finally, expectations that goods will not be available at any price will induce consumers to stock up now, increasing current demand.

MARKET SIZE (NUMBER OF POTENTIAL BUYERS) An increase in the number of potential buyers (holding buyers' incomes constant) at any given price shifts the market demand curve outward. Conversely, a reduction in the number of potential buyers at any given price shifts the market demand curve inward.

Changes in Demand versus Changes in Quantity Demanded

We have made repeated references to demand and to quantity demanded. It is important to realize that there is a difference between a *change in demand* and a *change in quantity demanded.*

Demand refers to a schedule of planned rates of purchase and depends on a great many *ceteris paribus* conditions, such as incomes, expectations, and the prices of substitutes or complements. Whenever there is a change in a *ceteris paribus* condition, there will be a change in demand—a shift in the entire demand curve to the right or to the left.

A quantity demanded is a specific quantity at a specific price, represented by a single point on a demand curve. When price changes, quantity demanded changes according to the law of demand, and there will be a movement from one point to another along the same demand curve. Look at Figure 3-5 on the following page. At a price of $3 per secure digital card, 6 million SD cards per year are demanded. If the price falls to $1, quantity demanded increases to 10 million per year. This movement occurs because the current market price for the product changes. In Figure 3-5, you can see the arrow pointing down the given demand curve D.

When you think of demand, think of the entire curve. Quantity demanded, in contrast, is represented by a single point on the demand curve.

A change or shift in demand is a movement of the entire curve. The only thing that can cause the entire curve to move is a change in a determinant other than its own price.

If the price of iPods goes down, what will happen to the demand for amplified speaker systems for iPods?

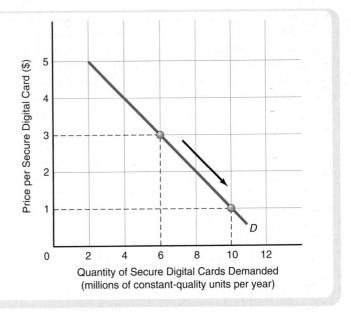

FIGURE 3-5

Movement Along a Given Demand Curve

A change in price changes the quantity of a good demanded. This can be represented as movement along a given demand schedule. If, in our example, the price of secure digital cards falls from $3 to $1 apiece, the quantity demanded will increase from 6 million to 10 million units per year.

In economic analysis, we cannot emphasize too much the following distinction that must constantly be made:

A change in a good's own price leads to a change in quantity demanded for any given demand curve, other things held constant. This is a movement along the curve.

A change in any of the ceteris paribus conditions for demand leads to a change in demand. This causes a shift of the curve.

QUICK QUIZ See page 81 for the answers. Review concepts from this section in MyEconLab.

Demand curves are drawn with determinants other than the price of the good held constant. These other determinants, called *ceteris paribus* conditions, are (1) _____; (2) _____; (3) _____; (4) _____; and (5) _____ at any given price. If any one of these determinants changes, the demand curve will shift to the right or to the left.

A change in demand comes about only because of a change in the _____ _____ conditions of demand. This change in demand is a shift in the demand curve to the left or to the right.

A change in the quantity demanded comes about when there is a change in the price of the good (other things held constant). Such a change in quantity demanded involves _____ _____ a given demand curve.

The Law of Supply

Supply
A schedule showing the relationship between price and quantity supplied for a specified period of time, other things being equal.

The other side of the basic model in economics involves the quantities of goods and services that firms will offer for sale to the market. The **supply** of any good or service is the amount that firms will produce and offer for sale under certain conditions during a specified time period. The relationship between price and quantity supplied, called the **law of supply,** can be summarized as follows:

> *At higher prices, a larger quantity will generally be supplied than at lower prices, all other things held constant. At lower prices, a smaller quantity will generally be supplied than at higher prices, all other things held constant.*

Law of supply
The observation that the higher the price of a good, the more of that good sellers will make available over a specified time period, other things being equal.

There is generally a direct relationship between price and quantity supplied. For supply, as the price rises, the quantity supplied rises; as price falls, the quantity supplied also falls. Producers are normally willing to produce and sell more of their product at a higher price than at a lower price, other things being constant. At $5 per secure digital card, manufacturers would almost certainly be willing to supply a larger quantity than at $1 per SD card, assuming, of course, that no other prices in the economy had changed.

As with the law of demand, millions of instances in the real world have given us confidence in the law of supply. On a theoretical level, the law of supply is based on a model in which producers and sellers seek to make the most gain possible from their activities. For example, as a manufacturer attempts to produce more and more SD cards over the same time period, it will eventually have to hire more workers, pay overtime wages (which are higher), and overutilize its machines. Only if offered a higher price per SD card will the manufacturer be willing to incur these higher costs. That is why the law of supply implies a direct relationship between price and quantity supplied.

How do you suppose that producers of minerals responded when prices of minerals rose during the 2000s?

EXAMPLE
Mining Production's Direct Response to Higher Prices for Minerals

Prices of minerals have jumped significantly during the 2000s. For instance, the price of uranium oxide, a mineral used as a key ingredient in fuel for nuclear power plants, has risen from just over $7 per pound in 2001 to more than $40 per pound today. Prices of other minerals, including nickel, zinc, copper, iron ore, and gold, have climbed as well. In response, mining companies have unveiled plans to carve out more mines. For instance, global minerals-producing firms such as BHP Billiton, Anglo American PLC, and OAO

Rusal have indicated that they intend to nearly double their mining production by 2011.

FOR CRITICAL ANALYSIS
Some observers of markets for minerals suggest that prices of minerals may decline during the 2010s. Other things being equal, how would you expect mining production to respond if this prediction holds true?

The Supply Schedule

Just as we were able to construct a demand schedule, we can construct a *supply schedule*, which is a table relating prices to the quantity supplied at each price. A supply schedule can also be referred to simply as *supply*. It is a set of planned production rates that depends on the price of the product. We show the individual supply schedule for a hypothetical producer in panel (a) of Figure 3-6 on the next page. At a price of $1 per secure digital card, for example, this producer will supply 20,000 SD cards per year. At a price of $5 per SD card, this producer will supply 55,000 SD cards per year.

FIGURE 3-6

The Individual Producer's Supply Schedule and Supply Curve for Secure Digital Cards

Panel (a) shows that at higher prices, a hypothetical supplier will be willing to provide a greater quantity of secure digital cards. We plot the various price-quantity combinations in panel (a) on the grid in panel (b). When we connect these points, we create the individual supply curve for SD cards. It is positively sloped.

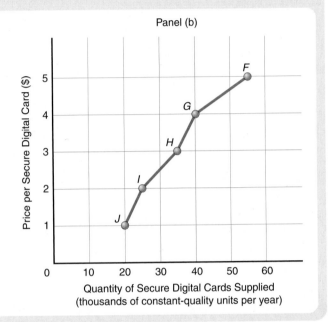

Panel (a)

Combination	Price per Constant-Quality Secure Digital Card	Quantity of Secure Digital Cards Supplied (thousands of constant-quality units per year)
F	$5	55
G	4	40
H	3	35
I	2	25
J	1	20

The Supply Curve

Supply curve

The graphical representation of the supply schedule; a line (curve) showing the supply schedule, which generally slopes upward (has a positive slope), other things being equal.

We can convert the supply schedule from panel (a) of Figure 3-6 into a **supply curve,** just as we earlier created a demand curve in Figure 3-1 on page 55. All we do is take the price-quantity combinations from panel (a) of Figure 3-6 and plot them in panel (b). We have labeled these combinations *F* through *J.* Connecting these points, we obtain an upward-sloping curve that shows the typically direct relationship between price and quantity supplied. Again, we have to remember that we are talking about quantity supplied *per year,* measured in constant-quality units.

The Market Supply Curve

Just as we summed the individual demand curves to obtain the market demand curve, we sum the individual producers' supply curves to obtain the market supply curve. Look at Figure 3-7, in which we horizontally sum two typical supply curves for manufacturers of SD cards. Supplier 1's data are taken from Figure 3-6. Supplier 2 is added. The numbers are presented in panel (a). The graphical representation of supplier 1 is in panel (b), of supplier 2 in panel (c), and of the summation in panel (d). The result, then, is the supply curve for SD cards, for suppliers 1 and 2. We assume that there are more suppliers of SD cards, however. The total market supply schedule and total market supply curve for SD cards are represented in Figure 3-8 on page 66, with the curve in panel (b) obtained by adding all of the supply curves such as those shown in panels (b) and (c) of Figure 3-7. Notice the difference between the market supply curve with only two suppliers in Figure 3-7 and the one with many suppliers—the entire true market—in panel (b) of Figure 3-8. (For simplicity, we assume that the true total market supply curve is a straight line.)

You Are There

To learn how the law of supply applies to the production of specialized insects, read **Beetle Factories Respond to Higher Demand for Weed-Eating Bugs,** on page 75.

FIGURE 3-7

Horizontal Summation of Supply Curves

In panel (a), we show the data for two individual suppliers of secure digital cards. Adding how much each is willing to supply at different prices, we come up with the combined quantities supplied in column 4. When we plot the values in columns 2 and 3 on grids from panels (b) and (c) and add them horizontally, we obtain the combined supply curve for the two suppliers in question, shown in panel (d).

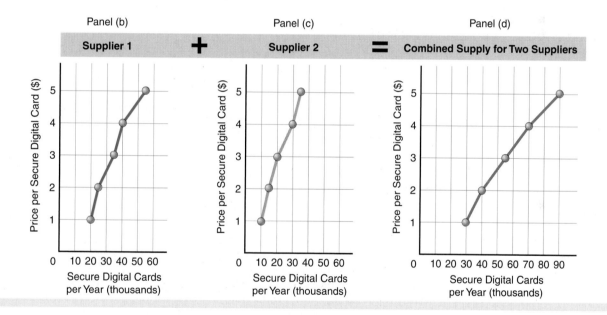

Panel (a)

(1) Price per Secure Digital Card	(2) Supplier 1's Quantity Supplied (thousands)	(3) Supplier 2's Quantity Supplied (thousands)	(4) = (2) + (3) Combined Quantity Supplied per Year (thousands)
$5	55	35	90
4	40	30	70
3	35	20	55
2	25	15	40
1	20	10	30

Note what happens at the market level when price changes. If the price is $3, the quantity supplied is 6 million. If the price goes up to $4, the quantity supplied increases to 8 million per year. If the price falls to $2, the quantity supplied decreases to 4 million per year. Changes in quantity supplied are represented by movements along the supply curve in panel (b) of Figure 3-8 on the following page.

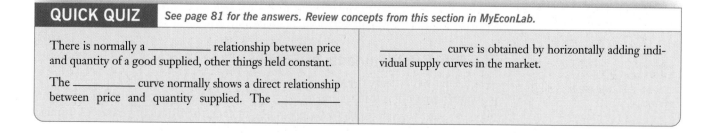

QUICK QUIZ   *See page 81 for the answers. Review concepts from this section in MyEconLab.*

There is normally a _____ relationship between price and quantity of a good supplied, other things held constant.

The _____ curve normally shows a direct relationship between price and quantity supplied. The _____

_____ curve is obtained by horizontally adding individual supply curves in the market.

FIGURE 3-8

The Market Supply Schedule and the Market Supply Curve for Secure Digital Cards

In panel (a), we show the summation of all the individual producers' supply schedules; in panel (b), we graph the resulting supply curve.

It represents the market supply curve for secure digital cards and is upward sloping.

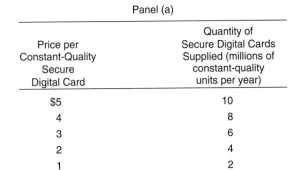

Panel (a)

Price per Constant-Quality Secure Digital Card	Quantity of Secure Digital Cards Supplied (millions of constant-quality units per year)
$5	10
4	8
3	6
2	4
1	2

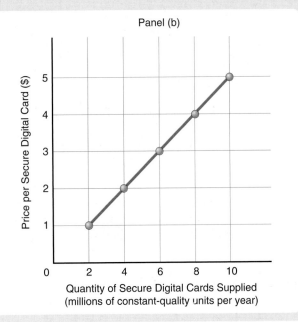

Panel (b)

Shifts in Supply

When we looked at demand, we found out that any change in anything relevant besides the price of the good or service caused the demand curve to shift inward or outward. The same is true for the supply curve. If something besides price changes and alters the willingness of suppliers to produce a good or service, we will see the entire supply curve shift.

Consider an example. There is a new method of manufacturing SD cards that significantly reduces the cost of production. In this situation, producers of SD cards will supply more product at *all* prices because their cost of so doing has fallen dramatically. Competition among manufacturers to produce more at each and every price will shift the supply curve outward to the right from S_1 to S_2 in Figure 3-9. At a price of $3, the number supplied was originally 6 million per year, but now the amount supplied (after the reduction in the costs of production) at $3 per SD card will be 9 million a year. (This is similar to what has happened to the supply curve of personal computers and cellphones in recent years as computer memory chip prices have fallen.)

Consider the opposite case. If the cost of making SD cards increases, the supply curve in Figure 3-9 will shift from S_1 to S_3. At each and every price, the quantity of SD cards supplied will fall due to the increase in the price of raw materials.

The Other Determinants of Supply

When supply curves are drawn, only the price of the good in question changes, and it is assumed that other things remain constant. The other things assumed constant are the *ceteris paribus* conditions of supply. They include the prices of resources (inputs)

FIGURE 3-9

A Shift in the Supply Curve

If the cost of producing secure digital cards were to fall dramatically, the supply curve would shift rightward from S_1 to S_2 such that at all prices, a larger quantity would be forthcoming from suppliers. Conversely, if the cost of production rose, the supply curve would shift leftward to S_3.

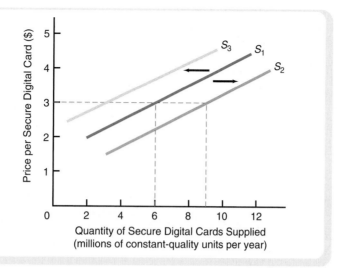

Quantity of Secure Digital Cards Supplied
(millions of constant-quality units per year)

used to produce the product, technology and productivity, taxes and subsidies, producers' price expectations, and the number of firms in the industry. If *any* of these *ceteris paribus* conditions changes, there will be a shift in the supply curve.

COST OF INPUTS USED TO PRODUCE THE PRODUCT   If one or more input prices fall, production costs fall, and the supply curve will shift outward to the right; that is, more will be supplied at each and every price. The opposite will be true if one or more inputs become more expensive. For example, when we draw the supply curve of new laptop computers, we are holding the price of microprocessors (and other inputs) constant. When we draw the supply curve of blue jeans, we are holding the cost of cotton fabric fixed.

How has a fall in an input price affected the supply of dentistry services?

E-COMMERCE EXAMPLE
Digital Imaging Boosts the Supply of Dentistry Services

To design a cap, crown, or denture, dentists use three-dimensional (3D) maps of the tooth that is to be restored. Traditionally, they have relied on 3D models that required 50 million wax and plaster impressions to be submitted each year to the dental labs that fabricate dental appliances such as crowns. Imperfections in impressions and damage to impressions in transit to labs were common. Consequently, U.S. dentists typically had to ask patients to return to their offices to redo about half of the impressions that they submitted to dental labs. Time devoted to redoing impressions could otherwise have been allocated to performing services for other patients. Hence, considering the opportunity costs the dentists incurred, the input prices of 3D models of teeth were relatively high.

Now, however, 3D maps of teeth can be produced at a much lower per-unit price using a technique called digital imaging. A dentist uses a wand about the size and shape of an electric toothbrush to scan a patient's tooth in order to create a detailed, lifelike 3D digital image stored in a computer file. The dentist then transmits this computer file, via the Internet, to a dental lab, where a technician can view the 3D tooth map from a variety of different angles for purposes of producing the appliance the dentist has ordered. Dentists utilizing this lower-priced input are already reporting soaring daily service output in their offices.

FOR CRITICAL ANALYSIS
Now that dentistry has entered the digital era, how are falling prices of computers, software, and Internet access likely to affect the supply of dentistry services?

TECHNOLOGY AND PRODUCTIVITY Supply curves are drawn by assuming a given technology, or "state of the art." When the available production techniques change, the supply curve will shift. For example, when a better production technique for SD cards becomes available, production costs decrease, and the supply curve will shift to the right. A larger quantity will be forthcoming at each and every price because the cost of production is lower.

How have new techniques utilizing poisonous venoms contributed to increased production of pharmaceuticals?

EXAMPLE
Integrating Poisons into Pharmaceuticals Production

The utilization of venomous secretions of reptiles has contributed to higher rates of production of pharmaceuticals used to treat multiple sclerosis, diabetes, and arterial disease. Technological advances have allowed the venom of cobras to be utilized in producing drugs for treatment of multiple sclerosis. In addition, a new technique employing the poisonous saliva of Gila monsters has given rise to drugs that help diabetics control their blood sugar levels. Furthermore, the use of the venom of the African saw-scaled viper has contributed to the development of new anticlotting heart medications. These and other efforts by drug companies to turn poisons into profits have boosted the amounts of pharmaceuticals produced.

FOR CRITICAL ANALYSIS
How are efforts to breed reptiles that produce larger amounts of venom likely to affect the supply of poison-based pharmaceuticals?

TAXES AND SUBSIDIES Certain taxes, such as a per-unit tax, are effectively an addition to production costs and therefore reduce the supply. If the supply curve is S_1 in Figure 3-9 on the previous page, a per-unit tax increase would shift it to S_3. A per-unit **subsidy** would do the opposite; it would shift the curve to S_2. Every producer would get a "gift" from the government for each unit produced.

How has the creation of a rail freight subsidy by European Union governments affected the supply of rail freight services in Europe?

Subsidy
A negative tax; a payment to a producer from the government, usually in the form of a cash grant per unit.

INTERNATIONAL POLICY EXAMPLE
Government Subsidies Generate More Train Traffic in Europe

Recently, governments of nations that are members of the European Union (EU) decided to shoulder most of the regular expenses associated with maintaining railroad track networks, thereby providing a significant subsidy per kilometer of track traversed by rail freight. European railroad companies have responded by increasing the amounts of freight transport services they provide. Hence, the provision of government subsidies has brought about an increase in the supply of European rail freight services.

FOR CRITICAL ANALYSIS
Have the EU governments' subsidies induced a movement along the rail freight supply curve or a shift in the supply curve?

PRICE EXPECTATIONS A change in the expectation of a future relative price of a product can affect a producer's current willingness to supply, just as price expectations affect a consumer's current willingness to purchase. For example, suppliers of SD cards may withhold from the market part of their current supply if they anticipate higher prices in the future. The current amount supplied at each and every price will decrease.

How is one company profiting from helping producers form expectations of the weather's influence on the prices of various items?

EXAMPLE
Keeping Price Expectations Updated with Forecasts of Forecasts

The prices of certain products often vary with the weather. The price of oranges, for instance, climbs whenever a cold snap grips Florida. Prices of natural gas drop when springlike weather settles into place during winter months. Consequently, forming accurate expectations of future prices of such items requires forecasting the weather.

The propensity for meteorologists to constantly revise weather forecasts complicates the process of forming expectations about future prices of products such as oranges or natural gas. To assist those producers who wish to continually update expectations about future prices of such products, WSI, the company that owns the Weather Channel, offers a new service. At a price of $90,000 per year, it sells subscriptions to its prediction about the daily weather

forecast provided by the National Oceanic and Atmospheric Administration (NOAA). Each day, one hour before NOAA meteorologists issue a weather forecast for the next several days, WSI provides its subscribers with a prediction of how the NOAA's forecast will change from its forecast the previous day. Then subscribing firms can use WSI's forecast of the NOAAs forecast to adjust their own expectations of the weather's likely effects on prices in the following days.

FOR CRITICAL ANALYSIS
If an item's price typically increases on days with good weather and decreases on days with bad weather, how would a producer of the item adjust today's output in light of an expectation of improved weather during the next few days?

NUMBER OF FIRMS IN THE INDUSTRY In the short run, when firms can change only the number of employees they use, we hold the number of firms in the industry constant. In the long run, the number of firms may change. If the number of firms increases, supply will increase, and the supply curve will shift outward to the right. If the number of firms decreases, supply will decrease, and the supply curve will shift inward to the left.

Changes in Supply versus Changes in Quantity Supplied

We cannot overstress the importance of distinguishing between a movement along the supply curve—which occurs only when the price changes for a given supply curve—and a shift in the supply curve—which occurs only with changes in *ceteris paribus* conditions. A change in the price of the good in question always (and only) brings about a change in the quantity supplied along a given supply curve. We move to a different point on the existing supply curve. This is specifically called a *change in quantity supplied*. When price changes, quantity supplied changes—there is a movement from one point to another along the same supply curve.

When you think of *supply*, think of the entire curve. Quantity supplied is represented by a single point on the supply curve.

Why are these people waiting in line for the new iPhone?

*A change, or shift, in supply is a movement of the entire curve. The **only** thing that can cause the entire curve to move is a change in one of the **ceteris paribus** conditions.*

Consequently,

*A change in price leads to a change in the quantity supplied, other things being constant. This is a movement **along** the curve.*

*A change in any **ceteris paribus** condition for supply leads to a change in supply. This causes a **shift of the curve.**ateful*

QUICK QUIZ *See page 81 for the answers. Review concepts from this section in MyEconLab.*

If the price changes, we _____ _____ a curve—there is a change in quantity demanded or supplied. If some other determinant changes, we _____ a curve—there is a change in demand or supply.

The **supply curve** is drawn with other things held constant. If these *ceteris paribus* conditions of supply change, the supply curve will shift. The major *ceteris paribus* conditions are (1) _____, (2) _____, (3) _____, (4) _____, and (5) _____.

Putting Demand and Supply Together

In the sections on demand and supply, we tried to confine each discussion to demand or supply only. But you have probably already realized that we can't view the world just from the demand side or just from the supply side. There is interaction between the two. In this section, we will discuss how they interact and how that interaction determines the prices that prevail in our economy and other economies in which the forces of demand and supply are allowed to work.

Let's first combine the demand and supply schedules and then combine the curves.

Demand and Supply Schedules Combined

Go to www.econtoday.com/chapter03 to see how the U.S. Department of Agriculture seeks to estimate demand and supply conditions for major agricultural products.

Let's place panel (a) from Figure 3-3 (the market demand schedule) on page 57 and panel (a) from Figure 3-8 (the market supply schedule) on page 66 together in panel (a) of Figure 3-10. Column 1 shows the price; column 2, the quantity supplied per year at any given price; and column 3, the quantity demanded. Column 4 is the difference between columns 2 and 3, or the difference between the quantity supplied and the quantity demanded. In column 5, we label those differences as either excess quantity supplied (called a *surplus*, which we shall discuss shortly) or excess quantity demanded (commonly known as a *shortage*, also discussed shortly). For example, at a price of $1, only 2 million secure digital cards would be supplied, but the quantity demanded would be 10 million. The difference would be −8 million, which we label excess quantity demanded (a shortage). At the other end, a price of $5 would elicit 10 million in quantity supplied, but quantity demanded would drop to 2 million, leaving a difference of +8 million units, which we call excess quantity supplied (a surplus).

Now, do you notice something special about the price of $3? At that price, both the quantity supplied and the quantity demanded per year are 6 million. The difference then is zero. There is neither excess quantity demanded (shortage) nor excess quantity

FIGURE 3-10

Putting Demand and Supply Together

In panel (a), we see that at the price of $3, the quantity supplied and the quantity demanded are equal, resulting in neither an excess quantity demanded nor an excess quantity supplied. We call this price the equilibrium, or market clearing, price. In panel (b), the intersection of the supply and demand curves is at *E*, at a price of $3 and a quantity of 6 million per year. At point *E*, there is neither an excess quantity demanded nor an excess quantity supplied. At a price of $1, the quantity supplied will be only 2 million per year, but the quantity demanded will be 10 million. The difference is excess quantity demanded at a price of $1. The price will rise, so we will move from point *A* up the supply curve and from point *B* up the demand curve to point *E*. At the other extreme, a price of $5 elicits a quantity supplied of 10 million but a quantity demanded of only 2 million. The difference is excess quantity supplied at a price of $5. The price will fall, so we will move down the demand curve and the supply curve to the equilibrium price, $3 per SD card.

Panel (a)

(1) Price per Constant-Quality Secure Digital Card	(2) Quantity Supplied (secure digital cards per year)	(3) Quantity Demanded (secure digital cards per year)	(4) Difference (2) − (3) (secure digital cards per year)	(5) Condition
$5	10 million	2 million	8 million	Excess quantity supplied (surplus)
4	8 million	4 million	4 million	Excess quantity supplied (surplus)
3	6 million	6 million	0	Market clearing price—equilibrium (no surplus, no shortage)
2	4 million	8 million	−4 million	Excess quantity demanded (shortage)
1	2 million	10 million	−8 million	Excess quantity demanded (shortage)

Panel (b)

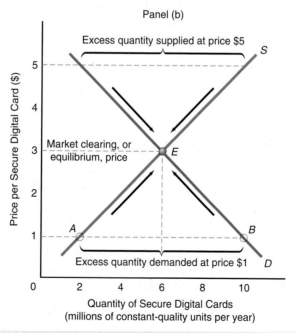

Market clearing, or **equilibrium, price**
The price that clears the market, at which quantity demanded equals quantity supplied; the price where the demand curve intersects the supply curve.

supplied (surplus). Hence the price of $3 is very special. It is called the **market clearing price**—it clears the market of all excess quantities demanded or supplied. There are no willing consumers who want to pay $3 per SD card but are turned away by sellers, and there are no willing suppliers who want to sell SD cards at $3 who cannot sell all they want at that price. Another term for the market clearing price is the **equilibrium price,** the price at which there is no tendency for change. Consumers are able to get all they want at that price, and suppliers are able to sell all they want at that price.

Equilibrium

Equilibrium
The situation when quantity supplied equals quantity demanded at a particular price.

We can define **equilibrium** in general as a point at which quantity demanded equals quantity supplied at a particular price. There tends to be no movement of the price or the quantity away from this point unless demand or supply changes. Any movement away from this point will set into motion forces that will cause movement back to it. Therefore, equilibrium is a stable point. Any point that is not an equilibrium is unstable and will not persist.

The equilibrium point occurs where the supply and demand curves intersect. The equilibrium price is given on the vertical axis directly to the left of where the supply and demand curves cross. The equilibrium quantity is given on the horizontal axis directly underneath the intersection of the demand and supply curves.

Panel (b) in Figure 3-3 and panel (b) in Figure 3-8 are combined as panel (b) in Figure 3-10 on the previous page. The demand curve is labeled D, the supply curve S. We have labeled the intersection of the supply curve with the demand curve as point E, for equilibrium. That corresponds to a market clearing price of $3, at which both the quantity supplied and the quantity demanded are 6 million units per year. There is neither excess quantity supplied nor excess quantity demanded. Point E, the equilibrium point, always occurs at the intersection of the supply and demand curves. This is the price *toward which* the market price will automatically tend to gravitate, because there is no outcome better than this price for both consumers and producers.

Shortages

Shortage
A situation in which quantity demanded is greater than quantity supplied at a price below the market clearing price.

The price of $3 depicted in Figure 3-10 represents a situation of equilibrium. If there were a non-market-clearing, or disequilibrium, price, this would put into play forces that would cause the price to change toward the market clearing price at which equilibrium would again be sustained. Look again at panel (b) in Figure 3-10. Suppose that instead of being at the equilibrium price of $3, for some reason the market price is $1. At this price, the quantity demanded of 10 million per year exceeds the quantity supplied of 2 million per year. We have a situation of excess quantity demanded at the price of $1. This is usually called a **shortage.** Consumers of SD cards would find that they could not buy all that they wished at $1 apiece. But forces will cause the price to rise: Competing consumers will bid up the price, and suppliers will increase output in response. (Remember, some buyers would pay $5 or more rather than do without SD cards. They do not want to be left out.) We would move from points A and B toward point E. The process would stop when the price again reached $3 per SD card.

At this point, it is important to recall a distinction made in Chapter 2:

Shortages and scarcity are not the same thing.

A shortage is a situation in which the quantity demanded exceeds the quantity supplied at a price that is somehow kept *below* the market clearing price. Our definition of scarcity was much more general and all-encompassing: a situation in which the resources available for producing output are insufficient to satisfy all wants. Any choice necessarily costs an opportunity, and the opportunity is lost. Hence, we will always live in a world of scarcity because we must constantly make choices, but we do not necessarily have to live in a world of shortages.

In what field is there currently a significant shortage of skilled workers?

EXAMPLE
In Nursing, Quantity Demanded Exceeds Quantity Supplied

At present, there are about 2.6 million positions filled or available for nurses at hospitals, physicians' offices, and other health care facilities across the land. Only about 2.2 million nurses are employed, however. Thus, at this time there is an excess quantity demanded—that is, a shortage—of nurses that is equal to approximately 0.4 million (at current wage rates, of course).

FOR CRITICAL ANALYSIS
What do you predict is likely to happen to the average hourly price of nurses' services—the average wage rate earned by nurses—within the next few years?

Surpluses

Now let's repeat the experiment with the market price at $5 rather than at the market clearing price of $3. Clearly, the quantity supplied will exceed the quantity demanded at that price. The result will be an excess quantity supplied at $5 per unit. This excess quantity supplied is often called a **surplus.** Given the curves in panel (b) in Figure 3-10 on page 71, however, there will be forces pushing the price back down toward $3 per SD card: Competing suppliers will cut prices and reduce output, and consumers will purchase more at these new lower prices. If the two forces of supply and demand are unrestricted, they will bring the price back to $3 per SD card.

Shortages and surpluses are resolved in unfettered markets—markets in which price changes are free to occur. The forces that resolve them are those of competition: In the case of shortages, consumers competing for a limited quantity supplied drive up the price; in the case of surpluses, sellers compete for the limited quantity demanded, thus driving prices down to equilibrium. The equilibrium price is the only stable price, and the (unrestricted) market price tends to gravitate toward it.

What happens when the price is set below the equilibrium price? Here come the scalpers.

Surplus
A situation in which quantity supplied is greater than quantity demanded at a price above the market clearing price.

POLICY EXAMPLE
Should Shortages in the Ticket Market Be Solved by Scalpers?

If you have ever tried to get tickets to a playoff game in sports, a popular Broadway play, or a superstar's rap concert, you know about "shortages." The standard Super Bowl ticket situation is shown in Figure 3-11 on the next page. At the face-value price of Super Bowl tickets ($800), the quantity demanded (175,000) greatly exceeds the quantity supplied

POLICY EXAMPLE (cont.)

(80,000). Because shortages last only as long as prices and quantities do not change, markets tend to exhibit a movement out of this disequilibrium toward equilibrium. Obviously, the quantity of Super Bowl tickets cannot change, but the price can go as high as $6,000.

Enter the scalper. This colorful term is used because when you purchase a ticket that is being resold at a price higher than face value, the seller is skimming an extra profit off the top ("taking your scalp"). If an event sells out and people who wished to purchase tickets at current prices were unable to do so, ticket prices by definition were lower than market clearing prices. People without tickets may be willing to buy high-priced tickets because they place a greater value on the entertainment event than the face value of the ticket. Without scalpers, those individuals would not be able to attend the event. In the case of the Super Bowl, various forms of scalping occur nationwide. Tickets for a seat on the 50-yard line have been sold for as much as $6,000 apiece. In front of every Super Bowl arena, you can find ticket scalpers hawking their wares.

In most states, scalping is illegal. In Pennsylvania, convicted scalpers are either fined $5,000 or sentenced to two years behind bars. For an economist, such legislation seems strange. As one New York ticket broker said, "I look at scalping like working as a stockbroker, buying low and selling high. If people are willing to pay me the money, what kind of problem is that?"

FOR CRITICAL ANALYSIS
What happens to ticket scalpers who are still holding tickets after an event has started?

FIGURE 3-11

Shortages of Super Bowl Tickets

The quantity of tickets for a Super Bowl game is fixed at 80,000. At the price per ticket of $800, the quantity demanded is 175,000. Consequently, there is an excess quantity demanded at the below-market clearing price. In this example, prices can go as high as $6,000 in the scalpers' market.

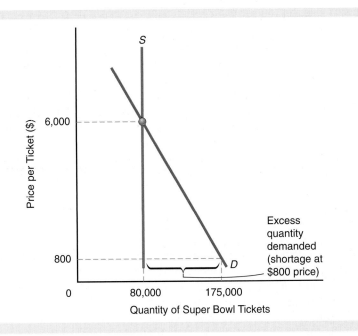

QUICK QUIZ
See page 81 for the answers. Review concepts from this section in MyEconLab.

The market clearing price occurs at the _____ of the market demand curve and the market supply curve. It is also called the _____ price, the price from which there is no tendency to change unless there is a change in demand or supply.

Whenever the price is _____ than the equilibrium price, there is an excess quantity supplied (a **surplus**).

Whenever the price is _____ than the equilibrium price, there is an excess quantity demanded (a **shortage**).

You Are There

Beetle Factories Respond to Higher Demand for Weed-Eating Bugs

Dan Palmer, production chief at the Phillip Alampi Beneficial Insect Rearing Laboratory in New Jersey, is struggling to handle new orders for one of the lab's products: *Galerucella*, which are brown beetles smaller than ladybugs. In the past, his lab mainly received daily orders for the beetles from private landowners and municipal governments in New Jersey, but now he is receiving numerous out-of-state orders as well.

The *Galerucella* beetles eat purple loosestrife, a weed imported from Europe 200 years ago that has spread throughout much of the United States and Canada. During the 1980s, environmentalists discovered that purple loosestrife chokes out native American flora and fills in spaces around lakes where wildlife such as ducks and turtles otherwise would thrive. Numerous landowners are now striving to halt and, if possible, reverse the spread of purple loosestrife. Weed-eating beetles such as *Galerucella* are increasingly regarded as a fundamental part of this effort—hence, the growing volume of orders placed for the beetles bred at labs such as Palmer's.

Dan Palmer contemplates the stack of orders that have arrived today. He concludes that the 12 people in his lab cannot possibly breed beetles in sufficient volumes to meet all his new orders. To increase daily beetle output, the lab must expand its staff, but to do that, it requires higher revenues and therefore must receive a higher price for each unit of beetles it ships. Otherwise, some of the orders that have been received today and that are likely to arrive in the days and weeks to come must go unfilled. He knows that the same situation exists at other labs that produce *Galerucella* and other weed-eating beetles. At current prices, these labs are simply unable to produce as many beetles as landowners would like to purchase.

CRITICAL ANALYSIS QUESTIONS

1. If the price of weed-eating beetles remains unchanged in the face of the recent rise in demand for these insects, what situation will exist in the market for the beetles?

2. If the price of the beetles increases, will there be a movement along the market supply curve, or will the market supply curve shift?

Issues and Applications

Why Are People Eating More?

CONCEPTS APPLIED

▶ Relative Price

▶ Law of Demand

▶ Normal Good

Being overweight or obese predisposes an individual to ailments such as arthritis, diabetes, heart disease, high blood pressure, respiratory problems, and strokes. Nevertheless, about two-thirds of the U.S. population is overweight. Nearly half of these people are classified as obese.

Undoubtedly, a generally more sedentary lifestyle helps to explain the increase in the body mass of the average U.S. resident. Panel (a) of Figure 3-12 suggests, however, that increased calorie consumption has contributed as well. Why are people ingesting so many more calories? To answer this question, one needs to look no further than two fundamental developments: (1) a falling relative price of food that has increased the quantity of food demanded and (2) rising incomes that have contributed to a higher demand for food.

FIGURE 3-12

U.S. Calorie Consumption and the Relative Price of Food

Panel (a) shows that the average U.S. resident's daily calorie consumption has surged since the late 1970s. Panel (b) shows that the price of food relative to the average price of all other items has declined since the 1970s.
Sources: U.S. Department of Agriculture; U.S. Department of Labor.

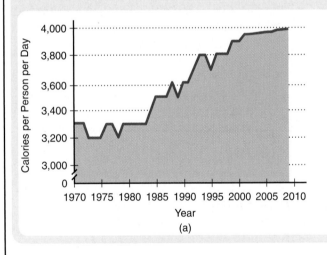

(a)

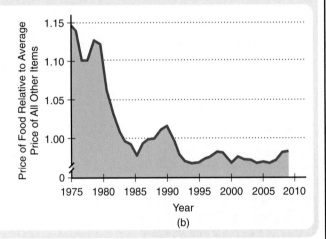

(b)

Moving Along the Food Demand Curve: Falling Relative Prices

Panel (b) of Figure 3-12 displays an index measure of the price of food relative to the average price of all other goods and services. This relative price measure indicates that the relative price of food has declined by almost 0.5 percent per year, which over the past three decades translates into an overall drop exceeding 17 percent.

The law of demand states that a decline in the relative price of an item leads to an increase in the quantity demanded of that item. With other things being equal, therefore, the significant decline in the relative price of food boosted desired food consumption. Hence, one reason that people today buy and eat more food is simply that food is cheaper than it used to be.

A Shift in the Food Demand Curve: Higher Incomes

Of course, other things have not remained unchanged since the mid-1970s. A key factor that has changed is incomes. The average inflation-adjusted income of a U.S. resident has increased by about 2 percent per year since the mid-1970s. The overall rise during the period has been more than 100 percent.

Some food items, such as canned beans and packaged macaroni and cheese, are inferior goods, so higher incomes have reduced consumption of these and similar foods. The vast majority of food items, however, are normal goods. Hence, the substantial rise in individual incomes has tended to raise the demand for foods as well as for other normal goods, such as personal computers and video games.

A Double-Whammy Effect on Food Consumption

Thus, two key factors have contributed to greater food consumption: the lower relative price of food and higher incomes. Increases in incomes have boosted demands for most food items, and declines in the relative prices have induced people to buy even more foods. Hence, people have been consuming more food and, with it, more calories. Without additional exercise, they have also been gaining more weight.

Test your understanding of this chapter by going online to **MyEconLab**.
In the Study Plan for this chapter, select Section N: News.

For Critical Analysis

1. If the demands for most food items have been rising as incomes have increased, what must have happened to the supplies of most food items to account for the declining relative price of food?

2. What factors might have accounted for the changes in food supplies discussed in Question 1? (Hint: What *ceteris paribus* conditions affect the position of a supply curve?)

Web Resources

1. For a review of the worldwide trend toward higher body masses, go to www.econtoday.com/chapter03.

2. To learn about various ways states and the federal government are trying to combat childhood obesity, click on the link to the National Center for Chronic Disease Prevention and Health Promotion, available at www.econtoday.com/chapter03.

Research Project

One way that the federal government seeks to assist low-income people is by issuing them food stamps, which they can use to purchase food items. Some observers have suggested that the government's food stamp program contributes to the higher obesity rates observed among low-income people as compared with rates observed among middle- and high-income individuals. Evaluate this argument. (Hint: Many of the least-expensive food items are often the highest-fat foods containing the most calories per unit of food.)

Here is what you should know after reading this chapter. **MyEconLab** will help you identify what you know, and where to go when you need to practice.

WHAT YOU SHOULD KNOW		WHERE TO GO TO PRACTICE
The Law of Demand According to the law of demand, other things being equal, individuals will purchase fewer units of a good at a higher price, and they will purchase more units of a good at a lower price.	market, 52 demand, 52 law of demand, 52	• **MyEconLab** Study Plan 3.1 • Audio introduction to Chapter 3

(*continued*)

 *(continued)*

WHAT YOU SHOULD KNOW

WHERE TO GO TO PRACTICE

Relative Prices versus Money Prices When determining the quantity of a good to purchase, people respond to changes in its relative price, which is the price of the good in terms of other goods. If the price of a unit of health care services rises by 50 percent next year while at the same time all other prices, including your wages, also increase by 50 percent, then the relative price of the health care services has not changed. Thus, in a world of generally rising prices, you have to compare the price of one good with the general level of prices of other goods in order to decide whether the relative price of that one good has gone up, gone down, or stayed the same.

relative price, 53
money price, 53

- **MyEconLab** Study Plan 3.1
- Video: The Difference Between Relative and Absolute Prices and the Importance of Looking at Only Relative Prices

A Change in Quantity Demanded versus a Change in Demand The demand schedule shows the relationship between various possible prices and respective quantities purchased per unit of time. Graphically, the demand schedule is a downward-sloping demand curve. A change in the price of the good generates a change in the quantity demanded, which is a movement along the demand curve. Factors other than the price of the good that affect the amount demanded are (1) income, (2) tastes and preferences, (3) the prices of related goods, (4) expectations, and (5) market size (the number of potential buyers). Whenever any of these *ceteris paribus* conditions of demand changes, there is a change in the demand for the good, and the demand curve shifts to a new position.

demand curve, 56
market demand, 56
ceteris paribus
  conditions, 59
normal goods, 59
inferior goods, 59
substitutes, 60
complements, 60

KEY FIGURE
Figure 3-2, 56
Figure 3-4, 58
Figure 3-5, 62

- **MyEconLab** Study Plans 3.2, 3.3
- Video: The Importance of Distinguishing Between a Shift in a Demand Curve and a Move Along the Demand Curve
- Animated Figures 3-2, 3-4, 3-5
- ABC News Video: What Drives the Market: Supply and Demand

The Law of Supply According to the law of supply, sellers will produce and offer for sale more units of a good at a higher price, and they will produce and offer for sale fewer units of the good at a lower price.

supply, 62
law of supply, 63

- **MyEconLab** Study Plan 3.4

A Change in Quantity Supplied versus a Change in Supply The supply schedule shows the relationship between various possible prices and respective quantities produced and sold per unit of time. On a graph, the supply schedule is a supply curve that slopes upward. A change in the price of the good generates a change in the quantity supplied, which is a movement along the supply curve. Factors other than the price of the good that affect the amount supplied are (1) input prices, (2) technology and productivity, (3) taxes and subsidies, (4) price expectations, and (5) the number of sellers. Whenever any of these *ceteris paribus* conditions changes, there is a change in the supply of the good, and the supply curve shifts to a new position.

supply curve, 64
subsidy, 68

KEY FIGURES
Figure 3-6, 64
Figure 3-7, 65
Figure 3-9, 67

- **MyEconLab** Study Plans 3.5, 3.6
- Video: The Importance of Distinguishing Between a Change in Supply versus a Change in Quantity Supplied
- Animated Figures 3-6, 3-7, 3-9

 (continued)

| WHAT YOU SHOULD KNOW | | WHERE TO GO TO PRACTICE |

Determining the Market Price and the Equilibrium Quantity
The equilibrium price of a good and the equilibrium quantity of the good that is produced and sold are determined by the intersection of the demand and supply curves. At this intersection point, the quantity demanded by buyers of the good just equals the quantity supplied by sellers. At the equilibrium price at this point of intersection, the plans of buyers and sellers mesh exactly. Hence, there is neither an excess quantity of the good supplied (surplus) nor an excess quantity of the good demanded (shortage) at this equilibrium point.

market clearing, or
equilibrium, price, 72
equilibrium, 72
shortage, 72
surplus, 73

KEY FIGURE
Figure 3-11, 74

- **MyEconLab** Study Plan 3.7
- Animated Figure 3-11
- ABC News Video: The Ripple Effects of Oil Prices

Log in to MyEconLab, take a chapter test, and get a personalized Study Plan that tells you which concepts you understand and which ones you need to review. From there, MyEconLab will give you further practice, tutorials, animations, videos, and guided solutions.
Log in to www.myeconlab.com

PROBLEMS

All problems are assignable in myeconlab. *Answers to odd-numbered problems appear at the back of the book.*

3-1. Suppose that in a recent market period, the following relationship existed between the price of prerecorded movie DVDs and the quantity supplied and quantity demanded.

Price	Quantity Demanded	Quantity Supplied
$19	100 million	40 million
$20	90 million	60 million
$21	80 million	80 million
$22	70 million	100 million
$23	60 million	120 million

Graph the supply and demand curves for movie DVDs given the information in the table. What are the equilibrium price and quantity? If the industry price is $20, is there a shortage or surplus of DVDs? How much is the shortage or surplus?

3-2. Suppose that in a later market period, the quantities supplied in the table in Problem 3-1 are unchanged. The quantity demanded, however, has increased by 30 million at each price. Construct the resulting demand curve in the illustration you made for Problem 3-1. Is this an increase or a decrease in demand? What are the new equilibrium quantity and the new market price? Give two examples of changes in *ceteris paribus* conditions that might cause such a change.

3-3. Consider the market for DSL high-speed Internet access service, which is a normal good. Explain whether the following events would cause an increase or a decrease in demand or an increase or a decrease in the quantity demanded.

a. Firms providing cable (an alternative to DSL) Internet access services reduce their prices.

b. Firms providing DSL high-speed Internet access services reduce their prices.

c. There is a decrease in the incomes earned by consumers of DSL high-speed Internet access services.

d. Consumers of DSL high-speed Internet access services anticipate a decline in the future price of these services.

3-4. In the market for flash memory drives (a normal good), explain whether the following events would cause an increase or a decrease in demand or an increase or a decrease in the quantity demanded. Also explain what happens to the equilibrium quantity and the market clearing price.

a. There are increases in the prices of storage racks and boxes for flash memory drives.

b. There is a decrease in the price of computer drives that read the information contained on flash memory drives.

c. There is a dramatic increase in the price of secure digital cards that, like flash memory drives, can be used to store digital data.

d. A booming economy increases the income of the typical buyer of flash memory drives.

e. Consumers of flash memory drives anticipate that the price of this good will decline in the future.

3-5. Give an example of a complement and a substitute in consumption for each of the following items.

a. Bacon

b. Tennis racquets

c. Coffee

d. Automobiles

3-6. At the beginning of the 2000s, the United States imposed high import taxes on a number of European goods due to a trade dispute. One of these goods was Roquefort cheese. Show how this tax affects the market for Roquefort cheese in the United States, shifting the appropriate curve and indicating a new equilibrium quantity and market price.

3-7. Consider the following diagram of a market for one-bedroom rental apartments in a college community.

a. At a rental rate of $1,000 per month, is there an excess quantity supplied, or is there an excess quantity demanded? What is the amount of the excess quantity supplied or demanded?

b. If the present rental rate of one-bedroom apartments is $1,000 per month, through what mechanism will the rental rate adjust to the equilibrium rental rate of $800?

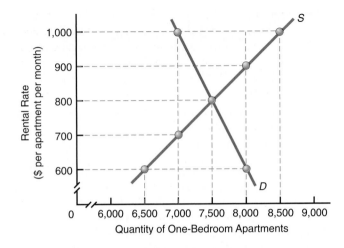

c. At a rental rate of $600 per month, is there an excess quantity supplied, or is there an excess quantity demanded? What is the amount of the excess quantity supplied or demanded?

d. If the present rental rate of one-bedroom apartments is $600 per month, through what mechanism will the rental rate adjust to the equilibrium rental rate of $800?

3-8. Consider the market for economics textbooks. Explain whether the following events would cause an increase or a decrease in supply or an increase or a decrease in the quantity supplied.

a. The market price of paper increases.

b. The market price of economics textbooks increases.

c. The number of publishers of economics textbooks increases.

d. Publishers expect that the market price of economics textbooks will increase next month.

3-9. Consider the market for laptop computers. Explain whether the following events would cause an increase or a decrease in supply or an increase or a decrease in the quantity supplied. Illustrate each, and show what would happen to the equilibrium quantity and the market price.

a. The price of memory chips used in laptop computers declines.

b. The price of machinery used to produce laptop computers increases.

c. The number of manufacturers of laptop computers increases.

d. There is a decrease in the demand for laptop computers.

3-10. The U.S. government offers significant per-unit subsidy payments to U.S. sugar growers. Describe the effects of the introduction of such subsidies on the market for sugar and the market for artificial sweeteners. Explain whether the demand curve or the supply curve shifts in each market, and if so, in which direction. Also explain what happens to the equilibrium quantity and the market price in each market.

3-11. Platinum's white luster has made the rare metal the chic look in engagement rings and wedding bands. Recently, however, the price of palladium, a more abundant metal with virtually identical characteristics, has declined considerably. Explain the likely effects that the drop in the price of palladium will have on the market for platinum.

3-12. Ethanol is a motor fuel manufactured from corn, barley, or wheat, and it can be used to power the engines of many autos and trucks. Suppose that the government decides to provide a large per-unit subsidy to ethanol producers. Explain the effects in the markets for the following items:

   a. Corn

   b. Gasoline

   c. Automobiles

3-13. If the price of processor chips used in manufacturing personal computers decreases, what will happen in the market for personal computers? How will the equilibrium price and equilibrium quantity of personal computers change?

3-14. Assume that the cost of aluminum used by soft-drink companies increases. Which of the following correctly describes the resulting effects in the market for soft drinks distributed in aluminum cans? (More than one statement may be correct.)

   a. The demand for soft drinks decreases.

   b. The quantity of soft drinks demanded decreases.

   c. The supply of soft drinks decreases.

   d. The quantity of soft drinks supplied decreases.

ECONOMICS ON THE NET

The U.S. Nursing Shortage For some years media stories have discussed a shortage of qualified nurses in the United States. This application explores some of the factors that have caused the quantity of newly trained nurses demanded to tend to exceed the quantity of newly trained nurses supplied.

Title: Nursing Shortage Resource Web Link

Navigation: Go to the Nursing Shortage Resource Web Link at **www.econtoday.com/chapter03**, and click on *Enrollment Increase Insufficient to Meet the Projected Increase in Demand for New Nurses*.

Application Read the discussion, and answer the following questions.

1. What has happened to the demand for new nurses in the United States? What has happened to the supply of new nurses? Why has the result been a shortage?

2. If there is a free market for the skills of new nurses, what can you predict is likely to happen to the wage rate earned by individuals who have just completed their nursing training?

For Group Study and Analysis Discuss the pros and cons of high schools and colleges trying to factor predictions about future wages into student career counseling. How might this potentially benefit students? What problems might high schools and colleges face in trying to assist students in evaluating the future earnings prospects of various jobs?

ANSWERS TO QUICK QUIZZES

p. 54: (i) inverse; (ii) demand

p. 58: (i) constant; (ii) market demand

p. 62: (i) income . . . tastes and preferences . . . prices of related goods . . . expectations about future prices and incomes . . . market size (the number of potential buyers in the market); (ii) *ceteris paribus*; (iii) movement along

p. 65: (i) direct; (ii) supply; (iii) market supply

p. 70: (i) move along . . . shift; (ii) input prices . . . technology and productivity . . . taxes and subsidies . . . expectations of future relative prices . . . the number of firms in the industry

p. 74: (i) intersection . . . equilibrium; (ii) greater; (iii) less

Extensions of Demand and Supply Analysis

4

About 100,000 U.S. residents possessing a malfunctioning organ, such as a liver, heart, or lung, are on waiting lists for transplants from deceased or living donors. A majority of the people waiting for organ transplants are individuals who are suffering from kidney failure. As they wait for donations of compatible kidneys, most people with failed kidneys must undergo years of dialysis, which is an artificial means of cleaning their bloodstreams of harmful toxins. Many never receive a kidney transplant, and a number of these individuals die each year. Why do people suffering from kidney failure have to wait for years to obtain transplants? Why are so many individuals never able to obtain transplants? By the end of this chapter, you will understand the answer to these questions.

LEARNING OBJECTIVES

MyEconLab helps you master each objective and study more efficiently. See end of chapter for details.

After reading this chapter, you should be able to:

- Discuss the essential features of the price system
- Evaluate the effects of changes in demand and supply on the market price and equilibrium quantity
- Understand the rationing function of prices
- Explain the effects of price ceilings
- Explain the effects of price floors
- Describe various types of government-imposed quantity restrictions on markets

? DID YOU KNOW THAT when the owner of a Wisconsin gasoline station recently offered a 2-cent-per-gallon price discount to senior citizens, the state's Department of Agriculture, Trade, and Consumer Protection objected? The state government agency informed the station owner that the price he had offered senior citizens was too low. Under state law, the station owner could not offer to sell gasoline to anyone at a price below a permissible minimum price, or price *floor*.

What effects can a price floor have on production and consumption of a good or service? As you will learn in this chapter, we can use the supply and demand analysis developed in Chapter 3 to answer this question. You will find that when a government sets a price floor above the equilibrium price, the result will be a surplus, in which quantity supplied remains above quantity demanded. Similarly, you will learn about how we can use supply and demand analysis to examine the "surplus" of various agricultural products, the "shortage" of apartments in certain cities, and many other phenomena. All of these examples are part of our economy, which we characterize as a *price system*.

The Price System and Markets

In a **price system,** otherwise known as a *market system*, relative prices are constantly changing to reflect changes in supply and demand for different commodities. The prices of those commodities are the signals to everyone within the system as to what is relatively scarce and what is relatively abundant. In this sense, prices provide information.

Indeed, it is the *signaling* aspect of the price system that provides the information to buyers and sellers about what should be bought and what should be produced. In a price system, there is a clear-cut chain of events in which any changes in demand and supply cause changes in prices that in turn affect the opportunities that businesses and individuals have for profit and personal gain. Such changes influence our use of resources.

Price system
An economic system in which relative prices are constantly changing to reflect changes in supply and demand for different commodities. The prices of those commodities are signals to everyone within the system as to what is relatively scarce and what is relatively abundant.

Exchange and Markets

The price system features **voluntary exchange,** acts of trading between individuals that make both parties to the trade subjectively better off. The **terms of exchange**—the prices we pay for the desired items—are determined by the interaction of the forces underlying supply and demand. In our economy, exchanges take place voluntarily in markets. A market encompasses the exchange arrangements of both buyers and sellers that underlie the forces of supply and demand. Indeed, one definition of a market is that it is a low-cost institution for facilitating exchange. A market increases incomes by helping resources move to their highest-valued uses.

Voluntary exchange
An act of trading, done on an elective basis, in which both parties to the trade expect to be better off after the exchange.

Terms of exchange
The conditions under which trading takes place. Usually, the terms of exchange are equal to the price at which a good is traded.

Transaction Costs

Individuals turn to markets because markets reduce the cost of exchanges. These costs are sometimes referred to as **transaction costs,** which are broadly defined as the costs associated with finding out exactly what is being transacted as well as the cost of enforcing contracts. If you were Robinson Crusoe and lived alone on an island, you would never incur a transaction cost. For everyone else, transaction costs are just as real as the costs of production. Today, high-speed computers have allowed us to reduce transaction costs by increasing our ability to process information and keep records.

How have real-time dating services via cellphone reduced the transaction costs of searching for a date?

Transaction costs
All of the costs associated with exchange, including the informational costs of finding out the price and quality, service record, and durability of a product, plus the cost of contracting and enforcing that contract.

E-COMMERCE EXAMPLE

Cellphone Services Reduce the Transaction Costs of Dating

Internet matchmaking is moving to a new level. Singles can now find potential dating partners in nearby locales via cellphone. Web dating services such as MeetMoi permit a registered user to indicate that she is available for text messaging within a ZIP code or at a nearby street address. The dating service's computer system then identifies other members who have indicated they are looking for a date in the specified area and sends back profiles matching the user's criteria. Match.com offers a cellphone service utilizing global-positioning-system technology to help users locate a nearby match. At another service, Zogo, a person can use a cellphone Web browser to view a list of potential matches. If the individual requests a phone conversation, a phone connection is initiated immediately if the requested party approves a text message request forwarded by Zogo. In these and other ways, Internet and telecommunication technologies continue to reduce the transaction costs of finding a date near you.

FOR CRITICAL ANALYSIS

How do you suppose that computer technology makes it possible for MeetMoi to charge only 99 cents for 10 anonymous text messages to potential dating partners who otherwise might take weeks of effort for a customer to identify on her own?

In what way does Costco reduce transaction costs?

Consider some simple examples of transaction costs. A club warehouse such as Sam's Club or Costco reduces the transaction costs of having to go to numerous specialty stores to obtain the items you desire. Financial institutions, such as commercial banks, have reduced the transaction costs of directing funds from savers to borrowers. In general, the more organized the market, the lower the transaction costs. Among those who constantly attempt to lower transaction costs are the much maligned middlemen.

The Role of Middlemen

As long as there are costs of bringing together buyers and sellers, there will be an incentive for intermediaries, normally called middlemen, to lower those costs. This means that middlemen specialize in lowering transaction costs. Whenever producers do not sell their products directly to the final consumer, by definition, one or more middlemen are involved. Farmers typically sell their output to distributors, who are usually called wholesalers, who then sell those products to retailers such as supermarkets.

As videos flood the Internet, are there profitable opportunities for middlemen?

E-COMMERCE EXAMPLE

Helping People Keep Up with the Flood of Online Videos

As video postings stream onto the Internet, consumers interested in seeing everything from the latest clip from *Saturday Night Live* to a professional baseball game that may alter league standings can find assistance from MeeVee. The company's Web service allows a user to store a list of interests as keywords or category listings. The service rummages through the Internet in search of relevant videos, which it automatically forwards to the client's hard drive, digital video recorder, or cellphone. MeeVee also notifies clients of future television shows or online broadcasts. Clients receive the services at no charge from MeeVee, which profits from deals with advertisers and revenue sharing with providers of pay-per-view video content.

FOR CRITICAL ANALYSIS

What would happen to the demand for the services of online video middlemen such as MeeVee if low-priced software enabling searches for video offerings via cellphones or home computers became available for purchase?

Changes in Demand and Supply

A key function of middlemen is to reduce transaction costs of buyers and sellers in markets for goods and services, and it is in markets that we see the results of changes in demand and supply. Market equilibrium can change whenever there is a *shock* caused by a change in a *ceteris paribus* condition for demand or supply. A shock to the supply and demand system can be represented by a shift in the supply curve, a shift in the demand curve, or a shift in both curves. Any shock to the system will result in a new set of supply and demand relationships and a new equilibrium. Forces will come into play to move the system from the old price-quantity equilibrium (now a disequilibrium situation) to the new equilibrium, where the new demand and supply curves intersect.

Effects of Changes in Either Demand or Supply

In many situations, it is possible to predict what will happen to both equilibrium price and equilibrium quantity when demand or supply changes. Specifically, whenever one curve is stable while the other curve shifts, we can tell what will happen to both price and quantity. Consider the possibilities in Figure 4-1. In panel (a), the supply curve remains unchanged, but demand increases from D_1 to D_2. Note that the results are an increase in the market clearing price from P_1 to P_2 and an increase in the equilibrium quantity from Q_1 to Q_2.

FIGURE 4-1

Shifts in Demand and in Supply: Determinate Results

In panel (a), the supply curve is unchanged at S. The demand curve shifts outward from D_1 to D_2. The equilibrium price and quantity rise from P_1, Q_1 to P_2, Q_2, respectively. In panel (b), again the supply curve is unchanged at S. The demand curve shifts inward to the left, showing a decrease in demand from D_1 to D_3. Both equilibrium price and equilibrium quantity fall. In panel (c), the demand curve now remains unchanged at D. The supply curve shifts from S_1 to S_2. The equilibrium price falls from P_1 to P_2. The equilibrium quantity increases, however, from Q_1 to Q_2. In panel (d), the demand curve is unchanged at D. Supply decreases as shown by a leftward shift of the supply curve from S_1 to S_3. The market clearing price increases from P_1 to P_3. The equilibrium quantity falls from Q_1 to Q_3.

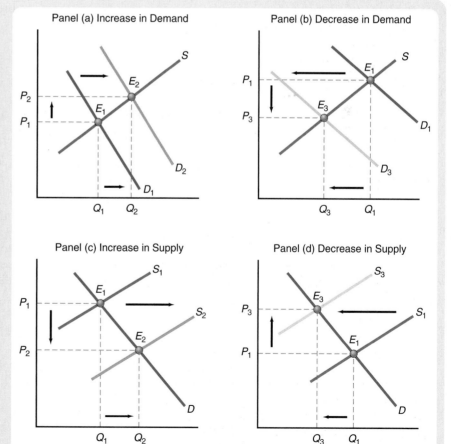

In panel (b) on the previous page, there is a decrease in demand from D_1 to D_3. This results in a decrease in both the equilibrium price of the good and the equilibrium quantity. Panels (c) and (d) show the effects of a shift in the supply curve while the demand curve is unchanged. In panel (c), the supply curve has shifted rightward. The equilibrium price of the product falls; the equilibrium quantity increases. In panel (d), supply has shifted leftward—there has been a supply decrease. The product's equilibrium price increases, and the equilibrium quantity decreases.

Why has the demand for decades-old music recently risen and pushed up the prices of hit songs from the past?

EXAMPLE
The Rising Price of Using Old Songs as Video Background Music

As video content pours onto televisions, cell-phones, and computers, producers of videos are scrambling for background music. Indeed, an increasing number of video creators are producing videos carefully synchronized with music, in some cases with videos scripted to fit storylines in song lyrics. The result has been a significant increase in the demand for background music, often purchased for these specific uses from catalogs of long-retired or deceased songwriters. As more producers seek to include hit songs from the past in their video productions, the prices of the rights to use the songs have increased, too. Nearly forgotten songs once available for a few hundred dollars now cost as much as $50,000.

FOR CRITICAL ANALYSIS
What do you suppose has happened to the market clearing price of copyrighted songs newly written for use as background music for video productions?

Situations in Which Both Demand and Supply Shift

The examples in Figure 4-1 show a theoretically determinate outcome of a shift either in the demand curve, holding the supply curve constant, or in the supply curve, holding the demand curve constant. When both the supply and demand curves change, the outcome is indeterminate for either equilibrium price or equilibrium quantity.

When both demand and supply increase, the equilibrium quantity unambiguously rises, because the increase in demand and the increase in supply *both* tend to generate a rise in quantity. The change in the equilibrium price is uncertain without more information, because the increase in demand tends to increase the equilibrium price, whereas the increase in supply tends to decrease the equilibrium price. Decreases in both demand and supply tend to generate a fall in quantity, so the equilibrium quantity falls. Again, the effect on the equilibrium price is uncertain without additional information, because a decrease in demand tends to reduce the equilibrium price, whereas a decrease in supply tends to increase the equilibrium price.

We can be certain that when demand decreases and supply increases at the same time, the equilibrium price will fall, because *both* the decrease in demand and the increase in supply tend to push down the equilibrium price. The change in the equilibrium quantity is uncertain without more information, because the decrease in demand tends to reduce the equilibrium quantity, whereas the increase in supply tends to increase the equilibrium quantity. If demand increases and supply decreases at the same time, both occurrences tend to push up the equilibrium price, so the equilibrium price definitely rises. The change in the equilibrium quantity cannot be determined without more information, because the increase in demand tends to raise the equilibrium quantity, whereas the decrease in supply tends to reduce the equilibrium quantity.

Why is one of the most common physical elements in the universe selling at a higher price here on planet Earth?

EXAMPLE
A Hot Market for a Cooling Element

The element helium is utilized by manufacturers of electronic components because its inert nature helps prevent other gases or impurities from lodging on microchips. In addition, helium readily absorbs heat, so it is very useful for cooling hot substances. Indeed, it can be used to cool metals to such low temperatures that they become superconductors. Even though helium is the second-most-abundant element in the known universe, on our world it is primarily found as a trace component of natural gas. Helium is extracted from natural gas by cooling it to the point at which component gases other than helium liquefy, leaving only helium gas.

The expanding range of industrial applications of helium has led to a rapidly expanding demand for the element. Thus, there has been a rightward shift in the demand curve

for helium, as shown in Figure 4-2. At the same time, however, breakdowns in aging equipment at natural gas fields in locales such as Qatar and Algeria have resulted in significant cutbacks in helium production. Thus, there has been a leftward shift in the helium supply curve. On net, the equilibrium quantity of helium produced and consumed has risen slightly, and the market clearing price of helium has also increased. Indeed, since early 2007 the world price of helium has risen by more than 20 percent.

FOR CRITICAL ANALYSIS
How do you suppose that the recent completion of a number of many new Asian factories that utilize helium as an input will affect the global price of helium?

FIGURE 4-2

The Effects of a Simultaneous Decrease in Helium Supply and Increase in Helium Demand

In the mid-2000s, various factors contributed to a reduction in the global supply of helium, depicted by the leftward shift in the helium supply curve from S_1 to S_2. At the same time, there was an increase in the demand for helium, as shown by the shift in the helium demand curve from D_1 to D_2. On net, the equilibrium quantity of helium produced and consumed rose slightly, from 100 million cubic feet per year at point E_1 to 110 million cubic feet per year at point E_2, and the equilibrium price of helium increased from about $0.04 per cubic foot to about $0.05 per cubic foot.

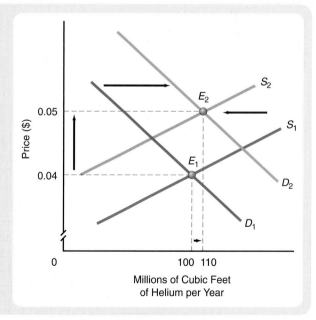

Price Flexibility and Adjustment Speed

We have used as an illustration for our analysis a market in which prices are quite flexible. Some markets are indeed like that. In others, however, price flexibility may take the form of subtle adjustments such as hidden payments or quality changes. For example, although the published price of bouquets of flowers may stay the same, the freshness of the flowers may change, meaning that the price per constant-quality unit changes. The published price of French bread might stay the same, but the quality could go up or down, perhaps through use of a different recipe, thereby changing the price per constant-quality unit. There are many ways to implicitly change prices without actually changing the published price for a *nominal* unit of a product or service.

We must also note that markets do not always return to equilibrium immediately. There may be a significant adjustment time. A shock to the economy in the form of an oil embargo, a drought, or a long strike will not be absorbed overnight. This means that even in unfettered market situations, in which there are no restrictions on changes in prices and quantities, temporary excess quantities supplied or excess quantities demanded may appear. Our analysis simply indicates what the market clearing price and equilibrium quantity ultimately will be, given a demand curve and a supply curve. Nowhere in the analysis is there any indication of the speed with which a market will get to a new equilibrium after a shock. The price may even temporarily overshoot the new equilibrium level. Remember this warning when we examine changes in demand and in supply due to changes in their *ceteris paribus* conditions.

QUICK QUIZ See page 106 for the answers. Review concepts from this section in MyEconLab.

The _____ of _____ in a voluntary exchange are determined by the interaction of the forces underlying demand and supply. These forces take place in markets, which tend to minimize _____ costs.

When the _____ curve shifts outward or inward with an unchanged _____ curve, equilibrium price and quantity increase or decrease, respectively. When the

_____ curve shifts outward or inward given an unchanged _____ curve, equilibrium price moves in the direction opposite to equilibrium quantity.

When there is a shift in demand or supply, the new equilibrium price is not obtained _____. Adjustment takes _____.

The Rationing Function of Prices

The synchronization of decisions by buyers and sellers that leads to equilibrium is called the *rationing function of prices*. Prices are indicators of relative scarcity. An equilibrium price clears the market. The plans of buyers and sellers, given the price, are not frustrated. It is the free interaction of buyers and sellers that sets the price that eventually clears the market. Price, in effect, rations a good to demanders who are willing and able to pay the highest price. Whenever the rationing function of prices is frustrated by government-enforced price ceilings that set prices below the market clearing level, a prolonged shortage results.

Methods of Nonprice Rationing

There are ways other than price to ration goods. *First come, first served* is one method. *Political power* is another. *Physical force* is yet another. Cultural, religious, and physical differences have been and are used as rationing devices throughout the world.

RATIONING BY WAITING Consider first come, first served as a rationing device. We call this *rationing by queues*, where *queue* means "line." Whoever is willing to wait in line the longest obtains the good that is being sold at less than the market clearing price. All who wait in line are paying a higher *total* price than the money price paid for the good. Personal time has an opportunity cost. To calculate the total price of the good, we must add up the money price plus the opportunity cost of the time spent waiting.

Rationing by waiting may occur in situations in which entrepreneurs are free to change prices to equate quantity demanded with quantity supplied but choose not to do so. This results in queues of potential buyers. It may seem that the price in the market is being held below equilibrium by some noncompetitive force. That is not true, however. Such queuing may arise in a free market when the demand for a good is subject to large or unpredictable fluctuations, and the additional costs to firms (and ultimately to consumers) of constantly changing prices or of holding sufficient inventories or providing sufficient excess capacity to cover peak demands are greater than the costs to consumers of waiting for the good. Common examples are waiting in line to purchase a fast-food lunch and queuing to purchase a movie ticket a few minutes before the next show.

RATIONING BY RANDOM ASSIGNMENT OR COUPONS *Random assignment* is another way to ration goods. You may have been involved in a rationing-by-random-assignment scheme in college if you were assigned a housing unit. Sometimes rationing by random assignment is used to fill slots in popular classes.

Rationing by *coupons* has also been used, particularly during wartime. In the United States during World War II, families were allotted coupons that allowed them to purchase specified quantities of rationed goods, such as meat and gasoline. To purchase such goods, they had to pay a specified price *and* give up a coupon.

The Essential Role of Rationing

In a world of scarcity, there is, by definition, competition for what is scarce. After all, any resources that are not scarce can be had by everyone at a zero price in as large a quantity as everyone wants, such as air to burn in internal combustion engines. Once scarcity arises, there has to be some method to ration the available resources, goods, and services. The price system is one form of rationing; the others that we mentioned are alternatives. Economists cannot say which system of rationing is "best." They can, however, say that rationing via the price system leads to the most efficient use of available resources. This means that generally in a freely functioning price system, all of the gains from mutually beneficial trade will be captured.

How is it that a number of summer internships for college students are now being rationed by the price system?

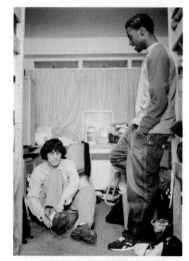

What are some alternative rationing methods to the ususal rationing-by-random-assignment schemes used for college housing units?

EXAMPLE
Summer Internships for Sale

Traditionally, college students have obtained summer internships with prestigious companies in two ways. One way is to apply for an internship administered through a school program and wait for university administrators to ration available internships to the students they deem most meritorious. Another is to apply to the companies directly and hope to be rated among the most desirable candidates.

In recent years, however, college students and their families have discovered a third method of securing a summer internship with a top firm: buy one at an auction. An increasing

EXAMPLE (cont.)

number of companies are now donating summer internships to charities, which raise funds by auctioning the internships to parents of college students looking for ways to obtain marketable experience for their children. Thus, a growing percentage of available summer college internships with highly regarded companies are now rationed by a freely functioning price system.

FOR CRITICAL ANALYSIS
How do you suppose that the auction price of a summer internship with investment bank Morgan Stanley would compare with the auction price of a summer internship with a small community bank?

QUICK QUIZ   *See page 106 for the answers. Review concepts from this section in MyEconLab.*

Prices in a market economy perform a rationing function because they reflect relative scarcity, allowing the market to clear. Other ways to ration goods include _____, _____ _____; _____ _____; _____ _____;

_____; and _____.

Even when businesspeople can change prices, some rationing by waiting may occur. Such _____ arises when there are large changes in demand coupled with high costs of satisfying those changes immediately.

The Policy of Government-Imposed Price Controls

Price controls
Government-mandated minimum or maximum prices that may be charged for goods and services.

Price ceiling
A legal maximum price that may be charged for a particular good or service.

Price floor
A legal minimum price below which a good or service may not be sold. Legal minimum wages are an example.

Nonprice rationing devices
All methods used to ration scarce goods that are price-controlled. Whenever the price system is not allowed to work, nonprice rationing devices will evolve to ration the affected goods and services.

The rationing function of prices is prevented when governments impose price controls. **Price controls** often involve setting a **price ceiling**—the maximum price that may be allowed in an exchange. The world has had a long history of price ceilings applied to product prices, wages, rents, and interest rates. Occasionally, a government will set a **price floor**—a minimum price below which a good or service may not be sold. Price floors have most often been applied to wages and agricultural products. Let's first consider price ceilings.

Price Ceilings and Black Markets

As long as a price ceiling is below the market clearing price, imposing a price ceiling creates a shortage, as can be seen in Figure 4-3. At any price below the market clearing, or equilibrium, price of $1,000, there will always be a larger quantity demanded than quantity supplied—a shortage, as you will recall from Chapter 3. Normally, whenever quantity demanded exceeds quantity supplied—that is, when a shortage exists—there is a tendency for the price to rise to its equilibrium level. But with a price ceiling, this tendency cannot be fully realized because everyone is forbidden to trade at the equilibrium price.

The result is fewer exchanges and **nonprice rationing devices.** Figure 4-3 illustrates the situation for portable electricity generators after a natural disaster: the equilibrium quantity of portable generators demanded and supplied (or traded) would be 10,000 units, and the market clearing price would be $1,000 per generator. But, if the government essentially imposes a price ceiling by requiring the price of portable

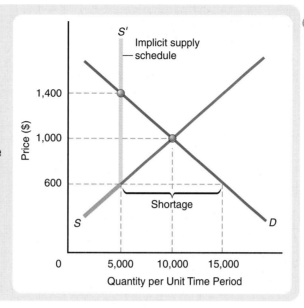

FIGURE 4-3

Black Markets

The demand curve is *D*. The supply curve is *S*. The equilibrium price is $1,000. The government, however, steps in and imposes a maximum price of $600. At that lower price, the quantity demanded will be 15,000, but the quantity supplied will be only 5,000. There is a "shortage." The implicit price (including time costs) tends to rise to $1,400. If black markets arise, as they generally will, the equilibrium black market price will end up somewhere between $600 and $1,400. The actual quantity transacted will be between 5,000 and 10,000.

You Are There

To consider the problems faced by government-sponsored public schools confronting salary scales that effectively create a ceiling on teachers' wages, read **Finding a Spanish Instructor in the Midst of a Teacher Shortage,** on page 99.

generators to remain at the predisaster level, which the government determines was a price of $600, the equilibrium quantity offered is only 5,000. Because frustrated consumers will be able to purchase only 5,000 units, there is a shortage. The most obvious nonprice rationing device to help clear the market is queuing, or physical lines, which we have already discussed. To avoid physical lines, waiting lists may be established.

Typically, an effective price ceiling leads to a **black market.** A black market is a market in which the price-controlled good is sold at an illegally high price through various methods. For example, if the price of gasoline is controlled at lower than the market clearing price, drivers who wish to fill up their cars may offer the gas station attendant a cash payment on the side (as happened in the United States in the 1970s and in China and India in the mid-2000s during price controls on gasoline). If the price of beef is controlled at below its market clearing price, a customer who offers the butcher good tickets to an upcoming football game may be allocated otherwise unavailable beef. Indeed, the true implicit price of a price-controlled good or service can be increased in an infinite number of ways, limited only by the imagination. (Black markets also occur when goods are made illegal.)

In what black market have long-distance runners been known to participate?

Black market
A market in which goods are traded at prices above their legal maximum prices or in which illegal goods are sold.

INTERNATIONAL EXAMPLE
The Global Black Market for Marathon Entry Numbers

The world's top marathons are held in Amsterdam, Berlin, Boston, Chicago, Honolulu, London, New York, Paris, Rotterdam, and Stockholm. When runners register for a marathon in one of these cities, they receive "bibs," or officially authorized paper numbers, which must be worn on their shirts

during the event. Marathon organizers typically set registration fees between $80 and $120, well below the equilibrium price. As a result, every year there are shortages of bibs. Even though most marathon organizers say that they ban the reselling of bibs, each year hundreds of individuals who have no intention

INTERNATIONAL EXAMPLE (cont.)

of participating in marathons register to run, obtain bibs, and put them up for sale on Web auction sites. Some black market bibs have fetched prices as high as $1,000.

FOR CRITICAL ANALYSIS
How could marathon organizers prevent bib shortages from occurring?

QUICK QUIZ   *See page 106 for the answers. Review concepts from this section in MyEconLab.*

Governments sometimes impose **price controls** in the form of price _____ and price _____.

An effective price _____ is one that sets the legal price below the market clearing price and is enforced.

Effective price _____ lead to nonprice rationing devices and black markets.

The Policy of Controlling Rents

Rent control
Price ceilings on rents.

More than 200 U.S. cities and towns, including Berkeley, California, and New York City, operate under some kind of rent control. **Rent control** is a system under which the local government tells building owners how much they can charge their tenants for rent. In the United States, rent controls date back to at least World War II. The objective of rent control is to keep rents below levels that would be observed in a freely competitive market.

The Functions of Rental Prices

In any housing market, rental prices serve three functions: (1) to promote the efficient maintenance of existing housing and stimulate the construction of new housing, (2) to allocate existing scarce housing among competing claimants, and (3) to ration the use of existing housing by current demanders. Rent controls interfere with all of these functions.

RENT CONTROLS AND CONSTRUCTION Rent controls discourage the construction of new rental units. Rents are the most important long-term determinant of profitability, and rent controls artificially depress them. Consider some examples. In a recent year in Dallas, Texas, with a 16 percent rental vacancy rate but no rent control laws, 11,000 new rental housing units were built. In the same year in San Francisco, California, only 2,000 units were built, despite a mere 1.6 percent vacancy rate. The major difference? San Francisco has had stringent rent control laws. In New York City, until changes in the law in 1997 and 2003, the only rental units being built were luxury units, which were exempt from controls.

EFFECTS ON THE EXISTING SUPPLY OF HOUSING When rental rates are held below equilibrium levels, property owners cannot recover the cost of maintenance, repairs, and capital improvements through higher rents. Hence, they curtail these activities. In the extreme situation, taxes, utilities, and the expenses of basic repairs exceed rental receipts. The result is abandoned buildings from Santa Monica, California, to New York City. Some owners have resorted to arson, hoping to collect the insurance on their empty buildings before the city claims them for back taxes.

RATIONING THE CURRENT USE OF HOUSING   Rent controls also affect the current use of housing because they restrict tenant mobility. Consider a family whose children have gone off to college. That family might want to live in a smaller apartment. But in a rent-controlled environment, giving up a rent-controlled unit can entail a substantial cost. In most rent-controlled cities, rents can be adjusted only when a tenant leaves. That means that a move from a long-occupied rent-controlled apartment to a smaller apartment can involve a hefty rent hike. In New York, this artificial preservation of the status quo came to be known as "housing gridlock."

Attempts to Evade Rent Controls

The distortions produced by rent controls lead to efforts by both property owners and tenants to evade the rules. This leads to the growth of expensive government bureaucracies whose job it is to make sure that rent controls aren't evaded. In New York City, because rent on an apartment can be raised only if the tenant leaves, property owners have had an incentive to make life unpleasant for tenants in order to drive them out or to evict them on the slightest pretext. The city has responded by making evictions extremely costly for property owners. Eviction requires a tedious and expensive judicial proceeding. Tenants, for their part, routinely try to sublet all or part of their rent-controlled apartments at fees substantially above the rent they pay to the owner. Both the city and the property owners try to prohibit subletting and often end up in the city's housing courts—an entire judicial system developed to deal with disputes involving rent-controlled apartments. The overflow and appeals from the city's housing courts sometimes clog the rest of New York's judicial system.

Go to **www.econtoday.com/chapter04** to learn more about New York City's rent controls from Tenant.net.

How have universities' policies of providing students' family members with tickets to graduation ceremonies at no charge provided some students with a profit incentive?

EXAMPLE
Zero-Priced Seats at Graduation Ceremonies Become Hot Items

Whenever you purchase a ticket to a concert or sporting event, you are effectively renting from the owner of the concert hall or sports center the space where you will sit during the time of the scheduled event. Likewise, a ticket to a college graduation ceremony grants the bearer the right to utilize space owned by the college for the duration of that particular occasion.

Colleges typically extend a few tickets at no charge to each graduating student to pass along for use by family members who wish to attend the student's graduation ceremony. Some students have more loved ones who would like to attend their graduation ceremonies than their allotments of no-charge tickets. Other students do not even wish to attend their own graduation ceremonies, let alone ask family members to attend. The latter students recognize, however, that some students are willing to pay positive prices for access to seats for loved ones lacking tickets. Many colleges threaten to discipline students who sell their graduation seating tickets, but to no avail. Each year at colleges across the nation, tickets to graduation ceremonies sell at prices ranging from as low as $5 per ticket to as high as $100 per ticket.

FOR CRITICAL ANALYSIS
Does anyone "lose out" as a result of black market exchanges of tickets to college graduation ceremonies?

Who Gains and Who Loses from Rent Controls?

The big losers from rent controls are clearly property owners. But there is another group of losers—low-income individuals, especially single mothers, trying to find their first apartment. Some observers now believe that rent controls have worsened the problem of homelessness in cities such as New York.

Often, owners of rent-controlled apartments charge "key money" before allowing a new tenant to move in. This is a large up-front cash payment, usually illegal but demanded nonetheless—just one aspect of the black market in rent-controlled apartments. Poor individuals have insufficient income to pay the hefty key money payment, nor can they assure the owner that their rent will be on time or even paid each month. Because controlled rents are usually below market clearing levels, apartment owners have little incentive to take any risk on low-income individuals as tenants. This is particularly true when a prospective tenant's chief source of income is a welfare check. Indeed, a large number of the litigants in the New York housing courts are welfare mothers who have missed their rent payments due to emergency expenses or delayed welfare checks. Their appeals often end in evictions and a new home in a temporary public shelter—or on the streets.

Who benefits from rent control? Ample evidence indicates that upper-income professionals benefit the most. These people can use their mastery of the bureaucracy and their large network of friends and connections to exploit the rent control system. Consider that in New York, actresses Mia Farrow and Cicely Tyson live in rent-controlled apartments, paying well below market rates. So do the former director of the Metropolitan Museum of Art and singer and children's book author Carly Simon.

QUICK QUIZ *See page 106 for the answers. Review concepts from this section in MyEconLab.*

_____ prices perform three functions: (1) allocating existing scarce housing among competing claimants, (2) promoting efficient maintenance of existing houses and stimulating new housing construction, and (3) rationing the use of existing houses by current demanders.

Effective rent _____ impede the functioning of rental prices. Construction of new rental units is discouraged. Rent _____ decrease spending on maintenance of existing ones and also lead to "housing gridlock."

There are numerous ways to evade rent controls; _____ _____ is one.

Price Floors in Agriculture

Another way that government can affect markets is by imposing price floors or price supports. In the United States, price supports are most often associated with agricultural products.

Price Supports

During the Great Depression, the federal government swung into action to help farmers. In 1933, it established a system of price supports for many agricultural products. Since then, there have been price supports for wheat, feed grains, cotton, rice, soybeans, sorghum, and dairy products, among other foodstuffs. The nature of the supports is quite simple: The government simply chooses a *support price* for an agricultural product

FIGURE 4-4

Agricultural Price Supports

Free market equilibrium occurs at *E*, with an equilibrium price of $250 per ton and an equilibrium quantity of 1.4 million tons. When the government sets a support price at $350 per ton, the quantity demanded is 1.0 million tons, and the quantity supplied is 2.2 million tons. The difference is the surplus, which the government buys. Farmers' income from consumers equals $350 × 1.0 million = $350 million. Farmers' additional income from taxpayers equals $350 × (2.2 million − 1.0 million) = $420 million.

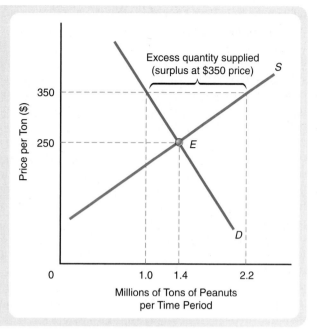

and then acts to ensure that the price of the product never falls below the support level. Figure 4-4 shows the market demand for and supply of peanuts. Without a price-support program, competitive forces would yield an equilibrium price of $250 per ton and an equilibrium quantity of 1.4 million tons per year. Clearly, if the government were to set the support price at or below $250 per ton, the quantity of peanuts demanded would equal the quantity of peanuts supplied at point *E*, because farmers could sell all they wanted at the market clearing price of $250 per ton.

But what happens when the government sets the support price *above* the market clearing price, at $350 per ton? At a support price of $350 per ton, the quantity demanded is only 1.0 million tons, but the quantity supplied is 2.2 million tons. The 1.2-million-ton difference between them is called the *excess quantity supplied*, or *surplus*. As simple as this program seems, its existence creates a fundamental question: How can the government agency charged with administering the price-support program prevent market forces from pushing the actual price down to $250 per ton?

If production exceeds the amount that consumers want to buy at the support price, what happens to the surplus? Quite simply, if the price-support program is to work, the government has to buy the surplus—the 1.2-million-ton difference. As a practical matter, the government acquires the 1.2-million-ton surplus indirectly through a government agency. The government either stores the surplus or sells it to foreign countries at a greatly reduced price (or gives it away free of charge) under the Food for Peace program.

Who Benefits from Agricultural Price Supports?

Although agricultural price supports have traditionally been promoted as a way to guarantee decent earnings for low-income farmers, most of the benefits have in fact gone to the owners of very large farms. Price-support payments are made on a per-bushel basis, not on a per-farm basis. Thus, traditionally, the larger the farm, the bigger

If this wheat farmer is guaranteed a high price, will he grow more or less wheat?

the benefit from agricultural price supports. In addition, *all* of the benefits from price supports ultimately accrue to *landowners* on whose land price-supported crops grow.

KEEPING PRICE SUPPORTS ALIVE UNDER A NEW NAME Back in the early 1990s, Congress indicated an intention to phase out most agricultural subsidies by the early 2000s. What Congress actually *did* throughout the 1990s, however, was to pass a series of "emergency laws" keeping farm subsidies alive. Some of these laws aimed to replace agricultural price supports with payments to many farmers for growing no crops at all, thereby boosting the market prices of crops by reducing supply. Nevertheless, the federal government and a number of state governments have continued to support prices of a number of agricultural products, such as peanuts, through "marketing loan" programs. These programs advance funds to farmers to help them finance the storage of some or all of their crops. The farmers can then use the stored produce as collateral for borrowing or sell it to the government and use the proceeds to repay debts. Marketing loan programs raise the effective price that farmers receive for their crops and commit federal and state governments to purchasing surplus production. Consequently, they lead to outcomes similar to traditional price-support programs.

How does the federal government's marketing loan program operate for U.S. cotton growers?

POLICY EXAMPLE
King Cotton Receives Royal Government Subsidies

Every year, before a U.S. cotton farmer plants a crop, the federal government extends a direct payment, based on the average size of the farmer's past planting, which the farmer uses to help finance the coming year's planting expenses. After the crop is planted, the farmer can borrow from the government, using the newly sown cotton as collateral. If the world price of cotton falls below a price floor of 65 cents per pound, the grower receives a payment from the government—effectively compensating the farmer for surplus cotton the farmer has planted—equal to 13 cents per pound. The world price of cotton has been less than 65 cents per pound for some time, so the government funds the production of surplus cotton in this manner every year. If the world price of cotton falls below 52 cents per pound, farmers turn their cotton over to the govern-

ment, which sells the cotton at the world price and absorbs the loan losses. In this way, the government effectively buys increased surpluses of cotton caused by unexpected drops in cotton prices well below the 65 cent price floor.

All told, total payments to cotton growers by the federal government amount to more than $3 billion per year. The entire U.S. cotton crop typically generates revenues to farmers of about $5 billion per year. Thus, the government usually provides at least 50 percent of all revenues received by cotton producers.

FOR CRITICAL ANALYSIS
What would happen to cotton farmers' revenues if the government raised the price floor?

The Main Beneficiaries of Agricultural Subsidies

In 2002, Congress enacted the Farm Security Act, which has perpetuated marketing loan programs and other subsidy and price-support arrangements for such farm products as wheat, corn, rice, peanuts, and soybeans. All told, the more than $9 billion in U.S. government payments for these and other products amounts to about 25 percent of the annual market value of all U.S. farm production.

The government seeks to cap the annual subsidy payment that an individual farmer can receive at $360,000 per year, but some farmers are able to garner higher annual amounts by exploiting regulatory loopholes. The greatest share of total agricultural subsidies goes to the owners of the largest farming operations. At present, 10 percent of U.S. farmers receive more than 70 percent of agricultural subsidies.

The 2007 Food, Security, and Bioenergy Act expanded on the 2002 legislation by giving farmers raising a number of crops a choice between federal subsidy programs. On the one hand, farmers can opt to participate in traditional programs involving a mix of direct payments and marketing loan programs. On the other hand, farmers can choose a program offering guaranteed revenues. If market clearing crop prices end up higher than those associated with the government's revenue guarantee, farmers sell their crops at the higher prices instead of collecting government subsidies. But if equilibrium crop prices end up below a level consistent with the government guarantee, farmers receive direct subsidies to bring their total revenues up to the guaranteed level.

Price Floors in the Labor Market

The **minimum wage** is the lowest hourly wage rate that firms may legally pay their workers. Proponents favor higher minimum wages to ensure low-income workers a "decent" standard of living. Opponents counter that higher minimum wages cause increased unemployment, particularly among unskilled minority teenagers.

Minimum wage
A wage floor, legislated by government, setting the lowest hourly rate that firms may legally pay workers.

Minimum Wages in the United States

The federal minimum wage started in 1938 at 25 cents an hour, about 40 percent of the average manufacturing wage at the time. Typically, its level has stayed at about 40 to 50 percent of average manufacturing wages. After holding the minimum wage at $5.15 per hour from 1997 to 2007, Congress enacted a series of phased increases in the hourly minimum wage, effective on July 24 of each year, to $5.85 in 2007, $6.55 in 2008, and $7.25 in 2009.

Go to www.econtoday.com/chapter04 for information from the U.S. Department of Labor about recent developments concerning the federal minimum wage.

Many states and cities have their own minimum wage laws that exceed the federal minimum. A number of municipalities refer to their minimum wage rules as "living wage" laws. Governments of these municipalities seek to set minimum wages consistent with living standards they deem to be socially acceptable—that is, overall wage income judged to be sufficient to purchase basic items such as housing and food.

Economic Effects of a Minimum Wage

What happens when the government establishes a floor on wages? The effects can be seen in Figure 4-5 on the next page. We start off in equilibrium with the equilibrium wage rate of W_e and the equilibrium quantity of labor equal to Q_e. A minimum wage, W_m, higher than W_e, is imposed. At W_m, the quantity demanded for labor is reduced to Q_d, and some workers now become unemployed. Some workers will become unemployed as a result of the minimum wage, but others will move to sectors where minimum wage laws do not apply; wages will be pushed down in these uncovered sectors.

Note that the reduction in employment from Q_e to Q_d, or the distance from B to A, is less than the excess quantity of labor supplied at wage rate W_m. This excess quantity supplied is the distance between A and C, or the distance between Q_d and Q_s. The reason the reduction in employment is smaller than the excess quantity of labor supplied at the minimum wage is that the excess quantity of labor supplied also includes the *additional* workers who would like to work more hours at the new, higher minimum wage.

FIGURE 4-5

The Effect of Minimum Wages

The market clearing wage rate is W_e. The market clearing quantity of employment is Q_e, determined by the intersection of supply and demand at point E. A minimum wage equal to W_m is established. The quantity of labor demanded is reduced to Q_d. The reduction in employment from Q_e to Q_d is equal to the distance between B and A. That distance is smaller than the excess quantity of labor supplied at wage rate W_m. The distance between B and C is the increase in the quantity of labor supplied that results from the higher minimum wage rate.

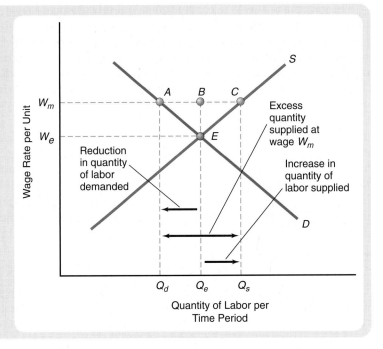

In the long run (a time period that is long enough to allow for full adjustment by workers and firms), some of the reduction in the quantity of labor demanded will result from a reduction in the number of firms, and some will result from changes in the number of workers employed by each firm. Economists estimate that a 10 percent increase in the minimum wage relative to the average prices of goods and services decreases total employment of those affected by 1 to 2 percent.

We can conclude from application of demand and supply analysis that a minimum wage established above the equilibrium wage rate typically has two fundamental effects. On the one hand, it boosts the wage earnings of those people who obtain employment. On the other hand, the minimum wage results in unemployment for other individuals. Thus, demand and supply analysis implies that the minimum wage makes some people better off while making others much worse off.

Quantity Restrictions

Governments can impose quantity restrictions on a market. The most obvious restriction is an outright ban on the ownership or trading of a good. It is currently illegal to buy and sell human organs. It is also currently illegal to buy and sell certain psychoactive drugs such as cocaine, heroin, and marijuana. In some states, it is illegal to start a new hospital without obtaining a license for a particular number of beds to be offered to patients. This licensing requirement effectively limits the quantity of hospital beds in some states. From 1933 to 1973, it was illegal for U.S. citizens to own gold except for manufacturing, medicinal, or jewelry purposes.

Some of the most common quantity restrictions exist in the area of international trade. The U.S. government, as well as many foreign governments, imposes import quotas on a variety of goods. An **import quota** is a supply restriction that prohibits

Import quota
A physical supply restriction on imports of a particular good, such as sugar. Foreign exporters are unable to sell in the United States more than the quantity specified in the import quota.

the importation of more than a specified quantity of a particular good in a one-year period. The United States has had import quotas on tobacco, sugar, and immigrant labor. For many years, there were import quotas on oil coming into the United States. There are also "voluntary" import quotas on certain goods. For instance, in 2005 the Chinese government agreed to "voluntarily" restrict the amount of textile products China sends to the United States and the European Union.

QUICK QUIZ   *See page 106 for the answers. Review concepts from this section in MyEconLab.*

With a price-_____ system, the government sets a minimum price at which, say, qualifying farm products can be sold. Any farmers who cannot sell at that price in the market can "sell" their surplus to the government. The only way a price-_____ system can survive is for the government or some other entity to buy up the excess quantity supplied at the support price.

When a _____ is placed on wages at a rate that is above market equilibrium, the result is an excess quantity of labor supplied at that minimum wage.

Quantity restrictions may take the form of _____ _____, which are limits on the quantity of specific foreign goods that can be brought into the United States for resale purposes.

You Are There

Finding a Spanish Instructor in the Midst of a Teacher Shortage

This year, average starting salaries for all college graduates have increased 5 percent. But the good news for college graduates only magnifies the problem faced by Jill Rogers, superintendent of schools in Martinsville, Illinois.

Like most public school superintendents across the land, Rogers must deal with what promises to be a wave of retirements by experienced teachers who entered the profession in the 1960s and 1970s. As schools scramble to replace these teachers, the demand for new teachers in sciences and languages is rising rapidly. On this late summer day, finding a Spanish teacher is the challenge that Rogers confronts. Classes begin in a week, and so far she has been unable to hire a qualified person to fill an open position. The source of her difficulty is a dollar figure—$28,352, the maximum permissible salary for an inexperienced teacher mandated under the government-sponsored school system's salary scale. As the day begins, Rogers is among the hundreds of public school superintendents nationwide trying to hire Spanish teachers at a salary at least $3,000 below the market clearing salary for new liberal arts graduates.

Fortunately, good news arrives before the end of the day. Rogers finally has landed a Spanish teacher. The new hire is a native Spanish-speaking woman from Argentina. She lacks teaching credentials, so Rogers quickly arranges for her to begin an accelerated teaching certification program at a local university. Rogers realizes that her school district is now among the fortunate few that will manage to hire a new Spanish teacher this year.

CRITICAL ANALYSIS QUESTIONS

1. Average nonteaching salaries for college graduates in the sciences are almost $20,000 higher than those for graduates in languages and other liberal arts fields. Given that teachers in all fields are paid similar salaries, how does this help to explain why the shortage of public school science teachers is particularly acute?

2. During the coming years, barring changes in public school salary structures, what is likely to happen to shortages of teachers in various fields as more experienced teachers retire?

Effects of the $0 Price Ceiling in the Market for Kidneys

CONCEPTS APPLIED

- Price Ceilings
- Nonprice Rationing Devices
- Black Markets

At any given moment, about 76,000 U.S. residents are waiting for kidneys for transplant from donors. Even though so many people suffering from kidney failure would like to obtain a transplant, there are only about 16,000 kidney transplants per year. Most people with two healthy kidneys could get by with only one without shortening their lives. In principle, almost any willing individual with a compatible kidney could provide it to someone on the kidney-transplant waiting list who has the same blood type. Nevertheless, nearly all transplanted kidneys obtained from living donors are donated by relatives or friends of the recipients. There are two key reasons for this. One is that relatives are more likely to have compatible kidneys. Another is that a person who cares about a recipient is more likely to be willing to incur the explicit and implicit costs associated with donating a kidney at the legal price ceiling of $0.

The Predictable Result of a $0 Price Ceiling: A Shortage

In the United States and most other nations, it is illegal to pay someone to provide an organ for transplantation. Hence, the only price at which an organ can be obtained is $0. Effectively, this is a price ceiling for organs such as kidneys.

Figure 4-6 provides a graphical representation of the market for kidneys for transplant. The quantity of kidneys demanded at the ceiling price of $0, at the point at which the demand curve touches the horizontal axis, is about 76,000. For most goods and services, a positive price is required to induce a positive quantity supplied, so supply curves usually touch the vertical axis. In the market for kidneys for transplantation, however, some people

are willing to provide kidneys at the legal price of $0, as evidenced by the fact that donors now provide an average of about 16,000 kidneys per year at this price. Thus, there is an excess quantity demanded equal to about 60,000 kidneys per year—that is, 60,000 people suffering from kidney failure and languishing on the transplant list.

Predictable Consequences of a Kidney Shortage

Because elimination of the kidney shortage through the price system is illegal, nonprice rationing devices are the main focus of efforts to direct available kidneys to people with failed kidneys. Most medical centers utilize three key criteria. First, the donor kidney must be compatible with the recipient's blood type and other

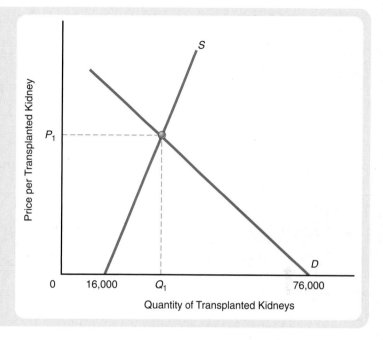

FIGURE 4-6

The Shortage of Kidneys for Transplantation at a Ceiling Price of $0

If kidneys for transplantation could be exchanged at an unregulated price, the equilibrium price would be equal to P_1, and the equilibrium quantity of transplants per year would be Q_1. At present, however, payments for organ transplants are illegal. Hence, there is a ceiling price of $0. At this price, about 16,000 kidneys for transplantation are supplied by donors each year. Approximately 76,000 kidneys for transplantation are demanded by people suffering from failed kidneys. Thus, there is a shortage of kidneys for transplantation equal to about 60,000 per year.

physical requirements. Second, a living donor must have a documented relationship—as a family member or friend—with a specially designated recipient. Third, if there is no clear relationship between a donor and a potential recipient, transplants take place strictly on a first-come, first-served basis.

For people with failed kidneys who are far down on the waiting list, the only legal option is to continue waiting. An illegal option is the black market. At fees starting at about $150,000, so-called organ brokers offer to locate a donor willing to provide a compatible kidney and a surgeon willing to perform a transplant (but often only for an additional fee). An estimated 6,000 kidney transplants worldwide are arranged by black market brokers.

Kidney Exchanges?

Economists have come up with a legal approach that may help reduce the size of the kidney shortage: organized "kidney exchanges" involving loved ones of people awaiting transplants. For instance, if a father with blood type A cannot donate a kidney to his daughter with blood type B, he may be amenable to donating a kidney to a young man with blood type A, whose sister with blood type B in turn donates a kidney to the father's daughter. Several medical centers are already utilizing kidney-exchange programs aimed at increasing the number of lifesaving transplants.

Test your understanding of this chapter by going online to **MyEconLab**.
In the Study Plan for this chapter, select Section N: News.

For Critical Analysis

1. Given normally shaped demand and supply curves, why does the maximum possible shortage of a good or service exist at a ceiling price of $0?

2. In recent years, an increasing number of medical facilities have struggled to prevent surgery patients from contracting infections caused by drug-resistant bacteria.

How do you suppose that the shortage of kidneys for transplantation would be affected if potential kidney donors become more fearful of such infections?

Web Resources

1. Read a description of the New England Program for Kidney Exchange at www.econtoday.com/chapter04.
2. To learn about the system of organized kidney exchange utilized by Johns Hopkins Medicine, go to www.econtoday.com/chapter04.

Research Project

Abstracting from normative issues relating to morals or ethics, what positive economic prediction can you make about the likely effect of legalized payments for transplanted kidneys on the size of the kidney shortage? Refer to Figure 4-6 on the previous page in explaining your answer.

 **myeconlab**

Here is what you should know after reading this chapter. **MyEconLab** will help you identify what you know, and where to go when you need to practice.

WHAT YOU SHOULD KNOW		WHERE TO GO TO PRACTICE
Essential Features of the Price System The price system, otherwise called the market system, allows prices to respond to changes in supply and demand for different commodities. Consumers' and business managers' decisions on resource use depend on what happens to prices. In the price system, exchange takes place in markets. The terms of exchange are communicated by prices in the marketplace, where middlemen reduce transaction costs by bringing buyers and sellers together.	price system, 83 voluntary exchange, 83 terms of exchange, 83 transaction costs, 83	• **MyEconLab** Study Plan 4.1 • Audio introduction to Chapter 4
How Changes in Demand and Supply Affect the Market Price and Equilibrium Quantity With a given supply curve, an increase in demand causes a rise in the market price and an increase in the equilibrium quantity, and a decrease in demand induces a fall in the market price and a decline in the equilibrium quantity. With a given demand curve, an increase in supply causes a fall in the market price and an increase in the equilibrium quantity, and a decrease in supply causes a rise in the market price and a decline in the equilibrium quantity. When both demand and supply shift at the same time, indeterminate results may occur. We must know the direction and degree of each shift in order to predict the change in the market price and the equilibrium quantity.	KEY FIGURE Figure 4-1, 85	• **MyEconLab** Study Plan 4.2 • Animated Figure 4-1 • ABC News Video: What Drives the Market: Supply and Demand
The Rationing Function of Prices In the market system, prices perform a rationing function—they ration scarce goods and services. Other ways of rationing include first come, first served; political power; physical force; random assignment; and coupons.		• **MyEconLab** Study Plan 4.3 • Video: Price Flexibility, the Essential Role of Rationing via Price and Alternative Rationing Systems

(continued)

 *(continued)*

WHAT YOU SHOULD KNOW

The Effects of Price Ceilings Government-imposed price controls that require prices to be no higher than a certain level are price ceilings. If a government sets a price ceiling below the market price, then at the ceiling price the quantity of the good demanded will exceed the quantity supplied. There will be a shortage of the good at the ceiling price. For instance, rent controls place a ceiling on permitted rental prices and create shortages in housing markets. Price ceilings can lead to nonprice rationing devices and black markets.

price controls, 90
price ceiling, 90
price floor, 90
nonprice rationing
  devices, 90
black market, 91
rent control, 92

KEY FIGURE
Figure 4-3, 91

WHERE TO GO TO PRACTICE

- **MyEconLab** Study Plans 4.4, 4.5
- Animated Figure 4-3

The Effects of Price Floors Government-mandated price controls that require prices to be no lower than a certain level are price floors. If a government sets a price floor above the market price, then at the floor price the quantity of the good supplied will exceed the quantity demanded. There will be a surplus of the good at the floor price. For instance, minimum wage laws that establish a price floor in the labor market and government price-support policies that set price floors in markets for agricultural goods often generate surpluses in these markets.

minimum wage, 97

KEY FIGURES
Figure 4-4, 95
Figure 4-5, 98

- **MyEconLab** Study Plans 4.6, 4.7
- Video: Minimum Wages
- Animated Figures 4-4, 4-5

Government-Imposed Restrictions on Market Quantities Quantity restrictions can take the form of outright government bans on the sale of certain goods, such as human organs or various psychoactive drugs. They can also arise from licensing requirements that limit the number of producers and thereby restrict the amount supplied of a good or service. Another example is an import quota, which limits the number of units of a foreign-produced good that can legally be sold domestically.

import quota, 98

- **MyEconLab** Study Plan 4.8

Log in to MyEconLab, take a chapter test, and get a personalized Study Plan that tells you which concepts you understand and which ones you need to review. From there, MyEconLab will give you further practice, tutorials, animations, videos, and guided solutions.
Log in to www.myeconlab.com

PROBLEMS

All problems are assignable in **myeconlab** . *Answers to odd-numbered problems appear at the back of the book.*

4-1. In recent years, technological improvements have greatly reduced the costs of producing music CDs, and a number of new firms have entered the music CD industry. At the same time, prices of substitutes for music CDs, such as Internet downloads and music DVDs, have declined considerably. Construct a supply and demand diagram of the market for music CDs. Illustrate the impacts of these developments, and evaluate the effects on the market price and equilibrium quantity.

4-2. Advances in research and development in the pharmaceutical industry have enabled manufacturers to identify potential cures more quickly and therefore at lower cost. At the same time, the aging of our society has increased the demand for new drugs. Construct a supply and demand diagram of the market for pharmaceutical drugs. Illustrate the impacts of these developments, and evaluate the effects on the market price and the equilibrium quantity.

4-3. The following table depicts the quantity demanded and quantity supplied of studio apartments in a small college town.

Monthly Rent	Quantity Demanded	Quantity Supplied
$600	3,000	1,600
$650	2,500	1,800
$700	2,000	2,000
$750	1,500	2,200
$800	1,000	2,400

What are the market price and equilibrium quantity of apartments in this town? If this town imposes a rent control of $650 per month, how many studio apartments will be rented?

4-4. The U.S. government imposes a price floor for U.S. sugar that is above the market clearing price. Illustrate the U.S. sugar market with the price floor in place. Discuss the effects of the price floor on conditions in the market for sugar in the United States.

4-5. The Canadian sugar industry has complained that U.S. sugar manufacturers "dump" sugar surpluses in the Canadian market. U.S. chocolate manufacturers have also complained about the high U.S. price of sugar. Explain how the imposition of a price floor for U.S. sugar, as described in Problem 4-4, affects each of these markets. What are the changes in equilibrium quantities and market prices due to the price floor?

4-6. Suppose that the U.S. government places a ceiling on the price of Internet access.

a. Show why there is a shortage of Internet access at the legal price.

b. Suppose that a black market for Internet providers arises, with Internet service providers developing hidden connections. Illustrate the black market for Internet access, including the implicit supply schedule, the legal price, the black market supply and demand, and the highest feasible black market price.

4-7. The table below illustrates the demand and supply schedules for seats on air flights between two cities:

Price	Quantity Demanded	Quantity Supplied
$200	2,000	1,200
$300	1,800	1,400
$400	1,600	1,600
$500	1,400	1,800
$600	1,200	2,000

What are the market price and equilibrium quantity in this market? Now suppose that federal authorities limit the number of flights between the two cities to ensure that no more than 1,200 passengers can be flown. Evaluate the effects of this quota if price adjusts. (Hint: How much are the 1,200 passengers willing to pay for their flights?)

4-8. The consequences of decriminalizing illegal drugs have long been debated. Some claim that legalization will lower the price of these drugs and reduce related crime. Others claim that more people will use these drugs. Suppose that some of these drugs are legalized so that anyone may sell them and use them. Now consider the two claims—that price will fall and quantity demanded will increase. Based on positive economic analysis, are these claims sound?

4-9. In recent years, the government of Pakistan has established a support price for wheat of about $0.20 per kilogram of wheat. At this price, consumers are willing to purchase 10 billion kilograms of wheat per year, while Pakistani farmers are willing to grow and harvest 18 billion kilograms of wheat per year. The government purchases and stores all surplus wheat.

a. What are annual consumer expenditures on the Pakistani wheat crop?

b. What are annual government expenditures on the Pakistani wheat crop?

c. How much, in total, do Pakistani wheat farmers receive for the wheat they produce?

4-10. Consider the information in Problem 4-9 and your answers to that question. Suppose that the market clearing price of Pakistani wheat in the absence of price supports is equal to $0.10 per kilogram. At this price, the quantity of wheat demanded is 12 billion kilograms. Under the government wheat price-support program, how much more is spent each year on wheat harvested in Pakistan than otherwise would have been spent in an unregulated market for Pakistani wheat?

4-11. Consider the diagram below, which depicts the labor market in a city that has adopted a "living wage law" requiring employers to pay a minimum wage rate of $9 per hour. Answer the questions that follow.

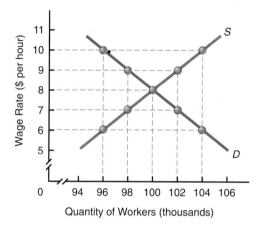

a. What condition exists in this city's labor market at the present minimum wage of $9 per hour? How many people are unemployed at this wage?

b. A city councilwoman has proposed amending the living wage law. She suggests reducing the minimum wage to $6 per hour. Assuming that the labor demand and supply curves were to remain in their present positions, how many people would be unemployed at a $6 minimum wage?

c. A councilman has offered a counterproposal. In his view, the current minimum wage is too low and should be increased to $10 per hour. Assuming that the labor demand and supply curves remain in their present positions, how many people would be unemployed at a $10 minimum wage?

4-12. Suppose that owners of high-rise office buildings are the main employers of custodial workers in a city. The city has decided to impose rent controls, and it has established a rent ceiling below the previous equilibrium rental rate for offices throughout the city.

a. How will the quantity of offices the building owners lease change?

b. How will the market wage and equilibrium quantity of labor services provided by custodial workers be affected by the imposition of rent controls?

4-13. In 2007, the government of a nation established a price support for wheat. The government's support price has been above the equilibrium price each year since, and the government has purchased all wheat over and above the amounts that consumers have bought at the support price. Every year since 2007, there has been an increase in the number of wheat producers in the market. No other factors affecting the market for wheat have changed. Predict what has happened every year since 2007 to each of the following:

a. Amount of wheat supplied by wheat producers

b. Amount of wheat demanded by wheat consumers

c. Amount of wheat purchased by the government

4-14. In advance of the recent increase in the U.S. minimum wage rate, the government of the state of Arizona decided to boost its own minimum wage by $1.60 per hour. This pushed the wage rate earned by Arizona teenagers above the equilibrium wage rate in the teen labor market. What is the predicted effect of this action by Arizona's government on each of the following?

a. The quantity of labor supplied by Arizona teenagers

b. The quantity of labor demanded by employers of Arizona teenagers

c. The number of unemployed Arizona teenagers

ECONOMICS ON THE NET

The Floor on Milk Prices At various times, the U.S. government has established price floors for milk. This application gives you an opportunity to apply what you have learned in this chapter to this real-world issue.

Title: Northeast Dairy Compact Commission

Navigation: Go to www.econtoday.com/chapter04 to visit the Web site of the Northeast Dairy Compact Commission.

Application Read the contents and answer these questions.

1. Based on the government-set price control concepts discussed in Chapter 4, explain the Northeast Dairy Compact that was once in place in the northeastern United States.

2. Draw a diagram illustrating the supply of and demand for milk in the Northeast Dairy Compact and the supply of and demand for milk outside the Northeast Dairy Compact. Illustrate how the compact affected the quantities demanded and supplied for participants in the compact. In addition, show how this affected the market for milk produced by those producers outside the dairy compact.

3. Economists have found that while the Northeast Dairy Compact functioned, midwestern dairy farmers lost their dominance of milk production and sales. In light of your answer to Question 2, explain how this occurred.

For Group Discussion and Analysis Discuss the impact of congressional failure to reauthorize the compact based on your above answers. Identify which arguments in your debate are based on positive economic analysis and which are normative arguments.

ANSWERS TO QUICK QUIZZES

p. 88: (i) terms . . . exchange . . . transaction; (ii) demand . . . supply . . . supply . . . demand; (iii) immediately . . . time

p. 90: (i) first come, first served . . . political power . . . physical force . . . random assignment . . . coupons; (ii) queuing

p. 92: (i) ceilings . . . floors; (ii) ceiling . . . controls

p. 94: (i) Rental; (ii) controls . . . controls; (iii) key money

p. 99: (i) support . . . support; (ii) floor; (iii) import quotas

Public Spending and Public Choice

5

I t is a clear, colorless liquid with a distinctive, sickly sweet odor. Chemists refer to it as an example of a "hydroxyl compound." To most of the rest of us, however, it is *ethanol*, a substance typically manufactured in the United States using corn as a key input. Combining 1 part ethanol with 9 parts gasoline yields a motor fuel, known as "E10," that can be used to power most existing vehicles. Many observers suggest that ethanol-based motor fuel offers a win–win situation: less reliance on gasoline derived largely from foreign oil and reduced carbon pollution from auto emissions. The U.S. government currently agrees—to the tune of more than $8 billion in annual government subsidies for ethanol production. In this chapter, you will learn about rationales for this and other government subsidies.

LEARNING OBJECTIVES

myeconlab

MyEconLab helps you master each objective and study more efficiently. See end of chapter for details.

After reading this chapter, you should be able to:

- Explain how market failures such as externalities might justify economic functions of government

- Distinguish between private goods and public goods and explain the nature of the free-rider problem

- Describe political functions of government that entail its involvement in the economy

- Analyze how Medicare affects the incentives to consume medical services

- Explain why increases in government spending on public education have not been associated with improvements in measures of student performance

- Discuss the central elements of the theory of public choice

? DID YOU KNOW THAT an auditor recently discovered that a New Jersey public school district had been transmitting salary payments totaling $130,000 per year to the account of an employee who had been deceased for more than 30 years? The same audit found that the school district had paid a company $953,000 for copy equipment even though the purchase order was for equipment valued only at $55,000. A media report quoted a local resident's complaint that the school district "needs to learn how to function like a private business" and "should care about taxpayers as much as companies care about their owners." As you will learn in this chapter, the incentives and institutional arrangements that condition the behavior of private firms and governments differ in some fundamental respects. One key distinction is that while firms function within the price system, a key rationale for the operations of government is to perform functions that the price system does not do well.

What a Price System Can and Cannot Do

Throughout the book so far, we have alluded to the advantages of a price system. High on the list is economic efficiency. In its ideal form, a price system allows all resources to move from lower-valued uses to higher-valued uses via voluntary exchange, by which mutually advantageous trades take place. In a price system, consumers are sovereign; that is to say, they have the individual freedom to decide what they wish to purchase. Politicians and even business managers do not ultimately decide what is produced; consumers decide. Some proponents of the price system argue that this is its most important characteristic. Competition among sellers protects consumers from coercion by one seller, and sellers are protected from coercion by one consumer because other consumers are available.

Sometimes, though, the price system does not generate these results, and too few or too many resources go to specific economic activities. Such situations are called **market failures.** Market failures prevent the price system from attaining economic efficiency and individual freedom. Market failures offer one of the strongest arguments in favor of certain economic functions of government, which we now examine.

Market failure
A situation in which the market economy leads to too few or too many resources going to a specific economic activity.

Correcting for Externalities

In a pure market system, competition generates economic efficiency only when individuals know and must bear the true opportunity cost of their actions. In some circumstances, the price that someone actually pays for a resource, good, or service is higher or lower than the opportunity cost that all of society pays for that same resource, good, or service.

Externalities

Consider a hypothetical world in which there is no government regulation against pollution. You are living in a town that until now has had clean air. A steel mill moves into town. It produces steel and has paid for the inputs—land, labor, capital, and entrepreneurship. The price the mill charges for the steel reflects, in this example, only the costs that it incurs. In the course of production, however, the mill utilizes one input—clean air—by simply using it. This is indeed an input because in making steel, the furnaces emit smoke. The steel mill doesn't have to pay the cost of dirtying the air. Rather, it is the people in the community who incur that cost in the form of dirtier clothes, dirtier cars and houses, and more respiratory illnesses. The effect is similar to

What externality is this family attempting to avoid?

what would happen if the steel mill could take coal or oil or workers' services without paying for them. There is an **externality,** an external cost. Some of the costs associated with the production of the steel have "spilled over" to affect **third parties,** parties other than the buyer and the seller of the steel.

A fundamental reason that air pollution creates external costs is that the air belongs to everyone and hence to no one in particular. Lack of clearly assigned **property rights,** or the rights of an owner to use and exchange property, prevents market prices from reflecting all the costs created by activities that generate spillovers onto third parties.

Why do some observers contend that negative externalities are associated with the growing use of digital billboards?

Externality
A consequence of an economic activity that spills over to affect third parties. Pollution is an externality.

Third parties
Parties who are not directly involved in a given activity or transaction.

Property rights
The rights of an owner to use and to exchange property.

EXAMPLE
Billboards That Catch Drivers' Eyes, Sometimes for Too Long

Outdoor advertising is now the second-fastest-growing form of advertising after Internet ads. Increasingly, advertisers are returning to old-fashioned roadside billboards. Not all billboards are so old-fashioned, however. Of the 500,000 billboards lining U.S. highways and city streets, approximately 2,000 are digital billboards. The number of digital billboards is likely to grow considerably in coming years, because the $500,000 cost of installing a digital billboard is more than outweighed by the ability to sell advertising space to multiple advertisers simultaneously.

For years, critics have regarded old-fashioned billboards as a form of visual pollution blocking views of scenery. In 1965, the federal Highway Beautification Act called for a reduction in the number of billboards but failed to provide sufficient funds to pay owners to remove them. Now, critics

deride billboards for more than just blocking scenic views. They suggest that the bright, eye-catching digital billboards are diverting drivers' eyes from roadways and causing accidents. The digital billboards' bright messages distract drivers, they argue, and thereby create a negative externality by making the roads less safe for drivers and for their passengers and occupants of other cars as well.

FOR CRITICAL ANALYSIS
Why might an owner of a digital billboard respond that assignment of property rights already solves the negative externality "problem" alleged by critics? (Hint: In most states, drivers must obtain liability insurance, and laws typically hold drivers solely responsible for accidents resulting from their being distracted while driving.)

External Costs in Graphical Form

To consider how market prices fail to take into account external costs in situations in which third-party spillovers exist without a clear assignment of property rights, look at panel (a) in Figure 5-1 on the following page. Here we show the demand curve for steel as D. The supply curve is S_1. The supply curve includes only the costs that the firms have to pay. Equilibrium occurs at point E, with a price of $500 per ton and a quantity equal to 110 million tons per year. But producing steel also involves externalities—the external costs that you and your neighbors pay in the form of dirtier clothes, cars, and houses and increased respiratory disease due to the air pollution emitted from the steel mill. In this case, the producers of steel use clean air without having to pay for it. Let's include these external costs in our graph to find out what the full cost of steel production would really be if property rights to the air around the steel mill could generate payments for "owners" of that air. We do this by imagining that steel producers have to pay the "owners" of the air for the input—clean air—that the producers previously used at a zero price.

FIGURE 5-1

External Costs and Benefits

In panel (a), we show a situation in which the production of steel generates external costs. If the steel mills ignore pollution, at equilibrium the quantity of steel will be 110 million tons. If the steel mills had to pay for the external costs that are caused by the mills' production but are currently borne by nearby residents, the supply curve would shift the vertical distance A–E_1, to S_2. If consumers of steel were forced to pay a price that reflected the spillover costs, the quantity demanded would fall to 100 million tons. In panel (b), we show a situation in which inoculations against communicable diseases generate external benefits to those individuals who may not be inoculated but who will benefit because epidemics will not occur. If each individual ignores the external benefit of inoculations, the market clearing quantity will be 150 million. If external benefits were taken into account by purchasers of inoculations, however, the demand curve would shift to D_2. The new equilibrium quantity would be 200 million inoculations, and the price of an inoculation would rise from $10 to $15.

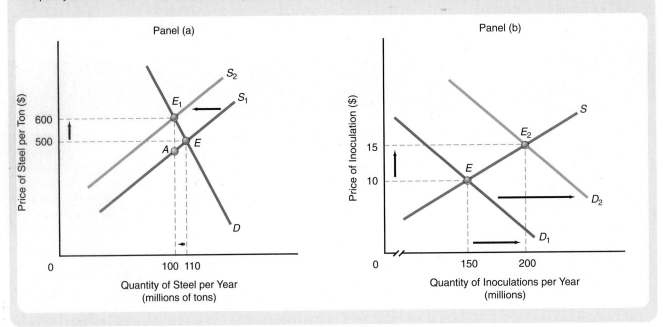

Panel (a)

Panel (b)

Recall from Chapter 3 that an increase in input prices shifts the supply curve up and to the left. Thus, in panel (a) of the figure, the supply curve shifts from S_1 to S_2. External costs equal the vertical distance between A and E_1. In this example, if steel firms had to take into account these external costs, the equilibrium quantity would fall to 100 million tons per year, and the price would rise to $600 per ton. Equilibrium would shift from E to E_1. In contrast, if the price of steel does not account for external costs, third parties bear those costs—represented by the distance between A and E_1—in the form of dirtier clothes, houses, and cars and increased respiratory illnesses.

External Benefits in Graphical Form

Externalities can also be positive. To demonstrate external benefits in graphical form, we will use the example of inoculations against communicable disease. In panel (b) of Figure 5-1, we show the demand curve as D_1 (without taking account of any external benefits) and the supply curve as S. The equilibrium price is $10 per inoculation, and the equilibrium quantity is 150 million inoculations.

We assume, however, that inoculations against communicable diseases generate external benefits to individuals who may not be inoculated but will benefit nevertheless because epidemics will not break out. If such external benefits were taken into account by those who purchase inoculations, the demand curve would shift from D_1 to D_2.

As a consequence of this shift in demand at point E_2, the new equilibrium quantity would be 200 million inoculations, and the new equilibrium price would be $15 per inoculation. If people who consider getting inoculations fail to take external benefits into account, this society is not devoting enough resources to inoculations against communicable diseases.

How do inoculations generate positive externalities?

Resource Misallocations of Externalities

When there are external costs, the market will tend to *overallocate* resources to the production of the good or service in question, for those goods or services are implicitly priced deceptively low. In the steel example, too many resources will be allocated to steel production, because the steel mill owners and managers are not required to take account of the external cost that steel production is imposing on the rest of society. In essence, the full cost of production is not borne by the owners and managers, so the price they charge the public for steel is lower than it would otherwise be. And, of course, the lower price means that buyers are willing and able to buy more. More steel is produced and consumed than if the sellers were to bear external costs.

In contrast, when there are external benefits, the price is too low to induce suppliers to allocate resources to the production of that good or service (because the demand, which fails to reflect the external benefits, is relatively too low). Thus, the market *underallocates* resources to producing the good or service. Hence, in a market system, too many of the goods that generate external costs are produced, and too few of the goods that generate external benefits are produced.

How the Government Can Correct Negative Externalities

In theory, the government can take action to try to correct situations in which a lack of property rights allows third-party spillovers to create an externality. In the case of negative externalities, at least two avenues are open to the government: special taxes and legislative regulation or prohibition.

SPECIAL TAXES In our example of the steel mill, the externality problem arises because using the air for waste disposal is costless to the firm but not to society. The government could attempt to tax the steel mill commensurate with the cost to third parties from smoke in the air. This, in effect, would be a pollution tax or an **effluent fee.** The ultimate effect would be to reduce the supply of steel and raise the price to consumers, ideally making the price equal to the full cost of production to society.

Effluent fee
A charge to a polluter that gives the right to discharge into the air or water a certain amount of pollution; also called a *pollution tax*

REGULATION Alternatively, to correct a negative externality arising from steel production, the government could specify a maximum allowable rate of pollution. This regulation would require that the steel mill install pollution abatement equipment at its facilities, reduce its rate of output, or some combination of the two. Note that the government's job would not be simple, for it would have to determine the appropriate level of pollution, which would require extensive knowledge of both the benefits and the costs of pollution control.

Go to **www.econtoday.com/chapter05** to learn more about how the Environmental Protection Agency uses regulations to try to protect the environment.

How the Government Can Correct Positive Externalities

What can the government do when the production of one good spills *benefits* over to third parties? It has several policy options: financing the production of the good or producing the good itself, subsidies (negative taxes), and regulation.

GOVERNMENT FINANCING AND PRODUCTION If the positive externalities seem extremely large, the government has the option of financing the desired additional production facilities so that the "right" amount of the good will be produced. Again consider inoculations against communicable diseases. The government could—and often does—finance campaigns to inoculate the population. It could (and does) even produce and operate inoculation centers where inoculations are given at no charge.

SUBSIDIES A subsidy is a negative tax; it is a payment made either to a business or to a consumer when the business produces or the consumer buys a good or a service. To generate more inoculations against communicable diseases, the government could subsidize everyone who obtains an inoculation by directly reimbursing those inoculated or by making payments to private firms that provide inoculations. Subsidies reduce the net price to consumers, thereby causing a larger quantity to be demanded.

How are governments seeking to help society capture the external benefits of transportation services that keep elderly drivers off the roads?

POLICY EXAMPLE
Incentives Coax Senior Citizens from Behind the Wheel

Many people continue driving even after their skills and senses falter. Drivers age 75 and older have higher crash rates per mile traveled than all age groups except 16- and 18-year-olds. Drivers age 85 and older are at fault in accidents more than twice as often as younger drivers. Members of the baby boom generation are already reaching the age of 65, when driving capabilities begin to falter, and many more will reach this age during the coming two decades. The Insurance Institute for Highway Safety estimates that if current U.S. population trends continue, by 2030 these drivers will account for 16 percent of all auto accidents and 25 percent of all fatal crashes.

Governments are already working to make roadways safer by providing incentives for aging baby boomers to park their cars and choose alternative modes of transportation. Many state governments are easing regulations that impede efforts by private firms to offer elderly people transportation. Some municipal governments, such as those in Atlanta and Oklahoma City, are providing vouchers that help cover most of the price of public transportation. A few cities, such as Portland, Maine, are supporting efforts by nonprofit organizations to provide transportation services to seniors. One Portland-supported nonprofit organization even accepts car trade-ins from seniors in return for credit toward future transportation services. Thus, governments are promoting alternative modes of transportation for seniors in an effort to attain the external benefit of getting more elderly residents out from behind the wheel.

FOR CRITICAL ANALYSIS
How do government subsidies for alternative modes of transportation affect seniors' demands for these alternative transportation services?

REGULATION In some cases involving positive externalities, the government can require by law that individuals in the society undertake a certain action. For example, regulations require that all school-age children be inoculated before entering public and private schools. Some people believe that a basic school education itself generates positive externalities. Perhaps as a result of this belief, we have regulations—laws—that require all school-age children to be enrolled in a public or private school.

QUICK QUIZ   *See page 133 for the answers. Review concepts from this section in MyEconLab.*

External _____ lead to an overallocation of resources to the specific economic activity. Two possible ways of correcting these spillovers are _____ and _____.

External _____ result in an underallocation of resources to the specific activity. Three possible government

corrections are _____ the production of the activity, _____ private firms or consumers to engage in the activity, and _____.

The Other Economic Functions of Government

Besides correcting for externalities, the government performs many other economic functions that affect the way exchange is carried out. In contrast, the political functions of government have to do with deciding how income should be redistributed among households and selecting which goods and services have special merits and should therefore be treated differently. The economic and political functions of government can and do overlap.

Let's look at four more economic functions of government.

Providing a Legal System

The courts and the police may not at first seem like economic functions of government. Their activities nonetheless have important consequences for economic activities in any country. You and I enter into contracts constantly, whether they be oral or written, expressed or implied. When we believe that we have been wronged, we seek redress of our grievances through our legal institutions. Moreover, consider the legal system that is necessary for the smooth functioning of our economic system. Our system has defined quite explicitly the legal status of businesses, the rights of private ownership, and a method of enforcing contracts. All relationships among consumers and businesses are governed by the legal rules of the game. In its judicial function, then, the government serves as the referee for settling disputes in the economic arena. In this role, the government often imposes penalties for violations of legal rules.

Much of our legal system is involved with defining and protecting property rights. One might say that property rights are really the rules of our economic game. When property rights are well defined, owners of property have an incentive to use that property efficiently. Any mistakes in their decisions about the use of property have negative consequences that the owners suffer. Furthermore, when property rights are well defined, owners of property have an incentive to maintain that property so that if they ever desire to sell it, it will fetch a better price.

Promoting Competition

Many people believe that the only way to attain economic efficiency is through competition. One of the roles of government is to serve as the protector of a competitive economic system. Congress and the various state governments have passed **antitrust legislation.** Such legislation makes illegal certain (but not all) economic activities that might restrain trade—that is, that might prevent free competition among actual and potential rival firms in the marketplace. The avowed aim of

Antitrust legislation
Laws that restrict the formation of monopolies and regulate certain anticompetitive business practices.

Monopoly
A firm that can determine the market price of a good. In the extreme case, a monopoly is the only seller of a good or service.

antitrust legislation is to reduce the power of **monopolies**—firms that can determine the market price of the goods they sell. A large number of antitrust laws have been passed that prohibit specific anticompetitive actions. Both the Antitrust Division of the Department of Justice and the Federal Trade Commission attempt to enforce these antitrust laws. Various state judicial agencies also expend efforts at maintaining competition.

Providing Public Goods

Private goods
Goods that can be consumed by only one individual at a time. Private goods are subject to the principle of rival consumption.

The goods used in our examples up to this point have been **private goods.** When I eat a cheeseburger, you cannot eat the same one. So you and I are rivals for that cheeseburger, just as much as contenders for the title of world champion are. When I use a DVD player, you cannot play some other disc at the same time. When I use the services of an auto mechanic, that person cannot work at the same time for you. That is the distinguishing feature of private goods—their use is exclusive to the people who purchase or rent them. The **principle of rival consumption** applies to all private goods by definition. Rival consumption is easy to understand. Either you use a private good or I use it.

Principle of rival consumption
The recognition that individuals are rivals in consuming private goods because one person's consumption reduces the amount available for others to consume.

There is an entire class of goods that are not private goods. These are called **public goods.** The principle of rival consumption does not apply to them. They can be consumed *jointly* by many individuals simultaneously, and no one can be excluded from consuming these goods even if they fail to pay to do so. National defense, police protection, and the legal system are examples of public goods.

Public goods
Goods for which the principle of rival consumption does not apply; they can be jointly consumed by many individuals simultaneously at no additional cost and with no reduction in quality or quantity. Also no one who fails to help pay for the good can be denied the benefit of the good.

CHARACTERISTICS OF PUBLIC GOODS Two fundamental characteristics of public goods set them apart from all other goods:

1. *Public goods can be used by more and more people at no additional opportunity cost and without depriving others of any of the services of the goods.* Once funds have been spent on national defense, the defense protection you receive does not reduce the amount of protection bestowed on anyone else. The opportunity cost of your receiving national defense once it is in place is zero because once national defense is in place to protect you, it also protects others.

2. *It is difficult to design a collection system for a public good on the basis of how much individuals use it.* Nonpayers can often utilize a public good without incurring any monetary cost, because the cost of excluding them from using the good is so high. Those who provide the public good find that it is not cost-effective to prevent nonpayers from utilizing it. For instance, taxpayers who pay to provide national defense typically do not incur the costs that would be entailed in excluding nonpayers from benefiting from national defense.

One of the problems of public goods is that the private sector has a difficult, if not impossible, time providing them. Individuals in the private sector have little or no incentive to offer public goods. It is difficult for them to make a profit doing so, because nonpayers cannot be excluded. Consequently, true public goods must necessarily be provided by government. Note, though, that economists do not categorize something as a public good simply because the government provides it.

When it comes to public goods, what's new about "dot-nu" on the Internet?

E-COMMERCE EXAMPLE

Is the "Nu" Internet Domain a Public Good?

With its closest neighbor, Tonga, more than 350 miles distant, the South Pacific island nation of Niue (pronounced "new-ay") is among the earth's most remote locales. Nevertheless, a key national objective is to be one of the most Web-connected countries on the planet. Niue's residents were the first to possess nationwide wireless Internet access; hence, Niue's self-proclaimed nickname—the "WiFi nation." Complete wireless access is provided by a private company based in Medfield, Massachusetts. In return, Niue's government has granted to that company most legal rights to the Internet domain name "dot-nu." Of course, "nu" sounds like "new" in English, and in Swedish "nu" happens to mean "now." Thus, firms in English-speaking nations and in Sweden have been rushing to purchase Web addresses with the "nu" domain name.

Now many residents are objecting to this arrangement. If the Niue government had retained control over Web addresses within the "nu" domain, they contend, the nation could have reaped benefits, such as a steady stream of registration fees that more and more of its residents could have received at no additional opportunity cost. Furthermore, they argue, none of Niue's residents could have been denied such benefits, even if they had not paid for them. Hence, critics of the deal with the U.S. company suggest that residents of Niue have been cheated out of control over what ought to be a public good—at least, by their logic.

FOR CRITICAL ANALYSIS

Is the "nu" domain on the Internet really a public good? (Hint: Is the "nu" domain name currently subject to the principle of rival consumption? Does possession of only one of the two characteristics of a public good mean that an item is a public good?)

FREE RIDERS The nature of public goods leads to the **free-rider problem,** a situation in which some individuals take advantage of the fact that others will assume the burden of paying for public goods such as national defense. Suppose that citizens were taxed directly in proportion to how much they tell an interviewer that they value national defense. Some people who actually value national defense will probably tell interviewers that it has no value to them—they don't want any of it. Such people are trying to be free riders. We may all want to be free riders if we believe that someone else will provide the commodity in question that we actually value.

The free-rider problem often arises in connection with sharing the burden of international defense. A country may choose to belong to a multilateral defense organization, such as the North Atlantic Treaty Organization (NATO), but then consistently attempt to avoid contributing funds to the organization. The nation knows it would be defended by others in NATO if it were attacked but would rather not pay for such defense. In short, it seeks a free ride.

Free-rider problem
A problem that arises when individuals presume that others will pay for public goods so that, individually, they can escape paying for their portion without causing a reduction in production.

Ensuring Economywide Stability

Our economy sometimes faces the problems of undesired unemployment and rising prices. The government, especially the federal government, has made an attempt to solve these problems by trying to stabilize the economy by smoothing out the ups and downs in overall business activity. The notion that the federal government should undertake actions to stabilize business activity is a relatively new idea in the United States, encouraged by high unemployment rates during the Great Depression of the 1930s and subsequent theories about possible ways that government could reduce unemployment. In 1946, Congress passed the Full-Employment Act, a landmark law concerning government responsibility for economic performance. It established three goals for government stabilization policy: full employment, price stability, and economic growth. These goals have provided the justification for many government economic programs during the post–World War II period.

QUICK QUIZ   See page 133 for the answers. Review concepts from this section in MyEconLab.

The economic activities of government include (1) correcting for _____, (2) providing a _____ _____, (3) promoting _____, (4) producing _____ goods, and (5) ensuring _____ _____.

The principle of _____ _____ does not apply to public goods as it does to private goods.

Public goods have two characteristics: (1) Once they are produced, there is no additional _____ _____ when additional consumers use them, because your use of a public good does not deprive others of its simultaneous use; and (2) consumers cannot conveniently be _____ on the basis of use.

The Political Functions of Government

At least two functions of government are political or normative functions rather than economic ones like those discussed in the first part of this chapter. These two areas are (1) the provision and regulation of government-sponsored and government-inhibited goods and (2) income redistribution.

Government-Sponsored and Government-Inhibited Goods

Through political processes, governments often determine that certain goods possess special merit and seek to promote their production and consumption. A **government-sponsored good** is defined as any good that the political process has deemed socially desirable. (Note that nothing inherent in any particular good makes it a government-sponsored good. The designation is entirely subjective.) Examples of government-sponsored goods in our society are sports stadiums, museums, ballets, plays, and concerts. In these areas, the government's role is the provision of these goods to the people in society who would not otherwise purchase them at market clearing prices or who would not purchase an amount of them judged to be sufficient. This provision may take the form of government production and distribution of the goods. It can also take the form of reimbursement for spending on government-sponsored goods or subsidies to producers or consumers for part of the goods' costs. Governments do indeed subsidize such goods as professional sports, concerts, ballets, museums, and plays. In most cases, those goods would not be so numerous without subsidization.

Government-inhibited goods are the opposite of government-sponsored goods. They are goods that, through the political process, have been deemed socially undesirable. Heroin, cigarettes, gambling, and cocaine are examples. The government exercises its role with respect to these goods by taxing, regulating, or prohibiting their manufacture, sale, and use. Governments justify the relatively high taxes on alcohol and tobacco by declaring that they are socially undesirable. The best-known example of governmental exercise of power in this area is the stance against certain psychoactive drugs. Most psychoactives (except nicotine, caffeine, and alcohol) are either expressly prohibited, as is the case for heroin, cocaine, and opium, or heavily regulated, as in the case of prescription psychoactives.

Government-sponsored good
A good that has been deemed socially desirable through the political process. Museums are an example.

Government-inhibited good
A good that has been deemed socially undesirable through the political process. Heroin is an example.

This drug bust represents what type of government activity?

What item is a government-inhibited good in the United States but a government-sponsored good in China?

INTERNATIONAL POLICY EXAMPLE
China's Government Struggles with How to Regard Tobacco

About 36 percent of all adults in China smoke, whereas only 21 percent of adults in the United States do. An estimated 10 percent of Chinese middle school students smoke, which is nearly double the U.S. rate. All told, the number of smokers in China—about 350 million—exceeds the entire U.S. population.

For China's government, the good news is that it owns the nation's cigarette manufacturing company, China National Tobacco Corporation. The government plows earnings from the firm's tobacco sales into a variety of activities, including constructing highways, hydroelectric dams, and railroads. The bad news is that all the smoking that the China National Tobacco Corporation has promoted in advertising campaigns is creating an epidemic of diseases, including lung cancer,

emphysema, and oral cancer. At present, more than 1 million Chinese residents die of tobacco-related diseases each year. The rate of growth of smoking is so high that this death toll is projected to more than double by 2025.

Consequently, even as the Chinese government sponsors tobacco production, the government's Center for Disease Control and Prevention has declared tobacco use to be the nation's biggest public health problem. China's government has regarded cigarettes as a government-sponsored good for 50 years. Now it is beginning to reconsider this designation.

FOR CRITICAL ANALYSIS
Who stands to lose if China's government ends tobacco's status as a government-sponsored good?

Income Redistribution

Another relatively recent political function of government has been the explicit redistribution of income. This redistribution uses two systems: the progressive income tax (described in Chapter 6) and transfer payments. **Transfer payments** are payments made to individuals for which no services or goods are rendered in return. The two primary money transfer payments in our system are Social Security old-age and disability benefits and unemployment insurance benefits. Income redistribution also includes a large amount of income **transfers in kind,** rather than money transfers. Some income transfers in kind are food stamps, Medicare and Medicaid, government health care services, and subsidized public housing.

The government has also engaged in other activities as a form of redistribution of income. For example, the provision of public education is at least in part an attempt to redistribute income by making sure that the poor have access to education.

Transfer payments
Money payments made by governments to individuals for which no services or goods are rendered in return. Examples are Social Security old-age and disability benefits and unemployment insurance benefits.

Transfers in kind
Payments that are in the form of actual goods and services, such as food stamps, subsidized public housing, and medical care, and for which no goods or services are rendered in return.

QUICK QUIZ   *See page 133 for the answers. Review concepts from this section in MyEconLab.*

Political, or normative, activities of the government include the provision and regulation of _____-_____ and _____-_____ goods and _____ redistribution.

Government-sponsored and government-inhibited goods do not have any inherent characteristics that qualify them as such; rather, collectively, through the _____ process,

we make judgments about which goods and services are "good" for society and which are "bad."

Income redistribution can be carried out by a system of progressive taxation, coupled with _____ payments, which can be made in money or in kind, such as food stamps and Medicare.

Public Spending and Transfer Programs

The size of the public sector can be measured in many different ways. One way is to count the number of public employees. Another is to look at total government outlays. Government outlays include all government expenditures on employees, rent, electricity, and the like. In addition, total government outlays include transfer payments, such as welfare and Social Security. In Figure 5-2, you see that government outlays prior to World War I did not exceed 10 percent of annual national income. There was a spike during World War I, a general increase during the Great Depression, and then a huge spike during World War II. Contrary to previous postwar periods, after World War II government outlays as a percentage of total national income rose steadily before dropping in the 1990s and rising again in the 2000s.

How do federal and state governments allocate their spending? A typical federal government budget is shown in panel (a) of Figure 5-3. The three largest categories are Medicare and other health-related spending, Social Security and other income-security programs, and national defense, which together constitute 78.4 percent of the total federal budget.

The makeup of state and local expenditures is quite different. As panel (b) shows, education is the biggest category, accounting for 34.2 percent of all expenditures.

Publicly Subsidized Health Care: Medicare

Figure 5-3 shows that health-related spending is a significant portion of total government expenditures. Certainly, medical expenses are a major concern for many elderly people. Since 1965, that concern has been reflected in the existence of the Medicare program, which pays hospital and physicians' bills for U.S. residents over the age of 65 (and for those younger than 65 in some instances). In return for paying a tax on their earnings while in the workforce (currently set at 2.9 percent of wages and salaries), retirees are assured that the majority of their hospital and physicians' bills will be paid for with public monies.

Go to www.econtoday.com/chapter05 to visit the U.S. government's official Medicare Web site.

FIGURE 5-2

Total Government Outlays over Time

Total government outlays (federal, state, and local combined) remained small until the 1930s, except during World War I. Since World War II, government outlays have not fallen back to their historical average.

Sources: Facts and Figures on Government Finance, various issues; Economic Indicators, various issues.

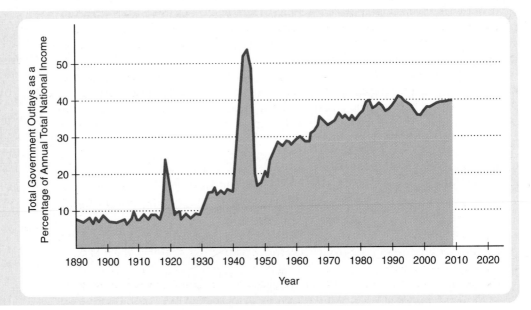

FIGURE 5-3

Federal Government Spending Compared to State and Local Spending

The federal government's spending habits are quite different from those of the states and cities. In panel (a), you can see that the most important categories in the federal budget are Medicare and other health-related spending, Social Security and other income-security programs, and national defense, which make up 78.4 percent. In panel (b), the most important category at the state and local level is education, which makes up 34.2 percent. "Other" includes expenditures in such areas as waste treatment, garbage collection, mosquito abatement, and the judicial system.

Sources: Budget of the United States government; government finances.

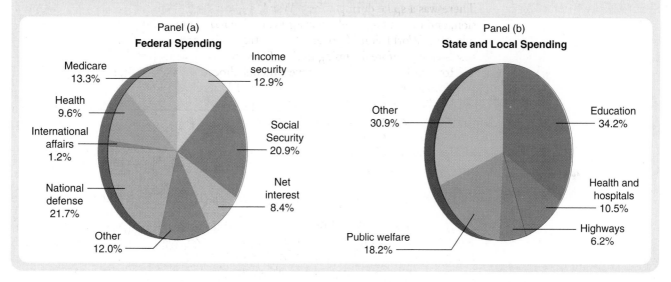

Panel (a)
Federal Spending

Medicare 13.3%
Health 9.6%
International affairs 1.2%
National defense 21.7%
Other 12.0%
Income security 12.9%
Social Security 20.9%
Net interest 8.4%

Panel (b)
State and Local Spending

Other 30.9%
Public welfare 18.2%
Education 34.2%
Health and hospitals 10.5%
Highways 6.2%

THE SIMPLE ECONOMICS OF MEDICARE To understand how, in less than 40 years, Medicare became the second-biggest domestic government spending program in existence, a bit of economics is in order. Consider Figure 5-4 on the following page, which shows the demand for and supply of medical care.

The initial equilibrium price is P_0 and equilibrium quantity is Q_0. Perhaps because the government believes that Q_0 is not enough medical care for these consumers, suppose that the government begins paying a subsidy that eventually is set at M for each unit of medical care consumed. This will simultaneously tend to raise the price per unit of care received by providers (physicians, hospitals, and the like) and lower the perceived price per unit that consumers see when they make decisions about how much medical care to consume. As presented in the figure, the price received by providers rises to P_s, while the price paid by consumers falls to P_d. As a result, consumers of medical care want to purchase Q_m units, and suppliers are quite happy to provide it for them.

MEDICARE INCENTIVES AT WORK We can now understand the problems that plague the Medicare system today. First, one of the things that people observed during the 20 years after the founding of Medicare was a huge upsurge in physicians' incomes and medical school applications, the spread of private for-profit hospitals, and the rapid proliferation of new medical tests and procedures. All of this was being encouraged by the rise in the price of medical services from P_0 to P_s, which encouraged entry into this market.

Second, government expenditures on Medicare have routinely turned out to be far in excess of the expenditures forecast at the time the program was put in place or was

How has the existence of Medicare changed seniors' consumption of medical services?

FIGURE 5-4

The Economic Effects of Medicare Subsidies

When the government pays a per-unit subsidy M for medical care, consumers pay the price of services P_d for the quantity of services Q_m. Providers receive the price P_s for supplying this quantity. Originally, the federal government projected that its total spending on Medicare would equal an amount such as the area $Q_0 \times (P_0 - P_d)$. Because actual consumption equals Q_m, however, the government's total expenditures equal $Q_m \times M$.

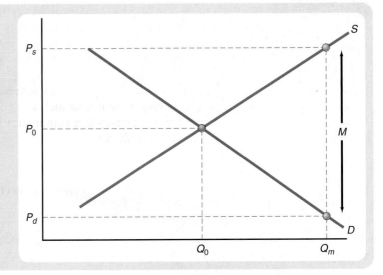

expanded. The reasons for this are easy to see. Bureaucratic planners often fail to recognize the incentive effects of government programs. On the demand side, they fail to account for the huge increase in consumption (from Q_0 to Q_m) that will result from a subsidy like Medicare. On the supply side, they fail to recognize that the larger amount of services can only be extracted from suppliers at a higher price, P_s. Consequently, original projected spending on Medicare was an area like $Q_0 \times (P_0 - P_d)$, because original plans for the program only contemplated consumption of Q_0 and assumed that the subsidy would have to be only $P_0 - P_d$ per unit. In fact, consumption rises to Q_m, and the additional cost per unit of service rises to P_s, implying an increase in the per-unit subsidy to M. Hence, actual expenditures turn out to be the far larger number $Q_m \times M$. Every expansion of the program, including the 2004 broadening of Medicare to cover obesity as a new illness eligible for coverage and the extension of Medicare to cover patients' prescription drug expenses beginning in 2006, has followed the same pattern.

Third, total spending on medical services soars, consuming far more income than initially expected. Originally, total spending on medical services was $P_0 \times Q_0$. In the presence of Medicare, spending rises to $P_s \times Q_m$.

HEALTH CARE SUBSIDIES CONTINUE TO GROW Just how fast are Medicare subsidies growing? Medicare's cost has risen from 0.7 percent of U.S. national income in 1970 to more than 2.8 percent today, which amounts to nearly $400 billion per year. Because Medicare spending is growing much faster than total employer and employee contributions, future spending guarantees far outstrip the taxes to be collected in the future to pay for the system. (The current Medicare tax rate is 2.9 percent on all earnings, with 1.45 percent paid by the employee and 1.45 percent paid by the employer.) Today, unfunded guarantees of Medicare spending in the future are estimated at more than $25 trillion (in today's dollars).

These amounts fail to reflect the costs of another federal health program called Medicaid. The Medicaid program is structured similarly to Medicare, in that the government also pays per-unit subsidies for health care to qualifying patients. Medicaid, however, provides subsidies only to people who qualify because they have lower incomes. At present, about 50 million people, or about one out of every six U.S. residents, qualify for Medicaid coverage. Medicaid is administered by state governments, but the federal government pays about 57 percent of the program's total cost from general tax revenues. The current cost of the program is more than $400 billion per year. In recent years, Medicaid spending has grown even faster than expenditures on Medicare, rising by more than 75 percent since 2000 alone. Current estimates indicate that spending on Medicaid is likely to increase at an annual rate of nearly 8 percent for the foreseeable future.

How have government health care subsidy programs such as Medicare contributed to a preference by physicians for expensive face-to-face communications with patients instead of less costly phone and e-mail consultations?

POLICY EXAMPLE
If the Government Doesn't Pay for It, Physicians Don't Do It

Lawyers, accountants, and most other professionals regard telephone and e-mail as indispensable tools for communicating with clients. In contrast, phone consultations with physicians are very rare, and only 2 percent of patients have regular e-mail contact with their physicians. Medicare pays for about 7,500 specific health-care-related services, including face-to-face visits with physicians. The program does not, however, recompense physicians for time they devote to telephone or e-mail consultations with patients. Hence, Medicare gives physicians incentives to schedule appointments with patients in their offices but provides no incentives to utilize modes of communication that would be more efficient in a number of situations. Physicians, in turn, have responded to these incentives by scheduling steady streams of office visits with patients and avoiding phone calls and e-mail communications.

FOR CRITICAL ANALYSIS
Who pays for the fact that Medicare's payment rules promote higher-priced, face-to-face physician-patient communications instead of lower-priced, remote communications?

Economic Issues of Public Education

In the United States, government involvement in health care is a relatively recent phenomenon. In contrast, state and local governments have assumed primary responsibility for public education for many years. Currently, these governments spend more than $700 billion on education—more than 4 percent of total U.S. national income. State and local sales, excise, property, and income taxes finance the bulk of these expenditures. In addition, each year the federal government provides tens of billions of dollars of support for public education through grants and other transfers to state and local governments.

THE NOW-FAMILIAR ECONOMICS OF PUBLIC EDUCATION State and local governments around the United States have developed a variety of complex mechanisms for funding public education. What all public education programs have in common, however, is the provision of educational services to primary, secondary, and college students at prices well below those that would otherwise prevail in the marketplace for these services.

So how do state and local governments accomplish this? The answer is that they operate public education programs that share some of the features of government-subsidized health care programs such as Medicare. Analogously to Figure 5-4, public schools provide educational services at a price below the market price. They are willing to produce the quantity of educational services demanded at this below-market price as long as they receive a sufficiently high per-unit subsidy from state and local governments.

THE INCENTIVE PROBLEMS OF PUBLIC EDUCATION Since the 1960s, various measures of the performance of U.S. primary and secondary students have failed to increase even as public spending on education has risen. Some measures of student performance have even declined.

Many economists argue that the incentive effects that have naturally arisen with higher government subsidies for public education help to explain this lack of improvement in student performance. A higher per-pupil subsidy creates a difference between the relatively high per-unit costs to schools of providing the amount of educational services that parents and students are willing to purchase and the relatively lower valuations of those services. As a consequence, some schools have provided services, such as after-school babysitting and various social services, that have contributed relatively little to student learning.

A factor that complicates efforts to assess the effects of education subsidies is that the public schools often face little or no competition from unsubsidized providers of educational services. In addition, public schools rarely compete against each other. In most locales, therefore, parents who are unhappy with the quality of services provided at the subsidized price cannot transfer their child to a different public school.

Have subsidies intended to promote public schools' Internet connectivity improved student learning outcomes?

You Are There

To contemplate the operation of a college as a private business, read **Aiming to Prevent Cost from Exceeding Value per Dollar in Higher Education,** on page 126.

E-COMMERCE EXAMPLE
The Minuscule Payoff from Public School Internet Subsidies

Among other things, the U.S. Telecommunications Act of 1996 created a program known as E-Rate, which provides subsidies to public schools for use in connecting classrooms to the Web. Under the E-Rate program, about $2 billion per year goes to subsidize between 20 and 90 percent of recipient schools' Internet-related telecommunications spending, depending on the schools' qualifying characteristics. On average, the E-Rate subsidy amounts to about $100 per pupil.

Although the immediate objective of this subsidy was to ensure that more students would have access to the Internet, E-Rate's creators also predicted that the program would improve student learning. Nevertheless, studies of student performances in two of the most populous states, Texas and California, find no concrete evidence that the program has improved outcomes. A decade after E-Rate was established, performances on standardized tests were virtually unchanged, as were student enrollments in advanced courses. High school dropout and graduation rates also remained the same. The E-Rate program has boosted Web access in the nation's public schools, but there is little evidence that more Internet connectivity has improved learning.

FOR CRITICAL ANALYSIS
Why might the $100-per-student E-Rate subsidy provide a minuscule learning payoff for students who already have Internet access at home?

QUICK QUIZ   See page 133 for the answers. Review concepts from this section in MyEconLab.

Medicare subsidizes the consumption of medical care by the elderly, thus increasing the amount of such care consumed. People tend to purchase large amounts of _____-value, _____-cost services in publicly funded health care programs such as Medicare, because they do not directly bear the full cost of their decisions.

Basic economic analysis indicates that higher subsidies for public education have widened the differential between parents' and students' relatively _____ per-unit valuations of the educational services of public schools and the _____ costs that schools incur in providing those services.

Collective Decision Making: The Theory of Public Choice

Governments consist of individuals. No government actually thinks and acts; rather, government actions are the result of decision making by individuals in their roles as elected representatives, appointed officials, and salaried bureaucrats. Therefore, to understand how government works, we must examine the incentives of the people in government as well as those who would like to be in government—avowed or would-be candidates for elective or appointed positions—and special-interest lobbyists attempting to get government to do something. At issue is the analysis of **collective decision making.** Collective decision making involves the actions of voters, politicians, political parties, interest groups, and many other groups and individuals. The analysis of collective decision making is usually called the **theory of public choice.** It has been given this name because it involves hypotheses about how choices are made in the public sector, as opposed to the private sector. The foundation of public-choice theory is the assumption that individuals will act within the political process to maximize their *individual* (not collective) well-being. In that sense, the theory is similar to our analysis of the market economy, in which we also assume that individuals act as though they are motivated by self-interest.

To understand public-choice theory, it is necessary to point out other similarities between the private market sector and the public, or government, sector; then we will look at the differences.

Collective decision making
How voters, politicians, and other interested parties act and how these actions influence nonmarket decisions.

Theory of public choice
The study of collective decision making.

Similarities in Market and Public-Sector Decision Making

In addition to the assumption of self-interest being the motivating force in both sectors, there are other similarities.

OPPORTUNITY COST Everything that is spent by all levels of government plus everything that is spent by the private sector must add up to the total income available at any point in time. Hence, every government action has an opportunity cost, just as in the market sector.

COMPETITION Although we typically think of competition as a private-market phenomenon, it is also present in collective action. Given the scarcity constraint government faces, bureaucrats, appointed officials, and elected representatives will always be in competition for available government funds. Furthermore, the individuals within any government agency or institution will act as individuals do in the private sector: They will try to obtain higher wages, better working conditions, and higher job-level classifications. We assume that they will compete and act in their own interest, not society's.

SIMILARITY OF INDIVIDUALS Contrary to popular belief, the types of individuals working in the private sector and working in the public sector are not inherently different. The difference, as we shall see, is that the individuals in government face a different **incentive structure** than those in the private sector. For example, the costs and benefits of being efficient or inefficient differ in the private and public sectors.

One approach to predicting government bureaucratic behavior is to ask what incentives bureaucrats face. Take the United States Postal Service (USPS) as an example. The bureaucrats running that government corporation are human beings with

Incentive structure
The system of rewards and punishments individuals face with respect to their own actions.

IQs not dissimilar to those possessed by workers in similar positions at Microsoft or American Airlines. Yet the USPS does not function like either of these companies. The difference can be explained in terms of the incentives provided for managers in the two types of institutions. When the bureaucratic managers and workers at Microsoft make incorrect decisions, work slowly, produce shoddy products, and are generally "inefficient," the profitability of the company declines. The owners—millions of shareholders—express their displeasure by selling some of their shares of company stock. The market value, as tracked on the stock exchange, falls. This induces owners of shares of stock to pressure managers to pursue strategies more likely to boost revenues and reduce costs.

But what about the USPS? If a manager, a worker, or a bureaucrat in the USPS gives shoddy service, the organization's owners—the taxpayers—have no straightforward mechanism for expressing their dissatisfaction. Despite the postal service's status as a "government corporation," taxpayers as shareholders do not really own shares of stock in the organization that they can sell.

Thus, to understand purported inefficiency in the government bureaucracy, we need to examine incentives and institutional arrangements—not people and personalities.

Differences Between Market and Collective Decision Making

There are probably more dissimilarities between the market sector and the public sector than there are similarities.

GOVERNMENT GOODS AND SERVICES AT ZERO PRICE The majority of goods that governments produce are furnished to the ultimate consumers without payment required. **Government,** or **political, goods** can be either private or public goods. The fact that they are furnished to the ultimate consumer free of charge does *not* mean that the cost to society of those goods is zero, however. It only means that the price *charged* is zero. The full opportunity cost to society is the value of the resources used in the production of goods produced and provided by the government.

For example, none of us pays directly for each unit of consumption of defense or police protection. Rather, we pay for all these items indirectly through the taxes that support our governments—federal, state, and local. This special feature of government can be looked at in a different way. There is no longer a one-to-one relationship between consumption of government-provided goods and services and payment for these items. Indeed, most taxpayers will find that their tax bill is the same whether or not they consume government-provided goods.

USE OF FORCE All governments can resort to using force in their regulation of economic affairs. For example, governments can use *expropriation*, which means that if you refuse to pay your taxes, your bank account and other assets may be seized by the Internal Revenue Service. In fact, you have no choice in the matter of paying taxes to governments. Collectively, we decide the total size of government through the political process, but individually, we cannot determine how much service we pay for during any one year.

VOTING VERSUS SPENDING In the private market sector, a dollar voting system is in effect. This dollar voting system is not equivalent to the voting system in the public sector. There are at least three differences:

1. In a political system, one person gets one vote, whereas in the market system, each dollar a person spends counts separately.

Government, or political, goods
Goods (and services) provided by the public sector; they can be either private or public goods.

2. The political system is run by **majority rule,** whereas the market system is run by **proportional rule.**

3. The spending of dollars can indicate intensity of want, whereas because of the all-or-nothing nature of political voting, a vote cannot.

Ultimately, the main distinction between political votes and dollar votes is that political outcomes may differ from economic outcomes. Remember that economic efficiency is a situation in which, given the prevailing distribution of income, consumers obtain the economic goods they want. There is no corresponding situation when political voting determines economic outcomes. Thus, a political voting process is unlikely to lead to the same decisions that a dollar voting process would yield in the marketplace.

Indeed, consider the dilemma every voter faces. Usually, a voter is not asked to decide on a single issue (although this happens); rather, a voter is asked to choose among candidates who present a large number of issues and state a position on each of them. Just consider the average U.S. senator, who has to vote on several thousand different issues during a six-year term. When you vote for that senator, you are voting for a person who must make thousands of decisions during the next six years.

How are economic outcomes in the world oil market affected by governmental involvement in extraction and distribution?

Majority rule

A collective decision-making system in which group decisions are made on the basis of more than 50 percent of the vote. In other words, whatever more than half of the electorate votes for, the entire electorate has to accept.

Proportional rule

A decision-making system in which actions are based on the proportion of the "votes" cast and are in proportion to them. In a market system, if 10 percent of the "dollar votes" are cast for blue cars, 10 percent of automobile output will be blue cars.

INTERNATIONAL EXAMPLE
Why a Synonym for "Big Oil" Is "Big Government"

Politicians and pundits commonly blame "big oil"—their shorthand for private oil companies—for higher oil prices. In fact, one factor contributing to the upward creep of inflation-adjusted oil prices is that an ever-greater share of oil is produced under government direction. In the early days of oil production, private firms produced the bulk of the world's oil. In contrast, today private companies such as Chevron, British Petroleum, ConocoPhillips, and ExxonMobil directly manage oil production from only 5 percent of the world's known reserves. Governments and government-owned companies coordinate production from the remaining 95 percent of reserves. To the extent that political factors influence governmentally managed oil production, output and price outcomes differ from those that privately directed production would have produced. Indeed, there is evidence that government-coordinated oil extraction and distribution is more costly than private oil production. These higher costs, in turn, lead to depressed oil output and higher oil prices.

FOR CRITICAL ANALYSIS
Why might dictators in totalitarian regimes make different oil production choices than private companies would have made?

QUICK QUIZ   *See page 133 for the answers. Review concepts from this section in MyEconLab.*

The theory of _____ _____ examines how voters, politicians, and other parties collectively reach decisions in the public sector of the economy.

As in private markets, _____ _____ and _____ have incentive effects that influence public-sector decision making. In contrast to private market situations, however, there is not a one-to-one relationship between consumption of a publicly provided good and the payment for that good.

You Are There

Aiming to Prevent Cost from Exceeding Value per Dollar in Higher Education

In 2001, Graham Doxey, Scott McKinley, and Marlow Einelund pooled their resources to start a new business: a private computer engineering college called Neumont University. Salt Lake City–based Neumont, which has operated since 2004, has no summer breaks. Instead, it offers students a year-round curriculum with a daily class schedule that stretches from 8 AM to 5 PM, thereby enabling students to graduate after two years instead of four years. Unlike a traditional university with a sprawling—and costly-to-maintain—campus, Neumont is housed in a glass-and-steel executive office building. Rather than residing in dorms, fraternities, or sororities on a campus quad, students live in nearby apartments.

These are not, however, the most dramatic differences between Neumont and other U.S. institutions of higher learning. Neumont's single goal is to provide students with training geared to meet the desires of employers. In contrast to students in computer engineering programs at most other universities, Neumont's students spend 30 percent of their time on theory and 70 percent on applications—essentially

a reversal of the percentages in traditional programs. Most Neumont students obtain professional certification as well as a bachelor's degree, which makes them both more employable and highly valued. Consequently, virtually all Neumont graduates obtain jobs, and most earn starting salaries 20 percent above the average for computer science graduates. In essence, Neumont seeks to ensure that the per-dollar cost of higher education is not higher than the per-dollar valuation that its graduates place on the tuition bills they pay for their education.

CRITICAL ANALYSIS QUESTIONS

1. Why might a university that is operated as a private firm be more likely than a traditional university to produce educational services at a cost per dollar that does not exceed students' per-dollar valuation of those services?

2. How could the entry of a number of other business-oriented universities such as Neumont induce traditional universities to alter their modes of operation?

An Ethanol Bonanza, or an Ethanol Boondoggle?

Issues and Applications

CONCEPTS APPLIED

- External Costs
- Government-Sponsored Good
- Subsidies

From the U.S. government's point of view, the use of gasoline as a motor fuel presents two problems. First, many reserves of the key input for refining gasoline, oil, are located in the politically unstable Middle East. Second, the utilization of gasoline as a motor fuel entails an external cost, because the burning of gasoline releases carbon dioxide and other pollutants into the air. In contrast, the key ingredients for manufacturing ethanol—corn and other grains—are readily grown domestically. Furthermore, burning ethanol may create a somewhat smaller "carbon footprint" in the atmosphere. These facts help to explain the government's fascination with ethanol-based fuel as a substitute for gasoline. What is unclear is whether there is a true economic rationale for government subsidies for ethanol.

Ethanol Is a Bonanza for Some

Motor fuels blended with ethanol, such as E10 (10 percent ethanol and 90 percent gasoline) and the more concentrated E85 (85 percent ethanol and 15 percent gasoline), have been available for a number of years. The U.S. government, however, had shown little interest in ethanol until the recent increase in gasoline prices and heightened worries over the potential global-warming impact of gasoline emissions.

Now, the government has effectively designated ethanol as a government-sponsored good. U.S. law currently requires U.S. refiners to blend 8 billion gallons of ethanol into motor fuels annually. The government provides a per-unit subsidy to ethanol producers of about $1 per gallon, or nearly half of the fuel's per-gallon production cost. Thus, annual government ethanol subsidies are about $8 billion. In phases through 2012, the ethanol requirement for U.S. refineries will rise to 36 billion gallons per year. Thus, total subsidies to ethanol producers are slated to increase to more than $36 billion.

All these government-generated revenues have certainly been a bonanza for ethanol manufacturers. Grain farmers have also been beneficiaries. The increased demand for corn as an ethanol input has boosted the market demand for corn and contributed to a nearly 40 percent increase in its inflation-adjusted price.

Others See Ethanol as a Boondoggle

The U.S. government's ethanol subsidies have certainly boosted production of ethanol. The cost is arguably very high relative to the benefits, however. Even if the 2012 target of 36 billion gallons of ethanol displaces an equal amount of gasoline, annual U.S. gasoline consumption will drop by less than 20 percent. As a consequence, U.S. dependence on volatile oil-producing nations will be reduced only slightly, and decreases in vehicular carbon emissions will be minor at best.

In fact, the ethanol production process releases pollutants into the atmosphere and fills the air surrounding ethanol refineries with a sickly sweet odor. One more implicit subsidy that the U.S. government has granted ethanol producers is looser air pollution regulations than those faced by other companies. The Environmental Protection Agency permits ethanol refineries to release 150 percent more emissions than other producers. Thus, emissions of pollutants from the nearly 200 ethanol refineries already operating or set to begin are likely to increase significantly during coming years.

Finally, some critics of ethanol subsidies suggest that producing ethanol from corn actually requires *more* energy than the ethanol ultimately creates. Whether or not this particular claim is correct, there is widespread agreement that given the energy expended to produce ethanol, the fuel is not the least costly source of energy for powering vehicles. This fact ultimately explains why the U.S. government requires its use and transmits billions of dollars of subsidies to producers each year to render ethanol a viable substitute for gasoline.

Test your understanding of this chapter by going online to **MyEconLab**.
In the Study Plan for this chapter, select Section N: News.

For Critical Analysis

1. In principle, could a higher per-unit tax on gasoline accomplish the U.S. government's objective of reducing gasoline consumption and related carbon emissions?

2. Who unambiguously benefits from the U.S. government's interventions in the ethanol market?

Web Resources

1. To contemplate a discussion of the pros and cons of ethanol and other so-called biofuels, go to www.econtoday.com/chapter05.

2. For information about vehicles equipped to operate using fuels with high concentrations of ethanol, go to www.econtoday.com/chapter05.

Research Project

Why is ethanol more appropriately classified as a government-sponsored good than as a public good? In your view, is there a strong *economic* argument for the government to continue to treat ethanol as a government-sponsored good and to promote ethanol output via explicit production requirements and subsidies? (Hint: In what situation does society underallocate resources to consumption of a good? Does this situation apply in the market for ethanol?)

myeconlab

Here is what you should know after reading this chapter. **MyEconLab** will help you identify what you know, and where to go when you need to practice.

WHAT YOU SHOULD KNOW

How Market Failures Such as Externalities Might Justify Economic Functions of Government A market failure is a situation in which an unhindered free market gives rise to too many or too few resources being directed to a specific form of economic activity. One market failure is an externality, which is a spillover effect on third parties not directly involved in producing or purchasing a good or service. In the case of a negative externality, firms do not pay for the costs arising from spillover effects that their production of a good imposes on others, so they produce too much of the good in question. Government may be able to improve the situation by restricting production or by imposing fees on producers. In the case of a positive externality, buyers fail to take into account the benefits that their consumption of a good yields to others, so they purchase too little of the good. Government may be able to induce more consumption of the good by regulating the market or subsidizing consumption. It can also provide a legal system to adjudicate disagreements about property rights, conduct antitrust policies to discourage monopoly and promote competition, provide public goods, and engage in policies designed to promote economic stability.

market failure, 108
externality, 109
third parties, 109
property rights, 109
effluent fee, 111
antitrust legislation, 113
monopoly, 114

KEY FIGURE
Figure 5-1, 110

WHERE TO GO TO PRACTICE

- **MyEconLab** Study Plans 5.1, 5.2
- Audio introduction to Chapter 5
- Animated Figure 5-1

(continued)

myeconlab *(Continued)*

WHAT YOU SHOULD KNOW   **WHERE TO GO TO PRACTICE**

Private Goods versus Public Goods and the Free-Rider Problem Private goods are subject to the principle of rival consumption, meaning that one person's consumption of such a good reduces the amount available for another person to consume. This is not so for public goods, which can be consumed by many people simultaneously at no additional opportunity cost and with no reduction in the quality or quantity of the good. In addition, no individual can be excluded from the benefits of a public good even if that person fails to help pay for it. This leads to the free-rider problem, which occurs when a person who thinks that others will pay for a public good seeks to avoid contributing to financing its production.

private goods, 114
principle of rival consumption, 114
public goods, 114
free-rider problem, 115

• **MyEconLab** Study Plan 5.3
• Video: Private Goods and Public Goods

Political Functions of Government That Lead to Its Involvement in the Economy Through the political process, government may determine that certain goods are deemed socially desirable and seek to promote their production and consumption. These are called government-sponsored goods. The government may also seek to restrict or even ban the production and sale of other goods that have been deemed socially undesirable through the political process, called government-inhibited goods. In addition, the political process may determine that income redistribution is socially desirable, and governments may become involved in supervising transfer payments or in-kind transfers in the form of nonmoney payments.

government-sponsored good, 116
government-inhibited good, 116
transfer payments, 117
transfers in kind, 117

• **MyEconLab** Study Plan 5.4

The Effect of Medicare on the Incentives to Consume Medical Services Medicare subsidizes the consumption of medical services by the elderly. As a result, the quantity consumed is higher, as is the price sellers receive per unit of those services. Medicare also encourages people to consume medical services that are very low in per-unit value relative to the cost of providing them. Medicare thereby places a substantial tax burden on other sectors of the economy.

KEY FIGURES
Figure 5-2, 118
Figure 5-4, 120

• **MyEconLab** Study Plan 5.5
• Video: Medicare
• Animated Figures 5-2, 5-4

Why Bigger Subsidies for Public Schools Do Not Necessarily Translate into Improved Student Performance When governments subsidize public schools, the last unit of educational services provided by public schools costs more than its valuation by parents and students. Thus, public schools provide services in excess of those best suited to promoting student learning. This helps explain why overall U.S. student performance has stagnated even as per-pupil subsidies have increased.

• MyEconLab Study Plan 5.5

 (continued)

| WHAT YOU SHOULD KNOW | | WHERE TO GO TO PRACTICE |

Central Elements of the Theory of Public Choice The theory of public choice applies to collective decision making, or the process through which voters and politicians interact to influence nonmarket choices. Public-choice theory emphasizes the incentive structures, or system of rewards or punishments, that affect the provision of government goods by the public sector. This theory points out that certain aspects of public-sector decision making, such as scarcity and competition, are similar to those that affect private-sector choices. Others, however, such as legal coercion and majority-rule decision making, differ from those involved in the market system.

collective decision making, 123
theory of public choice, 123
incentive structure, 123
government, or political, goods, 124
majority rule, 125
proportional rule, 125

- **MyEconLab** Study Plan 5.6

Log in to MyEconLab, take a chapter test, and get a personalized Study Plan that tells you which concepts you understand and which ones you need to review. From there, MyEconLab will give you further practice, tutorials, animations, videos, and guided solutions.
Log in to www.myeconlab.com

PROBLEMS

All problems are assignable in  *. Answers to odd-numbered problems appear at the back of the book.*

5-1. Many people who do not smoke cigars are bothered by the odor of cigar smoke. In the absence of any government involvement in the market for cigars, will too many or too few cigars be produced and consumed? From society's point of view, will the market price of cigars be too high or too low?

5-2. Suppose that repeated application of a pesticide used on orange trees causes harmful contamination of groundwater. The pesticide is applied annually in virtually all of the orange groves throughout the world. Most orange growers regard the pesticide as a key input in their production of oranges.

   a. Use a diagram of the market for the pesticide to illustrate the implications of a failure of orange producers' costs to reflect the social costs of groundwater contamination.

   b. Use your diagram from part (a) to explain a government policy that might be effective in achieving the amount of orange production that fully reflects all social costs.

5-3. Now draw a diagram of the market for oranges. Explain how the government policy you discussed in part (b) of Problem 5-2 is likely to affect the market price and equilibrium quantity in the orange market. In what sense do consumers of oranges now "pay" for dealing with the spillover costs of pesticide production?

5-4. Suppose that the U.S. government determines that cigarette smoking creates social costs not reflected in the current market price and equilibrium quantity of cigarettes. A study has recommended that the government can correct for the externality effect of cigarette consumption by paying farmers *not* to plant tobacco used to manufacture cigarettes. It also recommends raising the funds to make these payments by increasing taxes on cigarettes. Assuming that the government is correct that cigarette smoking creates external costs, evaluate whether the study's recommended policies might help correct this negative externality.

5-5. The government of a major city in the United States has determined that mass transit, such as bus lines, helps alleviate traffic congestion, thereby benefiting both individual auto commuters and companies that desire to move products and factors of production speedily along streets and highways. Nevertheless, even though several private bus lines are in service, commuters in the city are failing to take the social benefits of the use of mass transit into account.

   a. Discuss, in the context of demand-supply analysis, the essential implications of commuters' failure to take into account the social benefits associated with bus ridership.

   b. Explain a government policy that might be effective in achieving the socially efficient use of bus services.

5-6. Draw a diagram of the market for automobiles, which are a substitute for buses. Explain how the government policy you discussed in part (b) of Problem 5-5 is likely to affect the market price and equilibrium quantity in the auto market. How are auto consumers affected by this policy to attain the spillover benefits of bus transit?

5-7. Displayed in the next column are conditions in the market for residential Internet access in a small U.S. state. The government of this state has determined that access to the Internet improves the learning skills of children, which it has concluded is an external benefit of Internet access. The government has also concluded that if these external benefits were to be taken into account, 3 million residences would have Internet access. Suppose that the state government's judgments about the benefits of Internet access are correct and that it wishes to offer a per-unit subsidy just sufficient to increase total Internet access to 3 million residences. What per-unit subsidy should it offer? Use the diagram to explain how providing this subsidy would affect conditions in the state's market for residential Internet access.

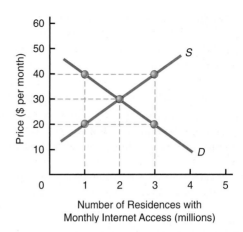

Number of Residences with Monthly Internet Access (millions)

5-8. The French government recently allocated the equivalent of more than $120 million in public funds to *Quaero* (Latin for "I search"), an Internet search engine analogous to Google or Yahoo. Does an Internet search engine satisfy the key characteristics of a public good? Why or why not? Based on your answer, is a publicly funded Internet search engine a public good or a government-sponsored good?

5-9. To promote increased use of port facilities in a major coastal city, a state government has decided to construct a state-of-the-art lighthouse at a projected cost of $10 million. The state proposes to pay half this cost and asks the city to raise the additional funds. Rather than raise its $5 million in funds via an increase in city taxes and fees, however, the city's government asks major businesses in and near the port area to contribute voluntarily to the project. Discuss key problems that the city is likely to face in raising the funds.

5-10. Governments of country A and country B spend the same amount each year. Spending on functions relating to dealing with market externalities and public goods accounts for 25 percent of government expenditures in country A but makes up 75 percent of government expenditures in country B. Funding to provide government-sponsored goods and efforts to restrict the production of government-inhibited goods account for 75 percent of government expenditures in country A but only 25 percent of government expenditures in country B. Which country's government is more heavily involved in the economy through economic functions of government as opposed to political functions? Explain.

5-11. A government offers to let a number of students at a public school transfer to a private school under two conditions: It will transmit to the private school the same per-pupil subsidy it provides the public school, and the private school will be required to admit the students at a below-market net tuition rate. Will the economic outcome be the same as the one that would have arisen if the government instead simply provided students with grants to cover the current market tuition rate at the private school? (Hint: Does it matter if schools receive payments directly from the government or from consumers?)

5-12. After a government implements a voucher program, granting funds that families can spend at schools of their choice, numerous students in public schools switch to private schools. Parents' and students' valuations of the services provided at both private and public schools adjust to equality with the true market price of educational services. Is anyone likely to lose out nonetheless? If so, who?

5-13. Suppose that the current price of a DVD drive is $100 and that people are buying 1 million drives per year. In order to improve computer literacy, the government decides to begin subsidizing the purchase of new DVD drives. The government believes that the appropriate price is $60 per drive, so the program offers to send people cash for the difference between $60 and whatever the people pay for each drive they buy.

  a. If no consumers change their DVD-drive-buying behavior, how much will this program cost the taxpayers?

  b. Will the subsidy cause people to buy more, fewer, or the same number of drives? Explain.

  c. Suppose that people end up buying 1.5 million drives once the program is in place. If the market price of drives does not change, how much will this program cost the taxpayers?

  d. Under the assumption that the program causes people to buy 1.5 million drives and also causes the market price of drives to rise to $120, how much will this program cost the taxpayers?

5-14. Scans of internal organs using magnetic resonance imaging (MRI) devices are often covered by subsidized health insurance programs such as Medicare. Consider the following table illustrating hypothetical quantities of individual MRI testing procedures demanded and supplied at various prices, and then answer the questions that follow.

Price	Quantity Demanded	Quantity Supplied
$100	100,000	40,000
$300	90,000	60,000
$500	80,000	80,000
$700	70,000	100,000
$900	60,000	120,000

  a. In the absence of a government-subsidized health plan, what is the equilibrium price of MRI tests? What is the amount of society's total spending on MRI tests?

  b. Suppose that the government establishes a health plan guaranteeing that all qualified participants can purchase MRI tests at an effective price (that is, out-of-pocket cost) to the individual of $100 per test. How many MRI tests will people consume?

  c. What is the per-unit price that induces producers to provide the amount of MRI tests demanded at the government-guaranteed price of $100? What is society's total spending on MRI tests?

  d. Under the government's coverage of MRI tests, what is the per-unit subsidy it provides? What is the total subsidy that the government pays to support MRI testing at its guaranteed price?

5-15. Suppose that, as part of an expansion of its State Care health system, a state government decides to offer a $50 subsidy to all people who, according to their physicians, should have their own blood pressure monitoring devices. Prior to this governmental decision, the market clearing price of blood pressure monitors in this state was $50, and the equilibrium quantity purchased was 20,000 per year.

  a. After the government expands its State Care plan, people in this state desire to purchase 40,000 devices each year. Manufacturers of blood pressure monitors are willing to provide 40,000 devices at a price of $60 per device. What out-of-pocket price does each consumer pay for a blood pressure monitor?

  b. What is the dollar amount of the increase in total expenditures on blood pressure monitors in this state following the expansion in the State Care program?

  c. Following the expansion of the State Care program, what *percentage* of total expenditures on blood pressure monitors is paid by the government? What percentage of total expenditures is paid by consumers of these devices?

5-16. A government agency is contemplating launching an effort to expand the scope of its activities. One rationale for doing so is that another government agency might make the same effort and, if successful, receive larger budget allocations in future years. Another rationale for expanding the agency's activities is that this will make the jobs of its workers more interesting, which may help the agency attract better-qualified employees. Nevertheless, to broaden its legal mandate, the agency will have to convince more than half of the House of Representatives and the Senate to approve a formal proposal to expand its activities. In addition, to expand its activities, the agency must have the authority to force private companies it does not currently regulate to be officially licensed by agency personnel. Identify which aspects of this problem are similar to those faced by firms that operate in private markets and which aspects are specific to the public sector.

ECONOMICS ON THE NET

Putting Tax Dollars to Work In this application, you will learn about how the U.S. government allocates its expenditures. This will enable you to conduct an evaluation of the current functions of the federal government.

Title: Historical Tables: Budget of the United States Government

Navigation: Go to **www.econtoday.com/chapter05** to visit the home page of the U.S. Government Printing Office. Select the most recent budget available, and then click on *Historical Tables*.

Application After the document downloads, examine Section 3, Federal Government Outlays by Function, and in particular Table 3.1, Outlays by Superfunction and Function. Then answer the following questions.

1. What government functions have been capturing growing shares of government spending in recent years? Which of these do you believe are related to the problem of addressing externalities, providing public goods, or dealing with other market failures? Which appear to be related to political functions instead of economic functions?

2. Which government functions are receiving declining shares of total spending? Are any of these related to the problem of addressing externalities, providing public goods, or dealing with other market failures? Are any related to political functions instead of economic functions?

For Group Study and Analysis Assign groups to the following overall categories of government functions: national defense, health, income security, and Social Security. Have each group prepare a brief report concerning long-term and recent trends in government spending on its category. Each group should take a stand on whether specific spending on items in its category is likely to relate to resolving market failures, public funding of government-sponsored goods, regulating the sale of government-inhibited goods, and so on.

ANSWERS TO QUICK QUIZZES

p. 113: (i) costs . . . taxation . . . regulation; (ii) benefits . . . financing . . . subsidizing . . . regulation
p. 116: (i) externalities . . . legal system . . . competition . . . public . . . economywide stability; (ii) rival consumption; (iii) opportunity cost . . . charged
p. 117: (i) government-sponsored . . . government-inhibited . . . income; (ii) political; (iii) transfer
p. 122: (i) low . . . high; (ii) low . . . higher
p. 125: (i) public choice; (ii) opportunity cost . . . competition

6

Funding the Public Sector

E ver since the U.S. federal income tax was established in 1913, there has been disagreement about how much income tax rates should differ across households based on their incomes. In recent years, various U.S. politicians and pundits have called for boosts in tax rates for higher-income individuals and cuts in tax rates for middle- and lower-income individuals. "The rich should pay their fair share" and "The middle class deserves a break" are typical rallying cries you may have encountered in media reports. Are tax rates currently low for higher-income households relative to those faced by lower-income households? To evaluate this question, you must understand more about the structure of tax systems, which is one issue that governments confront in paying for their operations.

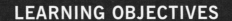

LEARNING OBJECTIVES

MyEconLab helps you master each objective and study more efficiently. See end of chapter for details.

After reading this chapter, you should be able to:

➤ Distinguish between average tax rates and marginal tax rates

➤ Explain the structure of the U.S. income tax system

➤ Understand the key factors influencing the relationship between tax rates and the tax revenues governments collect

➤ Explain how the taxes governments levy on purchases of goods and services affect market prices and equilibrium quantities

➤ Understand how the Social Security system works and explain the nature of the problems it poses for today's students

? DID YOU KNOW THAT since 1986, Congress has added 14,000 amendments containing 3 million words to U.S. tax laws? In addition, Congress has added 6 million words to regulations designed to implement all these amendments.

To obtain the funds required to finance their operations, governments collect taxes from many different sources—hence, the multitude of words written into a variety of legal statutes governing taxation. State and local governments assess sales taxes, property taxes, income taxes, hotel occupancy taxes, and electricity, gasoline, water, and sewage taxes. At the federal level, there are income taxes, Social Security taxes, Medicare taxes, and so-called excise taxes. When a person dies, state and federal governments also collect estate and inheritance taxes. Clearly, governments give considerable attention to their roles as tax collectors.

Paying for the Public Sector

There are three sources of funding available to governments. One source is explicit fees, called user *charges*, for government services. The second and main source of government funding is taxes. Nevertheless, sometimes federal, state, and local governments spend more than they collect in taxes. To do this, they must rely on a third source of financing, which is borrowing. During a specific interval, the **government budget constraint** expresses the key limitation on public expenditures. It states that the sum of public spending on goods, services, and transfer payments during a given period cannot exceed the sum of user charges, tax revenues, and borrowed funds.

A government cannot borrow unlimited amounts, however. After all, a government, like an individual or a firm, can convince others to lend it funds only if it can provide evidence that it will repay its debts. A government must ultimately rely on taxation and user charges, the sources of its own current and future revenues, to repay its debts. Over the long run, therefore, taxes and user charges are any government's *fundamental* sources of revenues. This long-term constraint indicates that the total amount that a government plans to spend and transfer today and into the future cannot exceed the total taxes and user charges that it currently earns and can reasonably anticipate collecting in future years. Taxation dwarfs user charges as a source of government resources, so let's begin by looking at taxation from a government's perspective.

Why are some states that rely on gasoline taxes to finance highway maintenance and construction contemplating a switch to "mileage taxes"?

Government budget constraint
The limit on government spending and transfers imposed by the fact that every dollar the government spends, transfers, or uses to repay borrowed funds must ultimately be provided by the user charges and taxes it collects.

POLICY EXAMPLE
States Consider Shifting Tax Gears to Satisfy Budget Constraints

A number of U.S. states earmark gasoline tax revenues to finance highway expansion and maintenance expenditures. Governments of these states are concerned that gasoline tax receipts will shrink as people respond to higher gasoline prices by switching from gas-guzzling sport utility vehicles to more fuel-efficient cars. State governments in North Carolina and Oregon are contemplating an alternative to taxing gasoline purchases: mileage taxation. Experiments are already under way in these states to equip autos with electronic odometers that record their mileage at gasoline stations. When drivers pump gasoline, specially equipped pumps read

the mileage and charge taxes based on miles driven. To ensure that drivers pay only for miles driven within state borders, the tax systems under consideration include global-positioning-system devices and automatically deduct out-of-state miles traveled. In this way, the states seek to raise funds to finance work on highways from drivers who traverse them the most.

FOR CRITICAL ANALYSIS
What is a one-sentence statement of the budget constraint for highway financing in states in which highway work is financed exclusively by gasoline taxes?

Systems of Taxation

In light of the government budget constraint, a major concern of any government is how to collect taxes. Jean-Baptiste Colbert, the seventeenth-century French finance minister, said the art of taxation was in "plucking the goose so as to obtain the largest amount of feathers with the least possible amount of hissing." In the United States, governments have designed a variety of methods of plucking the private-sector goose.

The Tax Base and the Tax Rate

Tax base
The value of goods, services, wealth, or incomes subject to taxation.

Tax rate
The proportion of a tax base that must be paid to a government as taxes.

To collect a tax, a government typically establishes a **tax base,** which is the value of goods, services, wealth, or incomes subject to taxation. Then it assesses a **tax rate,** which is the proportion of the tax base that must be paid to the government as taxes.

Federal, state, and local governments have established a number of tax bases and tax rates. How does a "dual-bracket" tax system with two different tax bases function?

POLICY EXAMPLE
The Same Tax Rate, but Different Tax Bases for Different People

Like municipalities in most states, city and county governments in Florida collect property taxes by applying a tax rate to assessed valuations of structures and surrounding properties. Unlike most states, Florida permits municipalities to establish a "dual-bracket" property tax system, meaning that municipalities can set the taxable values of properties at lower levels for permanent residents than for seasonal residents. To determine the property taxes owed, a municipality multiplies the differently assessed property values by the same property tax rate.

In some Florida communities, assessed values of properties owned by seasonal residents are up to 10 times higher than assessed values of virtually identical properties that permanent residents own on the same streets. Thus, the property taxes paid by seasonal residents are as much as 10 times higher than those paid by permanent residents.

FOR CRITICAL ANALYSIS
Why do you suppose that democratically elected municipal governments in Florida choose to value properties of permanent residents lower than properties of seasonal residents for purposes of establishing tax bases for property tax payments? (Hint: Seasonal residents typically register to vote in the cities and counties in which they reside most of the year.)

As we discuss shortly, for the federal government and many state governments, incomes are key tax bases. Therefore, to discuss tax rates and the structure of taxation systems in more detail, let's focus for now on income taxation.

Marginal and Average Tax Rates

If somebody says, "I pay 28 percent in taxes," you cannot really tell what that person means unless you know whether he or she is referring to average taxes paid or the tax rate on the last dollars earned. The latter concept refers to the **marginal tax rate,** where the word *marginal* means "incremental."

Marginal tax rate
The change in the tax payment divided by the change in income, or the percentage of additional dollars that must be paid in taxes. The marginal tax rate is applied to the highest tax bracket of taxable income reached.

The marginal tax rate is expressed as follows:

$$\text{Marginal tax rate} = \frac{\text{change in taxes due}}{\text{change in taxable income}}$$

It is important to understand that the marginal tax rate applies only to the income in the highest **tax bracket** reached, where a tax bracket is defined as a specified range of taxable income to which a specific and unique marginal tax rate is applied.

The marginal tax rate is not the same thing as the **average tax rate,** which is defined as follows:

$$\text{Average tax rate} = \frac{\text{total taxes due}}{\text{total taxable income}}$$

Taxation Systems

No matter how governments raise revenues—from income taxes, sales taxes, or other taxes—all of those taxes fit into one of three types of taxation systems: proportional, progressive, or regressive, according to the relationship between the tax rate and income. To determine whether a tax system is proportional, progressive, or regressive, we simply ask, What is the relationship between the average tax rate and the marginal tax rate?

PROPORTIONAL TAXATION **Proportional taxation** means that regardless of an individual's income, taxes comprise exactly the same proportion. In a proportional taxation system, the marginal tax rate is always equal to the average tax rate. If every dollar is taxed at 20 percent, then the average tax rate is 20 percent, and so is the marginal tax rate.

Under a proportional system of taxation, taxpayers at all income levels end up paying the same *percentage* of their income in taxes. With a proportional tax rate of 20 percent, an individual with an income of $10,000 pays $2,000 in taxes, while an individual making $100,000 pays $20,000. Thus, the identical 20 percent rate is levied on both taxpayers.

PROGRESSIVE TAXATION Under **progressive taxation,** as a person's taxable income increases, the percentage of income paid in taxes increases. In a progressive system, the marginal tax rate is above the average tax rate. If you are taxed 5 percent on the first $10,000 you earn, 10 percent on the next $10,000 you earn, and 30 percent on the last $10,000 you earn, you face a progressive income tax system. Your marginal tax rate is always above your average tax rate.

REGRESSIVE TAXATION With **regressive taxation,** a smaller percentage of taxable income is taken in taxes as taxable income increases. The marginal rate is *below* the average rate. As income increases, the marginal tax rate falls, and so does the average tax rate. The U.S. Social Security tax is regressive. Once the legislative maximum taxable wage base is reached, no further Social Security taxes are paid. Consider a simplified hypothetical example: Suppose that every dollar up to $100,000 is taxed at 10 percent. After $100,000 there is no Social Security tax. Someone making $200,000 still pays only $10,000 in Social Security taxes. That person's average Social Security tax is 5 percent. The person making $100,000, by contrast, effectively pays 10 percent. The person making $1 million faces an average Social Security tax rate of only 1 percent in our simplified example.

What form of voluntary yet regressive taxation is spreading throughout the U.S. states?

Tax bracket
A specified interval of income to which a specific and unique marginal tax rate is applied.

Average tax rate
The total tax payment divided by total income. It is the proportion of total income paid in taxes.

You Are There

To contemplate how marginal income tax rates can affect a person's job decisions, read **For This Physician, the Tax Rate Is Too High to Justify Working,** on pages 151 and 152.

Proportional taxation
A tax system in which, regardless of an individual's income, the tax bill comprises exactly the same proportion.

Progressive taxation
A tax system in which, as income increases, a higher percentage of the additional income is paid as taxes. The marginal tax rate exceeds the average tax rate as income rises.

Regressive taxation
A tax system in which as more dollars are earned, the percentage of tax paid on them falls. The marginal tax rate is less than the average tax rate as income rises.

POLICY EXAMPLE
State-Sponsored Gambling—Voluntary but Regressive Taxation

Increasingly, state governments are raising funds over and above traditional taxes and fees by operating lotteries and other legalized games of chance. State governments that supervise lotteries and other profitable gambling mechanisms regard them as forms of voluntary taxation. Economists have concluded that lower-income individuals usually pay larger percentages of their incomes to participate in state-run games of chance than do higher-income individuals. Thus, most state gambling operations involve *regressive* voluntary taxation.

FOR CRITICAL ANALYSIS
Why do you suppose that economists have found that slot-machine operations are among the most regressive forms of voluntary taxation conducted via state-run gambling operations? (Hint: Although each individual slot-machine bet is very small, people are equally tempted regardless of their incomes to feed large numbers of coins into the slots.)

QUICK QUIZ | *See page 158 for the answers. Review concepts from this section in MyEconLab.*

Governments collect taxes by applying a tax _____ to a tax _____, which refers to the value of goods, services, wealth, or incomes. Income tax rates are applied to tax brackets, which are ranges of income over which the tax rate is constant.

The _____ tax rate is the total tax payment divided by total income, and the _____ tax rate is the change in the tax payment divided by the change in income.

Tax systems can be _____, _____, or _____, depending on whether the marginal tax rate is the same as, greater than, or less than the average tax rate as income rises.

The Most Important Federal Taxes

What types of taxes do federal, state, and local governments collect? The two pie diagrams in Figure 6-1 show the percentages of receipts from various taxes obtained by the federal government and by state and local governments. For the federal government, key taxes are individual income taxes, corporate income taxes, Social Security taxes, and excise taxes on items such as gasoline and alcoholic beverages. For state and local governments, sales taxes, property taxes, and personal and corporate income taxes are the main types of taxes.

State-sponsored games of chance create what type of voluntary tax system?

The Federal Personal Income Tax

The most important tax in the U.S. economy is the federal personal income tax, which, as Figure 6-1 indicates, accounts for about 46.6 percent of all federal revenues. All U.S. citizens, resident aliens, and most others who earn income in the United States are required to pay federal income taxes on all taxable income, including income earned abroad.

The rates that are paid rise as income increases, as can be seen in Table 6-1 on page 140. Marginal income tax rates at the federal level have ranged from as low as 1 percent after the 1913 passage of the Sixteenth Amendment, which made the individual

FIGURE 6-1

Sources of Government Tax Receipts

As panel (a) shows, about 80 percent of federal revenues comes from income and Social Security and other social insurance taxes. State government revenues, shown in panel (b), are spread more evenly across sources, with less emphasis on taxes based on individual income.

Source: U.S. Department of Commerce, Bureau of Economic Analysis.

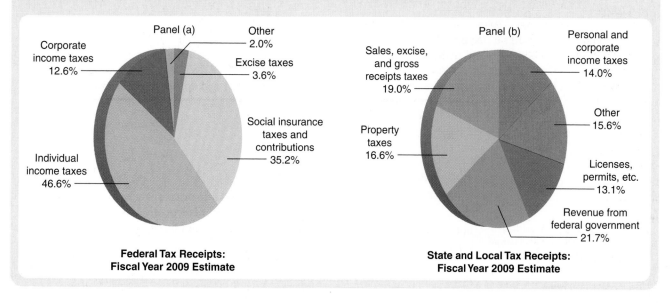

Panel (a)

- Corporate income taxes — 12.6%
- Other — 2.0%
- Excise taxes — 3.6%
- Social insurance taxes and contributions — 35.2%
- Individual income taxes — 46.6%

**Federal Tax Receipts:
Fiscal Year 2009 Estimate**

Panel (b)

- Sales, excise, and gross receipts taxes — 19.0%
- Personal and corporate income taxes — 14.0%
- Other — 15.6%
- Property taxes — 16.6%
- Licenses, permits, etc. — 13.1%
- Revenue from federal government — 21.7%

**State and Local Tax Receipts:
Fiscal Year 2009 Estimate**

income tax constitutional, to as high as 94 percent (reached in 1944). There were 14 separate tax brackets prior to the Tax Reform Act of 1986, which reduced the number to three (now six, as shown in Table 6-1 on the following page.).

Why is it somewhat surprising that many people among one particular group of U.S. residents pay federal income taxes?

Go to www.econtoday.com/chapter06 to learn from the National Center for Policy Analysis about what distinguishes recent flat tax proposals from a truly proportional income tax system. Click on "Flat Tax Proposals."

INTERNATIONAL POLICY EXAMPLE
Defying One Agency, Illegal Immigrants Pay Taxes to Another

No one knows exactly how many illegal immigrants reside in the United States, but most estimates put the number somewhere between 10 million and 15 million. As many as 1 out of every 20 U.S. workers may be in the country in defiance of efforts by the Department of Homeland Security to keep them out. Another U.S. government agency, the Department of the Treasury's Internal Revenue Service (IRS), makes it easy for these illegally residing but gainfully employed individuals to pay federal income taxes. All they have to do is obtain a special taxpayer identification number that begins with a "9" and indicates that they are unable to qualify for a Social Security number. Each year, the IRS collects an estimated $50 million in income taxes from illegal immigrants who obtain an identification number and pay income taxes through regular deductions from their wages.

FOR CRITICAL ANALYSIS

What is the marginal income tax rate for illegal workers who fail to report taxable earnings to the IRS because they fear their illegal status will be discovered?

TABLE 6-1

Federal Marginal Income Tax Rates

These rates became effective in 2008.

Single Persons		Married Couples	
Marginal Tax Bracket	Marginal Tax Rate	Marginal Tax Bracket	Marginal Tax Rate
$0–$8,025	10%	$0–$16,050	10%
$8,026–$32,550	15%	$16,051–$65,100	15%
$32,551–$78,850	25%	$65,101–$131,450	25%
$78,851–$164,550	28%	$131,451–$300,300	28%
$164,551–$357,700	33%	$300,301–$357,700	33%
$357,701 and up	35%	$357,701 and up	35%

Source: U.S. Department of the Treasury.

The Treatment of Capital Gains

Capital gain
A positive difference between the purchase price and the sale price of an asset. If a share of stock is bought for $5 and then sold for $15, the capital gain is $10.

Capital loss
A negative difference between the purchase price and the sale price of an asset.

The difference between the purchase price and sale price of an asset, such as a share of stock or a plot of land, is called a **capital gain** if it is a profit and a **capital loss** if it is not. The federal government taxes capital gains, and as of 2009, there were several capital gains tax rates.

What appear to be capital gains are not always real gains. If you pay $100,000 for a financial asset in one year and sell it for 50 percent more 10 years later, your nominal capital gain is $50,000. But what if during those 10 years inflation has driven average asset prices up by 50 percent? Your *real* capital gain would be zero, but you would still have to pay taxes on that $50,000. To counter this problem, many economists have argued that capital gains should be indexed to the rate of inflation. This is exactly what is done with the marginal tax brackets in the federal income tax code. Tax brackets for the purposes of calculating marginal tax rates each year are expanded at the rate of inflation, that is, the rate at which the average of all prices is rising. So, if the rate of inflation is 10 percent, each tax bracket is moved up by 10 percent. The same concept could be applied to capital gains and financial assets. So far, Congress has refused to enact such a measure.

The Corporate Income Tax

Figure 6-1 on page 139 shows that corporate income taxes account for about 12.6 percent of all federal taxes collected and about 2 percent of all state and local taxes collected. Corporations are generally taxed on the difference between their total revenues and their expenses. The federal corporate income tax structure is given in Table 6-2.

Retained earnings
Earnings that a corporation saves, or retains, for investment in other productive activities; earnings that are not distributed to stockholders.

DOUBLE TAXATION Because individual stockholders must pay taxes on the dividends they receive, and those dividends are paid out of *after-tax* profits by the corporation, corporate profits are taxed twice. If you receive $1,000 in dividends, you have to declare them as income, and you must normally pay taxes on them. Before the corporation was able to pay you those dividends, it had to pay taxes on all its profits, including any that it put back into the company or did not distribute in the form of dividends. Eventually, the new investment made possible by those **retained earnings**—profits not given out to stockholders—along with borrowed funds will be reflected in the value of the stock in that company. When you sell your stock in that company, you will have to pay taxes on the difference between what you paid for the stock and what you sold it for. In both cases, dividends and retained earnings (corporate profits) are taxed

TABLE 6-2

Federal Corporate Income Tax Schedule

These corporate tax rates were in effect through 2009.

Corporate Taxable Income	Corporate Tax Rate
$0–$50,000	15%
$50,001–$75,000	25%
$75,001–$100,000	34%
$100,001–$335,000	39%
$335,001–$10,000,000	34%
$10,000,001–$15,000,000	35%
$15,000,001–$18,333,333	38%
$18,333,334 and up	35%

Source: Internal Revenue Service.

twice. In 2003, Congress reduced the double taxation effect somewhat by enacting legislation that allowed most dividends to be taxed at lower rates than are applied to regular income, with this provision up for renewal in 2010.

WHO REALLY PAYS THE CORPORATE INCOME TAX? Corporations can function only as long as consumers buy their products, employees make their goods, stockholders (owners) buy their shares, and bondholders buy their bonds. Corporations per se do not do anything. We must ask, then, who really pays the tax on corporate income? This is a question of **tax incidence**. (The question of tax incidence applies to all taxes, including sales taxes and Social Security taxes.) The incidence of corporate taxation is the subject of considerable debate. Some economists suggest that corporations pass their tax burdens on to consumers by charging higher prices. Other economists argue that it is the stockholders who bear most of the tax. Still others contend that employees pay at least part of the tax by receiving lower wages than they would otherwise. Because the debate is not yet settled, we will not hazard a guess here as to what the correct conclusion may be. Suffice it to say that you should be cautious when you advocate increasing corporation income taxes. *People*—whether owners, consumers, or workers—ultimately end up paying the increase.

Tax incidence
The distribution of tax burdens among various groups in society.

Social Security and Unemployment Taxes

Each year, taxes levied on payrolls account for an increasing percentage of federal tax receipts. These taxes, which are distinct from personal income taxes, are for Social Security, retirement, survivors' disability, and old-age medical benefits (Medicare). Today, the Social Security tax is imposed on earnings up to roughly $105,000 at a rate of 6.2 percent on employers and 6.2 percent on employees. That is, the employer matches your "contribution" to Social Security. (The employer's contribution is really paid by the employees, at least in part, in the form of a reduced wage rate.) As Chapter 5 explained, a Medicare tax is imposed on all wage earnings at a combined rate of 2.9 percent. These taxes and the base on which they are levied are slated to rise in the next decade. Social Security taxes came into existence when the Federal Insurance Contributions Act (FICA) was passed in 1935. The future of Social Security is addressed later in this chapter.

There is also a federal unemployment tax, which helps pay for unemployment insurance. This tax rate is 0.6 percent on the first $7,000 of annual wages of each employee who earns more than $1,500. Only the employer makes this tax payment. This tax covers the costs of the unemployment insurance system. In addition to this federal tax, some states with an unemployment system impose their own tax of up to about 3 percent, depending on the past record of the particular employer. An employer who frequently lays off workers typically will have a slightly higher state unemployment tax rate than an employer who never lays off workers.

QUICK QUIZ   *See page 158 for the answers. Review concepts from this section in MyEconLab.*

The federal government raises most of its revenues through _____ taxes and social insurance taxes and contributions, and state and local governments raise most of their revenues from _____ taxes, _____ taxes, and income taxes.

Because corporations must first pay an income tax on most earnings, the personal income tax shareholders pay on dividends received (or realized capital gains) constitutes _____ taxation.

Both employers and employees must pay _____ _____ taxes and contributions at rates of 6.2 percent on roughly the first $105,000 in wage earnings, and a 2.9 percent _____ tax rate is applied to all wage earnings. The federal government and some state governments also assess taxes to pay for _____ insurance systems.

Tax Rates and Tax Revenues

For most state and local governments, income taxes yield fewer revenues than taxes imposed on sales of goods and services. Figure 6-1 on page 139 shows that sales taxes, gross receipts taxes, and excise taxes generate almost one-fifth of the total funds available to state and local governments. Thus, from the perspective of many state and local governments, a fundamental issue is how to set tax rates on sales of goods and services to extract desired total tax payments.

Sales Taxes

Sales taxes
Taxes assessed on the prices paid on most goods and services.

Ad valorem taxation
Assessing taxes by charging a tax rate equal to a fraction of the market price of each unit purchased.

Governments levy **sales taxes** on the prices that consumers pay to purchase each unit of a broad range of goods and services. Sellers collect sales taxes and transmit them to the government. Sales taxes are a form of *ad valorem* **taxation,** which means that the tax is applied "to the value" of the good. Thus, a government using a system of *ad valorem* taxation charges a tax rate equal to a fraction of the market price of each unit that a consumer buys. For instance, if the tax rate is 8 percent and the market price of an item is $100, then the amount of the tax on the item is $8.

A sales tax is therefore a proportional tax. The total amount of sales taxes a government collects equals the sales tax rate times the sales tax base, which is the market value of total purchases.

Static Tax Analysis

Static tax analysis
Economic evaluation of the effects of tax rate changes under the assumption that there is no effect on the tax base, meaning that there is an unambiguous positive relationship between tax rates and tax revenues.

There are two approaches to evaluating how changes in tax rates affect government tax collections. **Static tax analysis** assumes that changes in the tax rate have no effect on the tax base. Thus, this approach implies that if a state government desires to increase its sales tax collections, it can simply raise the tax rate. Multiplying the higher tax rate by the tax base thereby produces higher tax revenues.

Governments often rely on static tax analysis. Sometimes this yields unpleasant surprises. Consider, for instance, what happened in 1992 when Congress implemented a federal "luxury tax" on purchases of new pleasure boats priced at $100,000 or more. Applying the 10 percent luxury tax rate to the anticipated tax base—sales of new boats during previous years—produced a forecast of hundreds of million of dollars in revenues from the luxury tax. What actually happened, however, was an 80 percent plunge in sales of new luxury boats. People postponed boat purchases or bought used boats instead. Consequently, the tax base all but disappeared, and the federal government collected only a few tens of millions of dollars in taxes on boat sales. Congress repealed the tax a year later.

Dynamic Tax Analysis

The problem with static tax analysis is that it ignores incentive effects created by new taxes or hikes in existing tax rates. According to **dynamic tax analysis,** a likely response to an increase in a tax rate is a decrease in the tax base. When a government pushes up its sales tax rate, for example, consumers have an incentive to cut back on their purchases of goods and services subjected to the higher rate, perhaps by buying them in a locale where there is a lower sales tax rate or perhaps no tax rate at all. As shown in Figure 6-2 on the following page, the maximum sales tax rate varies considerably from state to state. Consider someone who lives in a state bordering Oregon. In such a border state, the sales tax rate can be as high as 8 percent, so a resident of that state has a strong incentive to buy higher-priced goods and services in Oregon, where there is no sales tax. Someone who lives in a high-tax county in Alabama has an incentive to buy an item online from an out-of-state firm to avoid paying sales taxes. Such shifts in expenditures in response to higher relative tax rates will reduce a state's sales tax base and thereby result in lower sales tax collections than the levels predicted by static tax analysis.

Dynamic tax analysis recognizes that increasing the tax rate could actually cause the government's total tax collections to *decline* if a sufficiently large number of consumers react to the higher sales tax rate by cutting back on purchases of goods and services included in the state's tax base. Some residents who live close to other states with lower sales tax rates might, for instance, drive across the state line to do more of their shopping. Other residents might place more orders with catalog companies or online firms located in other legal jurisdictions where their state's sales tax does not apply.

Why will the Connecticut state government probably receive less in estate tax revenues than state legislators anticipated?

Dynamic tax analysis
Economic evaluation of tax rate changes that recognizes that the tax base eventually declines with ever-higher tax rates, so that tax revenues may eventually decline if the tax rate is raised sufficiently.

If sales taxes are greatly increased only for luxury items, will anticipated tax revenues be fully realized?

POLICY EXAMPLE
Connecticut's "Death Tax" May Induce Changes in Residency

The Connecticut legislature recently passed a law imposing taxes on deceased individuals' estates valued in excess of $2 million. Under this law, an estate valued at $10 million typically will owe about $1 million in taxes to the state government. Based on estimates of the annual death rate among individuals with estates valued at more than $2 million, legislators anticipated that the law would generate an additional $150 million in annual tax revenues for Connecticut.

This static analysis, however, ignores the fact that thousands of wealthy Connecticut residents already own second homes in states without estate taxes. A Connecticut resident who anticipates an estate valued at $10 million when she dies

and already owns a second home in a state without an estate tax can save $1 million for her heirs by changing her residency. Economists cannot predict how many Connecticut residents may alter their state of residency to avoid the new estate tax. Economists agree, however, that dynamic tax analysis suggests that the tax law will generate fewer revenues than Connecticut legislators anticipated.

FOR CRITICAL ANALYSIS
Why would reducing Connecticut estate tax rates tend to decrease the likelihood of residency changes by people with second homes in other states?

FIGURE 6-2

States with the Highest and Lowest Sales Tax Rates

A number of states allow counties and cities to collect their own sales taxes in addition to state sales taxes. This figure shows the maximum sales tax rates for selected states, including county and municipal taxes. Delaware, Montana, New Hampshire, and Oregon have no sales taxes. All other states besides those in the figure and the District of Columbia have maximum sales tax rates between the 4 percent rate of Hawaii and the 9.875 percent rate in Arkansas.

Source: U.S. Department of Commerce.

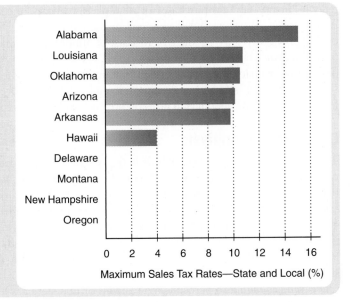

Maximizing Tax Revenues

Dynamic tax analysis indicates that whether a government's tax revenues ultimately rise or fall in response to a tax rate increase depends on exactly how much the tax base declines in response to the higher tax rate. On the one hand, the tax base may decline by a relatively small amount following an increase in the tax rate, or perhaps even imperceptibly, so that tax revenues rise. For instance, in the situation we imagine a government facing in Figure 6-3, a rise in the tax rate from 5 percent to 6 percent causes tax revenues to increase. Along this range, static tax analysis can provide a good approximation of the revenue effects of an increase in the tax rate. On the other hand, the tax base may decline so much that total tax revenues decrease. In Figure 6-3, for example, increasing the tax rate from 6 percent to 7 percent causes tax revenues to *decline*.

What is most likely is that when the tax rate is already relatively low, increasing the tax rate causes relatively small declines in the tax base. Within a range of relatively low sales tax rates, therefore, increasing the tax rate generates higher sales tax revenues, as illustrated along the upward-sloping portion of the curve depicted in Figure 6-3. If the government continues to push up the tax rate, however, people increasingly have an incentive to find ways to avoid purchasing taxable goods and services. Eventually, the tax base decreases sufficiently that the government's tax collections decline with ever-higher tax rates.

Consequently, governments that wish to maximize their tax revenues should not necessarily assess a high tax rate. In the situation illustrated in Figure 6-3, the government maximizes its tax revenues at T_{max} by establishing a sales tax rate of 6 percent. If the government were to raise the rate above 6 percent, it would induce a sufficient decline in the tax base that its tax collections would decline. If the government wishes to collect more than T_{max} in revenues to fund various government programs, it must somehow either expand its sales tax base or develop another tax.

How did Iceland discover that its corporate tax rates were above the revenue-maximizing level?

FIGURE 6-3

Maximizing the Government's Sales Tax Revenues

Dynamic tax analysis predicts that ever-higher tax rates bring about declines in the tax base, so that at sufficiently high tax rates the government's tax revenues begin to fall off. This implies that there is a tax rate, 6 percent in this example, at which the government can collect the maximum possible revenues, T_{max}.

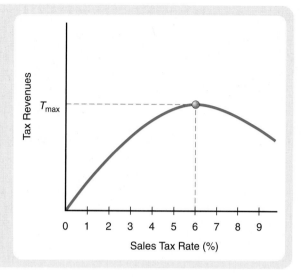

INTERNATIONAL POLICY EXAMPLE
How Iceland Slashed a Tax Rate and Boosted Tax Revenues

During the 1990s and 2000s, the Icelandic government phased in cuts in its corporate income tax rate from an initial rate of 45 percent to the current rate of 18 percent. In the process, the government's inflation-adjusted revenues from corporate income taxation more than doubled. Some in the Icelandic government suggest that the revenue-maximizing tax rate may be still lower, and a proposal to cut the rate to as low as 10 percent is under consideration. In any

event, it is now apparent to the government that the revenue-maximizing corporate income tax rate is considerably lower than 45 percent.

FOR CRITICAL ANALYSIS
What must have happened to the tax base relevant to Iceland's corporate income taxation system during the 1990s and 2000s?

QUICK QUIZ   *See page 158 for the answers. Review concepts from this section in MyEconLab.*

The _____ view of the relationship between tax rates and tax revenues implies that higher tax rates always generate increased government tax collections.

According to _____ tax analysis, higher tax rates cause the tax base to decrease. Tax collections will rise less than predicted by _____ tax analysis.

Dynamic tax analysis indicates that there is a tax rate that maximizes the government's tax collections. Setting the tax rate any higher would cause the tax base to _____ sufficiently that the government's tax revenues will _____.

Taxation from the Point of View of Producers and Consumers

Governments collect taxes on product sales at the source. They require producers to charge these taxes when they sell their output. This means that taxes on sales of goods and services affect market prices and quantities. Let's consider why this is so.

Taxes and the Market Supply Curve

Imposing taxes on final sales of a good or service affects the position of the market supply curve. To see why, consider panel (a) of Figure 6-4, which shows a gasoline market supply curve S_1 in the absence of taxation. At a price of $4.35 per gallon, gasoline producers are willing and able to supply 180,000 gallons of gasoline per week. If the price increases to $4.45 per gallon, firms increase production to 200,000 gallons of gasoline per week.

Both federal and state governments assess **excise taxes**—taxes on sales of particular commodities—on sales of gasoline. They levy gasoline excise taxes as a **unit tax,** or a constant tax per unit sold. On average, combined federal and state excise taxes on gasoline are about $0.40 per gallon.

Let's suppose, therefore, that a gasoline producer must transmit a total of $0.40 per gallon to federal and state governments for each gallon sold. Producers must

Excise tax
A tax levied on purchases of a particular good or service.

Unit tax
A constant tax assessed on each unit of a good that consumers purchase.

FIGURE 6-4

The Effects of Excise Taxes on the Market Supply and Equilibrium Price and Quantity of Gasoline

Panel (a) shows what happens if the government requires gasoline sellers to collect and transmit a $0.40 unit excise tax on gasoline. To be willing to continue supplying a given quantity, sellers must receive a price that is $0.40 higher for each gallon they sell, so the market supply curve shifts vertically by the amount of the tax. As illustrated in panel (b), this decline in market supply causes a reduction in the equilibrium quantity of gasoline produced and purchased. It also causes a rise in the market clearing price, to $4.75, so that consumers pay part of the tax. Sellers pay the rest in lower profits.

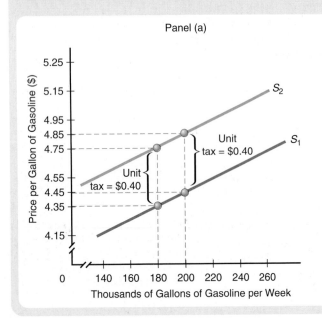

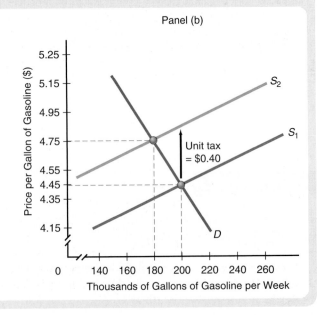

continue to receive a net amount of $4.35 per gallon to induce them to supply 180,000 gallons each week, so they must now receive $4.75 per gallon to supply that weekly quantity. Likewise, gasoline producers now will be willing to supply 200,000 gallons each week only if they receive $0.40 more per gallon, or a total amount of $4.85 per gallon.

As you can see, imposing the combined $0.40 per gallon excise taxes on gasoline shifts the supply curve vertically by exactly that amount to S_2 in panel (a). Thus, the effect of levying excise taxes on gasoline is to shift the supply curve vertically by the total per-unit taxes levied on gasoline sales. Hence, there is a decrease in supply. (In the case of an *ad valorem* sales tax, the supply curve would shift vertically by a proportionate amount equal to the tax rate.)

How Taxes Affect the Market Price and Equilibrium Quantity

Panel (b) of Figure 6-4 shows how imposing $0.40 per gallon in excise taxes affects the market price of gasoline and the equilibrium quantity of gasoline produced and sold. In the absence of excise taxes, the market supply curve S_1 crosses the demand curve D at a market price of $4.45 per gallon. At this market price, the equilibrium quantity of gasoline is 200,000 gallons of gasoline per week.

The excise tax levy of $0.40 per gallon shifts the supply curve to S_2. At the original $4.45 per gallon price, there is now an excess quantity of gasoline demanded, so the market price of gasoline rises to $4.75 per gallon. At this market price, the equilibrium quantity of gasoline produced and consumed each week is 180,000 gallons.

What factors determine how much the equilibrium quantity of a good or service declines in response to taxation? The answer to this question depends on how responsive quantities demanded and supplied are to changes in price.

Who Pays the Tax?

In our example, imposing excise taxes of $0.40 per gallon of gasoline causes the market price to rise to $4.75 per gallon from $4.45 per gallon. Thus, the price that each consumer pays is $0.30 per gallon higher. Consumers pay three-fourths of the excise tax levied on each gallon of gasoline produced and sold.

Gasoline producers must pay the rest of the tax. Their profits decline by $0.10 per gallon because costs have increased by $0.40 per gallon while consumers pay $0.30 more per gallon.

In the gasoline market, as in other markets for products subject to excise taxes and other taxes on sales, the shapes of the market demand and supply curves determine who pays most of a tax. The reason is that the shapes of these curves reflect the responsiveness to price changes of the quantity demanded by consumers and of the quantity supplied by producers.

In the example illustrated in Figure 6-4, the fact that consumers pay most of the excise taxes levied on gasoline reflects a relatively low responsiveness of quantity demanded by consumers to a change in the price of gasoline. Consumers pay most of the excise taxes on each gallon produced and sold because in this example the amount of gasoline they desire to purchase is relatively (but not completely) unresponsive to a change in the market price induced by excise taxes. We will revisit the issue of who pays excise taxes in Chapter 20.

If a state government increases the tax on a pack of cigarettes, who pays the tax?

QUICK QUIZ *See page 158 for the answers. Review concepts from this section in MyEconLab.*

When the government levies a tax on sales of a particular product, firms must receive a higher price to continue supplying the same quantity as before, so the supply curve shifts _____. If the tax is a unit excise tax, the supply curve shifts _____ by the amount of the tax.

Imposing a tax on sales of an item _____ the equilibrium quantity produced and consumed and _____ the market price.

When a government assesses a unit excise tax, the market price of the good or service typically rises by an amount _____ than the per-unit tax. Hence, consumers pay a portion of the tax, and firms pay the remainder.

Financing Social Security

In Chapter 5, you learned about Medicare, which is one of two major federal transfer programs. The other is Social Security, the federal system that transfers portions of the incomes of working-age people to elderly and disabled individuals. If current laws are maintained, Medicare's share of total national income will double over the next 20 years, as will the number of "very old" people—those over 85 and most in need of care. When Social Security is also taken into account, probably *half* of all federal government spending will go to the elderly by 2025. In a nutshell, senior citizens are the beneficiaries of an expensive and rapidly growing share of all federal spending.

Good Times for the First Retirees

The Social Security system was founded in 1935, as the United States was recovering from the Great Depression. The decision was made to establish Social Security as a means of guaranteeing a minimum level of pension benefits to all residents. Today, many people regard Social Security as a kind of "social compact"—a national promise to successive generations that they will receive support in their old age.

Social Security contributions
The mandatory taxes paid out of workers' wages and salaries.

Rate of return
The proportional annual benefit that results from making an investment.

Inflation-adjusted return
A rate of return that is measured in terms of real goods and services; that is, after the effects of inflation have been factored out.

BIG PAYOFFS FOR THE EARLIEST RECIPIENTS The first Social Security taxes (called "contributions") were collected in 1937, but it was not until 1940 that the first retirement benefits were paid. Ida May Fuller was the first person to receive a regular Social Security pension. She had paid a total of $25 in **Social Security contributions** before she retired. By the time she died in 1975 at age 100, she had received benefits totaling $23,000. Although Fuller perhaps did better than most, for the average retiree of 1940, the Social Security system was still more generous than any private investment plan anyone is likely to devise: After adjusting for inflation, the implicit **rate of return** on their contributions was an astounding 135 percent. (Roughly speaking, every $100 of combined employer and employee contributions yielded $135 *per year* during each and every year of that person's retirement. This is also called the **inflation-adjusted return**.)

Ever since the early days of Social Security, however, the implicit rate of return has decreased. Nonetheless, Social Security was an excellent deal for most retirees during the twentieth century. Figure 6-5 shows the implicit rate of return for people retiring in different years.

Given that the inflation-adjusted long-term rate of return on the stock market is about 7 to 9 percent, it is clear that for retirees, Social Security was a good deal until

FIGURE 6-5

Private Rates of Return on Social Security Contributions, by Year of Retirement

The rate of return on Social Security contributions has steadily declined.

Sources: Social Security Administration and author's estimates.

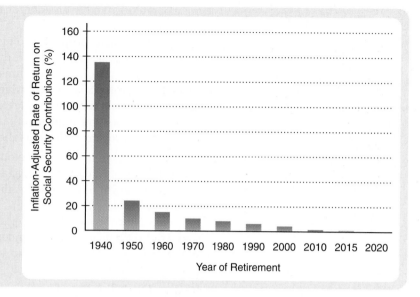

at least 1970. In fact, because Social Security benefits are a lot less risky than stocks, Social Security actually remained a pretty good "investment" for many people until around 1990.

SLOWING GROWTH IN WORKERS' CONTRIBUTIONS Social Security has managed to pay such high returns because at each point in time, current retirees are paid benefits out of the contributions of individuals who are currently working. (The contributions of today's retirees were long ago used to pay the benefits of previous retirees.) As long as Social Security was pulling in growing numbers of workers, either through a burgeoning workforce or by expanding its coverage of individuals in the workforce, the impressive rates of return during the early years of the program were possible.

But as birthrates declined beginning in the mid-1960s and the post–World War II baby boom generation began to reach retirement age, membership growth slowed, and the rate of return fell. Moreover, because the early participants received more than they contributed, it follows that if the number of participants stops growing, later participants must receive less—and that ultimately means a *negative* rate of return. And for today's college students—indeed for most people now under the age of 50 or so—that negative rate of return is what lies ahead, unless reforms are implemented.

What Will It Take to Salvage Social Security?

The United States now finds itself with a social compact—the Social Security system—that entails a flow of promised benefits that could exceed the inflow of taxes sometime between 2010 and 2015. What, if anything, might be done about this? There are five relevant options to consider.

1. **Raise Taxes.** The history of Social Security has been one of steadily increasing tax rates applied to an ever-larger portion of workers' wages. In 1935, a Social Security payroll tax rate of 2 percent was applied to the first $3,000 of an individual's earnings (more than $40,000 in today's dollars). Now the Social Security payroll tax rate is 10.4 percentage points higher, and the government applies

Go to **www.econtoday.com/chapter06** to learn more about Social Security at the official Web site of the Social Security Administration.

this tax rate to roughly an additional $65,000 of a worker's wages measured in today's dollars.

One prominent proposal promises an $80 billion increase in contributions via a 2.2 percentage-point hike in the payroll tax rate, to an overall rate of 14.6 percent. Another proposal is to eliminate the current cap on the level of wages to which the payroll tax is applied, which would also generate about $80 billion per year in additional tax revenues. Nevertheless, even a combined policy of eliminating the wage cap and implementing a 2.2 percentage-point tax increase would not, by itself, keep tax collections above benefit payments over the long run.

2. **Reduce Retirement Benefit Payouts**. Proposals are on the table to increase the age of full benefit eligibility, perhaps to as high as 70. Another option is to cut benefits to nonworking spouses. A third proposal is to impose "means testing" on some or all Social Security benefits. As things stand now, all individuals covered by the system collect benefits when they retire, regardless of their assets or other sources of retirement income. Under a system of means testing, individuals with substantial amounts of alternative sources of retirement income would receive reduced Social Security benefits.

3. **Reduce Disability Benefits**. In addition to old-age pension payments, the U.S. Social Security system also offers benefits to people with various types of disabilities. In 1984, Congress greatly liberalized the definition of "disability" for purposes of qualifying for these benefits, and the result has been a near doubling of disability beneficiaries, from 2.6 million to more than 5 million today. One way to help shore up Social Security's financial situation would be to tighten requirements for this program or perhaps separate it from the Social Security system.

4. **Reform Immigration Policies**. Many experts believe that significant changes in U.S. immigration laws could offer the best hope of dealing with the tax burdens and workforce shrinkage of the future. Currently, however, more than 90 percent of new immigrants are admitted on the basis of a selection system unchanged since 1952. This system ties immigration rights to family preference. That is why most people admitted to the United States happen to be the spouses, children, or siblings of earlier immigrants. Unless Congress makes skills or training that are highly valued in the U.S. workplace a criterion in the U.S. immigration preference system, new immigrants are unlikely to contribute significant payments to Social Security, because their incomes will remain relatively low. Without reforms, it is unlikely that immigration will relieve much of the pressure building due to our aging population.

5. **Find a Way to Increase Social Security's Implicit Rate of Return**. As noted earlier, a major current problem for Social Security is a low implicit rate of return. Looking into the future, however, the situation appears even worse. As Figure 6-6 indicates, implicit rates of return for the system will be *negative* by 2020.

The long-term inflation-adjusted return available in the stock market has been 7 to 9 percent since the 1930s. It is not surprising, therefore, that some observers have advocated that the Social Security system purchase stocks rather than Treasury bonds with the current excess of payroll taxes over current benefit payments. (Because this would necessitate the Treasury's borrowing more from the public, this amounts to having the government borrow from the public for purposes of investing in the stock market.)

Although the added returns on stock investments could help stave off tax increases or benefit cuts, there are a few potential problems with this proposal. Despite the stock market's higher long-term returns, the inherent uncertainty of those returns is not entirely

FIGURE 6-6

Projected Social Security Rates of Return for Future Retirees

Whereas workers who paid into Social Security in earlier years got a good deal, those who are now paying in and those who will pay in the future are facing low or negative implicit rates of return.

Sources: Social Security Administration and author's estimates.

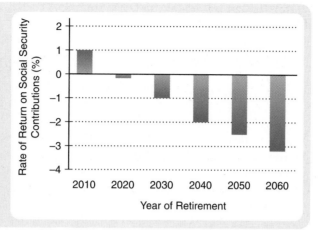

consistent with the function of Social Security as a source of *guaranteed* retirement income. Another issue is which stocks would be purchased. Political pressure to invest in companies that happened to be politically popular and to refrain from investing in those that were unpopular, regardless of their returns, would reduce the expected returns from the government's stock portfolio—possibly even below the returns on Treasury bonds.

QUICK QUIZ See page 158 for the answers. Review concepts from this section in MyEconLab.

Social Security and Medicare payments are using up a large and _____ portion of the federal budget. Because of a shrinking number of workers available to support each retiree, the per capita expense for future workers to fund these programs will _____ rapidly unless reforms are made.

During the early years of the Social Security system, taxes were _____ relative to benefits, resulting in a

_____ implicit rate of return for retirees. As taxes have risen relative to benefits, the implicit rate of return on Social Security has _____ steadily.

There are only five options—or combinations of these five options—for preserving the current social compact: _____ taxes, _____ retirement benefit payouts, _____ disability benefits, reform _____ policies, or _____ Social Security's rate of return.

You Are There

For This Physician, the Tax Rate Is Too High to Justify Working

John McGoldrick and his wife are physicians living in Brunswick, Maine. Their combined income puts them among higher-income U.S. households. Thus, every dollar that John earns over and above his wife's income is normally taxed at an effective top marginal income tax rate of 51.1 percent (including Medicare, Social Security, and state taxes). Today,

though, John has completed a tax worksheet indicating that the couple also owes the *alternative minimum tax (AMT)*. Congress created the AMT in 1969 to prevent very-high-income taxpayers from using numerous special deductions and credits to reduce their tax liabilities. When Congress created the AMT, however, it failed to take inflation into account.

You Are There (cont.)

Since 1969, inflation has pushed up current-dollar incomes. Hence, current-dollar incomes that were "very high" in 1969 are just "high" or even "middle" today. In addition, since then Congress has added numerous deductions and exemptions intended to benefit middle-income taxpayers. Both factors have had the effect of imposing the AMT on more households, including the McGoldricks', thereby pushing John's effective marginal income tax rate even higher.

John realizes that after he and his wife pay all federal taxes including the AMT, state and local taxes, malpractice insurance premiums, and the like, his net earnings do not cover expenses he and his wife incur for child care. The time has come, he decides, to quit his job as an emergency room physician and care for their children himself.

CRITICAL ANALYSIS QUESTIONS

1. How does John McGoldrick know that his effective marginal income tax rate for his year of labor has turned out to be higher than 51.1 percent?

2. Why does the AMT's existence make it difficult for someone contemplating employment or more hours of wage-earning work in her current job to assess her marginal income tax rate? (Hint: Individuals often do not know whether they face the AMT in a given year until after the year-end when they calculate their federal tax liability.)

Progressive Income Taxation in the United States

Issues and Applications

CONCEPTS APPLIED

➤ Progressive Taxation

➤ Tax Rate

➤ Average Tax Rate

On a regular basis, a number of members of the U.S. Congress propose decreasing income tax rates for middle- and lower-income households and increasing income tax rates for higher-income households. They argue that the federal income tax system places a disproportionate burden on middle- and lower-income households and that higher-income taxpayers do not pay "their fair share" of income taxes.

Just how progressive is the *current* U.S. income tax system? One way to evaluate this question is to look at the tax rates—percentages of incomes transmitted to the federal government as income taxes—that apply to different income groups. Another is to compare different income groups' shares of income to their shares of total tax payments.

FIGURE 6-7

Average Tax Rates and Shares of U.S. Federal Income Taxes for Different Income Groups

As panel (a) shows, average tax rates increase for groups with higher incomes. In addition, panel (b) indicates that among those who pay federal income taxes, lower-income taxpayers account for a much smaller portion of payments than higher-income taxpayers. These patterns indicate that the U.S. federal income tax system is progressive.

Source: Internal Revenue Service.

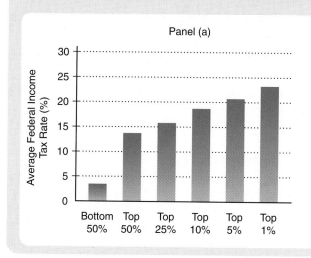

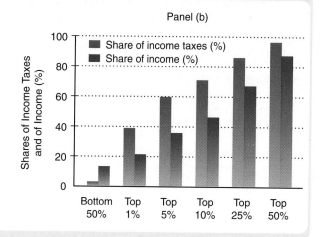

Average Tax Rates for Different Income Groups

Figure 6-7 displays the average federal income tax rates paid by various income groups in the United States. As you can see in panel (a), the average tax rate for all taxpayers in the lower half of the income distribution of taxpayers is about 3 percent. The average tax rate paid by those in the top half of income earners paying taxes is more than 10 percentage points higher.

Also shown in panel (a) are the average tax rates for those in the top 25, 10, 5, and 1 percent of income earners. The tax rate rises as incomes increase, so the U.S. income tax system is clearly progressive throughout the upper range of incomes.

The Distribution of Federal Income Tax Payments

Naturally, even if lower-income individuals faced the same income tax rates as higher-income individuals, the former group would pay a smaller share of total income taxes because they earn lower incomes. In a progressive income tax system, however, lower-income individuals also pay lower tax rates than those assessed against incomes of higher earners. Thus, under progressive taxation lower-income people typically pay a very small share of total tax payments.

Panel (b) of Figure 6-7 verifies that this is currently true in the United States. Taxpayers among the bottom 50 percent of income earners, who earn about 14 percent of all income, account for less than 4 percent of federal income taxes. Thus, the share of taxes paid by the lowest-income individuals is considerably less than their share of total income. Furthermore, panel (b) shows that the bulk of income tax payments is concentrated among the highest-income taxpayers. The top 10 percent of taxpaying income earners, who earn just about 45 percent of all income, pay almost 66 percent of federal income taxes. Those among the top 1 percent earn about 20 percent of all income but account for more than 38 percent of the government's total receipts.

In summary, U.S. income tax rates increase as incomes rise. Consequently, the highest-income taxpayers pay considerably larger shares of the nation's overall income tax bill than lower-income taxpayers.

The highest-income taxpayers also pay proportionately higher shares of taxes than their own shares of total income. Clearly, the United States has a progressive tax system.

Test your understanding of this chapter by going online to **MyEconLab**.
In the Study Plan for this chapter, select Section N: News.

For Critical Analysis

1. If the income tax system were made more progressive across all income groups, how would panel (a) of Figure 6-7 on the previous page change?

2. If the income tax system were made more progressive across all income groups, how would panel (b) of Figure 6-7 change?

Web Resources

1. To see the latest Internal Revenue Service statistics on U.S. income tax rates paid by different income groups, go to www.econtoday.com/chapter06.

2. For information about the increasing share of income earners who owe no federal income taxes at all, go to www.econtoday.com/chapter06.

Research Project

Figure 6-7 includes data only for U.S. income earners who actually paid taxes. Each year, a slightly larger portion—currently about one-third—of income earners in the United States owes zero federal income taxes. Other things being equal, does this trend tend to make the U.S. tax system more progressive? Explain. (Hint: Recall that by definition, 50 percent of all income earners are below the middle-income level.)

Here is what you should know after reading this chapter. **MyEconLab** will help you identify what you know, and where to go when you need to practice.

WHAT YOU SHOULD KNOW

WHERE TO GO TO PRACTICE

Average Tax Rates versus Marginal Tax Rates The average tax rate is the ratio of total tax payments to total income. In contrast, the marginal tax rate is the change in tax payments induced by a change in total taxable income. Thus, the marginal tax rate applies to the last dollar that a person earns.

government budget constraint, 135
tax base, 136
tax rate, 136
marginal tax rate, 136
tax bracket, 137
average tax rate, 137
proportional taxation, 137
progressive taxation, 137
regressive taxation, 137

- **MyEconLab** Study Plans 6.1, 6.2
- Audio introduction to Chapter 6
- Video: Types of Tax Systems
- ABC News Video: Big Government: Who Is Going to Pay the Bill?

(continued)

myeconlab *(continued)*

WHAT YOU SHOULD KNOW		WHERE TO GO TO PRACTICE
The U.S. Income Tax System The U.S. income tax system assesses taxes against both personal and business income. It is designed to be a progressive tax system, in which the marginal tax rate increases as income rises, so that the marginal tax rate exceeds the average tax rate. This contrasts with a regressive tax system, in which higher-income people pay lower marginal tax rates, resulting in a marginal tax rate that is less than the average tax rate. The marginal tax rate equals the average tax rate only under proportional taxation, in which the marginal tax rate does not vary with income.	capital gain, 140 capital loss, 140 retained earnings, 140 tax incidence, 141	• **MyEconLab** Study Plan 6.3 • Video: The Corporate Income Tax
The Relationship Between Tax Rates and Tax Revenues Static tax analysis assumes that the tax base does not respond significantly to an increase in the tax rate, so it seems to imply that a tax rate hike must always boost a government's total tax collections. Dynamic tax analysis reveals, however, that increases in tax rates cause the tax base to decline. Thus, there is a tax rate that maximizes the government's tax revenues. If the government pushes the tax rate higher, tax collections decline.	sales taxes, 142 *ad valorem* taxation, 142 static tax analysis, 142 dynamic tax analysis, 143 **KEY FIGURE** Figure 6-3, 145	• **MyEconLab** Study Plan 6.4 • Animated Figure 6-3
How Taxes on Purchases of Goods and Services Affect Market Prices and Quantities When a government imposes a per-unit tax on a good or service, a seller is willing to supply any given quantity only if the seller receives a price that is higher by exactly the amount of the tax. Hence, the supply curve shifts vertically by the amount of the tax per unit. In a market with typically shaped demand and supply curves, this results in a fall in the equilibrium quantity and an increase in the market price. To the extent that the market price rises, consumers pay a portion of the tax on each unit they buy. Sellers pay the remainder in lower profits.	excise tax, 146 unit tax, 146 **KEY FIGURE** Figure 6-4, 146	• **MyEconLab** Study Plan 6.5 • Animated Figure 6-4
How Social Security Works and Why It Poses Problems for Today's Students Since its inception, Social Security benefits have been paid out of taxes. Because of the growing mismatch between elderly and younger citizens, future scheduled benefits vastly exceed future scheduled taxes, so some combination of higher taxes and lower benefits will have to be implemented to maintain the current system. The situation might also be eased a bit if more skilled workers were permitted to immigrate and if Social Security contributions were invested in the stock market, where they could earn higher rates of return.	Social Security contributions, 148 rate of return, 148 inflation-adjusted return, 148 **KEY FIGURE** Figure 6-6, 151	• **MyEconLab** Study Plan 6.6 • Animated Figure 6-6

Log in to MyEconLab, take a chapter test, and get a personalized Study Plan that tells you which concepts you understand and which ones you need to review. From there, MyEconLab will give you further practice, tutorials, animations, videos, and guided solutions.
Log in to www.myeconlab.com

PROBLEMS

All problems are assignable in myeconlab *. Answers to odd-numbered problems appear at the back of the book.*

6-1. A senior citizen gets a part-time job at a fast-food restaurant. She earns $8 per hour for each hour she works, and she works exactly 25 hours per week. Thus, her total pretax weekly income is $200. Her total income tax assessment each week is $40, but she has determined that she is assessed $3 in taxes for the final hour she works each week.

   a. What is this person's average tax rate each week?

   b. What is the marginal tax rate for the last hour she works each week?

6-2. For purposes of assessing income taxes, there are three official income levels for workers in a small country: high, medium, and low. For the last hour on the job during a 40-hour workweek, a high-income worker pays a marginal income tax rate of 15 percent, a medium-income worker pays a marginal tax rate of 20 percent, and a low-income worker is assessed a 25 percent marginal income tax rate. Based only on this information, does this nation's income tax system appear to be progressive, proportional, or regressive?

6-3. Suppose that a state has increased its sales tax rate every other year since 2001. Assume that the state collected all sales taxes that residents legally owed. The following table summarizes its experience. What were total taxable sales in this state during each year displayed in the table?

Year	Sales Tax Rate	Sales Tax Collections
2001	0.03 (3 percent)	$9.0 million
2003	0.04 (4 percent)	$14.0 million
2005	0.05 (5 percent)	$20.0 million
2007	0.06 (6 percent)	$24.0 million
2009	0.07 (7 percent)	$29.4 million

6-4. The sales tax rate applied to all purchases within a state was 0.04 (4 percent) throughout 2008 but increased to 0.05 (5 percent) during all of 2009. The state government collected all taxes due, but its tax revenues were equal to $40 million each year. What happened to the sales tax base between 2008 and 2009? What could account for this result?

6-5. A city government imposes a proportional income tax on all people who earn income within its city

limits. In 2008, the city's income tax rate was 0.05 (5 percent), and it collected $20 million in income taxes. In 2009, it raised the income tax rate to 0.06 (6 percent), and its income tax collections declined to $19.2 million. What happened to the city's income tax base between 2008 and 2009? How could this have occurred?

6-6. An obscure subsidiary of Microsoft Corporation, Ireland-based Round Island One Limited, has only about 1,000 employees. Nevertheless, Microsoft has gradually been shifting more income-generating activities to Ireland, which has a lower corporate tax rate than nations such as the United States and the United Kingdom. In one year alone, shifting more of its operations to Ireland allowed Microsoft to reduce its worldwide corporate income tax rate by 6 percentage points. What has happened to Ireland's tax base as a result? What has happened to tax bases in nations such as the United States and the United Kingdom?

6-7. The British government recently imposed a unit excise tax of about $154 per ticket on airline tickets applying to flights to or from London airports. In answering the following questions, assume normally shaped demand and supply curves.

   a. Use an appropriate diagram to predict effects of the ticket tax on the market clearing price of London airline tickets and on the equilibrium number of flights into and out of London.

   b. What do you predict is likely to happen to the equilibrium price of tickets for air flights into and out of cities that are in close proximity to London but are not subject to the new ticket tax? Explain your reasoning.

6-8. To raise funds aimed at providing more support for public schools, a state government has just imposed a unit excise tax equal to $4 for each monthly unit of telephone services sold by each telephone company operating in the state. The diagram on the next page depicts the positions of the demand and supply curves for telephone services *before* the unit excise tax was imposed. Use this diagram to determine the position of the new market supply curve now that the tax hike has gone into effect.

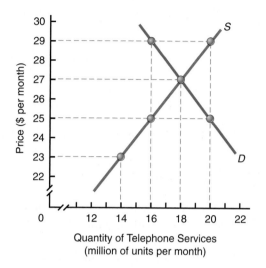

Quantity of Telephone Services
(million of units per month)

a. Does imposing the $4-per-month unit excise tax cause the market price of telephone services to rise by $4 per month? Why or why not?

b. What portion of the $4-per-month unit excise tax is paid by consumers? What portion is paid by providers of telephone services?

6-9. Suppose that the federal government imposes a unit excise tax of $2 per month on the monthly rates that Internet service providers charge for providing DSL high-speed Internet access to households and businesses. Draw a diagram of normally shaped market demand and supply curves for DSL Internet access services. Use this diagram to predict how the Internet service tax is likely to affect the market price and market quantity.

6-10. Consider the $2-per-month tax on DSL Internet access in Problem 6-9. Suppose that in the market for DSL Internet access services provided to households, the market price increases by $2 per month after the unit excise tax is imposed. If the market supply curve slopes upward, what can you say about the shape of the market demand curve over the relevant ranges of prices and quantities? Who pays the excise tax in this market?

6-11. Consider once more the DSL Internet access tax of $2 per month discussed in Problem 6-9. Suppose that in the market for DSL Internet access services provided to businesses, the market price does not change after the unit excise tax is imposed. If the market supply curve slopes upward, what can you say about the shape of the

market demand curve over the relevant ranges of prices and quantities? Who pays the excise tax in this market?

6-12. The following information applies to the market for a particular item in the *absence* of a unit excise tax:

Price ($ per unit)	Quantity Supplied	Quantity Demanded
4	50	200
5	75	175
6	100	150
7	125	125
8	150	100
9	175	75

a. According to the information above, in the *absence* of a unit excise tax, what is the market price? What is the equilibrium quantity?

b. Suppose that the government decides to subject producers of this item to a unit excise tax equal to $2 per unit sold. What is the new market price? What is the new equilibrium quantity?

c. What portion of the tax is paid by producers? What portion of the tax is paid by consumers?

6-13. In the following situations, what is the rate of return on the investment? (Hint: In each case, what is the percentage by which next year's benefit exceeds—or falls short of—this year's cost?)

a. You invest $100 today and receive in return $150 exactly one year from now.

b. You invest $100 today and receive in return $80 exactly one year from now.

6-14. Suppose that the following Social Security reform became law: All current Social Security recipients will continue to receive their benefits, but no increase will be made other than cost-of-living adjustments; U.S. citizens between age 40 and retirement not yet receiving Social Security can opt to continue with the current system; those who opt out can place what they would have contributed to Social Security into one or more government-approved investments; and those under 40 must place their contributions into one or more government-approved investments.

Now answer the following questions:

a. Who will be in favor of this reform and why?

b. Who will be against this reform and why?

c. What might happen to stock market indexes?

d. What additional risk is involved for those who end up in the private system?

e. What additional benefits are possible for the people in the private system?

f. Which firms in the investment industry might not be approved by the federal government and why?

ECONOMICS ON THE NET

Social Security Privatization There are many proposals for reforming Social Security, but only one fundamentally alters the nature of the current system: privatization. The purpose of this exercise is to learn more about what would happen if Social Security were privatized.

Title: Social Security Privatization

Navigation: Go to **www.econtoday.com/chapter06** to learn about Social Security privatization. Click on *FAQ on Social Security* in the left-hand column.

Application For each of the three entries noted here, read the entry and answer the question.

1. Click on *Is there really a Social Security crisis?* According to this article, when will the system begin to experience difficulties? Why?

2. Click on *What about raising the tax cap?* What does this article contend are the likely consequences of applying the Social Security payroll tax to more of a person's income? Why?

3. Click on *What about personal accounts in addition to Social Security?* Why does this article argue that simply adding personal accounts will not solve Social Security's problems?

For Group Study and Analysis It will be worthwhile for those not nearing retirement age to examine what the "older" generation thinks about the idea of privatizing the Social Security system in the United States. So create two groups—one for and one against privatization. Each group will examine the following Web site and come up with arguments in favor of or against the ideas expressed on it.

Go to **www.econtoday.com/chapter06** to read a proposal for Social Security reform. Accept or rebut the proposal, depending on the side to which you have been assigned. Be prepared to defend your reasons with more than just your feelings. At a minimum, be prepared to present arguments that are logical, if not entirely backed by facts.

Taking into account the characteristics of your group as a whole, is it likely to be made better off or worse off if Social Security is privatized? Should your decision to support or oppose privatization be based solely on how it affects you personally? Or should your decision take into account how it might affect others in your group?

ANSWERS TO QUICK QUIZZES

p. 138: (i) rate . . . base; (ii) average . . . marginal; (iii) proportional . . . progressive . . . regressive

p. 142: (i) income . . . sales . . . property; (ii) double; (iii) Social Security . . . Medicare . . . unemployment

p. 145: (i) static; (ii) dynamic . . . static; (iii) fall . . . decline

p. 148: (i) vertically . . . vertically; (ii) reduces . . . raises; (iii) less

p. 151: (i) rising . . . grow; (ii) low . . . high . . . decreased; (iii) raise . . . reduce . . . reduce . . . immigration . . . increase

The Macroeconomy: Unemployment and Inflation

7

S ince 2000, only U.S. residents aged 55 and over have increased their *labor force participation,* choosing either to obtain jobs or to actively seek employment. Among all other workers, labor force participation has generally trended downward since 2000.

Who can participate in the U.S. labor force? Among those individuals who can participate and choose to do so, how many are employed, and how many are unemployed? How is the U.S. unemployment rate calculated? All of these questions are answered in this chapter.

LEARNING OBJECTIVES

myeconlab

MyEconLab helps you master each objective and study more efficiently. See end of chapter for details.

After reading this chapter, you should be able to:

➤ Explain how the U.S. government calculates the official unemployment rate

➤ Discuss the types of unemployment

➤ Describe how price indexes are calculated and define the key types of price indexes

➤ Distinguish between nominal and real interest rates

➤ Evaluate who loses and who gains from inflation

➤ Understand key features of business fluctuations

? DID YOU KNOW THAT estimates indicate that each year, discount pricing by so-called big-box retailers, such as Wal-Mart, Target, and Kmart, helps to keep the overall U.S. *inflation rate*—the annual rate of increase in average prices of all goods and services—about 0.4 percentage point lower than it otherwise would be? Additionally, every year discount pricing by food superstores holds the annual rate of increase in average U.S. food prices an estimated 0.75 percentage point below the rate it otherwise would reach.

Trying to understand and better measure inflation and the overall performance of the national economy is a central objective of macroeconomics. This branch of economics seeks to explain and predict movements in the average level of prices, unemployment, and the total production of goods and services. This chapter introduces you to these key issues of macroeconomics.

Unemployment

Unemployment

The total number of adults (aged 16 years or older) who are willing and able to work and who are actively looking for work but have not found a job.

Unemployment is normally defined as the number of adults who are actively looking for work but do not have a job. Unemployment creates a cost to the entire economy in terms of lost output. One estimate indicates that at the beginning of the 2000s, when the unemployment rate rose by 2 percentage points and firms were operating below 80 percent of their capacity, the amount of output that the economy lost due to idle resources was roughly 2 percent of the total production throughout the United States. (In other words, we were somewhere inside the production possibilities curve that we talked about in Chapter 2.) That was the equivalent of more than an inflation-adjusted $200 billion of schools, houses, restaurant meals, cars, and movies that *could have been* produced. It is no wonder that policymakers closely watch the unemployment figures published by the Department of Labor's Bureau of Labor Statistics.

On a more personal level, the state of being unemployed often results in hardship and failed opportunities as well as a lack of self-respect. Psychological researchers believe that being fired creates at least as much stress as the death of a close friend. The numbers that we present about unemployment can never fully convey its true cost to the people of this or any other nation.

Labor force

Individuals aged 16 years or older who either have jobs or who are looking and available for jobs; the number of employed plus the number of unemployed.

Historical Unemployment Rates

The unemployment rate, defined as the proportion of the measured **labor force** that is unemployed, hit a low of 1.2 percent of the labor force at the end of World War II, after having reached 25 percent during the Great Depression in the 1930s. You can see in Figure 7-1 what has happened to the unemployment rate in the United States since 1890. The highest level ever was reached in the Great Depression, but the unemployment rate was also high during the Panic of 1893.

Employment, Unemployment, and the Labor Force

Figure 7-2 presents the population of individuals 16 years of age or older broken into three segments: (1) employed, (2) unemployed, and (3) not in the civilian labor force (a category that includes homemakers, full-time students, military personnel, persons in institutions, and retired persons). The employed and the unemployed, added together, make up the labor force. In 2009, the labor force amounted to 145.3 million + 10.4 million = 155.7 million people. To calculate the unemployment rate, we simply divide the number of unemployed by the number of people in the labor force and multiply by 100: 10.4 million/155.7 million × 100 = 6.7 percent.

What is the reason why large retailers, such as Wal-Mart and Costco, offer relatively low prices for their products, thereby keeping the overall inflation rate lower than it would be otherwise?

FIGURE 7-1

More Than a Century of Unemployment

Unemployment reached lows of less than 2 percent during World Wars I and II
and a high of more than 25 percent during the Great Depression.

Source: U.S. Department of Labor, Bureau of Labor Statistics.

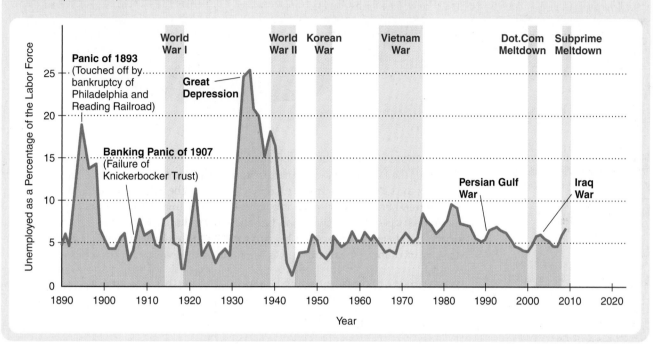

FIGURE 7-2

Adult Population

The population aged 16 and older can be broken down into three groups: people who are employed, those who are unemployed, and those not in the labor force.

Source: U.S. Department of Labor, Bureau of Labor Statistics.

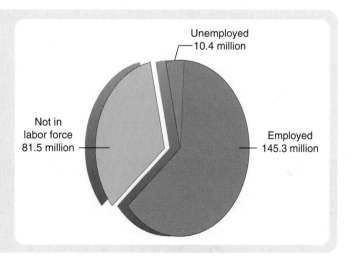

The Arithmetic Determination of Unemployment

Because there is a transition between employment and unemployment at any point in time—people are leaving jobs and others are finding jobs—there is a simple relationship between the employed and the unemployed, as can be seen in Figure 7-3 on page 162. Job

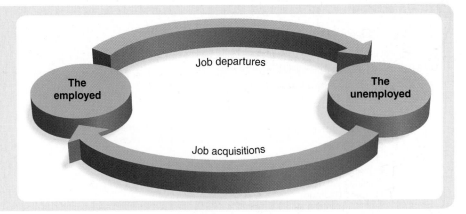

FIGURE 7-3

The Logic of the Unemployment Rate

Individuals who depart jobs but remain in the labor force are subtracted from the employed and added to the unemployed. When the unemployed acquire jobs, they are subtracted from the unemployed and added to the employed. In an unchanged labor force, if both flows are equal, the unemployment rate is stable. If more people depart jobs than acquire them, the unemployment rate increases, and vice versa.

Stock
The quantity of something, measured at a given point in time—for example, an inventory of goods or a bank account. Stocks are defined independently of time, although they are assessed at a point in time.

Flow
A quantity measured per unit of time; something that occurs over time, such as the income you make per week or per year or the number of individuals who are fired every month.

Job loser
An individual in the labor force whose employment was involuntarily terminated.

Reentrant
An individual who used to work full-time but left the labor force and has now reentered it looking for a job.

Job leaver
An individual in the labor force who quits voluntarily.

departures are shown at the top of the diagram, and job acquisitions are shown at the bottom. If the numbers of job departures and acquisitions are equal, the unemployment rate stays the same. If departures exceed acquisitions, the unemployment rate rises.

The number of unemployed is some number at any point in time. It is a **stock** of individuals who do not have a job but are actively looking for one. The same is true for the number of employed. The number of people departing jobs, whether voluntarily or involuntarily, is a **flow,** as is the number of people acquiring jobs.

CATEGORIES OF INDIVIDUALS WHO ARE WITHOUT WORK According to the Bureau of Labor Statistics, an unemployed individual will fall into any of four categories:

1. A **job loser,** whose employment was involuntarily terminated or who was laid off (40 to 60 percent of the unemployed)

2. A **reentrant,** who worked a full-time job before but has been out of the labor force (20 to 30 percent of the unemployed)

3. A **job leaver,** who voluntarily ended employment (less than 10 to around 15 percent of the unemployed)

4. A **new entrant,** who has never worked a full-time job for two weeks or longer (10 to 15 percent of the unemployed)

Which U.S. workers are now losing or leaving their jobs more rapidly than in previous years?

EXAMPLE
Why Older Men May Be More Anxious Than in Years Past

Since the early 1980s, average U.S. *job tenure* —the time a typical employee spends with the same employer—has risen by about six months, to 4 years. Average job tenure among women aged 35 to 44 has increased from just over 4 years in the early 1980s to a little over $4\frac{1}{2}$ years today. During the same period, average job tenure has also risen among women aged 45 to 54, from about 6 years to nearly 7 years. Average job tenure has also risen slightly for women and men under the age of 35.

Among older men, however, average job tenure has been *declining*. Since the early 1980s, average job tenure for men aged 35 to 44 has fallen from $7\frac{1}{2}$ years to about $5\frac{1}{2}$ years.

EXAMPLE (cont.)

For men aged 45 to 54, average job tenure has decreased even more, from almost 13 years in the early 1980s to only about 8 years today. Thus, older men tend to be categorized among job losers and job leavers more often than they were a generation ago.

FOR CRITICAL ANALYSIS
Why do you suppose that the average unemployment rate for older men has risen slightly, other things being equal?

DURATION OF UNEMPLOYMENT If you are out of a job for a week, your situation is typically much less serious than if you are out of a job for, say, 14 weeks. An increase in the duration of unemployment can increase the unemployment rate because workers stay unemployed longer, thereby creating a greater number of them at any given time. The most recent information on duration of unemployment paints the following picture: more than a third of those who become unemployed acquire a new job by the end of one month, approximately one-third more acquire a job by the end of two months, and only about a sixth are still unemployed after six months. Since the mid-1960s, the average annual duration of unemployment for all the unemployed has varied between 10 and 20 weeks. The overall average duration for the past 25 years has been about 15 weeks.

When overall business activity goes into a downturn, the duration of unemployment tends to rise, thereby accounting for much of the increase in the estimated unemployment rate. In a sense, then, it is the increase in the *duration* of unemployment during a downturn in national economic activity that generates the bad news that concerns policymakers in Washington, D.C. Furthermore, the individuals who stay unemployed longer than six months are the ones who create pressure on Congress to "do something." What Congress does, typically, is extend and supplement unemployment benefits.

THE DISCOURAGED WORKER PHENOMENON Critics of the published unemployment rate calculated by the federal government believe that it fails to reflect the true numbers of **discouraged workers** and "hidden unemployed." Though there is no agreed-on method to measure discouraged workers, the Department of Labor defines them as people who have dropped out of the labor force and are no longer looking for a job because they believe that the job market has little to offer them. To what extent do we want to include in the measured labor force individuals who voluntarily choose not to look for work or those who take only a few minutes a day to scan the want ads and then decide that there are no jobs?

Some economists argue that people who work part-time but are willing to work full-time should be classified as "semihidden" unemployed. Estimates range as high as 6 million workers at any one time. Offsetting this factor, though, is *overemployment*. An individual working 50 or 60 hours a week is still counted as only one full-time worker. Some people hold two or three jobs.

LABOR FORCE PARTICIPATION The way in which we define unemployment and membership in the labor force will affect the **labor force participation rate.** It is defined as the proportion of noninstitutionalized (i.e., not in prisons, mental institutions, etc.) working-age individuals who are employed or seeking employment.

New entrant
An individual who has never held a full-time job lasting two weeks or longer but is now seeking employment.

You Are There
To learn about how Denmark's government keeps the nation's unemployment level low, read **Staying Employed in Denmark —at the Taxpayers' Expense,** on pages 176 and 177.

Discouraged workers
Individuals who have stopped looking for a job because they are convinced that they will not find a suitable one.

Labor force participation rate
The percentage of noninstitutionalized working-age individuals who are employed or seeking employment.

The U.S. labor force participation rate has risen somewhat over time, from 60 percent in 1950 to about 66 percent today. The gender composition of the U.S. labor force has changed considerably during this time. In 1950, more than 83 percent of men and fewer than 35 percent of women participated in the U.S. labor force. Today, fewer than 75 percent of men and more than 60 percent of women are U.S. labor force participants.

QUICK QUIZ   *See page 183 for the answers. Review concepts from this section in MyEconLab.*

_____ persons are adults who are willing and able to work and are actively looking for a job but have not found one. The unemployment rate is computed by dividing the number of unemployed by the total _____ _____, which is equal to those who are employed plus those who are unemployed.

The unemployed are classified as _____ _____, _____, _____ _____, and _____

_____ to the labor force. The flow of people departing jobs and people acquiring jobs determines the stock of the unemployed as well as the stock of the employed.

The duration of unemployment affects the unemployment rate. If the duration of unemployment increases, the measured unemployment rate will _____, even though the number of unemployed workers may remain the same.

The Major Types of Unemployment

Unemployment has been categorized into four basic types: frictional, structural, cyclical, and seasonal.

Frictional Unemployment

Of the more than 155 million people in the labor force, more than 50 million will either change jobs or take new jobs during the year. In the process, more than 22 million persons will report themselves unemployed at one time or another. This continuous flow of individuals from job to job and in and out of employment is called **frictional unemployment.** There will always be some frictional unemployment as resources are redirected in the economy, because job-hunting costs are never zero, and workers never have full information about available jobs. To eliminate frictional unemployment, we would have to prevent workers from leaving their present jobs until they had already lined up other jobs at which they would start working immediately. And we would have to guarantee first-time job seekers a job *before* they started looking.

Frictional unemployment
Unemployment due to the fact that workers must search for appropriate job offers. This takes time, and so they remain temporarily unemployed.

Structural Unemployment

Structural changes in our economy cause some workers to become unemployed for very long periods of time because they cannot find jobs that use their particular skills. This is called **structural unemployment.** Structural unemployment is not caused by general business fluctuations, although business fluctuations may affect it. And unlike frictional unemployment, structural unemployment is not related to the movement of workers from low-paying to high-paying jobs.

At one time, economists thought about structural unemployment only from the perspective of workers. The concept applied to workers who did not have the ability, training, and skills necessary to obtain available jobs. Today, it still encompasses these

Structural unemployment
Unemployment resulting from a poor match of workers' abilities and skills with current requirements of employers.

workers. In addition, however, economists increasingly look at structural unemployment from the viewpoint of employers, many of whom face government mandates requiring them to take such steps as providing funds for social insurance programs for their employees and announcing plant closings months or even years in advance. There is now considerable evidence that government labor market policies influence how many positions businesses wish to create, thereby affecting structural unemployment. In the United States, many businesses appear to have adjusted to these policies by hiring more "temporary workers" or establishing short-term contracts with "private consultants." Such measures may have reduced the extent of U.S. structural unemployment in recent years.

Cyclical Unemployment

Cyclical unemployment is related to business fluctuations. It is defined as unemployment associated with changes in business conditions—primarily recessions and depressions. The way to lessen cyclical unemployment would be to reduce the intensity, duration, and frequency of downturns of business activity. Economic policymakers attempt, through their policies, to reduce cyclical unemployment by keeping business activity on an even keel.

How may construction firms' propensity to hire illegal aliens have helped cushion cyclical unemployment from the most recent drop in home-building activity?

Cyclical unemployment
Unemployment resulting from business recessions that occur when aggregate (total) demand is insufficient to create full employment.

INTERNATIONAL EXAMPLE
How Illegal Aliens Affect Measured U.S. Cyclical Unemployment

In 2007, home-building activity fell by more than 25 percent. In the past, the result would have been a rise in the number of people cyclically unemployed in the construction industry, typically by about the same percentage as the reduction in home-building activity. Thus, most economists predicted that cyclical unemployment in construction would increase by about 25 percent, or by about 900,000 people. In fact, the increase was only 4 percent, or 140,000 people.

What was different about this particular housing slump, economists determined, was that construction firms had hired large numbers of illegal immigrants alongside legal U.S. residents. When the downturn in house construction occurred, most home builders responded by discharging illegal workers and retaining employees who were legal U.S. residents. Because official unemployment measures include only legal U.S. residents, the number of workers officially classified as cyclically unemployed rose only slightly. Thus, illegal immigrants bore the brunt of the downturn. After losing their construction jobs, many of them presumably returned to their home nations.

FOR CRITICAL ANALYSIS
Why might construction firms' tendency to employ illegal aliens also prevent measured cyclical unemployment from declining as much as it otherwise might the next time there is a boom in home-building activity?

Seasonal Unemployment

Seasonal unemployment comes and goes with seasons of the year in which the demand for particular jobs rises and falls. In northern states, construction workers can often work only during the warmer months; they are seasonally unemployed during the winter. Summer resort workers can usually get jobs in resorts only during the summer season. They, too, become seasonally unemployed during the winter; the opposite is true for ski resort workers.

Seasonal unemployment
Unemployment resulting from the seasonal pattern of work in specific industries. It is usually due to seasonal fluctuations in demand or to changing weather conditions that render work difficult, if not impossible, as in the agriculture, construction, and tourist industries.

When this employee in a summer tourist area is laid off in the winter, she becomes part of what type of unemployment?

The unemployment rate that the Bureau of Labor Statistics releases each month is "seasonally adjusted." This means that the reported unemployment rate has been adjusted to remove the effects of variations in seasonal unemployment. Thus, the unemployment rate that the media dutifully announce reflects only the sum of frictional unemployment, structural unemployment, and cyclical unemployment.

Full Employment and the Natural Rate of Unemployment

Does full employment mean that everybody has a job? Certainly not, for not everyone is looking for a job—full-time students and full-time homemakers, for example, are not. Is it always possible for everyone who is looking for a job to find one? No, because transaction costs in the labor market are not zero. Transaction costs are those associated with any activity whose goal is to enter into, carry out, or terminate contracts. In the labor market, these costs involve time spent looking for a job, being interviewed, negotiating the terms of employment, and the like.

Full Employment

Full employment

An arbitrary level of unemployment that corresponds to "normal" friction in the labor market. In 1986, a 6.5 percent rate of unemployment was considered full employment. Today, it is assumed to be around 5 percent.

We will always have some frictional unemployment as individuals move in and out of the labor force, seek higher-paying jobs, and move to different parts of the country. **Full employment** is therefore a concept implying some sort of balance or equilibrium in an ever-shifting labor market. Of course, this general notion of full employment must somehow be put into numbers so that economists and others can determine whether the economy has reached the full-employment point.

The Natural Rate of Unemployment

Natural rate of unemployment

The rate of unemployment that is estimated to prevail in long-run macroeconomic equilibrium, when all workers and employers have fully adjusted to any changes in the economy.

To try to assess when a situation of balance has been attained in the labor market, economists estimate the **natural rate of unemployment,** the rate that is expected to prevail in the long run once all workers and employers have fully adjusted to any changes in the economy. If correctly estimated, the natural rate of unemployment should not include cyclical unemployment. When seasonally adjusted, the natural unemployment rate should include only frictional and structural unemployment.

A long-standing difficulty, however, has been a lack of agreement about how to estimate the natural unemployment rate. From the mid-1980s to the early 1990s, the President's Council of Economic Advisers (CEA) consistently estimated that the natural unemployment rate in the United States was about 6.5 percent. Even into the 2000s, Federal Reserve staff economists, employing an approach to estimating the natural rate of unemployment that was intended to improve on the CEA's traditional method, arrived at a natural rate just over 6 percent. When the measured unemployment rate fell to 4 percent in 2000, however, economists began to rethink their approach to estimating the natural unemployment rate. This led some to alter their estimation methods to take into account such factors as greater rivalry among domestic businesses and increased international competition, which led to an estimated natural rate of unemployment of roughly 5 percent. We shall return to the concept of the natural unemployment rate in Chapter 10.

QUICK QUIZ   See page 183 for the answers. Review concepts from this section in MyEconLab.

_____ **unemployment** occurs because of transaction costs in the labor market. For example, workers do not have full information about vacancies and must search for jobs.

_____ **unemployment** occurs when there is a poor match of workers' skills and abilities with available jobs,

perhaps because workers lack appropriate training or government labor rules reduce firms' willingness to hire.

The levels of frictional and structural unemployment are used in part to determine our (somewhat arbitrary) measurement of the _____ rate of unemployment.

Inflation and Deflation

During World War II, you could buy bread for 8 to 10 cents a loaf and have milk delivered fresh to your door for about 25 cents a half gallon. The average price of a new car was less than $700, and the average house cost less than $3,000. Today, bread, milk, cars, and houses all cost more—a lot more. Prices are about 14 times what they were in 1940. Clearly, this country has experienced quite a bit of *inflation* since then. We define **inflation** as an upward movement in the average level of prices. The opposite of inflation is **deflation,** defined as a downward movement in the average level of prices. Notice that these definitions depend on the *average* level of prices. This means that even during a period of inflation, some prices can be falling if other prices are rising at a faster rate. The prices of electronic equipment have dropped dramatically since the 1960s, even though there has been general inflation.

To discuss what has happened to prices here and in other countries, we have to know how to measure inflation.

Inflation
A sustained increase in the average of all prices of goods and services in an economy.

Deflation
A sustained decrease in the average of all prices of goods and services in an economy.

Inflation and the Purchasing Power of Money

The value of a dollar does not stay constant when there is inflation. The value of money is usually talked about in terms of **purchasing power.** A dollar's purchasing power is the real goods and services that it can buy. Consequently, another way of defining inflation is as a decline in the purchasing power of money. The faster the rate of inflation, the greater the rate of decline in the purchasing power of money.

One way to think about inflation and the purchasing power of money is to discuss dollar values in terms of *nominal* versus *real* values. The nominal value of anything is simply its price expressed in today's dollars. In contrast, the real value of anything is its value expressed in purchasing power, which varies with the overall price level. Let's say that you received a $100 bill from your grandparents this year. One year from now, the nominal value of that bill will still be $100. The real value will depend on what the purchasing power of money is after one year's worth of inflation. Obviously, if there is inflation during the year, the real value of that $100 bill will have diminished. For example, if you keep the $100 bill in your pocket for a year during which the rate of inflation is 3 percent, at the end of the year you will have to come up with $3 more to buy the same amount of goods and services that the $100 bill can purchase today.

Purchasing power
The value of money for buying goods and services. If your money income stays the same but the price of one good that you are buying goes up, your effective purchasing power falls, and vice versa.

Measuring the Rate of Inflation

How can we measure the rate of inflation? This is a thorny problem for government statisticians. It is easy to determine how much the price of an individual commodity has risen: If last year a light bulb cost 50 cents and this year it costs 75 cents, there has

If the price of women's shoes falls, can there still be inflation?

Price index
The cost of today's market basket of goods expressed as a percentage of the cost of the same market basket during a base year.

Base year
The year that is chosen as the point of reference for comparison of prices in other years.

been a 50 percent rise in the price of that light bulb over a one-year period. We can express the change in the individual light bulb price in one of several ways: The price has gone up 25 cents; the price is one and a half (1.5) times as high; the price has risen by 50 percent. An *index number* of this price rise is simply the second way (1.5) multiplied by 100, meaning that the index today would stand at 150. We multiply by 100 to eliminate decimals because it is easier to think in terms of percentage changes using whole numbers. This is the standard convention adopted for convenience in dealing with index numbers or price levels.

Computing a Price Index

The measurement problem becomes more complicated when it involves a large number of goods, especially if some prices have risen faster than others and some have even fallen. What we have to do is pick a representative bundle, a so-called market basket, of goods and compare the costs of that market basket of goods over time. When we do this, we obtain a **price index,** which is defined as the cost of a market basket of goods today, expressed as a percentage of the cost of that identical market basket of goods in some starting year, known as the **base year.**

$$\text{Price index} = \frac{\text{cost of market basket today}}{\text{cost of market basket in base year}} \times 100$$

In the base year, the price index will always be 100, because the year in the numerator and in the denominator of the fraction is the same; therefore, the fraction equals 1, and when we multiply it by 100, we get 100. A simple numerical example is given in Table 7-1. In the table, there are only two goods in the market basket—corn and computers. The *quantities* in the basket are the same in the base year, 2001, and the current year, 2011. Only the *prices* change. Such a *fixed-quantity* price index is the easiest to compute because the statistician need only look at prices of goods and services sold every year rather than observing how much of these goods and services consumers actually purchase each year.

Are women experiencing higher inflation rates than men?

EXAMPLE
Why Women Are Confronting Higher Inflation Than Men

In the past few years, the price index for the market basket of a typical U.S. female resident has increased at a rate at least 1 percentage point higher than the price index for a typical male's market basket. Why does this disparity exist? Compared with years past, more women are getting jobs. In addition, women are marrying and having children later in life. Higher-income single women tend to spend a larger percentage of their incomes than do single men. Demands for and hence prices of items in a typical female's market basket, such as cosmetics and jewelry, have risen at a faster pace than the demands for and prices of items in a typical male's market basket, such as big-screen TVs and premium cable sports channels. Hence, the typical female's price index has increased at a faster pace than the price index for a typical male.

FOR CRITICAL ANALYSIS
If price indexes for male and female market baskets have the same base year, in any given year following the base year, will the price index for the female market basket be greater or smaller than the price index for the male market basket?

TABLE 7-1

Calculating a Price Index for a Two-Good Market Basket

In this simplified example, there are only two goods—corn and computers. The quantities and base-year prices are given in columns 2 and 3. The cost of the 2001 market basket, calculated in column 4, comes to $1,400. The 2011 prices are given in column 5. The cost of the market basket in 2011, calculated in column 6, is $1,650. The price index for 2011 compared with 2001 is 117.86.

(1) Commodity	(2) Market Basket Quantity	(3) 2001 Price per Unit	(4) Cost of Market Basket in 2001	(5) 2011 Price per Unit	(6) Cost of Market Basket in 2011
Corn	100 bushels	$ 4	$ 400	$ 8	$ 800
Computers	2	500	1,000	425	850
Totals			$1,400		$1,650

$$\text{Price index} = \frac{\text{cost of market basket in 2011}}{\text{cost of market basket in base year 2001}} \times 100 = \frac{\$1,650}{\$1,400} \times 100 = 117.86$$

REAL-WORLD PRICE INDEXES Government statisticians calculate a number of price indexes. The most often quoted are the **Consumer Price Index (CPI),** the **Producer Price Index (PPI),** the **GDP deflator,** and the **Personal Consumption Expenditure (PCE) Index.** The CPI attempts to measure changes only in the level of prices of goods and services purchased by consumers. The PPI attempts to show what has happened to the average price of goods and services produced and sold by a typical firm. (There are also *wholesale price indexes* that track the price level for commodities that firms purchase from other firms.) The GDP deflator is the most general indicator of inflation because it measures changes in the level of prices of all new goods and services produced in the economy. The PCE Index measures average prices using weights from surveys of consumer spending.

THE CPI The Bureau of Labor Statistics (BLS) has the task of identifying a market basket of goods and services of the typical consumer. Today, the BLS uses the time period 1982–1984 as its base of market prices. It intends to change the base to 1993–1995 but has yet to do so. It has, though, updated the expenditure weights for its market basket of goods to reflect consumer spending patterns in 2001–2002. All CPI numbers since February 1998 reflect the new expenditure weights.

Economists have known for years that the way the BLS measures changes in the CPI is flawed. Specifically, the BLS has been unable to account for the way consumers substitute less expensive items for higher-priced items. The reason is that the CPI is a fixed-quantity price index, meaning that the BLS implicitly ignores changes in consumption patterns that occur between years in which it revises the index. Until recently, the BLS also has been unable to take quality changes into account as they occur. Now, though, it is subtracting from certain list prices estimated effects of qualitative improvements and adding to other list prices to account for deteriorations in quality. An additional flaw is that the CPI usually ignores successful new products until long after they have been introduced. Despite these flaws, the CPI is widely followed because its level is calculated and published monthly.

Why may efforts by the BLS to insulate the CPI from seasonal factors actually be adding to seasonal variations in the measurement of CPI inflation?

Consumer Price Index (CPI)
A statistical measure of a weighted average of prices of a specified set of goods and services purchased by typical consumers in urban areas.

Producer Price Index (PPI)
A statistical measure of a weighted average of prices of goods and services that firms produce and sell.

GDP deflator
A price index measuring the changes in prices of all new goods and services produced in the economy.

Personal Consumption Expenditure (PCE) Index
A statistical measure of average prices that uses annually updated weights based on surveys of consumer spending.

POLICY EXAMPLE
Are Seasonal Adjustments to the CPI Causing Seasonal Inflation?

The agency that calculates the CPI, the Bureau of Labor Statistics (BLS), seeks to prevent the CPI from being influenced by price movements that occur seasonally and hence are not related to any underlying economic trend. For example, gasoline prices usually rise in late spring as people begin driving more and then decline in the autumn months as people cut back on driving. To account for this, the BLS adjusts the gasoline component of the CPI downward in the spring and upward in the fall. The BLS designs these seasonal adjustments to cancel out exactly over a full year. In addition, the BLS makes "intervention" adjustments whenever a world event, such as a terrorist attack or a regional war flare-up, causes prices of gasoline and other items to vary in ways that the BLS deems to be unrelated to underlying economic trends.

Nevertheless, in nearly every year since 2000 the estimated CPI inflation rate for the first few months of each year has been noticeably higher than the estimated CPI inflation rate in later months. Some economists suggest that world events are occurring in seasonal cycles and that the BLS is *overreacting* in ways that actually *add* to seasonal inflation cycles. Hence, BLS interventions to keep seasonal effects from contaminating the CPI may actually be contributing to seasonal fluctuations in CPI inflation rates.

FOR CRITICAL ANALYSIS
Why do you think that policymakers desire to prevent seasonal factors from showing up in macroeconomic data?

THE PPI There are a number of Producer Price Indexes, including one for foodstuffs, another for intermediate goods (goods used in the production of other goods), and one for finished goods. Most of the producer prices included are in mining, manufacturing, and agriculture. The PPIs can be considered general-purpose indexes for nonretail markets.

Although in the long run the various PPIs and the CPI generally show the same rate of inflation, that is not the case in the short run. Most often the PPIs increase before the CPI because it takes time for producer price increases to show up in the prices that consumers pay for final products. Often changes in the PPIs are watched closely as a hint that inflation is going to increase or decrease.

Go to www.econtoday.com/chapter07 to obtain information about inflation and unemployment in other countries from the International Monetary Fund. Click on "World Economic Outlook Databases."

THE GDP DEFLATOR The broadest price index reported in the United States is the GDP deflator, where GDP stands for gross domestic product, or annual total national income. Unlike the CPI and the PPIs, the GDP deflator is *not* based on a fixed market basket of goods and services. The basket is allowed to change with people's consumption and investment patterns. In this sense, the changes in the GDP deflator reflect both price changes and the public's market responses to those price changes. Why? Because new expenditure patterns are allowed to show up in the GDP deflator as people respond to changing prices.

THE PCE INDEX Another price index that takes into account changing expenditure patterns is the Personal Consumption Expenditure (PCE) Index. The Bureau of Economic Analysis, an agency of the U.S. Department of Commerce, uses continuously updated annual surveys of consumer purchases to construct the weights for the PCE Index. Thus, an advantage of the PCE Index is that weights in the index are updated every year. The Federal Reserve has used the rate of change in the PCE Index as its primary inflation indicator because Fed officials believe that the updated weights in the PCE Index make it more accurate than the CPI as a measure of consumer price changes. Nevertheless, the CPI remains the most widely reported price index, and the U.S. government continues to use the CPI to adjust the value of Social Security benefits to account for inflation.

HISTORICAL CHANGES IN THE CPI Between World War II and the early 1980s, the Consumer Price Index showed a fairly dramatic trend upward. Figure 7-4 shows the annual rate of change in the CPI since 1860. Prior to World War II, there were numerous periods of deflation interspersed with periods of inflation. Persistent year-in and year-out inflation seems to be a post–World War II phenomenon, at least in this country. As far back as before the American Revolution, prices used to rise during war periods but then would fall back toward prewar levels afterward. This occurred

FIGURE 7-4

Inflation and Deflation in U.S. History

For 80 years after the Civil War, the United States experienced alternating inflation and deflation. Here we show them as reflected by changes in the Consumer Price Index. Since World War II, the periods of inflation have not been followed by periods of deflation; that is, even during peacetime, the price index has continued to rise. The shaded areas represent wartime.

Source: U.S. Department of Labor, Bureau of Labor Statistics.

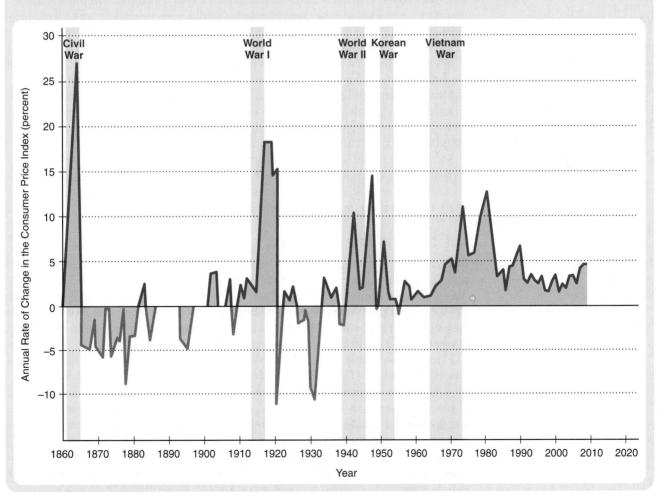

after the Revolutionary War, the War of 1812, the Civil War, and to a lesser extent World War I. Consequently, the overall price level in 1940 wasn't much different from 150 years earlier.

QUICK QUIZ *See page 183 for the answers. Review concepts from this section in MyEconLab.*

Once we pick a market basket of goods, we can construct a **price index** that compares the cost of that market basket today with the cost of the same market basket in a _____ year.

The _____ _____ **Index** is the most often used price index in the United States. The Producer Price Index (PPI) is also widely mentioned.

The _____ _____ measures what is happening to the average price level of *all* new, domestically produced final goods and services in our economy.

The _____ _____ _____ **Index** uses annually updated weights from consumer spending surveys to measure average prices faced by consumers.

Anticipated versus Unanticipated Inflation

To determine who is hurt by inflation and what the effects of inflation are in general, we have to distinguish between anticipated and unanticipated inflation. We will see that the effects on individuals and the economy are vastly different, depending on which type of inflation exists.

Anticipated inflation is the rate of inflation that most individuals believe will occur. If the rate of inflation this year turns out to be 5 percent, and that's about what most people thought it was going to be, we are in a situation of fully anticipated inflation.

Unanticipated inflation is inflation that comes as a surprise to individuals in the economy. For example, if the inflation rate in a particular year turns out to be 10 percent when on average people thought it was going to be 3 percent, there was unanticipated inflation—inflation greater than anticipated.

Some of the problems caused by inflation arise when it is unanticipated, because then many people are unable to protect themselves from its ravages. Keeping the distinction between anticipated and unanticipated inflation in mind, we can easily see the relationship between inflation and interest rates.

Inflation and Interest Rates

Let's start in a hypothetical world in which there is no inflation and anticipated inflation is zero. In that world, you may be able to borrow funds—to buy a house or a car, for example—at a **nominal rate of interest** of, say, 6 percent. If you borrow the funds to purchase a house or a car and your anticipation of inflation turns out to be accurate, neither you nor the lender will have been fooled. Each dollar you pay back in the years to come will be just as valuable in terms of purchasing power as the dollar that you borrowed.

What you ordinarily want to know when you borrow is the *real* rate of interest that you will have to pay. The **real rate of interest** is defined as the nominal rate of interest minus the anticipated rate of inflation. In effect, we can say that the nominal rate of interest is equal to the real rate of interest plus an *inflationary premium* to take account of anticipated inflation. That inflationary premium covers depreciation in the purchasing power of the dollars repaid by borrowers. (Whenever there are relatively high rates of anticipated inflation, we must add an additional factor to the inflationary premium—the product of the real rate of interest times the anticipated rate of inflation. Usually, this last term is omitted because the anticipated rate of inflation is not high enough to make much of a difference.)

Anticipated inflation
The inflation rate that we believe will occur; when it does, we are in a situation of fully anticipated inflation.

Unanticipated inflation
Inflation at a rate that comes as a surprise, either higher or lower than the rate anticipated.

Nominal rate of interest
The market rate of interest observed on contracts expressed in today's dollars.

Real rate of interest
The nominal rate of interest minus the anticipated rate of inflation.

Does Inflation Necessarily Hurt Everyone?

Most people think that inflation is bad. After all, inflation means higher prices, and when we have to pay higher prices, are we not necessarily worse off? The truth is that inflation affects different people differently. Its effects also depend on whether it is anticipated or unanticipated.

UNANTICIPATED INFLATION: CREDITORS LOSE AND DEBTORS GAIN In most situations, unanticipated inflation benefits borrowers because the nominal interest rate they are being charged does not fully compensate creditors for the inflation that actually occurred. In other words, the lender did not anticipate inflation correctly. Whenever inflation rates are underestimated for the life of a loan, creditors lose and debtors gain. Periods of considerable unanticipated (higher than anticipated) inflation occurred in the late 1960s and all of the 1970s. During those years, creditors lost and debtors gained.

PROTECTING AGAINST INFLATION Lenders attempt to protect themselves against inflation by raising nominal interest rates to reflect anticipated inflation. Adjustable-rate mortgages in fact do just that: The interest rate varies according to what happens to interest rates in the economy. Workers can protect themselves from inflation by obtaining **cost-of-living adjustments (COLAs),** which are automatic increases in wage rates to take account of increases in the price level.

> **Cost-of-living adjustments (COLAs)**
> Clauses in contracts that allow for increases in specified nominal values to take account of changes in the cost of living.

To the extent that you hold non-interest-bearing cash, you will lose because of inflation. If you have put $100 in a mattress and the inflation rate is 5 percent for the year, you will have lost 5 percent of the purchasing power of that $100. If you have your funds in a non-interest-bearing checking account, you will suffer the same fate. Individuals attempt to reduce the cost of holding cash by putting it into interest-bearing accounts, a wide variety of which often pay nominal rates of interest that reflect anticipated inflation.

THE RESOURCE COST OF INFLATION Some economists believe that the main cost of inflation is the opportunity cost of resources used to protect against distortions that inflation introduces as firms attempt to plan for the long run. Individuals have to spend time and resources to figure out ways to adjust their behavior in case inflation is different from what it has been in the past. That may mean spending a longer time working out more complicated contracts for employment, for purchases of goods in the future, and for purchases of raw materials.

Inflation requires that price lists be changed. This is called the **repricing,** or **menu, cost of inflation.** The higher the rate of inflation, the higher the repricing cost of inflation, because prices must be changed more often within a given period of time.

> **Repricing,** or **menu, cost of inflation**
> The cost associated with recalculating prices and printing new price lists when there is inflation.

QUICK QUIZ   *See page 183 for the answers. Review concepts from this section in MyEconLab.*

Whenever inflation is _____ than anticipated, creditors lose and debtors gain. Whenever the rate of inflation is _____ than anticipated, creditors gain and debtors lose.

Holders of cash lose during periods of inflation because the _____ _____ of their cash depreciates at the rate of inflation.

Households and businesses spend resources in attempting to protect themselves against the prospect of inflation, thus imposing a _____ cost on the economy.

Changing Inflation and Unemployment: Business Fluctuations

Business fluctuations
The ups and downs in business activity throughout the economy.

Expansion
A business fluctuation in which the pace of national economic activity is speeding up.

Contraction
A business fluctuation during which the pace of national economic activity is slowing down.

Recession
A period of time during which the rate of growth of business activity is consistently less than its long-term trend or is negative.

Depression
An extremely severe recession.

Some years unemployment goes up, and some years it goes down. Some years there is a lot of inflation, and other years there isn't. We have fluctuations in all aspects of our macroeconomy. The ups and downs in economywide economic activity are sometimes called **business fluctuations.** When business fluctuations are positive, they are called **expansions**—speedups in the pace of national economic activity. The opposite of an expansion is a **contraction,** which is a slowdown in the pace of national economic activity. The top of an expansion is usually called its *peak*, and the bottom of a contraction is usually called its *trough*. Business fluctuations used to be called *business cycles*, but that term no longer seems appropriate because *cycle* implies regular or automatic recurrence, and we have never had automatic recurrent fluctuations in general business and economic activity. What we have had are contractions and expansions that vary greatly in length. For example, the 10 post–World War II expansions have averaged 57 months, but three of those exceeded 90 months, and two lasted less than 25 months.

If the contractionary phase of business fluctuations becomes severe enough, we call it a **recession.** An extremely severe recession is called a **depression.** Typically, at the beginning of a recession, interest rates rise and as the recession gets worse, they fall. In addition, people's incomes start to fall, and the duration of unemployment increases so that the unemployment rate increases. In times of expansion, the opposite occurs.

In Figure 7-5, you see that typical business fluctuations occur around a growth trend in overall national business activity shown as a straight upward-sloping line. Starting out at a peak, the economy goes into a contraction (recession). Then an expansion starts that moves up to its peak, higher than the last one, and the sequence starts over again.

FIGURE 7-5

The Idealized Course of Business Fluctuations

A hypothetical business cycle would go from peak to trough and back again in a regular cycle. Real-world business cycles are not as regular as this hypothetical cycle.

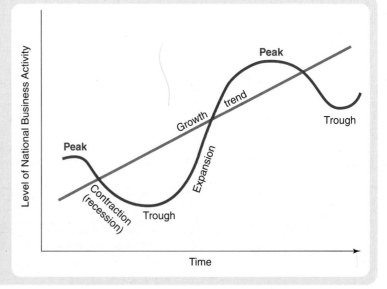

A Historical Picture of Business Activity in the United States

Figure 7-6 traces changes in U.S. business activity from 1880 to the present. Note that the long-term trend line is shown as horizontal, so all changes in business activity focus around that trend line. Major changes in business activity in the United States occurred during the Great Depression and World War II. Note that none of the actual business fluctuations that you see in Figure 7-6 exactly mirror the idealized course of a business fluctuation shown in Figure 7-5.

Go to **www.econtoday.com/chapter07** to learn about how economists at the National Bureau of Economic Research formally determine when a recession started.

Explaining Business Fluctuations: External Shocks

As you might imagine, because changes in national business activity affect everyone, economists for decades have attempted to understand and explain business fluctuations. For years, one of the most obvious explanations has been external events that tend to disrupt the economy. In many of the graphs in this chapter, you have seen that World War II was a critical point in this nation's economic history. A war is certainly an external shock—something that originates outside our economy.

To try to help account for shocks to economic activity that may induce business fluctuations and thereby make fluctuations easier to predict, the U.S. Department of Commerce and private firms and organizations tabulate indexes (weighted averages) of **leading indicators.** These are events that economists have noticed typically occur *before* changes in business activity. For example, economic downturns often follow such events

Leading indicators

Events that have been found to occur before changes in business activity.

FIGURE 7-6

National Business Activity, 1880 to the Present

Variations around the trend of U.S. business activity have been frequent since 1880.

Sources: American Business Activity from 1790 to Today, 67th ed., AmeriTrust Co., January 1996, plus author's estimates.

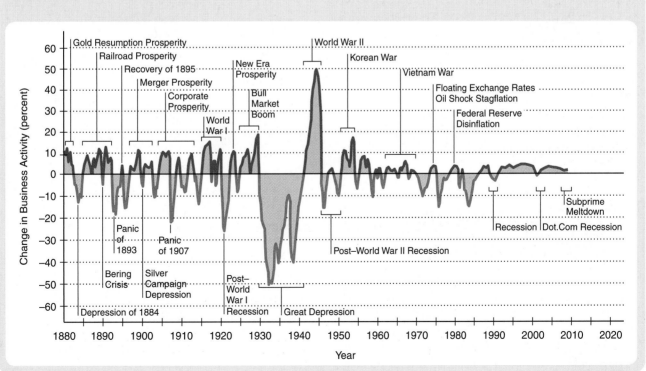

as a reduction in the average workweek, an increase in unemployment insurance claims, a decrease in the prices of raw materials, or a drop in the quantity of money in circulation.

To better understand the role of shocks in influencing business fluctuations, we need a theory of why national economic activity changes. The remainder of the macro chapters in this book develop the models that will help you understand the ups and downs of our business fluctuations.

Why has the year-to-year change in retail employment recently been a less reliable leading indicator than in years past?

EXAMPLE
A Flawless Leading Indicator Suddenly Reveals a Flaw

Since 1945, every time the year-to-year change in retail employment had a negative value, indicating a fall in retail employment, a recession either followed almost immediately or was already in progress. For this reason, business-cycle forecasters paid close attention to this particular leading indicator—until recently, that is. Each year since 2006, a wave of retail industry mergers and acquisitions has been accompanied by store closures around the country. Retailing jobs have disappeared, so year-to-year

changes in retail employment have been negative. Yet these declines in retail employment were not immediately followed by recessions. Consequently, this previously flawless leading indicator of a recession is now regarded as less reliable.

FOR CRITICAL ANALYSIS
Why do you suppose that business-cycle forecasters prefer to pay attention to an average of several leading indicators instead of only one or two leading indicators?

QUICK QUIZ
See page 183 for the answers. Review concepts from this section in MyEconLab.

The ups and downs in economywide business activity are called _____ _____, which consist of **expansions** and **contractions** in overall business activity.

The lowest point of a contraction is called the _____; the highest point of an expansion is called the _____.

A _____ is a downturn in business activity for some length of time.

One possible explanation for business fluctuations relates to _____ _____, such as wars, dramatic increases in the prices of raw materials, and earthquakes, floods, and droughts.

You Are There
Staying Employed in Denmark—at the Taxpayers' Expense

For just over 10 years, Danish resident Susanne Olsen has worked as an unskilled laborer in a slaughterhouse. Now, however, the company has halted its operations, and Olsen finds herself out of a job. It is not unusual to be unemployed in Denmark. Indeed, Danish workers change jobs more

frequently than workers in any other developed nation except the United States and Australia. What is different about Olsen's situation, as compared with the circumstances a U.S. or Australian worker would encounter, is that she can take advantage of one of the most generous government unem-

You Are There ▶ (cont.)

ployment programs on the planet. Now the Danish government's Public Employment Service has placed Olsen in a position as an apprentice golf landscaper. Her wages will be subsidized by the Danish government for the next four years. Many of her former slaughterhouse co-workers likewise have begun government-subsidized jobs with new employers.

Olsen knows that subsidizing jobs for all recent Danish job losers, including Olsen and her former co-workers, is very costly to taxpayers. In fact, the government spends about 4.4 percent of annual national income to support newly unemployed workers and subsidize their retraining. On average, therefore, every Danish resident contributes the

equivalent of about $1,600 per year in taxes that the government uses to subsidize recent job losers.

CRITICAL ANALYSIS QUESTIONS

1. What are the likely effects of Denmark's retraining subsidy program on the nation's average duration of unemployment?

2. Danish residents who are simply between jobs are not eligible for subsidies from the government, so does the retraining program have any effect on the nation's level of frictional unemployment?

Issues and Applications

Explaining the Downtrend in Labor Force Participation

The U.S. labor force participation rate is several percentage points higher today than it was a half-century ago. In recent years, however, labor force participation has fallen. What accounts for the decrease in U.S. labor force participation?

CONCEPTS APPLIED

▶ Labor Force

▶ Labor Force Participation Rate

▶ Discouraged Workers

The Downward Trend in Labor Force Participation

Figure 7-7 on the next page displays the U.S. labor force participation rate since 1995. As you can see, the rate of labor force participation trended upward during the latter part of the 1990s, reaching a peak of 67.3 percent in 2000. Since then, aside from short-lived upturns, it has trended downward, to about 66 percent today.

A drop in the labor force participation rate of about 1.3 percentage points does not seem large until it is

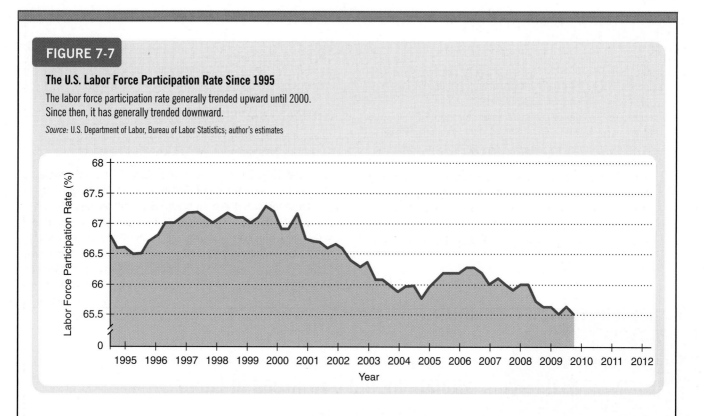

FIGURE 7-7

The U.S. Labor Force Participation Rate Since 1995

The labor force participation rate generally trended upward until 2000. Since then, it has generally trended downward.

Source: U.S. Department of Labor, Bureau of Labor Statistics; author's estimates

multiplied by just over 233 million people aged 16 and older. This yields an absolute drop in the labor force of just over 3 million people. If all these people who have left the labor force were located in a single city, it would be the third largest in the United States behind New York City and Los Angeles and just ahead of Chicago.

Why the Labor Force Participation Rate Has Dropped

Several factors have contributed to the decline in the labor force participation rate. One is that the number of new female entrants has been insufficient to replace women who have left the labor force. Hence, female labor force participation has tapered off very slightly in recent years.

Another factor is a dip in the labor force participation rate among teenagers. A smaller fraction of teens is opting to seek employment than in years past.

In addition, a number of people between the ages of 25 and 54 have dropped out of the labor force. Many of them have not graduated from high school or are high

school graduates without college training. Some economists suggest that at least some of these individuals have become discouraged by their lack of the skills desired by today's employers. If so, a part of the overall drop in labor force participation may reflect an increase in the number of discouraged workers.

Finally, altered legal rules have made it easier for all workers to receive disability benefits, and these changes undoubtedly help account for decreases in labor force participation among men and women under the age of 55. There is some evidence that these changes have encouraged people who otherwise might have worked with back pain or other problems to accept benefits and leave the labor force. There also is some evidence that some individuals now officially rated "disabled" actually are not and that a few of them earn incomes that they hide from taxation—and hence are not reported as part of the labor force. Some estimates indicate that greater access to disability benefits may account for as much as half of the decrease in the labor force during the 2000s.

Test your understanding of this chapter by going online to **MyEconLab**.
In the Study Plan for this chapter, select Section N: News.

For Critical Analysis

1. How might pressures felt by college-bound high school students to participate in academic-related organizations and activities contribute to a lower teen labor force participation rate?

2. Why are people receiving disability benefits not counted as part of the labor force?

Web Resources

1. To see how dramatically female labor force participation changed in the latter half of the twentieth century, go to www.econtoday.com/chapter07.

2. For the latest data regarding U.S. labor force participation, employment, and unemployment, go to www.econtoday.com/chapter07.

Research Project

If the United States had the same labor force participation rate today that it had in 1960 (about 60 percent) but with the same number of people aged 16 and older (about 238 million), roughly how many fewer people would be in the labor force? Based on this answer, at an unemployment rate of roughly 5 percent, how many people would be unemployed? How many fewer people would be employed? In light of this answer, why do you suppose that economists worry that a declining labor force participation rate may signal longer-term decreases in employment and production capability for the U.S. economy?

   Here is what you should know after reading this chapter. **MyEconLab** will help you identify what you know, and where to go when you need to practice.

WHAT YOU SHOULD KNOW

How the U.S. Government Calculates the Official Unemployment Rate The total number of workers who are officially unemployed consists of noninstitutionalized people aged 16 or older who are willing and able to work and who are actively looking for work but have not found a job. To calculate the unemployment rate, the government determines what percentage this quantity is of the labor force, which consists of all non-institutionalized people aged 16 years or older who either have jobs or are available for and actively seeking employment. Thus, the official unemployment rate does not include discouraged workers who have stopped looking for work because they are convinced that they will not find suitable employment. These individuals are not included in the labor force.

unemployment, 160
labor force, 160
stock, 162
flow, 162
job loser, 162
reentrant, 162
job leaver, 162
new entrant, 163
discouraged workers, 163
labor force participation rate, 163

KEY FIGURE
Figure 7-3, 162

WHERE TO GO TO PRACTICE

- **MyEconLab** Study Plan 7.1
- Audio introduction to Chapter 7
- Animated Figure 7-3
- ABC News Video: The Ripple Effect of Oil Prices

(continued)

 *(continued)*

WHAT YOU SHOULD KNOW

WHERE TO GO TO PRACTICE

The Types of Unemployment Workers who are temporarily unemployed because they are searching for appropriate job offers are frictionally unemployed. The structurally unemployed lack the skills currently required by prospective employers. People unemployed due to business contractions are said to be cyclically unemployed. And certain workers find themselves seasonally unemployed because of the seasonal patterns of occupations within specific industries. The natural unemployment rate is the seasonally adjusted rate of unemployment including only those who are frictionally and structurally unemployed during a given interval.

frictional unemployment, 164
structural unemployment, 164
cyclical unemployment, 165
seasonal unemployment, 165
full employment, 166
natural rate of unemployment, 166

- **MyEconLab** Study Plans 7.2, 7.3
- Video: Major Types of Unemployment

How Price Indexes Are Calculated and Key Price Indexes To calculate any price index, economists multiply 100 times the ratio of the cost of a market basket of goods and services in the current year to the cost of the same market basket in a base year. The market basket used to compute the Consumer Price Index (CPI) is a weighted set of goods and services purchased by a typical consumer in urban areas. The Producer Price Index (PPI) is a weighted average of prices of goods sold by a typical firm. The GDP deflator measures changes in the overall level of prices of all goods produced in the economy during a given interval. The Personal Consumption Expenditure (PCE) Index is a statistical measure of average prices using weights from annual surveys of consumer spending.

inflation, 167
deflation, 167
purchasing power, 167
price index, 168
base year, 168
Consumer Price Index (CPI), 169
Producer Price Index (PPI), 169
GDP deflator, 169
Personal Consumption Expenditure (PCE) Index, 169

KEY FIGURE
Figure 7-4, 171

- **MyEconLab** Study Plan 7.4
- Video: Measuring the Rate of Inflation
- Video: Inflation and Interest Rates
- Animated Figure 7-4

Nominal Interest Rate versus Real Interest Rate The nominal interest rate is the market rate of interest applying to contracts expressed in current dollars. The real interest rate is net of inflation that borrowers and lenders anticipate will erode the value of nominal interest payments during the period that a loan is repaid. Hence, the real interest rate equals the nominal interest rate minus the expected inflation rate.

anticipated inflation, 172
unanticipated inflation, 172
nominal rate of interest, 172
real rate of interest, 172

- **MyEconLab** Study Plan 7.5

Losers and Gainers from Inflation Creditors lose as a result of unanticipated inflation that comes as a surprise after they have made a loan, because the real value of the interest payments they receive will turn out to be lower than they had expected. Borrowers gain when unanticipated inflation occurs, because the real value of their interest and principal payments declines. Key costs of inflation are the expenses that people incur to protect themselves against inflation, costs of altering business plans because of unexpected changes in prices, and menu costs arising from expenses incurred in repricing goods and services.

cost-of-living adjustments (COLAs), 173
repricing, or menu, cost of inflation, 173

- **MyEconLab** Study Plan 7.5

(continued)

 *(continued)*

WHAT YOU SHOULD KNOW   **WHERE TO GO TO PRACTICE**

Key Features of Business Fluctuations Business fluctuations are increases and decreases in business activity. A positive fluctuation is an expansion, which is an upward movement in business activity from a trough, or low point, to a peak, or high point. A negative fluctuation is a contraction, which is a drop in the pace of business activity from a previous peak to a new trough.

business fluctuations, 174
expansion, 174
contraction, 174
recession, 174
depression, 174
leading indicators, 175

- **MyEconLab** Study Plan 7.6
- **Animated Figure 7-6**

KEY FIGURE
Figure 7-6, 175

Log in to MyEconLab, take a chapter test, and get a personalized Study Plan that tells you which concepts you understand and which ones you need to review. From there, MyEconLab will give you further practice, tutorials, animations, videos, and guided solutions.
Log in to www.myeconlab.com

PROBLEMS

All problems are assignable in myeconlab . *Answers to odd-numbered problems appear at the back of the book.*

7-1. Suppose that you are given the following information:

Total population	300.0 million
Adult, noninstitutionalized, nonmilitary population	200.0 million
Unemployment	7.5 million

a. If the labor force participation rate is 70 percent, what is the labor force?

b. How many workers are employed?

c. What is the unemployment rate?

7-2. Suppose that you are given the following information:

Labor force	206.2 million
Adults in the military	1.5 million
Nonadult population	48.0 million
Employed adults	196.2 million
Institutionalized adults	3.5 million
Nonmilitary, noninstitutionalized adults not in labor force	40.8 million

a. What is the total population?

b. How many people are unemployed, and what is the unemployment rate?

c. What is the labor force participation rate?

7-3. Suppose that the U.S. adult population is 224 million, the number employed is 156 million, and the number unemployed is 8 million.

a. What is the unemployment rate?

b. Suppose that there is a difference of 60 million between the adult population and the combined total of people who are employed and unemployed. How do we classify these 60 million people? Based on these figures, what is the U.S. labor force participation rate?

7-4. During the course of a year, the labor force consists of the same 1,000 people. Employers have chosen not to hire 20 of these people in the face of government regulations making it to costly to employ them. Hence, they remain unemployed throughout the year. At the same time, every month during the year, 30 different people become unemployed, and 30 other different people who were unemployed find jobs. There is no seasonal employment.

a. What is the frictional unemployment rate?

b. What is the unemployment rate?

c. Suppose that a system of unemployment compensation is established. Each month, 30 new people (not including the 20 that employers have chosen not to employ) continue to become unemployed, but each monthly group of newly unemployed now takes two months to find a job. After this change, what is the frictional unemployment rate?

d. After the change discussed in part (c), what is the unemployment rate?

7-5. Suppose that a nation has a labor force of 100 people. In January, Amy, Barbara, Carine, and Denise are unemployed; in February, those four find jobs, but Evan, Francesco, George, and Horatio become unemployed. Suppose further that every month, the previous four who were unemployed find jobs and four different people become unemployed. Throughout the year, however, the same three people—Ito, Jack, and Kelley—continually remain unemployed because firms facing government regulations view them as too costly to employ.

a. What is this nation's frictional unemployment rate?

b. What is its structural unemployment rate?

c. What is its unemployment rate?

7-6. In a country with a labor force of 200, a different group of 10 people becomes unemployed each month, but becomes employed once again a month later. No others outside these groups are unemployed.

a. What is this country's unemployment rate?

b. What is the average duration of unemployment?

c. Suppose that establishment of a system of unemployment compensation increases to two months the interval that it takes each group of job losers to become employed each month. Nevertheless, a different group of 10 people still becomes unemployed each month. Now what is the average duration of unemployment?

d. Following the change discussed in part (c), what is the country's unemployment rate?

7-7. A nation's frictional unemployment rate is 1 percent. Seasonal unemployment does not exist in this country. Its cyclical rate of unemployment is 3 percent, and its structural unemployment rate is 4 percent. What is this nation's overall rate of unemployment? What is its natural rate of unemployment?

7-8. In 2008, the cost of a market basket of goods was $2,000. In 2010, the cost of the same market basket of goods was $2,100. Use the price index formula to calculate the price index for 2010 if 2008 is the base year.

7-9. Consider the following price indexes: 90 in 2009, 100 in 2010, 110 in 2011, 121 in 2012, and 150 in 2013. Answer the following questions.

a. What is the base year?

b. What is the inflation rate from 2010 to 2011?

c. What is the inflation rate from 2011 to 2012?

d. If the cost of a market basket in 2010 is $2,000, what is the cost of the same basket of goods and services in 2009? In 2013?

7-10. The real interest rate is 4 percent, and the nominal interest rate is 6 percent. What is the anticipated rate of inflation?

7-11. Currently, the price index used to calculate the inflation rate is equal to 90. The general expectation throughout the economy is that next year its value will be 99. The current nominal interest rate is 12 percent. What is the real interest rate?

7-12. At present, the nominal interest rate is 7 percent, and the expected inflation rate is 5 percent. The current year is the base year for the price index used to calculate inflation.

a. What is the real interest rate?

b. What is the anticipated value of the price index next year?

7-13. Suppose that in 2013 there is a sudden, unanticipated burst of inflation. Consider the situations faced by the following individuals. Who gains and who loses?

a. A homeowner whose wages will keep pace with inflation in 2013 but whose monthly mortgage payments to a savings bank will remain fixed

b. An apartment landlord who has guaranteed to his tenants that their monthly rent payments during 2013 will be the same as they were during 2012

c. A banker who made an auto loan that the auto buyer will repay at a fixed rate of interest during 2013

d. A retired individual who earns a pension with fixed monthly payments from her past employer during 2013

7-14. Consider the diagram in the next column. The line represents the economy's growth trend, and the curve represents the economy's actual course of business fluctuations. For each part at the right, provide the letter label from the portion of the curve that corresponds to the associated term.

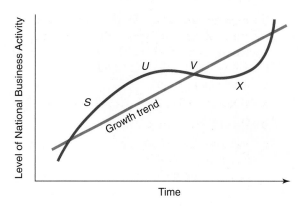

a. Contraction

b. Peak

c. Trough

d. Expansion

ECONOMICS ON THE NET

Looking at the Unemployment and Inflation Data This chapter reviewed key concepts relating to unemployment and inflation. In this application, you get a chance to examine U.S. unemployment and inflation data on your own.

Title: Bureau of Labor Statistics: Employment and Unemployment

Navigation: Use the link at **www.econtoday.com/chapter07** to visit the "Employment & Unemployment" page of the Bureau of Labor Statistics (BLS). Click on *Labor Force Statistics from the Current Population Survey.*

Application Perform the indicated operations, and answer the following questions.

1. Click checkmarks in the boxes for Civilian Labor Force Level, Employment Level, and Unemployment Level. Retrieve the data, and click a checkmark next to "include graphs." Can you identify periods of sharp cyclical swings? Do they show up in data for the labor force, employment, or unemployment?

2. Are cyclical factors important?

For Group Study and Analysis Divide the class into groups, and assign a price index to each group. Ask each group to take a look at the index for All Years at the link to the BLS statistics on inflation at **www.econtoday.com/chapter07**. Have each group identify periods during which their index accelerated or decelerated (or even fell). Do the indexes ever provide opposing implications about inflation and deflation?

ANSWERS TO QUICK QUIZZES

p. 164: (i) Unemployed . . . labor force; (ii) job losers . . . reentrants . . . job leavers . . . new entrants; (iii) increase; (iv) female

p. 167: (i) Frictional; (ii) Structural; (iii) natural

p. 172: (i) base; (ii) Consumer Price; (iii) GDP deflator; (iv) Personal Consumption Expenditure

p. 173: (i) greater . . . less; (ii) purchasing power; (iii) resource

p. 176: (i) business fluctuations; (ii) trough . . . peak; (iii) recession; (iv) external shocks

8

Measuring the Economy's Performance

For a number of years, measured U.S. business investment spending on capital goods has declined relative to total national expenditures on goods and services. On the surface, this trend appears to indicate a drop-off in growth of capital resources in relation to the rest of the U.S. economy—a decline with ominous implications for the nation's future economic growth. Some economists, however, contend that the apparent trend actually implies that U.S. capital investment is not being correctly measured. When less tangible, information-based forms of investment are added to the physical capital already included in the current measure of business investment spending, these economists conclude, growth in U.S. capital investment is very robust. How are capital investment and other aggregate economic quantities measured in the United States? Answering this question is the main objective of this chapter.

LEARNING OBJECTIVES

myeconlab

MyEconLab helps you master each objective and study more efficiently. See end of chapter for details.

After reading this chapter, you should be able to:

- ➤ Describe the circular flow of income and output
- ➤ Define gross domestic product (GDP)
- ➤ Understand the limitations of using GDP as a measure of national welfare
- ➤ Explain the expenditure approach to tabulating GDP
- ➤ Explain the income approach to computing GDP
- ➤ Distinguish between nominal GDP and real GDP

? DID YOU KNOW THAT during the past half-century, manufactured goods' share of total U.S. output of goods and services has declined by more than one-half? The value of manufactured goods as a percentage of *gross domestic product,* the government's key measure of overall annual economic activity, has fallen from about 28 percent in 1955 to less than 12 percent today.

The government conducts what has become known as **national income accounting** in an effort to measure the nation's overall economic performance over time. How this is done is the main focus of this chapter. But first we need to look at the flow of income within an economy, for it is the flow of goods and services from businesses to consumers and of payments from consumers to businesses that constitutes economic activity.

National income accounting
A measurement system used to estimate national income and its components; one approach to measuring an economy's aggregate performance.

The Simple Circular Flow

The concept of a circular flow of income (ignoring taxes) involves two principles:

1. In every economic exchange, the seller receives exactly the same amount that the buyer spends.
2. Goods and services flow in one direction and money payments flow in the other.

In the simple economy shown in Figure 8-1 on the following page, there are only businesses and households. It is assumed that businesses sell their *entire* output in the current period to households and that households spend their *entire* income in the current period on consumer products. Households receive their income by selling the use of whatever factors of production they own, such as labor services.

Profits Explained

We have indicated in Figure 8-1 that profit is a cost of production. You might be under the impression that profits are not part of the cost of producing goods and services, but profits are indeed a part of this cost because entrepreneurs must be rewarded for providing their services or they won't provide them. Their reward, if any, is profit. The reward—the profit—is included in the cost of the factors of production. If there were no expectations of profit, entrepreneurs would not incur the risk associated with the organization of productive activities. That is why we consider profits a cost of doing business.

Total Income or Total Output

The arrow that goes from businesses to households at the bottom of Figure 8-1 is labeled "Total income." What would be a good definition of **total income?** If you answered "the total of all individuals' income," you would be right. But all income is actually a payment for something, whether it be wages paid for labor services, rent paid for the use of land, interest paid for the use of capital, or profits paid to entrepreneurs. It is the amount paid to the resource suppliers. Therefore, total income is also defined as the annual *cost* of producing the entire output of **final goods and services.**

Total income
The yearly amount earned by the nation's resources (factors of production). Total income therefore includes wages, rent, interest payments, and profits that are received by workers, landowners, capital owners, and entrepreneurs, respectively.

The arrow going from households to businesses at the top of the figure represents the dollar value of output in the economy. This is equal to the total monetary value of all final goods and services for this simple economy. In essence, it represents the total business receipts from the sale of all final goods and services produced by businesses and consumed by households. Business receipts are the opposite side of household expenditures. When households purchase goods and services, those payments become a *business receipt.* Every transaction, therefore, simultaneously involves an expenditure and a receipt.

Final goods and services
Goods and services that are at their final stage of production and will not be transformed into yet other goods or services. For example, wheat ordinarily is not considered a final good because it is usually used to make a final good, bread.

FIGURE 8-1

The Circular Flow of Income and Product

Businesses provide final goods and services to households (upper clockwise loop), who in turn pay for them (upper counterclockwise loop). Payments flow in a counterclockwise direction and can be thought of as a circular flow. The dollar value of output is identical to total income because profits are defined as being equal to total business receipts minus business outlays for wages, rents, and interest. Households provide factor services to businesses and receive income (lower loops).

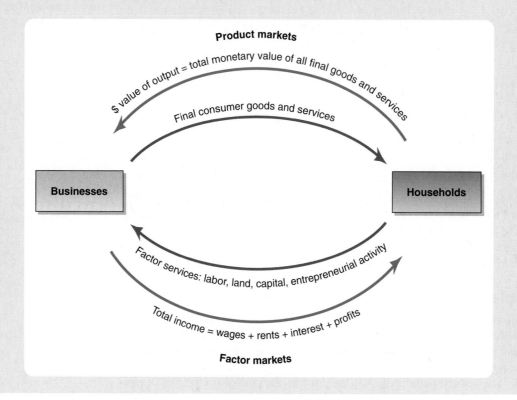

Product markets

$ value of output = total monetary value of all final goods and services

Final consumer goods and services

Businesses

Households

Factor services: labor, land, capital, entrepreneurial activity

Total income = wages + rents + interest + profits

Factor markets

PRODUCT MARKETS Transactions in which households buy goods take place in the product markets—that's where households are the buyers and businesses are the sellers of consumer goods. *Product market* transactions are represented in the upper loops in Figure 8-1. Note that consumer goods and services flow to household demanders, while money flows in the opposite direction to business suppliers.

FACTOR MARKETS *Factor market* transactions are represented by the lower loops in Figure 8-1. In the factor market, households are the sellers; they sell resources such as labor, land, capital, and entrepreneurial ability. Businesses are the buyers in factor markets; business expenditures represent receipts or, more simply, income for households. Also, in the lower loops of Figure 8-1, factor services flow from households to businesses, while the money paid for these services flows in the opposite direction from businesses to households. Observe also the flow of money (counterclockwise) from households to businesses and back again from businesses to households: It is an endless circular flow.

Why the Dollar Value of Total Output Must Equal Total Income

Total income represents the income received by households in payment for the production of goods and services. Why must total income be identical to the dollar value of total output? First, as Figure 8-1 shows, spending by one group is income to another. Second, it is a matter of simple accounting and the economic definition of profit as a cost of production. Profit is defined as what is *left over* from total business receipts after all other costs—wages, rents, interest—have been paid. If the dollar value of total output is $1,000 and the total of wages, rent, and interest for producing that output is $900, profit is $100. Profit is always the *residual* item that makes total income equal to the dollar value of total output.

QUICK QUIZ *See page 212 for the answers. Review concepts from this section in MyEconLab.*

In the circular flow model of income and output, households sell _____ services to businesses that pay for those services. The receipt of payments is total _____. Businesses sell goods and services to households that pay for them.

The dollar value of total output is equal to the total monetary value of all _____ goods and services produced.

The dollar value of final output must always equal total income; the variable that adjusts to make this so is known as _____.

National Income Accounting

We have already mentioned that policymakers require information about the state of the national economy. Economists use historical statistical records on the performance of the national economy in testing their theories about how the economy really works. Thus, national income accounting is important. Let's start with the most commonly presented statistic on the national economy.

Gross Domestic Product (GDP)

Gross domestic product (GDP) represents the total market value of the nation's annual final product, or output, produced by factors of production located within national borders. We therefore formally define GDP as the total market value of all final goods and services produced in an economy during a year. We are referring here to the value of a *flow of production*. A nation produces at a certain rate, just as you receive income at a certain rate. Your income flow might be at a rate of $20,000 per year or $100,000 per year. Suppose you are told that someone earns $5,000. Would you consider this a good salary? There is no way to answer that question unless you know whether the person is earning $5,000 per month or per week or per day. Thus, you have to specify a time period for all flows. Income received is a flow. You must contrast this with, for example, your total accumulated savings, which are a stock measured at a point in time, not over time. Implicit in just about everything we deal with in this chapter is a time period—usually one year. All the measures of domestic product and income are specified as *rates* measured in dollars per year.

Gross domestic product (GDP)
The total market value of all final goods and services produced during a year by factors of production located within a nation's borders.

Stress on Final Output

Intermediate goods
Goods used up entirely in the production of final goods.

Value added
The dollar value of an industry's sales minus the value of intermediate goods (for example, raw materials and parts) used in production.

GDP does not count **intermediate goods** (goods used up entirely in the production of final goods) because to do so would be to count them twice. For example, even though grain that a farmer produces may be that farmer's final product, it is not the final product for the nation. It is sold to make bread. Bread is the final product.

We can use a numerical example to clarify this point further. Our example will involve determining the value added at each stage of production. **Value added** is the amount of dollar value contributed to a product at each stage of its production. In Table 8-1, we see the difference between total value of all sales and value added in the production of a donut. We also see that the sum of the values added is equal to the sale price to the final consumer. It is the 45 cents that is used to measure GDP, not the 96 cents. If we used the 96 cents, we would be double counting from stages 2 through 5, for each intermediate good would be counted at least twice—once when it was produced and again when the good it was used in making was sold. Such double counting would grossly exaggerate GDP.

TABLE 8-1

Sales Value and Value Added at Each Stage of Donut Production

(1) Stage of Production	(2) Dollar Value of Sales	(3) Value Added
Stage 1: Fertilizer and seed	$.03	$.03
Stage 2: Growing	.06	.03
Stage 3: Milling	.12	.06
Stage 4: Baking	.30	.18
Stage 5: Retailing	.45	.15
	Total dollar value of all sales $.96	Total value added $.45

Stage 1: A farmer purchases 3 cents' worth of fertilizer and seed, which are used as factors of production in growing wheat.

Stage 2: The farmer grows the wheat, harvests it, and sells it to a miller for 6 cents. Thus, we see that the farmer has added 3 cents' worth of value. Those 3 cents represent income over and above expenses incurred by the farmer.

Stage 3: The miller purchases the wheat for 6 cents and adds 6 cents as the value added; that is, there is 6 cents for the miller as income. The miller sells the ground wheat flour to a donut-baking company.

Stage 4: The donut-baking company buys the flour for 12 cents and adds 18 cents as the value added. It then sells the donut to the final retailer.

Stage 5: The donut retailer sells donuts at 45 cents apiece, thus creating an additional value of 15 cents.

We see that the total value of the transactions involved in the production of one donut is 96 cents, but the total value added is 45 cents, which is exactly equal to the retail price. The total value added is equal to the sum of all income payments.

Exclusion of Financial Transactions, Transfer Payments, and Secondhand Goods

Remember that GDP is the measure of the dollar value of all final goods and services produced in one year. Many more transactions occur that have nothing to do with final goods and services produced. There are financial transactions, transfers of the ownership of preexisting goods, and other transactions that should not and do not get included in our measure of GDP.

FINANCIAL TRANSACTIONS There are three general categories of purely financial transactions: (1) the buying and selling of securities, (2) government transfer payments, and (3) private transfer payments.

Securities. When you purchase shares of existing stock in Microsoft Corporation, someone else has sold it to you. In essence, there was merely a *transfer* of ownership rights. You paid $100 to obtain the stock. Someone else received the $100 and gave up the stock. No producing activity was consummated at that time, unless a broker received a fee for performing the transaction, in which case only the fee is part of GDP. The $100 transaction is not included when we measure GDP.

Government Transfer Payments. Transfer payments are payments for which no productive services are concurrently provided in exchange. The most obvious government transfer payments are Social Security benefits, veterans' payments, and unemployment compensation. The recipients make no contribution to current production in return for such transfer payments (although they may have contributed in the past to be eligible to receive them). Government transfer payments are not included in GDP.

Private Transfer Payments. Are you receiving funds from your parents in order to attend school? Has a wealthy relative ever given you a gift of cash? If so, you have been the recipient of a private transfer payment. This is merely a transfer of funds from one individual to another. As such, it does not constitute productive activity and is not included in GDP.

TRANSFER OF SECONDHAND GOODS If I sell you my two-year-old laptop computer, no current production is involved. I transfer to you the ownership of a computer that was produced years ago; in exchange, you transfer to me $350. The original purchase price of the computer was included in GDP in the year I purchased it. To include the price again when I sell it to you would be counting the value of the computer a second time.

OTHER EXCLUDED TRANSACTIONS Many other transactions are not included in GDP for practical reasons:

- Household production—housecleaning, child care, and other tasks performed by people in their *own* households and for which they are not paid through the marketplace
- Otherwise legal underground transactions—those that are legal but not reported and hence not taxed, such as paying housekeepers in cash that is not declared as income
- Illegal underground activities—these include prostitution, illegal gambling, and the sale of illicit drugs

Go to **www.econtoday.com/chapter08** for the most up-to-date U.S. economic data at the Web site of the Bureau of Economic Analysis.

When this student bought her used computer, did that transaction add to the value of the nation's final goods and services?

You Are There

To contemplate gender differences in the performance of productive activities not included as part of gross domestic product, read **Housework's Exclusion from GDP Is Not Gender Neutral,** on pages 204 and 205.

What price did the Greek government pay for attempting to account for illegal activities in its GDP tabulations?

INTERNATIONAL POLICY EXAMPLE
Greece Pays a Price for Broadening Its GDP Definition

The government of Greece recently announced that its official tabulation of GDP would now include the total estimated value of production in black market industries, such as illegal gambling and prostitution. Consequently, the Greek government revised upward by about 25 percent its official GDP figures for every year since 2000. This change in GDP measurement came at a price, however. The European Union (EU), of which Greece is a member nation, makes regular payments to governments of the lowest-income EU members. As a result of the big jump in its annual GDP figures, Greece was no longer officially as "poor" in the eyes of the EU, which reduced its annual payments to the Greek government by almost $600 million.

FOR CRITICAL ANALYSIS
Why do you suppose that economists now have a harder time comparing Greek GDP to the levels of GDP in other nations, such as the United States?

Recognizing the Limitations of GDP

Like any statistical measure, gross domestic product is a concept that can be both well used and misused. Economists find it especially valuable as an overall indicator of a nation's economic performance. But it is important to realize that GDP has significant weaknesses. Because it includes only the value of goods and services traded in markets, it excludes *nonmarket* production, such as the household services of homemakers discussed earlier. This can cause some problems in comparing the GDP of an industrialized country with the GDP of a highly agrarian nation in which nonmarket production is relatively more important. It also causes problems if nations have different definitions of legal versus illegal activities. For instance, a nation with legalized gambling will count the value of gambling services, which has a reported market value as a legal activity. But in a country where gambling is illegal, individuals who provide such services will not report the market value of gambling activities, and so they will not be counted in that country's GDP. This can complicate comparing GDP in the nation where gambling is legal with GDP in the country that prohibits gambling.

Furthermore, although GDP is often used as a benchmark measure for standard-of-living calculations, it is not necessarily a good measure of the well-being of a nation. No measured figure of total national annual income can take account of changes in the degree of labor market discrimination, declines or improvements in personal safety, or the quantity or quality of leisure time. Measured GDP also says little about our environmental quality of life. As the now-defunct Soviet Union illustrated to the world, the large-scale production of such items as minerals, electricity, and irrigation for farming can have negative effects on the environment: deforestation from strip mining, air and soil pollution from particulate emissions or nuclear accidents at power plants, and erosion of the natural balance between water and salt in bodies of water such as the Aral Sea. Other nations, such as China and India, have also experienced greater pollution problems as their levels of GDP have increased. Hence, it is important to recognize the following point:

GDP is a measure of the value of production in terms of market prices and an indicator of economic activity. It is not a measure of a nation's overall welfare.

Nonetheless, GDP is a relatively accurate and useful measure to map *changes* in the economy's domestic economic activity. Understanding GDP is thus important for recognizing changes in economic activity over time.

QUICK QUIZ   *See page 212 for the answers. Review concepts from this section in MyEconLab.*

_____ _____ _____ is the total market value of final goods and services produced in an economy during a one-year period by factors of production within the nation's borders. It represents the dollar value of the flow of final production over a one-year period.

To avoid double counting, we look only at final goods and services produced or, equivalently, at _____ _____ .

In measuring GDP, we must _____ (1) purely financial transactions, such as the buying and selling of securities; (2) government transfer payments and private transfer payments; and (3) the transfer of secondhand goods.

Many other transactions are excluded from measured _____, among them household services rendered by homemakers, underground economy transactions, and illegal economic activities, even though many of these result in the production of final goods and services.

GDP is a useful measure for tracking changes in the _____ _____ of overall economic activity over time, but it is not a measure of the well-being of a nation's residents because it fails to account for nonmarket transactions, the amount and quality of leisure time, environmental or safety issues, labor market discrimination, and other factors that influence general welfare.

Two Main Methods of Measuring GDP

The definition of GDP is the total value of all final goods and services produced during a year. How, exactly, do we go about actually computing this number?

The circular flow diagram presented in Figure 8-1 on page 186 gave us a shortcut method for calculating GDP. We can look at the *flow of expenditures*, which consists of consumption, investment, government purchases of goods and services, and net expenditures in the foreign sector (net exports). In this **expenditure approach** to measuring GDP, we add the dollar value of all final goods and services. We could also use the *flow of income*, looking at the income received by everybody producing goods and services. In this **income approach,** we add the income received by all factors of production.

Deriving GDP by the Expenditure Approach

To derive GDP using the expenditure approach, we must look at each of the separate components of expenditures and then add them together. These components are consumption expenditures, investment, government expenditures, and net exports.

CONSUMPTION EXPENDITURES   How do we spend our income? As households or as individuals, we spend our income through consumption expenditure (*C*), which falls into three categories: **durable consumer goods, nondurable consumer goods,** and **services.** Durable goods are *arbitrarily* defined as items that last more than three years; they include automobiles, furniture, and household appliances. Nondurable goods are all the rest, such as food and gasoline. Services are intangible commodities: medical care, education, and the like.

Housing expenditures constitute a major proportion of anybody's annual expenditures. Rental payments on apartments are automatically included in consumption expenditure estimates. People who own their homes, however, do not make rental payments. Consequently, government statisticians estimate what is called the *implicit rental value* of

Expenditure approach
Computing GDP by adding up the dollar value at current market prices of all final goods and services.

Income approach
Measuring GDP by adding up all components of national income, including wages, interest, rent, and profits.

Durable consumer goods
Consumer goods that have a life span of more than three years.

Nondurable consumer goods
Consumer goods that are used up within three years.

Services
Mental or physical labor or help purchased by consumers. Examples are the assistance of physicians, lawyers, dentists, repair personnel, housecleaners, educators, retailers, and wholesalers; things purchased or used by consumers that do not have physical characteristics.

existing owner-occupied homes. It is roughly equal to the amount of rent you would have to pay if you did not own the home but were renting it from someone else.

GROSS PRIVATE DOMESTIC INVESTMENT We now turn our attention to **gross private domestic investment** (*I*) undertaken by businesses. When economists refer to investment, they are referring to additions to productive capacity. **Investment** may be thought of as an activity that uses resources today in such a way that they allow for greater production in the future and hence greater consumption in the future. When a business buys new equipment or puts up a new factory, it is investing; it is increasing its capacity to produce in the future.

In estimating gross private domestic investment, government statisticians also add consumer expenditures on *new* residential structures because new housing represents an addition to our future productive capacity in the sense that a new house can generate housing services in the future.

The layperson's notion of investment often relates to the purchase of stocks and bonds. For our purposes, such transactions simply represent the *transfer of ownership* of assets called stocks and bonds. Thus, you must keep in mind the fact that in economics, investment refers *only* to *additions* to productive capacity, not to transfers of assets.

FIXED VERSUS INVENTORY INVESTMENT In our analysis, we will consider the basic components of investment. We have already mentioned the first one, which involves a firm's buying equipment or putting up a new factory. These are called **producer durables, or capital goods.** A producer durable, or a capital good, is simply a good that is purchased not to be consumed in its current form but to be used to make other goods and services. The purchase of equipment and factories—capital goods—is called **fixed investment.**

The other type of investment has to do with the change in inventories of raw materials and finished goods. Firms do not immediately sell off all their products to consumers. Some of this final product is usually held in inventory waiting to be sold. Firms hold inventories to meet future expected orders for their products. When a firm increases its inventories of finished products, it is engaging in **inventory investment.** Inventories consist of all finished goods on hand, goods in process, and raw materials.

The reason that we can think of a change in inventories as being a type of investment is that an increase in such inventories provides for future increased consumption possibilities. When inventory investment is zero, the firm is neither adding to nor subtracting from the total stock of goods or raw materials on hand. Thus, if the firm keeps the same amount of inventories throughout the year, inventory *investment* has been zero.

GOVERNMENT EXPENDITURES In addition to personal consumption expenditures, there are government purchases of goods and services (*G*). The government buys goods and services from private firms and pays wages and salaries to government employees. Generally, we value goods and services at the prices at which they are sold. But many government goods and services are not sold in the market. Therefore, we cannot use their market value when computing GDP. The value of these goods is considered equal to their *cost*. For example, the value of a newly built road is considered equal to its construction cost and is included in the GDP for the year it was built.

NET EXPORTS (FOREIGN EXPENDITURES) To get an accurate representation of gross domestic product, we must include the foreign sector. As U.S. residents, we purchase foreign goods called *imports*. The goods that foreign residents purchase from us are our *exports*. To determine the *net* expenditures from the foreign sector, we subtract the value of imports from the value of exports to get net exports (*X*) for a year:

$$\text{Net exports } (X) = \text{total exports} - \text{total imports}$$

Gross private domestic investment
The creation of capital goods, such as factories and machines, that can yield production and hence consumption in the future. Also included in this definition are changes in business inventories and repairs made to machines or buildings.

Investment
Any use of today's resources to expand tomorrow's production or consumption.

Producer durables, or capital goods
Durable goods having an expected service life of more than three years that are used by businesses to produce other goods and services.

Fixed investment
Purchases by businesses of newly produced producer durables, or capital goods, such as production machinery and office equipment.

Inventory investment
Changes in the stocks of finished goods and goods in process, as well as changes in the raw materials that businesses keep on hand. Whenever inventories are decreasing, inventory investment is negative; whenever they are increasing, inventory investment is positive.

How are the expenditures on this recently built factory classified?

To understand why we subtract imports rather than ignoring them altogether, recall that we want to estimate *domestic* output, so we have to subtract U.S. expenditures on the goods produced in other nations.

Presenting the Expenditure Approach

We have just defined the components of GDP using the expenditure approach. When we add them all together, we get a definition for GDP, which is as follows:

$$GDP = C + I + G + X$$

where
C = consumption expenditures
I = investment expenditures
G = government expenditures
X = net exports

THE HISTORICAL PICTURE To get an idea of the relationship among C, I, G, and X, look at Figure 8-2 on the next page, which shows GDP, personal consumption expenditures, government purchases, and gross private domestic investment plus net exports since 1929. When we add up the expenditures of the household, business, government, and foreign sectors, we get GDP.

How does the Easter holiday's position in the calendar influence measured changes in Mexican GDP?

INTERNATIONAL EXAMPLE
How Easter Complicates Measuring Mexican GDP Growth

The Christian holiday Easter, which is a major holiday throughout Mexico, takes place on the first Sunday after the first full moon following the initial day of spring. In some years, Easter occurs before March 31 and hence during the first three-month period, or *quarter,* of the year. In other years, however, Easter falls after March 31 and hence during the second quarter.

Most Mexican companies halt operations and suspend sales for several days around the Easter holiday. This practice significantly depresses GDP during the affected quarter and influences percentage changes in GDP measured between quarters. Year-to-year measures of Mexican GDP growth are also affected. For instance, consider what happens when Easter happens to fall within the first quarter one year but the

second quarter of the following year. The percentage change in GDP between the first quarters of the two years is artificially lower as a result, but the percentage change in GDP between the second quarters of the two years is biased upward. Economists must always keep these Easter effects in mind when tracking Mexico's GDP from quarter to quarter or from year to year.

FOR CRITICAL ANALYSIS
How do you suppose that the Christmas holiday in the last week of December influences percentage changes in U.S. GDP from the third quarter to the fourth within a year and from the fourth quarter to the first quarter of the next year?

DEPRECIATION AND NET DOMESTIC PRODUCT We have used the terms *gross domestic product* and *gross private domestic investment* without really indicating what *gross* means. The dictionary defines it as "without deductions," the opposite of *net.* Deductions for what? you might ask. The deductions are for something we call **depreciation.** In the course of a year, machines and structures wear out or are used up in the production of domestic product. For example, houses deteriorate as they are occupied, and machines

Depreciation
Reduction in the value of capital goods over a one-year period due to physical wear and tear and also to obsolescence; also called *capital consumption allowance.*

FIGURE 8-2

GDP and Its Components

Here we see a display of gross domestic product, personal consumption expenditures, government purchases, and gross private domestic investment plus net exports for the years since 1929. Note that the scale of the vertical axis changes as we move up the axis. During the Great Depression of the 1930s, gross private domestic investment *plus* net exports was negative because we were investing very little at that time. During the early 2000s, gross private domestic investment declined and then recovered slowly. Net exports also became increasingly negative. Hence, the sum of these two items has grown at a slower pace in recent years.

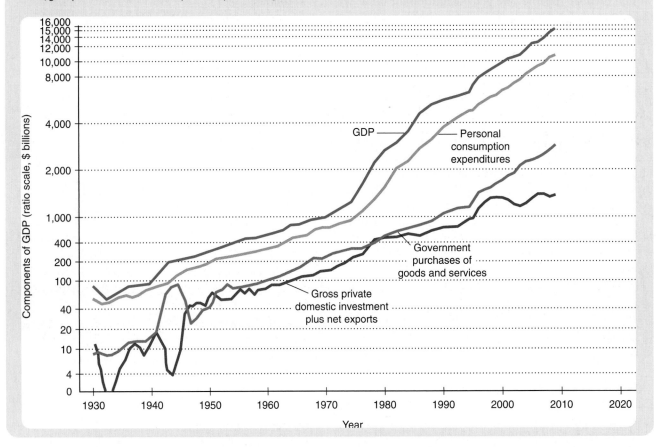

need repairs or they will fall apart and stop working. Most capital, or durable, goods depreciate.

An estimate of the amount that capital goods have depreciated during the year is subtracted from gross domestic product to arrive at a figure called **net domestic product (NDP),** which we define as follows:

Net domestic product (NDP)
GDP minus depreciation.

$$NDP = GDP - \text{depreciation}$$

Capital consumption allowance
Another name for depreciation, the amount that businesses would have to save in order to take care of deteriorating machines and other equipment.

Depreciation is also called **capital consumption allowance** because it is the amount of the capital stock that has been consumed over a one-year period. In essence, it equals the amount a business would have to put aside to repair and replace deteriorating machines. Because we know that

$$GDP = C + I + G + X$$

we know that the formula for NDP is

$$NDP = C + I + G + X - \text{depreciation}$$

Alternatively, because net $I = I -$ depreciation,

$$\text{NDP} = C + \text{net } I + G + X$$

Net investment measures *changes* in our capital stock over time and is positive nearly every year. Because depreciation does not vary greatly from year to year as a percentage of GDP, we get a similar picture of what is happening to our national economy by looking at either NDP or GDP data.

Net investment is an important variable to observe over time nonetheless. If everything else remains the same in an economy, changes in net investment can have dramatic consequences for future economic growth (a topic we cover in more detail in Chapter 9). Positive net investment by definition expands the productive capacity of our economy. This means that there is increased capital, which will generate even more income in the future. When net investment is zero, we are investing just enough to take account of depreciation. Our economy's productive capacity remains unchanged. Finally, when net investment is negative, we can expect negative economic growth prospects in the future. Negative net investment means that our productive capacity is actually declining—we are disinvesting. This actually occurred during the Great Depression.

Net investment
Gross private domestic investment minus an estimate of the wear and tear on the existing capital stock. Net investment therefore measures the change in the capital stock over a one-year period.

QUICK QUIZ   *See page 212 for the answers. Review concepts from this section in MyEconLab.*

The _____ approach to measuring GDP requires that we add up consumption expenditures, gross private investment, government purchases, and net exports. Consumption expenditures include consumer _____, consumer _____, and _____.

Gross private domestic investment *excludes* transfers of asset ownership. It includes only additions to the

productive _____ of a nation, repairs on existing capital goods, and changes in business _____.

We value government expenditures at their cost because we usually do not have _____ prices at which to value government goods and services.

To obtain **net domestic product (NDP)**, we subtract from GDP the year's _____ of the existing capital stock.

Deriving GDP by the Income Approach

If you go back to the circular flow diagram in Figure 8-1 on page 186, you see that product markets are at the top of the diagram and factor markets are at the bottom. We can calculate the value of the circular flow of income and product by looking at expenditures—which we just did—or by looking at total factor payments. Factor payments are called income. We calculate **gross domestic income (GDI)**, which we will see is identical to gross domestic product (GDP). Using the income approach, we have four categories of payments to individuals: wages, interest, rent, and profits.

Gross domestic income (GDI)
The sum of all income—wages, interest, rent, and profits—paid to the four factors of production.

1. *Wages.* The most important category is, of course, wages, including salaries and other forms of labor income, such as income in kind and incentive payments. We also count Social Security taxes (both the employees' and the employers' contributions).

2. *Interest.* Here interest payments do not equal the sum of all payments for the use of funds in a year. Instead, interest is expressed in *net* rather than in gross terms. The interest component of total income is only net interest received by households plus net interest paid to us by foreign residents. Net interest received by households is the difference between the interest they receive (from savings accounts, certificates of deposit, and the like) and the interest they pay (to banks for home mortgages, credit cards, and other loans).

Go to **www.econtoday.com/chapter08** to examine recent trends in U.S. GDP and its components.

3. *Rent.* Rent is all income earned by individuals for the use of their real (nonmonetary) assets, such as farms, houses, and stores. As stated previously, we have to include here the implicit rental value of owner-occupied houses. Also included in this category are royalties received from copyrights, patents, and assets such as oil wells.

4. *Profits.* Our last category includes total gross corporate profits plus *proprietors' income.* Proprietors' income is income earned from the operation of unincorporated businesses, which include sole proprietorships, partnerships, and producers' cooperatives. It is unincorporated business profit.

All of the payments listed are *actual* factor payments made to owners of the factors of production. When we add them together, though, we do not yet have gross domestic income. We have to take account of two other components: **indirect business taxes,** such as sales and business property taxes, and depreciation, which we have already discussed.

INDIRECT BUSINESS TAXES Indirect taxes are the (nonincome) taxes paid by consumers when they buy goods and services. When you buy a book, you pay the price of the book plus any state and local sales tax. The business is actually acting as the government's agent in collecting the sales tax, which it in turn passes on to the government. Such taxes therefore represent a business expense and are included in gross domestic income.

DEPRECIATION Just as we had to deduct depreciation to get from GDP to NDP, so we must *add* depreciation to go from net domestic income to gross domestic income. Depreciation can be thought of as the portion of the current year's GDP that is used to replace physical capital consumed in the process of production. Because somebody has paid for the replacement, depreciation must be added as a component of gross domestic income.

The last two components of GDP—indirect business taxes and depreciation—are called **nonincome expense items.**

Figure 8-3 on page 198 shows a comparison between estimated gross domestic product and gross domestic income for 2009. Whether you decide to use the expenditure approach or the income approach, you will come out with the same number. There are sometimes statistical discrepancies, but they are usually relatively small.

Why has measured gross domestic income exceeded measured gross domestic product in recent years?

Indirect business taxes
All business taxes except the tax on corporate profits. Indirect business taxes include sales and business property taxes.

Nonincome expense items
The total of indirect business taxes and depreciation.

EXAMPLE
The Upward Bias in Gross Domestic Income Relative to GDP

The Bureau of Economic Analysis (BEA), the agency that computes gross domestic income (GDI) and gross domestic product (GDP), draws the data used to calculate the two measures from different sources. Consequently, measured GDI is rarely exactly equal to measured GDP. From 2004 to 2006, the difference between GDI and GDP was very slight. Since then, however, GDI has been noticeably larger than GDP.

The main explanation for the higher level of GDI is that GDI includes income that corporate managers receive from stock options. When corporations' profits increase, so do the values of stock options. When managers exercise their

---

EXAMPLE (cont.)

options to trade stock holdings for cash, some of the higher corporate profits flow to the managers. Corporations sometimes underreport the portions of their profits that flow to managers through stock options. Thus, when corporate profits rise, double counting occurs. Higher reported profits push up GDI. Any of these profits that are not reported as payments to managers via stock options then add to labor

income and show up in GDI a second time. In this way, measured GDI is raised above the measured level of GDP.

FOR CRITICAL ANALYSIS

If all measurement errors in national income accounting could be eliminated, what would be true of the relationship between GDI and GDP?

QUICK QUIZ   *See page 212 for the answers. Review concepts from this section in MyEconLab.*

To derive GDP using the income approach, we add up all factor payments, including _____, _____, _____, and _____.

To get an accurate measure of GDP using the income approach, we must also add _____ _____ _____ and _____ to those total factor payments.

Other Components of National Income Accounting

Gross domestic income or product does not really tell us how much income people have access to for spending purposes. To get to those kinds of data, we must make some adjustments, which we now do.

National Income (NI)

We know that net domestic product (NDP) is the total market value of goods and services available to consume and to add to the capital stock. NDP, however, includes indirect business taxes and transfers, which should not count as part of income earned by U.S. factors of production, but does not include various business incomes that should. We therefore subtract from NDP indirect taxes and transfers and add other business income adjustments. Because U.S. residents earn income abroad and foreign residents earn income in the United States, we also add net U.S. income earned abroad. The result is what we define as **national income (NI)**—income earned by all U.S. factors of production.

National income (NI)
The total of all factor payments to resource owners. It can be obtained from net domestic product (NDP) by subtracting indirect business taxes and transfers and adding net U.S. income earned abroad and other business income adjustments.

Personal Income (PI)

National income does not actually represent what is available to individuals to spend because some people obtain income for which they have provided no concurrent good or service and others earn income but do not receive it. In the former category are mainly recipients of transfer payments from the government, such as Social Security, welfare, and food stamps. These payments represent shifts of funds within the economy by way of the government, with no goods or services concurrently rendered in exchange. For the other category, income earned but not received, the most obvious examples are corporate retained earnings that are plowed back into the business, contributions to social insurance, and corporate income taxes. When transfer payments

FIGURE 8-3

Gross Domestic Product and Gross Domestic Income, 2009 (in billions of 2009 dollars per year)

By using the two different methods of computing the output of the economy, we come up with gross domestic product and gross domestic income, which are by definition equal. One approach focuses on expenditures, or the flow of product; the other approach concentrates on income, or the flow of costs.

Sources: U.S. Department of Commerce and author's estimates.

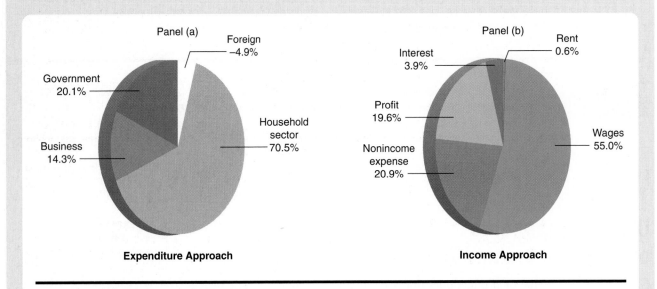

Expenditure Approach

Income Approach

Expenditure Point of View—Product Flow Expenditure by Different Sectors:		Income Point of View—Cost Flow Domestic Income (at Factor Cost):	
Household sector		*Wages*	
Personal consumption expenses	$10,618.6	All wages, salaries, and supplemental employee compensation	$8,275.8
Government sector		*Rent*	
Purchase of goods and services	3,037.4	All rental income of individuals plus implicit rent on owner-occupied dwellings	87.2
Business sector			
Gross private domestic investment (including depreciation)	2,149.6	*Interest*	
		Net interest paid by business	611.4
Foreign sector		*Profit*	
Net exports of goods and services	−760.1	Proprietorial income	1,341.0
		Corporate profits before taxes deducted	1,610.3
		Nonincome expense items	
		Indirect business taxes	842.1
		Depreciation	2,367.3
		Statistical discrepancy	−89.6
Gross domestic product	$15,045.5	Gross domestic income	$15,045.5

TABLE 8-2

Going from GDP to Disposable
Income, 2009

	Billions of Dollars
Gross domestic product (GDP)	15,045.5
Minus depreciation	−2,367.3
Net domestic product (NDP)	12,678.2
Minus indirect business taxes and transfers	−1,339.7
Plus other business income adjustments	1,391.7
Plus net U.S. income earned abroad	71.2
National income (NI)	12,801.4
Minus corporate taxes, Social Security contributions, corporate retained earnings	−1,874.4
Plus government transfer payments	1,165.3
Personal income (PI)	12,092.3
Minus personal income taxes	−1,152.5
Disposable personal income (DPI)	10,939.8

Sources: U.S. Department of Commerce and author's estimates.

are added and when income earned but not received is subtracted, we end up with **personal income (PI)**—income *received* by the factors of production prior to the payment of personal income taxes.

Disposable Personal Income (DPI)

Everybody knows that you do not get to take home all your salary. To get **disposable personal income (DPI),** we subtract all personal income taxes from personal income. This is the income that individuals have left for consumption and saving.

Deriving the Components of GDP

Table 8-2 shows how to derive the various components of GDP. It explains how to go from gross domestic product to net domestic product to national income to personal income and then to disposable personal income. On the frontpapers of your book, you can see the historical record for GDP, NDP, NI, PI, and DPI for selected years since 1929.

We have completed our rundown of the different ways that GDP can be computed and of the different variants of national income and product. What we have not yet touched on is the difference between national income measured in this year's dollars and national income representing real goods and services.

Personal income (PI)
The amount of income that households actually receive before they pay personal income taxes.

Disposable personal income (DPI)
Personal income after personal income taxes have been paid.

QUICK QUIZ *See page 212 for the answers. Review concepts from this section in MyEconLab.*

To obtain _____ _____, we subtract indirect business taxes and transfers from net domestic product and add other business income adjustments and net U.S. income earned abroad.

To obtain _____ _____, we must add government transfer payments, such as Social Security benefits and food stamps. We must subtract income earned but not

received by factor owners, such as corporate retained earnings, Social Security contributions, and corporate income taxes.

To obtain disposable personal income, we subtract all personal _____ _____ from personal income. Disposable personal income is income that individuals actually have for consumption or saving.

Distinguishing Between Nominal and Real Values

Nominal values
The values of variables such as GDP and investment expressed in current dollars, also called *money values;* measurement in terms of the actual market prices at which goods and services are sold.

Real values
Measurement of economic values after adjustments have been made for changes in the average of prices between years.

So far, we have shown how to measure *nominal* income and product. When we say "nominal," we are referring to income and product expressed in the current "face value" of today's dollar. Given the existence of inflation or deflation in the economy, we must also be able to distinguish between the **nominal values** that we will be looking at and the **real values** underlying them. Nominal values are expressed in current dollars. Real income involves our command over goods and services—purchasing power—and therefore depends on money income and a set of prices. Thus, real income refers to nominal income corrected for changes in the weighted average of all prices. In other words, we must make an adjustment for changes in the price level. Consider an example. Nominal income *per person* in 1960 was only about $2,800 per year. In 2009, nominal income per person was about $49,000. Were people really that bad off in 1960? No, for nominal income in 1960 is expressed in 1960 prices, not in the prices of today. In today's dollars, the per-person income of 1960 would be closer to $14,700, or about 30 percent of today's income per person. This is a meaningful comparison between income in 1960 and income today. Next we will show how we can translate nominal measures of income into real measures by using an appropriate price index, such as the Consumer Price Index or the GDP deflator discussed in Chapter 7.

Correcting GDP for Price Changes

If a DVD movie costs $20 this year, 10 DVDs will have a market value of $200. If next year they cost $25 each, the same 10 DVDs will have a market value of $250. In this case, there is no increase in the total quantity of DVDs, but the market value will have increased by one-fourth. Apply this to every single good and service produced and sold in the United States, and you realize that changes in GDP, measured in *current* dollars, may not be a very useful indication of economic activity. If we are really interested in variations in the *real* output of the economy, we must correct GDP (and just about everything else we look at) for changes in the average of overall prices from year to year. Basically, we need to generate an index that approximates the changes in average prices and then divide that estimate into the value of output in current dollars to adjust the value of output to what is called **constant dollars,** or dollars corrected for general price level changes. This price-corrected GDP is called *real GDP.*

Constant dollars
Dollars expressed in terms of real purchasing power using a particular year as the base or standard of comparison, in contrast to current dollars.

How much has correcting for price changes caused real GDP to differ from nominal GDP during the past few years?

EXAMPLE
Correcting GDP for Price Index Changes, 1999–2009

Let's take a numerical example to see how we can adjust GDP for changes in the price index. We must pick an appropriate price index in order to adjust for these price level changes. We mentioned the Consumer Price Index, the Producer Price Index, and the GDP deflator in Chapter 7. Let's use the GDP deflator to adjust our figures. Table 8-3 gives 11 years of GDP figures. Nominal GDP figures are shown in column 2. The price index (GDP deflator) is in column 3, with base year of 2005, when the GDP deflator equals 100. Column 4 shows real (inflation-adjusted) GDP in 2005 dollars.

The formula for real GDP is

$$\text{Real GDP} = \frac{\text{nominal GDP}}{\text{price index}} \times 100$$

EXAMPLE (cont.)

The step-by-step derivation of real (constant-dollar) GDP is as follows: The base year is 2005, so the price index for that year must equal 100. In 2005, nominal GDP was $12,433.9 billion, and so was real GDP expressed in 2005 dollars. In 2006, the price index increased to 103.157. Thus, to correct 2006's nominal GDP for inflation, we divide the price index, 103.157, into the nominal GDP figure of $13,194.7 billion and then multiply it by 100. The rounded result is $12,790.9 billion, which is 2006 GDP expressed in terms of the purchasing power of dollars in 2005. What about a situation when the price index is lower than in 2005? Look at 1999. Here the price index shown in column

3 is only 86.609. That means that in 1999, the average of all prices was just below 87 percent of prices in 2005. To obtain 1999 GDP expressed in terms of 2005 purchasing power, we divide nominal GDP, $9,268.4 billion, by 86.609 and then multiply by 100. The rounded result is a larger number—$10,701.5 billion. Column 4 in Table 8-3 is a better measure of how the economy has performed than column 2, which shows nominal GDP changes.

FOR CRITICAL ANALYSIS

A few years ago, the base year for the GDP deflator was 2000. What does a change in the base year for the price index affect?

TABLE 8-3

Correcting GDP for Price Index Changes

To correct GDP for price index changes, we first have to pick a price index (the GDP deflator) with a specific year as its base. In our example, the base level is 2005 prices; the price index for that year is 100. To obtain 2005 constant-dollar GDP, we divide the price index into nominal GDP and multiply by 100. In other words, we divide column 3 into column 2 and multiply by 100. This gives us column 4, which (taking into account rounding of the deflator) is a measure of real GDP expressed in 2005 purchasing power.

(1) Year	(2) Nominal GDP (billions of dollars per year)	(3) Price Index (base year 2005 = 100)	(4) = [(2) ÷ (3)] × 100 Real GDP (billions of dollars per year, in constant 2005 dollars)
1999	9,268.4	86.609	10,701.5
2000	9,817.0	88.496	11,093.2
2001	10,128.0	90.619	11,176.5
2002	10,469.6	92.201	11,355.2
2003	10,960.8	94.163	11,640.3
2004	11,685.9	96.869	12,063.6
2005	12,433.9	100.000	12,433.9
2006	13,194.7	103.157	12,790.9
2007	13,841.3	105.897	13,070.5
2008	14,421.0	109.295	13,194.6
2009	15,045.5	112.792	13,338.7

Sources: U.S. Department of Commerce, Bureau of Economic Analysis, and author's estimates.

Plotting Nominal and Real GDP

Nominal GDP and real GDP since 1970 are plotted in Figure 8-4 on the following page. There is quite a big gap between the two GDP figures, reflecting the amount of inflation that has occurred. Note that the choice of a base year is arbitrary. We have chosen 2005 as the base year in our example. This happens to be the base year that is currently used by the government for the GDP deflator.

Per Capita Real GDP

Looking at changes in real GDP may be deceiving, particularly if the population size has changed significantly. If real GDP over a 10-year period went up 100 percent, you might

FIGURE 8-4

Nominal and Real GDP

Here we plot both nominal and real GDP. Real GDP is expressed in the purchasing power of 2005 dollars. The gap between the two represents price level changes.

Source: U.S. Department of Commerce.

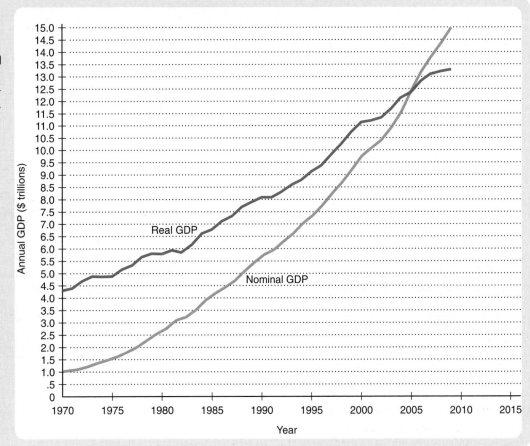

jump to the conclusion that the real income of a typical person in the economy had increased by that amount. But what if during the same period the population increased by 200 percent? Then what would you say? Certainly, the amount of real GDP per person, or *per capita real GDP*, would have fallen, even though *total* real GDP had risen. To account not only for price changes but also for population changes, we must first deflate GDP and then divide by the total population, doing this for each year. If we were to look at certain less developed countries, we would find that in many cases, even though real GDP has risen over the past several decades, per capita real GDP has remained constant or fallen because the population has grown just as rapidly or even more rapidly.

QUICK QUIZ *See page 212 for the answers. Review concepts from this section in MyEconLab.*

To correct **nominal GDP** for price changes, we first select a base year for our price index and assign it the number _____. Then we construct an index based on how a weighted average of prices has changed relative to that base year. For example, if in the next year a weighted average of the prices indicates that prices have increased by 10 percent,

we would assign it the number _____. We then divide each year's price index, so constructed, into its respective nominal GDP figure (and multiply by 100).

We can divide the _____ into real GDP to obtain per capita real GDP.

Comparing GDP Throughout the World

It is relatively easy to compare the standard of living of a family in Los Angeles with that of one living in Boston. Both families get paid in dollars and can buy the same goods and services at Wal-Mart, McDonald's, and Costco. It is not so easy, however, to make a similar comparison between a family living in the United States and one in, say, Indonesia. The first problem concerns money. Indonesian residents get paid in rupiah, their national currency, and buy goods and services with those rupiah. How do we compare the average standard of living measured in rupiah with that measured in dollars?

Foreign Exchange Rates

In earlier chapters, you have encountered international examples that involved local currencies, but the dollar equivalent has always been given. The dollar equivalent is calculated by looking up the **foreign exchange rate** that is published daily in major newspapers throughout the world. If you know that you can exchange $1.50 per euro, the exchange rate is 1.50 to 1 (or otherwise stated, a dollar is worth 0.67 euros). So, if French incomes per capita are, say, 24,120 euros, that translates, at an exchange rate of $1.50 per euro, to $36,180. For years, statisticians calculated relative GDPs by simply adding up each country's GDP in its local currency and dividing by the respective dollar exchange rate.

True Purchasing Power

The problem with simply using foreign exchange rates to convert other countries' GDPs and per capita GDPs into dollars is that not all goods and services are bought and sold in a world market. Restaurant food, housecleaning services, and home repairs do not get exchanged across countries. In countries that have very low wages, those kinds of services are much cheaper than foreign exchange rate computations would imply. Government statistics claiming that per capita income in some poor country is only $300 a year seem shocking. But such a statistic does not tell you the true standard of living of people in that country. Only by looking at what is called **purchasing power parity** can you determine other countries' true standards of living compared to ours.

Given that nations use different currencies, how can we compare nations' levels of real GDP per capita?

Foreign exchange rate
The price of one currency in terms of another.

If lawn-care services are very cheap in some countries, how can that affect cross-country comparisons of living standards?

Purchasing power parity
Adjustment in exchange rate conversions that takes into account differences in the true cost of living across countries.

INTERNATIONAL EXAMPLE
Purchasing Power Parity Comparisons of World Incomes

A few years ago, the International Monetary Fund accepted the purchasing power parity approach as the correct one. It started presenting international statistics on each country's GDP relative to every other's based on purchasing power parity relative to the U.S. dollar. The results were surprising. As you can see from Table 8-4 on the following page, China's per capita GDP is higher based on purchasing power parity than when measured at market foreign exchange rates.

FOR CRITICAL ANALYSIS
What is the percentage increase in China's per capita GDP when one switches from foreign exchange rates to purchasing power parity?

INTERNATIONAL EXAMPLE (cont.)

TABLE 8-4

Comparing GDP Internationally

Country	Annual GDP Based on Purchasing Power Parity (billions of U.S. dollars)	Per Capita GDP Based on Purchasing Power Parity (U.S. dollars)	Per Capita GDP Based on Foreign Exchange Rates (U.S. dollars)
United States	12,398	41,813	41,813
Japan	3,870	30,290	35,742
China	5,333	4,088	1,717
Germany	2,511	30,445	33,794
France	1,862	30,591	35,180
Russia	1,698	11,858	5,336
Indonesia	708	3,209	1,316
Italy	1,626	27,750	30,248
United Kingdom	1,889	31,371	37,018
Brazil	1,583	8,474	4,745

Source: World Bank.

QUICK QUIZ

See page 212 for the answers. Review concepts from this section in MyEconLab.

The foreign _____ _____ is the price of one currency in terms of another.

Statisticians often calculate relative GDP by adding up each country's GDP in its local currency and dividing by the dollar _____ _____.

Because not all goods and services are bought and sold in the world market, we must correct exchange rate conversions of other countries' GDP figures to take into account differences in the true _____ of _____ across countries.

You Are There ▸ Housework's Exclusion from GDP Is Not Gender Neutral

Ann Barlow of San Ramon, California, and her husband have aimed for a "gender-neutral" approach when assigning paid chores to their teenage son and daughter. Nevertheless, Ann has noticed that her daughter devotes significantly more time per week to housework than her son, even though both receive the same weekly payment.

It turns out that Barlow's experience is not unique. Indeed, studies by economists and sociologists indicate that parents are likely to pay girls less for doing housework than boys. Even when teens of both genders receive

the same weekly pay from their parents, girls tend to spend more hours per week on housework than boys do. There is considerable evidence indicating that this gender-based housework gap grows as young women and young men become adults. Adult women typically devote more than 19 hours per week to household activities, whereas adult men spend less than 10 hours per week.

Uncompensated housework by either women or men is not a market activity and hence fails to be included in U.S.

You Are There (cont.)

GDP. Thus, to the extent that parents may accidentally be requiring daughters to do more housework than sons, they may be perpetuating a tendency for women to direct more of their time to activities that do not contribute to measured GDP.

CRITICAL ANALYSIS QUESTIONS

1. What would happen to the level of GDP if economists could find a feasible way of assigning dollar values to nonmarket housework when computing GDP?

2. Why is it difficult for economists to assign values to nonmarket housework?

Issues and Applications

Is U.S. Fixed Investment Understated?

One key component of GDP is gross private domestic investment. In most years through the early 1990s, gross private domestic investment was a larger percentage of GDP than government spending. Since the early 1990s, however, gross private domestic investment's share of GDP has been smaller than the percentage accounted for by government expenditures. Some economists argue that, in part, this is because U.S. business fixed investment is significantly understated.

CONCEPTS APPLIED

- Gross Private Domestic Investment
- Investment
- Fixed Investment

Tangible versus Intangible Investment

As now defined, business fixed investment consists of new purchases of producer durables, or capital goods. Included among these producer durables are *tangible*—that is, material, or concrete—items such as production machinery, office equipment, and computer software.

Some economists suggest that limiting business fixed investment only to tangible items is inappropriate. After all, they argue, investment is broadly defined as any use of today's resources to expand tomorrow's production or consumption. These economists contend that business expenditures include several forms of *intangible* investment that should also be counted as business fixed investment. Examples are spending on research into new processes or products, improvements in business organization, and businesses' tuition payments for employees' job-related education. Currently, national income accountants classify these and other business expenditures as spending on inputs, not as business fixed investment.

FIGURE 8-5

U.S. Business Fixed Investment as a Percentage of GDP Since 1950, Excluding and Including Intangible Forms of Investment

The current measure of business fixed investment, which excludes intangible investments, trended upward as a share of GDP from 1950 to 1981 but has since trended downward. If intangible forms of investment were included, business fixed investment would instead exhibit a generally consistent upward trend since 1950.

Source: Carol Corrado, Dan Sickel, and Charles Hulten, "Intangible Capital and Economic Growth," Finance and Economics Discussion Series, Board of Governors of the Federal Reserve System, 2006; author's estimates.

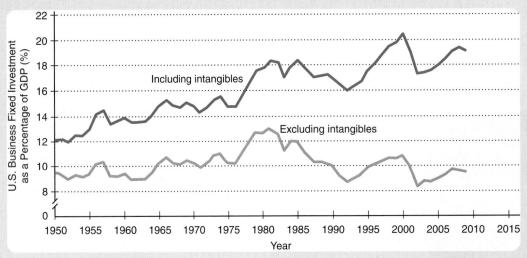

Business Fixed Investment with and without "Intangibles"

Figure 8-5 illustrates how altering the present definition of business fixed investment by adding intangible forms of investment would change business fixed investment's share of GDP since 1950. These estimates indicate that through the 1980s, including intangible investment would have boosted business fixed investment's share of GDP by a factor of about one-half. Since the 1990s, however, including intangibles would have increased business fixed investment's share of GDP by an even larger factor. If intangibles were included today, business fixed investment's share of GDP would more than double, from just over 8 percent to more than 17 percent. Economists

pressing for redefining business fixed investment suggest that this reflects the increased importance of intangible forms of investment in today's knowledge-driven, information-technology-based economy.

Currently, gross private domestic investment is about 14 percent of GDP, compared with 20 percent of GDP for government spending. If intangible forms of investment were counted as part of business fixed investment, gross private domestic investment's share of GDP would rise to about 24 percent. Thus, including intangible forms of investment as part of business fixed investment would once again push the share of GDP going to gross private domestic investment above the share for which government spending accounts.

Test your understanding of this chapter by going online to **MyEconLab**.
In the Study Plan for this chapter, select Section N: News.

For Critical Analysis

1. What would happen to the level of GDP if intangible forms of investment were included within the current official definition of business fixed investment? (Hint: Recall that gross domestic investment is added to government expenditures, consumption spending, and net exports to obtain GDP.)

2. Why are tangible forms of investment likely to be easier for national income accountants to measure accurately than intangible forms of investment?

Web Resources

1. For a detailed economic analysis of the effects of counting intangible forms of investment within business fixed investment, go to www.econtoday.com/chapter08.

2. To review issues associated with the current exclusion of intangible investment from business fixed investment, go to www.econtoday.com/chapter08.

Research Project

Some estimates indicate that including intangible investments would boost measured U.S. business fixed investment by about $1 trillion per year. Adding intangible investments would also increase the official measure of the nation's capital stock, which at present excludes these forms of investment. Would adding intangible forms of investment to the definition of business fixed investment imply that the net annual growth in the capital stock would also be about $1 trillion higher? Explain your reasoning.

Here is what you should know after reading this chapter. **MyEconLab** will help you identify what you know, and where to go when you need to practice.

WHAT YOU SHOULD KNOW		WHERE TO GO TO PRACTICE
The Circular Flow of Income and Output The circular flow of income and output captures two key principles: (1) In every transaction, the seller receives exactly the same amount that the buyer spends; and (2) goods and services flow in one direction, and money payments flow in the other direction. In the circular flow, households ultimately purchase the nation's total output of final goods and services. They make these purchases using income—wages, rents, interest, and profits—earned from selling labor, land, capital, and entrepreneurial services, respectively. Hence, the values of total income and total output must be the same in the circular flow.	national income accounting, 185 total income, 185 final goods and services, 185 **KEY FIGURE** Figure 8-1, 186	• **MyEconLab** Study Plan 8.1 • Audio introduction to Chapter 8 • Animated Figure 8-1 • ABC News Video: Economic Growth: How Much, How Fast?
Gross Domestic Product (GDP) A nation's gross domestic product is the total market value of its final output of goods and services produced within a given year using factors of production located within the nation's borders. Because GDP measures the value of a flow of production during a year in terms of market prices, it is not a measure of a nation's wealth.	gross domestic product (GDP), 187 intermediate goods, 188 value added, 188	• **MyEconLab** Study Plan 8.2
The Limitations of Using GDP as a Measure of National Welfare Gross domestic product is a useful measure for tracking year-to-year changes in the value of a nation's overall economic activity in terms of market prices. But it excludes nonmarket transactions that may contribute to or detract from general welfare. It also fails to account for factors such as labor market discrimination, personal safety, environmental quality, and the amount and quality of leisure time. That is why GDP is not a perfect measure of national well-being.		• **MyEconLab** Study Plan 8.2 • Video: What GDP Excludes

(continued)

 *(continued)*

WHAT YOU SHOULD KNOW		WHERE TO GO TO PRACTICE

The Expenditure Approach to Tabulating GDP To calculate GDP using the expenditure approach, we sum consumption spending, investment expenditures, government spending, and net export expenditures. Thus, we add up the total amount spent on newly produced goods and services during the year to obtain the dollar value of the output produced and purchased during the year.

expenditure approach, 191
income approach, 191
durable consumer goods, 191
nondurable consumer goods, 191
services, 191
gross private domestic investment, 192
investment, 192
producer durables, or capital goods, 192
fixed investment, 192
inventory investment, 192
depreciation, 193
net domestic product (NDP), 194
capital consumption allowance, 194
net investment, 195

KEY FIGURE
Figure 8-2, 194

- **MyEconLab** Study Plan 8.3
- Video: Investment and GDP
- Animated Figure 8-2

The Income Approach to Computing GDP To tabulate GDP using the income approach, we add total wages and salaries, rental income, interest income, profits, and nonincome expense items—indirect business taxes and depreciation—to obtain gross domestic income, which is equivalent to gross domestic product. Thus, the total value of all income earnings (equivalent to total factor costs) equals GDP.

gross domestic income (GDI), 195
indirect business taxes, 196
nonincome expense items, 196
national income (NI), 197
personal income (PI), 199
disposable personal income (DPI), 199

- **MyEconLab** Study Plans 8.3, 8.4
- Video: Investment and GDP

Distinguishing Between Nominal GDP and Real GDP Nominal GDP is the value of newly produced output during the current year measured at current market prices. Real GDP adjusts the value of current output into constant dollars by correcting for changes in the overall level of prices from year to year. To calculate real GDP, we divide nominal GDP by the price index (the GDP deflator) and multiply by 100.

nominal values, 200
real values, 200
constant dollars, 200
foreign exchange rate, 203
purchasing power parity, 203

KEY FIGURE
Figure 8-4, 202

- **MyEconLab** Study Plans 8.5, 8.6
- Animated Figure 8-4

Log in to MyEconLab, take a chapter test, and get a personalized Study Plan that tells you which concepts you understand and which ones you need to review. From there, MyEconLab will give you further practice, tutorials, animations, videos, and guided solutions.
Log in to www.myeconlab.com

PROBLEMS

All problems are assignable in **myeconlab** . *Answers to odd-numbered problems appear at the back of the book.*

8-1. Each year after a regular spring cleaning, Juanita spruces up her home a little by retexturing and repainting the walls of one room in her house. In a given year, she spends $25 on magazines to get ideas about wall textures and paint shades, $45 on newly produced texturing materials and tools, $35 on new paintbrushes and other painting equipment, and $175 on newly produced paint. Normally, she preps the walls, a service that a professional wall-texturing specialist would charge $200 to do, and applies two coats of paint, a service that a painter would charge $350 to do, on her own.

   a. When she purchases her usual set of materials and does all the work on her home by herself in a given spring, how much does Juanita's annual spring texturing and painting activity contribute to GDP?

   b. Suppose that Juanita hurt her back this year and is recovering from surgery. Her surgeon has instructed her not to do any texturing work, but he has given her the go-ahead to paint a room as long as she is cautious. Thus, she buys all the equipment required to both texture and paint a room. She hires someone else to do the texturing work but does the painting herself. How much would her spring painting activity add to GDP?

   c. As a follow-up to part (b), suppose that as soon as Juanita bends down to dip her brush into the paint, she realizes that painting will be too hard on her back after all. She decides to hire someone else to do all the work using the materials she has already purchased. In this case, how much will her spring painting activity contribute to GDP?

8-2. Each year, Johan typically does all his own landscaping and yard work. He spends $200 per year on mulch for his flower beds, $225 per year on flowers and plants, $50 on fertilizer for his lawn, and $245 on gasoline and lawn mower maintenance. The lawn and garden store where he obtains his mulch and fertilizer charges other customers $500 for the service of spreading that much mulch in flower beds and $50 for the service of distributing fertilizer over a yard the size of Johan's. Paying a professional yard care service to mow his lawn would require an expenditure of $1,200 per year, but in that case Johan would not have to buy gasoline or maintain his own lawn mower.

   a. In a normal year, how much does Johan's landscaping and yard work contribute to GDP?

   b. Suppose that Johan has developed allergy problems this year and will have to reduce the amount of his yard work. He can wear a mask while running his lawn mower, so he will keep mowing his yard, but he will pay the lawn and garden center to spread mulch and distribute fertilizer. How much will all the work on Johan's yard contribute to GDP this year?

   c. As a follow-up to part (b), at the end of the year, Johan realizes that his allergies are growing worse and that he will have to arrange for all his landscaping and yard work to be done by someone else next year. How much will he contribute to GDP next year?

8-3. Consider the following hypothetical data for the U.S. economy in 2012 (all amounts are in trillions of dollars).

Consumption	11.0
Indirect business taxes	.8
Depreciation	1.3
Government spending	2.8
Imports	2.7
Gross private domestic investment	3.0
Exports	2.5

   a. Based on the data, what is GDP? NDP? NI?

   b. Suppose that in 2013, exports fall to $2.3 trillion, imports rise to $2.85 trillion, and gross private domestic investment falls to $2.25 trillion. What will GDP be in 2013, assuming that other values do not change between 2012 and 2013?

8-4. Look back at Table 8-3 on page 201, which explains how to calculate real GDP in terms of 2005 constant dollars. Change the base year to 2000. Recalculate the price index, and then recalculate real GDP—that is, express column 4 of Table 8-3 in terms of 2000 dollars instead of 2005 dollars.

8-5. Consider the following hypothetical data for the U.S. economy in 2012 (in trillions of dollars), and assume that there are no statistical discrepancies or other adjustments.

Profit	2.8
Indirect business taxes and transfers	.8
Rent	.7
Interest	.8
Wages	8.2
Depreciation	1.3
Consumption	11.0
Exports	1.5
Government transfer payments	2.0
Personal income taxes and nontax payments	1.7
Imports	1.7
Corporate taxes and retained earnings	.5
Social Security contributions	2.0
Government spending	1.8

a. What is gross domestic income? GDP?

b. What is gross private domestic investment?

c. What is personal income? Personal disposable income?

8-6. Which of the following are production activities that are included in GDP? Which are not?

a. Mr. King performs the service of painting his own house instead of paying someone else to do it.

b. Mr. King paints houses for a living.

c. Mrs. King earns income from parents by taking baby photos in her home photography studio.

d. Mrs. King takes photos of planets and stars as part of her astronomy hobby.

e. E*Trade charges fees to process Internet orders for stock trades.

f. Mr. Ho spends $10,000 on shares of stock via an Internet trade order and pays a $10 brokerage fee.

g. Mrs. Ho receives a Social Security payment.

h. Ms. Hernandez makes a $300 payment for an Internet-based course on stock trading.

i. Mr. Langham sells a used laptop computer to his neighbor.

8-7. Explain what happens to contributions to GDP in each of the following situations.

a. A woman who makes a living charging for investment advice on her Internet Web site marries one of her clients, to whom she now provides advice at no charge.

b. A tennis player wins two top professional tournaments as an unpaid amateur, meaning the tournament sponsor does not have to pay out his share of prize money.

c. A company that had been selling used firearms illegally finally gets around to obtaining an operating license and performing background checks as specified by law prior to each gun sale.

8-8. Explain what happens to the official measure of GDP in each of the following situations.

a. Air quality improves significantly throughout the United States, but there are no effects on aggregate production or on market prices of final goods and services.

b. The U.S. government spends considerably less on antipollution efforts this year than it did in recent years.

c. The quality of cancer treatments increases, so patients undergo fewer treatments, which hospitals continue to provide at the same price per treatment as before.

8-9. Which of the following activities of a computer manufacturer during the current year are included in this year's measure of GDP?

a. The manufacturer purchases a chip in June, uses it as a component in a computer in August, and sells the computer to a customer in November.

b. A retail outlet of the company sells a computer manufactured during the current year.

c. A marketing arm of the company receives fee income during the current year when a buyer of one of its computers elects to use the computer manufacturer as her Internet service provider.

8-10. A number of economists contend that official measures of U.S. gross private investment expenditures are understated. Answer parts (a) and (b) below to determine just how understated these economists believe that officially measured investment spending may be.

a. Household spending on education, such as college tuition expenditures, is counted as consumption spending. Some economists suggest that these expenditures, which amount to 6 percent of GDP, should be counted as investment spending instead. Based on this 6 percent estimate and the GDP computations detailed in Figure 8-3 on page 198, how many billions of dollars would shift from consumption to investment if this suggestion was adopted?

b. Some economists argue that intangible forms of investment—business research spending, educational expenses for employees, and the like—should be included in the official measure of gross private domestic investment. These expenditures, which amount to about 12 percent of GDP, currently are treated as business input expenses and are not included in GDP. Based on this 12 percent estimate and the GDP computations detailed in Figure 8-3 on page 198, how much higher would gross private domestic investment be if intangible investment expenditures were counted as investment spending?

c. Based on your answers to parts (a) and (b), what is the total amount that gross private domestic investment may be understated, according to economists who argue that household education spending and business intangible investments should be added? How much may GDP be understated?

8-11. Consider the following table for the economy of a nation whose residents produce five final goods.

Good	2009		2013	
	Price	Quantity	Price	Quantity
Shampoo	$ 2	15	$ 4	20
DVD drives	200	10	250	10
Books	40	5	50	4
Milk	3	10	4	3
Candy	1	40	2	20

Assuming a 2009 base year:

a. What is nominal GDP for 2009 and 2013?

b. What is real GDP for 2009 and 2013?

8-12. Consider the following table for the economy of a nation whose residents produce four final goods.

Good	2011		2012	
	Price	Quantity	Price	Quantity
Computers	$1,000	10	$800	15
Bananas	6	3,000	11	1,000
Televisions	100	500	150	300
Cookies	1	10,000	2	10,000

Assuming a 2012 base year:

a. What is nominal GDP for 2011 and 2012?

b. What is real GDP for 2011 and 2012?

8-13. In the table for Problem 8-12, if 2012 is the base year, what is the price index for 2011? (Round decimal fractions to the nearest tenth.)

8-14. Suppose that early in a year, a hurricane hits a town in Florida and destroys a substantial number of homes. A portion of this stock of housing, which had a market value of $100 million (not including the market value of the land), was uninsured. The owners of the residences spent a total of $5 million during the rest of the year to pay salvage companies to help them save remaining belongings. A small percentage of uninsured owners had sufficient resources to spend a total of $15 million during the year to pay construction companies to rebuild their homes. Some were able to devote their own time, the opportunity cost of which was valued at $3 million, to work on rebuilding their homes. The remaining people, however, chose to sell their land at its market value and abandon the remains of their houses. What was the combined effect of these transactions on GDP for this year? (Hint: Which transactions took place in the markets for *final* goods and services?) In what ways, if any, does the effect on GDP reflect a loss in welfare for these individuals?

8-15. Suppose that in 2013, geologists discover large reserves of oil under the tundra in Alaska. These reserves have a market value estimated at $50 billion at current oil prices. Oil companies spend $1 billion to hire workers and move and position equipment to begin exploratory pumping during that same year. In the process of loading some of the oil onto tankers at a port, one company accidentally spills some of the oil into a bay and by the end of the year pays $1 billion to other companies to clean it up. The oil spill kills thousands of birds, seals, and other wildlife. What was the combined effect of these events on GDP for this year? (Hint: Which transactions took place in the markets for *final* goods and services?) In what ways, if any, does the effect on GDP reflect a loss in national welfare?

8-16. Consider the diagram in the next column, and answer the following questions.

   a. What is the base year? Explain

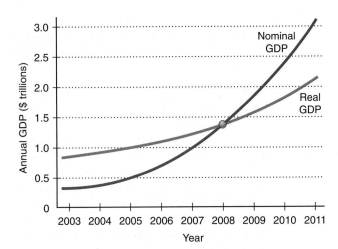

b. Has this country experienced inflation or deflation since the base year? How can you tell?

ECONOMICS ON THE NET

Tracking the Components of Gross Domestic Product One way to keep tabs on the components of GDP is via the FRED database at the Web site of the Federal Reserve Bank of St. Louis.

Title: Gross Domestic Product and Components

Navigation: Use the link at **www.econtoday.com/chapter08** to visit the home page of the Federal Reserve Bank of St. Louis. Click on *Gross Domestic Product (GDP) and Components.*

Application

1. Click on *GDP/GNP,* and then click a checkmark next to *GDP (Gross Domestic Product).* Write down nominal GDP data for the past 10 quarters.

2. Back up to *GDPCA (Real Gross Domestic Product) Dollars.* Write down the amounts for the past 10 quarters. Use the formula on page 200 to calculate the price level for each quarter. Has the price level decreased or increased in recent quarters?

For Group Study and Analysis Divide the class into "consumption," "investment," "government sector," and "foreign sector" groups. Have each group evaluate the contribution of each category of spending to GDP and to its quarter-to-quarter volatility. Reconvene the class, and discuss the factors that appear to create the most variability in GDP.

ANSWERS TO QUICK QUIZZES

p. 187: (i) factor . . . income; (ii) final; (iii) profit
p. 191: (i) Gross domestic product; (ii) value added; (iii) exclude; (iv) GDP; (v) market value
p. 195: (i) expenditure . . . durables . . . nondurables . . . services; (ii) capacity . . . inventories; (iii) market; (iv) depreciation
p. 197: (i) wages . . . interest . . . rent . . . profits; (ii) indirect business taxes . . . depreciation
p. 199: (i) national income; (ii) personal income; (iii) income taxes
p. 202: (i) 100 . . . 110; (ii) population
p. 204: (i) exchange rate; (ii) exchange rate; (iii) cost . . . living

Global Economic Growth and Development

9

What do Australia, Bulgaria, Germany, and Japan all have in common? The answer is that they are among more than 20 nations throughout the world that now offer significant financial incentives for women to bear children. These nations' efforts to boost birthrates are aimed both at halting current population declines and at generating net population increases over the longer term. In all these nations, the ultimate objective of giving women incentives to have more babies is to provide a stronger foundation for future *economic growth*. In this chapter, you will learn about the measurement of economic growth, the importance of growth rates, and the key factors that determine economic growth.

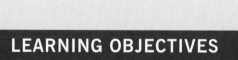

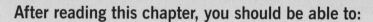

LEARNING OBJECTIVES

myeconlab

MyEconLab helps you master each objective and study more efficiently. See end of chapter for details.

After reading this chapter, you should be able to:

➤ Define economic growth

➤ Recognize the importance of economic growth rates

➤ Explain why productivity increases are crucial for maintaining economic growth

➤ Describe the fundamental determinants of economic growth

➤ Understand the basis of new growth theory

➤ Discuss the fundamental factors that contribute to a nation's economic development

DID YOU KNOW THAT only one European nation, Luxembourg, has per capita real GDP—real GDP divided by the population—higher than the U.S. per capita real GDP? Luxembourg's per capita real GDP is nearly 50 percent greater than overall U.S. per capita real GDP, which puts its residents' incomes on a par with those of the U.S. states of Connecticut and Delaware. In Belgium, France, Germany, and Italy, however, per capita real GDP is only slightly higher than in the U.S. states of Arkansas and Montana, where per capita real GDP is less than 75 percent of the overall U.S. level. In fact, per capita real GDP in these four European nations is only about 14 percent higher than in Mississippi and West Virginia, the U.S. states with the lowest per capita real GDP.

A few decades ago, per capita real GDP in Arkansas, Mississippi, Montana, and West Virginia was far below the levels in Belgium, France, Germany, and Italy. Since then, per capita real GDP has grown more rapidly in the four U.S. states than in the four European nations. Thus, the four U.S. states have experienced a higher rate of *economic growth,* which is the topic of this chapter.

How Do We Define Economic Growth?

Recall from Chapter 2 that we can show economic growth graphically as an outward shift of a production possibilities curve, as is seen in Figure 9-1. If there is economic growth between 2011 and 2035, the production possibilities curve will shift outward toward the red curve. The distance that it shifts represents the amount of economic growth, defined as the increase in the productive capacity of a nation. Although it is possible to come up with a measure of a nation's increased productive capacity, it would not be easy. Therefore, we turn to a more readily obtainable definition of economic growth.

Most people have a general idea of what economic growth means. When a nation grows economically, its citizens must be better off in at least some ways, usually in terms of their material well-being. Typically, though, we do not measure the well-being of any nation solely in terms of its total output of real goods and services or in terms of real GDP without making some adjustments. After all, India

How does spending on this new research and development facility add to economic growth in the future?

FIGURE 9-1

Economic Growth

If there is growth between 2011 and 2035, the production possibilities curve for the entire economy will shift outward from the blue line labeled 2011 to the red line labeled 2035. The distance that it shifts represents an increase in the productive capacity of the nation.

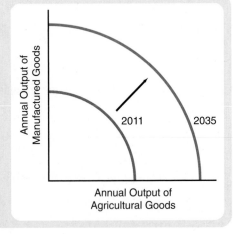

has a real GDP more than 15 times as large as that of Denmark. The population in India, though, is about 200 times greater than that of Denmark. Consequently, we view India as a relatively poor country and Denmark as a relatively rich country. Thus, when we measure economic growth, we must adjust for population growth. Our formal definition becomes this: **Economic growth** occurs when there are increases in *per capita* real GDP, measured by the rate of change in per capita real GDP per year. Figure 9-2 presents the historical record of real GDP per person in the United States.

Economic growth
Increases in per capita real GDP measured by its rate of change per year.

Problems in Definition

Our definition of economic growth says nothing about the *distribution* of output and income. A nation might grow very rapidly in terms of increases in per capita real output, while its poor people remain poor or become even poorer. Therefore, in assessing the economic growth record of any nation, we must be careful to pinpoint which income groups have benefited the most from such growth. How much does economic growth differ across countries?

FIGURE 9-2

The Historical Record of U.S. Economic Growth

The graph traces per capita real GDP in the United States since 1900. Data are given in 2005 dollars.

Source: U.S. Department of Commerce.

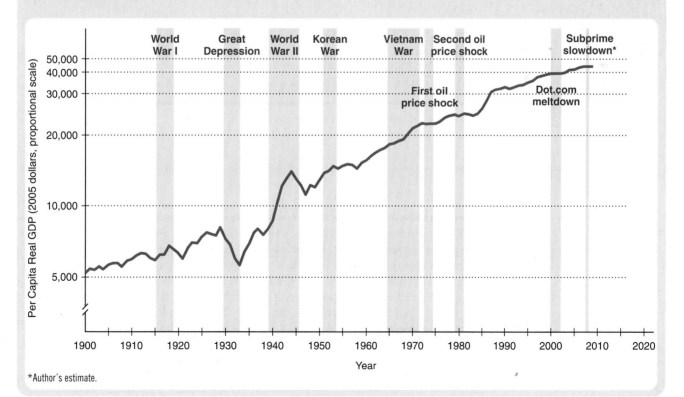

*Author's estimate.

INTERNATIONAL EXAMPLE
Growth Rates Around the World

Table 9-1 shows the average annual rate of growth of real GDP per person in selected countries for the period since 1990. Notice that during the time period under study, the United States is positioned about midway in the pack. Thus, even though we are one of the world's richest countries, our rate of economic growth in recent decades has been in the middle range. The reason that U.S. per capita real GDP has remained higher than per capita real GDP in most other nations is that the United States has been able to sustain growth over many decades. This is something that most other countries have so far been unable to accomplish.

FOR CRITICAL ANALYSIS
"The largest change is from zero to one." Does this statement have anything to do with relative growth rates in poorer versus richer countries?

TABLE 9-1

Per Capita Real GDP Growth Rates in Various Countries

Country	Average Annual Rate of Growth of Real GDP Per Capita, 1990–2009 (%)
France	2.9
Brazil	3.0
Japan	3.3
Germany	3.4
Canada	3.5
Sweden	3.8
United States	4.4
Turkey	5.5
Malaysia	5.6
India	5.7
Indonesia	5.9
China	10.1

Sources: World Bank, International Monetary Fund, and author's estimates.

Real standards of living can go up without any positive economic growth. This can occur if individuals are, on average, enjoying more leisure by working fewer hours but producing as much as they did before. For example, if per capita real GDP in the United States remained at $45,000 a year for a decade, we could not automatically jump to the conclusion that U.S. residents were, on average, no better off. What if, during that same 10-year period, average hours worked fell from 37 per week to 33 per week? That would mean that during the 10 years under study, individuals in the labor force were "earning" 4 more hours of leisure a week.

Nothing so extreme as this example has occurred in this country, but something similar has. Average hours worked per week fell steadily until the 1960s, when they leveled off. That means that during much of the history of this country, the increase

Go to www.econtoday.com/chapter09 to get the latest figures and estimates on economic growth throughout the world.

in per capita real GDP *understated* the actual economic growth that we were experiencing because we were enjoying more and more leisure as time passed.

Why are economists reexamining officially reported rates of economic growth in China and India?

POLICY EXAMPLE
Are Growth Rates in China and India Overstated?

No one doubts that per capita real GDP has been growing very rapidly in China and India in recent years. Nevertheless, preliminary evidence from an ongoing World Bank study suggests that errors in measuring prices used to adjust GDP figures for China and India may have led to overstatements in their per capita real GDP for a number of years. New estimates indicate that per capita real GDP in China may be as much as 40 percent lower than the figures listed in World Bank reports. In India, per capita real GDP could be up to 38 percent lower.

Consequently, per capita real GDP in these two nations has not grown at the officially reported rates. As you read this page, economists are undoubtedly in the process of recalculating recent economic growth rates in China, India, and a number of other nations.

FOR CRITICAL ANALYSIS
Why must economists recalculate a nation's annual rates of economic growth after revising annual estimates of per capita real GDP for that country?

Is Economic Growth Bad?

Some commentators on our current economic situation believe that the definition of economic growth ignores its negative effects. Some psychologists even contend that economic growth makes us worse off. They say that the more the economy grows, the more "needs" are created so that we feel worse off as we become richer. Our expectations are rising faster than reality, so we presumably always suffer from a sense of disappointment. Also, economists' measurement of economic growth does not take into account the spiritual and cultural aspects of the good life. As with all activities, both costs and benefits are associated with growth. You can see some of those listed in Table 9-2.

Any measure of economic growth that we use will be imperfect. Nonetheless, the measures that we do have allow us to make comparisons across countries and over

What phenomenon now allows a larger percentage of Indian citizens to purchase expensive clothes?

TABLE 9-2		
Costs and Benefits of Economic Growth	**Benefits**	**Costs**
	Reduction in illiteracy	Environmental pollution
	Reduction in poverty	Breakdown of the family
	Improved health	Isolation and alienation
	Longer lives	Urban congestion
	Political stability	

TABLE 9-3

One Dollar Compounded Annually at Different Interest Rates

Here we show the value of a dollar at the end of a specified period during which it has been compounded annually at a specified interest rate. For example, if you took $1 today and invested it at 5 percent per year, it would yield $1.05 at the end of one year. At the end of 10 years, it would equal $1.63, and at the end of 50 years, it would equal $11.50.

Number of Years	Interest Rate						
	3%	4%	5%	6%	8%	10%	20%
1	1.03	1.04	1.05	1.06	1.08	1.10	1.20
2	1.06	1.08	1.10	1.12	1.17	1.21	1.44
3	1.09	1.12	1.16	1.19	1.26	1.33	1.73
4	1.13	1.17	1.22	1.26	1.36	1.46	2.07
5	1.16	1.22	1.28	1.34	1.47	1.61	2.49
6	1.19	1.27	1.34	1.41	1.59	1.77	2.99
7	1.23	1.32	1.41	1.50	1.71	1.94	3.58
8	1.27	1.37	1.48	1.59	1.85	2.14	4.30
9	1.30	1.42	1.55	1.68	2.00	2.35	5.16
10	1.34	1.48	1.63	1.79	2.16	2.59	6.19
20	1.81	2.19	2.65	3.20	4.66	6.72	38.30
30	2.43	3.24	4.32	5.74	10.00	17.40	237.00
40	3.26	4.80	7.04	10.30	21.70	45.30	1,470.00
50	4.38	7.11	11.50	18.40	46.90	117.00	9,100.00

time and, if used judiciously, can enable us to gain important insights. Per capita real GDP, used so often, is not always an accurate measure of economic well-being, but it is a serviceable measure of productive activity.

The Importance of Growth Rates

Notice in Table 9-1 on page 216 that the growth rates in real per capita income for most countries differ very little—generally by only a few percentage points. You might want to know why such small differences in growth rates are important. What does it matter if we grow at 3 percent rather than at 4 percent per year? The answer is that in the long run, it matters a lot.

A small difference in the rate of economic growth does not matter very much for next year or the year after. For the more distant future, however, it makes considerable difference. The power of *compounding* is impressive. Let's see what happens with three different annual rates of growth: 3 percent, 4 percent, and 5 percent. We start with $1 trillion per year of U.S. GDP at some time in the past. We then compound this $1 trillion, or allow it to grow at these three different growth rates. The difference is huge. In 50 years, $1 trillion per year becomes $4.38 trillion per year if compounded at 3 percent per year. Just one percentage point more in the growth rate, 4 percent, results in a real GDP of $7.11 trillion per year in 50 years, almost double the previous amount. Two percentage points' difference in the growth rate—5 percent per year—results in a real GDP of $11.5 trillion per year in 50 years, or nearly three times as much. Obviously, very small differences in annual growth rates result in great differences in cumulative economic growth. That is why nations are concerned if the growth rate falls even a little in absolute percentage terms.

Thus, when we talk about growth rates, we are talking about compounding. In Table 9-3, we show how $1 compounded annually grows at different interest rates. We see in the 3 percent column that $1 in 50 years grows to $4.38. We merely multiplied $1 trillion times 4.38 to get the growth figure in our earlier example. In the 5 percent column, $1 grows to $11.50 after 50 years. Again, we multiplied $1 trillion times 11.50 to get the growth figure for 5 percent in the preceding example.

How do economists measure the pace of world economic growth?

INTERNATIONAL EXAMPLE
An Upswing in Global Economic Growth

Calculating aggregate world per capita real GDP is complicated by the fact that prices of goods and services are measured in terms of various nations' currencies, such as the dollar, the euro, and the yen. To measure global GDP, economists commonly start by converting the value of every country's GDP into U.S. dollars, which is accomplished by multiplying the country's GDP by the exchange rate of the dollar for its currency. Then they adjust for the fact that price levels vary across countries relative to the United States. Next, they develop worldwide GDP deflators to adjust the resulting global GDP measure for inflation, thereby computing a measure of world *real* GDP. Dividing world real GDP by the estimated world population yields world per capita real GDP. Finally, by computing annual percentage changes in world per capita real GDP, economists measure global economic growth.

Between 1870 and 1913, world per capita real GDP increased at an average annual rate of only 1.3 percent per year. Prior to the current century, the highest average global economic growth rate ever recorded was 2.9 percent, which occurred during the period 1950–1973. Since 2000, world per capita real GDP has grown at an average annual rate of 3.2 percent. Thus, the first decade of this century is on track to record the highest average pace of measured economic growth in human history.

FOR CRITICAL ANALYSIS
Based on Table 9-3, if the pace of global economic growth continues through 2010, about how much higher will world per capita real GDP be in 2010 than in 2000?

THE RULE OF 70 Table 9-3 indicates that how quickly the level of a nation's per capita real GDP increases depends on the rate of economic growth. A formula called the **rule of 70** provides a shorthand way to calculate approximately how long it will take a country to experience a significant increase in per capita real GDP. According to the rule of 70, the approximate number of years necessary for a nation's per capita real GDP to increase by 100 percent—that is, to *double*—is equal to 70 divided by the average rate of economic growth. Thus, at an annual growth rate of 10 percent, per capita real GDP should double in about 7 years. As you can see in Table 9-3, at a 10 percent growth rate, in 7 years per capita real GDP would rise by a factor of 1.94, which is very close to 2, or very nearly the doubling predicted by the rule of 70. At an annual growth rate of 8 percent, the rule of 70 predicts that nearly 9 years will be required for a nation's per capita real GDP to double. Table 9-3 verifies that this prediction is correct. Indeed, the table shows that after 9 years an exact doubling will occur at a growth rate of 8 percent.

The rule of 70 implies that at lower rates of economic growth, much more time must pass before per capita real GDP will double. At a 3 percent growth rate, just over 23 (70/3) years must pass before per capita real income doubles. At a rate of growth of only 1 percent per year, 70 (70/1) years must pass. This means that if a nation's average rate of economic growth is 1 percent instead of 3 percent, 47 more years—about two generations—must pass for per capita real GDP to double. Clearly, the rule of 70 verifies that even very slight differences in economic growth rates are important.

Rule of 70
A rule stating that the approximate number of years required for per capita real GDP to double is equal to 70 divided by the average rate of economic growth.

QUICK QUIZ See page 238 for the answers. Review concepts from this section in *MyEconLab*.

Economic growth can be defined as the increase in _____ _____ real GDP, measured by its rate of change per year.

The _____ of economic growth are reductions in illiteracy, poverty, and illness and increases in life spans and political stability. The _____ of economic growth

may include environmental pollution, alienation, and urban congestion.

Small percentage-point differences in growth rates lead to _____ differences in per capita real GDP over time. These differences can be seen by examining a compound interest table such as the one in Table 9-3 on page 218.

Productivity Increases:
The Heart of Economic Growth

Let's say that you are required to type 10 term papers and homework assignments a year. You have a computer, but you do not know how to touch-type. You end up spending an average of two hours per typing job. The next summer, you buy a touch-typing tutorial to use on your computer and spend a few minutes a day improving your speed. The following term, you spend only one hour per typing assignment, thereby saving 10 hours a semester. You have become more productive. This concept of productivity summarizes your ability (and everyone else's) to produce the same output with fewer inputs. Thus, **labor productivity** is normally measured by dividing the total real domestic output (real GDP) by the number of workers or the number of labor hours. By definition, labor productivity increases whenever average output produced per worker during a specified time period increases.

Why has labor productivity grown faster in the United States than in other developed nations?

Labor productivity
Total real domestic output (real GDP) divided by the number of workers (output per worker).

EXAMPLE
Explaining the U.S. Lead in Labor Productivity Growth

During the past decade, labor productivity has increased by about 9 percent in nations in the European Monetary Union (the member nations of the European Union that use the euro as their currency), 13 percent in Japan, 18 percent in the United Kingdom, and more than 27 percent in the United States. Economists offer three explanations for why labor productivity has grown more in the United States than in other developed nations. First, U.S. firms face fewer legal restrictions on opening or closing operations and hiring and firing workers, so that private markets have more freedom to direct workers from lower-productivity jobs to higher-productivity positions. Second, U.S. producers face more competition, which induces them

to adopt new technologies that make workers more productive. Third, lower tax rates on labor income give U.S. workers greater incentives to direct more time to developing skills on the job. Taken together, these three factors have boosted the overall growth of labor productivity in the United States as compared with the world's other highly developed nations.

FOR CRITICAL ANALYSIS
How do you suppose that the higher growth of U.S. labor productivity has contributed to the rise in U.S. per capita real GDP relative to per capita real GDP in European nations?

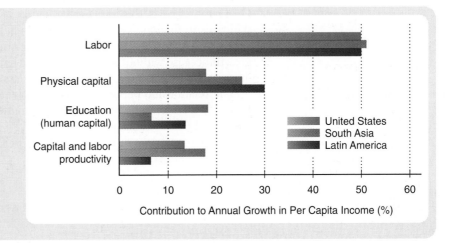

FIGURE 9-3

Factors Accounting for Economic Growth in Selected Regions

In the United States, South Asia, and Latin America, growth in labor resources is the main contributor to economic growth.

Source: International Monetary Fund.

Clearly, there is a relationship between economic growth and increases in labor productivity. If you divide all resources into just capital and labor, economic growth can be defined simply as the cumulative contribution to per capita GDP growth of three components: the rate of growth of capital, the rate of growth of labor, and the rate of growth of capital and labor productivity. If everything else remains constant, improvements in labor productivity ultimately lead to economic growth and higher living standards.

Figure 9-3 displays estimates of the relative contributions of the growth of labor and capital and the growth of labor and capital productivity to economic growth in the United States, nations in South Asia, and Latin American countries. The growth of labor resources, through associated increases in labor force participation, has contributed to the expansion of output that has accounted for at least half of economic growth in all three regions. Total capital is the sum of physical capital, such as tools and machines, and human capital, which is the amount of knowledge acquired from research and education. Figure 9-3 shows the separate contributions of the growth of these forms of capital, which together have accounted for roughly a third of the growth rate of per capita incomes in the United States, South Asia, and Latin America. In these three parts of the world, growth in overall capital and labor productivity has contributed the remaining 7 to 18 percent.

Go to www.econtoday.com/chapter09 for information about the latest trends in U.S. labor productivity.

Saving: A Fundamental Determinant of Economic Growth

Economic growth does not occur in a vacuum. It is not some predetermined fate of a nation. Rather, economic growth depends on certain fundamental factors. One of the most important factors that affects the rate of economic growth and hence long-term living standards is the rate of saving.

A basic proposition in economics is that if you want more tomorrow, you have to consume less today.

To have more consumption in the future, you have to consume less today and save the difference between your consumption and your income.

On a national basis, this implies that higher saving rates eventually mean higher living standards in the long run, all other things held constant. Concern has been growing in the United States that we are not saving enough. Saving is important for economic growth because without saving, we cannot have investment. If there is no investment in our capital stock, there would be much less economic growth.

The relationship between the rate of saving and per capita real GDP is shown in Figure 9-4. Among the nations with the highest rates of saving are China, Germany, Japan, and Saudi Arabia.

How has the propensity for residents of China to save helped to fuel economic growth in that nation?

INTERNATIONAL EXAMPLE
Saving and Growth in China

Since the late 1980s, residents of China have consistently directed at least 35 percent of their real GDP to saving. Indeed, since 2001 saving in China has exceeded 40 percent of real GDP, and currently this percentage hovers near 50 percent. The bulk of this saving has been channeled into investment in capital. Today, investment spending accounts for more than 44 percent of that nation's total expenditures on final goods and services. These consistently high rates of saving and capital investment in China help to explain why the nation's economy maintains an annual rate of growth of per capita real GDP of about 10 percent.

FOR CRITICAL ANALYSIS

Why do you suppose that economists who predict that consumption's share of real GDP in China is likely to increase in future years also project an eventual falloff in the nation's rate of economic growth?

FIGURE 9-4

Relationship Between Rate of Saving and Per Capita Real GDP

This diagram shows the relationship between per capita real GDP and the rate of saving expressed as the average share of annual real GDP saved.

Source: World Bank.

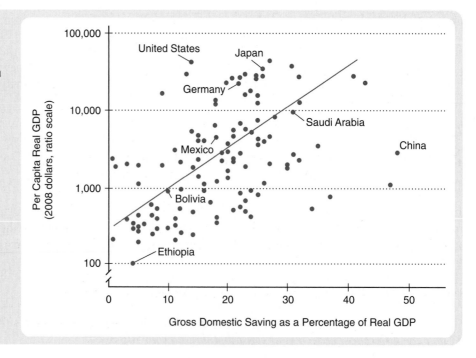

QUICK QUIZ   *See page 238 for the answers. Review concepts from this section in MyEconLab.*

Economic growth is numerically equal to the rate of growth of _____ plus the rate of growth of _____ plus the rate of growth in the productivity of _____ and of _____. Improvements in labor productivity, all other things being equal, lead to greater economic growth and higher living standards.

One fundamental determinant of the rate of growth is the rate of _____. To have more consumption in the future, we have to _____ rather than consume. In general, countries that have had higher rates of _____ have had higher rates of growth in per capita real GDP.

New Growth Theory and the Determinants of Growth

A simple arithmetic definition of economic growth has already been given. The per capita growth rates of capital and labor plus the per capita growth rate of their productivity constitute the rate of economic growth. Economists have had good data on the growth of the physical capital stock in the United States as well as on the labor force. But when you add those two growth rates together, you still do not get the total economic growth rate in the United States. The difference has to be due to improvements in productivity. Economists typically labeled this "improvements in technology," and that was that. More recently, proponents of what is now called **new growth theory** argue that technology cannot simply be looked at as an outside factor without explanation. Technology must be understood in terms of what drives it. What are the forces that make productivity grow in the United States and elsewhere?

New growth theory
A theory of economic growth that examines the factors that determine why technology, research, innovation, and the like are undertaken and how they interact.

Growth in Technology

Consider some startling statistics about the growth in technology. Microprocessor speeds may increase from 4,000 megahertz to 10,000 megahertz by the year 2015. By that same year, the size of the thinnest circuit line within a transistor may decrease by 90 percent. The typical memory capacity (RAM) of computers will jump from 2 gigabytes, or about 32 times the equivalent text in the Internal Revenue Code, to more than 300 gigabytes. Recent developments in phase-change memory technologies and in new techniques for storing bits of data on molecules and even individual atoms promise even greater expansions of computer memory capacities. Predictions are that computers may become as powerful as the human brain by 2020.

Technology: A Separate Factor of Production

We now recognize that technology must be viewed as a separate factor of production that is sensitive to rewards. Otherwise stated, one of the major foundations of new growth theory is this:

> *When the rewards are greater, more technological advances will occur.*

Let's consider several aspects of technology here, the first one being research and development.

Research and Development

A certain amount of technological advance results from research and development (R&D) activities that have as their goal the development of specific new materials, new products, and new machines. How much spending a nation devotes to R&D can have an impact on its long-term economic growth. Part of how much a nation spends depends on what businesses decide is worth spending. That in turn depends on their expected rewards from successful R&D. If your company develops a new way to produce computer memory chips, how much will it be rewarded? The answer depends on what you can charge others to use the new technique.

Patent

A government protection that gives an inventor the exclusive right to make, use, or sell an invention for a limited period of time (currently, 20 years).

PATENTS To protect new techniques developed through R&D, we have a system of **patents,** in which the federal government gives the patent holder the exclusive right to make, use, and sell an invention for a period of 20 years. One can argue that this special protection given to owners of patents increases expenditures on R&D and therefore adds to long-term economic growth. Figure 9-5 shows that U.S. patent grants fell during the 1970s, increased steadily after 1982, surged from 1995 until 2001, and increased again during the past few years.

POSITIVE EXTERNALITIES AND R&D As we discussed in Chapter 5, positive externalities are benefits from an activity that are not enjoyed by the instigator of the activity. In the case of R&D spending, a certain amount of the benefits go to other companies that do not have to pay for them. In particular, according to economists David Coe of the International Monetary Fund and Elhanan Helpman of Tel Aviv University, about a quarter of the global productivity gains of R&D investment in the top seven industrialized countries goes to other nations. For every 1 percent rise in the stock of R&D in the United States alone, for example, productivity in the rest of the world increases by about 0.25 percent. One country's R&D expenditures benefit other countries because they are able to import capital goods—computers, telecommunications networks—from technologically advanced countries and then use them as inputs in making their own industries more efficient. In addition, countries that import high-tech goods are able to imitate the technology.

FIGURE 9-5

U.S. Patent Grants

The U.S. Patent and Trademark Office gradually began awarding more patent grants between the early 1980s and the mid-1990s. Since 1995, the number of patents granted each year has risen in most years.

Source: U.S. Patent and Trademark Office.

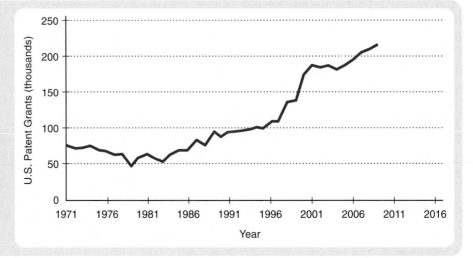

The Open Economy and Economic Growth

People who study economic growth today emphasize the importance of the openness of the economy. Free trade encourages a more rapid spread of technology and industrial ideas. Moreover, open economies may experience higher rates of economic growth because their own industries have access to a bigger market. When trade barriers are erected in the form of tariffs and the like, domestic industries become isolated from global technological progress. This occurred for many years in Communist countries and in most developing countries in Africa, Latin America, and elsewhere. Figure 9-6 on the following page shows the relationship between economic growth and openness as measured by the level of tariff barriers.

How have relative per capita incomes in Latin America and Asia changed since most Latin American countries opted for much higher trade barriers?

INTERNATIONAL EXAMPLE
A Story of Different Choices Regarding Trade—and Economic Growth

In 1950, per capita real GDP in Latin America exceeded the Asian level by 75 percent. Today, Latin America's per capita real GDP is almost 20 percent *less* than Asia's per capita real GDP. One factor that contributed to the Asian turnaround relative to Latin America stands out sharply: much greater Asian openness to international trade. Since the late 1950s, a number of Asian nations, including Hong Kong, Japan, and Singapore, have adopted low trade barriers. In contrast, the majority of Latin American countries have maintained some of the highest trade barriers in the world. For nearly 60 years, trade barriers in nations such as Argentina, Brazil, and Chile have been up to 100 times greater than those in Asia. Hence, residents of most Latin American countries have been denied the benefits of economic growth resulting from openness to trade that have been experienced by many Asian residents.

FOR CRITICAL ANALYSIS
In light of the evidence that low trade barriers promote economic growth, why do you suppose that some people in every nation favor high barriers to trade?

Innovation and Knowledge

We tend to think of technological progress as, say, the invention of the transistor. But invention means nothing by itself; **innovation** is required. Innovation involves the transformation of something new, such as an invention, into something that benefits the economy either by lowering production costs or by providing new goods and services. Indeed, the new growth theorists believe that real wealth creation comes from innovation and that invention is but a facet of innovation.

Historically, technologies have moved relatively slowly from invention to innovation to widespread use, and the dispersion of new technology remains for the most part slow and uncertain. The inventor of the transistor thought it might be used to make better hearing aids. At the time it was invented, the *New York Times*'s sole reference to it was in a small weekly column called "News of Radio." When the laser was invented, no one really knew what it could be used for. It was initially used to help in navigation, measurement, and chemical research. Today, it is used in the reproduction of music, printing, surgery, telecommunications, and optical data transmittal and storage. Tomorrow, who knows?

Innovation
Transforming an invention into something that is useful to humans.

You Are There

To contemplate a real-world example of how an innovation can take place slowly and even unexpectedly, consider **An Invention Becomes a Market Innovation—by Accident,** on page 233.

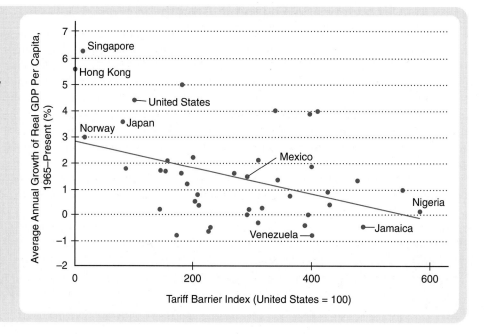

FIGURE 9-6

The Relationship Between Economic Growth and Tariff Barriers to International Trade

Nations with low tariff barriers are relatively open to international trade and have tended to have higher average annual rates of real GDP per capita growth since 1965.

Source: World Bank.

Typically, thousands of raw ideas emerge each year at a large firm's R&D laboratories. Only a few hundred of these ideas develop into formal proposals for new processes or products. Of these proposals, the business selects perhaps a few dozen that it deems suitable for further study to explore their feasibility. After careful scrutiny, the firm concludes that only a handful of these ideas are inventions worthy of being integrated into actual production processes or launched as novel products. The firm is fortunate if one or two ultimately become successful marketplace innovations.

The Importance of Ideas and Knowledge

Economist Paul Romer has added at least one important factor that determines the rate of economic growth. He contends that production and manufacturing knowledge is just as important as the other determinants and perhaps even more so. He considers knowledge a factor of production that, like capital, has to be paid for by forgoing current consumption. Economies must therefore invest in knowledge just as they invest in machines. Because past investment in capital may make it more profitable to acquire more knowledge, there may be an investment-knowledge cycle in which investment spurs knowledge and knowledge spurs investment. A once-and-for-all increase in a country's rate of investment may permanently raise that country's growth rate. (According to traditional theory, a once-and-for-all increase in the rate of saving and therefore in the rate of investment simply leads to a new steady-state standard of living, not one that continues to increase.)

Another way of looking at knowledge is that it is a store of ideas. According to Romer, ideas are what drive economic growth. We have become, in fact, an idea economy. Consider Microsoft Corporation. A relatively small percentage of that company's labor force is involved in actually building products. Rather, a majority of Microsoft employees are attempting to discover new ideas that can be translated into

Does the existence of a Segway involve an invention or an innovation?

computer code that can then be turned into products. The major conclusion that Romer and other new growth theorists draw is this:

Economic growth can continue as long as we keep coming up with new ideas.

The Importance of Human Capital

Knowledge, ideas, and productivity are all tied together. One of the threads is the quality of the labor force. Increases in the productivity of the labor force are a function of increases in human capital, the fourth factor of production discussed in Chapter 2. Recall that human capital consists of the knowledge and skills that people in the workforce acquire through education, on-the-job training, and self-teaching. To increase your own human capital, you have to invest by forgoing income-earning activities while you attend school. Society also has to invest in the form of teachers and education.

According to the new growth theorists, human capital is at least as important as physical capital, particularly when trying to explain international differences in living standards. It is therefore not surprising that one of the most effective ways that developing countries can become developed is by investing in secondary schooling.

One can argue that policy changes that increase human capital will lead to more technological improvements. One of the reasons that concerned citizens, policymakers, and politicians are looking for a change in the U.S. schooling system is that our educational system seems to be falling behind those of other countries. This lag is greatest in science and mathematics—precisely the areas required for developing better technology.

QUICK QUIZ   *See page 238 for the answers. Review concepts from this section in MyEconLab.*

_____ _____ theory argues that the greater the rewards, the more rapid the pace of technology. And greater rewards spur research and development.

The openness of a nation's economy to international _____ seems to correlate with its rate of economic growth.

Invention and innovation are not the same thing. _____ are useless until _____ transforms them into goods and services that people find valuable.

According to _____ _____ theory, economic growth can continue as long as we keep coming up with new ideas.

Increases in _____ capital can lead to greater rates of economic growth. These come about by increased education, on-the-job training, and self-teaching.

Immigration, Property Rights, and Growth

New theories of economic growth have also shed light on two additional factors that play important roles in influencing a nation's rate of growth of per capita real GDP: immigration and property rights.

Population and Immigration as They Affect Economic Growth

There are several ways to view population growth as it affects economic growth. On the one hand, population growth can result in a larger labor force and increases in human capital, which contribute to economic growth. On the other hand, population growth can be seen as a drain on the economy because for any given amount of GDP, more population means lower per capita GDP. According to MIT economist Michael Kremer, the first of these effects is historically more important. His conclusion is that population growth drives technological progress, which then increases economic growth. The theory is simple: If there are 50 percent more people in the United States, there will be 50 percent more geniuses. And with 50 percent more people, the rewards for creativity are commensurately greater. Otherwise stated, the larger the potential market, the greater the incentive to become ingenious.

A larger market also provides an incentive for well-trained people to immigrate, which undoubtedly helps explain why the United States attracts a disproportionate number of top scientists from around the globe.

Does immigration help spur economic growth? Yes, according to the late economist Julian Simon, who pointed out that "every time our system allows in one more immigrant, on average, the economic welfare of American citizens goes up. . . . Additional immigrants, both the legal and the illegal, raise the standard of living of U.S. natives and have little or no negative impact on any occupational or income class." He further argued that immigrants do not displace natives from jobs but rather create jobs through their purchases and by starting new businesses. Immigrants' earning and spending simply expand the economy.

Not all researchers agree with Simon, and few studies have tested the theories he and Kremer have advanced. This area is currently the focus of much research.

Property Rights and Entrepreneurship

If you were in a country where bank accounts and businesses were periodically expropriated by the government, how willing would you be to leave your financial assets in a savings account or to invest in a business? Certainly, you would be less willing than if such actions never occurred. In general, the more securely private property rights (see page 109) are assigned, the more capital accumulation there will be. People will be willing to invest their savings in endeavors that will increase their wealth in future years. This requires that property rights in their wealth be sanctioned and enforced by the government. In fact, some economic historians have attempted to show that it was the development of well-defined private property rights and legal structures that allowed Western Europe to increase its growth rate after many centuries of stagnation. The ability and certainty with which they can reap the gains from investing also determine the extent to which business owners in other countries will invest capital in developing countries. The threat of loss of property rights that hangs over some developing nations probably stands in the way of foreign investments that would allow these nations to develop more rapidly.

The legal structure of a nation is closely tied to the degree with which its citizens use their own entrepreneurial skills. In Chapter 2, we identified entrepreneurship as the fifth factor of production. Entrepreneurs are the risk takers who seek out new ways to do things and create new products. To the extent that entrepreneurs are allowed to capture the rewards from their entrepreneurial activities, they will seek to engage in those activities. In countries where such rewards cannot be captured because of a lack of property rights, there will be less entrepreneurship. Typically, this results in fewer investments and a lower rate of growth. We shall examine the implications this has for policymakers in Chapter 18.

QUICK QUIZ   *See page 238 for the answers. Review concepts from this section in MyEconLab.*

While some economists argue that population growth reduces _____ growth, others contend that the opposite is true. The latter economists consequently believe that immigration should be encouraged rather than discouraged.

Well-defined and protected _____ rights are important for fostering entrepreneurship. In the absence of well-defined _____ rights, individuals have less incentive to take risks, and economic growth rates suffer.

Economic Development

How did developed countries travel paths of growth from extreme poverty to relative riches? That is the essential issue of **development economics,** which is the study of why some countries grow and develop and others do not and of policies that might help developing economies get richer. It is not enough simply to say that people in different countries are different and that is why some countries are rich and some countries are poor. Economists do not deny that different cultures have different work ethics, but they are unwilling to accept such a pat and fatalistic answer.

Look at any world map. About four-fifths of the countries you will see on the map are considered relatively poor. The goal of economists who study development is to help the more than 4 billion people today with low living standards join the more than 2 billion people who have at least moderately high living standards.

Development economics
The study of factors that contribute to the economic growth of a country.

Putting World Poverty into Perspective

Most U.S. residents cannot even begin to understand the reality of poverty in the world today. At least one-half, if not two-thirds, of the world's population lives at subsistence level, with just enough to eat for survival. Indeed, the World Bank estimates that nearly 20 percent of the world's people live on less than $1.50 per day. The official poverty line in the United States is set above the average income of at least half the human beings on the planet. This is not to say that we should ignore domestic problems with the poor and homeless simply because they are living better than many people elsewhere in the world. Rather, it is necessary for us to maintain an appropriate perspective on what are considered problems for this country relative to what are considered problems elsewhere.

The Relationship Between Population Growth and Economic Development

The world's population is growing at the rate of about 2.3 people a second. That amounts to 198,720 a day or 72.5 million a year. Today, there are nearly 7 billion people on earth. By 2050, according to the United Nations, the world's population will be close to leveling off at around 9.1 billion. Panel (a) of Figure 9-7 on page 230 shows population growth. Panel (b) emphasizes an implication of panel (a), which is that virtually all the growth in population is occurring in developing nations. Many developed countries are expected to lose population over the next several decades.

Ever since the Reverend Thomas Robert Malthus wrote *An Essay on the Principle of Population* in 1798, excessive population growth has been a concern. Modern-day Malthusians are able to generate great enthusiasm for the concept that population growth is bad. Over and over, media pundits and a number of scientists tell us that rapid population growth threatens economic development and the quality of life.

FIGURE 9-7

Expected Growth in World Population by 2050

Panel (a) displays the percentages of the world's population residing in the various continents by 2050 and shows projected population growth for these continents and for selected nations. It indicates that Asia and Africa are expected to gain the most in population by the year 2050. Panel (b) indicates that population will increase in developing countries before beginning to level off around 2050, whereas industrially advanced nations will grow very little in population in the first half of this century.

Source: United Nations.

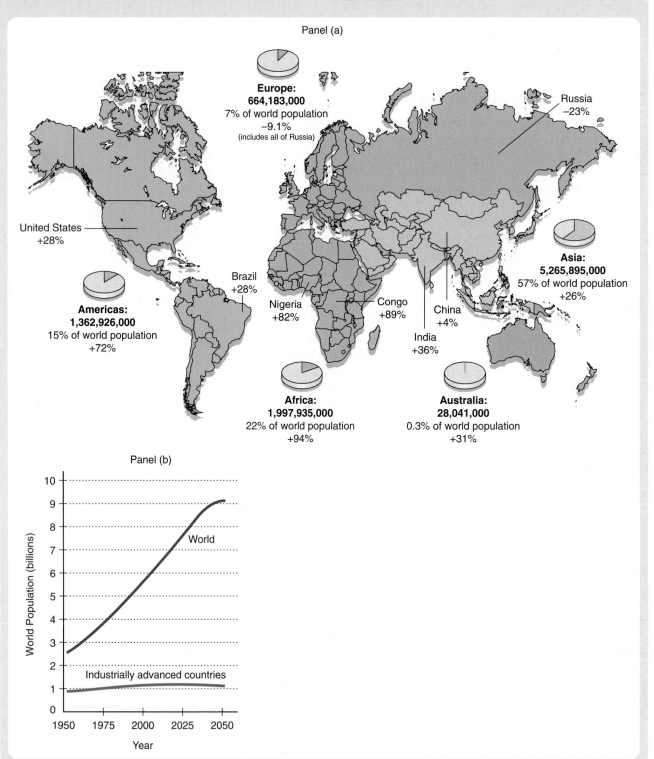

Panel (a)

Europe:
664,183,000
7% of world population
−9.1%
(includes all of Russia)

Russia
−23%

United States
+28%

Asia:
5,265,895,000
57% of world population
+26%

Brazil
+28%

Nigeria
+82%

Congo
+89%

China
+4%

India
+36%

Americas:
1,362,926,000
15% of world population
+72%

Africa:
1,997,935,000
22% of world population
+94%

Australia:
28,041,000
0.3% of world population
+31%

Panel (b)

World

Industrially advanced countries

World Population (billions)

Year

MALTHUS WAS PROVED WRONG Malthus predicted that population would outstrip food supplies. This prediction has never been supported by the facts, according to economist Nicholas Eberstadt of the Harvard Center for Population Studies. As the world's population has grown, so has the world's food supply, measured by calories per person. Furthermore, the price of food, corrected for inflation, has generally been falling for more than a century. That means that the supply of food has been expanding faster than the rise in demand caused by increased population.

GROWTH LEADS TO SMALLER FAMILIES Furthermore, economists have found that as nations become richer, average family size declines. Otherwise stated, the more economic development occurs, the slower the population growth rate becomes. This has certainly been true in Western Europe and in the former Soviet Union, where populations in some countries are actually declining. Predictions of birthrates in developing countries have often turned out to be overstated if those countries experience rapid economic growth. This was the case in Chile, Hong Kong, Mexico, and Taiwan. Recent research on population and economic development has revealed that social and economic modernization has been accompanied by a decline in childbearing significant enough that it might be called a fertility revolution. Modernization reduces infant mortality, which in turn reduces the incentive for couples to have many children to make sure that a certain number survive to adulthood. Modernization also lowers the demand for children for a variety of reasons, not the least being that couples in more developed countries do not need to rely on their children to take care of them in old age.

The Stages of Development: Agriculture to Industry to Services

If we analyze the development of modern rich nations, we find that they went through three stages. First is the agricultural stage, when most of the population is involved in agriculture. Then comes the manufacturing stage, when much of the population becomes involved in the industrialized sector of the economy. And finally there is a shift toward services. That is exactly what happened in the United States: The so-called tertiary, or service, sector of the economy continues to grow, whereas the manufacturing sector (and its share of employment) is declining in relative importance.

Of particular significance, however, is the requirement for early specialization in a nation's comparative advantage (see Chapter 2). The doctrine of comparative advantage is particularly appropriate for the developing countries of the world. If trading is allowed among nations, a country is best off if it produces what it has a comparative advantage in producing and imports the rest (for more details, see Chapter 33). This means that many developing countries should continue to specialize in agricultural production or in labor-intensive manufactured goods.

Keys to Economic Development

One theory of development states that for a country to develop, it must have a large natural resource base. This theory goes on to assert that much of the world is running out of natural resources, thereby limiting economic growth and development. Only the narrowest definition of a natural resource, however, could lead to such an opinion. In broader terms, a natural resource is something occurring in nature that we can use for our own purposes. As emphasized by new growth theory, natural resources therefore include human capital—education and experience. Also, the natural resources that we could define several hundred years ago did not, for example, include hydroelectric power—no one knew that such a natural resource existed or how to bring it into existence.

Natural resources by themselves are not a prerequisite for or a guarantee of economic development, as demonstrated by Japan's extensive development despite a lack

Go to www.econtoday.com/chapter09 to contemplate whether there may be a relationship between inequality and a nation's growth and to visit the home page of the World Bank's Thematic Group on Inequality, Poverty, and Socioeconomic Performance.

of domestic oil resources and by Brazil's slow pace of development in spite of a vast array of natural resources. Resources must be transformed into something usable for either investment or consumption.

Economists have found that four factors seem to be highly related to the pace of economic development:

1. *Establishing a system of property rights.* As noted earlier, if you were in a country where bank accounts and businesses were periodically expropriated by the government, you would be reluctant to leave some of your wealth in a savings account or to invest in a business. Expropriation of private property rarely takes place in developed countries. It has occurred in numerous developing countries, however. For example, private property was once nationalized in Chile and still is for the most part in Cuba. Economists have found that other things being equal, the more secure private property rights are, the more private capital accumulation and economic growth there will be.

2. *Developing an educated population.* Both theoretically and empirically, we know that a more educated workforce aids economic development because it allows individuals to build on the ideas of others. Thus, developing countries can advance more rapidly if they increase investments in education. Or, stated in the negative, economic development is difficult to sustain if a nation allows a sizable portion of its population to remain uneducated. Education allows impoverished young people to acquire skills that enable them to avoid poverty as adults.

3. *Letting "creative destruction" run its course.* The twentieth-century Harvard economist Joseph Schumpeter championed the concept of "creative destruction," through which new businesses ultimately create new jobs and economic growth after first destroying old jobs, old companies, and old industries. Such change is painful and costly, but it is necessary for economic advancement. Nowhere is this more important than in developing countries, where the principle is often ignored. Many governments in developing nations have had a history of supporting current companies and industries by discouraging new technologies and new companies from entering the marketplace. The process of creative destruction has not been allowed to work its magic in these countries.

4. *Limiting protectionism.* Open economies experience faster economic development than economies closed to international trade. Trade encourages individuals and businesses to discover ways to specialize so that they can become more productive and earn higher incomes. Increased productivity and subsequent increases in economic growth are the results. Thus, having fewer trade barriers promotes faster economic development.

Go to www.econtoday.com/chapter09 to link to a World Trade Organization explanation of how free trade promotes greater economic growth and higher employment.

QUICK QUIZ   See page 238 for the answers. Review concepts from this section in MyEconLab.

Although many people believe that population growth hinders economic development, there is little evidence to support that notion. What is clear is that economic development tends to lead to a reduction in the rate of _____ growth.

Historically, there are three stages of economic development: the _____ stage, the _____ stage, and the _____-_____ stage, when a large part of the workforce is employed in providing services.

Although one theory of economic development holds that a sizable natural resource base is the key to a nation's development,

this fails to account for the importance of the human element: The _____ _____ must be capable of using a country's natural resources.

Fundamental factors contributing to the pace of economic development are a well-defined system of _____ _____, training and _____, allowing new generations of companies and industries to _____ older generations, and promoting an open economy by allowing _____ _____.

You Are There An Invention Becomes a Market Innovation—by Accident

Several years ago, Richard Bracke was working as a bodyguard and chef. He happened to meet Robert Cotton and Mark Zickel, who were making hammocks and marketing them on the Web site of Amazon.com. The three men agreed that portable audio products were likely to become popular, and they began developing flat-panel speakers for use with laptop computers. Together, they formed a company called Sonic Impact Technologies, based in San Diego.

In 2003, the three businessmen learned about a small amplifier utilizing a tiny microchip. They decided to power it with two AA batteries and sell it for $39 as a child's beach plaything called the T-Amp. A couple of years later, sales suddenly took off. Adults, it turned out, were buying T-Amps at the $39 price as fast as the company could get them to stores. Some adult customers reported that they were connecting the "toy" amplifiers to $6,000 CD players and

$18,000 speakers. Purely by accident, the T-Amp had become a major innovation in the stereo-amplifier market.

Today, Sonic Impact Technologies sells a line of products that includes speakers for iPods, mini-subwoofers and portable speakers for stereo systems, and speaker bags and cases. Nevertheless, the T-Amp remains a major product, undoubtedly still purchased for use by some children but mainly by adults.

CRITICAL ANALYSIS QUESTIONS

1. How does the experience of Sonic Impact Technologies provide support for the view that invention is only one facet of innovation?

2. How does the T-Amp story bolster the argument that technologies often move relatively slowly from initial invention to widespread use?

Issues and Applications

Governments Get Serious About "Child Support"

CONCEPTS APPLIED

- Economic Growth
- Labor Productivity
- Immigration and Growth

In the United States and the United Kingdom, the current birthrate of slightly less than 2.0 children per woman is just below the level of 2.1 children per woman that would be necessary to maintain the current populations of those countries. In a number of other nations, such as Canada, Estonia, Germany, Italy, Japan, and South Korea, the birthrate has dropped below 1.5 children per woman. Consequently, the populations of these nations are tending to *shrink*—leading their governments to worry that prospects for economic growth likewise are dwindling.

Government-Funded Incentives to Have Babies

In an effort to reverse population downturns, the governments of more than 20 countries are offering compensation to women who bear children. For instance, new mothers receive lump-sum payments in Italy (about $1,500), Australia (just under $4,000), and Russia ($9,200). The French government promises the mother of a third child about $1,125 per month for the child's first year. South Korea's government provides fertility treatments for women seeking to have children, tax breaks and grants to help cover child care, and extra grants for those women who choose to bear several children.

Some national governments offer explicit wage compensation to women who have babies. The Bulgarian government offers 315 days of compensation equal to 90 percent of the average market wage rate, and under many circumstances, the stipend can be extended to two years. Estonia's government pays mothers 100 percent of the average market wage for 15 months, and Lithuania offers 100 percent wage compensation for 6 months followed by a payment of 85 percent of the market wage rate for another 6 months. In Germany, even fathers receive wage compensation for up to two months.

Can the Baby-Subsidy Fad Regenerate Labor Growth?

Both the number of hours that a nation's residents work and the average units of output they produce per hour determine the country's overall labor productivity. Thus, in the long run, increasing population growth could pay off in higher economic growth in countries where governments are rushing to offer child-bearing inducements.

During a single decade or so, however, more babies will not translate into larger, more productive workforces.

Countries with shrinking populations that are seeking to maintain or boost labor growth—and, hence, economic growth rates—in the near term must consider additional options.

Other Options: Human Capital Development and Immigration

For governments of nations with shrinking native-born populations, one alternative way to boost overall labor productivity is to adopt policies that promote greater individual productivity—higher output per existing worker. For instance, in France, Germany, and other European nations with declining populations, national governments have taken tentative steps toward reversing policies that have had the effect of reducing output per worker. Governments in these and other nations have also boosted subsidies aimed at increasing human capital investments. Many subsidies have been aimed explicitly at forms of education, on-the-job training, and self-teaching most likely to yield immediate productivity payoffs.

Another near-term alternative is to boost national labor forces through immigration. Governments of European nations have permitted more immigrants from Africa and the Middle East, where women on average bear about five children. The Japanese, South Korean, and Taiwanese governments have also loosened restrictions on immigration from the rest of Asia, where women bear an average of about three children each.

Over the next decade, policies aimed at raising labor productivity via investments in human capital and greater openness to immigration are more likely than baby subsidies to boost economic growth in nations with shrinking populations. Indeed, it remains to be seen whether offering incentives to women to have more children in order to raise native-born populations will succeed in reenergizing economic growth.

Test your understanding of this chapter by going online to **MyEconLab**.
In the Study Plan for this chapter, select Section N: News.

For Critical Analysis

1. Why is steady population growth, by itself, unable to assure steadily increasing overall economic growth?

2. Why is it at least possible that in some cases allowing more immigration will not necessarily boost economic growth? (Hint: Recall that economic growth is measured as the rate of change in real GDP *per capita.*)

Web Resources

1. For a discussion of recent shifts in global population growth, go to www.econtoday.com/chapter09.

2. To learn about why population growth in much of Eastern Europe has been negative in recent years, go to www.econtoday.com/chapter09.

Research Project

Suppose that you have been appointed to a commission charged with recommending policies for promoting economic growth in a nation experiencing a shrinking native-born population, lagging labor productivity, and stagnant growth in per capita real GDP. Develop a list of three policies, and rank them on the basis of their likely success in boosting long-run economic growth. Briefly defend your ranking.

 Here is what you should know after reading this chapter. **MyEconLab** will help you identify what you know, and where to go when you need to practice.

WHAT YOU SHOULD KNOW		WHERE TO GO TO PRACTICE
Economic Growth The rate of economic growth is the annual rate of change in per capita real GDP. This measure of the rate of growth of a nation's economy takes into account both its growth in overall production of goods and services and the growth rate of its population. It is an average measure that does not account for possible changes in the distribution of income or various welfare costs or benefits that may accompany growth of the economy.	economic growth, 215 KEY FIGURES Figure 9-1, 214 Figure 9-2, 215	• **MyEconLab** Study Plan 9.1 • Audio introduction to Chapter 9 • Animated Figures 9-1, 9-2 • ABC News Video: Economic Growth: How Much, How Fast?
Why Economic Growth Rates Are Important Over long intervals, relatively small differences in the rate of economic growth can accumulate to produce large disparities in per capita incomes. The reason is that like accumulations of interest, economic growth compounds over time. Thus, if a nation's rate of per capita real GDP growth rises by 3 percentage points per year, it will have a level of per capita real GDP that is more than four times higher after 50 years. But a country with a per capita real GDP growth rate 4 percentage points higher per year ends up with per capita real GDP more than seven times higher.	rule of 70, 219	• **MyEconLab** Study Plan 9.1 • Video: Growth Rates and Compound Interest
Why Productivity Increases Are Crucial for Maintaining Economic Growth For a nation with a relatively stable population and a steady rate of capital accumulation, productivity growth emerges as a fundamental factor influencing near-term changes in economic growth. Higher productivity growth unambiguously contributes to greater annual increases in a nation's per capita real GDP.	labor productivity, 220	• **MyEconLab** Study Plan 9.2

(continued)

 (continued)

WHAT YOU SHOULD KNOW		WHERE TO GO TO PRACTICE
The Key Determinants of Economic Growth The fundamental factors contributing to economic growth are growth in a nation's pool of labor, growth of its capital stock, and growth in the productivity of its capital and labor. A key determinant of capital accumulation is a nation's saving rate. Higher saving rates contribute to greater investment and hence increased capital accumulation and economic growth.		• **MyEconLab** Study Plan 9.3 • Video: Saving and Economic Growth
New Growth Theory This is a theory that examines why individuals and businesses conduct research into inventing and developing new technologies and how this process interacts with the rate of economic growth. This theory emphasizes how rewards to technological innovation contribute to higher economic growth rates. A key implication of the theory is that ideas and knowledge are crucial elements of the growth process.	new growth theory, 223 patent, 224 innovation, 225 **KEY FIGURES** Figure 9-5, 224 Figure 9-6, 226	• **MyEconLab** Study Plan 9.4 • Video: The Importance of Human Capital • Animated Figures 9-5, 9-6
Fundamental Factors That Contribute to a Nation's Economic Development Key features shared by nations that attain higher levels of economic development are protection of property rights, significant opportunities for their residents to obtain training and education, policies that permit new companies and industries to replace older ones, and the avoidance of protectionist barriers that hinder international trade.	development economics, 229 **KEY FIGURE** Figure 9-7, 230	• **MyEconLab** Study Plans 9.5, 9.6 • Animated Figure 9-7

Log in to MyEconLab, take a chapter test, and get a personalized Study Plan that tells you which concepts you understand and which ones you need to review. From there, MyEconLab will give you further practice, tutorials, animations, videos, and guided solutions.
Log in to www.myeconlab.com

PROBLEMS

All problems are assignable in **myeconlab** . *Answers to odd-numbered problems appear at the back of the book.*

9-1. The graph shows a production possibilities curve for 2012 and two potential production possibilities curves for 2013, denoted 2013$_A$ and 2013$_B$.

    a. Which of the labeled points corresponds to maximum feasible 2012 production that is more likely to be associated with the curve denoted 2013$_A$?

    b. Which of the labeled points corresponds to maximum feasible 2012 production that is more likely to be associated with the curve denoted 2013$_B$?

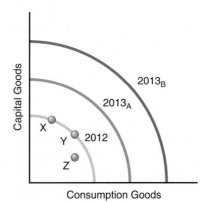

9-2. A nation's capital goods wear out over time, so a portion of its capital goods become unusable every year. Last year, its residents decided to produce no capital goods. It has experienced no growth in its population or in the amounts of other productive resources during the past year. In addition, the nation's technology and resource productivity have remained unchanged during the past year. Will the nation's economic growth rate for the current year be negative, zero, or positive?

9-3. In the situation described in Problem 9-2, suppose that educational improvements during the past year enable the people of this nation to repair all capital goods so that they continue to function as well as new. All other factors are unchanged, however. In light of this single change to the conditions faced in this nation, will the nation's economic growth rate for the current year be negative, zero, or positive?

9-4. Consider the following data. What is the per capita real GDP in each of these countries?

Country	Population (millions)	Real GDP ($ billions)
A	10	55
B	20	60
C	5	70

9-5. Suppose that during the next 10 years, real GDP triples and population doubles in each of the nations in Problem 9-4. What will per capita real GDP be in each country after 10 years have passed?

9-6. Consider the following table displaying annual growth rates for nations X, Y, and Z, each of which entered 2009 with real per capita GDP equal to $20,000:

	Annual Growth Rate (%)			
Country	2009	2010	2011	2012
X	7	1	3	4
Y	4	5	7	9
Z	5	4	3	2

a. Which nation most likely experienced a sizable earthquake in late 2009 that destroyed a significant portion of its stock of capital goods, but was followed by speedy investments in rebuilding the nation's capital stock? What is this nation's per capita real GDP at the end of 2012, rounded to the nearest dollar?

b. Which nation most likely adopted policies in 2009 that encouraged a gradual shift in production from capital goods to consumption goods? What is this nation's per capita real GDP at the end of 2012, rounded to the nearest dollar?

c. Which nation most likely adopted policies in 2009 that encouraged a quick shift in production from consumption goods to capital goods? What is this nation's per capita real GDP at the end of 2012, rounded to the nearest dollar?

9-7. Per capita real GDP grows at a rate of 3 percent in country F and at a rate of 6 percent in country G. Both begin with equal levels of per capita real GDP. Use Table 9-3 on page 218 to determine how much higher per capita real GDP will be in country G after 20 years. How much higher will real GDP be in country G after 40 years?

9-8. Per capita real GDP in country L is three times as high as in country M. The economic growth rate in country M, however, is 8 percent, while country L's economy grows at a rate of 5 percent. Use Table 9-3 on page 218 to determine approximately how many years will pass before per capita real GDP in country M surpasses per capita real GDP in country L.

9-9. Per capita real GDP in country S is only half as great as per capita real GDP in country T. Country T's rate of economic growth is 4 percent. The government of country S, however, enacts policies that achieve a growth rate of 20 percent. Use Table 9-3 on page 218 to determine how long country S must maintain this growth rate before its per capita real GDP surpasses that of country T.

9-10. In 2010, a nation's population was 10 million. Its nominal GDP was $40 billion, and its price index was 100. In 2011, its population had increased to 12 million, its nominal GDP had risen to $57.6 billion, and its price index had increased to 120. What was this nation's economic growth rate during the year?

9-11. Between the start of 2010 and the start of 2011, a country's economic growth rate was 4 percent. Its population did not change during the year, nor did its price level. What was the rate of increase of the country's nominal GDP during this one-year interval?

9-12. In 2010, a nation's population was 10 million, its real GDP was $1.21 billion, and its GDP deflator had a value of 121. By 2011, its population had increased to 12 million, its real GDP had risen to $1.5 billion, and its GDP deflator had a value of 125. What was the percentage change in per capita real GDP between 2010 and 2011?

9-13. A nation's per capita real GDP was $2,000 in 2009, and the nation's population was 5 million in that year. Between 2009 and 2010, the inflation rate in this country was 5 percent, and the nation's annual rate of economic growth was 10 percent. Its population remained unchanged. What was per capita real GDP in 2010? What was the *level* of real GDP in 2010?

9-14. Brazil has a population of about 190 million, with about 140 million over the age of 15. Of these, an estimated 25 percent, or 35 million people, are functionally illiterate. The typical literate individual reads only about two nonacademic books per year, which is less than half the number read by the typical literate U.S. or European resident. Answer the following questions solely from the perspective of new growth theory:

a. Discuss the implications of Brazil's literacy and reading rates for its growth prospects in light of the key tenets of new growth theory.

b. What types of policies might Brazil implement to improve its growth prospects? Explain.

ECONOMICS ON THE NET

Multifactor Productivity and Its Growth Growth in productivity is a key factor determining a nation's overall economic growth.

Title: Bureau of Labor Statistics: Multifactor Productivity Trends

Navigation: Use the link at **www.econtoday.com/ chapter09** to visit the multifactor productivity home page of the Bureau of Labor Statistics.

Application Read the summary, and answer the following questions.

1. What does multifactor productivity measure? Based on your reading of this chapter, how does multifactor productivity relate to the determination of economic growth?

2. Click on *Multifactor Productivity Trends in Manufacturing*, and then click on *Manufacturing Industries: Multifactor Productivity Trends*. According to these data, which industries have exhibited the greatest productivity growth in recent years?

For Group Study and Analysis Divide the class into three groups to examine multifactor productivity data for the private business sector, the private nonfarm business sector, and the manufacturing sector. Have each group identify periods when multifactor productivity growth was particularly fast or slow. Then compare notes. Does it appear to make a big difference which sector one looks at when evaluating periods of greatest and least growth in multifactor productivity?

ANSWERS TO QUICK QUIZZES

p. 220: (i) per capita; (ii) benefits . . . costs; (iii) large

p. 223: (i) capital . . . labor . . . capital . . . labor; (ii) saving . . . save . . . saving

p. 227: (i) New growth; (ii) trade; (iii) Inventions . . . innovation; (iv) new growth; (v) human

p. 229: (i) economic; (ii) property . . . property

p. 232: (i) population; (ii) agricultural . . . manufacturing . . . service-sector; (iii) labor force; (iv) property rights . . . education . . . replace . . . international trade

Real GDP and the Price Level in the Long Run

10

From the 1930s until the early 1960s, the annual rate of U.S. real GDP growth steadily increased, but it generally trended downward in the 1970s and 1980s. During the 1990s, annual real GDP growth recovered somewhat. Nevertheless, during the 2000s there has been yet another decline. What factors determine variations in real GDP growth rates over long periods of time? How are long-run changes in the rate of real GDP growth related to rates of change in the level of prices—that is, the inflation rate? In this chapter, you will learn the answers to these questions.

LEARNING OBJECTIVES

MyEconLab helps you master each objective and study more efficiently. See end of chapter for details.

After reading this chapter, you should be able to:

➤ Understand the concept of long-run aggregate supply

➤ Describe the effect of economic growth on the long-run aggregate supply curve

➤ Explain why the aggregate demand curve slopes downward and list key factors that cause this curve to shift

➤ Discuss the meaning of long-run equilibrium for the economy as a whole

➤ Evaluate why economic growth can cause deflation

➤ Evaluate likely reasons for persistent inflation in recent decades

? DID YOU KNOW THAT between 1920 and 1929—the period known in the United States as the "Roaring Twenties"—the U.S. price level declined? Between 1920 and 1922, the price level fell at an average annual rate of 8.2 percent. From 1923 to 1926, however, the level of prices rose at an annual rate of about 1.4 percent. Then, from 1927 to 1929, the price level fell once more, at an average annual rate of decline equal to 1.1 percent. In the meantime, the average prices of shares of stock in U.S. corporations more than doubled, and real GDP increased.

Why did the United States experience periods of deflation even as the nation experienced economic growth during the 1920s? Why did deflation continue even when economic growth turned negative in the 1930s, a time we now call the Great Depression? To answer these questions, you must learn about factors that influence the long-run stability of the price level.

Output Growth and the Long-Run Aggregate Supply Curve

In Chapter 2, we showed the derivation of the production possibilities curve (PPC). At any point in time, the economy can be inside or on the PPC but never outside it. Along the PPC, a country's resources are fully employed in the production of goods and services, and the sum total of the inflation-adjusted value of all final goods and services produced is the nation's real GDP. Economists refer to the total of all planned production for the entire economy as the **aggregate supply** of real output.

Aggregate supply
The total of all planned production for the economy.

Long-run aggregate supply curve
A vertical line representing the real output of goods and services after full adjustment has occurred. It can also be viewed as representing the real GDP of the economy under conditions of full employment—the full-employment level of real GDP.

The Long-Run Aggregate Supply Curve

Put yourself in a world in which nothing has been changing, year in and year out. The price level has not changed. Technology has not changed. The prices of inputs that firms must purchase have not changed. Labor productivity has not changed. All resources are fully employed, so the economy operates on its production possibilities curve, such as the one depicted in panel (a) of Figure 10-1. This is a world that is fully adjusted and in which people have all the information they are ever going to have about that world. The **long-run aggregate supply curve** (*LRAS*) in this world is some amount of real GDP—say,

FIGURE 10-1

The Production Possibilities Curve and the Economy's Long-Run Aggregate Supply Curve

At a point in time, a nation's base of resources and its technological capabilities define the position of its production possibilities curve (PPC), as shown in panel (a). This defines the real GDP that the nation can produce when resources are fully employed, which determines the position of the long-run aggregate supply curve (*LRAS*) displayed in panel (b). Because people have complete information and input prices adjust fully in the long run, the *LRAS* is vertical.

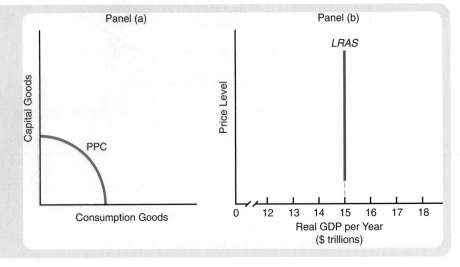

$15 trillion of real GDP—which is the value of the flow of production of final goods and services measured in **base-year dollars.** We can represent long-run aggregate supply by a vertical line at $15 trillion of real GDP. This is what you see in panel (b) of the figure. That curve, labeled *LRAS*, is a vertical line determined by technology and **endowments,** or resources that exist in our economy. It is the full-information and full-adjustment level of real output of goods and services. It is the level of real GDP that will continue being produced year after year, forever, if nothing changes.

Another way of viewing the *LRAS* is to think of it as the full-employment level of real GDP. When the economy reaches full employment along its production possibilities curve, no further adjustments will occur unless a change occurs in the other variables that we are assuming constant and stable. Some economists suggest that the *LRAS* occurs at the level of real GDP consistent with the natural rate of unemployment, the unemployment rate that occurs in an economy with full adjustment in the long run. As we discussed in Chapter 7, many economists like to think of the natural rate of unemployment as consisting of frictional and structural unemployment.

To understand why the *LRAS* is vertical, think about the long run, which is a sufficiently long period that all factors of production and prices, including wages and other input prices, can change. A change in the level of prices of goods and services has no effect on real GDP per year in the long run, because higher prices will be accompanied by comparable changes in input prices. Suppliers will therefore have no incentive to increase or decrease their production of goods and services. Remember that in the long run, everybody has full information, and there is full adjustment to price level changes. (Of course, this is not necessarily true in the short run, as we shall discuss in Chapter 11.)

Base-year dollars
The value of a current sum expressed in terms of prices in a base year.

Endowments
The various resources in an economy, including both physical resources and such human resources as ingenuity and management skills.

Go to **www.econtoday.com/chapter10** to find out how fast wages are adjusting. Click on "Employment Costs," and then on "Employment Cost Index."

Economic Growth and Long-Run Aggregate Supply

In Chapter 9, you learned about the determinants of the growth in per capita real GDP: the annual growth rate of labor, the rate of year-to-year capital accumulation, and the rate of growth of the productivity of labor and capital. As time goes by, population gradually increases, and labor force participation rates may even rise. The capital stock typically grows as businesses add such capital equipment as new information-technology hardware. Furthermore, technology improves. Thus, the economy's production possibilities increase, and the production possibilities curve shifts outward, as shown in panel (a) of Figure 10-2.

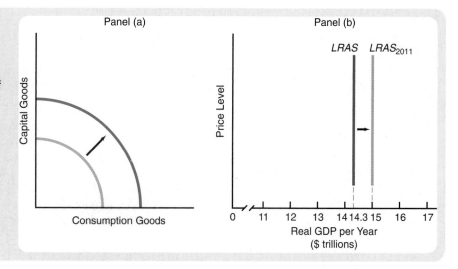

FIGURE 10-2

The Long-Run Aggregate Supply Curve and Shifts in It

In panel (a), we repeat a diagram that we used in Chapter 2, on page 38, to show the meaning of economic growth. Over time, the production possibilities curve shifts outward. In panel (b), we demonstrate the same principle by showing the long-run aggregate supply curve as initially a vertical line at $14.3 trillion of real GDP per year. As our productive abilities increase, the *LRAS* moves outward to *LRAS*$_{2011}$ at $15 trillion.

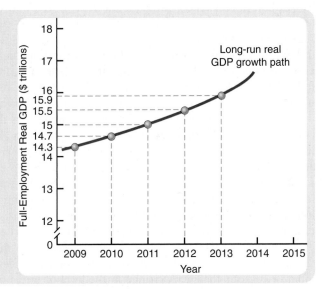

FIGURE 10-3

A Sample Long-Run Growth Path for Real GDP

Year-to-year shifts in the long-run aggregate supply curve yield a long-run trend path for real GDP growth. In this example, from 2011 onward, real GDP grows by a steady 3 percent per year.

The result is economic growth: Aggregate real GDP and per capita real GDP increase. This means that in a growing economy such as ours, the *LRAS* will shift outward to the right, as in panel (b). We have drawn the *LRAS* for the year 2011 to the right of our original *LRAS* of $14.3 trillion of real GDP. We assume that between now and 2011, real GDP increases to $15 trillion, to give us the position of the $LRAS_{2011}$ curve. Thus, it is to the right of today's *LRAS* curve.

We may conclude that in a growing economy, the *LRAS* shifts ever farther to the right over time. If the *LRAS* happened to shift rightward at a constant pace, real GDP would increase at a steady annual rate. As shown in Figure 10-3, this means that real GDP would increase along a long-run, or *trend*, path that is an upward-sloping line. Thus, if the *LRAS* shifts rightward from $14.3 trillion to $15 trillion between now and 2011 and then increases at a steady 3 percent annual rate every year thereafter, in 2012 long-run real GDP will equal $15.5 trillion, in 2013 it will equal $15.9 trillion, and so on.

How is a net outflow of skilled workers threatening to make Germany's long-run real GDP growth path less steeply sloped?

INTERNATIONAL EXAMPLE
Will a "Brain Drain" Flatten Germany's Trend Growth Path?

When a nation loses some of its best-educated workers, it experiences a *brain drain*. A nation undergoing a brain drain experiences an outflow of human capital and hence loses a portion of a key productive resource. As a result, the nation's economic growth slows. Its long-run aggregate supply curve shifts rightward at a slower pace, and its long-run real GDP growth path becomes less steeply sloped.

Germany has been experiencing a brain drain since the early 2000s. In recent years, nearly 150,000 residents, including numerous engineers, physicians, and university professors, have departed from Germany annually. Their departures have left the nation with more than 20,000 open jobs in engineering, 5,000 unfilled positions for physicians, and hundreds of vacant academic posts. An insufficient number of German residents are choosing to be trained in these fields,

INTERNATIONAL EXAMPLE (cont.)

and immigration rules hinder efforts by engineers, physicians, and professors from other countries to move to Germany. Consequently, a net outflow of human capital appears likely to continue. If so, we can predict that Germany's economic growth will probably continue to slow, and a shallower long-run real GDP growth path is likely to result.

FOR CRITICAL ANALYSIS

How is a declining birthrate in Germany likely to affect the nation's long-run real GDP growth path?

QUICK QUIZ *See page 260 for the answers. Review concepts from this section in MyEconLab.*

The **long-run aggregate supply curve,** *LRAS*, is a _____ line determined by amounts of available resources such as labor and capital and by technology and resource productivity. The position of the *LRAS* gives the full-information and full-adjustment level of real GDP.

The _____ rate of unemployment occurs at the long-run level of real GDP given by the position of the *LRAS*.

If labor or capital increases from year to year or if the productivity of either of these resources rises from one year to the next, the *LRAS* shifts _____. In a growing economy, therefore, real GDP gradually _____ over time.

Total Expenditures and Aggregate Demand

In equilibrium, individuals, businesses, and governments purchase all the goods and services produced, valued in trillions of real dollars. As explained in Chapters 7 and 8, GDP is the dollar value of total expenditures on domestically produced final goods and services. Because all expenditures are made by individuals, firms, or governments, the total value of these expenditures must be what these market participants decide it shall be.

The decisions of individuals, managers of firms, and government officials determine the annual dollar value of total expenditures. You can certainly see this in your role as an individual. You decide what the total dollar amount of your expenditures will be in a year. You decide how much you want to spend and how much you want to save. Thus, if we want to know what determines the total value of GDP, the answer is clear: the spending decisions of individuals like you; firms; and local, state, and national governments. In an open economy, we must also include foreign individuals, firms, and governments (foreign residents, for short) that decide to spend their money income in the United States.

Simply stating that the dollar value of total expenditures in this country depends on what individuals, firms, governments, and foreign residents decide to do really doesn't tell us much, though. Two important issues remain:

1. What determines the total amount that individuals, firms, governments, and foreign residents want to spend?

2. What determines the equilibrium price level and the rate of inflation (or deflation)?

The *LRAS* tells us only about the economy's long-run real GDP. To answer these additional questions, we must consider another important concept. This is **aggregate demand,** which is the total of all *planned* real expenditures in the economy.

Because there is a net outflow of graduates and researchers from German universities like this one, what can you predict about Germany's long-run GDP growth path?

Aggregate demand
The total of all planned expenditures in the entire economy.

The Aggregate Demand Curve

Aggregate demand curve
A curve showing planned purchase rates for all final goods and services in the economy at various price levels, all other things held constant.

The **aggregate demand curve**, *AD*, gives the various quantities of all final commodities demanded at various price levels, all other things held constant. Recall the components of GDP that you studied in Chapter 8: consumption spending, investment expenditures, government purchases, and net foreign demand for domestic production. They are all components of aggregate demand. Throughout this chapter and the next, whenever you see the aggregate demand curve, realize that it is a shorthand way of talking about the components of GDP that are measured by government statisticians when they calculate total economic activity each year. In Chapter 12, you will look more closely at the relationship between these components and, in particular, at how consumption spending depends on income.

The aggregate demand curve gives the total amount, measured in base-year dollars, of *real* domestic final goods and services that will be purchased at each price level—everything produced for final use by households, businesses, the government, and foreign residents. It includes iPhones, socks, shoes, medical and legal services, computers, and millions of other goods and services that people buy each year.

A graphical representation of the aggregate demand curve is seen in Figure 10-4. On the horizontal axis, real GDP is measured. For our measure of the price level, we use the GDP price deflator on the vertical axis. The aggregate demand curve is labeled *AD*. If the GDP deflator is 110, aggregate quantity demanded is $15 trillion per year (point *A*). At the price level 115, it is $14 trillion per year (point *B*). At the price level 120, it is $13 trillion per year (point *C*). The higher the price level, the lower the total real amount of final goods and services demanded in the economy, everything else remaining constant, as shown by the arrow along *AD* in Figure 10-4. Conversely, the lower the price level, the higher the total real GDP demanded by the economy, everything else staying constant.

Let's take the year 2009. Estimates based on U.S. Department of Commerce preliminary statistics reveal the following information:

- Nominal GDP was estimated to be $15,045.5 billion.

- The price level as measured by the GDP deflator was about 109.3 (base year is 2005, for which the index equals 100).

- Real GDP (output) was approximately $13,194.6 billion in 2005 dollars.

FIGURE 10-4

The Aggregate Demand Curve

The aggregate demand curve, *AD*, slopes downward. If the price level is 110, we will be at point *A* with $15 trillion of real GDP demanded per year. As the price level increases to 115 and to 120, we move up the aggregate demand curve to points *B* and *C*.

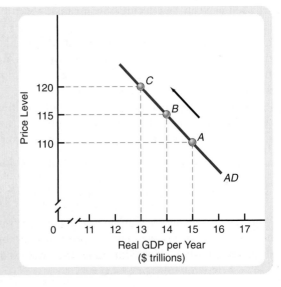

What can we say about 2009? Given the dollar cost of buying goods and services and all of the other factors that go into spending decisions by individuals, firms, governments, and foreign residents, the total amount of planned spending on final goods and services by firms, individuals, governments, and foreign residents was $13,194.6 billion in 2009 (in terms of 2005 dollars).

What Happens When the Price Level Rises?

What if the price level in the economy rose to 160 tomorrow? What would happen to the amount of real goods and services that individuals, firms, governments, and foreigners wish to purchase in the United States? We know from Chapter 3 that when the price of one good or service rises, the quantity of it demanded will fall. But here we are talking about the *price level*—the average price of *all* goods and services in the economy. The answer is still that the total quantities of real goods and services demanded would fall, but the reasons are different. When the price of one good or service goes up, the consumer substitutes other goods and services. For the entire economy, when the price level goes up, the consumer doesn't simply substitute one good for another, for now we are dealing with the demand for *all* goods and services in the nation. There are *economywide* reasons that cause the aggregate demand curve to slope downward. They involve at least three distinct forces: the *real-balance effect*, the *interest rate effect*, and the *open economy effect*.

THE REAL-BALANCE EFFECT A rise in the price level will have an effect on spending. Individuals, firms, governments, and foreign residents carry out transactions using money, a portion of which consists of currency and coins that you have in your pocket (or stashed away) right now. Because people use money to purchase goods and services, the amount of money that people have influences the amount of goods and services they want to buy. For example, if you find a $100 bill on the sidewalk, the amount of money you have will rise. Given your now greater level of money, or cash, balances—currency in this case—you will almost surely increase your spending on goods and services. Similarly, if your pocket is picked while you are at the mall, your desired spending would be affected. For example, if your wallet had $150 in it when it was stolen, the reduction in your cash balances—in this case, currency—would no doubt cause you to reduce your planned expenditures. You would ultimately buy fewer goods and services.

This response is sometimes called the **real-balance effect** (or *wealth effect*) because it relates to the real value of your cash balances. While your *nominal* cash balances may remain the same, any change in the price level will cause a change in the *real* value of those cash balances—hence the real-balance effect on total planned expenditures.

When you think of the real-balance effect, just think of what happens to your real wealth if you have, say, a $100 bill hidden under your mattress. If the price level increases by 5 percent, the purchasing power of that $100 bill drops by 5 percent, so you have become less wealthy. You will reduce your purchases of all goods and services by some small amount.

Real-balance effect
The change in expenditures resulting from a change in the real value of money balances when the price level changes, all other things held constant; also called the *wealth effect*.

THE INTEREST RATE EFFECT There is a more subtle but equally important effect on your desire to spend. A higher price level leaves people with too few money balances. Hence, they try to borrow more (or lend less) to replenish their cash. This drives up interest rates. Higher interest rates raise borrowing costs for consumers and businesses. They will borrow less and consequently spend less. The fact that a higher price level pushes up interest rates and thereby reduces borrowing and spending is known as the **interest rate effect**.

Interest rate effect
One of the reasons that the aggregate demand curve slopes downward: Higher price levels increase the interest rate, which in turn causes businesses and consumers to reduce desired spending due to the higher cost of borrowing.

Higher interest rates make it more costly for people to finance purchases of houses and cars. Higher interest rates also make it less profitable for firms to install new equipment and to erect new office buildings. Whether we are talking about individuals or firms, a rise in the price level will cause higher interest rates, which in turn reduce the amount of goods and services that people are willing to purchase. Therefore, an increase in the price level will tend to reduce total planned expenditures. (The opposite occurs if the price level declines.)

THE OPEN ECONOMY EFFECT: THE SUBSTITUTION OF FOREIGN GOODS   Recall from Chapter 8 that GDP includes net exports—the difference between exports and imports. In an open economy, we buy imports from other countries and ultimately pay for them through the foreign exchange market. The same is true for foreign residents who purchase our goods (exports). Given any set of exchange rates between the U.S. dollar and other currencies, an increase in the price level in the United States makes U.S. goods more expensive relative to foreign goods. Foreign residents have downward-sloping demand curves for U.S. goods. When the relative price of U.S. goods goes up, foreign residents buy fewer U.S. goods and more of their own. At home, relatively cheaper prices for foreign goods cause U.S. residents to want to buy more foreign goods instead of domestically produced goods. Thus, when the domestic price level rises, the result is a fall in exports and a rise in imports. That means that a price level increase tends to reduce net exports, thereby reducing the amount of real goods and services purchased in the United States. This is known as the **open economy effect.**

Open economy effect
One of the reasons that the aggregate demand curve slopes downward: Higher price levels result in foreign residents desiring to buy fewer U.S.-made goods, while U.S. residents now desire more foreign-made goods, thereby reducing net exports. This is equivalent to a reduction in the amount of real goods and services purchased in the United States.

What Happens When the Price Level Falls?

What about the reverse? Suppose now that the GDP deflator falls to 100 from an initial level of 120. You should be able to trace the three effects on desired purchases of goods and services. Specifically, how do the real-balance, interest rate, and open economy effects cause people to want to buy more? You should come to the conclusion that the lower the price level, the greater the total planned spending on goods and services.

The aggregate demand curve, *AD*, shows the quantity of aggregate output that will be demanded at alternative price levels. It is downward sloping, just like the demand curve for individual goods. The higher the price level, the lower the real amount of total planned expenditures, and vice versa.

Demand for All Goods and Services versus Demand for a Single Good or Service

Even though the aggregate demand curve, *AD*, in Figure 10-4 on page 244 looks similar to the one for individual demand, *D*, for a single good or service that you encountered in Chapters 3 and 4, the two are not the same. When we derive the aggregate demand curve, we are looking at the entire economic system. The aggregate demand curve, *AD*, differs from an individual demand curve, *D*, because we are looking at total planned expenditures on *all* goods and services when we construct *AD*.

Shifts in the Aggregate Demand Curve

In Chapter 3, you learned that any time a nonprice determinant of demand changes, the demand curve will shift inward to the left or outward to the right. The same analysis holds for the aggregate demand curve, except we are now talking about the non-price-level determinants of aggregate demand. So, when we ask the question, "What determines the position of the aggregate demand curve?" the fundamental proposition is as follows:

*Any non-price-level change that increases aggregate spending (on domestic goods) shifts **AD** to the right. Any non-price-level change that decreases aggregate spending (on domestic goods) shifts **AD** to the left.*

The list of potential determinants of the position of the aggregate demand curve is long. Some of the most important "curve shifters" for aggregate demand are presented in Table 10-1.

TABLE 10-1

Determinants of Aggregate Demand

Aggregate demand consists of the demand for domestically produced consumption goods, investment goods, government purchases, and net exports. Consequently, any change in total planned spending on any one of these components of real GDP will cause a change in aggregate demand. Some possibilities are listed here.

Changes That Cause an Increase in Aggregate Demand	Changes That Cause a Decrease in Aggregate Demand
An increase in the amount of money in circulation	A decrease in the amount of money in circulation
Increased security about jobs and future income	Decreased security about jobs and future income
Improvements in economic conditions in other countries	Declines in economic conditions in other countries
A reduction in real interest rates (nominal interest rates corrected for inflation) not due to price level changes	A rise in real interest rates (nominal interest rates corrected for inflation) not due to price level changes
Tax decreases	Tax increases
A drop in the foreign exchange value of the dollar	A rise in the foreign exchange value of the dollar

---

QUICK QUIZ   *See page 260 for the answers. Review concepts from this section in MyEconLab.*

Aggregate demand is the total of all planned _____ in the economy, and **aggregate supply** is the total of all planned _____ in the economy. The aggregate demand curve shows the various quantities of total planned _____ on final goods and services at various price levels; it is downward sloping.

There are three reasons why the aggregate demand curve is downward sloping: the _____ - _____ effect, the _____ _____ effect, and the _____ _____ effect.

The _____ - _____ effect occurs because price level changes alter the real value of cash balances, thereby causing people to desire to spend more or less, depending on whether the price level decreases or increases.

The _____ _____ effect is caused by interest rate changes that mimic price level changes. At higher interest rates, people seek to buy _____ houses and cars, and at lower interest rates, they seek to buy _____ .

The **open economy effect** occurs because of a shift away from expenditures on _____ goods and a shift toward expenditures on _____ goods when the domestic price level increases.

Long-Run Equilibrium and the Price Level

As noted in Chapter 3, equilibrium occurs where the demand and supply curves intersect. The same is true for the economy as a whole, as shown in Figure 10-5: The equilibrium price level occurs at the point where the aggregate demand curve *(AD)* crosses the long-run aggregate supply curve *(LRAS)*. At this equilibrium price level of 120, the total of all planned real expenditures for the entire economy is equal to actual real GDP produced by firms after all adjustments have taken place. Thus, the equilibrium depicted in Figure 10-5 is the economy's *long-run equilibrium.*

The Long-Run Equilibrium Price Level

Note in Figure 10-5 that if the price level were to increase to 140, actual real GDP would exceed total planned real expenditures. Inventories of unsold goods would begin to accumulate, and firms would stand ready to offer more services than people wish to purchase. As a result, the price level would tend to fall.

In contrast, if the price level were 100, then total planned real expenditures by individuals, businesses, and the government would exceed actual real GDP. Inventories of unsold goods would begin to be depleted. The price level would rise toward 120, and higher prices would encourage firms to expand production and replenish inventories of goods available for sale.

The Effects of Economic Growth on the Price Level

We now have a basic theory of how real GDP and the price level are determined in the long run when all of a nation's resources can change over time and all input prices can adjust fully to changes in the overall level of prices of goods and services that firms produce. Let's begin by evaluating the effects of economic growth on the nation's price level.

ECONOMIC GROWTH AND SECULAR DEFLATION Take a look at panel (a) of Figure 10-6, which shows what happens, other things being equal, when the *LRAS* shifts rightward over time. If the economy were to grow steadily during, say, a 10-year

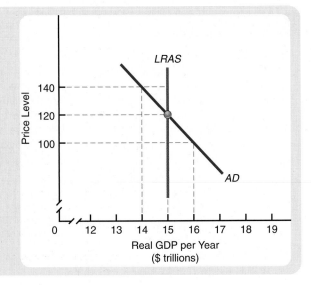

FIGURE 10-5

Long-Run Economywide Equilibrium

For the economy as a whole, long-run equilibrium occurs at the price level where the aggregate demand curve crosses the long-run aggregate supply curve. At this long-run equilibrium price level, which is 120 in the diagram, total planned real expenditures equal real GDP at full employment, which in our example is a real GDP of $15 trillion.

FIGURE 10-6

Secular Deflation versus Long-Run Price Stability in a Growing Economy

Panel (a) illustrates what happens when economic growth occurs without a corresponding increase in aggregate demand. The result is a decline in the price level over time, known as *secular deflation*. Panel (b) shows that, in principle, secular deflation can be eliminated if the aggregate demand curve shifts rightward at the same pace that the long-run aggregate supply curve shifts to the right.

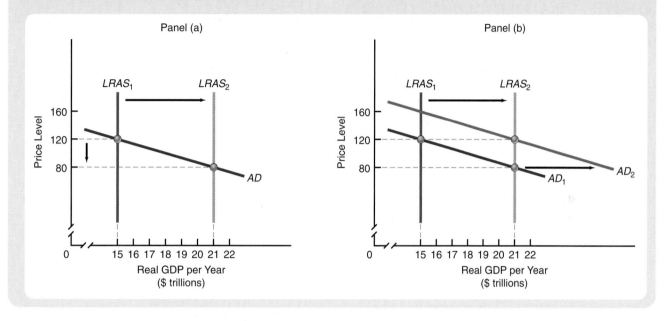

interval, the long-run aggregate supply schedule would shift to the right, from $LRAS_1$ to $LRAS_2$. In panel (a), this results in a downward movement along the aggregate demand schedule. The equilibrium price level falls, from 120 to 80.

Thus, if all factors that affect total planned real expenditures are unchanged, so that the aggregate demand curve does not noticeably move during the 10-year period of real GDP growth, the growing economy in the example would experience deflation. This is known as **secular deflation,** or a persistently declining price level resulting from economic growth in the presence of relatively unchanged aggregate demand.

SECULAR DEFLATION IN THE UNITED STATES In the United States, between 1872 and 1894, the price of bricks fell by 50 percent, the price of sugar by 67 percent, the price of wheat by 69 percent, the price of nails by 70 percent, and the price of copper by nearly 75 percent. Founders of a late-nineteenth-century political movement called *populism* offered a proposal for ending deflation: They wanted the government to issue new money backed by silver. As noted in Table 10-1 on page 247, an increase in the quantity of money in circulation causes the aggregate demand curve to shift to the right. It is clear from panel (b) of Figure 10-6 that the increase in the quantity of money would indeed have pushed the price level back upward, because the AD curve would shift from AD_1 to AD_2.

Nevertheless, money growth remained low for several more years. Not until the early twentieth century would the United States put an end to secular deflation, namely, by creating a new monetary system.

Secular deflation
A persistent decline in prices resulting from economic growth in the presence of stable aggregate demand.

Go to **www.econtoday.com/chapter10** to learn about how the price level has changed during recent years. Then click on "Gross Domestic Product and Components" (for GDP deflators) or "Consumer Price Indexes."

In what country is a warming climate boosting the pace at which the long-run aggregate supply curve is shifting rightward?

INTERNATIONAL EXAMPLE
For Greenland, a Warming Climate Is Good Economic News

Greenland is the world's largest island by surface area, but its population is only about 60,000. The island nation is located at the meeting point of the Atlantic and Arctic oceans. Greenland owes its name to the fact that when it was discovered in the thirteenth century, the Medieval Warm Period was in progress, so birch trees, grass, and willows lined its shores. Global temperatures declined slightly in later centuries, and today more than 80 percent of the country is covered with ice. During the past 30 years, however, the nation's average temperature has risen by 2.7 degrees Fahrenheit. Some climatologists project that Greenland's average temperature could rise by more than 10 addi-

tional degrees by the end of this century. Warmer days allow farmers to take advantage of the extended sunlight and raise more crops and animals, and fishermen have begun catching large numbers of warm-water cod that previously had been absent from the region. Thus, the general warming trend has boosted Greenland's productive capabilities and shifted its long-run aggregate supply curve rightward.

FOR CRITICAL ANALYSIS
If growth of aggregate demand in Greenland were to fail to keep pace with the climate-induced increase in long-run aggregate supply, what would happen to the nation's price level?

Causes of Inflation

Of course, so far during your lifetime, deflation has not been a problem in the United States. Instead, what you have experienced is inflation. Figure 10-7 shows annual U.S. inflation rates for the past few decades. Clearly, inflation rates have been variable. The other obvious fact, however, is that inflation rates have been consistently *positive*. The price level in the United States has *risen* almost every year. For today's United States, secular deflation has not been a big political issue. If anything, it is secular *inflation* that has plagued the nation.

FIGURE 10-7

Inflation Rates in the United States

U.S. inflation rates rose considerably during the 1970s but declined to lower levels since the 1980s. Nevertheless, the United States has experienced inflation every year since 1959.

Sources: *Economic Report of the President; Economic Indicators*, various issues.

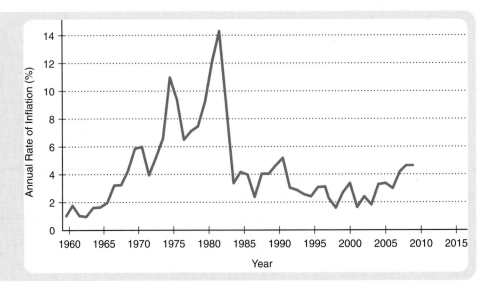

Supply-Side Inflation?

What causes such persistent inflation? The model of aggregate demand and long-run aggregate supply provides two possible explanations for inflation. One potential rationale is depicted in panel (a) of Figure 10-8. This panel shows a rise in the price level caused by a *decline in long-run aggregate supply.* Hence, one possible reason for persistent inflation would be continual reductions in economywide production.

A leftward shift in the aggregate supply schedule could be caused by several factors, such as reductions in labor force participation, higher marginal tax rates on wages, or the provision of government benefits that give households incentives *not* to supply labor services to firms. Tax rates and government benefits have increased during recent decades, but so has the U.S. population. The significant overall rise in real GDP that has taken place during the past few decades tells us that population growth and productivity gains undoubtedly have dominated other factors. In fact, the aggregate supply schedule has actually shifted *rightward,* not leftward, over time. Consequently, this supply-side explanation for persistent inflation *cannot* be the correct explanation.

How has global warming changed the position of Greenland's long-run aggregate supply curve?

Demand-Side Inflation

This leaves only one other explanation for the persistent inflation that the United States has experienced in recent decades. This explanation is depicted in panel (b) of Figure 10-8. If aggregate demand increases for a given level of long-run aggregate supply, the price level must increase. The reason is that at an initial price level such as 120, people desire to purchase more goods and services than firms are willing and able to produce given currently available resources and technology. As a result, the rise in

You Are There

To contemplate what life is like in a country experiencing a very high rate of inflation, read **Another Day's Battle with Inflation in Zimbabwe,** on pages 253 and 254.

FIGURE 10-8

Explaining Persistent Inflation

As shown in panel (a), it is possible for a decline in long-run aggregate supply to cause a rise in the price level. Long-run aggregate supply *increases* in a growing economy, however, so this cannot explain the observation of persistent U.S. inflation. Panel (b) provides the actual explanation of persistent inflation in the United States and most other nations today, which is that increases in aggregate demand push up the long-run equilibrium price level. Thus, it is possible to explain persistent inflation if the aggregate demand curve shifts rightward at a faster pace than the long-run aggregate supply curve.

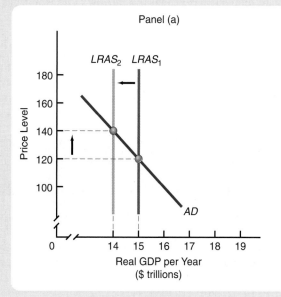

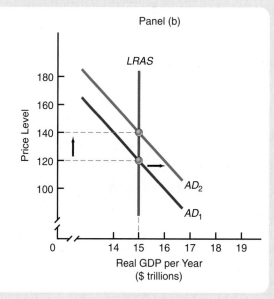

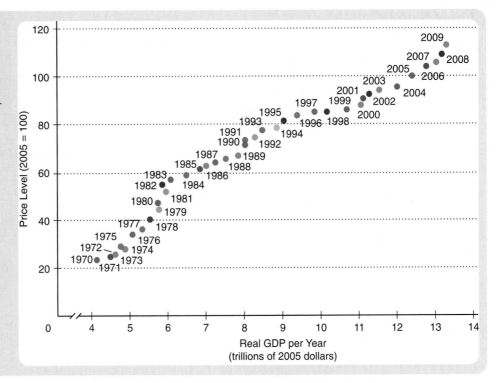

FIGURE 10-9

Real GDP and the Price Level in the United States, 1970 to the Present

This figure shows the points where aggregate demand and aggregate supply have intersected each year from 1970 to the present. The United States has experienced economic growth over this period, but not without inflation.

Sources: Economic Report of the President; Economic Indicators, various issues; author's estimates.

aggregate demand leads only to a general rise in the price level, such as the increase to a value of 140 depicted in the figure.

From a long-run perspective, we are left with only one possibility: Persistent inflation in a growing economy is possible only if the aggregate demand curve shifts rightward over time at a faster pace than the rightward progression of the long-run aggregate supply curve. Thus, in contrast to the experience of people who lived in the latter portion of the nineteenth century, when aggregate demand grew too slowly relative to aggregate supply to maintain price stability, your grandparents, parents, and you have lived in times when aggregate demand has grown too *speedily*. The result has been a continual upward drift in the price level, or long-term inflation.

Figure 10-9 shows that U.S. real GDP has grown in most years since 1970. Nevertheless, this growth has been accompanied by higher prices every single year.

Figure 10-9 indicates a steady but generally restrained upward drift in the price level over time. Thus, annual rates of inflation have been positive but have been relatively low. Is persistent but low inflation benign in its effects on the economy, or can even small rates of inflation have a negative impact on real GDP?

EXAMPLE
Does Sustained Low Inflation Depress Real GDP?

Economists agree that inflation imposes two fundamental types of costs that can reduce real GDP. First, because unexpected inflation reduces real rates of return on financial assets, people have an incentive to divert resources away from producing goods and services to more carefully managing their financial assets. Second, inflation hinders efforts to distinguish temporary variations in prices of goods and services from permanent price changes, which

EXAMPLE (cont.)

complicates firms' efforts to determine profitable rates of production of goods and services.

These resource costs of inflation are naturally larger at higher inflation rates. Most studies show that negative effects on real GDP are most significant at annual inflation rates above 15 percent. They also indicate that even low sustained inflation can depress real GDP. Nevertheless, most research has concluded that the currently low rates of inflation reduce U.S. real GDP by no more than $500 million per year—when total real GDP exceeds $13 *trillion* per year.

Some recent estimates, however, take into account a third cost of inflation. Several forms of taxation, such as the federal government's alternative minimum tax, are not indexed to

inflation. Thus, sustained low inflation eventually pushes more and more people into higher tax brackets. As their marginal tax rates increase, people cut back on productive activities. Estimates that take into account this supplemental effect of inflation suggest that each additional percentage point of annual inflation depresses annual real GDP by as much as 0.5 to 1.0 percent, which amounts to as much as tens of *billions* of base-year dollars per year.

FOR CRITICAL ANALYSIS

What does the government have to gain from failing to index its taxes to inflation?

QUICK QUIZ   *See page 260 for the answers. Review concepts from this section in MyEconLab.*

When the economy is in long-run equilibrium, the price level adjusts to equate total planned real _____ by individuals, businesses, and the government with total planned _____ by firms.

Economic growth causes the long-run aggregate supply schedule to shift _____ over time. If the position of the aggregate demand curve does not change, the long-run

equilibrium price level tends to _____, and there is **secular deflation.**

Because the U.S. economy has grown in recent decades, the persistent inflation during those years has been caused by the aggregate demand curve shifting _____ at a faster pace than the long-run aggregate supply curve.

 # You Are There Another Day's Battle with Inflation in Zimbabwe

Ayina Musoni and her daughter and two grandchildren share a house in Harare, Zimbabwe, with three lodgers who pay weekly rent totaling 3 million Zimbabwean dollars. In light of her high costs of equipping the house with basic items, she is raising the rent she charges her lodgers. At the grocery this morning, she had to pay nearly 150,000 Zimbabwean dollars to purchase one roll of toilet paper. Thus, one two-ply sheet of toilet paper cost almost 500 Zimbabwean dollars, which is the value of the lowest-denomination currency note now issued in Zimbabwe. Musoni anticipates that within three months the price will be about twice as high, because Zimbabwe's price level has been doubling four times per year. At this time, the nation's inflation rate is nearly 1,000 percent per year.

To an economist, one key factor contributing to Zimbabwe's bout with inflation is apparent from just a glance at people as they shop. Instead of carrying wallets or purses, shoppers carry bags of cash. There is so much paper money in circulation that instead of making transactions using individual currency bills, people deal in currency "bricks"—stacks of 10 million Zimbabwean dollars. And Zimbabwe's government continues to churn out more money into circulation, thereby generating still more inflation.

During her morning trip to the grocery, Musoni noticed that her cash bag was beginning to run low on "bricks." She sighs as she contemplates the lengthy line she will face at the cash machine at her bank this afternoon. It takes a long

You Are There (cont.)

time for the machine to discharge the daily maximum of 250,000 Zimbabwean dollars that she is allowed to withdraw from her bank account.

CRITICAL ANALYSIS QUESTIONS

1. In Zimbabwe, which curve has been shifting rapidly rightward—the *AD* curve or the *LRAS* curve?

2. Can the rapid pace at which new money is being placed into circulation in Zimbabwe indirectly help to explain why the nation's real GDP has also been steadily declining in recent years? (Hint: Can people produce as many goods and services while waiting in lines to obtain cash?)

Is U.S. Long-Run Real GDP Growth Declining?

Issues and Applications

CONCEPTS APPLIED

- Aggregate Supply
- Long-Run Aggregate Supply
- Long-Run Aggregate Supply Curve

Since the 1930s, U.S. real GDP has increased in all but a few years. This implies that the long-run growth path for real GDP has sloped upward. The steepness of the nation's long-run real GDP growth path depends on the pace at which the total of all planned production for the economy, or aggregate supply, rises under conditions of full employment. To gauge the speed of growth of long-run aggregate supply, economists and policymakers utilize a concept known as *potential real GDP,* which is a concrete measure of the position of the long-run aggregate supply curve. The rate at which potential real GDP increases each year, or the potential annual rate of real GDP growth, indicates how fast the long-run aggregate supply curve shifts rightward over time.

Estimated U.S. Potential Real GDP Growth Rates

To estimate the potential annual rate of real GDP growth, economists must develop projections of long-run growth paths for three key factors: the capital stock, labor employment, and productivity of labor and capital. Based on such projections, most economists agree that potential real GDP growth in the United States rose from about 3.5 percent per year during the 1930s and 1940s to just above 4 percent in the early 1960s. This upsurge in growth followed an unprecedented wave of innovations—the development and use of new products and novel production techniques—that came on the heels of major inventions during the 1930s and 1940s. As a consequence, U.S. long-run aggregate supply increased during the 1950s and 1960s.

Most estimates indicate that from the early 1960s to the early 1990s, potential annual rates of growth of real GDP steadily declined to somewhere between 2.8 and 2.9 percent. The main factors driving this decline were a reduction in the long-run rate of growth in investment and a diminished long-run rate of productivity growth.

Of course, between the 1980s and 1990s, rapid innovations in the utilization of computer and communications technologies occurred. To some extent, these developments may help explain why the estimated annual rate of potential U.S. real GDP growth rose sharply during the 1990s, to around 3.1 or 3.2 percent. Indeed, during those years some economists suggested that long-run growth of capital investment and long-run productivity growth might eventually rise closer to the levels observed in the 1950s and 1960s. A few observers even suggested that the United States might be on the cusp of a "golden age" of growth.

Lower Potential Real GDP Growth in the 2000s

Since 2000, however, estimated potential annual rates of U.S. real GDP growth have been steadily declining once again. Long-run productivity growth appears to have held steady. Long-run growth in measured capital investment has tapered off, however, and returned to the levels observed during the 1980s.

In addition, a new factor has pushed down potential real GDP growth during the 2000s. The U.S. labor force participation rate has trended downward, reducing the growth of labor employment. According to most estimates, the current potential real GDP growth rate is between 2.5 and 2.7 percent—the lowest for the United States since the 1920s. Thus, these estimates indicate that the U.S. long-run aggregate supply curve is currently shifting rightward at the slowest pace in more than 80 years.

Test your understanding of this chapter by going online to **MyEconLab.** In the Study Plan for this chapter, select Section N: News.

For Critical Analysis

1. If the rate at which the long-run aggregate supply curve shifts rightward decreases but aggregate demand continues increasing at the same rate, what must happen to the rate of change in the long-run equilibrium price level?

2. Could your answer to Question 1 assist in explaining why the average annual U.S. inflation rate has been higher in the 2000s than in the 1990s? Why or why not?

Web Resources

1. To learn how the U.S. Congressional Budget Office estimates potential U.S. real GDP growth, go to www.econtoday.com/chapter10.

2. For a discussion of the difficulties economists confront in estimating the potential growth of real GDP, use the link available at www.econtoday.com/chapter10.

Research Project

Explain how it might be possible for the estimated annual rate of U.S. potential real GDP growth to increase even if projections indicate that the growth of labor employment and productivity growth are both likely to decline over time. In what sense is it true that estimates of U.S. potential real GDP growth are based on other estimates?

Here is what you should know after reading this chapter. **MyEconLab** will help you identify what you know, and where to go when you need to practice.

WHAT YOU SHOULD KNOW		WHERE TO GO TO PRACTICE
Long-Run Aggregate Supply The long-run aggregate supply curve is vertical at the amount of real GDP that firms plan to produce when they have full information and when complete adjustment of input prices to any changes in output prices has taken place. This is the full-employment level of real GDP, or the economywide output level at which the natural rate of unemployment—the sum of frictional and structural unemployment as a percentage of the labor force—occurs.	aggregate supply, 240 long-run aggregate supply curve, 240 base-year dollars, 241 endowments, 241 **KEY FIGURE** Figure 10-1, 240	• **MyEconLab** Study Plan 10.1 • Audio introduction to Chapter 10 • Video: The Long-Run Aggregate Supply Curve • Animated Figure 10-1
Economic Growth and the Long-Run Aggregate Supply Curve Economic growth is an expansion of a country's production possibilities. Thus, the production possibilities curve shifts rightward when the economy grows, and so does the nation's long-run aggregate supply curve. In a growing economy, the changes in full-employment real GDP defined by the shifting long-run aggregate supply curve define the nation's long-run, or trend, growth path.	**KEY FIGURES** Figure 10-2, 241 Figure 10-3, 242	• **MyEconLab** Study Plan 10.1 • Video: The Long-Run Aggregate Supply Curve • Animated Figures 10-2, 10-3
Why the Aggregate Demand Curve Slopes Downward and Factors That Cause It to Shift A rise in the price level reduces the real value of cash balances in the hands of the public, which induces people to cut back on planned spending. This is the real-balance effect. In addition, higher interest rates typically accompany increases in the price level, and this interest rate effect induces people to cut back on borrowing and, consequently, spending. Finally, a rise in the price level at home causes domestic goods to be more expensive relative to foreign goods, so there is a fall in exports and a rise in imports, both of which cause domestic planned expenditures to fall. These three factors together account for the downward slope of the aggregate demand curve. A shift in the aggregate demand curve results from a change in total planned real expenditures at any given price level.	aggregate demand, 243 aggregate demand curve, 244 real-balance effect, 245 interest rate effect, 245 open economy effect, 246 **KEY FIGURE** Figure 10-4, 244	• **MyEconLab** Study Plans 10.2, 10.3 • Video: The Aggregate Demand Curve and What Happens When the Price Level Rises • Video: Shifts in the Aggregate Demand Curve • Animated Figure 10-4

(continued)

 *(continued)*

WHAT YOU SHOULD KNOW		WHERE TO GO TO PRACTICE

Long-Run Equilibrium for the Economy In a long-run economywide equilibrium, the price level adjusts until total planned real expenditures equal actual real GDP. Thus, the long-run equilibrium price level is determined at the point where the aggregate demand curve intersects the long-run aggregate supply curve. If the price level is below its long-run equilibrium value, total planned real expenditures exceed actual real GDP, and the level of prices of goods and services will rise back toward the long-run equilibrium price level. In contrast, if the price level is above its long-run equilibrium value, actual real GDP is greater than total planned real expenditures, and the price level declines in the direction of the long-run equilibrium price level.

KEY FIGURE
Figure 10-5, 248

- **MyEconLab** Study Plan 10.4
- Animated Figure 10-5

Why Economic Growth Can Cause Deflation If the aggregate demand curve is stationary during a period of economic growth, the long-run aggregate supply curve shifts rightward along the aggregate demand curve. The long-run equilibrium price level falls, so there is deflation. Historically, economic growth has in this way generated secular deflation, or relatively long periods of declining prices.

secular deflation, 249

KEY FIGURE
Figure 10-6, 249

- **MyEconLab** Study Plan 10.4
- Animated Figure 10-6

Likely Reasons for Recent Persistent Inflation One event that can induce inflation is a decline in long-run aggregate supply, because this causes the long-run aggregate supply curve to shift leftward. In a growing economy, however, the long-run aggregate supply curve generally shifts rightward. This indicates that a much more likely cause of persistent inflation is a pace of aggregate demand growth that exceeds the pace at which long-run aggregate supply increases.

KEY FIGURES
Figure 10-7, 250
Figure 10-8, 251

- **MyEconLab** Study Plan 10.5
- Animated Figures 10-7, 10-8

Log in to MyEconLab, take a chapter test, and get a personalized Study Plan that tells you which concepts you understand and which ones you need to review. From there, MyEconLab will give you further practice, tutorials, animations, videos, and guided solutions.
Log in to www.myeconlab.com

PROBLEMS

All problems are assignable in **myeconlab**. *Answers to odd-numbered problems appear at the back of the book.*

10-1. Many economists view the natural rate of unemployment as the level observed when real GDP is given by the position of the long-run aggregate supply curve. How can there be positive unemployment in this situation?

10-2. Suppose that the long-run aggregate supply curve is positioned at a real GDP level of $15 trillion in base-year dollars, and the long-run equilibrium price level (in index number form) is 115. What is the full-employment level of *nominal* GDP?

10-3. Continuing from Problem 10-2, suppose that the full-employment level of *nominal* GDP in the following year rises to $17.7 trillion. The long-run equilibrium price level, however, remains unchanged. By how much (in real dollars) has the long-run aggregate supply curve shifted to the right in the following year? By how much, if any, has the aggregate demand curve shifted to the right? (Hint: The equilibrium price level can stay the same only if *LRAS* and *AD* shift rightward by the same amount.)

10-4. Suppose that the position of a nation's long-run aggregate supply curve has not changed, but its long-run equilibrium price level has increased. Which of the following factors might account for this event?

  a. A rise in the value of the domestic currency relative to other world currencies

  b. An increase in the quantity of money in circulation

  c. An increase in the labor force participation rate

  d. A decrease in taxes

  e. A rise in real incomes of countries that are key trading partners of this nation

  f. Increased long-run economic growth

10-5. Suppose that during a given year, the quantity of U.S. real GDP that can be produced in the long run rises from $14.9 trillion to $15.0 trillion, measured in base-year dollars. During the year, no change occurs in the various factors that influence aggregate demand. What will happen to the U.S. long-run equilibrium price level during this particular year?

10-6. Assume that the position of a nation's aggregate demand curve has not changed, but the long-run equilibrium price level has declined. Other things being equal, which of the following factors might account for this event?

  a. An increase in labor productivity

  b. A decrease in the capital stock

  c. A decrease in the quantity of money in circulation

  d. The discovery of new mineral resources used to produce various goods

  e. A technological improvement

10-7. Suppose that there is a sudden rise in the price level. What will happen to economywide planned spending on purchases of goods and services? Why?

10-8. Assume that the economy is in long-run equilibrium with complete information and that input prices adjust rapidly to changes in the prices of goods and services. If there is a sudden rise in the price level induced by an increase in aggregate demand, what happens to real GDP?

10-9. Consider the accompanying diagram when answering the questions that follow.

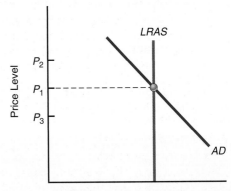

Real GDP per Year (base-year dollars)

  a. Suppose that the current price level is P_2. Explain why the price level will decline toward P_1.

  b. Suppose that the current price level is P_3. Explain why the price level will rise toward P_1.

10-10. Explain whether each of the following events would cause a movement along or a shift in the position of the *LRAS* curve, other things being equal. In each case, explain the direction of the movement along the curve or shift in its position.

a. Last year, businesses invested in new capital equipment, so this year the nation's capital stock is higher than it was last year.

b. There has been an 8 percent increase in the quantity of money in circulation that has shifted the *AD* curve.

c. A hurricane of unprecedented strength has damaged oil rigs, factories, and ports all along the nation's coast.

d. Inflation has occurred during the past year as a result of rightward shifts of the *AD* curve.

10-11. Explain whether each of the following events would cause a movement along or a shift in the position of the *AD* curve, other things being equal. In each case, explain the direction of the movement along the curve or shift in its position.

a. Deflation has occurred during the past year.

b. Real GDP levels of all the nation's major trading partners have declined.

c. There has been a decline in the foreign exchange value of the nation's currency.

d. The price level has increased this year.

10-12. This year, a nation's long-run equilibrium real GDP and price level both increased. Which of the following combinations of factors might simultaneously account for *both* occurrences?

a. An isolated earthquake at the beginning of the year destroyed part of the nation's capital stock, and the nation's government significantly reduced its purchases of goods and services.

b. There was a minor technological improvement at the end of the previous year, and the quantity of money in circulation rose significantly during the year.

c. Labor productivity increased somewhat throughout the year, and consumers significantly increased their total planned purchases of goods and services.

d. The capital stock increased somewhat during the year, and the quantity of money in circulation declined considerably.

10-13. Explain how, if at all, each of the following events would affect equilibrium real GDP and the long-run equilibrium price level.

a. A reduction in the quantity of money in circulation

b. An income tax rebate (the return of previously paid taxes) from the government to house-

holds, which they can apply only to purchases of goods and services

c. A technological improvement

d. A decrease in the value of the home currency in terms of the currencies of other nations

10-14. For each question below, suppose that the economy *begins* at the long-run equilibrium point *A*. Identify which of the other points on the diagram—points *B*, *C*, *D*, or *E*—could represent a *new* long-run equilibrium after the described events take place and move the economy away from point *A*.

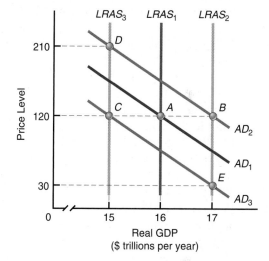

a. Significant productivity improvements occur, and the quantity of money in circulation increases.

b. No new capital investment takes place, and a fraction of the existing capital stock depreciates and becomes unusable. At the same time, the government imposes a large tax increase on the nation's households.

c. More efficient techniques for producing goods and services are adopted throughout the economy at the same time that the government reduces its spending on goods and services.

10-15. In Ciudad Barrios, El Salvador, the latest payments from relatives working in the United States have finally arrived. When the credit unions open for business, up to 150 people are already waiting in line. After receiving the funds their relatives have transmitted to these institutions, customers go off to outdoor markets to stock up on food or clothing or to appliance stores to purchase new stereos or televisions. Similar scenes occur throughout the developing world, as each year migrants working in higher-income, developed nations send around $200 billion of their earnings back to their relatives in less developed nations. Evidence indicates that the relatives, such as those in Ciudad Barrios, typically spend nearly all of the funds on current consumption.

a. Based on the information supplied, are developing countries' income inflows transmitted by migrant workers primarily affecting their economies' long-run aggregate supply curves or aggregate demand curves?

b. How are equilibrium price levels in nations that are recipients of large inflows of funds from migrants likely to be affected? Explain your reasoning.

ECONOMICS ON THE NET

Wages, Productivity, and Aggregate Supply How much firms pay their employees and the productivity of those employees influence firms' total planned production, so changes in these factors affect the position of the aggregate supply curve. This application gives you the opportunity to examine recent trends in measures of the overall wages and productivity of workers.

Title: Bureau of Labor Statistics: Economy at a Glance

Navigation: Use the link at **www.econtoday.com/chapter10** to visit the Bureau of Labor Statistics (BLS) Web site.

Application Perform the indicated operations, and answer the following questions.

1. Click on *Employment Costs*, and then click on *Employment Cost Index—NAICS Basis*. Choose the first data series in the list. What are the recent trends in wages and salaries and in benefits? In the long run, how should these trends be related to movements in the overall price level?

2. Back up to the home page, and click on *Productivity and Costs* and then on *PDF* next to "Economic News

Releases: Productivity and Costs." How has labor productivity behaved recently? What does this imply for the long-run aggregate supply curve?

3. Back up to U.S. Economy at a Glance, and now click on *National Employment* and then on *PDF* next to "Economic News Releases: Employment Situation Summary." Does it appear that the U.S. economy is currently in a long-run growth equilibrium?

For Group Study and Analysis

1. Divide the class into aggregate demand and long-run aggregate supply groups. Have each group search the Internet for data on factors that influence its assigned curve. For which factors do data appear to be most readily available? For which factors are data more sparse or more subject to measurement problems?

2. The BLS home page displays a map of the United States. Assign regions of the nation to different groups, and have each group develop a short report about current and future prospects for economic growth within its assigned region. What similarities exist across regions? What regional differences are there?

ANSWERS TO QUICK QUIZZES

p. 243: (i) vertical; (ii) natural; (iii) rightward . . . increases

p. 247: (i) expenditures . . . production . . . spending; (ii) real-balance . . . interest rate . . . open economy; (iii) real-balance; (iv) interest rate . . . fewer . . . more; (v) domestic . . . foreign

p. 253: (i) expenditures . . . production; (ii) rightward . . . decline; (iii) rightward

Classical and Keynesian Macro Analyses

11

L ike a rerun of a bad TV show, the same basic pattern has repeated four times in recent U.S. history: 1973–1974, 1979–1980, 1990, and 2000–2001. First, world oil prices jump. Then companies start to scale back production plans. Finally, the price level rises even as real GDP begins to slide. Within a few weeks, the word *recession* is in the air, and within a few more months, a committee of economists at the National Bureau of Economic Research announces that a recession is actually under way. Why have oil price increases so often preceded recessions? Do recessions necessarily follow a run-up in the world price of oil? Before you can answer these questions, you must learn about how changes in the price of oil and other key inputs can exert short-run effects on real GDP and the price level.

LEARNING OBJECTIVES

myeconlab

MyEconLab helps you master each objective and study more efficiently. See end of chapter for details.

After reading this chapter, you should be able to:

➤ Discuss the central assumptions of the classical model

➤ Describe the short-run determination of equilibrium real GDP and the price level in the classical model

➤ Explain circumstances under which the short-run aggregate supply curve may be either horizontal or upward sloping

➤ Understand what factors cause shifts in the short-run and long-run aggregate supply curves

➤ Evaluate the effects of aggregate demand and supply shocks on equilibrium real GDP in the short run

➤ Determine the causes of short-run variations in the inflation rate

DID YOU KNOW THAT the price of a bottle containing 6.5 ounces of Coca-Cola remained unchanged at 5 cents from 1886 to 1959? The prices of many other goods and services changed at least slightly during that 73-year period, and since then the prices of most items, including Coca-Cola, have generally moved in an upward direction. Nevertheless, prices of final goods and services have not always adjusted immediately in response to changes in aggregate demand. Consequently, one approach to understanding the determination of real GDP and the price level emphasizes *incomplete* adjustment in the prices of many goods and services. The simplest version of this approach was first developed by a twentieth-century economist named John Maynard Keynes (pronounced like *canes*). It assumes that in the short run, prices of most goods and services are nearly as rigid as the price of Coca-Cola from 1886 to 1959. Although the modern version of the Keynesian approach allows for greater flexibility of prices in the short run, incomplete price adjustment still remains a key feature of the modern Keynesian approach.

The Keynesian approach does not retain the long-run assumption, which you encountered in Chapter 10, of fully adjusting prices. Economists who preceded Keynes employed this assumption in creating an approach to understanding variations in real GDP and the price level that Keynes called the *classical model*. Like Keynes, we shall begin our study of variations in real GDP and the price level by considering the earlier, classical approach.

The Classical Model

The classical model, which traces its origins to the 1770s, was the first systematic attempt to explain the determinants of the price level and the national levels of real GDP, employment, consumption, saving, and investment. Classical economists— Adam Smith, J. B. Say, David Ricardo, John Stuart Mill, Thomas Malthus, A. C. Pigou, and others—wrote from the 1770s to the 1930s. They assumed, among other things, that all wages and prices were flexible and that competitive markets existed throughout the economy.

Say's Law

Every time you produce something for which you receive income, you generate the income necessary to make expenditures on other goods and services. That means that an economy producing $15 trillion of real GDP, measured in base-year dollars, simultaneously produces the income with which these goods and services can be purchased. As an accounting identity, *actual* aggregate output always equals *actual* aggregate income. Classical economists took this accounting identity one step further by arguing that total national supply creates its own national demand. They asserted what has become known as **Say's law:**

> **Say's law**
> A dictum of economist J. B. Say that supply creates its own demand; producing goods and services generates the means and the willingness to purchase other goods and services.

Supply creates its own demand; hence, it follows that desired *expenditures will equal* actual *expenditures.*

What does Say's law really mean? It states that the very process of producing specific goods (supply) is proof that other goods are desired (demand). People produce more goods than they want for their own use only if they seek to trade them for other goods. Someone offers to supply something only because he or she has a demand for something else. The implication of this, according to Say, is that no general glut, or overproduction, is possible in a market economy. From this reasoning, it seems to follow that full employment of labor and other resources would be the normal state of affairs in such an economy.

FIGURE 11-1

Say's Law and the Circular Flow

Here we show the circular flow of income and output. The very act of supplying a certain level of goods and services necessarily equals the level of goods and services demanded, in Say's simplified world.

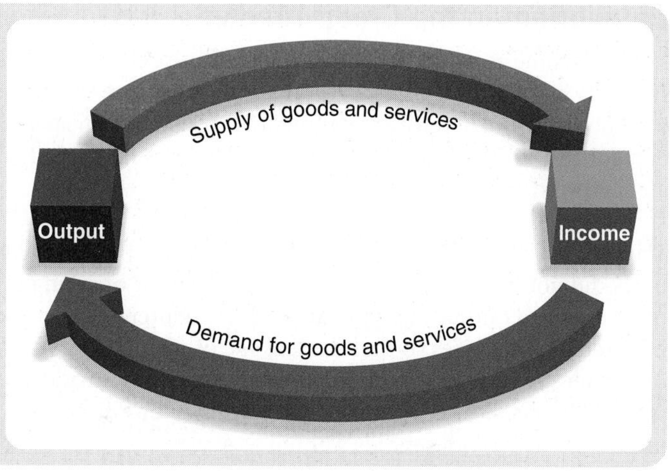

Say acknowledged that an oversupply of some goods might occur in particular markets. He argued that such surpluses would simply cause prices to fall, thereby decreasing production as the economy adjusted. The opposite would occur in markets in which shortages temporarily appeared.

All this seems reasonable enough in a simple barter economy in which households produce most of the goods they want and trade for the rest. This is shown in Figure 11-1, where there is a simple circular flow. But what about a more sophisticated economy in which people work for others and money is used instead of barter? Can these complications create the possibility of unemployment? And does the fact that laborers receive money income, some of which can be saved, lead to unemployment? No, said the classical economists to these last two questions. They based their reasoning on a number of key assumptions.

Assumptions of the Classical Model

The classical model makes four major assumptions:

1. *Pure competition exists.* No single buyer or seller of a commodity or an input can affect its price.

2. *Wages and prices are flexible.* The assumption of pure competition leads to the notion that prices, wages, interest rates, and the like are free to move to whatever level supply and demand dictate (as the economy adjusts). Although no *individual* buyer can set a price, the community of buyers or sellers can cause prices to rise or to fall to an equilibrium level.

3. *People are motivated by self-interest.* Businesses want to maximize their profits, and households want to maximize their economic well-being.

4. *People cannot be fooled by money illusion.* Buyers and sellers react to changes in relative prices. That is to say, they do not suffer from **money illusion.** For example, workers will not be fooled into thinking that a doubling of wages makes them better off if the price level has also doubled during the same time period.

Money illusion
Reacting to changes in money prices rather than relative prices. If a worker whose wages double when the price level also doubles thinks he or she is better off, that worker is suffering from money illusion.

The classical economists concluded, after taking account of the four major assumptions, that the role of government in the economy should be minimal. If pure competition prevails, if all prices and wages are flexible, and if people are self-interested and do not experience money illusion, then any problems in the macroeconomy will be temporary. The market will correct itself.

According to the classical model, what will happen to the prices of these canned goods if aggregate demand increases?

Go to **www.econtoday.com/chapter11** to link to Federal Reserve data on U.S. interest rates.

Equilibrium in the Credit Market

When income is saved, it is not reflected in product demand. It is a type of *leakage* from the circular flow of income and output because saving withdraws funds from the income stream. Therefore, total planned consumption spending *can* fall short of total current real GDP. In such a situation, it appears that supply does not necessarily create its own demand.

THE RELATIONSHIP BETWEEN SAVING AND INVESTMENT   The classical economists did not believe that the complicating factor of saving in the circular flow model of income and output was a problem. They contended that each dollar saved would be invested by businesses so that the leakage of saving would be matched by the injection of business investment. *Investment* here refers only to additions to the nation's capital stock. The classical economists believed that businesses as a group would intend to invest as much as households wanted to save.

THE EQUILIBRIUM INTEREST RATE   Equilibrium between the saving plans of consumers and the investment plans of businesses comes about, in the classical economists' model, through the working of the credit market. In the credit market, the *price* of credit is the interest rate. At equilibrium, the price of credit—the interest rate—ensures that the amount of credit demanded equals the amount of credit supplied. Planned investment just equals planned saving, so there is no reason to be concerned about the leakage of saving. This is illustrated graphically in Figure 11-2.

In the figure, the vertical axis measures the rate of interest in percentage terms, and the horizontal axis measures amounts of desired saving and desired investment per unit time period. The desired saving curve is really a supply curve of saving. It shows that people wish to save more at higher interest rates than at lower interest rates.

In contrast, the higher the rate of interest, the less profitable it is to invest and the lower is the level of desired investment. Thus, the desired investment curve slopes downward. In this simplified model, the equilibrium rate of interest is 5 percent, and the equilibrium quantity of saving and investment is $2 trillion per year.

FIGURE 11-2

Equating Desired Saving and Investment in the Classical Model

The schedule showing planned investment is labeled "Desired investment." The desired saving curve is shown as an upward-sloping supply curve of saving. The equilibrating force here is, of course, the interest rate. At higher interest rates, people desire to save more. But at higher interest rates, businesses wish to engage in less investment because it is less profitable to invest. In this model, at an interest rate of 5 percent, planned investment just equals planned saving, which is $2 trillion per year.

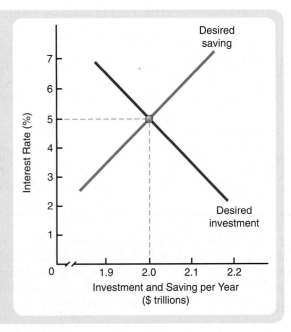

How does globalization of the world economy help to explain why saving and investment are not necessarily equalized within an individual nation's borders?

INTERNATIONAL EXAMPLE
In a Global Economy, World Saving Equals World Investment

In the classical model, saving equals investment when the interest rate is at an equilibrium value. At a given time when full adjustment to equilibrium may not yet have occurred, however, saving will not equal investment.

Nevertheless, even in full equilibrium, saving and investment may not always be equal *within* individual countries. In our increasingly globalized economy, saving and investment flow across national borders. Thus, the classical model implies that if the entire world economy is considered, the world interest rate should adjust until world saving equals world investment.

Take a look at Figure 11-3, which displays investment and saving as shares of world GDP for both industrialized nations and so-called emerging nations whose economies are gradually becoming more industrialized. Notice the pattern of the curves in the two panels: During periods in which investment exceeds saving in one group, saving exceeds investment in the other group. Since 1998, for example, investment has

exceeded saving in the industrialized nations in panel (a), while saving has exceeded investment in the emerging nations in panel (b). This indicates that some saving in the emerging nations during this period flowed to the industrialized nations to help finance investment in those countries. Indeed, in most years, the sums of investment and saving as percentages of world GDP for the two groups are equal. For example, in 2009, saving for both groups of nations summed to an estimated 20.4 percent of world GDP, and investment for both groups added up to an estimated 20.4 percent of world GDP. Hence, world saving was equal to world investment in that year, as predicted by the classical model for the global economy.

FOR CRITICAL ANALYSIS

Why does the classical model predict that world saving should end up being equal to world investment even if no funds flow across nations' borders? (Hint: Interest rate.)

FIGURE 11-3

Saving and Investment in Industrialized and Emerging Nations Since 1970

Saving and investment as percentages of world GDP since 1970 are shown for industrialized nations in panel (a) and for emerging nations in panel (b).

Source: International Monetary Fund.

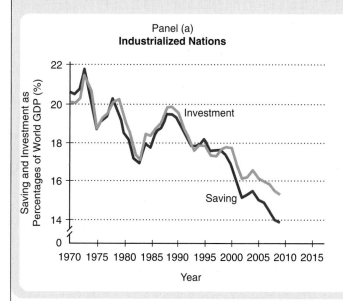

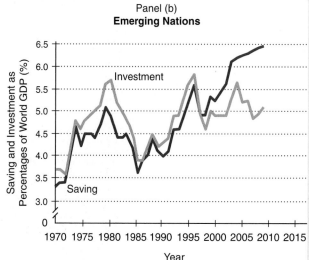

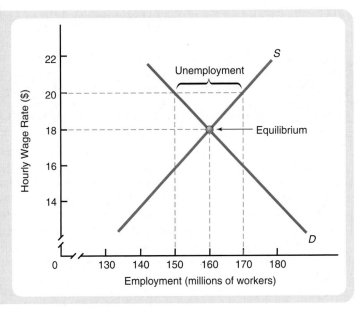

FIGURE 11-4

Equilibrium in the Labor Market

The demand for labor is downward sloping; at higher wage rates, firms will employ fewer workers. The supply of labor is upward sloping; at higher wage rates, more workers will work longer, and more people will be willing to work. The equilibrium wage rate is $18 with an equilibrium employment per year of 160 million workers.

Equilibrium in the Labor Market

Go to www.econtoday.com/chapter11 to find out the latest U.S. saving rate from the Bureau of Economic Analysis. Select "Personal saving as a percentage of disposable personal income."

Now consider the labor market. If an excess quantity of labor is supplied at a particular wage level, the wage level must be above equilibrium. By accepting lower wages, unemployed workers will quickly be put back to work. We show equilibrium in the labor market in Figure 11-4.

Assume that equilibrium exists at $18 per hour and 160 million workers employed. If the wage rate were $20 per hour, there would be unemployment—170 million workers would want to work, but businesses would want to hire only 150 million. In the classical model, this unemployment is eliminated rather rapidly by wage rates dropping back to $18 per hour, as seen in Figure 11-4.

THE RELATIONSHIP BETWEEN EMPLOYMENT AND REAL GDP Employment is not to be regarded simply as some isolated figure that government statisticians estimate. Rather, the level of employment in an economy determines its real GDP (output), other things held constant. A hypothetical relationship between input (number of employees) and the value of output (real GDP per year) is shown in Table 11-1. The row that has 160 million workers per year as the labor input is highlighted. That might be considered a hypothetical level of full employment, and it is related to a rate of real GDP, in base-year dollars, of $15 trillion per year.

TABLE 11-1

The Relationship Between Employment and Real GDP

Other things being equal, an increase in the quantity of labor input increases real GDP. In this example, if 160 million workers are employed, real GDP is $15 trillion in base-year dollars.

Labor Input per Year (millions of workers)	Real GDP per Year ($ trillions)
150	12
154	13
158	14
160	15
164	16
166	17

Classical Theory, Vertical Aggregate Supply, and the Price Level

In the classical model, greater than the natural unemployment rate is impossible. Say's law, coupled with flexible interest rates, prices, and wages, would always tend to keep workers fully employed so that the aggregate supply curve, as shown in Figure 11-5, is vertical at the real GDP of $15 trillion, in base-year dollars. We have labeled the supply curve *LRAS*, which is the long-run aggregate supply curve introduced in Chapter 10. It was defined there as the real GDP that would be produced in an economy with full information and full adjustment of wages and prices year in and year out. *LRAS* therefore corresponds to the long-run rate of unemployment. In the classical model, this happens to be the *only* aggregate supply curve. The classical economists made little distinction between the long run and the short run. Prices adjust so fast that the economy is essentially always on or quickly moving toward *LRAS*. Furthermore, because the labor market adjusts rapidly, real GDP is always at, or soon to be at, full employment. Full employment does not mean zero unemployment because there is always some frictional and structural unemployment (discussed in Chapter 7), which yields the natural rate of unemployment.

EFFECT OF AN INCREASE IN AGGREGATE DEMAND IN THE CLASSICAL MODEL

In this model, any change in aggregate demand will quickly cause a change in the price level. Consider starting at E_1, at price level 120, in Figure 11-5. If aggregate demand shifts to AD_2, the economy will tend toward point *A*, but because this is beyond full employment, real GDP prices will rise, and the economy will find itself back on the vertical *LRAS* at point E_2 at a higher price level, 130. The price level will increase as a result of the increase in *AD* because employers will end up bidding up wages for workers, as well as bidding up the prices of other inputs.

The level of real GDP per year clearly does not depend on the level of aggregate demand. Hence, we say that in the classical model, the equilibrium level of real GDP per year is completely *supply determined*. Changes in aggregate demand affect only the price level, not real GDP.

FIGURE 11-5

Classical Theory and Increases in Aggregate Demand

The classical theorists believed that Say's law and flexible interest rates, prices, and wages would always lead to full employment at real GDP of $15 trillion, in base-year dollars, along the vertical aggregate supply curve, *LRAS*. With aggregate demand AD_1 the price level is 120. An increase in aggregate demand shifts AD_1 to AD_2. At price level 120, the quantity of real GDP demanded per year would be $15.5 trillion at point *A* on AD_2. But $15.5 trillion in real GDP per year is greater than real GDP at full employment. Prices rise, and the economy quickly moves from E_1 to E_2, at the higher price level of 130.

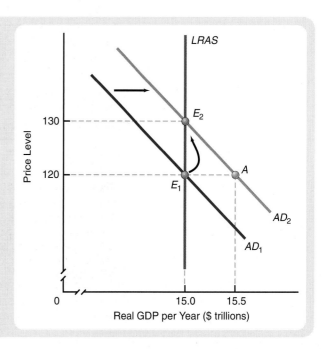

FIGURE 11-6

Effect of a Decrease in Aggregate Demand in the Classical Model

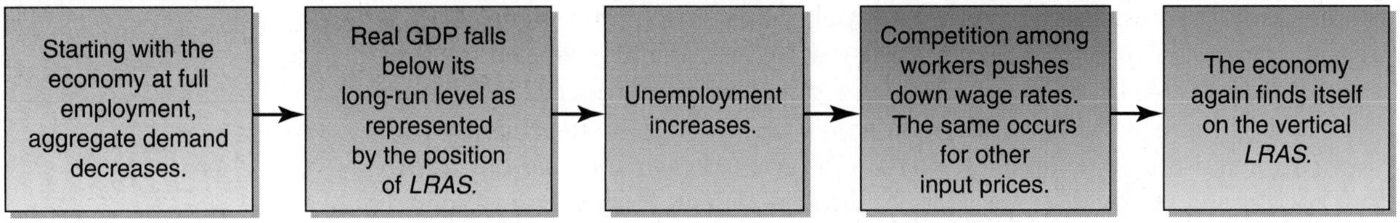

| Starting with the economy at full employment, aggregate demand decreases. | → | Real GDP falls below its long-run level as represented by the position of *LRAS*. | → | Unemployment increases. | → | Competition among workers pushes down wage rates. The same occurs for other input prices. | → | The economy again finds itself on the vertical *LRAS*. |

EFFECT OF A DECREASE IN AGGREGATE DEMAND IN THE CLASSICAL MODEL
The effect of a decrease in aggregate demand in the classical model is the converse of the analysis just presented for an increase in aggregate demand. You can simply reverse AD_2 and AD_1 in Figure 11-5 on the preceding page. To help you see how this analysis works, consider the flowchart in Figure 11-6.

QUICK QUIZ *See page 286 for the answers. Review concepts from this section in MyEconLab.*

Say's law states that _____ creates its own _____ and therefore *desired* expenditures will equal *actual* expenditures.

The classical model assumes that (1) _____ _____ exists, (2) _____ and _____ are completely flexible, (3) individuals are motivated by _____-_____, and (4) they cannot be fooled by _____ _____.

When saving is introduced into the model, equilibrium occurs in the credit market through changes in the interest rate such that desired _____ equals desired _____ at the equilibrium rate of interest.

In the labor market, full employment occurs at a _____ _____ at which quantity demanded equals quantity supplied. That particular level of employment is associated with the full-employment level of real GDP per year.

In the classical model, because *LRAS* is _____, the equilibrium level of real GDP is supply determined. Any changes in aggregate demand simply change the _____ _____.

Keynesian Economics and the Keynesian Short-Run Aggregate Supply Curve

The classical economists' world was one of fully utilized resources. There would be no unused capacity and no unemployment. But then in the 1930s Europe and the United States entered a period of economic decline that seemingly could not be explained by the classical model. John Maynard Keynes developed an explanation that has since become known as the Keynesian model. Keynes and his followers argued that prices, especially the price of labor (wages), were inflexible downward due to the existence of unions and long-term contracts between businesses and workers. That meant that prices were "sticky." Keynes contended that in such a world, which has large amounts of excess capacity and unemployment, an increase in aggregate demand will not raise the price level, and a decrease in aggregate demand will not cause firms to lower prices.

FIGURE 11-7

Demand-Determined Equilibrium Real GDP at Less Than Full Employment

Keynes assumed that prices will not fall when aggregate demand falls and that there is excess capacity, so prices will not rise when aggregate demand increases. Thus, the short-run aggregate supply curve is simply a horizontal line at the given price level, 120, represented by *SRAS.* An aggregate demand shock that increases aggregate demand to AD_2 will increase the equilibrium level of real GDP per year to $15.5 trillion. An aggregate demand shock that decreases aggregate demand to AD_3 will decrease the equilibrium level of real GDP to $14.5 trillion. The equilibrium price level will not change.

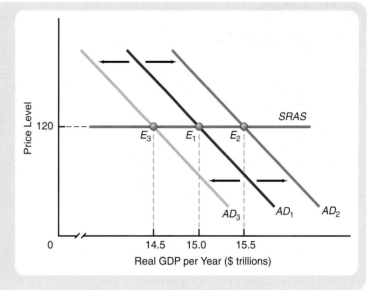

Demand-Determined Real GDP

This situation is depicted in Figure 11-7. For simplicity, Figure 11-7 does not show the point where the economy reaches capacity, and that is why the *short-run aggregate supply curve* (to be discussed later) never starts to slope upward and is simply the horizontal line labeled *SRAS.* Moreover, we don't show *LRAS* in Figure 11-7 either. It would be a vertical line at the level of real GDP per year that is consistent with full employment. If we start out in equilibrium with aggregate demand at AD_1, the equilibrium level of real GDP per year, measured in base-year dollars, is $15 trillion at point E_1, and the equilibrium price level is 120. If there is a rise in aggregate demand, so that the aggregate demand curve shifts outward to the right to AD_2, the equilibrium price level at point E_2 will not change; only the equilibrium level of real GDP per year will increase, to $15.5 trillion. Conversely, if there is a fall in aggregate demand that shifts the aggregate demand curve to AD_3, the equilibrium price level will again remain at 120 at point E_3, but the equilibrium level of real GDP per year will fall to $14.5 trillion.

Under such circumstances, the equilibrium level of real GDP per year is completely *demand determined.*

The Keynesian Short-Run Aggregate Supply Curve

The horizontal short-run aggregate supply curve represented in Figure 11-7 is often called the **Keynesian short-run aggregate supply curve.** According to Keynes, unions and long-term contracts are real-world factors that explain the inflexibility of *nominal* wage rates. Such stickiness of wages makes *involuntary* unemployment of labor a distinct possibility, because leftward movements along the Keynesian short-run aggregate supply curve reduce real production and, hence, employment. The classical assumption of everlasting full employment no longer holds.

A good example of a horizontal short-run aggregate supply curve can be seen by examining data from the 1930s. Look at Figure 11-8 on the following page, where you see real GDP in trillions of 2005 dollars on the horizontal axis and the price level

Keynesian short-run aggregate supply curve
The horizontal portion of the aggregate supply curve in which there is excessive unemployment and unused capacity in the economy.

FIGURE 11-8

Real GDP and the Price Level, 1934–1940

Keynes suggested that in a depressed economy, increased aggregate spending can increase output without raising prices. The data for the United States' recovery from the Great Depression seem to bear this out. In such circumstances, real GDP is demand determined.

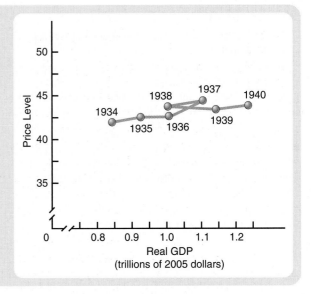

index on the vertical axis. From the early days of recovery from the Great Depression to the outbreak of World War II, real GDP increased without much rise in the price level. During this period, the economy experienced neither supply constraints nor any dramatic changes in the price level. The most simplified Keynesian model in which prices do not change is essentially an immediate post-Depression model that fits the data very well during this period.

Why has the horizontal Keynesian short-run aggregate supply curve been making a comeback?

EXAMPLE
Are the U.S. and European *SRAS* Curves Horizontal?

Today, economists called *New Keynesians* contend that the short-run aggregate supply curve is essentially flat. The New Keynesians know that some firms change their prices every day, but they contend that price changes are, on average, relatively infrequent. Research in the early 2000s provided some support for this hypothesis. These studies indicated that, on average, U.S. firms adjusted their prices only about once each year. More recent studies, however, suggest that the average period between U.S. price changes may be as brief as six months. It may be even shorter in a number of industries.

There is much stronger evidence of slow price adjustment in Europe. In contrast to U.S. firms, European sellers rarely place goods "on sale," and prices of services in Europe are particularly slow to change. This explains why economists continue to find strong evidence that at least a year passes, on average, between changes in prices of European goods and services. To New Keynesians, this is strong evidence that European aggregate supply curves are flat in the short run. Indeed, most New Keynesians contend that price-adjustment intervals as short as a few months are still sufficiently lengthy to justify viewing the U.S. short-run aggregate supply curve as horizontal. If so, changes in aggregate demand can exert significant near-term effects on real GDP without affecting the price level.

FOR CRITICAL ANALYSIS
If the short-run aggregate supply curve were really horizontal, how could the price level ever increase? (Hint: Over the longer term, the short-run aggregate supply curve can shift.)

Output Determination Using Aggregate Demand and Aggregate Supply: Fixed versus Changing Price Levels in the Short Run

The underlying assumption of the simplified Keynesian model is that the relevant range of the short-run aggregate supply schedule (*SRAS*) is horizontal, as depicted in panel (a) of Figure 11-9. There you see that short-run aggregate supply is fixed at price level 120. If aggregate demand is AD_1, then the equilibrium level of real GDP, in base-year dollars, is $15 trillion per year. If aggregate demand increases to AD_2, then the equilibrium level of real GDP increases to $16 trillion per year.

As discussed in Chapter 10, the price level has drifted upward during recent decades. Hence, prices are not totally sticky. Modern Keynesian analysis recognizes that *some*—but not complete—price adjustment takes place in the short run. Panel (b) of Figure 11-9 displays a more general **short-run aggregate supply curve** (*SRAS*). This curve represents the relationship between the price level and real GDP with incomplete price adjustment and in the absence of complete information in the short run. Allowing for partial price adjustment implies that *SRAS* slopes upward, and its slope is steeper after it crosses long-run aggregate supply, *LRAS*. This is because higher and higher prices are required to induce firms to raise their production of goods and services to levels that temporarily exceed full-employment real GDP.

Short-run aggregate supply curve
The relationship between total planned economywide production and the price level in the short run, all other things held constant. If prices adjust incompletely in the short run, the curve is positively sloped.

FIGURE 11-9

Real GDP Determination with Fixed versus Flexible Prices

In panel (a), the price level index is fixed at 120. An increase in aggregate demand from AD_1 to AD_2 moves the equilibrium level of real GDP from $15 trillion per year to $16 trillion per year in base-year dollars. In panel (b), *SRAS* is upward sloping. The same shift in aggregate demand yields an equilibrium level of real GDP of only $15.5 trillion per year and a higher price level index at 130.

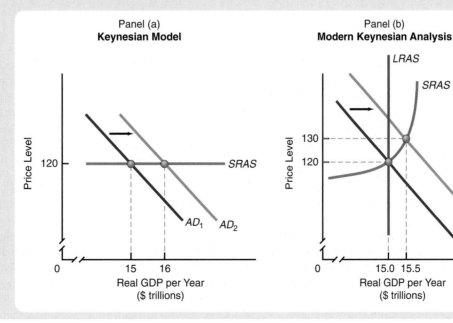

With partial price adjustment in the short run, if aggregate demand is AD_1 then the equilibrium level of real GDP in panel (b) is also $15 trillion per year, at a price level of 120, too. An increase in aggregate demand to AD_2 such as occurred in panel (a) produces a different equilibrium, however. Equilibrium real GDP increases to $15.5 trillion per year, which is less than in panel (a) because an increase in the price level to 130 causes planned purchases of goods and services to decline.

In the modern Keynesian short run, when the price level rises partially, real GDP can be expanded beyond the level consistent with its long-run growth path, discussed in Chapter 10, for a variety of reasons:

1. In the short run, most labor contracts implicitly or explicitly call for flexibility in hours of work at the given wage rate. Therefore, firms can use existing workers more intensively in a variety of ways: They can get workers to work harder, to work more hours per day, and to work more days per week. Workers can also be switched from *uncounted* production, such as maintenance, to *counted* production, which generates counted production of goods and services. The distinction between counted and uncounted is simply what is measured in the marketplace, particularly by government statisticians and accountants. If a worker cleans a machine, there is no measured output. But if that worker is put on the production line and helps increase the number of units produced each day, measured output will go up. That worker's production has then been counted.

2. Existing capital equipment can be used more intensively. Machines can be worked more hours per day. Some can be made to operate faster. Maintenance can be delayed.

3. Finally, if wage rates are held constant, a higher price level leads to increased profits from additional production, which induces firms to hire more workers. The duration of unemployment falls, and thus the unemployment rate falls. And people who were previously not in the labor force (homemakers and younger or older workers) can be induced to enter it.

All these adjustments cause real GDP to rise as the price level increases.

Shifts in the Aggregate Supply Curve

Just as non-price-level factors can cause a shift in the aggregate demand curve, there are non-price-level factors that can cause a shift in the aggregate supply curve. The analysis here is more complicated than the analysis for the non-price-level determinants for aggregate demand, for here we are dealing with both the short run and the long run—*SRAS* and *LRAS*. Still, anything other than the price level that affects the production of final goods and services will shift aggregate supply curves.

Shifts in Both Short- and Long-Run Aggregate Supply

There is a core class of events that cause a shift in both the short-run aggregate supply curve and the long-run aggregate supply curve. These include any change in our endowments of the factors of production. Any change in these factors of production—labor, capital, or technology—that influence economic growth will shift *SRAS* and *LRAS*. Look at Figure 11-10. Initially, the two curves are $SRAS_1$ and $LRAS_1$. Now consider a major discovery of mineral deposits in Idaho, in an area where no one thought deposits of mineral inputs existed. This shifts $LRAS_1$ to $LRAS_2$ at $15.5 trillion of real GDP, measured in base-year dollars. $SRAS_1$ also shifts outward horizontally to $SRAS_2$.

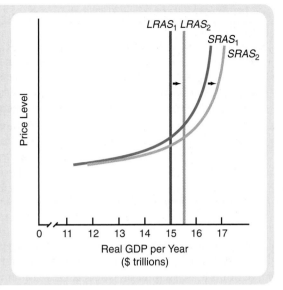

FIGURE 11-10

Shifts in Both Short- and Long-Run Aggregate Supply

Initially, the two supply curves are $SRAS_1$ and $LRAS_1$. Now consider a discovery of mineral deposits in Idaho in an area where no one thought such production inputs existed. This shifts $LRAS_1$ to $LRAS_2$ at $15.5 trillion of real GDP, in base-year dollars. $SRAS_1$ also shifts outward horizontally to $SRAS_2$.

Shifts in *SRAS* Only

Some events, particularly those that are short-lived, will temporarily shift *SRAS* but not *LRAS*. One of the most obvious is a change in production input prices, particularly those caused by external events that are not expected to last forever. Consider a major hurricane that temporarily shuts down a significant portion of U.S. oil production, as happened after Hurricane Katrina. Oil is an important input in many production activities. The resulting drop in oil production will cause at least a temporary increase in the price of this input. You can see what happens in Figure 11-11. *LRAS* remains fixed, but $SRAS_1$ shifts to $SRAS_2$, reflecting the increase in input prices—the higher price of oil. This is because the rise in the costs of production at each level of real GDP per year requires a higher price level to cover those increased costs.

You Are There

To contemplate why a nation might face a trade-off between reducing its exposure to aggregate supply shocks and providing a foundation for aggregate supply growth, consider **Putting More Weight on Stability Than Growth in Denmark,** on pages 279 and 280.

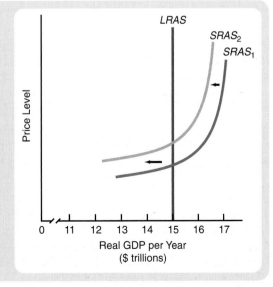

FIGURE 11-11

Shifts in *SRAS* Only

A temporary increase in an input price will shift the short-run aggregate supply curve from $SRAS_1$ to $SRAS_2$.

TABLE 11-2

Determinants of Aggregate Supply

The determinants listed here can affect short-run or long-run aggregate supply (or both), depending on whether they are temporary or permanent.

Changes That Cause an Increase in Aggregate Supply	Changes That Cause a Decrease in Aggregate Supply
Discoveries of new raw materials	Depletion of raw materials
Increased competition	Decreased competition
A reduction in international trade barriers	An increase in international trade barriers
Fewer regulatory impediments to business	More regulatory impediments to business
An increase in the supply of labor	A decrease in labor supplied
Increased training and education	Decreased training and education
A decrease in marginal tax rates	An increase in marginal tax rates
A reduction in input prices	An increase in input prices

We summarize the possible determinants of aggregate supply in Table 11-2. These determinants will cause a shift in the short-run or the long-run aggregate supply curve or both, depending on whether they are temporary or permanent.

How much does the federal government estimate that its 2003 tax rate cuts have shifted the U.S. short-run and long-run aggregate supply curves?

POLICY EXAMPLE
The Aggregate Supply Impact of Cuts in U.S. Marginal Tax Rates

In 2003, Congress reduced marginal tax rates applicable to earned income, capital gains, and dividend income. The U.S. Treasury estimates that the long-run effect of these tax rate cuts has been a 0.7 percent increase in annual real GDP. Thus, these marginal tax rate cuts together generated rightward shifts in the *LRAS* and *SRAS* curves of about $96 billion, in constant dollars, per year.

FOR CRITICAL ANALYSIS
How would the U.S. Treasury's estimate of the aggregate supply effects of the 2003 tax rate cuts be altered if Congress follows through with proposals to raise marginal tax rates back to pre-2003 levels?

QUICK QUIZ   *See page 286 for the answers. Review concepts from this section in MyEconLab.*

If we assume that the economy is operating on a horizontal short-run aggregate supply curve, the equilibrium level of real GDP per year is completely _____ determined.

The horizontal short-run aggregate supply curve has been called the **Keynesian short-run aggregate supply curve** because Keynes believed that many prices, especially wages, would not be _____ even when aggregate demand decreased.

In modern Keynesian theory, the **short-run aggregate supply curve, SRAS,** shows the relationship between the price level and real GDP without full adjustment or full information. It is upward sloping because it allows for only _____ price adjustment in the short run.

Real GDP can be expanded in the short run because firms can use existing workers and capital equipment more _____. Also, in the short run, when input prices are fixed, a higher price level means _____ profits, which induce firms to hire more workers.

Any change in factors influencing long-run output, such as labor, capital, or technology, will shift both *SRAS* and *LRAS*. A temporary change in input prices, however, will shift only_____ .

Consequences of Changes in Aggregate Demand

We now have a basic model to apply when evaluating short-run adjustments of the equilibrium price level and equilibrium real GDP when there are shocks to the economy. Whenever there is a shift in the aggregate demand or supply curves, the equilibrium price level or real GDP level (or both) may change. These shifts are called **aggregate demand shocks** on the demand side and **aggregate supply shocks** on the supply side.

When Aggregate Demand Falls While Aggregate Supply Is Stable

Now we can show what happens in the short run when aggregate supply remains stable but aggregate demand falls. The short-run outcome will be a rise in the unemployment rate. In Figure 11-12, you see that with AD_1, both long-run and short-run equilibrium are at $15 trillion (in base-year dollars) of real GDP per year (because $SRAS$ and $LRAS$ also intersect AD_1 at that level of real GDP). The long-run equilibrium price level is 120. A reduction in aggregate demand shifts the aggregate demand curve to AD_2. The new intersection with $SRAS$ is at $14.8 trillion per year, which is less than the long-run equilibrium level of real GDP. The difference between $15 trillion and $14.8 trillion is called a **recessionary gap,** defined as the difference between the short-run equilibrium level of real GDP and real GDP if the economy were operating at full employment on its $LRAS$.

In effect, at E_2, the economy is in short-run equilibrium at less than full employment. With too many unemployed inputs, input prices will begin to fall. Eventually, $SRAS$ will have to shift down. Where will it intersect AD_2?

Aggregate demand shock
Any event that causes the aggregate demand curve to shift inward or outward.

Aggregate supply shock
Any event that causes the aggregate supply curve to shift inward or outward.

Recessionary gap
The gap that exists whenever equilibrium real GDP per year is less than full-employment real GDP as shown by the position of the long-run aggregate supply curve.

FIGURE 11-12

The Short-Run Effects of Stable Aggregate Supply and a Decrease in Aggregate Demand: The Recessionary Gap

If the economy is at equilibrium at E_1, with price level 120 and real GDP per year of $15 trillion, a shift inward of the aggregate demand curve to AD_2 will lead to a new short-run equilibrium at E_2. The equilibrium price level will fall to 115, and the short-run equilibrium level of real GDP per year will fall to $14.8 trillion. There will be a recessionary gap of $200 billion.

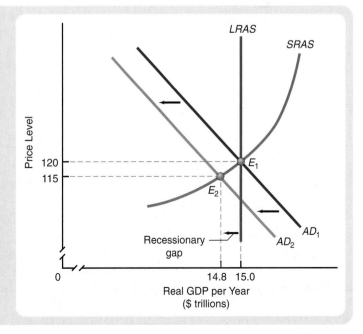

FIGURE 11-13

The Effects of Stable Aggregate Supply with an Increase in Aggregate Demand: The Inflationary Gap

The economy is at equilibrium at E_1. An increase in aggregate demand to AD_2 leads to a new short-run equilibrium at E_2 with the price level rising from 120 to 125 and equilibrium real GDP per year rising from $15 trillion to $15.2 trillion. The difference, $200 billion, is called the inflationary gap.

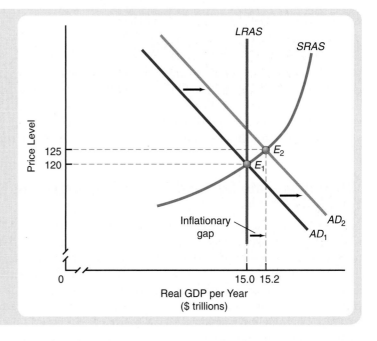

Short-Run Effects When Aggregate Demand Increases

We can reverse the situation and have aggregate demand increase to AD_2, as is shown in Figure 11-13. The initial equilibrium conditions are exactly the same as in Figure 11-12. The move to AD_2 increases the short-run equilibrium from E_1 to E_2 such that the economy is operating at $15.2 trillion of real GDP per year, which exceeds *LRAS*. This is a condition of an overheated economy, typically called an **inflationary gap.**

At E_2 in Figure 11-13, the economy is at a short-run equilibrium that is beyond full employment. In the short run, more can be squeezed out of the economy than occurs in the long-run, full-information, full-adjustment situation. Firms will be operating beyond long-run capacity. Inputs will be working too hard. Input prices will begin to rise. That will eventually cause *SRAS* to shift upward. At what point on AD_2 in Figure 11-13 will the new *SRAS* stop shifting?

Inflationary gap

The gap that exists whenever equilibrium real GDP per year is greater than full-employment real GDP as shown by the position of the long-run aggregate supply curve.

Explaining Short-Run Variations in Inflation

In Chapter 10, we noted that in a growing economy, the explanation for persistent inflation is that aggregate demand rises over time at a faster pace than the full-employment level of real GDP. Short-run variations in inflation, however, can arise as a result of both demand *and* supply factors.

Demand-Pull versus Cost-Push Inflation

Figure 11-13 presents a demand-side theory explaining a short-run jump in prices, sometimes called *demand-pull inflation*. Whenever the general level of prices rises in the short run because of increases in aggregate demand, we say that the economy is experiencing **demand-pull inflation**—inflation caused by increases in aggregate demand.

An alternative explanation for increases in the price level comes from the supply side. Look at Figure 11-14. The initial equilibrium conditions are the same as in

Demand-pull inflation

Inflation caused by increases in aggregate demand not matched by increases in aggregate supply.

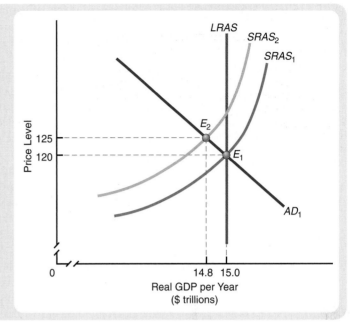

FIGURE 11-14

Cost-Push Inflation

If aggregate demand remains stable but $SRAS_1$ shifts to $SRAS_2$, equilibrium changes from E_1 to E_2. The price level rises from 120 to 125. If there are continual decreases in aggregate supply of this nature, the situation is called cost-push inflation.

Figure 11-13. Now, however, there is a leftward shift in the aggregate supply curve, from $SRAS_1$ to $SRAS_2$. Equilibrium shifts from E_1 to E_2. The price level increases from 120 to 125, while the equilibrium level of real GDP per year decreases from $15 trillion to $14.8 trillion. Such a decrease in aggregate supply causes what is called **cost-push inflation.**

As the example of cost-push inflation shows, if the economy is initially in equilibrium on its *LRAS*, a decrease in *SRAS* will lead to a rise in the price level. Thus, any abrupt change in one of the factors that determine aggregate supply will alter the equilibrium level of real GDP and the equilibrium price level. If the economy is for some reason operating to the left of its *LRAS*, an increase in *SRAS* will lead to a simultaneous *increase* in the equilibrium level of real GDP per year and a *decrease* in the price level. You should be able to show this in a graph similar to Figure 11-14.

Cost-push inflation
Inflation caused by decreases in short-run aggregate supply.

Aggregate Demand and Supply in an Open Economy

In many of the international examples in the early chapters of this book, we had to translate foreign currencies into dollars when the open economy was discussed. We used the exchange rate, or the dollar price of other currencies. In Chapter 10, you also learned that the open economy effect was one of the reasons why the aggregate demand curve slopes downward. When the domestic price level rises, U.S. residents want to buy cheaper-priced foreign goods. The opposite occurs when the U.S. domestic price level falls. Currently, the foreign sector of the U.S. economy constitutes more than 14 percent of all economic activities.

HOW A WEAKER DOLLAR AFFECTS AGGREGATE SUPPLY Assume that the dollar becomes weaker in international foreign exchange markets. If last year the dollar could buy 130 *naira*, the Nigerian currency, but this year it buys only 120 naira, the dollar has become weaker. To the extent that U.S. companies import raw and partially processed goods from Nigeria, a weaker dollar can lead to higher input prices. For instance, in a typical year, U.S. natural gas distributors purchase about 10,000 million

(10 billion) cubic feet of natural gas from suppliers in Nigeria. Suppose that the price of Nigerian natural gas, quoted in Nigerian naira, is 0.910 naira per million cubic feet. At a rate of exchange of 130 naira per dollar, this means that the U.S. dollar price is $0.0070 per million cubic feet (0.910 naira divided by 130 naira per dollar equals $0.0070), so that 10 billion cubic feet of Nigerian natural gas imports cost U.S. distributors $70 million. If the U.S. dollar weakens against the Nigerian naira, so that a dollar purchases only 120 naira, then the U.S. dollar price rises to $0.0076 per million cubic feet (0.910 naira divided by 120 naira per dollar equals $0.0076). As a consequence, the U.S. dollar price of 10 billion cubic feet of Nigerian natural gas imports increases to $76 million.

Go to www.econtoday.com/chapter11 for Federal Reserve Bank of New York data showing how the dollar's value is changing relative to other currencies.

Thus, a general weakening of the dollar against the naira and other world currencies will lead to a shift inward to the left in the short-run aggregate supply curve as shown in panel (a) of Figure 11-15. In that simplified model, equilibrium real GDP would fall, and the price level would rise. Employment would also tend to decrease.

HOW A WEAKER DOLLAR AFFECTS AGGREGATE DEMAND A weaker dollar has another effect that we must consider. Foreign residents will find that U.S.-made goods are now less expensive, expressed in their own currency. Suppose that as a result of the dollar's weakening, the dollar, which previously could buy 0.70 euros, can now buy only 0.67 euros. Before the dollar weakened, a U.S.-produced $10 compact disc cost a French resident 7.00 euros at the exchange rate of 0.70 euro per $1. After the dollar weakens and the exchange rate changes to 0.67 euro per $1, that same $10 CD will cost 6.70 euros. Conversely, U.S. residents will find that the weaker dollar

FIGURE 11-15

The Two Effects of a Weaker Dollar

When the dollar decreases in value in the international currency market, there are two effects. The first is higher prices for imported inputs, causing a shift inward to the left in the short-run aggregate supply schedule from $SRAS_1$ to $SRAS_2$ in panel (a). Equilibrium tends to move from E_1 to E_2 at a higher price level and a lower equilibrium real GDP per year. Second, a weaker dollar can also affect the aggregate demand curve because it will lead to more net exports and cause AD_1 to rise to AD_2 in panel (b). Due to this effect, equilibrium will move from E_1 to E_2 at a higher price level and a higher equilibrium real GDP per year. On balance, the combined effects of the increase in aggregate demand and decrease in aggregate supply will be to push up the price level, but real GDP may rise or fall.

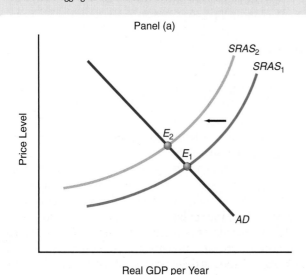

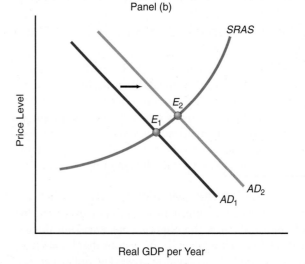

makes imported goods more expensive. The result for U.S. residents is more exports and fewer imports, or higher net exports (exports minus imports). If net exports rise, employment in export industries will rise: This is represented in panel (b) of Figure 11-15 on the facing page. After the dollar becomes weaker, the aggregate demand curve shifts outward from AD_1 to AD_2. The result is a tendency for equilibrium real GDP and the price level to rise and for unemployment to decrease.

What happens to the quantity demanded of American-made dresses when the dollar becomes weaker?

THE NET EFFECTS ON INFLATION AND REAL GDP. We have learned, then, that a weaker dollar *simultaneously* leads to a decrease in *SRAS* and an increase in *AD*. In such situations, the equilibrium price level definitely rises. A weaker dollar contributes to inflation.

The effect of a weaker dollar on real GDP depends on which curve—*AD* or *SRAS*— shifts more. If the aggregate demand curve shifts more than the short-run aggregate supply curve, equilibrium real GDP will rise. Conversely, if the aggregate supply curve shifts more than the aggregate demand curve, equilibrium real GDP will fall.

You should be able to redo this entire analysis for a stronger dollar.

QUICK QUIZ   *See page 286 for the answers. Review concepts from this section in MyEconLab.*

_____-run equilibrium occurs at the intersection of the aggregate demand curve, *AD*, and the short-run aggregate supply curve, *SRAS*. _____-run equilibrium occurs at the intersection of *AD* and the long-run aggregate supply curve, *LRAS*. Any unanticipated shifts in aggregate demand or supply are called aggregate demand _____ or aggregate supply _____.

When aggregate demand decreases while aggregate supply is stable, a _____ gap can occur, defined as the difference between the equilibrium level of real GDP and how much the economy could be producing if it were operating on its *LRAS*. An increase in aggregate demand leads to an _____ gap.

With stable aggregate supply, an abrupt outward shift in *AD* may lead to what is called _____-_____ inflation. With stable aggregate demand, an abrupt shift inward in *SRAS* may lead to what is called _____-_____ inflation.

A _____ dollar will raise the cost of imported inputs, thereby causing *SRAS* to shift inward to the left. At the same time, a _____ dollar will also lead to higher net exports, causing the aggregate demand curve to shift outward. The equilibrium price level definitely rises, but the net effect on equilibrium real GDP depends on which shift is larger.

You Are There ➤ Putting More Weight on Stability Than Growth in Denmark

Dalum Papir A/S is almost halfway through its second century as a Danish paper manufacturer. Years ago, the firm was one of many paper companies, but now it constitutes one-half of Denmark's two-firm paper industry. The company utilizes highly energy-efficient techniques to manufacture glossy paper from recycled materials for magazines. Dalum Papir has had little choice but to conserve energy. Government taxation has boosted energy prices more than 45 percent above the U.S. level. In addition, like other Danish

firms, Dalum Papir must meet government-mandated standards for energy conservation.

Ever since the 1970s, when a worldwide spike in oil prices set off a prolonged recession, Denmark's government has sought to shield the nation's economy from future aggregate supply shocks induced by jumps in energy prices. Toward that end, it has enacted high energy taxes and tough regulatory conservation measures. A consequence is that Danish oil consumption per $1 million of real GDP has

You Are There (cont.)

declined by more than 30 percent—to 120 tons of oil per $1 million of real GDP—over the last 30 years. Indeed, Denmark's *total* oil consumption has remained unchanged since the late 1970s. Thus, consistent with the government's intent, whenever oil prices suddenly shoot up, Denmark's economy tends to experience smaller aggregate supply shocks than it did in years past.

As the experience of Dalum Papir and the dwindling Danish paper industry illustrates, however, the government's quest for aggregate supply stability has come at the cost of growth in production of goods and services. Since the late 1970s, Denmark's real GDP has doubled, whereas U.S. real GDP has *quadrupled*. During that period, total U.S. oil consumption has increased by more than 40 percent, yet because U.S. real GDP has increased fourfold, U.S. oil consumption per $1 million of real GDP has fallen

by more than 25 percent—almost as much as the percentage decline in Danish oil consumption per $1 million in real GDP. Thus, although the Danish economy is less susceptible than the U.S. economy to aggregate supply shocks, Denmark's aggregate supply is growing at about half the pace at which U.S. aggregate supply is expanding.

CRITICAL ANALYSIS QUESTIONS

1. Why do unexpected variations in energy prices generate aggregate supply shocks, while sudden changes in total planned expenditures do not?

2. Other things being equal, why might we expect the Danish price level to be more stable over time than the U.S. price level?

Higher Oil Prices and (Usually) U.S. Recessionary Gaps

Issues and Applications

CONCEPTS APPLIED

- Aggregate Supply Shock
- Short-Run Aggregate Supply Curve
- Recessionary Gap

During the past four decades, sudden increases in oil prices have been associated with onsets of recessions. The U.S. economy recently has been more resilient to oil price hikes, but the latest oil price increase contributed to a slowdown.

A Recurring History of Oil Price Jumps and Recessions

Figure 11-16 displays the real, inflation-adjusted price per barrel of oil since 1970 in blue. The figure also shows rates of growth in a measure of real consumption expenditures in red. The shaded intervals indicate U.S.

FIGURE 11-16

Real Oil Prices and Year-to-Year Growth in U.S. Personal Consumption Expenditures Since 1970

Real oil prices rose in advance of or coincided with four of the past six recession periods (indicated by shaded intervals). In the late 2000s, the real price of oil rose considerably. The rate of growth of U.S. real consumption expenditures dropped but did not become negative.

Sources: Federal Reserve Bank of St. Louis, Bureau of Economic Analysis, National Bureau of Economic Research.

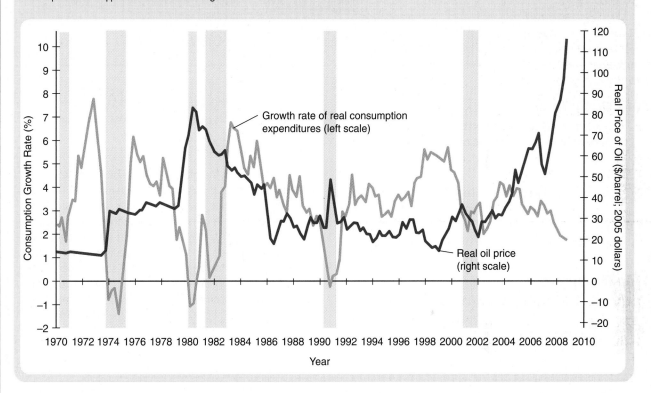

recession periods. As you can see, the price of oil increased noticeably in late 1973 and early 1974. The result was an aggregate supply shock. The U.S. aggregate supply curve shifted leftward, generating a recessionary gap. Real expenditures on goods and services declined, as indicated in the figure by the negative rate of change in real consumption expenditures. The economy experienced a recession that lasted just over a year before concluding in early 1975.

Analogous patterns, in which an oil price increase was followed in succession by an aggregate supply shock, a recessionary gap, a consumption spending decline, and a recession, repeated in 1979–1980, 1990, and 2000–2001. Out of the past six recessions, only two

(1970 and 1981–1982) were not linked to oil price increases and resulting aggregate supply shocks.

An Oil Price Run-Up But Not an Immediate Recessionary Outcome

As Figure 11-16 indicates, the real price of oil trended significantly higher from late 2001 through 2008. This gain in inflation-adjusted oil prices certainly generated an aggregate supply shock, and real consumption expenditure growth dropped in response.

Nevertheless, the rate of change of real consumption expenditures remained positive. In contrast to the similarly large oil price run-up that took place in the late 1970s, there was not an immediate, deep recession, even though the real price of oil surpassed levels seen in the last quarter of a century. Most economists agree that the main reason that a rapid, steep recession did not occur is that today U.S. production processes are less reliant on oil. Back in the early 1970s, nearly 1.4 barrels of oil were required to produce $1,000 worth of

U.S. real GDP. By 2000, less than 0.8 barrel of oil was used to produce that amount of real GDP, and today less than 0.6 barrel of oil is utilized. Thus, oil price jumps have smaller effects on short-run aggregate supply today than in preceding years.

Test your understanding of this chapter by going online to **MyEconLab**.
In the Study Plan for this chapter, select Section N: News.

For Critical Analysis

1. Would the comparison of the oil price increases of the 2000s with those of the 1970s be affected by choosing, say, 1975 as the base year for inflation adjustment? Why or why not?

2. In light of the reduced role of oil as a factor of production in the U.S. economy, would you expect an aggregate supply shock as large as in 1979 to occur as a result of the recent run-up in oil prices? Why or why not?

Web Resources

1. To see how nominal and inflation-adjusted oil prices have varied since the end of World War II, go to www.econtoday .com/chapter11.

2. For a very detailed discussion of historical and current factors affecting oil prices, go to www.econtoday.com/chapter11.

Research Project

When we consider the effects of oil price increases on the short-run aggregate supply curve, equilibrium real GDP, and the equilibrium price level, we usually engage in *ceteris paribus* reasoning. That is, we assume that everything else, including any other factor affecting short-run aggregate supply and aggregate demand, is unchanged. Evaluate why our analysis of effects of aggregate supply shocks, particularly during the run-up of inflation-adjusted oil prices during the 2000s, may be incomplete or misleading if we forget that more than one condition can change at the same time.

---

myeconlab Here is what you should know after reading this chapter. **MyEconLab** will help you identify what you know, and where to go when you need to practice.

WHAT YOU SHOULD KNOW		WHERE TO GO TO PRACTICE
Central Assumptions of the Classical Model The classical model makes four key assumptions: (1) pure competition prevails, so no individual buyer or seller of a good or service or of a factor of production can affect its price; (2) wages and prices are completely flexible; (3) people are motivated by self-interest; and (4) buyers and sellers do not experience money illusion, meaning that they respond only to changes in relative prices.	Say's law, 262 money illusion, 263	• **MyEconLab** Study Plan 11.1 • Audio introduction to Chapter 11 • Video: Say's Law

(continued)

 *(continued)*

WHAT YOU SHOULD KNOW		WHERE TO GO TO PRACTICE
Short-Run Determination of Equilibrium Real GDP and the Price Level in the Classical Model Under the four assumptions of the classical model, the short-run aggregate supply curve is vertical at full-employment real GDP and thus corresponds to the long-run aggregate supply curve. So, even in the short run, real GDP cannot increase in the absence of changes in factors of production, such as labor, capital, and technology, which induce longer-term economic growth. Given the position of the classical aggregate supply curve, movements in the equilibrium price level are generated by variations in the position of the aggregate demand curve.	KEY FIGURES Figure 11-2, 264 Figure 11-4, 266 Figure 11-5, 267 Figure 11-6, 268	• **MyEconLab** Study Plan 11.1 • Audio introduction to Chapter 11 • Animated Figures 11-2, 11-4, 11-5, 11-6
Circumstances Under Which the Short-Run Aggregate Supply Curve May Be Horizontal or Upward Sloping If product prices and wages and other input prices are "sticky," perhaps because of labor and other contracts, the short-run aggregate supply schedule can be horizontal over much of its range. This is the Keynesian short-run aggregate supply curve. More generally, however, to the extent that there is incomplete adjustment of prices in the short run, the short-run aggregate supply curve slopes upward.	Keynesian short-run aggregate supply curve, 269 short-run aggregate supply curve, 271 KEY FIGURES Figure 11-7, 269 Figure 11-9, 271	• **MyEconLab** Study Plans 11.2, 11.3 • Video: The Short-Run Aggregate Supply Curve • Animated Figures 11-7, 11-9
Factors That Induce Shifts in the Short-Run and Long-Run Aggregate Supply Curves Both the long-run aggregate supply curve and the short-run aggregate supply curve shift in response to changes in the availability of labor or capital or to changes in technology and productivity. Because output prices may adjust only partially to changing input prices in the short run, however, a widespread change in the prices of factors of production, such as an economywide change in wages, can cause a shift in the short-run aggregate supply curve without affecting the long-run aggregate supply curve.	KEY TABLE Table 11-2, 274 KEY FIGURES Figure 11-10, 273 Figure 11-11, 273	• **MyEconLab** Study Plan 11.4 • Animated Figures 11-10, 11-11
Effects of Aggregate Demand and Supply Shocks on Equilibrium Real GDP in the Short Run An aggregate demand shock that causes the aggregate demand curve to shift leftward pushes equilibrium real GDP below full-employment real GDP in the short run, so there is a recessionary gap. An aggregate demand shock that induces a rightward shift in the aggregate demand curve results in an inflationary gap, in which short-run equilibrium real GDP exceeds full-employment real GDP.	aggregate demand shock, 275 aggregate supply shock, 275 recessionary gap, 275 inflationary gap, 276 KEY FIGURES Figure 11-12, 275 Figure 11-13, 276	• **MyEconLab** Study Plan 11.5 • Video: Shifts in the Short-Run Aggregate Supply Curve • Animated Figures 11-12, 11-13

(continued)

 *(continued)*

WHAT YOU SHOULD KNOW

Causes of Short-Run Variations in the Inflation Rate In the short run, demand-pull inflation can occur when the aggregate demand curve shifts rightward along an upward-sloping short-run aggregate supply curve. Cost-push inflation can arise in the short run when the short-run aggregate supply curve shifts leftward along the aggregate demand curve. A weakening of the dollar shifts the short-run aggregate supply curve leftward and the aggregate demand curve rightward, which causes inflation but has uncertain effects on real GDP.

demand-pull inflation, 276
cost-push inflation, 277

KEY FIGURE
Figure 11-14, 277

WHERE TO GO TO PRACTICE

- **MyEconLab** Study Plan 11.6
- Animated Figure 11-14

Log in to MyEconLab, take a chapter test, and get a personalized Study Plan that tells you which concepts you understand and which ones you need to review. From there, MyEconLab will give you further practice, tutorials, animations, videos, and guided solutions.
Log in to www.myeconlab.com

PROBLEMS

All problems are assignable in **myeconlab** *. Answers to odd-numbered problems appear at the back of the book.*

11-1. Consider a country whose economic structure matches the assumptions of the classical model. After reading a recent best-seller documenting a growing population of low-income elderly people who were ill-prepared for retirement, most residents of this country decide to increase their saving at any given interest rate. Explain whether or how this could affect the following:

    a. The current equilibrium interest rate

    b. Current equilibrium real GDP

    c. Current equilibrium employment

    d. Current equilibrium investment

    e. Future equilibrium real GDP (see Chapter 9)

11-2. Consider a country with an economic structure consistent with the assumptions of the classical model. Suppose that businesses in this nation suddenly anticipate higher future profitability from investments they undertake today. Explain whether or how this could affect the following:

    a. The current equilibrium interest rate

    b. Current equilibrium real GDP

    c. Current equilibrium employment

    d. Current equilibrium saving

    e. Future equilibrium real GDP (see Chapter 9)

11-3. "There is *absolutely no distinction* between the classical model and the model of long-run equilibrium discussed in Chapter 10." Is this statement true or false? Support your answer.

11-4. A nation in which the classical model applies experiences a decline in the quantity of money in circulation. Use an appropriate aggregate demand and aggregate supply diagram to explain what happens to equilibrium real GDP and to the equilibrium price level.

11-5. Suppose that the classical model is appropriate for a country that has suddenly experienced an influx of immigrants who possess a wide variety of employable skills and who have reputations for saving relatively large portions of their incomes, compared with native-born residents, at any given interest rate. Evaluate the effects of this event on the following:

    a. Current equilibrium employment

    b. Current equilibrium real GDP

    c. The current equilibrium interest rate

d. Current equilibrium investment

e. Future equilibrium real GDP (See Chapter 9)

11-6. Suppose that the Keynesian short-run aggregate supply curve is applicable for a nation's economy. Use appropriate diagrams to assist in answering the following questions:

a. What are two factors that can cause the nation's real GDP to increase in the short run?

b. What are two factors that can cause the nation's real GDP to increase in the long run?

11-7. What determines how much real GDP responds to changes in the price level along the short-run aggregate supply curve?

11-8. At a point along the short-run aggregate supply curve that is to the right of the point where it crosses the long-run aggregate supply curve, what must be true of the unemployment rate relative to the long-run, full-employment rate of unemployment? Why?

11-9. Suppose that the stock market crashes in an economy with an upward-sloping short-run aggregate supply curve, and consumer and business confidence plummets. What are the short-run effects on equilibrium real GDP and the equilibrium price level?

11-10. Suppose that there is a temporary, but significant, increase in oil prices in an economy with an upward-sloping *SRAS* curve. If policymakers wish to prevent the equilibrium price level from changing in response to the oil price increase, should they increase or decrease the quantity of money in circulation? Why?

11-11. As in Problem 11-10, suppose that there is a temporary, but significant, increase in oil prices in an economy with an upward-sloping *SRAS* curve. In this case, however, suppose that policymakers wish to prevent equilibrium real GDP from changing in response to the oil price increase. Should they increase or decrease the quantity of money in circulation? Why?

11-12. Based on your answers to Problems 11-10 and 11-11, can policymakers stabilize *both* the price level *and* real GDP simultaneously in response to a short-lived but sudden rise in oil prices? Explain briefly.

11-13. For each question that follows, suppose that the economy *begins* at the short-run equilibrium point *A*. Identify which of the other points on the diagram—

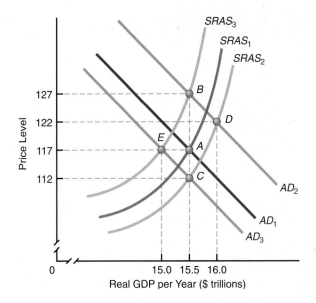

point *B*, *C*, *D*, or *E*—could represent a *new* short-run equilibrium after the described events take place and move the economy away from point *A*. Briefly explain your answers.

a. Most workers in this nation's economy are union members, and unions have successfully negotiated large wage boosts. At the same time, economic conditions suddenly worsen abroad, reducing real GDP and disposable income in other nations of the world.

b. A major hurricane has caused short-term halts in production at many firms and created major bottlenecks in the distribution of goods and services that had been produced prior to the storm. At the same time, the nation's central bank has significantly pushed up the rate of growth of the nation's money supply.

c. A strengthening of the value of this nation's currency in terms of other countries' currencies affects both the *SRAS* curve and the *AD* curve.

11-14. Consider an open economy in which the aggregate supply curve slopes upward in the short run. Firms in this nation do not import raw materials or any other productive inputs from abroad, but foreign residents purchase many of the nation's goods and services. What is the most likely short-run effect on this nation's economy if there is a significant downturn in economic activity in other nations around the world?

ECONOMICS ON THE NET

Money, the Price Level, and Real GDP The classical and Keynesian theories have differing predictions about how changes in the money supply should affect the price level and real GDP. Here you get to look at data on growth in the money supply, the price level, and real GDP.

Title: Federal Reserve Bank of St. Louis Monetary Trends

Navigation: Use the link at **www.econtoday.com/chapter11** to visit the Federal Reserve Bank of St. Louis. Click on *Gross Domestic Product and M2*.

Application Read the article; then answer these questions.

1. Classical theory indicates that, *ceteris paribus*, changes in the price level should be closely related to changes in aggregate demand induced by variations in the quantity of money. Click on *Gross Domestic Product and M2*, and take a look at the charts labeled "Gross Domestic Product Price Index" and "M2." (M2 is a measure of the quantity of money in circulation.) Are annual percentage changes in these variables closely related?

2. Keynesian theory predicts that, *ceteris paribus*, changes in GDP and the quantity of money should be directly related. Take a look at the charts labeled "Real Gross Domestic Product" and "M2." Are annual percentage changes in these variables closely related?

For Group Study and Analysis Both classical and Keynesian theories of relationships among real GDP, the price level, and the quantity of money hinge on specific assumptions. Have class groups search through the FRED database (accessible at **www.econtoday.com/chapter11**) to evaluate factors that provide support for either theory's predictions. Which approach appears to receive greater support from recent data? Does this necessarily imply that this is the "true theory"? Why or why not?

ANSWERS TO QUICK QUIZZES

p. 268: (i) supply . . . demand; (ii) pure competition . . . wages . . . prices . . . self-interest . . . money illusion; (iii) saving . . . investment; (iv) wage rate; (v) vertical . . . price level

p. 274: (i) demand; (ii) reduced; (iii) partial; (iv) intensively . . . higher; (v) *SRAS*

p. 279: (i) Short . . . Long . . . shocks . . . shocks; (ii) recessionary . . . inflationary; (iii) demand-pull . . . cost-push; (iv) weaker . . . weaker

Consumption, Real GDP, and the Multiplier

12

I n theory, higher interest rates should boost households' borrowing costs and give them an incentive to cut back on their consumption spending. Between 1945 and 1989, this is exactly what U.S. consumers did. During these years, a given 1-percentage-point increase in the interest rate would cause U.S. consumption expenditures to decline by 1 to 2 percent. In the years since 1989, however, the impact of interest rate changes on household consumption has decreased substantially. Why has this happened? What are the implications for U.S. aggregate demand and real GDP? To be able to answer these questions, you must learn more about the determinants of consumption spending and about consumption's role in influencing aggregate demand and equilibrium real GDP. These are key topics of this chapter.

LEARNING OBJECTIVES

X myeconlab

MyEconLab helps you master each objective and study more efficiently. See end of chapter for details.

After reading this chapter, you should be able to:

▶ Distinguish between saving and savings and explain how saving and consumption are related

▶ Explain the key determinants of consumption and saving in the Keynesian model

▶ Identify the primary determinants of planned investment

▶ Describe how equilibrium real GDP is established in the Keynesian model

▶ Evaluate why autonomous changes in total planned expenditures have a multiplier effect on equilibrium real GDP

▶ Understand the relationship between total planned expenditures and the aggregate demand curve

? DID YOU KNOW THAT at the end of the 1990s, some businesspeople, numerous media pundits, and even a few economists were speculating that the adoption of new information technologies might have made recessions obsolete? By early 2001, of course, it had become clear that recessions could not be relegated to the dustbin of history. Indeed, most economists blame a nearly 15 percent drop in information-technology investment between the middle of 2000 and the middle of 2001 for the recession that formally lasted from March 2001 until November 2001.

Instead of putting an end to recessions, variations in investment in new information technologies arguably have had a lot to do with fluctuations in real GDP during the first decade of the 2000s. John Maynard Keynes focused much of his research on how unanticipated changes in investment spending affect a nation's aggregate spending and real GDP. The key to determining the broader economic effects of investment fluctuations, Keynes reasoned, was to understand the relationship between how much people earn and their willingness to engage in personal consumption spending. Thus, Keynes argued that a prerequisite to understanding how investment affects a nation's economy is to understand the determinants of household consumption. In this chapter, you will learn how an understanding of consumption expenditures can assist you in evaluating the effects of variations in business investment on real GDP.

Some Simplifying Assumptions in a Keynesian Model

Continuing in the Keynesian tradition, we will assume that the short-run aggregate supply curve within the current range of real GDP is horizontal. That is, we assume that it is similar to Figure 11-7 on page 269. Thus, the equilibrium level of real GDP is demand determined. This is why Keynes wished to examine the elements of desired aggregate expenditures. Because of the Keynesian assumption of inflexible prices, inflation is not a concern. Hence, real values are identical to nominal values.

To simplify the income determination model that follows, a number of assumptions are made:

1. Businesses pay no indirect taxes (for example, sales taxes).
2. Businesses distribute all of their profits to shareholders.
3. There is no depreciation (capital consumption allowance), so gross private domestic investment equals net investment.
4. The economy is closed—that is, there is no foreign trade.

Given all these simplifying assumptions, **real disposable income,** or after-tax real income, will be equal to real GDP minus net taxes—taxes paid less transfer payments received.

Another Look at Definitions and Relationships

You can do only two things with a dollar of disposable income: consume it or save it. If you consume it, it is gone forever. If you save the entire dollar, however, you will be able to consume it (and perhaps more if it earns interest) at some future time. That is the distinction between **consumption** and **saving.** Consumption is the act of using income for the purchase of consumption goods. **Consumption goods** are goods

Real disposable income
Real GDP minus net taxes, or after-tax real income.

Consumption
Spending on new goods and services to be used up out of a household's current income. Whatever is not consumed is saved. Consumption includes such things as buying food and going to a concert.

Saving
The act of not consuming all of one's current income. Whatever is not consumed out of spendable income is, by definition, saved. *Saving* is an action measured over time (a flow), whereas *savings* are a stock, an accumulation resulting from the act of saving in the past.

Consumption goods
Goods bought by households to use up, such as food and movies.

purchased by households for immediate satisfaction. (These also include services.) Consumption goods are such things as food and movies. By definition, whatever you do not consume you save and can consume at some time in the future.

STOCKS AND FLOWS: THE DIFFERENCE BETWEEN SAVING AND SAVINGS It is important to distinguish between *saving* and *savings*. *Saving* is an action that occurs at a particular rate—for example, $40 per week or $2,080 per year. This rate is a flow. It is expressed per unit of time, usually a year. Implicitly, then, when we talk about saving, we talk about a *flow*, or rate, of saving. *Savings*, by contrast, is a *stock* concept, measured at a certain point or instant in time. Your current *savings* are the result of past *saving*. You may currently have *savings* of $8,000 that are the result of four years' *saving* at a rate of $2,000 per year. Consumption is also a flow concept. You consume from after-tax income at a certain rate per week, per month, or per year.

When this person deposits his payroll check at the bank, what decision does he have to make next?

RELATING INCOME TO SAVING AND CONSUMPTION A dollar of take-home income can be allocated either to consumption or to saving. Realizing this, we can see the relationship among saving, consumption, and disposable income from the following expression:

$$\text{Consumption} + \text{saving} \equiv \text{disposable income}$$

This is called an *accounting identity*, meaning that it has to hold true at every moment in time. (To indicate that the relationship is always true, we use the $\equiv$ symbol.)

From this relationship, we can derive the following definition of saving:

$$\text{Saving} \equiv \text{disposable income} - \text{consumption}$$

Hence, saving is the amount of disposable income that is not spent to purchase consumption goods.

Investment

Investment is also a flow concept. As noted in Chapter 8, *investment* as used in economics differs from the common use of the term. In common speech, it is often used to describe putting funds into the stock market or real estate. In economic analysis, investment is defined to include expenditures on new machines and buildings—**capital goods**—that are expected to yield a future stream of income. This is called *fixed investment*. We also include changes in business inventories in our definition. This we call *inventory investment*.

Investment
Spending on items such as machines and buildings, which can be used to produce goods and services in the future. The investment part of real GDP is the portion that will be used in the process of producing goods in the future.

Capital goods
Producer durables; nonconsumable goods that firms use to make other goods.

QUICK QUIZ See page 316 for the answers. Review concepts from this section in MyEconLab.

If we assume that we are operating on a _____ short-run aggregate supply curve, the equilibrium level of real GDP per year is completely demand determined.

_____ is a flow, something that occurs over time. It equals disposable income minus consumption.

_____ is a stock. It is the accumulation resulting from saving.

_____ is also a flow. It includes expenditures on new machines, buildings, and equipment and changes in business inventories.

Determinants of Planned Consumption and Planned Saving

In the classical model discussed in Chapter 11 on pages 262–268, the supply of saving was determined by the rate of interest. Specifically, the higher the rate of interest, the more people wanted to save and therefore the less people wanted to consume.

In contrast, according to Keynes, the interest rate is *not* the most important determinant of an individual's real saving and consumption decisions. In his view, income, not the interest rate, is the main determinant of saving. Thus:

> *Keynes argued that real saving and consumption decisions depend primarily on a household's present real disposable income.*

Consumption function

The relationship between amount consumed and disposable income. A consumption function tells us how much people plan to consume at various levels of disposable income.

The relationship between planned real consumption expenditures of households and their current level of real disposable income has been called the **consumption function.** It shows how much all households plan to consume per year at each level of real disposable income per year. Columns (1) and (2) of Table 12-1 illustrate a consumption function for a hypothetical household.

We see from Table 12-1 that as real disposable income rises, planned consumption also rises, but by a smaller amount, as Keynes suggested. Planned saving also increases with disposable income. Notice, however, that below an income of $60,000, the

TABLE 12-1

Real Consumption and Saving Schedules: A Hypothetical Case

Column 1 presents real disposable income from zero up to $120,000 per year; column 2 indicates planned consumption per year; column 3 presents planned saving per year. At levels of disposable income below $60,000, planned saving is negative. In column 4, we see the average propensity to consume, which is merely planned consumption divided by disposable income. Column 5 lists average propensity to save, which is planned saving divided by disposable income. Column 6 is the marginal propensity to consume, which shows the proportion of *additional* income that will be consumed. Finally, column 7 shows the proportion of *additional* income that will be saved, or the marginal propensity to save. (Δ represents "change in.")

Combination	(1) Real Disposable Income per Year (Y_d)	(2) Planned Real Consumption per Year (C)	(3) Planned Real Saving per Year ($S \equiv Y_d - C$) (1) − (2)	(4) Average Propensity to Consume ($APC \equiv C/Y_d$) (2) ÷ (1)	(5) Average Propensity to Save ($APS \equiv S/Y_d$) (3) ÷ (1)	(6) Marginal Propensity to Consume ($MPC \equiv \Delta C/\Delta Y_d$)	(7) Marginal Propensity to Save ($MPS \equiv \Delta S/\Delta Y_d$)
A	$ 0	$12,000	$−12,000	–	–	–	–
B	12,000	21,600	−9,600	1.8	−0.8	0.8	0.2
C	24,000	31,200	−7,200	1.3	−0.3	0.8	0.2
D	36,000	40,800	−4,800	1.133	−0.133	0.8	0.2
E	48,000	50,400	−2,400	1.05	−0.05	0.8	0.2
F	60,000	60,000	0	1.0	0.0	0.8	0.2
G	72,000	69,600	2,400	0.967	0.033	0.8	0.2
H	84,000	79,200	4,800	0.943	0.057	0.8	0.2
I	96,000	88,800	7,200	0.925	0.075	0.8	0.2
J	108,000	98,400	9,600	0.911	0.089	0.8	0.2
K	120,000	108,000	12,000	0.9	0.1	0.8	0.2

planned saving of this hypothetical household is actually negative. The farther that income drops below that level, the more the household engages in **dissaving,** either by going into debt or by using up some of its existing wealth.

Graphing the Numbers

We now graph the consumption and saving relationships presented in Table 12-1. In the upper part of Figure 12-1 on the following page, the vertical axis measures the level of planned real consumption per year, and the horizontal axis measures the level of real disposable income per year. In the lower part of the figure, the horizontal axis is again real disposable income per year, but now the vertical axis is planned real saving per year. All of these are on a dollars-per-year basis, which emphasizes the point that we are measuring flows, not stocks.

As you can see, we have taken income-consumption and income-saving combinations *A* through *K* and plotted them. In the upper part of Figure 12-1, the result is called the *consumption function.* In the lower part, the result is called the *saving function.* Mathematically, the saving function is the *complement* of the consumption function because consumption plus saving always equals disposable income. What is not consumed is, by definition, saved. The difference between actual disposable income and the planned rate of consumption per year *must* be the planned rate of saving per year.

How can we find the rate of saving or dissaving in the upper part of Figure 12-1? We begin by drawing a line that is equidistant from both the horizontal and the vertical axes. This line is 45 degrees from either axis and is often called the **45-degree reference line.** At every point on the 45-degree reference line, a vertical line drawn to the income axis is the same distance from the origin as a horizontal line drawn to the consumption axis. Thus, at point *F,* where the consumption function intersects the 45-degree line, real disposable income equals planned real consumption. Point *F* is sometimes called the *break-even income point* because there is neither positive nor negative real saving. This can be seen in the lower part of Figure 12-1 as well. The planned annual rate of real saving at a real disposable income level of $60,000 is indeed zero.

Dissaving and Autonomous Consumption

To the left of point *F* in either part of Figure 12-1, this hypothetical family engages in dissaving, either by going into debt or by consuming existing assets. The rate of real saving or dissaving in the upper part of the figure can be found by measuring the vertical distance between the 45-degree line and the consumption function. This simply tells us that if our hypothetical household sees its real disposable income fall to less than $60,000, it will not limit its consumption to this amount. It will instead go into debt or consume existing assets in some way to compensate for part of the lost income.

Now look at the point on the diagram where real disposable income is zero but planned consumption is $12,000. This amount of real planned consumption, which does not depend at all on actual real disposable income, is called **autonomous consumption.** The autonomous consumption of $12,000 is *independent* of disposable income. That means that no matter how low the level of real income of our hypothetical household falls, the household will always attempt to consume at least $12,000 per year. (We are, of course, assuming here that the household's real disposable income does not equal zero year in and year out. There is certainly a limit to how long our hypothetical household could finance autonomous consumption without any

Dissaving
Negative saving; a situation in which spending exceeds income. Dissaving can occur when a household is able to borrow or use up existing assets.

45-degree reference line
The line along which planned real expenditures equal real GDP per year.

Autonomous consumption
The part of consumption that is independent of (does not depend on) the level of disposable income. Changes in autonomous consumption shift the consumption function.

FIGURE 12-1

The Consumption and Saving Functions

If we plot the combinations of real disposable income and planned real consumption from columns 1 and 2 in Table 12-1 on page 290, we get the consumption function.

At every point on the 45-degree line, a vertical line drawn to the income axis is the same distance from the origin as a horizontal line drawn to the consumption axis. Where the consumption function crosses the 45-degree line at *F*, we know that planned real consumption equals real disposable income and there is zero saving. The vertical distance between the 45-degree line and the consumption function measures the rate of real saving or dissaving at any given income level. If we plot the relationship between column 1—real disposable income—and column 3—planned real saving—from Table 12-1 on page 290, we arrive at the saving function shown in the lower part of this diagram. It is the complement of the consumption function presented above it.

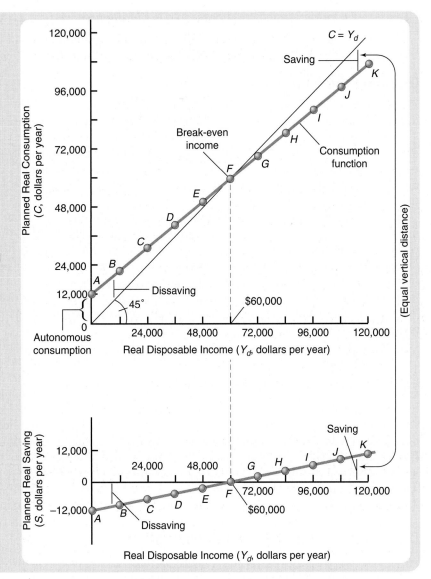

income.) That $12,000 of yearly consumption is determined by things other than the level of income. We don't need to specify what determines autonomous consumption; we merely state that it exists and that in our example it is $12,000 per year.

Just remember that the word *autonomous* means "existing independently." In our model, autonomous consumption exists independently of the hypothetical household's level of real disposable income. (Later we will review some of the determinants of consumption other than real disposable income.) There are many possible types of autonomous expenditures. Hypothetically, we can assume that investment is autonomous—independent of income. We can assume that government expenditures are autonomous. We will do just that at various times in our discussions to simplify our analysis of income determination.

Average Propensity to Consume and to Save

Let's now go back to Table 12-1 on page 290, and this time let's look at columns 4 and 5: **average propensity to consume (APC)** and **average propensity to save (APS).** They are defined as follows:

$$APC \equiv \frac{\text{real consumption}}{\text{real disposable income}}$$

$$APS \equiv \frac{\text{real saving}}{\text{real disposable income}}$$

Average propensity to consume (APC)

Real consumption divided by real disposable income; for any given level of real income, the proportion of total real disposable income that is consumed.

Average propensity to save (APS)

Real saving divided by real disposable income; for any given level of real income, the proportion of total real disposable income that is saved.

Notice from column 4 in Table 12-1 that for this hypothetical household, the average propensity to consume decreases as real disposable income increases. This decrease simply means that the fraction of the household's real disposable income going to consumption falls as income rises. Column 5 shows that the average propensity to save, which at first is negative, finally hits zero at an income level of $60,000 and then becomes positive. In this example, the APS reaches a value of 0.1 at income level $120,000. This means that the household saves 10 percent of a $120,000 income.

It's quite easy for you to figure out your own average propensity to consume or to save. Just divide the value of what you consumed by your total real disposable income for the year, and the result will be your personal APC at your current level of income. Also, divide your real saving during the year by your real disposable income to calculate your own APS.

How low is the U.S. average propensity to save, and why is it so low?

EXAMPLE
Explaining the Low U.S. "Saving Rate"

The media do not refer to the ratio of real household saving to real disposable income as the "average propensity to save (APS)." Instead, they call this ratio, after it has been converted into a percentage, the nation's "saving rate." During the 1980s, the measured U.S. saving rate averaged 9.0 percent, so the average value of the APS was 0.090. During the 1990s, the average saving rate dropped to 5.2 percent, so the average value of the APS declined to 0.052. Since 2000, the saving rate has averaged only 1.8 percent, implying an average APS value of 0.018.

Why have the measured saving rate and the APS declined? One reason may be that the official measure of household saving understates actual saving because it fails to include capital gains on financial assets, which had been higher in many recent years than previously. In addition, improved access to credit cards and other sources of credit has induced many households to opt to borrow in order to expand their consumption and, hence, reduce their saving.

Finally, there is evidence that many households view increases in values of residential property as a form of saving. As inflation-adjusted house values increased during the 1990s and into the mid-2000s, therefore, real saving declined relative to disposable income. When real residential property values began falling throughout much of the nation in 2007 and 2008, there was a slight rise in the saving rate and the APS. If the decline in housing values continues, therefore, the saving rate and the APS may continue to increase.

FOR CRITICAL ANALYSIS
Why do you suppose that the government officially calculates saving as the residual difference between disposable income and consumption instead of computing consumption as the residual difference between disposable income and saving? (Hint: Which do you think is likely to be easier to measure—total household expenditures on goods and services or total household saving?)

Marginal Propensity to Consume and to Save

Marginal propensity to consume (MPC)
The ratio of the change in consumption to the change in disposable income. A marginal propensity to consume of 0.8 tells us that an additional $100 in take-home pay will lead to an additional $80 consumed.

Marginal propensity to save (MPS)
The ratio of the change in saving to the change in disposable income. A marginal propensity to save of 0.2 indicates that out of an additional $100 in take-home pay, $20 will be saved. Whatever is not saved is consumed. The marginal propensity to save plus the marginal propensity to consume must always equal 1, by definition.

Now we go to the last two columns in Table 12-1 on page 290: **marginal propensity to consume (MPC)** and **marginal propensity to save (MPS)**. The term *marginal* refers to a small incremental or decremental change (represented by the Greek letter delta, Δ, in Table 12-1). The marginal propensity to consume, then, is defined as

$$\text{MPC} \equiv \frac{\text{change in real consumption}}{\text{change in real disposable income}}$$

The marginal propensity to save is defined similarly as

$$\text{MPS} \equiv \frac{\text{change in real saving}}{\text{change in real disposable income}}$$

MARGINAL VERSUS AVERAGE PROPENSITIES What do MPC and MPS tell you? They tell you what percentage of a given increase or decrease in real income will go toward consumption and saving, respectively. The emphasis here is on the word *change*. The marginal propensity to consume indicates how much you will change your planned real consumption if there is a change in your actual real disposable income. If your marginal propensity to consume is 0.8, that does *not* mean that you consume 80 percent of *all* disposable income. The percentage of your total real disposable income that you consume is given by the average propensity to consume, or APC. As Table 12-1 indicates, the APC is not equal to 0.8. Instead, an MPC of 0.8 means that you will consume 80 percent of any *increase* in your disposable income. Hence, the MPC cannot be less than zero or greater than one. It follows that households increase their planned real consumption by more than zero and less than 100 percent of any increase in real disposable income that they receive.

If the market value of this couple's newly purchased house goes up significantly in the next ten years, do you think that the couple's measured saving rate will go up or down?

DISTINGUISHING THE MPC FROM THE APC Consider a simple example in which we show the difference between the average propensity to consume and the marginal propensity to consume. Assume that your consumption behavior is exactly the same as our hypothetical household's behavior depicted in Table 12-1. You have an annual real disposable income of $108,000. Your planned consumption rate, then, from column 2 of Table 12-1 is $98,400. So your average propensity to consume is $98,400/$108,000 = 0.911. Now suppose that at the end of the year, your boss gives you an after-tax bonus of $12,000. What would you do with that additional $12,000 in real disposable income? According to the table, you would consume $9,600 of it and save $2,400. In that case, your *marginal* propensity to consume would be $9,600/$12,000 = 0.8 and your marginal propensity to save would be $2,400/$12,000 = 0.2. What would happen to your *average* propensity to consume? To find out, we add $9,600 to $98,400 of planned consumption, which gives us a new consumption rate of $108,000. The average propensity to consume is then $108,000 divided by the new higher salary of $120,000. Your APC drops from 0.911 to 0.9.

In contrast, your MPC remains, in our simplified example, 0.8 all the time. Look at column 6 in Table 12-1 on page 290. The MPC is 0.8 at every level of income. (Therefore, the MPS is always equal to 0.2 at every level of income.) The constancy of MPC reflects the assumption that the amount that you are willing to consume out of additional income will remain the same in percentage terms no matter what level of real disposable income is your starting point.

Some Relationships

Consumption plus saving must equal income. Both your total real disposable income and the change in total real disposable income are either consumed or saved. The proportions of either measure must equal 1, or 100 percent. This allows us to make the following statements:

$$\text{APC} + \text{APS} \equiv 1 \; (= 100 \text{ percent of total income})$$

$$\text{MPC} + \text{MPS} \equiv 1 \; (= 100 \text{ percent of the } \textit{change} \text{ in income})$$

The average propensities as well as the marginal propensities to consume and save must total 1, or 100 percent. Check the two statements by adding the figures in columns 4 and 5 for each level of real disposable income in Table 12-1. Do the same for columns 6 and 7.

Causes of Shifts in the Consumption Function

A change in any other relevant economic variable besides real disposable income will cause the consumption function to shift. The number of such nonincome determinants of the position of the consumption function is virtually unlimited. Real household **wealth** is one determinant of the position of the consumption function. An increase in the real wealth of the average household will cause the consumption function to shift upward. A decrease in real wealth will cause it to shift downward. So far we have been talking about the consumption function of an individual or a household. Now let's move on to the national economy.

Are some wealth effects on consumption larger than others?

> ### You Are There
>
> To think about why a government might try to convince its nation's residents to increase their autonomous consumption expenditures, read **Listen to the German Chancellor: It's Time to Go Shopping!** on page 310.

Wealth

The stock of assets owned by a person, household, firm, or nation. For a household, wealth can consist of a house, cars, personal belongings, stocks, bonds, bank accounts, and cash.

EXAMPLE
Consumption Effects of Changes in Housing versus Financial Wealth

In the United States, about 62 percent of household wealth is in the form of home ownership. Tax rates on this household wealth are relatively low compared with tax rates on financial wealth (stocks, bonds, and other financial assets). In addition, when home equity is offered as collateral, the costs of borrowing are usually lower than when financial assets are used as collateral. Thus, a rise in the real value of housing wealth generates a larger effect on real consumption spending than a rise in the real value of financial wealth. Most estimates indicate that a constant-dollar increase in real housing wealth boosts real consumption spending by 6 cents. In contrast, a constant-dollar rise in real financial wealth pushes up real consumption by only about 2 cents. Thus, a given increase in real housing wealth shifts the consumption function upward by about three times as much as an identical increase in real financial wealth.

FOR CRITICAL ANALYSIS

In nations such as Finland and Italy, in which more than 80 percent of household wealth is in the form of housing, would you expect the wealth effect on consumption of a change in real housing wealth to be greater or smaller than in the United States?

QUICK QUIZ   *See page 316 for the answers. Review concepts from this section in MyEconLab.*

The **consumption function** shows the relationship between planned rates of real consumption and real _____ _____ per year. The saving function is the complement of the consumption function because real saving plus real _____ must equal real disposable income.

The _____ propensity to consume is equal to real consumption divided by real disposable income. The _____ propensity to save is equal to real saving divided by real disposable income.

The _____ propensity to consume is equal to the change in planned real consumption divided by the change in real disposable income. The _____ propensity to save is equal to the change in planned real saving divided by the change in real disposable income.

Any change in real disposable income will cause the planned rate of consumption to change; this is represented by a_____ _____ the consumption function. Any change in a nonincome determinant of consumption will cause a _____ _____ the consumption function.

Determinants of Investment

Investment, you will remember, consists of expenditures on new buildings and equipment and changes in business inventories. Historically, real gross private domestic investment in the United States has been extremely volatile over the years, relative to real consumption. If we were to look at net private domestic investment (investment after depreciation has been deducted), we would see that in the depths of the Great Depression and at the peak of the World War II effort, the figure was negative. In other words, we were eating away at our capital stock—we weren't even maintaining it by completely replacing depreciated equipment.

If we compare real investment expenditures historically with real consumption expenditures, we find that the latter are less variable over time than the former. Why is this so? One possible reason is that the real investment decisions of businesses are based on highly variable, subjective estimates of how the economic future looks.

The Planned Investment Function

Consider that at all times, businesses perceive an array of investment opportunities. These investment opportunities have rates of return ranging from zero to very high, with the number (or dollar value) of all such projects inversely related to the rate of return. Because a project is profitable only if its rate of return exceeds the opportunity cost of the investment—the rate of interest—it follows that as the interest rate falls, planned investment spending increases, and vice versa. Even if firms use retained earnings (internal financing) to fund an investment, the lower the market rate of interest, the smaller the *opportunity cost* of using those retained earnings.

Thus, it does not matter in our analysis whether the firm must seek financing from external sources or can obtain such financing by using retained earnings. Whatever the method of financing, as the interest rate falls, more investment opportunities will be profitable, and planned investment will be higher.

It should be no surprise, therefore, that the investment function is represented as an inverse relationship between the rate of interest and the value of planned real investment. A hypothetical investment schedule is given in panel (a) of Figure 12-2 and plotted in panel (b). We see from this schedule that if, for example, the rate of interest is 5 percent, the dollar value of planned investment will be $2 trillion per year. Notice that planned investment is also given on a per-year basis, showing that it represents

Does the spending on computers for this new high-tech company represent additions to net private domestic investment?

FIGURE 12-2

Planned Real Investment

As shown in the hypothetical planned investment schedule in panel (a), the rate of planned real investment is inversely related to the rate of interest. If we plot the data pairs from panel (a), we obtain the investment function, *I*, in panel (b). It is negatively sloped.

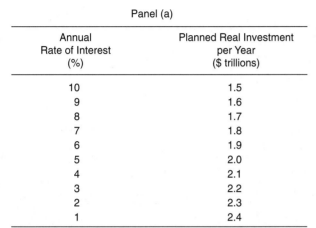

Panel (a)

Annual Rate of Interest (%)	Planned Real Investment per Year ($ trillions)
10	1.5
9	1.6
8	1.7
7	1.8
6	1.9
5	2.0
4	2.1
3	2.2
2	2.3
1	2.4

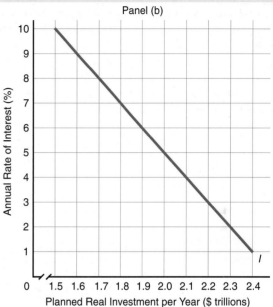

Panel (b)

a flow, not a stock. (The stock counterpart of investment is the stock of capital in the economy measured in inflation-adjusted dollars at a point in time.)

What Causes the Investment Function to Shift?

Because planned real investment is assumed to be a function of the rate of interest, any non-interest-rate variable that changes can have the potential of shifting the investment function. One of those variables is the expectations of businesses. If higher profits are expected, more machines and bigger plants will be planned for the future. More investment will be undertaken because of the expectation of higher profits. In this case, the investment schedule, *I*, would shift outward to the right, meaning that more investment would be desired at all rates of interest. Any change in productive technology can potentially shift the investment function. A positive change in productive technology would stimulate demand for additional capital goods and shift *I* outward to the right. Changes in business taxes can also shift the investment schedule. If they increase, we predict a leftward shift in the planned investment function because higher taxes imply a lower (after-tax) rate of return.

How have changes in anticipated profitability of investments in information technology (IT) caused IT investment's share of total business investment to change between the 1990s and the 2000s?

Go to economic data provided by the Federal Reserve Bank of St. Louis via the link at **www.econtoday.com/chapter12** to see how U.S. real private investment has varied in recent years.

EXAMPLE

The Rise and Decline of IT Investment's Share of Total Investment

Between 1991 and 2000, the share of business investment spending going to information-technology (IT) goods such as computers and software rose from 31 percent to nearly 45 percent. Since 2000, however, the IT share of investment expenditures has declined steadily, to slightly less than 40 percent at present. A key factor driving IT investment's changing share of total business investment has been variations in the average price of IT goods. Between 1991 and 2000, the average price of IT goods declined by nearly 8 percent per year. Naturally, anticipated profits from IT investments soared, which increased the incentive for firms to engage in IT

investments during the 1990s. Since 2000, the average price of IT goods has continued to decline, but at a slower pace of about 4 percent per year. The expected profitability of IT investments in the 2000s has remained high—but not so high as during the 1990s. Consequently, IT investment's share of total investment has dropped during the 2000s.

FOR CRITICAL ANALYSIS

What do you suppose would happen to IT investment's share of total business investment if the average price of IT goods began to rise each year?

QUICK QUIZ   *See page 316 for the answers. Review concepts from this section in MyEconLab.*

The planned investment schedule shows the relationship between real investment and the _____ _____; it slopes _____.

The non-interest-rate determinants of planned investment are _____, innovation and technological changes, and _____ _____.

Any change in the non-interest-rate determinants of planned investment will cause a _____ _____ the planned investment function so that at each and every rate of interest a different amount of planned investment will be made.

Determining Equilibrium Real GDP

We are interested in determining the equilibrium level of real GDP per year. But when we examined the consumption function earlier in this chapter, it related planned real consumption expenditures to the level of real disposable income per year. We have already shown where adjustments must be made to GDP in order to get real disposable income (see Table 8-2 on page 199). Real disposable income turns out to be less than real GDP because real net taxes (real taxes minus real government transfer payments) are usually about 14 to 21 percent of GDP. A representative average is about 18 percent, so disposable income, on average, has in recent years been around 82 percent of GDP.

Consumption as a Function of Real GDP

To simplify our model, assume that real disposable income, Y_d, differs from real GDP by the same absolute amount every year. Therefore, we can relatively easily substitute real GDP for real disposable income in the consumption function.

FIGURE 12-3

Consumption as a Function of Real GDP

This consumption function shows the rate of planned expenditures for each level of real GDP per year. In this example, there is an autonomous component of consumption equal to $0.2 trillion. Along the 45-degree reference line, planned real consumption expenditures per year, *C*, are identical to real GDP per year, *Y*. The consumption curve intersects the 45-degree reference line at a value of $1 trillion per year in base-year dollars.

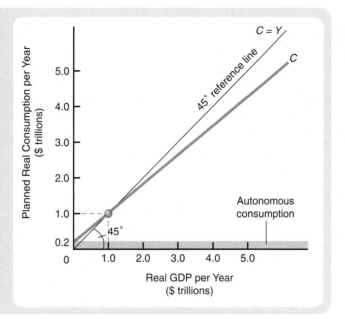

We can now plot any consumption function on a diagram in which the horizontal axis is no longer real disposable income but rather real GDP, as in Figure 12-3. Notice that there is an autonomous part of real consumption that is so labeled. The difference between this graph and the graphs presented earlier in this chapter is the change in the horizontal axis from real disposable income to real GDP per year. For the rest of this chapter, assume that the MPC out of real GDP equals 0.8, suggesting that 20 percent of changes in real disposable income is saved: In other words, of an additional after-tax $100 earned, an additional $80 will be consumed.

The 45-Degree Reference Line

As in the earlier graphs, Figure 12-3 shows a 45-degree reference line. The 45-degree line bisects the quadrant into two equal spaces. Thus, along the 45-degree reference line, planned real consumption expenditures, *C*, equal real GDP per year, *Y*. One can see, then, that at any point where the consumption function intersects the 45-degree reference line, planned real consumption expenditures will be exactly equal to real GDP per year, or *C* = *Y*. Note that in this graph, because we are looking only at planned real consumption on the vertical axis, the 45-degree reference line is where planned real consumption, *C*, is always equal to real GDP per year, *Y*. Later, when we add real investment, government spending, and net exports to the graph, *all* planned real expenditures will be labeled along the vertical axis. In any event, real consumption and real GDP are equal at $1 trillion per year. That is where the consumption curve, *C*, intersects the 45-degree reference line. At that GDP level, all real GDP is consumed.

Adding the Investment Function

Another component of private aggregate demand is, of course, real investment spending, *I*. We have already looked at the planned investment function, which related real investment, which includes changes in inventories of final products, to

FIGURE 12-4

Combining Consumption and Investment

In panel (a), we show determination of real investment in trillions of dollars per year, occurring where the investment schedule intersects the saving schedule at an interest rate of 5 percent and equal to $2 trillion per year. In panel (b), investment is a constant $2 trillion per year. When we add this amount to the consumption line, we obtain in panel (c) the $C + I$ line, which is vertically higher than the C line by exactly $2 trillion. Real GDP is equal to $C + I$ at $11 trillion per year where total planned real expenditures, $C + I$, are equal to actual real GDP, for this is where the $C + I$ line intersects the 45-degree reference line, on which $C + I$ is equal to Y at every point. (For simplicity, we ignore the fact that the dependence of saving on income can influence investment.)

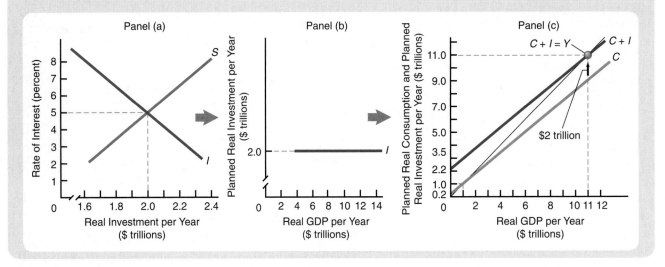

the rate of interest. You see that as the downward-sloping curve in panel (a) of Figure 12-4. Recall from Figure 11-2 (on page 264) that the equilibrium rate of interest is determined at the intersection of the desired saving schedule, which is labeled S and is upward sloping. The equilibrium rate of interest is 5 percent, and the equilibrium rate of real investment is $2 trillion per year. The $2 trillion of real investment per year is *autonomous* with respect to real GDP—that is, it is independent of real GDP. In other words, given that we have a determinant investment level of $2 trillion at a 5 percent rate of interest, we can treat this level of real investment as constant, regardless of the level of GDP. This is shown in panel (b) of Figure 12-4. The vertical distance of real investment spending is $2 trillion. Businesses plan on investing a particular amount—$2 trillion per year—and will do so no matter what the level of real GDP.

How do we add this amount of real investment spending to our consumption function? We simply add a line above the C line that we drew in Figure 12-3 that is higher by the vertical distance equal to $2 trillion of autonomous real investment spending. This is shown by the arrow in panel (c) of Figure 12-4. Our new line, now labeled $C + I$, is called the *consumption plus investment line*. In our simple economy without real government expenditures and net exports, the $C + I$ curve represents total planned real expenditures as they relate to different levels of real GDP per year. Because the 45-degree reference line shows all the points where planned real expenditures (now $C + I$) equal real GDP, we label it $C + I = Y$. Thus, in equilibrium, the sum of consumption spending (C) and investment spending (I) equals real GDP (Y), which is $11 trillion per year. Equilibrium occurs when total

FIGURE 12-5

Planned and Actual Rates of Saving and Investment

Only at the equilibrium level of real GDP of $11 trillion per year will planned saving equal actual saving, planned investment equal actual investment, and hence planned saving equal planned investment.

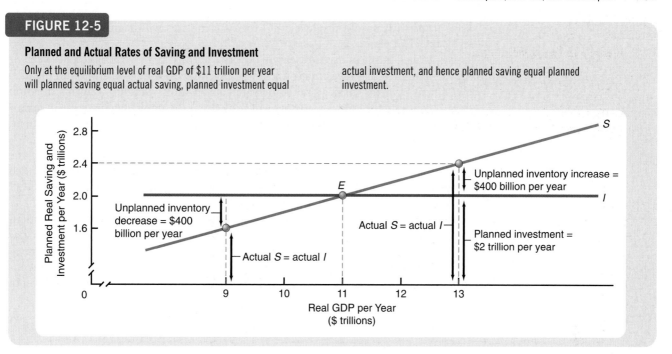

planned real expenditures equal real GDP (given that any amount of production of goods and services in this model in the short run can occur without a change in the price level).

Saving and Investment: Planned versus Actual

Figure 12-5 shows the planned investment curve as a horizontal line at $2 trillion per year in base-year dollars. Real investment is completely autonomous in this simplified model—it does not depend on real GDP.

The planned saving curve is represented by *S*. Because in our model whatever is not consumed is, by definition, saved, the planned saving schedule is the complement of the planned consumption schedule, represented by the *C* line in Figure 12-3 (on page 299). For better exposition, we look at only a part of the saving and investment schedules—annual levels of real GDP between $9 trillion and $13 trillion.

Why does equilibrium have to occur at the intersection of the planned saving and planned investment schedules? If we are at *E* in Figure 12-5, planned saving equals planned investment. All anticipations are validated by reality. There is no tendency for businesses to alter the rate of production or the level of employment because they are neither increasing nor decreasing their inventories in an unplanned way.

UNPLANNED CHANGES IN BUSINESS INVENTORIES If real GDP is $13 trillion instead of $11 trillion, planned investment, as usual, is $2 trillion per year. It is exceeded, however, by planned saving, which is $2.4 trillion per year. The additional $0.4 trillion ($400 billion) in saving by households over and above planned investment represents less consumption spending and will translate into unsold goods that accumulate as unplanned business inventory investment. Thus, consumers will *actually* purchase fewer goods and services than businesses had *anticipated*. This will leave firms with unsold products, and their inventories will begin to rise above the levels they had planned.

Unplanned business inventories will now rise at the rate of $400 billion per year, or $2.4 trillion in actual investment (including inventories) minus $2 trillion in planned investment by firms that had not anticipated an inventory buildup. But this situation cannot continue for long. Businesses will respond to the unplanned increase in inventories by cutting back production of goods and services and reducing employment, and we will move toward a lower level of real GDP.

Naturally, the adjustment process works in reverse if real GDP is less than the equilibrium level. For instance, if real GDP is $9 trillion per year, an unintended inventory decrease of $0.4 trillion ultimately brings about an increase in real GDP toward the equilibrium level of $11 trillion.

Every time the saving rate planned by households differs from the investment rate planned by businesses, there will be a shrinkage or an expansion in the circular flow of income and output (introduced in Chapter 8) in the form of unplanned inventory changes. Real GDP and employment will change until unplanned inventory changes are again zero—that is, until we have attained the equilibrium level of real GDP.

QUICK QUIZ   *See page 316 for the answers. Review concepts from this section in MyEconLab.*

We assume that the consumption function has an _____ part that is independent of the level of real GDP per year. It is labeled "_____ consumption."

For simplicity, we assume that real investment is _____ with respect to real GDP and therefore unaffected by the level of real GDP per year.

The _____ level of real GDP can be found where planned saving equals planned investment.

Whenever planned saving exceeds planned investment, there will be unplanned inventory _____, and real GDP will fall as producers cut production of goods and services. Whenever planned saving is less than planned investment, there will be unplanned inventory _____, and real GDP will rise as producers increase production of goods and services.

Keynesian Equilibrium with Government and the Foreign Sector Added

To this point, we have ignored the role of government in our model. We have also left out the foreign sector of the economy. Let's think about what happens when we also consider these as elements of the model.

Government

To add real government spending, G, to our macroeconomic model, we assume that the level of resource-using government purchases of goods and services (federal, state, and local), *not* including transfer payments, is determined by the political process. In other words, G will be considered autonomous, just like real investment (and a certain component of real consumption). In the United States, resource-using federal government expenditures account for about 20 percent of real GDP.

The other side of the coin, of course, is that there are real taxes, which are used to pay for much of government spending. We will simplify our model greatly by assuming that there is a constant **lump-sum tax** of $2.3 trillion a year to finance $2.3 trillion of government spending. This lump-sum tax will reduce disposable income by the same amount. We show this in Table 12-2 (column 2), where we give the numbers for a complete model.

Lump-sum tax
A tax that does not depend on income. An example is a $1,000 tax that every household must pay, irrespective of its economic situation.

The Foreign Sector

For years, the media have focused attention on the nation's foreign trade deficit. We have been buying merchandise and services from foreign residents—real imports—the value of which exceeds the value of the real exports we have been selling to them. The difference between real exports and real imports is *real net exports*, which we will label X in our graphs. The level of real exports depends on international economic conditions, especially in the countries that buy our products. Real imports depend on economic conditions here at home. For simplicity, assume that real imports exceed real exports (real net exports, X, is negative) and furthermore that the level of real net exports is autonomous—independent of real national income. Assume a level of X of −$0.8 trillion per year, as shown in column 8 of Table 12-2.

Determining the Equilibrium Level of GDP per Year

We are now in a position to determine the equilibrium level of real GDP per year under the continuing assumptions that the price level is unchanging; that investment, government, and the foreign sector are autonomous; and that planned consumption

---

TABLE 12-2

The Determination of Equilibrium Real GDP with Government and Net Exports Added
Figures are trillions of dollars.

(1)	(2)	(3)	(4)	(5)	(6)	(7)	(8)	(9)	(10)	(11)
Real GDP	Real Taxes	Real Disposable Income	Planned Real Consumption	Planned Real Saving	Planned Real Investment	Real Government Spending	Real Net Exports (exports minus imports)	Total Planned Real Expenditures (4)+(6)+(7)+(8)	Unplanned Inventory Changes	Direction of Change in Real GDP
9.0	2.3	6.7	6.7	0.0	2.0	2.3	−0.8	10.2	−1.2	Increase
10.0	2.3	7.7	7.5	0.2	2.0	2.3	−0.8	11.0	−1.0	Increase
11.0	2.3	8.7	8.3	0.4	2.0	2.3	−0.8	11.8	−0.8	Increase
12.0	2.3	9.7	9.1	0.6	2.0	2.3	−0.8	12.6	−0.6	Increase
13.0	2.3	10.7	9.9	0.8	2.0	2.3	−0.8	13.4	−0.4	Increase
14.0	2.3	11.7	10.7	1.0	2.0	2.3	−0.8	14.2	−0.2	Increase
15.0	2.3	12.7	11.5	1.2	2.0	2.3	−0.8	15.0	0	Neither (equilibrium)
16.0	2.3	13.7	12.3	1.4	2.0	2.3	−0.8	15.8	+0.2	Decrease
17.0	2.3	14.7	13.1	1.6	2.0	2.3	−0.8	16.6	+0.4	Decrease

FIGURE 12-6

The Equilibrium Level of Real GDP

The consumption function, with no government and thus no taxes, is shown as *C*. When we add autonomous investment, government spending, and net exports, we obtain *C + I + G + X*. We move from E_1 to E_2. Equilibrium real GDP is $15 trillion per year.

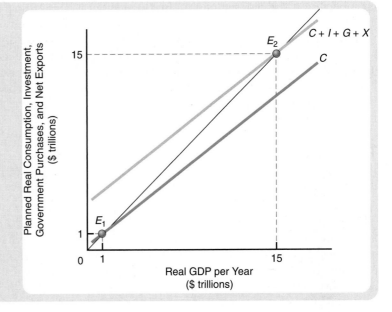

expenditures are determined by the level of real GDP. As can be seen in Table 12-2 on the preceding page, total planned real expenditures of $15 trillion per year equal real GDP of $15 trillion per year, and this is where we reach equilibrium.

Remember that equilibrium always occurs when total planned real expenditures equal real GDP. Now look at Figure 12-6, which shows the equilibrium level of real GDP. There are two curves, one showing the consumption function, which is the exact duplicate of the one shown in Figure 12-3 on page 299, and the other being the *C + I + G + X* curve, which intersects the 45-degree reference line (representing equilibrium) at $15 trillion per year.

Whenever total planned real expenditures differ from real GDP, there are unplanned inventory changes. When total planned real expenditures are greater than real GDP, inventory levels drop in an unplanned manner. To get inventories back up, firms seek to expand their production of goods and services, which increases real GDP. Real GDP rises toward its equilibrium level. Whenever total planned real expenditures are less than real GDP, the opposite occurs. There are unplanned inventory increases, causing firms to cut back on their production of goods and services in an effort to push inventories back down to planned levels. The result is a drop in real GDP toward the equilibrium level.

QUICK QUIZ See page 316 for the answers. Review concepts from this section in MyEconLab.

When we add autonomous investment, *I*, and autonomous government spending, *G*, to the consumption function, we obtain the *C + I + G* curve, which represents total _____ _____ for a closed economy. In an open economy, we add the foreign sector, which consists of exports minus imports, or net exports, *X*. Total planned expenditures are thus represented by the *C + I + G + X* curve.

Equilibrium real GDP can be found by locating the intersection of the total planned real expenditures curve with the _____-_____ reference line. At that level of real GDP per year, planned real consumption plus planned real investment plus real government expenditures plus real net exports will equal real GDP.

> **QUICK QUIZ** | (continued)
>
> Whenever total planned real expenditures exceed real GDP, there will be unplanned _____ in inventories; production of goods and services will increase, and a higher level of equilibrium real GDP will prevail. Whenever total
>
> planned real expenditures are less than real GDP, there will be unplanned _____ in inventories; production of goods and services will decrease, and equilibrium real GDP will decrease.

The Multiplier

Look again at panel (c) of Figure 12-4 on page 300. Assume for the moment that the only real expenditures included in real GDP are real consumption expenditures. Where would the equilibrium level of real GDP be in this case? It would be where the consumption function (C) intersects the 45-degree reference line, which is at $1 trillion per year. Now we add the autonomous amount of planned real investment, $2 trillion, and then determine what the new equilibrium level of real GDP will be. It turns out to be $11 trillion per year. Adding $2 trillion per year of investment spending increased equilibrium real GDP by *five* times that amount, or by $10 trillion per year.

The Multiplier Effect

What is operating here is the multiplier effect of changes in autonomous spending. The **multiplier** is the number by which a permanent change in autonomous real investment or autonomous real consumption is multiplied to get the change in the equilibrium level of real GDP. Any permanent increases in autonomous real investment or in any autonomous component of consumption will cause an even larger increase in real GDP. Any permanent decreases in autonomous real spending will cause even larger decreases in real GDP per year. To understand why this multiple expansion (or contraction) in equilibrium real GDP occurs, let's look at a simple numerical example.

Multiplier
The ratio of the change in the equilibrium level of real GDP to the change in autonomous real expenditures; the number by which a change in autonomous real investment or autonomous real consumption, for example, is multiplied to get the change in equilibrium real GDP.

We'll use the same figures we used for the marginal propensity to consume and to save. MPC will equal 0.8, or $\frac{4}{5}$, and MPS will equal 0.2, or $\frac{1}{5}$. Now let's run an experiment and say that businesses decide to increase planned real investment permanently by $100 billion a year. We see in Table 12-3 on page 306 that during what we'll call the first round in column 1, investment is increased by $100 billion; this also means an increase in real GDP of $100 billion, because the spending by one group represents income for another, shown in column 2. Column 3 gives the resultant increase in consumption by households that received this additional $100 billion in income. This is found by multiplying the MPC by the increase in real GDP. Because the MPC equals 0.8, real consumption expenditures during the first round will increase by $80 billion.

But that's not the end of the story. This additional household consumption is also spending, and it will provide $80 billion of additional income for other individuals. Thus, during the second round, we see an increase in real GDP of $80 billion. Now, out of this increased real GDP, what will be the resultant increase in consumption expenditures? It will be 0.8 times $80 billion, or $64 billion. We continue these induced expenditure rounds and find that an initial increase in autonomous investment expenditures of $100 billion will eventually cause the equilibrium level of real GDP to increase by $500 billion. A permanent $100 billion increase in autonomous real investment spending has induced an additional $400 billion increase in real consumption spending, for a total increase in real GDP of $500 billion. In other words, equilibrium real GDP will change by an amount equal to five times the change in real investment.

TABLE 12-3

The Multiplier Process

We trace the effects of a permanent $100 billion increase in autonomous real investment spending on real GDP per year. If we assume a marginal propensity to consume of 0.8, such an increase will eventually elicit a $500 billion increase in equilibrium real GDP per year.

	Assumption: MPC = 0.8, or $\frac{4}{5}$		
(1)	(2)	(3)	(4)
	Annual Increase in Real GDP	Annual Increase in Planned Real Consumption	Annual Increase in Planned Real Saving
Round	($ billions)	($ billions)	($ billions)
1 ($100 billion per year increase in I)	100.00 →	80.000	20.000
2	80.00 ←	64.000	16.000
3	64.00 ←	51.200	12.800
4	51.20 ←	40.960	10.240
5	40.96 ←	32.768	8.192
.	.	.	.
All later rounds	163.84	131.072	32.768
Totals ($C + I + G$)	500.00	400.000	100.000

The Multiplier Formula

It turns out that the autonomous spending multiplier is equal to the reciprocal of the marginal propensity to save. In our example, the MPC was $\frac{4}{5}$; therefore, because MPC + MPS = 1, the MPS was equal to $\frac{1}{5}$. The reciprocal is 5. That was our multiplier. A $100 billion increase in real planned investment led to a $500 billion increase in the equilibrium level of real GDP. Our multiplier will always be the following:

$$\text{Multiplier} \equiv \frac{1}{1 - \text{MPC}} \equiv \frac{1}{\text{MPS}}$$

You can always figure out the multiplier if you know either the MPC or the MPS. Let's consider an example. If MPS = $\frac{1}{4}$,

$$\text{Multiplier} = \frac{1}{\frac{1}{4}} = 4$$

Because MPC + MPS = 1, it follows that MPS = 1 − MPC. Hence, we can always figure out the multiplier if we are given the marginal propensity to consume. In this example, if the marginal propensity to consume is given as $\frac{3}{4}$,

$$\text{Multiplier} = \frac{1}{1 - \frac{3}{4}} = \frac{1}{\frac{1}{4}} = 4$$

By taking a few numerical examples, you can demonstrate to yourself an important property of the multiplier:

The smaller the marginal propensity to save, the larger the multiplier.

Otherwise stated:

The larger the marginal propensity to consume, the larger the multiplier.

Demonstrate this to yourself by computing the multiplier when the marginal propensity to save equals $\frac{3}{4}$, $\frac{1}{2}$, and $\frac{1}{4}$. What happens to the multiplier as the MPS gets smaller?

When you have the multiplier, the following formula will then give you the change in equilibrium real GDP due to a permanent change in autonomous spending:

$$\text{Change in equilibrium real GDP} = \text{multiplier} \times \text{change in autonomous spending}$$

The multiplier, as noted earlier, works for a permanent increase or a permanent decrease in autonomous spending per year. In our earlier example, if the autonomous component of real consumption had fallen permanently by $100 billion, the reduction in equilibrium real GDP would have been $500 billion per year.

Significance of the Multiplier

Depending on the size of the multiplier, it is possible that a relatively small change in planned investment or in autonomous consumption can trigger a much larger change in equilibrium real GDP per year. In essence, the multiplier magnifies the fluctuations in equilibrium real GDP initiated by changes in autonomous spending.

As was just noted, the larger the marginal propensity to consume, the larger the multiplier. If the marginal propensity to consume is $\frac{1}{2}$, the multiplier is 2. In that case, a $1 billion decrease in (autonomous) real investment will elicit a $2 billion decrease in equilibrium real GDP per year. Conversely, if the marginal propensity to consume is $\frac{9}{10}$, the multiplier will be 10. That same $1 billion decrease in planned real investment expenditures with a multiplier of 10 will lead to a $10 billion decrease in equilibrium real GDP per year.

How a Change in Real Autonomous Spending Affects Real GDP When the Price Level Can Change

So far, our examination of how changes in real autonomous spending affect equilibrium real GDP has considered a situation in which the price level remains unchanged. Thus, our analysis has only indicated how much the aggregate demand curve shifts in response to a change in investment, government spending, net exports, or lump-sum taxes.

Of course, when we take into account the aggregate supply curve, we must also consider responses of the equilibrium price level to a multiplier-induced change in aggregate demand. We do so in Figure 12-7 on the next page. The intersection of AD_1 and $SRAS$ is at a price level of 120 with equilibrium real GDP of $15 trillion per year. An increase in autonomous spending shifts the aggregate demand curve outward to the right to AD_2. If the price level remained at 120, the short-run equilibrium level of real GDP would increase to $15.5 trillion per year because, for the $100 billion increase in autonomous spending, the multiplier would be 5, as it was in Table 12-3.

The price level does not stay fixed, however, because ordinarily the $SRAS$ curve is positively sloped. In this diagram, the new short-run equilibrium level of real GDP is hypothetically $15.3 trillion. The ultimate effect on real GDP is smaller than the multiplier effect on nominal income because part of the additional income is used to

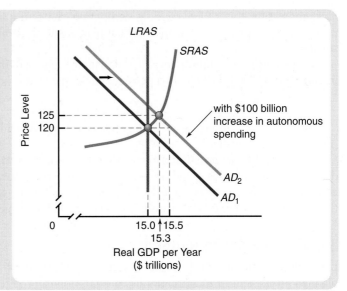

FIGURE 12-7

Effect of a Rise in Autonomous Spending on Equilibrium Real GDP

A $100 billion increase in autonomous spending (investment, government, or net exports) moves AD_1 to AD_2. If the price index increases from 120 to 125, equilibrium real GDP goes up only to, say, $15.3 trillion per year instead of $15.5 trillion per year.

pay higher prices. Not all is spent on additional goods and services, as is the case when the price level is fixed.

If the economy is at an equilibrium level of real GDP that is greater than *LRAS*, the implications for the eventual effect on real GDP are even more severe. Look again at Figure 12-7. The *SRAS* curve starts to slope upward more dramatically after $15 trillion of real GDP per year. Therefore, any increase in aggregate demand will lead to a proportionally greater increase in the price level and a smaller increase in equilibrium real GDP per year. The ultimate effect on real GDP of any increase in autonomous spending will be relatively small because most of the changes will be in the price level. Moreover, any increase in the short-run equilibrium level of real GDP will tend to be temporary because the economy is temporarily above *LRAS*—the strain on its productive capacity will raise the price level.

The Relationship Between Aggregate Demand and the *C + I + G + X* Curve

There is clearly a relationship between the aggregate demand curves that you studied in Chapters 10 and 11 and the *C + I + G + X* curve developed in this chapter. After all, aggregate demand consists of consumption, investment, and government purchases, plus the foreign sector of our economy. There is a major difference, however, between the aggregate demand curve, *AD*, and the *C + I + G + X* curve: The latter is drawn with the price level held constant, whereas the former is drawn, by definition, with the price level changing. To derive the aggregate demand curve from the *C + I + G + X* curve, we must now allow the price level to change. Look at the upper part of Figure 12-8. Here we see the *C + I + G + X* curve at a price level equal to 100, and at $15 trillion of real GDP per year, planned real expenditures exactly equal real GDP. This gives us point *A* in the lower graph, for it shows what real GDP would be at a price level of 100.

FIGURE 12-8

The Relationship Between *AD* and the *C + I + G + X* Curve

In the upper graph, the *C + I + G + X* curve at a price level equal to 100 intersects the 45-degree reference line at E_1, or $15 trillion of real GDP per year. That gives us point *A* (price level = 100; real GDP = $15 trillion) in the lower graph. When the price level increases to 125, the *C + I + G + X* curve shifts downward, and the new level of real GDP at which planned real expenditures equal real GDP is at E_2 at $13 trillion per year. This gives us point *B* in the lower graph. Connecting points *A* and *B*, we obtain the aggregate demand curve.

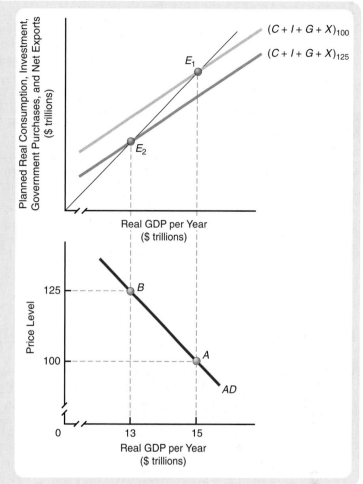

Now let's assume that in the upper graph, the price level increases to 125. What are the effects?

1. A higher price level can decrease the purchasing power of any cash that people hold (the real-balance effect). This is a decrease in real wealth, and it causes consumption expenditures, *C*, to fall, thereby putting downward pressure on the *C + I + G + X* curve.

2. Because individuals attempt to borrow more to replenish their real cash balances, interest rates will rise, which will make it more costly for people to buy houses and cars (the interest rate effect). Higher interest rates also make it less profitable to install new equipment and to erect new buildings. Therefore, the rise in the price level indirectly causes a reduction in total planned spending on goods and services.

3. In an open economy, our higher price level causes foreign spending on our goods to fall (the open economy effect). Simultaneously, it increases our demand for others' goods. If the foreign exchange price of the dollar stays constant for a while, there will be an increase in imports and a decrease in exports, thereby reducing the size of *X*, again putting downward pressure on the *C + I + G + X* curve.

The result is that a new $C + I + G + X$ curve at a price level equal to 125 generates an equilibrium at E_2 at $13 trillion of real GDP per year. This gives us point B in the lower part of Figure 12-8 on the previous page. When we connect points A and B, we obtain the aggregate demand curve, AD.

QUICK QUIZ   See page 316 for the answers. Review concepts from this section in MyEconLab.

Any change in autonomous spending shifts the expenditure curve and causes a _____ effect on equilibrium real GDP per year.

The **multiplier** is equal to the reciprocal of the _____ propensity to _____.

The smaller is the marginal propensity to _____, the larger is the **multiplier.** Otherwise stated, the larger is the

marginal propensity to _____, the larger is the **multiplier.**

The $C + I + G + X$ curve is drawn with the price level held constant, whereas the AD curve allows the price level to _____. Each different price level generates a new $C + I + G + X$ curve.

You Are There    **Listen to the German Chancellor: It's Time to Go Shopping!**

Angela Merkel has been in office as chancellor of Germany for only a few weeks, and her government's approval rating has been soaring in anticipation of improved economic policies. Merkel recently directed her finance minister, Peer Steinbrück, to consider policies the government might adopt in an effort to boost real GDP growth above 2 percent and push the unemployment rate down from the current 11 percent. As Merkel reviews Steinbrück's response, her spirits drop. The finance ministry forecasts a real budget deficit equal to 3.3 percent of real GDP for the coming fiscal year. Under the terms of its membership in the European Monetary Union, the group of nations using the euro as a common currency, Germany's real budget deficit cannot exceed 3.0 percent of real GDP. Thus, the government must either reduce its real expenditures or find a way to collect more taxes.

After meeting with her cabinet ministers, Merkel reaches a conclusion. Her government must find a way to convince Germany's residents to increase their consumption spending. If household consumption increases, so will real GDP and taxable real incomes of the nation's residents, which in turn will boost the government's income tax revenues and

reduce its budget deficit. Merkel instructs Steinbrück and her other ministers to develop a public relations effort aimed at encouraging the nation's residents, whose average saving rate is among the world's highest, to spend a larger share of their disposable incomes. Essentially, her plan is that the German government will engage in a nationwide "marketing effort" aimed at generating a rise in household consumption spending. This path, Merkel has determined, is the best one to pursue in an effort to bring about higher real GDP, lower unemployment, and a smaller government budget deficit.

CRITICAL ANALYSIS QUESTIONS

1. Why would a decrease in government spending or an increase in taxes have been inconsistent with all of the German government's goals? (Hint: Could these actions have *simultaneously* boosted real GDP *and* reduced the budget deficit?)

2. If the German government's "marketing effort" turns out to be successful, through what economic process will it have brought about higher equilibrium real GDP per year?

The Diminishing Effect of Interest Rate Changes on U.S. Real Consumption Spending

CONCEPTS APPLIED

In the Keynesian theory of real income determination, the main determinant of real consumption spending is real disposable income. As noted in this chapter, there are also other determinants of real consumption expenditures. One important determinant is real household wealth. Another determinant is the interest rate. In recent years, however, the impact of interest rate changes on real consumption spending has been declining.

- Consumption
- Consumption Function
- Autonomous Consumption

Interest Rate Changes and Consumption Spending

Recall from Chapter 10 that interest rate changes affect total planned expenditures and aggregate demand. For instance, when a rise in the price level pushes up the interest rate, businesses and households respond to higher borrowing costs by decreasing their desired spending. This is the interest rate effect that helps explain why the aggregate demand curve slopes downward. Furthermore, increases in real interest rates (nominal interest rates corrected for inflation) not due to price level changes also raise borrowing costs for businesses and households and induce them to decrease spending. The result is a decrease in aggregate demand.

Any decreases in real household spending induced by a higher real interest rate translate into lower consumption expenditures at any given level of real disposable income. Autonomous consumption falls in response to a rise in the real interest rate.

The Declining Impact of Interest Rate Changes on Consumption

Figure 12-9 depicts estimated effects, given a constant price level, of a 1-percentage-point increase in the interest rate on real U.S. consumption expenditures

FIGURE 12-9

Estimated Impacts of a 1-Percentage-Point Interest Rate Increase on Real U.S. Consumption Spending Since 1945

The estimated effects of a 1-percentage-point increase in the interest rate on real consumption spending have declined over time, indicating that consumption expenditures have become less sensitive to interest rate changes.

Source: Board of Governors of the Federal Reserve System.

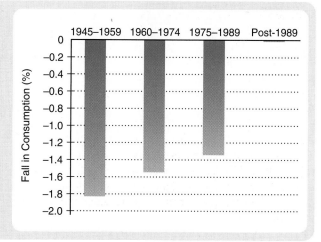

over four periods: 1945–1959, 1960–1974, 1975–1989, and post-1989. During the earliest period, a 1-percentage-point interest rate increase led on average to a decline of almost 2 percent in real consumption spending. Since the 1950s, however, the responsiveness of real consumption expenditures to a change in the interest rate has fallen. For the most recent period since 1990, the estimated impact of an interest rate increase on real consumption spending is negligible.

Federal Reserve economists suggest that one explanation for the reduced sensitivity of real consumption to interest rate changes is that more U.S. employers are able to cushion their responses to higher U.S. interest rates by borrowing internationally. As a consequence, employers are less likely than in years past to reduce workers' hours or engage in layoffs when U.S. interest rates increase. Thus, households' disposable incomes are less likely to decline in the face of a higher U.S. interest rate, and they are better able to maintain their consumption levels.

Test your understanding of this chapter by going online to **MyEconLab.**
In the Study Plan for this chapter, select Section N: News.

For Critical Analysis

1. Does an interest rate change cause a movement along or a shift in the consumption function?

2. How does reduced sensitivity of consumption spending to interest rate changes likely make real GDP less volatile in the face of variations in market interest rates? (Hint: If autonomous consumption is less responsive to interest rate changes, what must be true of variations in equilibrium real GDP in the face of those interest rate changes?)

Web Resources

1. To take a look at how assorted interest rates have changed over time, go to www.econtoday.com/chapter12.

2. Examine data on various measures of U.S. consumption expenditures at www.econtoday.com/chapter12.

Research Project

Figure 12-9 on the previous page indicates that the estimated effect of interest rate changes on autonomous consumption has become much smaller. Look back at the relationship between the *AD* curve and the *C + I + G + X* curve displayed in Figure 12-8 on page 309, and suppose that it applies to a period before 1990. Explain how today's smaller interest rate impact on autonomous consumption affects the size of the shift in the *C + I + G + X* curve depicted in Figure 12-8. What does your analysis imply about the size of the interest rate effect that helps to explain the downward slope of the *AD* curve?

Here is what you should know after reading this chapter. **MyEconLab** will help you identify what you know, and where to go when you need to practice.

WHAT YOU SHOULD KNOW

WHERE TO GO TO PRACTICE

The Difference Between Saving and Savings and the Relationship Between Saving and Consumption Saving is a flow over time, whereas savings is a stock of resources at a point in time. Thus, the portion of your disposable income that you do not consume during a week, a month, or a year is an addition to your stock of savings. By definition, saving during a year plus consumption during that year must equal total disposable (after-tax) income earned that year.

real disposable income, 288
consumption, 288
saving, 288
consumption goods, 288
investment, 289
capital goods, 289

- **MyEconLab** Study Plan 12.1
- Audio introduction to Chapter 12

(continued)

 *(continued)*

WHAT YOU SHOULD KNOW

WHERE TO GO TO PRACTICE

Key Determinants of Consumption and Saving in the Keynesian Model In the classical model, the interest rate is the main determinant of saving, but in the Keynesian model, the primary determinant is disposable income. The reason is that as real disposable income increases, so do real consumption expenditures. Consumption plus saving equal disposable income, so saving must also vary with changes in disposable income. Of course, factors other than disposable income can affect consumption and saving. The portion of consumption unrelated to disposable income is called autonomous consumption. The ratio of saving to disposable income is the average propensity to save (APS), and the ratio of consumption to disposable income is the average propensity to consume (APC). A change in saving divided by the corresponding change in disposable income is the marginal propensity to save (MPS), and a change in consumption divided by the corresponding change in disposable income is the marginal propensity to consume (MPC).

consumption function, 290
dissaving, 291
45-degree reference line, 291
autonomous consumption, 291
average propensity to consume (APC), 293
average propensity to save (APS), 293
marginal propensity to consume (MPC), 294
marginal propensity to save (MPS), 294
wealth, 295

KEY FIGURE
Figure 12-1, 292

- **MyEconLab** Study Plan 12.2
- Video: The Marginal Propensity to Consume
- Animated Figure 12-1

Key Determinants of Planned Investment A rise in the interest rate reduces the profitability of investment, so planned investment varies inversely with the interest rate. Hence, the investment schedule slopes downward. Changes in business expectations, productive technology, or business taxes cause the investment schedule to shift. In the basic Keynesian model, changes in real GDP do not affect planned investment, meaning that investment is autonomous with respect to real GDP.

- **MyEconLab** Study Plan 12.3
- Video: The Determinates of Investment

How Equilibrium Real GDP Is Established in the Keynesian Model In equilibrium, total planned real consumption, investment, government, and net export expenditures equal real GDP, so $C + I + G + X = Y$. This occurs at the point where the $C + I + G + X$ curve crosses the 45-degree reference line. In a world without government spending and taxes, equilibrium also occurs when planned saving is equal to planned investment. Furthermore, at equilibrium real GDP, there is no tendency for business inventories to expand or contract.

lump-sum tax, 303
KEY FIGURE
Figure 12-5, 301

- **MyEconLab** Study Plans 12.4, 12.5
- Animated Figure 12-5

Why Autonomous Changes in Total Planned Real Expenditures Have a Multiplier Effect on Equilibrium Real GDP Any increase in autonomous expenditures, such as an increase in autonomous investment, causes a direct rise in real GDP. The resulting increase in disposable income in turn stimulates

multiplier, 305
KEY TABLE
Table 12-3, 306

- **MyEconLab** Study Plans 12.6 and 12.7
- Animated Table 12-3
- Video: The Multiplier

(continued)

 *(continued)*

WHAT YOU SHOULD KNOW	WHERE TO GO TO PRACTICE

increased consumption by an amount equal to the marginal propensity to consume multiplied by the rise in disposable income that results. As consumption increases, so does real GDP, which induces a further increase in consumption spending. The ultimate expansion of real GDP is equal to the multiplier, $1/(1 - MPC)$, times the increase in autonomous expenditures. Because $MPS \equiv 1 - MPC$, the multiplier can also be written as $1/MPS$.

The Relationship Between Total Planned Expenditures and the Aggregate Demand Curve An increase in the price level decreases the purchasing power of cash holdings, which induces households and businesses to cut back on spending. As individuals and firms seek to borrow to replenish their cash balances, the interest rate tends to rise, which further discourages spending. A higher price level also reduces exports as foreign residents cut back on purchases of domestically produced goods. These combined effects shift the $C + I + G + X$ curve downward following a rise in the price level, so that equilibrium real GDP falls. This yields the downward-sloping aggregate demand curve.

KEY FIGURES
Figure 12-7, 308
Figure 12-8, 309

- **MyEconLab** Study Plan 12.8
- Animated Figures 12-7, 12-8

Log in to MyEconLab, take a chapter test, and get a personalized Study Plan that tells you which concepts you understand and which ones you need to review. From there, MyEconLab will give you further practice, tutorials, animations, videos, and guided solutions.
Log in to www.myeconlab.com

PROBLEMS

All problems are assignable in myeconlab. *Answers to odd-numbered problems appear at the back of the book.*

12-1. Classify each of the following as either a stock or a flow.

a. Myung Park earns $850 per week.

b. Time Warner purchases $100 million in new computer equipment this month.

c. Sally Schmidt has $1,000 in a savings account at a credit union.

d. XYZ, Inc., produces 200 units of output per week.

e. Giorgio Giannelli owns three private jets.

f. General Motors' production declines by 750 autos per month.

g. Russia owes $25 billion to the International Monetary Fund.

12-2. Consider the table below when answering the following questions. For this hypothetical economy, the marginal propensity to save is constant at all levels of real GDP, and investment spending is autonomous. There is no government.

Real GDP	Consumption	Saving	Investment
$ 2,000	$2,200	$_____	$400
4,000	4,000	_____	_____
6,000	_____	_____	_____
8,000	_____	_____	_____
10,000	_____	_____	_____
12,000	_____	_____	_____

a. Complete the table. What is the marginal propensity to save? What is the marginal propensity to consume?

b. Draw a graph of the consumption function. Then add the investment function to obtain $C + I$.

c. Under the graph of $C + I$, draw another graph showing the saving and investment curves. Note that the $C + I$ curve crosses the 45-degree reference line in the upper graph at the same level of real GDP where the saving and investment curves cross in the lower graph. (If not, redraw your graphs.) What is this level of real GDP?

d. What is the numerical value of the multiplier?

e. What is equilibrium real GDP without investment? What is the multiplier effect from the inclusion of investment?

f. What is the average propensity to consume at equilibrium real GDP?

g. If autonomous investment declines from $400 to $200, what happens to equilibrium real GDP?

12-3. Consider the table below when answering the following questions. For this hypothetical economy, the marginal propensity to consume is constant at all levels of real GDP, and investment spending is autonomous. Equilibrium real GDP is equal to $8,000. There is no government.

Real GDP	Consumption	Saving	Investment
$ 2,000	$2,000	_____	_____
4,000	3,600	_____	_____
6,000	5,200	_____	_____
8,000	6,800	_____	_____
10,000	8,400	_____	_____
12,000	10,000	_____	_____

a. Complete the table. What is the marginal propensity to consume? What is the marginal propensity to save?

b. Draw a graph of the consumption function. Then add the investment function to obtain $C + I$.

c. Under the graph of $C + I$, draw another graph showing the saving and investment curves. Does the $C + I$ curve cross the 45-degree reference line in the upper graph at the same level of real GDP where the saving and investment curves cross in the lower graph, at the equilibrium real GDP of $8,000? (If not, redraw your graphs.)

d. What is the average propensity to save at equilibrium real GDP?

e. If autonomous consumption were to rise by $100, what would happen to equilibrium real GDP?

12-4. Calculate the multiplier for the following cases.

   a. MPS = 0.25

   b. MPC = $\frac{5}{6}$

   c. MPS = 0.125

   d. MPC = $\frac{6}{7}$

12-5. Assume that the multiplier in a country is equal to 4 and that autonomous real consumption spending is $1 trillion. If current real GDP is $15 trillion, what is the current value of real consumption spending?

12-6. The multiplier in a country is equal to 5, and households pay no taxes. At the current equilibrium real GDP of $14 trillion, total real consumption spending by households is $12 trillion. What is real autonomous consumption in this country?

12-7. At an initial point on the aggregate demand curve, the price level is 125, and real GDP is $15 trillion. When the price level falls to a value of 120, total autonomous expenditures increase by $250 billion. The marginal propensity to consume is 0.75. What is the level of real GDP at the new point on the aggregate demand curve?

12-8. At an initial point on the aggregate demand curve, the price level is 100, and real GDP is $15 trillion. After the price level rises to 110, however, there is an upward movement along the aggregate demand curve, and real GDP declines to $14 trillion. If total autonomous spending declined by $200 billion in response to the increase in the price level, what is the marginal propensity to consume in this economy?

12-9. In an economy in which the multiplier has a value of 3, the price level has decreased from 115 to 110. As a consequence, there has been a movement along the aggregate demand curve from $15 trillion in real GDP to $15.9 trillion in real GDP.

   a. What is the marginal propensity to save?

   b. What was the amount of the change in autonomous expenditures generated by the decline in the price level?

12-10. Consider the accompanying diagram, which applies to a nation with no government spending, taxes, and net exports. Use the information in the diagram to answer the following questions, and explain your answers.

a. What is the marginal propensity to save?

b. What is the present level of planned investment spending for the present period?

c. What is the equilibrium level of real GDP for the present period?

d. What is the equilibrium level of saving for the present period?

e. If planned investment spending for the present period increases by $25 billion, what will be the resulting *change* in equilibrium real GDP? What will be the new equilibrium level of real GDP if other things, including the price level, remain unchanged?

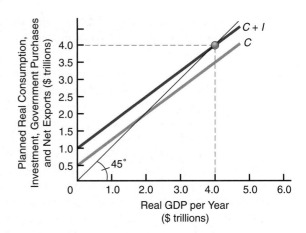

ECONOMICS ON THE NET

The Relationship Between Consumption and Real GDP According to the basic consumption function we considered in this chapter, consumption rises at a fixed rate when both disposable income and real GDP increase. Your task here is to evaluate how reasonable this assumption is and to determine the relative extent to which variations in consumption appear to be related to variations in real GDP.

Title: Gross Domestic Product and Components

Navigation: Use the link at **www.econtoday.com/chapter12** to visit the Federal Reserve Bank of St. Louis's Web page on *Gross Domestic Product and Components*. Then click on *Personal Income and Outlays*.

Application

1. Scan down the alphabetical list, and click on *Personal Consumption Expenditure (Bil. of $; Q)*. Then click on "Download Data." Write down consumption expenditures for the past eight quarters. Now back up to

Gross Domestic Product and Components, click on *Gross Domestic Product, 1 Decimal (Bil. $; Q)*, click on "Download Data," and write down GDP for the past eight quarters. Use these data to calculate implied values for the marginal propensity to consume, assuming that taxes do not vary with income. Is there any problem with this assumption?

2. Back up to *Gross Domestic Product and Components*. Now click on *Gross Domestic Product: Implicit Price Deflator*. Scan through the data since the mid-1960s. In what years did the largest variations in GDP take place? What component or components of GDP appear to have accounted for these large movements?

For Group Study and Analysis Assign groups to use the FRED database to try to determine the best measure of aggregate U.S. disposable income for the past eight quarters. Reconvene as a class, and discuss each group's approach to this issue.

ANSWERS TO QUICK QUIZZES

p. 289: (i) horizontal; (ii) Saving . . . Savings; (iii) Investment

p. 296: (i) disposable income . . . consumption; (ii) average . . . average; (iii) marginal . . . marginal; (iv) movement along . . . shift in

p. 298: (i) interest rate . . . downward; (ii) expectations . . . business taxes; (iii) shift in

p. 302: (i) autonomous . . . autonomous; (ii) autonomous; (iii) equilibrium; (iv) increase . . . decrease

p. 304: (i) planned expenditures; (ii) 45-degree; (iii) decreases . . . increases

p. 310: (i) multiplier; (ii) marginal . . . save; (iii) save . . . consume; (iv) change

The Keynesian Model and the Multiplier

We can see the multiplier effect more clearly if we look at Figure B-1, in which we see only a small section of the graphs that we used in Chapter 12. We start with equilibrium real GDP of $14.5 trillion per year. This equilibrium occurs with total planned real expenditures represented by $C + I + G + X$. The $C + I + G + X$ curve intersects the 45-degree reference line at $14.5 trillion per year. Now we increase real investment, I, by $100 billion. This increase in investment shifts the entire $C + I + G + X$ curve vertically to $C + I' + G + X$. The vertical shift represents that $100 billion increase in autonomous investment. With the higher level of planned expenditures per year, we are no longer in equilibrium at E. Inventories are falling. Production of goods and services will increase as firms try to replenish their inventories. Eventually, real GDP will catch up with total planned expenditures. The new equilibrium level of real GDP is established at E' at the intersection of the new $C + I' + G + X$ curve and the 45-degree reference line, along which $C + I + G + X = Y$ (total planned expenditures equal real GDP). The new equilibrium level of real GDP is $15 trillion per year. Thus, the increase in equilibrium real GDP is equal to five times the permanent increase in planned investment spending.

FIGURE B-1

Graphing the Multiplier

We can translate Table 12-3 on page 306 into graphic form by looking at each successive round of additional spending induced by an autonomous increase in planned investment of $100 billion. The total planned expenditures curve shifts from $C + I + G + X$, with its associated equilibrium level of real GDP of $14.5 trillion, to a new curve labeled $C + I' + G + X$. The new equilibrium level of real GDP is $15 trillion. Equilibrium is again established.

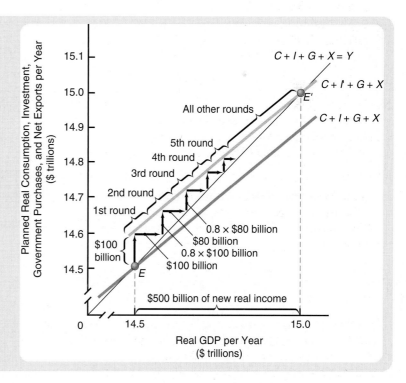

13

Fiscal Policy

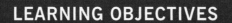

G overnment expenditures on health care services have grown significantly since federal and state governments began covering payments for various types of health-related expenses in the mid-1960s. Today, government health care expenditures account for more than 30 percent of all federal government spending and as much as 35 percent of all state government spending. These percentages may increase as both the U.S. Congress and individual state governments continue to expand programs that pay for health care services. Other things being equal, do ongoing increases in government health care spending generate dollar-for-dollar increases in total planned expenditures in the United States? Or do higher government health care expenditures displace a portion of private health care spending? Why do the answers to these questions matter? You will find out in this chapter.

LEARNING OBJECTIVES

After reading this chapter, you should be able to:

➤ Use traditional Keynesian analysis to evaluate the effects of discretionary fiscal policies

➤ Discuss ways in which indirect crowding out and direct expenditure offsets can reduce the effectiveness of fiscal policy actions

➤ Explain why the Ricardian equivalence theorem calls into question the usefulness of tax changes

➤ List and define fiscal policy time lags and explain why they complicate efforts to engage in fiscal "fine-tuning"

➤ Describe how certain aspects of fiscal policy function as automatic stabilizers for the economy

myeconlab

MyEconLab helps you master each objective and study more efficiently. See end of chapter for details.

? DID YOU KNOW THAT when President Woodrow Wilson signed the U.S. federal income tax into law in October 1913, only about 1 percent of the U.S. population owed any income taxes? Nevertheless, during a floor debate prior to passage of the law, one lawmaker predicted that if the law passed, eventually "a hand from Washington will stretch out to every man's house." Of course, not every income-earning household pays some kind of federal taxes today, but most do. How much taxpayers get back from the federal government in return, in the form of income transfers such as Social Security and Medicare or services such as national defense, police protection, and education, depends on their incomes. The Tax Foundation estimates that for every dollar that households earning less than about $24,000 per year pay in taxes, they get back transfers and services valued at $8.21. Households earning between $42,000 and $62,000 per year receive transfers and services valued at an estimated $1.30 for each tax dollar they pay. Households earning more than about $100,000 per year get back an estimated $0.41 for each dollar of taxes.

All told, U.S. taxpayers transmit nearly $3 trillion in tax payments to the federal government each year, and the federal government spends about $0.8 trillion more than this by borrowing the additional funds. Total federal tax receipts and federal government expenditures each exceed 20 percent of GDP. In this chapter, you will learn about how variations in federal taxes and government spending affect real GDP and the price level.

Why do the income tax returns that U.S. residents file on April 15th not tell a complete story?

Discretionary Fiscal Policy

The making of deliberate, discretionary changes in federal government expenditures or taxes (or both) to achieve certain national economic goals is the realm of **fiscal policy.** Some national goals are high employment (low unemployment), price stability, and economic growth. Fiscal policy can be thought of as a deliberate attempt to cause the economy to move to full employment and price stability more quickly than it otherwise might.

Fiscal policy has typically been associated with the economic theories of John Maynard Keynes and what is now called *traditional* Keynesian analysis. Recall from Chapter 11 that Keynes's explanation of the Great Depression was that there was insufficient aggregate demand. Because he believed that wages and prices were "sticky downward," he argued that the classical economists' picture of an economy moving automatically and quickly toward full employment was inaccurate. To Keynes and his followers, government had to step in to increase aggregate demand. Expansionary fiscal policy initiated by the federal government was the way to ward off recessions and depressions.

Changes in Government Spending

In Chapter 11, we looked at the recessionary gap and the inflationary gap (see Figures 11-12 and 11-13 on pages 275 and 276). The recessionary gap was defined as the amount by which the current level of real GDP falls short of the economy's potential production if it were operating on its *LRAS* curve. The inflationary gap was defined as the amount by which the short-run equilibrium level of real GDP exceeds the long-run equilibrium level as given by *LRAS*. Let us examine fiscal policy first in the context of a recessionary gap.

WHEN THERE IS A RECESSIONARY GAP The government, along with firms, individuals, and foreign residents, is one of the spending agents in the economy. When the government decides to spend more, all other things held constant, the dollar value of total spending must rise. Look at panel (a) of Figure 13-1 on page 320. We begin by

Fiscal policy
The discretionary changing of government expenditures or taxes to achieve national economic goals, such as high employment with price stability.

FIGURE 13-1

Expansionary and Contractionary Fiscal Policy:
Changes in Government Spending

If there is a recessionary gap and short-run equilibrium is at E_1, in panel (a), fiscal policy can presumably increase aggregate demand to AD_2. The new equilibrium is at E_2 at higher real GDP per year and a higher price level. In panel (b), the economy is at short-run equilibrium at E_1, which is at a higher real GDP than the *LRAS*. To reduce this inflationary gap, fiscal policy can be used to decrease aggregate demand from AD_1 to AD_2. Eventually, equilibrium will fall to E_2, which is on the *LRAS*.

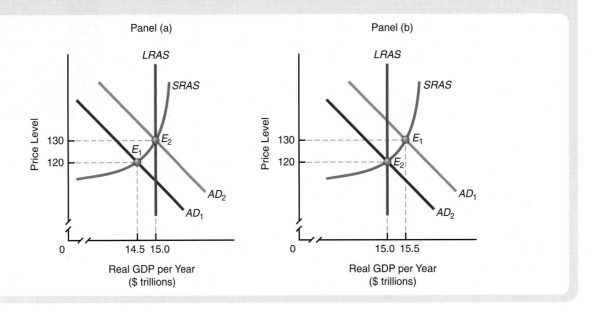

assuming that some negative shock in the near past has left the economy at point E_1, which is a short-run equilibrium in which AD_1 intersects *SRAS* at $14.5 trillion of real GDP per year. There is a recessionary gap of $500 billion of real GDP per year—the difference between *LRAS* (the economy's long-run potential) and the short-run equilibrium level of real GDP per year. When the government decides to spend more (expansionary fiscal policy), the aggregate demand curve shifts to the right to AD_2. Here we assume that the government knows exactly how much more to spend so that AD_2 intersects *SRAS* at $15 trillion, or at *LRAS*. Because of the upward-sloping *SRAS*, the price level rises from 120 to 130 as real GDP goes to $15 trillion per year.

Why has Peru's national government experienced difficulty engaging in discretionary fiscal policy?

INTERNATIONAL POLICY EXAMPLE
Struggling to Boost Government Spending in Peru

When a new president of Peru recently took office, he promised speedy action on a discretionary government spending "shock" aimed at preventing the nation's economy from slipping further into recession. The president sought $1 billion in new expenditures on roads, drinking-water facilities, and improvements in schools and hospitals. Within days, the president's finance ministry had allocated $520 million for immediate spending. Five months later,

INTERNATIONAL POLICY EXAMPLE (cont.)

however, only about $160 million had actually been spent, even though Peru's finance ministry had opened offices to facilitate expenditures in each of the nation's separately governed regions.

The reason for the delay is that Peru has a complex system of laws requiring national government spending to be coordinated with regional governments. When the new president took office at the national level, so did new governors in 23 of the nation's 25 separate regions. Most of these

regional governors had little previous experience with the intricacies of the nation's government spending rules. These complicated legal rules, Peru's new president discovered, severely limit the national government's spending discretion.

FOR CRITICAL ANALYSIS
Why did the $160 million in government spending after five months likely shift Peru's aggregate demand curve rightward by more than that amount?

WHEN THERE IS AN INFLATIONARY GAP The entire process shown in panel (a) of Figure 13-1 can be reversed, as shown in panel (b). There, we assume that a recent shock has left the economy at point E_1, at which an inflationary gap exists at the intersection of *SRAS* and AD_1. Real GDP cannot be sustained at $15.5 trillion indefinitely, because this exceeds long-run aggregate supply, which in real terms is $15 trillion. If the government recognizes this and reduces its spending (pursues a contractionary fiscal policy), this action reduces aggregate demand from AD_1 to AD_2. Equilibrium will fall to E_2 on the *LRAS*, where real GDP per year is $15 trillion. The price level will fall from 130 to 120.

Changes in Taxes

The spending decisions of firms, individuals, and other countries' residents depend on the taxes levied on them. Individuals in their role as consumers look to their disposable (after-tax) income when determining their desired rates of consumption. Firms look at their after-tax profits when deciding on the levels of investment to undertake. Foreign residents look at the tax-inclusive cost of goods when deciding whether to buy in the United States or elsewhere. Therefore, holding all other things constant, a rise in taxes causes a reduction in aggregate demand because it reduces consumption, investment, or net exports.

WHEN THE CURRENT SHORT-RUN EQUILIBRIUM IS TO THE RIGHT OF *LRAS*
Assume that aggregate demand is AD_1 in panel (a) of Figure 13-2 on the following page. It intersects *SRAS* at E_1, which yields real GDP greater than *LRAS*. In this situation, an increase in taxes shifts the aggregate demand curve inward to the left. For argument's sake, assume that it intersects *SRAS* at E_2, or exactly where *LRAS* intersects AD_2. In this situation, the level of real GDP falls from $15.5 trillion per year to $15 trillion per year. The price level falls from 120 to 100.

WHEN THE CURRENT SHORT-RUN EQUILIBRIUM IS TO THE LEFT OF *LRAS*
Look at panel (b) in Figure 13-2. AD_1 intersects *SRAS* at E_1, with real GDP at $14.5 trillion, less than the *LRAS* of $15 trillion. In this situation, a decrease in taxes shifts the aggregate demand curve outward to the right. At AD_2, equilibrium is established at E_2, with the price level at 120 and equilibrium real GDP at $15 trillion per year.

FIGURE 13-2

Contractionary and Expansionary Fiscal Policy: Changes in Taxes

In panel (a), the economy is initially at E_1, where real GDP exceeds long-run equilibrium real GDP. Contractionary fiscal policy via a tax increase can move aggregate demand to AD_2 so that the new equilibrium is at E_2 at a lower price level. Real GDP is now consistent with *LRAS,* which eliminates the inflationary gap. In panel (b), with a recessionary gap (in this case of $500 billion), taxes are cut. AD_1 moves to AD_2. The economy moves from E_1 to E_2, and real GDP is now at $15 trillion per year, the long-run equilibrium level.

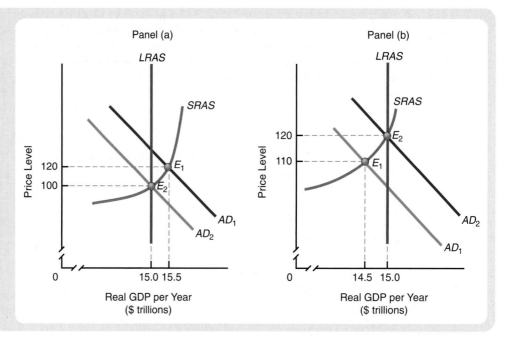

QUICK QUIZ

See page 338 for the answers. *Review concepts from this section in MyEconLab.*

Fiscal policy is defined as making discretionary changes in government _____ or _____ to achieve such national goals as high employment or reduced inflation.

To address a situation in which there is a _____ gap and the economy is operating at less than long-run aggregate supply (*LRAS*), the government can _____ its spending and thereby shift the aggregate demand curve to the right, causing the equilibrium level of real GDP per year to increase.

To address a situation in which there is an _____ gap, the government can _____ its spending and cause the aggregate demand curve to shift to the left, which reduces the equilibrium level of real GDP per year.

Changes in taxes can have similar effects on the equilibrium rate of real GDP and the price level. A _____ in taxes can lead to an increase in the equilibrium level of real GDP per year. In contrast, if there is an inflationary gap, an _____ in taxes can decrease equilibrium real GDP.

Possible Offsets to Fiscal Policy

Fiscal policy does not operate in a vacuum. Important questions have to be answered: If government expenditures increase, how are those expenditures financed, and by whom? If taxes are increased, what does the government do with the taxes? What will happen if individuals worry about increases in *future* taxes because the government is spending more today without raising current taxes? All of these questions involve *offsets* to the effects of current fiscal policy. We will look at each of them and others in detail.

Indirect Crowding Out

Let's take the first example of fiscal policy in this chapter—an increase in government expenditures. If government expenditures rise and taxes are held constant, something has to give. Our government does not simply take goods and services when it wants them. It has to pay for them. When it pays for them and does not simultaneously collect the same amount in taxes, it must borrow. That means that an increase in government spending without raising taxes creates additional government borrowing from the private sector (or from other countries' residents).

INDUCED INTEREST RATE CHANGES If the government attempts to borrow more from the private sector, it will have to offer a higher interest rate to lure the additional funds from savers. This is the interest rate effect of expansionary fiscal policy financed by borrowing from the public. Consequently, when the federal government finances increased spending by additional borrowing, it will push interest rates up. When interest rates go up, it is less profitable for firms to finance new construction, equipment, and inventories. It is also more expensive for individuals to finance purchases of cars and homes.

Thus, a rise in government spending, holding taxes constant (that is, deficit spending), tends to crowd out private spending, dampening the positive effect of increased government spending on aggregate demand. This is called the **crowding-out effect.** In the extreme case, the crowding out may be complete, with the increased government spending having no net effect on aggregate demand. The final result is simply more government spending and less private investment and consumption. Figure 13-3 shows how the crowding-out effect occurs.

THE FIRM'S INVESTMENT DECISION To understand the crowding-out effect better, consider a firm that is contemplating borrowing $100,000 to expand its business. Suppose that the interest rate is 5 percent. The interest payments on the debt will be 5 percent times $100,000, or $5,000 per year ($417 per month). A rise in the interest rate to 8 percent will push the payments to 8 percent of $100,000, or $8,000 per year ($667 per month). The extra $250 per month in interest expenses will discourage some firms from making the investment. Consumers face similar decisions when they purchase houses and cars. An increase in the interest rate causes their monthly payments to go up, thereby discouraging some of them from purchasing cars and houses.

GRAPHICAL ANALYSIS You see in Figure 13-4 on the following page that the economy is in a situation in which, at point E_1, equilibrium real GDP is below the long-run level consistent with the position of the *LRAS* curve. But suppose that government

Crowding-out effect
The tendency of expansionary fiscal policy to cause a decrease in planned investment or planned consumption in the private sector; this decrease normally results from the rise in interest rates.

FIGURE 13-3

The Crowding-Out Effect, Step by Step

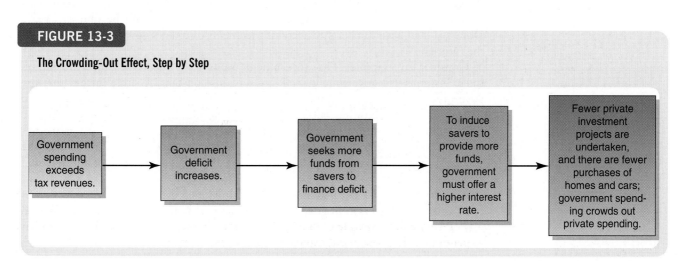

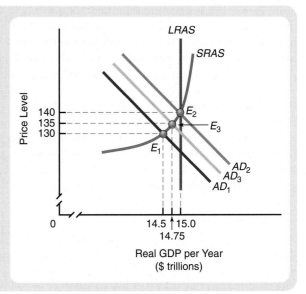

FIGURE 13-4

The Crowding-Out Effect

Expansionary fiscal policy that causes deficit financing initially shifts AD_1 to AD_2. Equilibrium initially moves toward E_2. But expansionary fiscal policy pushes up interest rates, thereby reducing interest-sensitive spending. This effect causes the aggregate demand curve to shift inward to AD_3, and the new short-run equilibrium is at E_3.

expansionary fiscal policy in the form of increased government spending (without increasing current taxes) attempts to shift aggregate demand from AD_1 to AD_2. In the absence of the crowding-out effect, real GDP would increase to $15 trillion per year, and the price level would rise to 140 (point E_2). With the (partial) crowding-out effect, however, as investment and consumption decline, partly offsetting the rise in government spending, the aggregate demand curve shifts inward to the left to AD_3. The new short-run equilibrium is now at E_3, with real GDP of $14.75 trillion per year at a price level of 135. In other words, crowding out dilutes the effect of expansionary fiscal policy, and a recessionary gap remains.

Planning for the Future: The Ricardian Equivalence Theorem

Economists have often implicitly assumed that people look at changes in taxes or changes in government spending only in the present. What if people actually think about the size of *future* tax payments? Does this have an effect on how they react to an increase in government spending with no current tax increases? Some economists believe that the answer is yes. What if people's horizons extend beyond this year? Don't we then have to take into account the effects of today's government policies on the future?

Consider an example. The government wants to reduce taxes by $100 billion today. Assume that government spending remains constant. Assume further that the government initially has a balanced budget. Thus, the only way for the government to pay for this $100 billion tax cut is to borrow $100 billion today. The public will owe $100 billion plus interest later. Realizing that a $100 billion tax cut today is mathematically equivalent to $100 billion plus interest later, people may wish to save the proceeds from the tax cut to meet future tax liabilities—payment of interest and repayment of debt.

Consequently, a tax cut may not affect total planned expenditures. A reduction in taxes without a reduction in government spending may therefore have no impact on aggregate demand. Similarly, an increase in taxes without an increase in government spending may not have a large impact on aggregate demand.

Suppose that a decrease in taxes shifts the aggregate demand curve from AD_1 to AD_2 in Figure 13-4. If consumers partly compensate for a higher future tax liability by saving more, the aggregate demand curve shifts leftward, to a position such as AD_3. In the extreme case in which individuals fully take into account their increased tax liabilities, the aggregate demand curve shifts all the way back to AD_1, so that there is no effect on the economy. This is known as the **Ricardian equivalence theorem,** after the nineteenth-century economist David Ricardo, who first developed the argument publicly.

According to the Ricardian equivalence theorem, it does not matter how government expenditures are financed—by taxes or by borrowing. Is the theorem correct? Research indicates that Ricardian equivalence effects likely exist but has not provided much compelling evidence about their magnitudes.

Ricardian equivalence theorem
The proposition that an increase in the government budget deficit has no effect on aggregate demand.

Direct Expenditure Offsets

Government has a distinct comparative advantage over the private sector in certain activities such as diplomacy and national defense. Otherwise stated, certain resource-using activities in which the government engages do not compete with the private sector. In contrast, some of what government does, such as public education, competes directly with the private sector. When government competes with the private sector, **direct expenditure offsets** to fiscal policy may occur. For example, if the government starts providing milk at no charge to students who are already purchasing milk, there is a direct expenditure offset. Direct household spending on milk decreases, but government spending on milk increases.

Normally, the impact of an increase in government spending on aggregate demand is analyzed by implicitly assuming that government spending is *not* a substitute for private spending. This is clearly the case for a cruise missile. Whenever government spending is a substitute for private spending, however, a rise in government spending causes a direct reduction in private spending to offset it.

How has a Florida state insurance program largely created a direct expenditure offset?

Direct expenditure offsets
Actions on the part of the private sector in spending income that offset government fiscal policy actions. Any increase in government spending in an area that competes with the private sector will have some direct expenditure offset.

POLICY EXAMPLE
Direct Expenditure Offsets in Florida Insurance Coverage

In 2002, Florida's legislature created Citizens Property Insurance Corporation (CPIC), a state government insurance agency offering taxpayer-subsidized insurance policies to homeowners. In addition, the legislature placed ceilings on the premium rates that private insurance companies could charge for homeowners' insurance policies. Today, more than 1.5 million people have policies with CPIC. About 0.1 million of these CPIC policyholders previously were uninsured. The rest, however, have switched to CPIC from private insurers, either because they were attracted by CPIC's lower premium rates or because private insurers canceled their policies when prohibited from raising premium rates. Thus, about 1.4 million homeowners who previously paid private insurers for insurance coverage now pay, with Florida taxpayers' assistance, a state government agency for that coverage. In addition, when they receive compensation for losses from CPIC following the next big hurricane, these homeowners will receive about the same amount of insurance proceeds that private insurers otherwise would have provided.

FOR CRITICAL ANALYSIS
Are there any aspects of CPIC's operations that do not involve a direct expenditure offset?

THE EXTREME CASE In the extreme case, the direct expenditure offset is dollar for dollar, so we merely end up with a relabeling of spending from private to public. Assume that you have decided to spend $100 on groceries. Upon your arrival at the checkout counter, you find a U.S. Department of Agriculture official. She announces that she will pay for your groceries—but only the ones in the cart. Here increased government spending is $100. You leave the store in bliss. But just as you are deciding how to spend the $100, an Internal Revenue Service agent appears. He announces that as a result of the current budgetary crisis, your taxes are going to rise by $100. You have to pay right now. Increases in taxes have now been $100. We have a balanced-budget increase in government spending. In this scenario, *total* spending does not change. We simply end up with higher government spending, which directly offsets exactly an equal reduction in consumption. Aggregate demand and GDP are unchanged. Otherwise stated, if there is a full direct expenditure offset, the government spending multiplier is zero.

THE LESS EXTREME CASE Much government spending has a private-sector substitute. When government expenditures increase, private spending tends to decline somewhat (but generally not dollar for dollar), thereby mitigating the upward impact on total aggregate demand. To the extent that there are some direct expenditure offsets to expansionary fiscal policy, predicted changes in aggregate demand will be lessened. Consequently, real GDP and the price level will be less affected.

The Supply-Side Effects of Changes in Taxes

We have talked about changing taxes and changing government spending, the traditional tools of fiscal policy. We have not really talked about the possibility of changing *marginal* tax rates. Recall from Chapter 6 that the marginal tax rate is the rate applied to the last, or highest, bracket of taxable income. In our federal tax system, higher marginal tax rates are applied as income rises. In that sense, the United States has a progressive federal individual income tax system. Expansionary fiscal policy could involve reducing marginal tax rates. Advocates of such changes argue that lower tax rates will lead to an increase in productivity because individuals will work harder and longer, save more, and invest more and that increased productivity will lead to more economic growth, which will lead to higher real GDP. The government, by applying lower marginal tax rates, will not necessarily lose tax revenues, for the lower marginal tax rates will be applied to a growing tax base because of economic growth—after all, tax revenues are the product of a tax rate times a tax base.

The relationship between tax rates and tax revenues, which you may recall from the discussion of sales taxes in Chapter 6, is sometimes called the *Laffer curve*, named after economist Arthur Laffer, who explained the relationship to some journalists and politicians in 1974. It is reproduced in Figure 13-5. On the vertical axis are tax revenues, and on the horizontal axis is the marginal tax rate. As you can see, total tax revenues initially rise but then eventually fall as the tax rate continues to increase after reaching some unspecified tax-revenue-maximizing rate at the top of the curve.

People who support the notion that reducing taxes does not necessarily lead to reduced tax revenues are called supply-side economists. **Supply-side economics** involves changing the tax structure to create incentives to increase productivity. Due to a shift in the aggregate supply curve to the right, there can be greater real GDP without upward pressure on the price level.

Consider the supply-side effects of changes in marginal tax rates on labor. An increase in tax rates reduces the opportunity cost of leisure, thereby inducing individuals to

You Are There

To learn about whether the federal government takes the Laffer curve into account in its analysis of tax policy, take a look at **A Derailed Effort to Move Toward Accounting for the Laffer Curve**, on page 331.

Supply-side economics
The suggestion that creating incentives for individuals and firms to increase productivity will cause the aggregate supply curve to shift outward.

FIGURE 13-5

Laffer Curve

The Laffer curve indicates that tax revenues initially rise with a higher tax rate. Eventually, however, tax revenues decline as the tax rate increases.

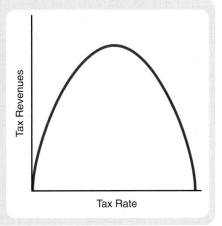

reduce their work effort and to consume more leisure. But an increase in tax rates will also reduce spendable income, thereby shifting the demand curve for leisure inward to the left, which tends to increase work effort. The outcome of these two effects on the choice of leisure (and thus work) depends on which of them is stronger. Supply-side economists argue that at various times, the first effect has dominated: Increases in marginal tax rates have caused workers to work less, and decreases in marginal tax rates have caused workers to work more.

Is it possible that the U.S. economy was operating at a tax rate higher than the revenue-maximizing tax rate before the tax rate cuts of 2003?

POLICY EXAMPLE
A Laffer Curve in the Mid-2000s?

In May 2003, at the urging of the administration of George W. Bush, Congress reduced the top tax rate on corporate dividends, from 39.6 percent to 15 percent, and the tax rate on capital gains, from 20 percent to 15 percent. In addition, Congress cut personal income tax rates slightly.

Many critics of the 2003 tax rate cuts predicted that the federal government's tax revenues would plummet after the rates were cut. Nevertheless, by the beginning of 2008, after four years of higher real GDP growth, total federal income tax receipts from corporations and individuals had increased by nearly 50 percent.

FOR CRITICAL ANALYSIS

Why do you suppose that it is difficult to determine exactly which factors are most responsible for increases or decreases in income tax revenues? (Hint: Income tax revenues depend on income, which in turn varies with equilibrium real GDP, which in turn changes with variations in aggregate demand and aggregate supply.)

QUICK QUIZ   *See page 338 for the answers. Review concepts from this section in MyEconLab.*

Indirect crowding out occurs because of an interest rate effect in which the government's efforts to finance its

deficit spending cause interest rates to _____, thereby crowding out private investment and spending,

QUICK QUIZ *(continued)*

particularly on cars and houses. This is called the **crowding-out effect.**

_____ _____ _____ occur when government spending competes with the private sector and is increased. A direct crowding-out effect may occur.

The _____ _____ theorem holds that an increase in the government budget deficit has no effect on aggregate demand because individuals anticipate that their

future taxes will increase and therefore save more today to pay for them.

Changes in marginal tax rates may cause _____-_____ effects if a reduction in marginal tax rates induces enough additional work, saving, and investing. Government tax receipts can actually increase. This is called _____-_____ economics.

Discretionary Fiscal Policy in Practice: Coping with Time Lags

We can discuss fiscal policy in a relatively precise way. We draw graphs with aggregate demand and supply curves to show what we are doing. We could even in principle estimate the offsets that we just discussed. Even if we were able to measure all of these offsets exactly, however, would-be fiscal policymakers still face a problem: The conduct of fiscal policy involves a variety of time lags.

Policy Time Lags

Policymakers must be concerned with time lags. Quite apart from the fact that it is difficult to measure economic variables, it takes time to collect and assimilate such data. Thus, policymakers must contend with the **recognition time lag,** the months that may elapse before national economic problems can be identified.

After an economic problem is recognized, a solution must be formulated; thus, there will be an **action time lag** between the recognition of a problem and the implementation of policy to solve it. For fiscal policy, the action time lag is particularly long. Such policy must be approved by Congress and is subject to political wrangling and infighting. The action time lag can easily last a year or two. Then it takes time to actually implement the policy. After Congress enacts fiscal policy legislation, it takes time to decide such matters as who gets new federal construction contracts.

Finally, there is the **effect time lag:** After fiscal policy is enacted, it takes time for the policy to affect the economy. To demonstrate the effects, economists need only shift curves on a chalkboard, a whiteboard, or a piece of paper, but in real time, such effects take quite a while to work their way through the economy. ·

Problems Posed by Time Lags

Because the various fiscal policy time lags are long, a policy designed to combat a recession might not produce results until the economy is already out of that recession and perhaps experiencing inflation, in which case the fiscal policy would worsen the situation. Or a fiscal policy designed to eliminate inflation might not produce effects until the economy is in a recession; in that case, too, fiscal policy would make the economic problem worse rather than better.

Furthermore, because fiscal policy time lags tend to be *variable* (each lasting anywhere from one to three years), policymakers have a difficult time fine-tuning the economy. Clearly, fiscal policy is more guesswork than science.

Recognition time lag
The time required to gather information about the current state of the economy.

Action time lag
The time between recognizing an economic problem and implementing policy to solve it. The action time lag is quite long for fiscal policy, which requires congressional approval.

Effect time lag
The time that elapses between the implementation of a policy and the results of that policy.

Automatic Stabilizers

Not all changes in taxes (or in tax rates) or in government spending (including government transfers) constitute discretionary fiscal policy. There are several types of automatic (or nondiscretionary) fiscal policies. Such policies do not require new legislation on the part of Congress. Specific automatic fiscal policies—called **automatic, or built-in, stabilizers**—include the tax system itself, unemployment compensation, and income transfer payments.

The Tax System as an Automatic Stabilizer

You know that if you work less, you are paid less, and therefore you pay fewer taxes. The amount of taxes that our government collects falls automatically during a recession. Basically, incomes and profits fall when business activity slows down, and the government's tax revenues drop, too. Some economists consider this an automatic tax cut, which therefore stimulates aggregate demand. It reduces the extent of any negative economic fluctuation.

The progressive nature of the federal personal and corporate income tax systems magnifies any automatic stabilization effect that might exist. If your hours of work are reduced because of a recession, you still pay some federal personal income taxes. But because of our progressive system, you may drop into a lower tax bracket, thereby paying a lower marginal tax rate. As a result, your disposable income falls by a smaller percentage than your before-tax income falls.

Unemployment Compensation and Income Transfer Payments

Like our tax system, unemployment compensation payments stabilize aggregate demand. Throughout the course of business fluctuations, unemployment compensation reduces *changes* in people's disposable income. When business activity drops, most laid-off workers automatically become eligible for unemployment compensation from their state governments. Their disposable income therefore remains positive, although at a lower level than when they were employed. During boom periods, there is less unemployment, and consequently fewer unemployment payments are made to the labor force. Less purchasing power is being added to the economy because fewer unemployment checks are paid out. In contrast, during recessions the opposite is true.

Income transfer payments act similarly as an automatic stabilizer. When a recession occurs, more people become eligible for income transfer payments, such as Supplemental Security Income and temporary assistance to needy families. Therefore, those people do not experience so dramatic a drop in disposable income as they otherwise would have.

Stabilizing Impact

The key stabilizing impact of our tax system, unemployment compensation, and income transfer payments is their ability to mitigate changes in disposable income, consumption, and the equilibrium level of real GDP. If disposable income is prevented from falling as much as it otherwise would during a recession, the downturn will be moderated. In contrast, if disposable income is prevented from rising as rapidly as it otherwise would during a boom, the boom is less likely to get out of hand. The progressive income tax and unemployment compensation thus provide automatic stabilization to the economy. We present the argument graphically in Figure 13-6 on the following page.

Automatic, or built-in, stabilizers
Special provisions of certain federal programs that cause changes in desired aggregate expenditures without the action of Congress and the president. Examples are the federal progressive tax system and unemployment compensation.

Why do we consider that the unemployment compensation system in the United States is an automatic, rather than discretionary, stabilizer?

FIGURE 13-6

Automatic Stabilizers

Here we assume that as real GDP rises, tax revenues rise and government transfers fall, other things remaining constant. Thus, as the economy expands from Y_f to Y_1, a budget surplus automatically arises; as the economy contracts from Y_f to Y_2, a budget deficit automatically arises. Such automatic changes tend to drive the economy back toward its full-employment real GDP.

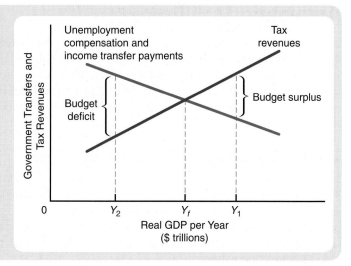

What Do We Really Know About Fiscal Policy?

There are two ways of looking at fiscal policy. One prevails during normal times and the other during abnormal times.

Fiscal Policy During Normal Times

Go to www.econtoday.com/chapter13 to learn about the current outlook for the budget of the U.S. government.

During normal times (without "excessive" unemployment, inflation, or unusual problems in the national economy), we know that due to the recognition time lag and the modest size of any fiscal policy action that Congress will actually take, discretionary fiscal policy is probably not very effective. Congress ends up doing too little too late to help in a minor recession. Moreover, fiscal policy that generates repeated tax changes (as has happened) creates uncertainty, which may do more harm than good. To the extent that fiscal policy has any effect during normal times, it probably achieves this by way of automatic stabilizers rather than by way of discretionary policy.

Fiscal Policy During Abnormal Times

During abnormal times, fiscal policy may be effective. Consider some classic examples: the Great Depression and war periods.

Why might discretionary fiscal policy work during another "great depression" whereas it probably works very little during normal times?

THE GREAT DEPRESSION When there is a catastrophic drop in real GDP, as there was during the Great Depression, fiscal policy may be able to stimulate aggregate demand. Because so many people have few assets left and thus are income-constrained during such periods, government spending is a way to get income into their hands—income that they are likely to spend immediately.

WARTIME Wars are in fact reserved for governments. War expenditures are not good substitutes for private expenditures—they have little or no direct expenditure offsets. Consequently, war spending as part of expansionary fiscal policy usually has noteworthy effects, such as occurred while we were waging World War II, when real

GDP increased dramatically (though much of the output of new goods and services was expended for military uses).

The "Soothing" Effect of Keynesian Fiscal Policy

One view of traditional Keynesian fiscal policy does not call for it to be used on a regular basis but nevertheless sees it as potentially useful. As you have learned in this chapter, many problems are associated with attempting to use fiscal policy. But if we should encounter a severe downturn, fiscal policy is available. Knowing this may reassure consumers and investors. Thus, the availability of fiscal policy may induce more buoyant and stable expectations of the future, thereby smoothing investment spending.

QUICK QUIZ   *See page 338 for the answers. Review concepts from this section in MyEconLab.*

Time lags of various sorts reduce the effectiveness of fiscal policy. These include the _____ time lag, the _____ time lag, and the _____ time lag.

Two _____, or built-in, stabilizers are the progressive income tax and unemployment compensation.

Built-in stabilizers automatically tend to _____ changes in disposable income resulting from changes in overall business activity.

Although discretionary fiscal policy may not necessarily be a useful policy tool in normal times because of time lags, it may work well during _____ times, such as depressions and wartimes. In addition, the existence of fiscal policy may have a soothing effect on consumers and investors.

You Are There   ▶ A Derailed Effort to Move Toward Accounting for the Laffer Curve

Robert Carroll, deputy assistant secretary for tax analysis, tries one more time to explain why the U.S. Department of the Treasury has proposed allocating $513,000 for a Division of Dynamic Analysis within the department's Office of Tax Analysis. At present, he notes, the Treasury routinely considers how taxpayers are likely to respond to changes in tax rates, but it does not evaluate how the overall economy might be affected by these changes. The proposed division would regularly evaluate the broader economic effects of increases or decreases in tax rates. In effect, the proposed new division would seek to take into account the Laffer curve by evaluating how broader responses of the economy to an altered tax rate might feed back to affect tax revenues.

During the next weeks, Carroll and his Treasury colleagues watch with dismay as TV panelists and Internet bloggers criticize the proposed Division of Dynamic Analysis as a political tool aimed at reducing tax rates of high-income taxpayers. Soon, several key members of Congress begin parroting the same criticisms. Within a few months, discussion of the proposal comes to an abrupt halt in Congress. For now, the proposal is dead.

CRITICAL ANALYSIS QUESTIONS

1. Is it possible that reducing tax rates of high-income taxpayers could, at least in principle, actually boost tax payments by these individuals?

2. Why might failure to consider the Laffer curve cause Congress to overestimate how much revenue the federal government will take in when it raises a tax rate?

Does Government Spending Crowd Out Private Health Care Expenditures?

CONCEPTS APPLIED

- Fiscal Policy
- Crowding-Out Effect
- Direct Expenditure Offsets

Since the mid-1960s, the federal government has directed an increasing share of tax dollars to expenditures on health care services for U.S. residents. Today, nearly one-third of all federal government expenditures are related to health care. Hence, health care spending cannot be ignored in any evaluation of U.S. fiscal policy.

A Continuing Expansion of Government Health Care Spending

When most people are asked about U.S. government spending on health care, they think first of Medicare, the federal government program that covers many health care expenses incurred by elderly U.S. residents. The nearly $500 billion per year that the government spends on Medicare is about 20 percent of total—combined public and private—health care spending. In the one-year period between 2005 and 2006, Medicare spending on prescription drugs jumped from 2 percent to 22 percent of the nation's total expenditures on pharmaceuticals.

Much of the recent growth in federal health care spending, however, has occurred through expansion of two other programs. One of these is Medicaid, which pays for health care for low-income individuals. During the 1980s and 1990s, Congress gradually expanded Medicaid to cover virtually all health care spending for children and pregnant women in families with incomes below the official poverty line (about $22,000). Medicaid has also expanded as longer-lived elderly individuals are outliving their savings and falling below the income ceiling for Medicaid coverage. The program now pays at least part of the health care expenses of more than 60 percent of all people in nursing homes. Annual Medicaid spending has expanded to close to $400 billion per year.

Adding to Taxpayers' Medicaid Bill

In addition, in 1997 Congress augmented the Medicaid program by creating the jointly federal- and state-subsidized State Children's Health Insurance Program (SCHIP).

Today, through SCHIP 38 states and the District of Columbia pay the health care expenses of children in families with incomes as high as 350 percent of the official poverty income. Congress is considering an expansion of SCHIP that could increase annual spending on the program from less than $10 billion to $50 billion, or perhaps even more.

The Crowding-Out Effect of Government Health Care Spending

Congress typically justifies increases in health care spending as necessary to provide for U.S. residents who cannot obtain private insurance and are unable to pay for health care from their own resources. Nevertheless, there is considerable evidence that government health care expenditures crowd out a significant amount of health care spending that otherwise would be undertaken from private funds.

For instance, Jonathan Gruber of the Massachusetts Institute of Technology and Kosali Simon of Cornell University have studied the crowding-out effect of various expansions of government health care spending between 1996 and 2002. They estimate that new government spending on health care during that period reduced private health care expenditures by about 60 percent. In other words, every $1.00 of government expenditures on health care in the 1996–2002 period offset $0.60 of private spending. Thus, a significant direct expenditure offset is associated with government spending on health care.

Test your understanding of this chapter by going online to **MyEconLab.**
In the Study Plan for this chapter, select Section N: News.

For Critical Analysis

1. Based on Gruber and Simon's estimate, has increased government health care spending succeeded in covering some people who otherwise might not have had insurance coverage of health care expenses?

2. If we assume that 60 percent of *all* Medicare and Medicaid spending directly offsets private spending, about how many dollars of private health care spending are crowded out by combined Medicare and Medicaid expenditures by the federal government?

Web Resources

1. For information about Medicare spending, go to www. econtoday.com/chapter13.

2. For updates on Medicaid expenditures, go to www. econtoday.com/chapter13.

Research Project

Suppose that you are involved in designing yet another new government health care spending program. One of your goals is to limit the direct expenditure offset of the new program. How might you go about designing the program to attain this objective? (Hint: Think of incentives that might induce people without private insurance to utilize the government program and disincentives that would prevent people who now possess private insurance from switching to the government program.)

Here is what you should know after reading this chapter. **MyEconLab** will help you identify what you know, and where to go when you need to practice.

WHAT YOU SHOULD KNOW

WHERE TO GO TO PRACTICE

The Effects of Discretionary Fiscal Policies Using Traditional Keynesian Analysis In short-run Keynesian analysis, a deliberate increase in government spending or a reduction in taxes shifts the aggregate demand curve outward and thereby closes a recessionary gap in which current real GDP is less than the long-run level of real GDP. Likewise, an intentional reduction in government spending or a tax increase shifts the aggregate demand curve inward and closes an inflationary gap in which current real GDP exceeds the long-run level of real GDP.

fiscal policy, 319

KEY FIGURES
Figure 13-1, 320
Figure 13-2, 322

- **MyEconLab** Study Plan 13.1
- Audio introduction to Chapter 13
- Animated Figures 13-1, 13-2

(continued)

 *(continued)*

WHAT YOU SHOULD KNOW		WHERE TO GO TO PRACTICE

How Indirect Crowding Out and Direct Expenditure Offsets Can Reduce the Effectiveness of Fiscal Policy Actions Indirect crowding out occurs when the government engages in expansionary fiscal policy by increasing government spending or reducing taxes. When government spending exceeds tax revenues, the government must borrow from the private sector. To obtain the necessary funds, the government must offer a higher interest rate, thereby driving up market interest rates. This reduces, or crowds out, interest-sensitive private spending, thereby reducing the net effect of the fiscal expansion on aggregate demand. As a result, the aggregate demand curve shifts by a smaller amount than it would have in the absence of the crowding-out effect, and fiscal policy has a somewhat lessened net effect on equilibrium real GDP. Increased government spending may also substitute directly for private expenditures, and the resulting decline in private spending directly offsets the increase in total planned expenditures that the government had intended to bring about. This also reduces the net change in aggregate demand brought about by a fiscal policy action.

crowding-out effect, 323
direct expenditure
  offsets, 325
supply-side economics,
  326

KEY FIGURES
Figure 13-3, 323
Figure 13-4, 324
Figure 13-5, 327

- **MyEconLab** Study Plan 13.2
- Video: The Crowding-Out Effect
- Animated Figures 13-3, 13-4, 13-5

The Ricardian Equivalence Theorem According to this proposition, when the government cuts taxes and borrows to finance the tax reduction, people realize that eventually the government will have to repay the loan. Thus, they anticipate that taxes will have to increase in the future. This induces them to save the proceeds of the tax cut to meet their future tax liabilities. Thus, a tax cut fails to induce an increase in aggregate consumption spending and consequently has no effect on total planned expenditures and aggregate demand.

Ricardian equivalence
  theorem, 325

KEY FIGURE
Figure 13-4, 324

- **MyEconLab** Study Plan 13.2
- Animated Figure 13-4

Fiscal Policy Time Lags and the Effectiveness of Fiscal "Fine-Tuning" Efforts to engage in fiscal policy actions intended to bring about changes in aggregate demand are complicated by policy time lags. One of these is the recognition time lag, which is the time required to collect information about the economy's current situation. Another is the action time lag, the period between recognition of a problem and implementation of a policy intended to address it. Finally, there is the effect time lag, which is the interval between the implementation of a policy and its having an effect on the economy. For fiscal policy, all of these lags can be lengthy and variable, often lasting one to three years. Hence, fiscal "fine-tuning" may be a poor choice of words.

recognition time lag, 328
action time lag, 328
effect time lag, 328

- **MyEconLab** Study Plan 13.3
- Video: Time Lags

(continued)

 (continued)

WHAT YOU SHOULD KNOW		WHERE TO GO TO PRACTICE

Automatic Stabilizers In our tax system, income taxes diminish automatically when economic activity drops, and unemployment compensation and income transfer payments increase. Thus, when there is a decline in real GDP, the automatic reduction in income tax collections and increases in unemployment compensation and income transfer payments tend to minimize the reduction in total planned expenditures that would otherwise have resulted. The existence of these programs thereby helps to stabilize the economy automatically in the face of variations in autonomous expenditures that induce fluctuations in economic activity.

automatic, or built-in, stabilizers, 329

KEY FIGURE
Figure 13-6, 330

- **MyEconLab** Study Plans 13.4, 13.5
- Animated Figure 13-6

Log in to MyEconLab, take a chapter test, and get a personalized Study Plan that tells you which concepts you understand and which ones you need to review. From there, MyEconLab will give you further practice, tutorials, animations, videos, and guided solutions.
Log in to www.myeconlab.com

PROBLEMS

All problems are assignable in *. Answers to odd-numbered problems appear at the back of the book.*

13-1. Suppose that Congress and the president decide that the nation's economic performance is weakening and that the government should "do something" about the situation. They make no tax changes but do enact new laws increasing government spending on a variety of programs.

   a. Prior to the congressional and presidential action, careful studies by government economists indicated that the direct multiplier effect of a rise in government expenditures on equilibrium real GDP is equal to 6. In the 12 months since the increase in government spending, however, it has become clear that the actual ultimate effect on real GDP will be less than half of that amount. What factors might account for this?

   b. Another year and a half elapses following passage of the government spending boost. The government has undertaken no additional policy actions, nor have there been any other events of significance. Nevertheless, by the end of the second year, real GDP has returned to its

original level, and the price level has increased sharply. Provide a possible explanation for this outcome.

13-2. Suppose that Congress enacts a significant tax cut with the expectation that this action will stimulate aggregate demand and push up real GDP in the short run. In fact, however, neither real GDP nor the price level changes significantly as a result of the tax cut. What might account for this outcome?

13-3. Explain how time lags in discretionary fiscal policymaking could thwart the efforts of Congress and the president to stabilize real GDP in the face of an economic downturn. Is it possible that these time lags could actually cause discretionary fiscal policy to *destabilize* real GDP?

13-4. Determine whether each of the following is an example of a direct expenditure offset to fiscal policy.

   a. In an effort to help rejuvenate the nation's railroad system, a new government agency buys unused track, locomotives, and passenger and freight cars, many of which private companies would otherwise have purchased and put into regular use.

b. The government increases its expenditures without raising taxes; to cover the resulting budget deficit, it borrows more funds from the private sector, thereby pushing up the market interest rate and discouraging private planned investment spending.

c. The government finances the construction of a classical music museum that otherwise would never have received private funding.

13-5. Determine whether each of the following is an example of indirect crowding out resulting from an expansionary fiscal policy action.

a. The government provides a subsidy to help keep an existing firm operating, even though a group of investors otherwise would have provided a cash infusion that would have kept the company in business.

b. The government reduces its taxes without decreasing its expenditures; to cover the resulting budget deficit, it borrows more funds from the private sector, thereby pushing up the market interest rate and discouraging private planned investment spending.

c. Government expenditures fund construction of a high-rise office building on a plot of land where a private company otherwise would have constructed an essentially identical building.

13-6. The U.S. government is in the midst of spending more than $1 billion on seven buildings containing more than 100,000 square feet of space to be used for study of infectious diseases. Prior to the government's decision to construct these buildings, a few universities had been planning to build essentially the same facilities using privately obtained funds. After construction on the government buildings began, however, the universities dropped their plans. Evaluate whether the government's $1 billion expenditure is actually likely to push U.S. real GDP above the level it would have reached in the absence of the government's construction spree.

13-7. Determine whether each of the following is an example of a discretionary fiscal policy action.

a. A recession occurs, and government-funded unemployment compensation is paid to laid-off workers.

b. Congress votes to fund a new jobs program designed to put unemployed workers to work.

c. The Federal Reserve decides to reduce the quantity of money in circulation in an effort to slow inflation.

d. Under powers authorized by an act of Congress, the president decides to authorize an emergency release of funds for spending programs intended to head off economic crises.

13-8. Determine whether each of the following is an example of an automatic fiscal stabilizer.

a. A government agency arranges to make loans to businesses whenever an economic downturn begins.

b. As the economy heats up, the resulting increase in equilibrium real GDP immediately results in higher income tax payments, which dampen consumption spending somewhat.

c. As the economy starts to recover from a recession and more people go back to work, government-funded unemployment compensation payments begin to decline.

d. To stem an overheated economy, the president, using special powers granted by Congress, authorizes emergency impoundment of funds that Congress had previously authorized for spending on government programs.

13-9. Consider the diagram below, in which the current short-run equilibrium is at point *A*, and answer the questions that follow.

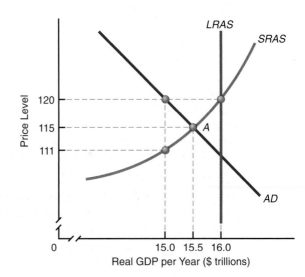

   a. What type of gap exists at point *A*?

   b. If the marginal propensity to save equals 0.20, what change in government spending could eliminate the gap identified in part (a)? Explain.

13-10. Consider the diagram below, in which the current short-run equilibrium is at point *A*, and answer the questions that follow.

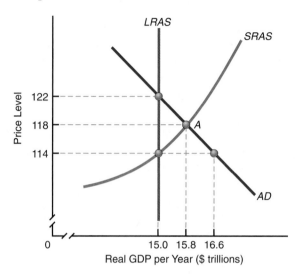

   a. What type of gap exists at point *A*?

   b. If the marginal propensity to consume equals 0.75, what change in government spending could eliminate the gap identified in part (a)? Explain.

13-11. Currently, a government's budget is balanced. The marginal propensity to consume is 0.80. The government has determined that each additional $10 billion it borrows to finance a budget deficit pushes up the market interest rate by 0.1 percentage point. It has also determined that every 0.1-percentage-point change in the market interest rate generates a change in planned investment

expenditures equal to $2 billion. Finally, the government knows that to close a recessionary gap and take into account the resulting change in the price level, it must generate a net rightward shift in the aggregate demand curve equal to $200 billion. Assuming that there are no direct expenditure offsets to fiscal policy, how much should the government increase its expenditures? (Hint: How much private investment spending will each $10 billion increase in government spending crowd out?)

13-12. A government is currently operating with an annual budget deficit of $40 billion. The government has determined that every $10 billion reduction in the amount it borrows each year would reduce the market interest rate by 0.1 percentage point. Furthermore, it has determined that every 0.1-percentage-point change in the market interest rate generates a change in planned investment expenditures in the opposite direction equal to $5 billion. The marginal propensity to consume is 0.75. Finally, the government knows that to eliminate an inflationary gap and take into account the resulting change in the price level, it must generate a net leftward shift in the aggregate demand curve equal to $40 billion. Assuming that there are no direct expenditure offsets to fiscal policy, how much should the government increase taxes? (Hint: How much new private investment spending is induced by each $10 billion decrease in government spending?)

13-13. Assume that the Ricardian equivalence theorem is not relevant. Explain why an income-tax-rate cut should affect short-run equilibrium real GDP.

13-14. Suppose that Congress enacts a lump-sum tax cut of $750 billion. The marginal propensity to consume is equal to 0.75. Assuming that Ricardian equivalence holds true, what is the effect on equilibrium real GDP? On saving?

ECONOMICS ON THE NET

Federal Government Spending and Taxation A quick way to keep up with the federal government's spending and taxation is by examining federal budget data at the White House Internet address.

Title: Historical Tables: Budget of the United States Government

Navigation: Use the link at **www.econtoday.com/chapter13** to visit the Office of Management and Budget. Select the most recent budget. Then click on *Historical Tables*.

Application After the document downloads, perform the indicated operations and answer the questions.

1. Go to section 2, "Composition of Federal Government Receipts." Take a look at Table 2.2, "Percentage Composition of Receipts by Source." Before World War II, what was the key source of revenues of the federal government? What has been the key revenue source since World War II?

2. Now scan down the document to Table 2.3, "Receipts by Source as Percentages of GDP." Have any government revenue sources declined as a percentage of GDP? Which ones have noticeably risen in recent years?

For Group Study and Analysis Split into four groups, and have each group examine section 3, "Federal Government Outlays by Function," and in particular Table 3.1, "Outlays by Superfunction and Function." Assign groups to the following functions: national defense, health, income security, and Social Security. Have each group prepare a brief report concerning recent and long-term trends in government spending on each function. Which functions have been capturing growing shares of government spending in recent years? Which have been receiving declining shares of total spending?

ANSWERS TO QUICK QUIZZES

p. 322: (i) expenditures . . . taxes; (ii) recessionary . . . increase; (iii) inflationary . . . decrease; (iv) decrease . . . increase

p. 327: (i) increase; (ii) Direct expenditure offsets; (iii) Ricardian equivalence; (iv) supply-side . . . supply-side

p. 331: (i) recognition . . . action . . . effect; (ii) automatic; (iii) moderate; (iv) abnormal

Fiscal Policy: A Keynesian Perspective

The traditional Keynesian approach to fiscal policy differs in three ways from that presented in Chapter 13. First, it emphasizes the underpinnings of the components of aggregate demand. Second, it assumes that government expenditures are not substitutes for private expenditures and that current taxes are the only taxes taken into account by consumers and firms. Third, the traditional Keynesian approach focuses on the short run and so assumes that as a first approximation, the price level is constant.

Changes in Government Spending

Figure C-1 measures real GDP along the horizontal axis and total planned real expenditures (aggregate demand) along the vertical axis. The components of aggregate demand are real consumption (C), investment (I), government spending (G), and net exports (X). The height of the schedule labeled $C + I + G + X$ shows total planned real expenditures (aggregate demand) as a function of real GDP. This schedule slopes upward because consumption depends positively on real GDP. Everywhere along the 45-degree reference line, planned real spending equals real GDP. At the point Y^*, where the $C + I + G + X$ line intersects the 45-degree line, planned real spending is consistent with real GDP per year. At any income less than Y^*, spending exceeds real GDP, and so real GDP and thus real spending will tend to rise. At any level of real GDP greater than Y^*, planned spending is less than real GDP, and so real GDP and thus spending will tend to decline. Given the determinants of C, I, G, and X, total real spending (aggregate demand) will be Y^*.

The Keynesian approach assumes that changes in government spending cause no direct offsets in either consumption or investment spending because G is not a substitute

---

FIGURE C-1

The Impact of Higher Government Spending on Aggregate Demand

Government spending increases, causing $C + I + G + X$ to move to $C + I + G' + X$. Equilibrium real GDP per year increases to Y^{**}.

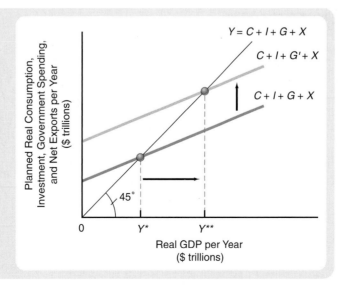

for *C*, *I*, or *X*. Hence, a rise in government spending from *G* to *G'* causes the *C* + *I* + *G* + *X* line to shift upward by the full amount of the rise in government spending, yielding the line *C* + *I* + *G'* + *X*. The rise in real government spending causes real GDP to rise, which in turn causes consumption spending to rise, which further increases real GDP. Ultimately, aggregate demand rises to Y^{**}, where spending again equals real GDP. A key conclusion of the traditional Keynesian analysis is that total spending rises by *more* than the original rise in government spending because consumption spending depends positively on real GDP.

Changes in Taxes

According to the Keynesian approach, changes in current taxes affect aggregate demand by changing the amount of real disposable (after-tax) income available to consumers. A rise in taxes reduces disposable income and thus reduces real consumption; conversely, a tax cut raises disposable income and thus causes a rise in consumption spending. The effects of a tax increase are shown in Figure C-2. Higher taxes cause consumption spending to decline from *C* to *C'*, causing total spending to shift downward to *C'* + *I* + *G* + *X*. In general, the decline in consumption will be less than the increase in taxes because people will also reduce their saving to help pay the higher taxes.

The Balanced-Budget Multiplier

One interesting implication of the Keynesian approach concerns the impact of a balanced-budget change in government real spending. Suppose that the government increases spending by $1 billion and pays for it by raising current taxes by $1 billion. Such a policy is called a *balanced-budget increase in real spending*. Because the higher spending tends to push aggregate demand *up* by *more* than $1 billion while the higher taxes tend to push aggregate demand *down* by *less* than $1 billion, a most remarkable thing happens: A balanced-budget increase in *G* causes total spending to rise by *exactly* the amount of the rise in *G*—in this case, $1 billion. We say that the *balanced-budget*

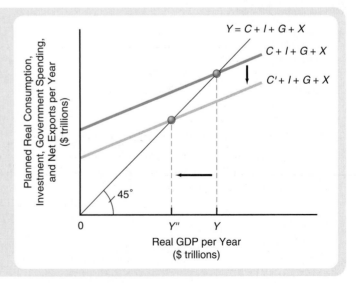

FIGURE C-2

The Impact of Higher Taxes on Aggregate Demand

Higher taxes cause consumption to fall to *C'*. Equilibrium real GDP per year decreases to *Y"*.

multiplier is equal to 1. Similarly, a balanced-budget reduction in government spending will cause total spending to fall by exactly the amount of the government spending cut.

The Fixed Price Level Assumption

The final key feature of the traditional Keynesian approach is that it typically assumes that as a first approximation, the price level is fixed. Recall that nominal GDP equals the price level multiplied by real GDP. If the price level is fixed, an increase in government spending that causes nominal GDP to rise will show up exclusively as a rise in *real* GDP. This will in turn be accompanied by a decline in the unemployment rate because the additional real GDP can be produced only if additional factors of production, such as labor, are utilized.

PROBLEMS

All problems are assignable in myeconlab. *Answers to odd-numbered problems appear at the back of the book.*

C-1. Assume that equilibrium real GDP is $15.2 trillion and full-employment equilibrium (*FE*) is $15.55 trillion. The marginal propensity to save is $\frac{1}{7}$. Answer the questions using the data in the following graph.

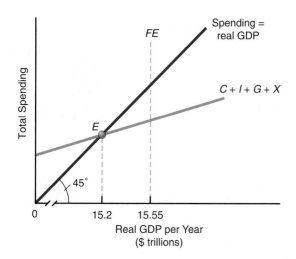

a. What is the marginal propensity to consume?

b. By how much must new investment or government spending increase to bring the economy up to full employment?

c. By how much must government cut personal taxes to stimulate the economy to the full-employment equilibrium?

C-2. Assume that MPC = $\frac{4}{5}$ when answering the following questions.

a. If government expenditures rise by $2 billion, by how much will the aggregate expenditure curve shift upward? By how much will equilibrium real GDP per year change?

b. If taxes increase by $2 billion, by how much will the aggregate expenditure curve shift downward? By how much will equilibrium real GDP per year change?

C-3. Assume that MPC = $\frac{4}{5}$ when answering the following questions.

a. If government expenditures rise by $1 billion, by how much will the aggregate expenditure curve shift upward?

b. If taxes rise by $1 billion, by how much will the aggregate expenditure curve shift downward?

c. If both taxes and government expenditures rise by $1 billion, by how much will the aggregate expenditure curve shift? What will happen to the equilibrium level of real GDP?

d. How does your response to the second question in part (c) change if MPC = $\frac{3}{4}$? If MPC = $\frac{1}{2}$?

14

Deficit Spending and the Public Debt

T he federal *budget deficit*—the amount that the federal government spends each year over and above what it collects in taxes and fees—often has appeared to move in tandem with the *trade deficit,* which is the amount by which imports of goods and services exceed exports of those items. In years past, the two deficits were sufficiently closely related that economists began to call them the "twin deficits." In recent years, however, the U.S. trade deficit increased even when the U.S. government's budget deficit was shrinking. Why has this divergence occurred? Are the two deficits no longer twins? To be able to evaluate these questions, you must first learn about the government's budget deficit and its relationship to other key variables, including the public debt, real GDP, the price level, and, of course, the trade deficit.

LEARNING OBJECTIVES

MyEconLab helps you master each objective and study more efficiently. See end of chapter for details.

After reading this chapter, you should be able to:

- Explain how federal government budget deficits occur
- Define the public debt and understand alternative measures of the public debt
- Evaluate circumstances under which the public debt could be a burden to future generations
- Discuss why the federal budget deficit might be measured incorrectly
- Analyze the macroeconomic effects of government budget deficits
- Describe possible ways to reduce the government budget deficit

?

DID YOU KNOW THAT the U.S. federal government spends a total of more than $3 billion *per day* on Social Security, Medicare, and Medicaid? Federal spending on each of these guaranteed spending programs, often called government *entitlements*, is *individually* nearly as great as the entire discretionary portion of the federal government's budget.

Every year since 2001, the U.S. government has spent more than it collected in taxes. The government anticipates continuing to spend more than it takes in until at least 2012. Should you be worried about this? The answer, as you will see in this chapter, is both yes and no. First, let's examine what the government actually does when it spends more than it receives.

Public Deficits and Debts: Flows versus Stocks

A **government budget deficit** exists if the government spends more than it receives in taxes during a given period of time. The government has to finance this shortfall somehow. Barring any resort to money creation (the subject matter of Chapters 15, 16, and 17), the U.S. Treasury sells IOUs on behalf of the U.S. government, in the form of securities that are normally called bonds. In effect, the federal government asks U.S. and foreign households, businesses, and governments to lend funds to the government to cover its deficit. For example, if the federal government spends $100 billion more than it receives in revenues, the Treasury will raise that $100 billion by selling $100 billion of new Treasury bonds. Those who buy the Treasury bonds (lend funds to the U.S. government) will receive interest payments over the life of the bond plus eventual repayment of the entire amount lent. In return, the U.S. Treasury receives immediate purchasing power. In the process, it also adds to its indebtedness to bondholders.

Government budget deficit
An excess of government spending over government revenues during a given period of time.

Distinguishing Between Deficits and Debts

You have already learned about flows. GDP, for instance, is a flow because it is a dollar measure of the total amount of final goods and services produced within a given period of time, such as a year.

The federal deficit is also a flow. Suppose that the current federal deficit is $500 billion. This means that the federal government is currently spending at a rate of $500 billion *per year* more than it is collecting in taxes and other revenues.

Of course, governments do not always spend more each year than the revenues they receive. If a government spends an amount exactly equal to the revenues it collects during a given period, then during this interval the government operates with a **balanced budget**. If a government spends less than the revenues it receives during a given period, then during this interval it experiences a **government budget surplus.**

Balanced budget
A situation in which the government's spending is exactly equal to the total taxes and other revenues it collects during a given period of time.

Government budget surplus
An excess of government revenues over government spending during a given period of time.

The Public Debt

You have also learned about stocks, which are measured at a point in time. Stocks change between points in time as a result of flows. The amount of unemployment, for example, is a stock. It is the total number of people looking for work but unable to find it at a given point in time. Suppose that the stock of unemployed workers at the beginning of the month is 7.3 million and that at the end of the month the stock of unemployed workers has increased to 7.5 million. This means that during the month, assuming an unchanged labor force, there was a net flow of 0.2 million individuals away from the state of being employed into the state of being out of work but seeking employment.

Public debt
The total value of all outstanding federal government securities.

Go to www.econtoday.com/chapter14 to learn more about the activities of the Congressional Budget Office, which reports to the legislative branch of the U.S. government about the current state of the federal government's spending and receipts.

Likewise, the total accumulated **public debt** is a stock measured at a given point in time, and it changes from one time to another as a result of government budget deficits or surpluses. For instance, on December 31, 2007, one measure of the public debt was about $5 trillion. During 2008, the federal government operated at a deficit of nearly $0.5 trillion. As a consequence, on December 31, 2008, this measure of the public debt had increased to nearly $5.5 trillion.

Government Finance: Spending More Than Tax Collections

Following four consecutive years—1998 through 2001—of official budget surpluses, the federal government began to experience budget deficits once more beginning in 2002. Since then, government spending has increased considerably, and tax revenues have failed to keep pace. Consequently, the federal government has operated with a deficit each year since 2002, and most observers anticipate a steady flow of government red ink for the foreseeable future.

The Historical Record of Federal Budget Deficits

Figure 14-1 charts inflation-adjusted expenditures and revenues of the federal government since 1940. The *real* annual budget deficit is the arithmetic difference between real expenditures and real revenues during years in which the government's spending has exceeded its revenues. As you can see, there is nothing out of the ordinary about federal budget deficits. Indeed, the annual budget surpluses of 1998 through 2001 were somewhat out of the ordinary. The 1998 budget surplus was the first since 1968, when the government briefly operated with a surplus. Before the 1998–2001 budget surpluses, the U.S. government had not experienced back-to-back annual surpluses since the 1950s.

Indeed, since 1940 the U.S. government has operated with an annual budget surplus for a total of only 13 years. In all other years, it has collected insufficient taxes and other revenues to fund its spending. Every year this has occurred, the federal government has borrowed to finance its additional expenditures.

Even though Figure 14-1 accounts for inflation, it does not give a clear picture of the size of the federal government's deficits or surpluses in relation to overall economic activity in the United States. Figure 14-2 provides a clearer view of the size of government deficits or surpluses relative to the size of the U.S. economy by expressing them as percentages of GDP. As you can see, the federal budget deficit reached a peak of nearly 6 percent of GDP in the early 1980s. It then fell back, increased once again during the late 1980s and early 1990s, and then declined steadily into the budget surplus years of 1998–2001. Since 2001, the government budget has increased to 3.5 percent of GDP, dropped below 3 percent of GDP, and then risen once more, to about 6 percent of GDP.

The Resurgence of Federal Government Deficits

Why has the government's budget slipped from a surplus equal to nearly 2.5 percent of GDP into a deficit of about 3 percent of GDP? The answer is that the government has been spending much more than its revenues. Spending has increased at a faster pace since the early 2000s—particularly in light of the on-going bailout of financial institutions that will eventually total hundreds of billions of dollars—than during any other decade since World War II.

FIGURE 14-1

Federal Budget Deficits and Surpluses Since 1940

Federal budget deficits (expenditures in excess of receipts, in red) have been much more common than federal budget surpluses (receipts in excess of expenditures, in green).*

*Budgeted items not including 2008–2009 financial institutions bailout expenditures.
Source: Office of Management and Budget.

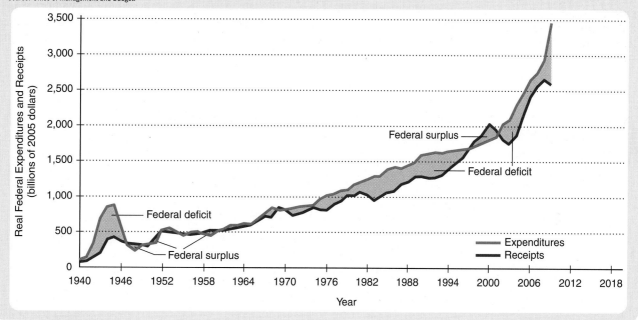

FIGURE 14-2

The Federal Budget Deficit Expressed as a Percentage of GDP

Beginning in 2000, the federal budget deficit rose as a share of GDP before declining in recent years. (Note that the negative values for the 1998–2001 period designate budget surpluses as a percentage of GDP during those years.)*

*Budgeted items not including 2008–2009 financial institutions bailout expenditures.
Sources: Economic Report of the President; Economic Indicators, various issues.

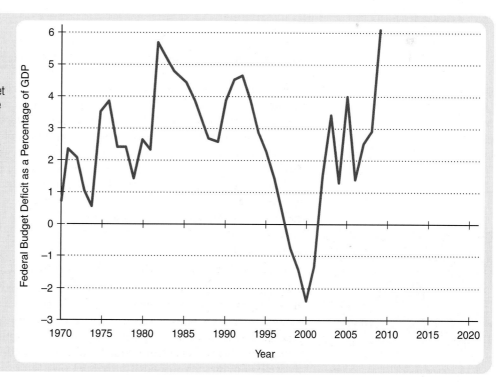

The more complex answer also considers government revenues. In 2001, Congress and the executive branch slightly reduced income tax rates, and in 2003 they also cut federal capital gains taxes and estate taxes. Because tax rates were reduced toward the end of a recession when real income growth was relatively low, government tax revenues were stagnant for a time. When economic activity began to expand into the mid-2000s, tax revenues started rising at a pace closer to the rapid rate of growth of government spending. Then in the late 2000s, economic activity grew more slowly, and the growth in annual federal expenditures exceeded growth in annual tax collections. As long as this situation persists, the U.S. government will operate with a budget deficit, just as it did so often during the previous six decades.

QUICK QUIZ | *See page 364 for the answers. Review concepts from this section in MyEconLab.*

Whenever the federal government spends more than it receives during a given year, it operates with a _____ _____. If federal government spending exactly equals government revenues, then the government experiences a _____ _____. If the federal government collects more revenues than it spends, then it operates with a _____ _____.

The federal budget deficit is a flow, whereas accumulated budget deficits represent a _____, called the **public debt.**

The federal budget deficit expressed as a percentage of GDP hit its most recent peak of around 6 percent in the early 1980s. Between 1998 and 2001, the federal government experienced a budget _____, but since then its budget has once more been in _____. Currently, the budget _____ exceeds 6 percent of GDP.

Evaluating the Rising Public Debt

Gross public debt
All federal government debt irrespective of who owns it.

Net public debt
Gross public debt minus all government interagency borrowing.

All federal public debt, taken together, is called the **gross public debt.** We arrive at the **net public debt** when we subtract from the gross public debt the portion that is held by government agencies (in essence, what the federal government owes to itself). For instance, if the Social Security Administration holds U.S. Treasury bonds, the U.S. Treasury makes debt payments to another agency of the government. On net, therefore, the U.S. government owes these payments to itself.

The net public debt increases whenever the federal government experiences a budget deficit. That is, the net public debt increases when government outlays are greater than total government receipts.

Accumulation of the Net Public Debt

Why does the number on this "national debt clock" exaggerate the true public debt?

Table 14-1 displays, for various years since 1940, real values, in base-year 2005 dollars, of the federal budget deficit, the total and per capita net public debt (the amount owed on the net public debt by a typical individual), and the net interest cost of the public debt in total and as a percentage of GDP. It shows that the level of the real net public debt and the real net public debt per capita grew following the early 1980s and again in the late 2000s. Thus, the real, inflation-adjusted amount that a typical individual owes to holders of the net public debt has varied over time.

TABLE 14-1

The Federal Deficit, Our Public Debt, and the Interest We Pay on It

Net public debt in column 3 is defined as total federal debt *excluding* all loans between federal government agencies. Per capita net public debt is obtained by dividing the net public debt by the population.*

(1) Year	(2) Federal Budget Deficit (billions of 2005 dollars)	(3) Net Public Debt (billions of 2005 dollars)	(4) Per Capita Net Public Debt (2005 dollars)	(5) Net Interest Costs (billions of 2005 dollars)	(6) Net Interest as a Percentage of GDP
1940	8.9	97.3	736.2	2.1	0.9
1945	492.9	2,150.7	15,372.8	28.3	1.45
1950	21.1	1,490.7	9,788.0	32.7	1.68
1955	18.0	1,360.8	8,202.8	29.4	1.23
1960	1.6	1,253.5	6,937.0	36.5	1.37
1965	7.9	1,287.7	6,627.5	42.3	1.26
1970	11.5	1,169.1	5,700.1	59.1	1.47
1975	134.1	1,180.0	5,463.1	69.3	1.52
1980	154.3	1,482.6	6,564.3	109.7	1.92
1985	344.1	2,430.0	10,247.4	209.7	3.22
1990	306.5	3,337.4	13,349.4	243.1	3.23
1995	201.2	4,421.6	16,585.2	284.7	3.24
2000	−267.1	3,853.1	13,644.1	252.0	2.34
2005	318.3	4,592.2	15,480.8	184.0	1.38
2006	240.6	4,681.2	15,915.5	219.7	1.36
2007	153.0	4,754.7	16,382.5	223.9	1.34
2008	416.3	5,006.3	16,322.8	223.2	1.33
2009	758.9	5,192.0	17,003.8	233.7	1.34

*Budgeted items not including 2008–2009 financial institutions bailout expenditures.
Sources: U.S. Department of the Treasury; Office of Management and Budget. *Note:* Data for 2008 and 2009 are estimates.

The net public debt levels reported in Table 14-1 do not provide a basis of comparison with the overall size of the U.S. economy. Figure 14-3 on the following page does this by displaying the net public debt as a percentage of GDP. We see that after World War II, this ratio fell steadily until the early 1970s (except for a small rise in the late 1950s) and then leveled off until the 1980s. After that, the ratio of the net public debt to GDP more or less continued to rise to around 50 percent of GDP, before dropping slightly in the late 1990s and early 2000s. With the reappearance of budget deficits since 2001, the ratio has been rising once again.

Annual Interest Payments on the Public Debt

Columns 5 and 6 of Table 14-1 show an important consequence of the net public debt. This is the interest that the government must pay to those who hold the bonds it has issued to finance past budget deficits. Those interest payments started rising dramatically around 1975 and then declined in the 1990s and early 2000s. Government deficits have recently been higher than in the late 1990s and early 2000s, so interest payments expressed as a percentage of GDP might rise in the years to come.

If U.S. residents were the sole owners of the government's debts, the interest payments on the net public debt would go only to U.S. residents. In this situation, we would owe the debt to ourselves, with most people being taxed so that the government could pay interest to others (or to ourselves). During the 1970s, however, the share of the net public debt owned by foreign individuals, businesses, and governments started to rise, reaching 20 percent in 1978. From there it declined until the late 1980s, when it began to rise rapidly. Today, foreign residents, businesses, and governments hold nearly 50 percent of the net public debt. Thus, we do not owe the debt just to ourselves.

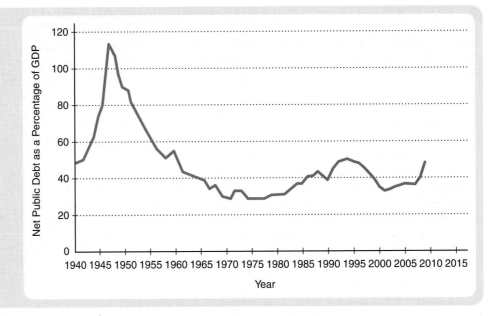

FIGURE 14-3

Net U.S. Public Debt as a Percentage of GDP

During World War II, the net public debt grew dramatically. After the war, it fell until the 1970s, started rising in the 1980s, declined once more in the 1990s, and recently has been increasing again.

Source: U.S. Department of the Treasury.

Why has the U.S. Treasury's financing of the debt that the government has accumulated since the early 2000s been criticized as wasteful misuse of taxpayers' funds?

POLICY EXAMPLE
What Was the U.S. Treasury Thinking?

Between 2001 and 2004, as the U.S. federal deficit increased, market interest rates were declining. Even though the U.S. Treasury had eliminated 30-year bonds in 2001, it still could have borrowed funds to cover the higher deficits by issuing 20-year bonds paying interest rates that were very low by historical standards. Instead, the Treasury chose to fund the higher deficits primarily by issuing bonds with maturities of less than 10 years. (A bond's *maturity* is when it comes due. Thus, a 30-year bond has a maturity of 30 years.) As a consequence, the share of the public debt with a maturity of 20 years or more dropped from 11 percent in 2001 to about 5 percent in 2004.

Beginning in 2004, interest rates started rising again. Since then, the Treasury has been refinancing much of the debt accumulated during the deficit years of the early 2000s at higher interest rates. Who paid the higher interest expense from refinancing this debt at the higher rates of interest? Taxpayers did, of course. By 2006, the Treasury had brought back the 30-year bond, just in time for higher market interest rates on these longest-maturity bonds. Thus, taxpayers are now paying much more interest on the new 30-year bonds than they otherwise would have been paying if the Treasury had issued 20-year bonds when deficits first began rising in 2001.

FOR CRITICAL ANALYSIS

Why do you suppose that one critic has compared the Treasury's handling of deficit financing to an individual homeowner opting for a variable-rate mortgage loan at a 5 percent interest rate instead of a fixed-rate mortgage loan at a lower rate of 4.5 percent?

Burdens of the Public Debt

Do current budget deficits and the accumulating public debt create social burdens? One perspective on this question considers possible burdens on future generations. Another focuses on transfers from U.S. residents to residents of other nations.

HOW TODAY'S BUDGET DEFICITS MIGHT BURDEN FUTURE GENERATIONS If the federal government wishes to purchase goods and services valued at $100 billion, it can finance this expenditure either by raising taxes by $100 billion or by selling $100 billion in bonds. Many economists maintain that the second option, deficit spending, would lead to a higher level of national consumption and a lower level of national saving than the first option.

The reason, say these economists, is that if people are taxed, they will have to forgo private consumption now as society substitutes government goods for private goods. If the government does not raise taxes but instead sells bonds to finance the $100 billion in expenditures, the public's disposable income remains the same. Members of the public have merely shifted their allocations of assets to include $100 billion in additional government bonds. There are two possible circumstances that could cause people to treat government borrowing differently than they treat taxes. One is that people will fail to realize that their liabilities (in the form of higher future taxes due to increased interest payments on the public debt) have *also* increased by $100 billion. Another is that people will believe that they can consume the governmentally provided goods without forgoing any private consumption because the bill for the government goods will be paid by *future* taxpayers.

THE CROWDING-OUT EFFECT But if full employment exists, and society raises its present consumption by adding consumption of government-provided goods to the original quantity of privately provided goods, then something must be *crowded out*. In a closed economy, investment expenditures on capital goods must decline. As you learned in Chapter 13, the mechanism by which investment is crowded out is an increase in the interest rate. Deficit spending increases the total demand for credit but leaves the total supply of credit unaltered. The rise in interest rates causes a reduction in the growth of investment and capital formation, which in turn slows the growth of productivity and improvement in society's living standard.

This perspective suggests that deficit spending can impose a burden on future generations in two ways. First, unless the deficit spending is allocated to purchases that lead to long-term increases in real GDP, future generations will have to be taxed at a higher rate. That is, only by imposing higher taxes on future generations will the government be able to retire the higher public debt resulting from the present generation's consumption of governmentally provided goods. Second, the increased level of consumption by the present generation crowds out investment and reduces the growth of capital goods, leaving future generations with a smaller capital stock and thereby reducing their wealth.

PAYING OFF THE PUBLIC DEBT IN THE FUTURE Suppose that after 50 years of running deficits financed by selling bonds to U.S. residents, the public debt becomes so large that each adult person's implicit share of the net public debt liability is $50,000. Suppose further that the government chooses (or is forced) to pay off the debt at that time. Will that generation be burdened with our government's overspending? Assume that a large portion of the debt is owed to ourselves. It is true that every adult will have to come up with $50,000 in taxes to pay off the debt, but then the government will use these funds to pay off the bondholders. Sometimes the bondholders and taxpayers will be the same people. Thus, *some* people will be burdened because they owe $50,000 and own less than $50,000 in government bonds. Others, however, will receive more than $50,000 for the bonds they own. Nevertheless, as a generation within society, they will pay and receive about the same amount of funds.

If this government highway project increases the deficit, what might be the effect on private investment expenditures?

Of course, there could be a burden on some low-income adults who will find it difficult or impossible to obtain $50,000 to pay off the tax liability. Still, nothing says that taxes to pay off the debt must be assessed equally. Indeed, it seems likely that a special tax would be levied, based on the ability to pay.

OUR DEBT TO FOREIGN RESIDENTS So far we have been assuming that we owe all of the public debt to ourselves. But, as we saw earlier, that is not the case. What about the nearly 50 percent owned by foreign residents?

It is true that if foreign residents buy U.S. government bonds, we do not owe that debt to ourselves. Thus, when debts held by foreign residents come due, future U.S. residents will be taxed to repay these debts plus accumulated interest. Portions of the incomes of future U.S. residents will then be transferred abroad. In this way, a potential burden on future generations may result.

But this transfer of income from U.S. residents to residents of other nations will not necessarily be a burden. It is important to realize that if the rate of return on projects that the government funds by operating with deficits exceeds the interest rate paid to foreign residents, both foreign residents and future U.S. residents will be better off. If funds obtained by selling bonds to foreign residents are expended on wasteful projects, however, a burden may well be placed on future generations.

We can apply the same reasoning to the problem of current investment and capital creation being crowded out by current deficits. If deficits lead to slower growth rates, future generations will be poorer. But if the government expenditures are really investments, and if the rate of return on such public investments exceeds the interest rate paid on the bonds, both present and future generations will be economically better off.

What rule of thumb do many economists use to spot foreign purchases of U.S. government bonds?

INTERNATIONAL EXAMPLE
Who Is Most Likely to Buy U.S. Government Bonds "Indirectly"?

The U.S. Treasury typically auctions new debt securities once or twice per week. Within a few minutes after the close of each auction, the Treasury reports information about the quantities sold to those who made *direct* and *indirect* bids. The difference between the two types of bids is that direct bidders submit their bids directly to the Treasury, whereas indirect bidders submit their bids through direct bidders. Most direct bids come from so-called *primary dealers* of government securities, which have special payments accounts with the Federal Reserve Bank of New York, which is part of the Federal Reserve System, the U.S. central bank (see Chapter 15). These institutions also submit indirect bids on behalf of their clients.

In a typical auction, there are various indirect bidders, including private pension funds, securities brokers and dealers, and insurance companies. Many indirect bids also come from international sources. Private foreign residents and companies submit indirect bids through private U.S. banks. Foreign central banks and international institutions, such as the International Monetary Fund and the World Bank, place indirect bids through the Federal Reserve Bank of New York. Normally, about half of all indirect bids originate internationally. Thus, traders normally assume that roughly 50 percent of indirect bids reported following a Treasury auction were placed by foreign bidders.

FOR CRITICAL ANALYSIS
Why do you suppose that the U.S. Treasury does not report each bidder by name? (Hint: The Treasury's objective is to raise funds by selling bonds at the lowest interest cost, and it may feel that to achieve this goal it must satisfy many other preferences of bidders.)

QUICK QUIZ   *See page 364 for the answers. Review concepts from this section in MyEconLab.*

When we subtract the funds that government agencies borrow from each other from the ___gross___ public debt, we obtain the ___net___ public debt.

The public debt may impose a burden on ___future___ generations if they have to be taxed at higher rates to pay for the ___current___ generation's increased consumption of governmentally provided goods. In addition, there may be a burden if the debt leads to crowding out of current investment, resulting in _____ capital formation and hence a _____ economic growth rate.

If foreign residents hold a significant part of our public debt, then we no longer "owe it to ourselves." If the rate of return on the borrowed funds is _____ than the interest to be paid to foreign residents, future generations can be made better off by government borrowing. Future generations will be worse off, however, if the opposite is true.

Federal Budget Deficits in an Open Economy

Many economists believe that it is no accident that foreign residents hold such a large portion of the U.S. public debt. Their reasoning suggests that a U.S. trade deficit—a situation in which the value of U.S. imports of goods and services exceeds the value of its exports—will often accompany a government budget deficit.

Trade Deficits and Government Budget Deficits

Figure 14-4 on the following page shows U.S. trade deficits and surpluses compared to federal budget deficits and surpluses. In 1983, imports of goods and services began to consistently exceed exports of those items on an annual basis in the United States. At the same time, the federal budget deficit rose dramatically. Beginning in the early 2000s, both deficits increased once again.

Thus, it appears that there is a relationship between trade deficits and government budget deficits: Larger trade deficits tend to accompany larger government budget deficits.

Why the Two Deficits Are Related

Intuitively, there is a reason why we would expect federal budget deficits to be associated with trade deficits. You might call this the unpleasant arithmetic of trade and budget deficits.

Suppose that, initially, the government's budget is balanced; government expenditures are matched by an equal amount of tax collections and other government revenues. Now assume that the federal government begins to operate with a budget deficit; it increases its spending, collects fewer taxes, or both. Assume further that domestic consumption and domestic investment do not decrease relative to GDP. Where, then, do the funds come from to finance the government's budget deficit? A portion of these funds must come from abroad. That is to say, dollar holders abroad will have to purchase newly created government bonds.

Of course, foreign dollar holders will choose to hold the new government bonds only if there is an economic inducement to do so, such as an increase in U.S. interest rates. Given that private domestic spending and other factors are unchanged, interest rates will indeed rise whenever there is an increase in deficits financed by increased borrowing.

FIGURE 14-4

The Related U.S. Deficits

The United States exported more than it imported until 1983. Then it started experiencing large trade deficits, as shown in this diagram. The federal budget has been in deficit most years since the 1960s.

The question is, has the federal budget deficit created the trade deficit?

Sources: Economic Report of the President; Economic Indicators, various issues; author's estimates.

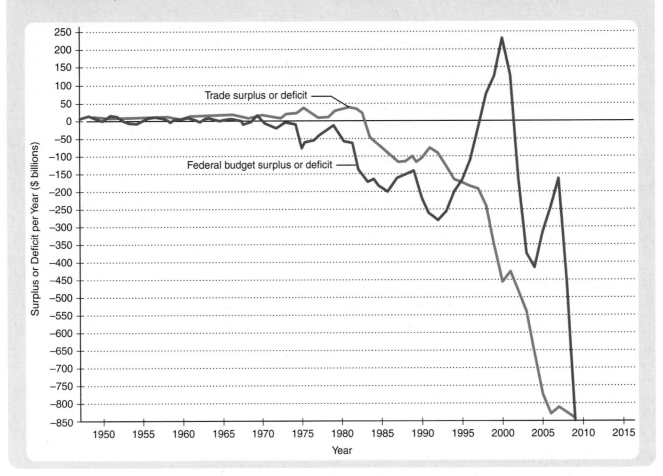

When foreign dollar holders purchase the new U.S. government bonds, they will have fewer dollars to spend on U.S. items, including U.S. export goods. Hence, when our nation's government operates with a budget deficit, we should expect to see foreign dollar holders spending more on U.S. government bonds and less on U.S.-produced goods and services. As a consequence of the U.S. government deficit, therefore, we should anticipate a decline in U.S. exports relative to U.S. imports, or a higher U.S. trade deficit.

Growing U.S. Government Deficits: Implications for U.S. Economic Performance

We have seen that one consequence of higher U.S. government budget deficits is higher international trade deficits. Higher budget deficits are also likely to have broader consequences for the economy. Reaching a consensus about these broader consequences, however, requires agreement about exactly how to measure deficits within the government's overall budget.

Which Government Deficit Is the "True" Deficit?

Assessing the implications of higher government deficits is complicated by the fact that the government may report distorted measures of its own budget. One problem is that the U.S. government has never adopted a particularly business-like approach to tracking its expenditures and receipts. Another is that even within its own accounting system, the government persists in choosing "official" measures that yield the lowest reported deficits and highest reported surpluses.

CAPITAL BUDGETING THEORY The federal government has only one budget to guide its spending and taxing each fiscal year. It does not distinguish between current spending for upkeep of the grounds of the U.S. Capitol building, for example, and spending for a new aircraft carrier that will last for many years to come. In contrast, businesses, as well as state and local governments, have two budgets. One, called the *operating budget*, includes expenditures for current operations, such as salaries and interest payments. The other, called a *capital budget*, includes expenditures on investment items, such as machines, buildings, roads, and dams. Municipal governments, for example, may pay for items on the capital budget by long-term borrowing.

Why do some economists argue that expenditures on a new aircraft carrier should not be mixed up with federal expenditures on, say, welfare payments?

If the federal government used a capital budgeting system, we would see that a large portion of the more than $850 billion deficit estimated for fiscal year 2009 was being used to finance activities or assets yielding long-term returns. According to Office of Management and Budget (OMB) estimates for 2009, investment-type outlays such as payments for military equipment and subsidies for research and development exceeded $220 billion.

For years, many economists have recommended that Congress create a capital budget and remove investment outlays from its operating budget. Opponents of such a change point out that it would allow the government to grow even faster than currently. After all, many new expenditures could be placed in the capital budget, thereby cutting the size of the operating budget deficit and reducing pressure on Congress to curtail the growth of federal government spending.

PICK A DEFICIT, ANY DEFICIT Even using standard accounting techniques, the "official" U.S. government budget deficit can vary drastically, depending on what the government chooses to include or not include. Every year, the OMB makes predictions about the federal budget deficit. So does the Congressional Budget Office. The two budget agencies each produce several deficit estimates for each fiscal year. They give them names such as the "baseline deficit," the "policy deficit," or the "on-budget deficit."

There is also a deficit that is reduced by the amount of the Social Security surplus—for 2007 and 2008 combined a reduction on the order of $500 billion—even though Congress supposedly regards the Social Security surplus as a pool of funds set aside for future disbursement rather than a source of funds for current spending. We could go on, but the point is not to know the details of these various measures of "the government deficit," but rather to understand that no one number gives a complete picture of the total amount of the government budget deficit.

Public discourse might be simplified if everyone could agree on a single measure of the deficit, but the government's accounting system does not make it easy to determine which deficit figure is clearly "best." Thus, we should probably anticipate that

For more information about the role of the Office of Management and Budget in the government's budgeting process, go to www.econtoday.com/chapter14.

for years to come, politicians and government officials will continue to bandy about whatever deficit figures best advance their own particular causes.

The Macroeconomic Consequences of Budget Deficits

No matter how we choose to measure the federal government's deficit, everyone can agree that it has been rising in recent years. Let's consider, therefore, the broader effects of higher government budget deficits on the U.S. economy. When evaluating additional macroeconomic effects of government deficits, two important points must be kept well in mind. First, given the level of government expenditures, the main alternative to the deficit is higher taxes. Therefore, the effects of a deficit should be compared to the effects of higher taxes, not to zero. Second, it is important to distinguish between the effects of deficits when full employment exists and the effects when substantial unemployment exists.

SHORT-RUN MACROECONOMIC EFFECTS OF HIGHER BUDGET DEFICITS How do increased government budget deficits affect the economy in the short run? The answer depends on the initial state of the economy. Recall from Chapter 13 that higher government spending and lower taxes that generate budget deficits typically add to total planned expenditures, even after taking into account direct and indirect expenditure offsets. When there is a recessionary gap, the increase in aggregate demand can eliminate the recessionary gap and push the economy toward its full-employment real GDP level. In the presence of a short-run recessionary gap, therefore, government deficit spending can influence both real GDP and employment.

If the economy is at the full-employment level of real GDP, however, increased total planned expenditures and higher aggregate demand generated by a larger government budget deficit create an inflationary gap. Although greater deficit spending temporarily raises equilibrium real GDP above the full-employment level, the price level also increases.

LONG-RUN MACROECONOMIC EFFECTS OF HIGHER BUDGET DEFICITS In a long-run macroeconomic equilibrium, the economy has fully adjusted to changes in all factors. These factors include changes in government spending and taxes and, consequently, the government budget deficit. Although increasing the government budget deficit raises aggregate demand, in the long run equilibrium real GDP remains at its full-employment level. Further increases in the government deficit via higher government expenditures or tax cuts can only be inflationary. They have no effect on equilibrium real GDP, which remains at the full-employment level in the long run.

The fact that long-run equilibrium real GDP is unaffected in the face of increased government deficits has an important implication:

> *In the long run, higher government budget deficits have no effect on equilibrium real GDP. Ultimately, therefore, government spending in excess of government receipts simply redistributes a larger share of real GDP to government-provided goods and services.*

Thus, if the government operates with higher deficits over an extended period, the ultimate result is a shrinkage in the share of privately provided goods and services. By continually spending more than it collects in taxes and other revenue sources, the government takes up a larger portion of economic activity.

Why did Congress recently enact one law aimed at expanding the federal deficit even as it implemented a tax plan aimed at reducing the deficit?

POLICY EXAMPLE
A Short-Run Deficit-Boosting Stimulus Is Set to Give Way to Deficit-Fighting Tax Increases

In early 2008, in response to a decline in the U.S. real GDP growth rate, Congress passed the Economic Stimulus Act. This law provided for about $45 billion in government spending. It also authorized tax "rebates." The term *rebate* was something of a misnomer, because individual taxpayers with incomes exceeding $87,000 and households with joint incomes exceeding $162,000 received no rebate. In contrast, people who paid as little as $1 in taxes were eligible for $300 "rebate" checks. Nevertheless, the "rebate" program dispersed more than $100 billion in funds aimed at stimulating consumption spending and preventing a short-run recessionary gap from expanding. Thus, the legislation expanded the federal deficit by about $150 billion in total.

Within weeks after the law's passage, worries over an increasing budget deficit induced Congress to authorize a significant increase in personal income tax rates at the end of 2010. The scheduled tax rate increases promised to raise the overall U.S. personal income tax burden by 25 percent. Estimates at the time indicated that as a result, the ratio of personal income taxes to GDP could climb to its highest level since World War II. Of course, even if higher personal income tax rates help to bring down the deficit in the 2010s, the higher marginal tax rates will also tend to reduce long-run aggregate supply and dampen future real GDP growth. The result could be lower incomes and hence reduced income tax revenues in later years.

FOR CRITICAL ANALYSIS
Why do you suppose that most economists contend that changes in tax rates have larger and longer-lasting effects on economic activity than one-time tax rebates?

QUICK QUIZ   *See page 364 for the answers. Review concepts from this section in MyEconLab.*

Given constant shares of domestic consumption and domestic investment relative to GDP, funds to finance higher government budget deficits must come from abroad. To obtain the dollars required to purchase newly issued government bonds, foreign residents must sell _____ goods and services in the United States than U.S. residents sell abroad; thus, U.S. imports must _____ U.S. exports. For this reason, the federal budget deficit and the international trade _____ tend to be related.

Some people argue that the federal budget deficit is measured incorrectly because it lumps together spending on capital and spending on consumption. Establishing separate _____ and _____ budgets might, according to this view, promote more accurate measurement of federal finances.

Higher government deficits arise from increased government spending or tax cuts, which raise aggregate demand. Thus, larger government budget deficits can raise real GDP in a _____ gap situation. If the economy is already at the full-employment level of real GDP, however, higher government deficits can only temporarily push equilibrium real GDP _____ the full-employment level.

In the long run, higher government budget deficits cause the equilibrium price level to rise but fail to raise equilibrium real GDP above the full-employment level. Thus, the long-run effect of increased government deficits is simply a redistribution of real GDP from _____ provided goods and services to _____-provided goods and services.

How Could the Government Reduce All Its Red Ink?

There have been many suggestions about how to reduce the government deficit. One way to reduce the deficit is to increase tax collections.

INCREASING TAXES FOR EVERYONE From an arithmetic point of view, a federal budget deficit can be wiped out by simply increasing the amount of taxes collected. Let's see what this would require. Projections for 2009 are instructive. The Office of Management and Budget estimated the 2009 federal budget deficit at about $850 billion. To have prevented this deficit from occurring by raising taxes, in 2009 the government would have had to collect at least $5,000 more in taxes from *every worker* in the United States. Needless to say, reality is such that we will never see annual federal budget deficits wiped out by simple tax increases.

TAXING THE RICH Some people suggest that the way to eliminate the deficit is to raise taxes on the rich. What does it mean to tax the rich more? If you talk about taxing "millionaires," you are referring to those who pay taxes on more than $1 million in income per year. There are fewer than 100,000 of them. Even if you were to double the taxes they currently pay, the reduction in the deficit would be relatively trivial. Changing marginal tax rates at the upper end will produce similarly unimpressive results. The Internal Revenue Service (IRS) has determined that an increase in the top marginal tax rate from 35 percent to 45 percent would raise, at best, only about $35 billion in additional taxes. (This assumes that people do not figure out a way to avoid the higher tax rate.) Extra revenues of $35 billion per year represent less than 9 percent of the estimated 2009 federal budget deficit.

The reality is that the data do not support the notion that tax increases can completely *eliminate* deficits. Although eliminating a deficit in this way is possible arithmetically, politically just the opposite has occurred. When more tax revenues have been collected, Congress has usually responded by increasing government spending.

REDUCING EXPENDITURES Reducing expenditures is another way to decrease the federal budget deficit. Figure 14-5 shows various components of government spending as a percentage of total expenditures. There you see that military spending as a share of total federal expenditures has risen slightly in recent years, though it remains much lower than in most previous years.

During the period from the conclusion of World War II until 1972, military spending was the most important aspect of the federal budget. Figure 14-5 shows that it no longer is, even taking into account the war on terrorism that began in late 2001. **Entitlements,** which are legislated federal government payments that anyone who qualifies is entitled to receive, are now the most important component of the federal budget. These include payments for Social Security and other income security programs and for Medicare and other health programs such as Medicaid. Entitlements are consequently often called **noncontrollable expenditures,** or nondiscretionary expenditures unrelated to national defense that automatically change without any direct action by Congress.

IS IT TIME TO BEGIN WHITTLING AWAY AT ENTITLEMENTS? In 1960, spending on entitlements represented about 20 percent of the total federal budget. Today, entitlement expenditures make up more than half of total federal spending. Consider Social Security, Medicare, and Medicaid. In constant 2005 dollars, in 2009 Social Security, Medicare, and Medicaid represented about $1,350 billion of estimated federal expenditures, or slightly more than the total of all other spending by the federal government. (This excludes military and international payments and interest on the government debt.)

Entitlements
Guaranteed benefits under a government program such as Social Security, Medicare, or Medicaid.

Noncontrollable expenditures
Government spending that changes automatically without action by Congress.

FIGURE 14-5

**Components of Federal Expenditures as Percentages
of Total Federal Spending**

Although military spending as a percentage of total federal spending has risen
and fallen with changing national defense concerns, national defense expenditures as a percentage of total spending have generally trended downward
since the mid-1950s. Social Security and other income security programs and

Medicare and other health programs now account for larger shares of total
federal spending than any other programs.

Source: Office of Management and Budget.

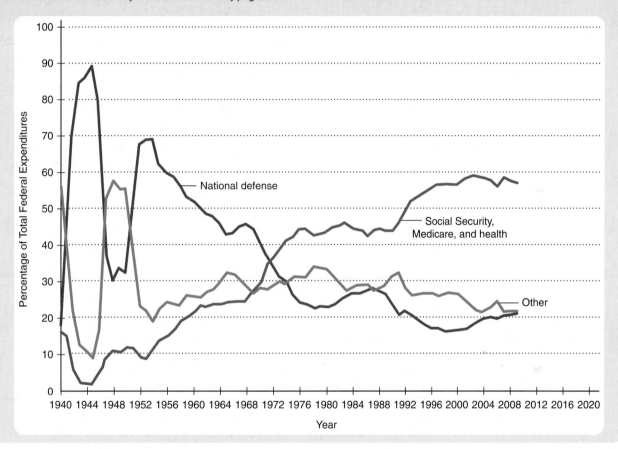

Entitlement payments for Social Security, Medicare, and Medicaid now exceed all
other domestic spending. Entitlements are growing faster than any other part of the
federal government budget. During the past two decades, real spending on entitlements (adjusted for inflation) grew between 7 and 8 percent per year, while the economy grew less than 3 percent per year. Social Security payments are growing in real
terms at about 6 percent per year, but Medicare and Medicaid are growing at double-
digit rates. The passage of Medicare prescription drug benefits in 2003 simply added
to the already rapid growth of these health care entitlements.

Many people believe that entitlement programs are "necessary" federal expenditures. Interest on the public debt must be paid, but Congress can change just about
every other federal expenditure labeled "necessary." The federal budget deficit is not
expected to drop in the near future because entitlement programs are not likely to be
eliminated. Governments have trouble cutting government benefit programs once
they are established. This means that containing federal budget deficits is likely to
prove to be a difficult task.

You Are There

To think further about the long-
term budgetary issues posed by
health care entitlements, take a
look at **Facing a Future Medicare
Meltdown?** on the next two pages.

How does the existence of "trust funds" for entitlement programs complicate the measurement of the deficit and the public debt?

POLICY EXAMPLE
Should Entitlement "Trust Funds" Be Included in Deficits and the Net Public Debt?

Congress has set up a number of entitlement "trust funds." Social Security, Medicare, and military and civil service retirement programs all have their own trust funds. Each year these accounts typically receive a total of about $200 billion from general revenues, which Congress earmarks as "belonging" to the various entitlement programs for future use. Congress requires managers of the trust funds to purchase Treasury securities. In effect, therefore, Congress first allocates revenues to the trust funds and then turns around and borrows from them to finance other expenditures.

The entitlement trust funds' holdings of Treasury securities are intragovernmental debt counted in the gross public debt. Changes in these holdings are not included, however, in the official measure of the federal deficit, nor are the holdings counted as part of the net public debt. Some economists contend that they should be, at least if Congress seriously views these entitlement accounts as "trust funds." Eventually, they point out, Congress will have to draw on the trust funds to make payments to retirees. When this happens, Congress will have to reduce other government spending, raise taxes, or borrow more from the public. Thus, annual allocations to the trust funds arguably constitute a form of current government spending and a debt owed to the public at the present time.

FOR CRITICAL ANALYSIS
How much would the annual deficit increase if trust funds' allocations from Congress were counted as current expenditures?

QUICK QUIZ
See page 364 for the answers. Review concepts from this section in MyEconLab.

One way to reduce federal budget _____ is to increase taxes. Proposals to reduce deficits by raising taxes on the highest-income individuals will not appreciably reduce budget deficits, however.

Another way to decrease federal budget _____ is to cut back on government spending, particularly on _____, defined as benefits guaranteed under government programs such as Social Security and Medicare.

You Are There ➤ Facing a Future Medicare Meltdown?

Thomas Saving, a public trustee of the Social Security and Medicare system, has been looking at the future of Medicare, and he does not like what he sees. Social Security's total payout over the next 75 years is projected to be nearly $7 trillion (measured in 2005 dollars). Medicare's anticipated payout over the same period is even larger: in excess of $24 trillion, or more than four times today's official public debt. Saving concludes that the nation cannot wait to solve the problem decades from now. After all, the Social Security and Medicare programs already are operating at a combined deficit equal to more than 5 percent of federal income tax revenues. At their current rates of growth, in 15 years covering the deficits in the two programs will require more than *25 percent* of all income tax revenues.

Saving considers possible courses of action. One is to do nothing, which would mean that by 2040 the Social Security

You Are There (cont.)

and Medicare deficits will eat up one out of every two income tax dollars collected by the federal government. Another alternative is to gradually raise the Medicare premiums paid by the elderly to cover the program's shortfalls. The 75-year projection indicates that eventually the elderly would have to spend all their Social Security income on Medicare premiums, however. A third possibility, assuming payroll tax rates remain unchanged, is to allocate some nonpayroll taxes to Social Security and Medicare. But then a 10 percent increase in all nonpayroll taxes would be required to close the Social Security and Medicare deficits by 2020. A 50 percent increase in nonpayroll taxes would be required by 2080.

Ultimately, Saving decides, there is only one reasonable solution: The cost of the Medicare program to the government must be reduced. This could be accomplished by rationing Medicare coverage, either through government-directed rationing or by imposing fixed budgets on seniors

and allowing them to ration their own care. Alternatively, the government could seek to give health care providers incentives to produce their services at lower costs. One way or another, Saving concludes, the growth of Medicare expenses must be contained, starting now.

CRITICAL ANALYSIS QUESTIONS

1. Barring U.S. government cuts in nonentitlement spending (e.g., a cut in military expenditures) or increases in taxes, why will unchecked growth of entitlement spending eventually lead to even higher federal deficits than the nation is currently observing?

2. Why is it arguable, in light of government promises of future payments through entitlement programs, that the official measure of the public debt understates the overall indebtedness of the government?

Issues and Applications

Are the Budget and Trade Deficits Twins or Distant Cousins?

CONCEPTS APPLIED

► Government Budget Deficit

► Balanced Budget

► Government Budget Surplus

In principle, an increase in the U.S. government budget deficit should be related to lower U.S. exports and hence a higher U.S. trade deficit. For this reason, economists sometimes refer to the U.S. government budget deficit and the U.S. trade deficit as *twin deficits*.

There is not always a direct relationship between the twin deficits, however, as you can see by looking back at Figure 14-4 on page 352. During the 1980s and the early 2000s, the two deficits definitely moved together. During most of the 1990s and mid-2000s, however, they generally moved in opposite directions. Why was this so?

Other Things Are Not Always Equal

Let's recall why we might predict a relationship between U.S. government budget deficits and trade deficits. If the government moves from a position of a balanced budget to a situation in which it operates with a budget deficit, some funds to finance the deficit typically come from abroad. Other things being equal, when foreign residents allocate funds to holding new U.S. government bonds—which they will opt to do when U.S. interest rates rise—they can no longer spend those funds on U.S. exports. Hence, with all other factors unchanged, when the U.S. budget falls deeper into deficit, the U.S. trade deficit will increase. In contrast, when the U.S. budget moves toward a surplus, the U.S. trade deficit will tend to decline, other things being equal.

Note that key phrases in the above explanation are "other things being equal" and "with all other factors unchanged." In the real world, other things are not always equal. Other factors that influence the trade deficit can change. Indeed, changes in other factors explain the diverging movements in the U.S. budget deficit and trade deficit in the 1990s and the mid-2000s.

Why the Twin Deficits Diverged in the 1990s and the Mid-2000s

A key factor that changed during the 1990s and the early 2000s was U.S. real GDP. In 1990 and 2001, there were recessions. When real GDP declined, so did incomes and hence income tax revenues, which caused federal budget deficits to increase. During the post-recession expansions, real GDP increased, and so did taxable incomes. Federal income tax revenues surged throughout the 1990s and again in the mid-2000s. Federal spending increased at a slower pace, so the federal budget deficit shrank.

Higher disposable incomes in the 1990s and mid-2000s also induced households to purchase more imported goods and services, which helped to fuel trade deficits. Thus, economic expansions during the 1990s and mid-2000s brought about declines in the budget deficit, but at the same time the expansions boosted the trade deficit. The two deficits diverged.

Other factors can also contribute to divergences of the budget deficit and the trade deficit. For instance, during the late 1990s U.S. labor and capital productivity increased significantly, which induced firms to increase their investment spending. One source of funds to finance these expenditures was borrowings from abroad. Thus, even as the federal government's budget moved into a surplus at the end of the 1990s, resulting in less government borrowing from abroad, U.S. companies increased their borrowings from foreign residents. This helped contribute to a continuing U.S. trade deficit even as the government budget operated with a surplus through 2001.

Measuring How Much Government Budget Deficits Contribute to Trade Deficits

Leonardo Bartolini and Amartya Lahiri of the Federal Reserve Bank of New York have examined the strength of the relationship between government budget deficits and trade deficits. They conclude that there is unambiguously a relationship: On average, each $1 increase in the government budget deficit is associated with a $0.30 increase in the trade deficit. Hence, there is definitely a tendency for the two deficits to move together over time.

The fact that other factors influencing the two deficits, such as real GDP and investment expenditures, change over time explains why there is not a dollar-for-dollar relationship between the two deficits. Nevertheless, over long periods of time the trade deficit should tend to rise when the government budget deficit increases, and vice versa, and in fact this pattern is what we observe.

Test your understanding of this chapter by going online to **MyEconLab**.
In the Study Plan for this chapter, select Section N: News.

For Critical Analysis

1. If the government's budget is initially balanced, but then the government begins operating with a budget surplus, why would we expect the trade deficit to shrink, other things being equal?

2. Why might variations in the dollar's value in terms of other currencies cause the trade deficit to move independently from the changes in the government budget deficit? (Hint: If the value of the dollar increases, do exports become more or less expensive to U.S. residents? Do imports become more or less expensive?)

Web Resources

1. To take a look at a summary of Bartolini and Lahiri's study of the twin deficits, go to www.econtoday.com/chapter14.

2. For more discussion of the relationship between government budget deficits and trade deficits, go to www.econtoday.com/chapter14.

Research Project

Recently, a number of economists have suggested that a decrease in the U.S. saving rate may be contributing to a weaker relationship between the government budget deficit and the trade deficit. How might a decrease in saving by U.S. households affect the relationship between the twin deficits? (Hint: A reduction in autonomous saving corresponds to a rise in autonomous consumption that boosts equilibrium real income and hence causes import spending to rise, independently of the budget deficit.)

---

myeconlab

Here is what you should know after reading this chapter. **MyEconLab** will help you identify what you know, and where to go when you need to practice.

WHAT YOU SHOULD KNOW

Federal Government Budget Deficits Whenever the flow of government expenditures exceeds the flow of government revenues during a period of time, a budget deficit occurs. If government expenditures are less than government revenues during a given interval, a budget surplus occurs. The government operates with a balanced budget during a specific period if its expenditures equal its revenues. The federal budget deficit expressed as a percentage of GDP reached about 6 percent in the early 1980s. The federal government operated with a surplus between 1998 and 2001. The government budget went into deficit once more in 2002. The deficit recently has risen to more than 6 percent of GDP.

government budget deficit, 343
balanced budget, 343
government budget surplus, 343
public debt, 344

KEY FIGURES
Figure 14-1, 345
Figure 14-2, 345

WHERE TO GO TO PRACTICE

- **MyEconLab** Study Plans 14.1, 14.2
- Audio introduction to Chapter 14
- ABC News Video: Big Government: Who is Going to Pay the Bill?
- Animated Figures 14-1, 14-2

The Public Debt The federal budget deficit is a flow, whereas accumulated budget deficits are a stock, called the public debt. The gross public debt is the stock of total government bonds, and the net public debt is the difference between the gross public debt and the amount of government agencies' holdings of government bonds. In recent years, the net public debt as a share of GDP has been running at around 40 percent of GDP.

gross public debt, 346
net public debt, 346

KEY FIGURE
Figure 14-3, 348

- **MyEconLab** Study Plan 14.3

(continued)

 *(continued)*

WHAT YOU SHOULD KNOW		WHERE TO GO TO PRACTICE

How the Public Debt Might Prove a Burden to Future Generations If people are taxed, they must forgo private consumption as society substitutes government goods for private goods. Thus, if future generations must be taxed at higher rates to pay for the current generation's increased consumption of governmentally provided goods, future generations may experience a burden from the public debt. Any current crowding out of investment as a consequence of additional debt accumulation can reduce capital formation and future economic growth. Furthermore, if capital invested by foreign residents who purchase some of the U.S. public debt has not been productively used, future generations will be worse off.

KEY FIGURE
Figure 14-4, 352

- **MyEconLab** Study Plans 14.3, 14.4
- Animated Figure 14-4

Why the Federal Budget Deficit Might Be Incorrectly Measured Some people contend that the federal budget deficit is measured incorrectly because it combines government capital and consumption expenditures. They argue that the federal government should have an operating budget and a capital budget.

- **MyEconLab** Study Plan 14.5

The Macroeconomic Effects of Government Budget Deficits Because higher government deficits are caused by increased government spending or tax cuts, they contribute to a rise in total planned expenditures and aggregate demand. If there is a short-run recessionary gap, higher government deficits can thereby push equilibrium real GDP toward the full-employment level. If the economy is already at the full-employment level of real GDP, however, then a higher deficit creates a short-run inflationary gap.

- **MyEconLab** Study Plan 14.5

Possible Ways to Reduce the Government Budget Deficit Suggested ways to reduce the deficit are to increase taxes, particularly on the rich, and to reduce expenditures, particularly on entitlements, defined as guaranteed benefits under government programs such as Social Security and Medicare.

entitlements, 356
noncontrollable
  expenditures, 356
KEY FIGURE
Figure 14-5, 357

- **MyEconLab** Study Plan 14.5
- Animated Figure 14-5

Log in to MyEconLab, take a chapter test, and get a personalized Study Plan that tells you which concepts you understand and which ones you need to review. From there, MyEconLab will give you further practice, tutorials, animations, videos, and guided solutions.
Log in to www.myeconlab.com

PROBLEMS

All problems are assignable in myeconlab *. Answers to odd-numbered problems appear at the back of the book.*

14-1. In 2011, government spending is $3.3 trillion, and taxes collected are $2.9 trillion. What is the federal government deficit in that year?

14-2. Suppose that the Office of Management and Budget provides the following estimates of federal budget receipts, federal budget spending, and GDP, all expressed in billions of dollars. Calculate the implied estimates of the federal budget deficit as a percentage of GDP for each year.

Year	Federal Budget Receipts	Federal Budget Spending	GDP
2011	2,829.8	3,382.6	15,573.2
2012	2,892.4	3,441.6	16,316.0
2013	2,964.2	3,529.3	16,852.1
2014	3,013.5	3,600.1	17,454.4

14-3. It may be argued that the effects of a higher public debt are the same as the effects of a higher deficit. Why?

14-4. What happens to the net public debt if the federal government operates next year with a:

a. budget deficit?

b. balanced budget?

c. budget surplus?

14-5. What is the relationship between the gross public debt and the net public debt?

14-6. Explain how each of the following will affect the net public debt, other things being equal.

a. Previously, the government operated with a balanced budget, but recently there has been a sudden increase in federal tax collections.

b. The federal government had been operating with a very small annual budget deficit until three successive hurricanes hit the Atlantic Coast, and now government spending has risen substantially.

c. The General National Mortgage Association, a federal government agency that purchases certain types of home mortgages, buys U.S. Treasury bonds from another government agency.

14-7. Explain in your own words why there is likely to be a relationship between federal budget deficits and U.S. international trade deficits.

14-8. Suppose that the share of U.S. GDP going to domestic consumption remains constant. Initially, the federal government was operating with a balanced budget, but this year it has increased its spending well above its collections of taxes and other sources of revenues. To fund its deficit spending, the government has issued bonds. So far, very few foreign residents have shown any interest in purchasing the bonds.

a. What must happen to induce foreign residents to buy the bonds?

b. If foreign residents desire to purchase the bonds, what is the most important source of dollars to buy them?

14-9. Suppose that the economy is experiencing the short-run equilibrium position depicted at point *A* in the diagram below. Then the government raises its spending and thereby runs a budget deficit in an effort to boost equilibrium real GDP to its long-run equilibrium level of $15 trillion (in base-year dollars). Explain the effects of an increase in the government deficit on equilibrium real GDP and the equilibrium price level. In addition, given that many taxes and government benefits vary with real GDP, discuss what change we might

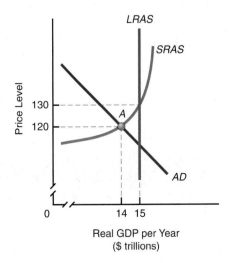

expect to see in the budget deficit as a result of the effects on equilibrium real GDP.

14-10. Suppose that the economy is experiencing the short-run equilibrium position depicted at point *B* in the diagram to the right. Explain the short-run effects of an increase in the government deficit on equilibrium real GDP and the equilibrium price level. What will be the long-run effects?

14-11. To reduce the size of the deficit (and reduce the growth of the net public debt), a politician suggests that "we should tax the rich." The politician makes a simple arithmetic calculation in which he applies the higher tax rate to the total income reported by "the rich" in a previous year. He says that this is how much the government could receive from increasing taxes on "the rich." What is the major fallacy in such calculations?

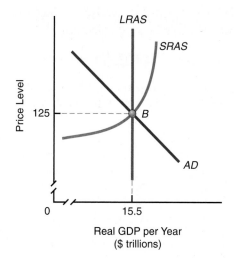

ECONOMICS ON THE NET

The Public Debt By examining the federal government's budget data, its current estimates of the public debt can be determined.

Title: Historical Tables: Budget of the United States Government

Navigation: Use the link at **www.econontoday.com/chapter14** to visit the Office of Management and Budget. Select the most recent budget. Then select *Historical Tables*.

Application After the document downloads, perform the indicated operations and answer the following questions.

1. In the Table of Contents in the left-hand margin of the Historical Tables, click on Table 7.1, "Federal Debt at the End of the Year, 1940–2009." In light of the discussion in this chapter, which column shows the net public debt? What is the conceptual difference between the gross public debt and the net public debt? Last year, what was the dollar difference between these two amounts?

2. Table 7.1 includes estimates of the gross and net public debt over the next several years. Suppose that these estimates turn out to be accurate. Calculate how much the net public debt would increase on average each year. What are possible ways that the government could prevent these predicted increases from occurring?

For Group Study and Analysis Divide into two groups, and have each group take one side in answering the question, "Is the public debt a burden or a blessing?" Have each group develop rationales for supporting its position. Then reconvene the entire class, and discuss the relative merits of the alternative positions and rationales.

ANSWERS TO QUICK QUIZZES

p. 346: (i) budget deficit . . . balanced budget . . . budget surplus; (ii) stock; (iii) surplus . . . deficit . . . deficit
p. 351: (i) gross . . . net; (ii) future . . . current . . . less . . . lower; (iii) higher
p. 355: (i) more . . . exceed . . . deficit; (ii) operating . . . capital; (iii) recessionary . . . above; (iv) privately . . . government
p. 358: (i) deficits; (ii) deficits . . . entitlements

Money, Banking, and Central Banking

15

F or years, they were the big names of Wall Street: Bear Stearns, Goldman Sachs, Lehman Brothers, Merrill Lynch, and Morgan Stanley. Known as "investment banks," these firms were created during the dark days of the Great Depression of the 1930s. Over the years, they grew into financial powerhouses. In 2008, however, they met their match: mortgage-related securities issued by government-supported companies with the harmless-sounding nicknames "Fannie Mae" and "Freddie Mac." When values of mortgage loans and securities issued by Fannie Mae and Freddie Mac plummeted, so did the fortunes of the previously rock-solid U.S. investment banks. In this chapter, you will learn about firms called *financial intermediaries*, which no longer include investment banks but which continue to include very important institutions we call commercial banks.

LEARNING OBJECTIVES

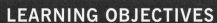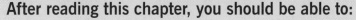

After reading this chapter, you should be able to:

- Define the fundamental functions of money
- Identify key properties that any good that functions as money must possess
- Explain official definitions of the quantity of money in circulation
- Understand why financial intermediaries such as banks exist
- Explain the essential features of federal deposit insurance
- Describe the basic structure and functions of the Federal Reserve System

myeconlab

MyEconLab helps you master each objective and study more efficiently. See end of chapter for details.

? DID YOU KNOW THAT it is now illegal to carry on your person more than $5 worth of pennies or nickels out of the United States? It is also against the law to transport more than $100 worth of pennies or nickels out of the country via truck, ship, or plane, and melting pennies and nickels is prohibited. Penalties for violating these restrictions may include prison terms as long as five years and fines as high as $10,000.

Pennies and nickels contain zinc, copper, and nickel, all of which have seen recent upswings in prices. As a result, the value of the metals used in the coins now exceeds the coins' face values. The penny is composed mostly of zinc, and the amount of zinc in a penny has had a market value as high as 1.8 cents in recent years. Nickels are 70 percent copper and 25 percent nickel, and the market value of a nickel's metal content has reached as high as 8.4 cents. Consequently, people who can gather up large numbers of these coins at their face values potentially can earn significant rates of return—as much as 80 percent on pennies and more than 65 percent on nickels. This explains why the U.S. government has banned the international transport and melting of pennies and nickels. The government is already incurring more costs to produce these coins than their value in exchange for goods and services. By banning the international transport and melting of pennies and nickels, the government is trying to prevent people from profiting from selling coins that are already generating losses to taxpayers.

Coins, paper currency, and bank accounts from which people transmit debit-card and check payments are all included in the Federal Reserve's measure of the total amount of *money* that we can use to purchase goods and services. Money has been important to society for thousands of years. In the fourth century B.C., Aristotle claimed that everything had to "be accessed in money, for this enables men always to exchange their services, and so makes society possible." Money is indeed a part of our everyday existence. Nevertheless, we have to be careful when we talk about money. Often we hear a person say, "I wish I had more money," instead of "I wish I had more wealth," thereby confusing the concepts of money and wealth. Economists use the term **money** to mean anything that people generally accept in exchange for goods and services. Table 15-1 provides a list of some items that various civilizations have used as money. The best way to understand how these items served this purpose is to examine the functions of money.

Why did the U.S. government outlaw the transportation of pennies and nickels out of the United States?

Money

Any medium that is universally accepted in an economy both by sellers of goods and services as payment for those goods and services and by creditors as payment for debts.

TABLE 15-1

Types of Money

This is a partial list of items that have been used as money. Native Americans used *wampum*, beads made from shells. Fijians used whale teeth. The early colonists in North America used tobacco. And cigarettes were used in post–World War II Germany and in Poland during the breakdown of Communist rule in the late 1980s.

Iron	Boar tusk	Playing cards
Copper	Red woodpecker scalps	Leather
Brass	Feathers	Gold
Wine	Glass	Silver
Corn	Polished beads (wampum)	Knives
Salt	Rum	Pots
Horses	Molasses	Boats
Sheep	Tobacco	Pitch
Goats	Agricultural implements	Rice
Tortoise shells	Round stones with centers removed	Cows
Porpoise teeth	Crystal salt bars	Paper
Whale teeth	Snail shells	Cigarettes

Source: Roger LeRoy Miller and David D. VanHoose, *Money, Banking, and Financial Markets,* 3rd ed. (Cincinnati: South-Western, 2007), p. 7.

The Functions of Money

Money traditionally has four functions. The one that most people are familiar with is money's function as a *medium of exchange*. Money also serves as a *unit of accounting*, a *store of value* or *purchasing power*, and a *standard of deferred payment*. Anything that serves these four functions is money. Anything that could serve these four functions could be considered money.

Money as a Medium of Exchange

When we say that money serves as a **medium of exchange,** we mean that sellers will accept it as payment in market transactions. Without some generally accepted medium of exchange, we would have to resort to *barter*. In fact, before money was used, transactions took place by means of barter. **Barter** is simply a direct exchange of goods for goods. In a barter economy, the shoemaker who wants to obtain a dozen water glasses must seek out a glassmaker who at exactly the same time is interested in obtaining a pair of shoes. For this to occur, there has to be a high likelihood of a *double coincidence of wants* for each specific item to be exchanged. If there isn't, the shoemaker must go through several trades in order to obtain the desired dozen glasses—perhaps first trading shoes for jewelry, then jewelry for some pots and pans, and then the pots and pans for the desired glasses.

Money facilitates exchange by reducing the transaction costs associated with means-of-payment uncertainty. That is, the existence of money means that individuals no longer have to hold a diverse collection of goods as an exchange inventory. As a medium of exchange, money allows individuals to specialize in producing those goods for which they have a comparative advantage and to receive money payments for their labor. Money payments can then be exchanged for the fruits of other people's labor. The use of money as a medium of exchange permits more specialization and the inherent economic efficiencies that come with it (and hence greater economic growth).

How is a Web site helping those interested in engaging in barter increase the probability of finding a double coincidence of wants?

Medium of exchange
Any item that sellers will accept as payment.

Barter
The direct exchange of goods and services for other goods and services without the use of money.

E-COMMERCE EXAMPLE
A Web Site That Specializes in Identifying Double Coincidences of Wants

At the Web site Swaptree.com, money is not an acceptable medium of exchange. Suppose that you have an item, such as a book you do not care to read again or a movie DVD you know you will never watch again. You can go to Swaptree, indicate your item's availability, and provide a list of items you would be willing to accept in exchange. Then Swaptree's system compiles a list of matching items that others have made available for a barter trade. If there are no double coincidences of wants involving only two people, Swaptree's system can engineer three-way and even four-way trades among users who want different things. When people agree to make an exchange, they must pay for shipping, but no money changes hands.

Thus, Swaptree reduces the costs of finding a double coincidence of wants and thereby improves the feasibility of barter exchange for people who desire to trade goods without using money. The company's owners seek to earn profits—which they do accept in the form of money—from selling advertising space on the firm's Web site.

FOR CRITICAL ANALYSIS
How does Swaptree's specialized ability to identify double coincidences of wants enable potential barter traders to avoid having to hold a diverse collection of goods as an exchange inventory?

Money as a Unit of Accounting

Unit of accounting
A measure by which prices are expressed; the common denominator of the price system; a central property of money.

A **unit of accounting** is a way of placing a specific price on economic goods and services. It is the common denominator, the commonly recognized measure of value. The dollar is the unit of accounting in the United States. It is the yardstick that allows individuals easily to compare the relative value of goods and services. Accountants at the U.S. Department of Commerce use dollar prices to measure national income and domestic product, a business uses dollar prices to calculate profits and losses, and a typical household budgets regularly anticipated expenses using dollar prices as its unit of accounting.

Another way of describing money as a unit of accounting is to say that it serves as a *standard of value* that allows people to compare the relative worth of various goods and services. This allows for comparison shopping, for example.

Money as a Store of Value

Store of value
The ability to hold value over time; a necessary property of money.

One of the most important functions of money is that it serves as a **store of value** or purchasing power. The money you have today can be set aside to purchase things later on. In the meantime, money retains its nominal value, which you can apply to those future purchases. If you have $1,000 in your checking account, you can choose to spend it today on goods and services, spend it tomorrow, or spend it a month from now. In this way, money provides a way to transfer value (wealth) into the future.

Why are some $100 bills worth less than others outside the United States?

INTERNATIONAL EXAMPLE
Why Musical Chairs in the U.S. Treasury Make the $100 Bill a Weaker Store of Value Abroad

A cabin attendant on an Italian cruise ship about to dock in the city of Antananarivo, Madagascar, hurries to get in line to collect his monthly pay: seven U.S. $100 bills. To his dismay, he finds himself several spots from the front of the line. He worries that this means his seven $100 bills will not be signed by one of the two most recent U.S. Treasury secretaries, Henry Paulson or John Snow. If the cabin attendant is unlucky enough to receive bills signed by an earlier Treasury secretary, such as Robert Rubin, his pay effectively will be reduced by up to $10 per each bill bearing Rubin's signature.

The cabin attendant listens as a crewmate complains that a $100 bill he has just received, which was signed by Snow, will likely be worth no more than $95 in port. This crewmate says there is a rumor circulating that a new U.S. Treasury secretary has taken office. People assume that the rumor is true, so $100 bills signed by Snow are regarded as "old." Like residents of many countries, Madagascar residents worry that aged U.S. bills have been around long enough for foreign counterfeiters to have produced good likenesses of the bills. Hence, Madagascar businesses will not provide $100 of goods or services in exchange for an old $100 bill. The cabin attendant sighs. Clearly, U.S. $100 bills are losing some of their value outside the United States each time a new U.S. Treasury secretary takes office.

FOR CRITICAL ANALYSIS
How might a recent redesign of $100 bills that makes them harder to counterfeit help these bills maintain their value outside the United States?

Money as a Standard of Deferred Payment

Standard of deferred payment
A property of an item that makes it desirable for use as a means of settling debts maturing in the future; an essential property of money.

The fourth function of the monetary unit is as a **standard of deferred payment.** This function involves the use of money both as a medium of exchange and as a unit of accounting. Debts are typically stated in terms of a unit of accounting; they are paid with a monetary medium of exchange. That is to say, a debt is specified in a dollar amount and paid in currency (or by check). A corporate bond, for example, has a face value—the dollar value stated on it, which is to be paid upon maturity. The periodic interest payments on that corporate bond are specified and paid in dollars, and when the bond comes due (at maturity), the corporation pays the face value in dollars to the holder of the bond.

Properties of Money

Money is an asset—something of value—that accounts for part of personal wealth. Wealth in the form of money can be exchanged later for other assets, goods, or services. Although money is not the only form of wealth that can be exchanged for goods and services, it is the most widely and readily accepted one.

Money—The Most Liquid Asset

Money's attribute as the most readily tradable asset is called **liquidity.** We say that an asset is *liquid* when it can easily be acquired or disposed of without high transaction costs and with relative certainty as to its value. Money is by definition the most liquid asset. People can easily convert money to other asset forms. Therefore, most individuals hold at least a part of their wealth in the form of the most liquid of assets, money. You can see how assets rank in liquidity relative to one another in Figure 15-1.

When we hold money, however, we incur a cost for this advantage of liquidity. Because cash in your pocket and many checking or debit account balances do not earn interest, that cost is the interest yield that could have been obtained had the asset been held in another form—for example, in the form of stocks and bonds.

> *The cost of holding money (its opportunity cost) is measured by the alternative interest yield obtainable by holding some other asset.*

Liquidity
The degree to which an asset can be acquired or disposed of without much danger of any intervening loss in *nominal* value and with small transaction costs. Money is the most liquid asset.

Monetary Standards, or What Backs Money

In the past, many different monetary standards have existed. For example, commodity money, which is a physical good that may be valued for other uses it provides, has been used (see Table 15-1 on page 366). The main forms of commodity money were gold and silver. Today, though, most people throughout the world accept coins, paper

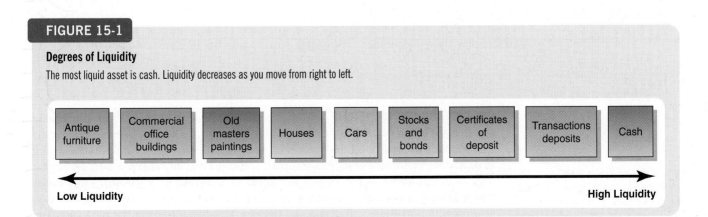

FIGURE 15-1

Degrees of Liquidity
The most liquid asset is cash. Liquidity decreases as you move from right to left.

Antique furniture | Commercial office buildings | Old masters paintings | Houses | Cars | Stocks and bonds | Certificates of deposit | Transactions deposits | Cash

Low Liquidity ←———————————————————→ **High Liquidity**

Transactions deposits
Checkable and debitable account balances in commercial banks and other types of financial institutions, such as credit unions and savings banks; any accounts in financial institutions from which you can easily transmit debit-card and check payments without many restrictions.

Fiduciary monetary system
A system in which money is issued by the government and its value is based uniquely on the public's faith that the currency represents command over goods and services.

currency, and balances held on deposit as **transactions deposits** (debitable and checkable accounts with banks and other financial institutions) in exchange for items sold, including labor services.

But these forms of money raise a question: Why are we willing to accept as payment something that has no intrinsic value? After all, you could not sell checks or debit cards to very many producers for use as a raw material in manufacturing. The reason is that payments in the modern world arise from a **fiduciary monetary system.** This means that the value of the payments rests on the public's confidence that such payments can be exchanged for goods and services. *Fiduciary* comes from the Latin *fiducia*, which means "trust" or "confidence." In our fiduciary monetary system, there is no legal requirement for money, in the form of currency or transactions deposits, to be convertible to a fixed quantity of gold, silver, or some other precious commodity. The bills are just pieces of paper. Usually, coins have a value stamped on them that today is greater than the market value of the metal in them. Nevertheless, currency and transactions deposits are money because of their acceptability and predictability of value.

ACCEPTABILITY Transactions deposits and currency are money because they are accepted in exchange for goods and services. They are accepted because people have confidence that these items can later be exchanged for other goods and services. This confidence is based on the knowledge that such exchanges have occurred in the past without problems.

How has an electronic medium of exchange issued by a Hong Kong videogame company gained widespread acceptance as a form of money?

You Are There

To consider why acceptability is such an important property for money, read **Would You Like Your Change in Fives, Tens, Melvilles, or Rockwells?** on page 387.

INTERNATIONAL EXAMPLE
A Virtual Money Becomes Widely Acceptable in China

In China, almost 250 million people regularly conduct exchanges using electronic "QQ coins" issued by Tencent Holdings, Limited, a Hong Kong–based company that sells online videogames. Originally, QQ coins, each of which sells for one Chinese yuan (about 13 cents), were a company marketing ploy. Tencent provided them to customers to finance purchases of virtual flowers, cellphone ringtones, and virtual equipment such as magical swords used in Web-based videogames. Recently, people have begun accepting QQ coins in exchange for physical items, such as CDs, movie DVDs, and cosmetics, and many gamblers now place bets using

QQ coins. Some businesses operate services that exchange the virtual QQ coins for real Chinese currency. A few economists have suggested that QQ coins are so widely accepted that they should be counted as part of China's money supply. This would pose a measurement problem, however, because Tencent so far has been unwilling to disclose how many QQ coins are in circulation.

FOR CRITICAL ANALYSIS
Is there any particular reason that moneys that people find acceptable in exchange must be issued by a government?

PREDICTABILITY OF VALUE Money retains its usefulness even if its purchasing power is declining year in and year out, as in periods of inflation, if it still retains the characteristic of predictability of value. If you anticipate that the inflation rate is going to be around 3 percent during the next year, you know that any dollar you receive a year from now will have a purchasing power equal to 3 percent less than that same dollar today. Thus, you will not necessarily refuse to accept money in exchange simply because you know that its value will decline by the rate of inflation during the next year. You may, however, wish to be compensated for that *expected* decline in money's real value.

QUICK QUIZ   *See page 393 for the answers. Review concepts from this section in MyEconLab.*

Money is defined by its functions, which are as a _____ of _____, _____ of _____, _____ of _____, and _____ of _____ _____.

Money is a highly _____ asset because it can be disposed of with low transaction costs and with relative certainty as to its value.

Modern nations have _____ monetary systems—national currencies are not convertible into a fixed quantity of a commodity such as gold or silver.

Money is accepted in exchange for goods and services because people have confidence that it can later be exchanged for other goods and services. In addition, money has _____ value.

Defining Money

Money is important. Changes in the total **money supply**—the amount of money in circulation—and changes in the rate at which the money supply increases or decreases affect important economic variables, such as the rate of inflation, interest rates, and (at least in the short run) employment and the level of real GDP. Although there is widespread agreement among economists that money is indeed important, they have struggled to reach agreement about how to define and measure it. There are two basic approaches: the **transactions approach,** which stresses the role of money as a medium of exchange, and the **liquidity approach,** which stresses the role of money as a temporary store of value.

Money supply
The amount of money in circulation.

The Transactions Approach to Measuring Money: M1

Using the transactions approach to measuring money, the money supply consists of currency, transactions deposits, and traveler's checks not issued by banks. One key designation of the money supply, including currency, transactions deposits, and traveler's checks not issued by banks, is **M1.** The various elements of M1 for a typical year are presented in panel (a) of Figure 15-2 on the following page.

Transactions approach
A method of measuring the money supply by looking at money as a medium of exchange.

Liquidity approach
A method of measuring the money supply by looking at money as a temporary store of value.

CURRENCY The largest component of U.S. currency is paper bills called Federal Reserve notes, which are designed and printed by the U.S. Bureau of Engraving and Printing. U.S. currency also consists of coins minted by the U.S. Treasury. Federal Reserve banks (to be discussed shortly) issue paper notes and coins throughout the U.S. banking system.

M1
The money supply, measured as the total value of currency plus transactions deposits plus traveler's checks not issued by banks.

TRANSACTIONS DEPOSITS Individuals conduct most of their larger transactions with debit cards and checks. The convenience and safety of using debit cards and checks have made transactions deposits the most important component of the money supply. Debit and checking transactions are a means of transferring the ownership of deposits in financial institutions. Hence, transactions deposits are normally acceptable as a medium of exchange. The financial institutions that offer transactions deposits are numerous and include commercial banks and virtually all **thrift institutions**—savings banks, savings and loan associations (S&Ls), and credit unions.

Thrift institutions
Financial institutions that receive most of their funds from the savings of the public; they include savings banks, savings and loan associations, and credit unions.

TRAVELER'S CHECKS **Traveler's checks** are paid for by the purchaser at the time of transfer. The total quantity of traveler's checks outstanding issued by institutions other than banks is part of the M1 money supply. American Express, Cook's, and other institutions issue traveler's checks.

Traveler's checks
Financial instruments obtained from a bank or a nonbanking organization and signed during purchase that can be used as cash upon a second signature by the purchaser.

FIGURE 15-2

Composition of the U.S. M1 and M2 Money Supply, 2009

Panel (a) shows estimates of the M1 money supply, of which the largest component (over 55 percent) is currency. M2 consists of M1 plus three other components, the most important of which is savings deposits at all depository institutions.

Sources: Federal Reserve Bulletin; Economic Indicators, various issues; author's estimates.

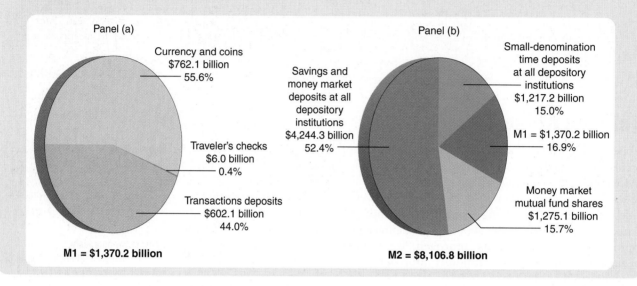

Panel (a)

Currency and coins
$762.1 billion
55.6%

Traveler's checks
$6.0 billion
0.4%

Transactions deposits
$602.1 billion
44.0%

M1 = $1,370.2 billion

Panel (b)

Small-denomination time deposits at all depository institutions
$1,217.2 billion
15.0%

Savings and money market deposits at all depository institutions
$4,244.3 billion
52.4%

M1 = $1,370.2 billion
16.9%

Money market mutual fund shares
$1,275.1 billion
15.7%

M2 = $8,106.8 billion

M2
M1 plus (1) savings and small-denomination time deposits at all depository institutions, (2) balances in retail money market mutual funds, and (3) money market deposit accounts (MMDAs).

Savings deposits
Interest-earning funds that can be withdrawn at any time without payment of a penalty.

Depository institutions
Financial institutions that accept deposits from savers and lend funds from those deposits out at interest.

Money market deposit accounts (MMDAs)
Accounts issued by banks yielding a market rate of interest with a minimum balance requirement and a limit on transactions. They have no minimum maturity.

Time deposit
A deposit in a financial institution that requires notice of intent to withdraw or must be left for an agreed period. Withdrawal of funds prior to the end of the agreed period may result in a penalty.

The Liquidity Approach to Measuring Money: M2

The liquidity approach to defining and measuring the U.S. money supply involves taking into account not only the most liquid assets that people use as money, which are already included in the definition of M1, but also other assets that are highly liquid—that is, assets that can be converted into money quickly without loss of nominal dollar value and without much cost. Thus, the liquidity approach to the definition of the money supply views money as a temporary store of value and so includes all of M1 *plus* several other highly liquid assets. Panel (b) of Figure 15-2 above shows the components of **M2**—money as a temporary store of value. We examine each of these components in turn.

SAVINGS DEPOSITS Total **savings deposits** in all **depository institutions** (such as commercial banks, savings banks, savings and loan associations, and credit unions) are part of the M2 money supply. A savings deposit has no set maturity.

  Money market deposit accounts (MMDAs) are one popular form of savings deposit. These deposits usually require a minimum balance and set limits on the number of monthly transactions (deposits and withdrawals by check).

SMALL-DENOMINATION TIME DEPOSITS A basic distinction has always been made between a transactions deposit, from which check or debit-card payments may be transmitted, and a **time deposit**, which theoretically requires notice of withdrawal and on which the financial institution pays the depositor interest. The name indicates that there is an agreed period during which the funds must be left in the financial institution. If the deposit holder withdraws funds before the end of that period, the institution issuing the deposit may apply a penalty. Time deposits include savings certificates and small **certificates of deposit (CDs).** The owner of a savings certificate is given a receipt indicating the amount deposited, the interest rate to be paid, and the maturity date. A CD is an actual certificate that indicates the date of issue, its maturity date, and other relevant contractual matters.

The distinction between transactions deposits and time deposits has generally become blurred, but it is still used in the official definition of the money supply. To be included in the M2 definition of the money supply, however, time deposits must be less than $100,000—hence, the designation *small-denomination time deposits.* A variety of small-denomination time deposits are available from depository institutions, ranging in maturities from one month to 10 years.

Certificate of deposit (CD)
A time deposit with a fixed maturity date offered by banks and other financial institutions.

MONEY MARKET MUTUAL FUND BALANCES Many individuals keep part of their assets in the form of shares in **money market mutual funds.** These retail mutual funds invest only in short-term credit instruments. The majority of these money market funds allow check-writing privileges, provided that the size of the check exceeds some minimum amount, usually $100. All money market mutual fund balances except those held by large institutions (which typically use them more like large time deposits) are included in M2.

Money market mutual funds
Funds obtained from the public that investment companies hold in common and use to acquire short-maturity credit instruments, such as certificates of deposit and securities sold by the U.S. government.

M2 AND OTHER MONEY SUPPLY DEFINITIONS When all of these assets are added together, the result is M2, as shown in panel (b) of Figure 15-2.

Economists and other researchers have come up with additional definitions of money. Some are simply broader than M2. Just remember that there is no best definition of the money supply. For different purposes and under varying institutional circumstances, different definitions are appropriate. The definition that seems to correlate best with economic activity on an economywide basis for most countries is probably M2, although some businesspeople and policymakers prefer a monetary aggregate known as *MZM.* The MZM aggregate is the so-called money-at-zero-maturity money stock. Obtaining MZM entails adding to M1 those deposits without set maturities, such as savings deposits, that are included in M2. MZM includes *all* money market funds, however, and it excludes all deposits with fixed maturities, such as small-denomination time deposits.

For Federal Reserve data concerning the latest trends in the monetary aggregates, go to www .econtoday.com/chapter15 and click on "Money Stock Measures—H.6" under Money Stock and Reserve Balances.

QUICK QUIZ   *See page 393 for the answers. Review concepts from this section in MyEconLab.*

The **money supply** can be defined in a variety of ways, depending on whether we use the transactions approach or the liquidity approach. Using the _____ approach, the money supply consists of currency, **transactions deposits,** and traveler's checks. This is called _____ .

_____ deposits are any deposits in financial institutions from which the deposit owner can transfer funds using a debit card or checks.

When we add savings deposits, small-denomination time deposits (certificates of deposit), money market deposit accounts, and retail money market mutual fund balances to _____, we obtain the measure known as _____.

Financial Intermediation and Banks

Most nations, including the United States, have a banking system that encompasses two types of institutions. One type consists of private banking institutions. These include commercial banks, which are privately owned profit-seeking institutions, and thrift institutions, such as savings banks, savings and loan associations (S&Ls), and credit unions. Thrift institutions may be profit-seeking institutions, or they may be *mutual* institutions that are owned by their depositors. The other type of institution is a **central bank,** which typically serves as a banker's bank and as a bank for the national treasury or finance ministry.

Direct versus Indirect Financing

When individuals choose to hold some of their savings in new bonds issued by a corporation, their purchases of the bonds are in effect direct loans to the business. This is an example of *direct finance*, in which people lend funds directly to a business. Business financing is not always direct. Individuals might choose instead to hold a time deposit at a bank. The bank may then lend to the same company. In this way, the same people can provide *indirect finance* to a business. The bank makes this possible by *intermediating* the financing of the company.

Financial Intermediation

Banks and other financial institutions are all in the same business—transferring funds from savers to investors. This process is known as **financial intermediation,** and its participants, such as banks and savings institutions, are **financial intermediaries.** The process of financial intermediation is illustrated in Figure 15-3.

ASYMMETRIC INFORMATION, ADVERSE SELECTION, AND MORAL HAZARD Why might people wish to direct their funds through a bank instead of lending them directly to a business? One important reason is **asymmetric information**—the fact

Central bank
A banker's bank, usually an official institution that also serves as a country's treasury's bank. Central banks normally regulate commercial banks.

Financial intermediation
The process by which financial institutions accept savings from businesses, households, and governments and lend the savings to other businesses, households, and governments.

Financial intermediaries
Institutions that transfer funds between ultimate lenders (savers) and ultimate borrowers.

Asymmetric information
Information possessed by one party in a financial transaction but not by the other party.

FIGURE 15-3

The Process of Financial Intermediation

The process of financial intermediation is depicted here. Note that ultimate lenders and ultimate borrowers are the same economic units—households, businesses, and governments—but not necessarily the same individuals. Whereas individual households can be net lenders or borrowers, households as an economic unit typically are net lenders. Specific businesses or governments similarly can be net lenders or borrowers; as economic units, both are net borrowers.

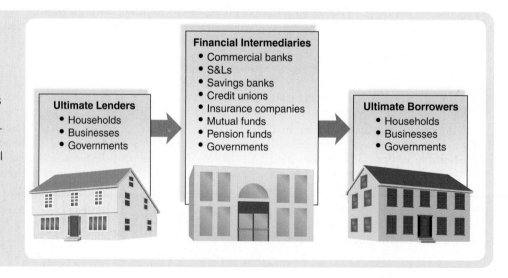

that the business may have better knowledge of its own current and future prospects than potential lenders do. For instance, the business may know that it intends to use borrowed funds for projects with a high risk of failure that would make repaying the loan difficult. This potential for borrowers to use the borrowed funds in high-risk projects is known as **adverse selection.** Alternatively, a business that had intended to undertake low-risk projects may change management after receiving a loan, and the new managers may use the borrowed funds in riskier ways. The possibility that a borrower might engage in behavior that increases risk after borrowing funds is called **moral hazard.**

To minimize the possibility that a business might fail to repay a loan, people thinking about lending funds directly to the business must study the business carefully before making the loan, and they must continue to monitor its performance afterward. Alternatively, they can choose to avoid the trouble by holding deposits with financial intermediaries, which then specialize in evaluating the creditworthiness of business borrowers and in keeping tabs on their progress until loans are repaid. Thus, adverse selection and moral hazard both help explain why people use financial intermediaries.

LARGER SCALE AND LOWER MANAGEMENT COSTS Another important reason that financial intermediaries exist is that they make it possible for many people to pool their funds, thereby increasing the size, or *scale*, of the total amount of savings managed by an intermediary. This centralization of management reduces costs and risks below the levels savers would incur if all were to manage their savings alone. *Pension fund companies*, which are institutions that specialize in managing funds that individuals save for retirement, owe their existence largely to their abilities to provide such cost savings to individual savers. Likewise, *investment companies*, which are institutions that manage portfolios of financial instruments called mutual funds on behalf of shareholders, also exist largely because of cost savings from their greater scale of operations.

How are online firms allowing borrowers to match up with lenders without any involvement by banks or other traditional financial intermediaries?

Adverse selection
The likelihood that individuals who seek to borrow may use the funds that they receive for high-risk projects.

Moral hazard
The possibility that a borrower might engage in riskier behavior after a loan has been obtained.

E-COMMERCE EXAMPLE
Watch Out Banks! Here Come Zopa and Circleone

At Zopa.com and Circleone.com, lenders and borrowers can engage in transactions without dealing with traditional financial intermediaries. Borrowers can apply for loans, and lenders can provide funds directly. Both Web sites' systems rate prospective borrowers according to credit scores and provide estimated loan default rates. Thus, lenders can charge less creditworthy applicants higher interest rates. Each site has some distinctive features. Zopa divides loans into separate shares, so that a lender can share the risks of a loan with other lenders. Circleone allows borrowers to form groups with collective ratings, so that lenders can better distinguish between groups with differing risks. Nevertheless, both sites directly match borrowers and lenders, thereby eliminating any role for traditional financial intermediaries, such as banks. These electronic financial intermediaries profit by charging fees ranging from 1 to 1.5 percent of the total amount of a borrower's loan.

FOR CRITICAL ANALYSIS
How does Zopa's practice of dividing loans among several lenders potentially help limit each lender's exposure to moral hazard risk?

TABLE 15-2

Financial Intermediaries and Their Assets and Liabilities

Financial Intermediary	Assets	Liabilities
Commercial banks	Car loans and other consumer debt, business loans, government securities, home mortgages	Transactions deposits, savings deposits, various other time deposits, money market deposit accounts
Savings and loan associations and savings banks	Home mortgages, some consumer and business debt	Savings and loan shares, transactions deposits, various time deposits, money market deposit accounts
Credit unions	Consumer debt, long-term mortgage loans	Credit union shares, transactions deposits
Insurance companies	Mortgages, stocks, bonds, real estate	Insurance contracts, annuities, pension plans
Pension and retirement funds	Stocks, bonds, mortgages, time deposits	Pension plans
Money market mutual funds	Short-term credit instruments such as large-denomination CDs, Treasury bills, and high-grade commercial paper	Fund shares with limited checking privileges

Liabilities
Amounts owed; the legal claims against a business or household by nonowners.

Assets
Amounts owned; all items to which a business or household holds legal claim.

FINANCIAL INSTITUTION LIABILITIES AND ASSETS Every financial intermediary has its own sources of funds, which are **liabilities** of that institution. When you place $100 in your transactions deposit at a bank, the bank creates a liability—it owes you $100—in exchange for the funds deposited. A commercial bank gets its funds from transactions and savings accounts; an insurance company gets its funds from insurance policy premiums.

Each financial intermediary has a different primary use of its **assets.** For example, a credit union usually makes small consumer loans, whereas a savings bank makes mainly mortgage loans. Table 15-2 lists the assets and liabilities of typical financial intermediaries. Be aware, though, that the distinctions between different types of financial institutions are becoming more and more blurred. As laws and regulations change, there will be less need to make any distinction. All may ultimately be treated simply as financial intermediaries.

Payment Intermediaries

Payment intermediaries
Institutions that facilitate transfers of funds between depositors who hold transactions deposits with those institutions.

A commercial bank is an example of a type of financial intermediary that performs another important function. Together with savings and loan associations and credit unions, commercial banks operate as **payment intermediaries,** which are institutions that facilitate payments on behalf of holders of transactions deposits.

TRANSMITTING PAYMENTS VIA DEBIT-CARD TRANSACTIONS Since 2006, the dollar volume of payments transmitted using debit cards has exceeded the value of checking transactions. To see how a debit-card transaction clears, take a look at Figure 15-4. Suppose that Bank of America has provided a debit card to a college student named Jill Jones, who in turn uses the card to purchase $200 worth of clothing

FIGURE 15-4

How a Debit-Card Transaction Clears

When a college student named Jill Jones uses a debit card issued by Bank of America to purchase clothing valued at $200 from Macy's, which has an account with Citibank, the debit-card transaction creates an electronic record that is transmitted to Citibank. The debit-card system forwards this record to Bank of America, which deducts $200 from Jill Jones's transactions deposit account. Then the debit-card system transmits the $200 payment to Citibank, which credits the $200 to Macy's account.

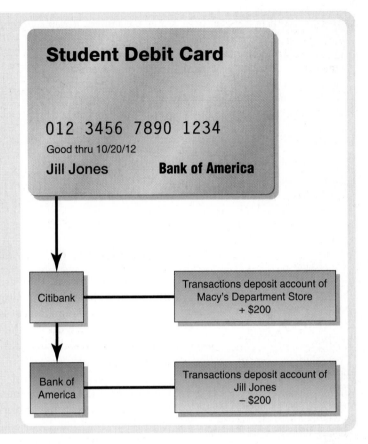

from Macy's, which has an account at Citibank. The debit-card transaction generates an electronic record, which Macy's transmits to Citibank.

The debit-card system automatically uses the electronic record to determine the bank that issued the debit card used to purchase the clothing. It transmits this information to Bank of America. Then Bank of America verifies that Jill Jones is an account holder, deducts $200 from her transactions deposit account, and transmits these funds electronically, via the debit-card system, to Citibank. Finally, Citibank credits $200 to Macy's transactions deposit account, and payment for the clothing purchase is complete.

THE PAYOFF FROM PAYMENT INTERMEDIATION Payment intermediation has traditionally been a key activity of banks. Until recently, however, the impact of this aspect of their operations on their bottom line has often been hard for economists to determine.

A Federal Reserve Bank of New York study recently attempted to determine banks' payoffs from providing payments-related services to their customers. This study of the income statements of the 25 largest U.S. banking companies revealed that revenues derived from debit-card and checking transfer services accounted for 28 percent of the banks' total earnings. Another 10 percent of the institutions' earnings were generated from processing payments for credit cards, stocks, and bonds. Thus, payment intermediation is a fundamental aspect of the banking business.

QUICK QUIZ   *See page 393 for the answers. Review concepts from this section in MyEconLab.*

_____ intermediaries, including depository institutions such as commercial banks and savings institutions, insurance companies, mutual funds, and pension funds, transfer funds from ultimate lenders (savers) to ultimate borrowers. Depository institutions also operate as _____ intermediaries that transfer funds on behalf of holders of transactions deposits.

Financial intermediaries specialize in tackling problems of _____ information. They address the _____

_____ problem by carefully reviewing the creditworthiness of loan applicants, and they deal with the _____ _____ problem by monitoring borrowers after they receive loans. Many financial intermediaries also take advantage of cost reductions arising from the centralized management of funds pooled from the savings of many individuals.

Federal Deposit Insurance

When businesses fail, they create hardships for creditors, owners, and customers. But when a depository institution fails, an even greater hardship results, because many individuals and businesses depend on the safety and security of banks. As Figure 15-5 shows, during the 1920s an average of about 600 banks failed each year. In the early 1930s, during the Great Depression, that average soared to nearly 3,000 failures each year.

In 1933, at the height of such bank failures, the **Federal Deposit Insurance Corporation (FDIC)** was founded to insure the funds of depositors and remove the reason for ruinous runs on banks. In 1934, federal deposit insurance was extended to deposits in savings and loan associations and mutual savings banks, and in 1971 it was offered for deposits in credit unions.

As can be seen in Figure 15-5, bank failure rates dropped dramatically after passage of the early federal legislation. The long period from 1935 until the 1980s was relatively quiet. From World War II to 1984, fewer than nine banks failed per year. From 1985 until the beginning of 1993, however, 1,065 commercial banks failed—an average of nearly 120 bank failures per year, more than 10 times the average for the preceding 40 years! We will examine the reasons shortly. But first we need to understand how deposit insurance works.

The Rationale for Deposit Insurance

Federal deposit insurance was established to mitigate the primary cause of bank failures, **bank runs**—the simultaneous rush of depositors to convert their demand deposits or time deposits into currency.

Consider the following scenario. A bank begins to look shaky; its assets may not seem sufficient to cover its liabilities. If the bank has no deposit insurance, depositors in this bank (and any banks associated with it) will all want to withdraw their funds from the bank at the same time. Their concern is that this shaky bank will not have enough assets to return their deposits to them in the form of currency. Indeed, this is what happens in a bank failure when insurance doesn't exist. Just as when a regular business fails, the creditors of the bank may not all get paid, or if they do, they will get paid less than 100 percent of what they are owed. Depositors are creditors of a bank because their funds are on loan to the bank. As Chapter 16 will explain in detail, however, banks do not hold 100 percent of their depositors' funds as cash. Instead, banks lend out most of their deposit funds to borrowers. Consequently, all depositors cannot

Federal Deposit Insurance Corporation (FDIC)
A government agency that insures the deposits held in banks and most other depository institutions; all U.S. banks are insured this way.

Bank runs
Attempts by many of a bank's depositors to convert transactions and time deposits into currency out of fear that the bank's liabilities may exceed its assets.

FIGURE 15-5

Bank Failures

A tremendous number of banks failed prior to creation of federal deposit insurance in 1933. Thereafter, bank failures were few until an upsurge between 1984 and 1989 and jumps in annual failure rates in the early and late 2000s.

Source: Federal Deposit Insurance Corporation.

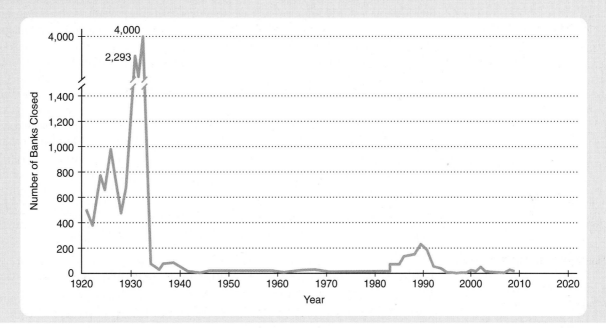

withdraw all their funds simultaneously. Hence, the intent of the legislation enacted in the 1930s was to assure depositors that they could have their deposits converted into cash when they wished, no matter how serious the financial situation of the bank.

Federal deposit insurance provided this assurance. The FDIC charged premiums to depository institutions based on their total deposits, and these premiums went into funds that would reimburse depositors in the event of bank failures. By insuring deposits, the FDIC bolstered depositors' trust in the banking system and provided depositors with the incentive to leave their deposits with the bank, even in the face of widespread talk of bank failures. In 1933, it was sufficient for the FDIC to cover each account up to $2,500. The current maximum is $250,000 per depositor per institution.

To keep up with the latest issues in deposit insurance and banking with the assistance of the FDIC, go to **www.econtoday.com/ chapter15**.

How Deposit Insurance Causes Increased Risk Taking by Bank Managers

Until the 1990s, all insured depository institutions paid the same small fee for coverage. The fee that they paid was completely unrelated to how risky their assets were. A depository institution that made loans to companies such as Dell, Inc., and Microsoft Corporation paid the same deposit insurance premium as another depository institution that made loans (at higher interest rates) to the governments of developing countries that were teetering on the brink of financial collapse. Although deposit insurance premiums for a while were adjusted somewhat in response to the riskiness of a depository institution's assets, they never reflected all of the relative risk. Indeed, since the late 1990s, very few depository institutions have paid *any* deposit insurance premiums. This lack of correlation between risk and premiums can be considered a fundamental flaw in the deposit insurance scheme.

Because bank managers do not have to pay higher insurance premiums when they make riskier loans, they have an incentive to invest in more assets of higher yield, and therefore necessarily higher risk, than they would if there were no deposit insurance. The insurance premium rate is artificially low, permitting institution managers to obtain deposits at less than full cost (because depositors will accept a lower interest payment on insured deposits). Consequently, depository institution managers can increase their profits by using insured deposits to purchase higher-yield, higher-risk assets. The gains to risk taking accrue to the managers and stockholders of the depository institutions; the losses go to the deposit insurer (and, as we will see, ultimately to taxpayers).

To combat these flaws in the financial industry and in the deposit insurance system, a vast regulatory apparatus oversees depository institutions. The FDIC and other federal deposit insurance agencies possess regulatory powers to offset the risk-taking temptations to depository institution managers. Those powers include the ability to require higher capital investment; the ability to regulate, examine, and supervise bank affairs; and the ability to enforce regulatory decisions. Still higher capital requirements were imposed in the early 1990s and then adjusted somewhat beginning in 2000, but a recent jump in bank failures reveals that basic flaws remain.

Deposit Insurance, Adverse Selection, and Moral Hazard

As a deposit insurer, the FDIC effectively acts as a government-run insurance company. This means that the FDIC's operations expose the federal government to the same kinds of asymmetric information problems that other financial intermediaries face.

ADVERSE SELECTION IN DEPOSIT INSURANCE One of these problems is *adverse selection*, which is often a problem when insurance is involved because people or firms that are relatively poor risks are sometimes able to disguise that fact from insurers. It is instructive to examine the way this works with the deposit insurance provided by the FDIC. Deposit insurance shields depositors from the potential adverse effects of risky decisions and so makes depositors willing to accept riskier investment strategies by their banks. Clearly, this encourages more high-flying, risk-loving entrepreneurs to become managers of banks. Moreover, because depositors have so little incentive to monitor the activities of insured banks, it is also likely that the insurance actually encourages outright crooks—embezzlers and con artists—to enter the industry. The consequences for the FDIC—and for taxpayers—are larger losses.

MORAL HAZARD IN DEPOSIT INSURANCE Moral hazard is also an important phenomenon in the presence of insurance contracts, such as the deposit insurance provided by the FDIC. Insured depositors know that they will not suffer losses if their bank fails. Hence, they have little incentive to monitor their bank's investment activities or to punish their bank by withdrawing their funds if the bank assumes too much risk. This means that insured banks have incentives to take on more risks than they otherwise would.

With those risks come higher losses for the FDIC and taxpayers, as first revealed in the late 1980s when more than 1,500 savings institutions failed at a taxpayer cost of about $200 billion. In the late 2000s, taxpayers learned even more about risks of losses when dozens of banks failed and when hundreds more banks and thousands of their borrowers received taxpayer bailouts totaling more than $1 trillion.

Two major pieces of legislation were enacted to try to rein in some of the moral hazard risks exposed by this episode. One, the Financial Institutions Reform, Recovery, and Enforcement Act of 1989, provided the tax funds required to reimburse depositors and subjected weak institutions to tougher regulatory oversight. The other, the FDIC Improvement Act of 1991, toughened regulatory standards and required the FDIC to close weak depository institutions promptly, rather than letting their managers continue to roll the dice with taxpayers' dollars at stake.

A Deposit Insurance Reform Effort in Progress

In February 2006, President George W. Bush signed into law the Federal Deposit Insurance Reform Act of 2005, which represents a new effort to reform the federal deposit insurance system. On the one hand, this law expanded the coverage of federal deposit insurance and hence potentially increased the system's moral hazard problems. The legislation increased deposit insurance coverage for Individual Retirement Accounts offered by banks and other depository institutions from $100,000 to $250,000. In addition, it authorized the FDIC to adjust, at five-year intervals beginning in 2010, the $100,000 limit on all other types of deposits to reflect inflation, as measured by the rate of change in the Personal Consumption Expenditures (PCE) Index.

On the other hand, the act provides the FDIC with improved tools for addressing moral hazard risks. The law combined the accumulated premium payments by banks and savings institutions into a single Deposit Insurance Fund (DIF), thereby formalizing identical treatment of all institutions covered by federal deposit insurance. In addition, the law altered a rule concerning FDIC deposit insurance premiums. Now the FDIC can charge premiums if total DIF funds are less than 1.5 percent of all deposits. Furthermore, the legislation eliminated a limit on how often the FDIC could change deposit insurance premiums, so now the FDIC can also adjust deposit insurance premiums at any time. Finally, the law gave the FDIC more leeway to place institutions in any risk category it deems appropriate, irrespective of each institution's size.

Thus, the Federal Deposit Insurance Reform Act broadened the coverage of federal deposit insurance. At the same time, it expanded the discretion of the FDIC to combat the moral hazard risks that naturally arise from the existence of the deposit insurance system.

QUICK QUIZ *See page 393 for the answers. Review concepts from this section in MyEconLab.*

To limit the fallout from systemwide failures and bank runs, Congress created the _____ _____ _____ _____ in 1933. Since the advent of federal deposit insurance, there have been no true bank runs at federally insured banks.

Federal insurance of bank deposits insulates depositors from risks, so depositors are _____ concerned about riskier investment strategies by depository institutions. Thus, bank managers have an incentive to invest in _____ assets to make _____ rates of return.

On the one hand, the Federal Deposit Insurance Reform Act of 2005 expanded the _____ hazard risks associated with deposit insurance by increasing limits for insured retirement deposits and indexing limits for other deposits to inflation. On the other hand, the law granted the FDIC greater discretion to assess risk-based deposit insurance _____ intended to restrain _____ hazard risks.

The Federal Reserve System: The U.S. Central Bank

Federal deposit insurance and bank regulation constitute one level of government involvement in the banking system. Another key banking institution, which in the United States is partly a creature of government and partly privately directed, is the Federal Reserve System, which serves as the nation's central bank.

Central Banks and Their Roles

The first central bank, which began operations in 1668, was Sweden's Sveriges Riksbank (called the Risens Standers Bank until 1867). In 1694, the English Parliament established the most historically famous of central banks, the Bank of England. It authorized the Bank of England to issue currency notes redeemable in silver, and initially the Bank of England's notes circulated alongside currency notes issued by the government and private finance companies. Until 1800, the Riksbank and the Bank of England were the only central banks. The number of central banks worldwide was less than 10 as late as 1873. The number expanded toward the end of the nineteenth century and again considerably during the second half of the twentieth century. Today, there are about 180 central banks.

The duties of central banks fall into three broad categories:

1. They perform banking functions for their nations' governments.

2. They provide financial services for private banks.

3. They conduct their nations' monetary policies.

The third is the area of central banking that receives the most media attention, even though most central banks devote the bulk of their resources to the other two tasks.

The Federal Reserve System

The Fed
The Federal Reserve System; the central bank of the United States.

The Federal Reserve System, also known simply as **the Fed,** is the most important regulatory agency in the United States' monetary system and is usually considered the monetary authority. The Fed was established by the Federal Reserve Act, signed on December 13, 1913, by President Woodrow Wilson. The act was the outgrowth of recommendations from the National Monetary Commission, which had been authorized by the Aldridge-Vreeland Act of 1908. Basically, the commission had attempted to find a way to counter the periodic financial panics that had occurred in our country. Based on the commission's recommendations, which were developed after considerable study of the Bank of England and other central banks, Congress established the Federal Reserve System to aid and supervise banks and also to provide banking services for the U.S. Treasury.

What role does the Federal Reserve System play in the U.S. monetary system?

ORGANIZATION OF THE FEDERAL RESERVE SYSTEM Figure 15-6 shows how the Federal Reserve System is organized. It is managed by the Board of Governors, composed of seven full-time members appointed by the U.S. president with the approval of the Senate. The chair of the Board of Governors is the leading official of the Board of Governors and of the Federal Reserve System. Since 2006, Ben Bernanke has held this position.

The 12 Federal Reserve district banks have a total of 25 branches. The boundaries of the 12 Federal Reserve districts and the cities in which Federal Reserve banks are located are shown in Figure 15-7 on the following page. The Federal Open Market

FIGURE 15-6

Organization of the Federal Reserve System

The 12 Federal Reserve district banks are headed by 12 separate presidents. The main authority of the Fed resides with the Board of Governors of the Federal Reserve System, whose seven members are appointed for 14-year terms by the president of the United States and confirmed by the Senate. Open market operations are carried out through the Federal Open Market Committee (FOMC), consisting of the seven members of the Board of Governors plus five presidents of the district banks (always including the president of the New York bank, with the others rotating).

Source: Board of Governors of the Federal Reserve System, *The Federal Reserve System: Purposes and Functions,* 7th ed. (Washington, D.C., 1984), p. 5.

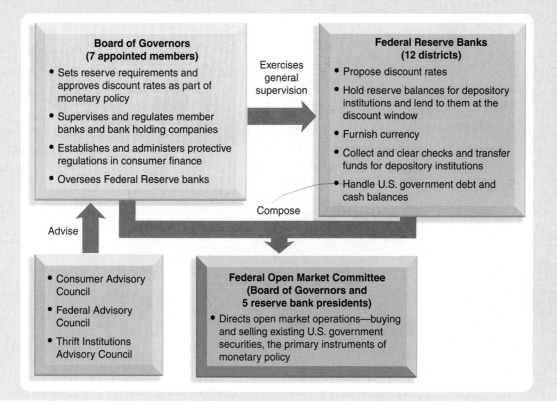

Committee (FOMC) determines the future growth of the money supply and other important variables. This committee is composed of the members of the Board of Governors, the president of the New York Federal Reserve Bank, and presidents of four other Federal Reserve banks, rotated periodically. The chair of the Board of Governors also chairs the FOMC.

DEPOSITORY INSTITUTIONS Depository institutions—all financial institutions that accept deposits—that comprise our monetary system consist of about 7,300 commercial banks, 1,100 savings and loan associations and savings banks, and 10,000 credit unions. All depository institutions may purchase services from the Federal Reserve System on an equal basis. Also, almost all depository institutions are required to keep a certain percentage of their deposits in reserve at the Federal Reserve district banks or as vault cash. This percentage depends on the bank's volume of business. (For further discussion, see Chapter 16.)

FUNCTIONS OF THE FEDERAL RESERVE SYSTEM Here we present in detail what the Federal Reserve does.

FIGURE 15-7

The Federal Reserve System

The Federal Reserve System is divided into 12 districts, each served by one of the Federal Reserve district banks, located in the cities indicated. The Board of Governors meets in Washington, D.C.

Source: Board of Governors of the Federal Reserve System.

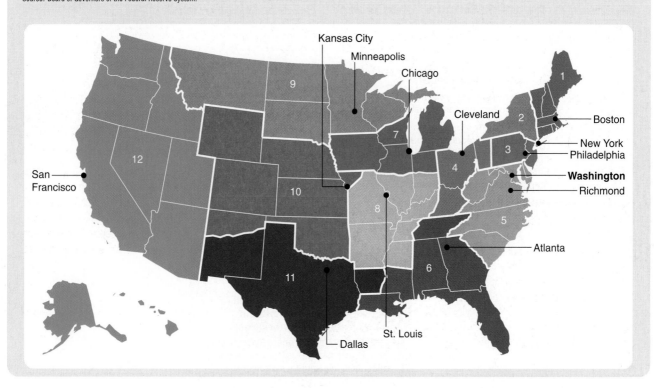

1. *The Fed supplies the economy with fiduciary currency.* The Federal Reserve banks supply the economy with paper currency called Federal Reserve notes. For example, during holiday seasons, when very large numbers of currency transactions take place, more paper currency is desired. Commercial banks respond to the increased number and dollar amounts of depositors' currency withdrawals by turning to the Federal Reserve banks to replenish vault cash. Hence, the Federal Reserve banks must have on hand a sufficient amount of cash to accommodate the demands for paper currency at different times of the year. Note that even though all Federal Reserve notes are printed at the Bureau of Engraving and Printing in Washington, D.C., each note is assigned a code indicating which of the 12 Federal Reserve banks first introduced the note into circulation. Moreover, each of these notes is an obligation (liability) of the Federal Reserve System, *not* the U.S. Treasury.

2. *The Fed provides payment-clearing systems.* The Federal Reserve System has long operated systems for transmitting and clearing payments. Federal Reserve banks all offer check-clearing services to commercial banks, savings institutions, and credit unions.

   In addition, the Federal Reserve System operates an electronic payments transfer system called *Fedwire*, which about 2,000 U.S. depository institutions use to process interbank payments. For instance, when a bank extends a loan to another institution, it typically transmits the payment using Fedwire. The other institution repays the loan the next day or a few days later by transmitting a payment on the same system. The average payment transfer on Fedwire exceeds $3 million, and the typical daily volume of all payments processed on this system is greater than $1 trillion.

The Fed charges fees to depository institutions to clear checks and transmit electronic payments, and its clearing operations compete with private clearinghouses. At present, the Fed clears a little less than one-third of all U.S. checks and transmits almost half of U.S. large-value electronic payments.

Is it possible that the Fed's days of clearing checks are numbered?

E-COMMERCE EXAMPLE
Private Electronic Check Clearing May Clear Out the Fed

Today, more than half of all paper check clearing is accomplished electronically. Banks scan the checks and then transmit digital images as verification of receipt. The Fed anticipates that by 2011, it will no longer handle any paper checks but instead will provide only data-processing services relating to electronic check clearing. These Fed services face considerable private competition from lower-cost private check-clearing operations. Many large banks already have formed independent clearing associations that enable them to clear checks without using Federal Reserve banks as intermediaries. One of these, the National Automated Clearing House Association, is testing a nationwide, privately operated electronic check-clearing system.

In 2003, the Fed operated 45 check-processing centers, but it has since closed more than two-thirds of the centers and plans by 2011 to maintain centers only in Atlanta, Cleveland, Dallas, and Philadelphia. Eventually, though, if the new private system is able to clear checks at lower cost than the Fed's streamlined system, the Fed may close all of its centers and exit the check-clearing business.

FOR CRITICAL ANALYSIS
Why do you suppose that Federal Reserve banks have eliminated thousands of jobs since 2003?

3. *The Fed holds depository institutions' reserves.* The 12 Federal Reserve district banks hold the reserves (other than vault cash) of depository institutions. As you will see in Chapter 16, depository institutions are required by law to keep a certain percentage of their transactions deposits as reserves. Even if they weren't required to do so by law, they would still wish to keep some reserves on which thay can draw funds as needed for expected and unexpected transactions.

4. *The Fed acts as the government's fiscal agent.* The Federal Reserve is the banker and fiscal agent for the federal government. The government, as we are all aware, collects large sums of funds through taxation. The government also spends and distributes equally large sums. Consequently, the U.S. Treasury has a transactions account with the Federal Reserve. Thus, the Fed acts as the government's banker, along with commercial banks that hold government deposits. The Fed also helps the government collect certain tax revenues and aids in the purchase and sale of government securities.

5. *The Fed supervises depository institutions.* The Fed (along with the Comptroller of the Currency, the Federal Deposit Insurance Corporation, the Office of Thrift Supervision in the Treasury Department, and the National Credit Union Administration) is a supervisor and regulator of depository institutions. The Fed and other regulators periodically and without warning examine depository institutions

to see what kinds of loans have been made, what has been used as security for the loans, and who has received them. Whenever such an examination indicates that a bank is not conforming to current banking rules and standards, the Fed can require the bank to alter its banking practices.

6. **The Fed acts as the "lender of last resort."** From time to time, an individual bank that is otherwise in good financial condition can find itself temporarily low on cash and other liquid assets. Such an institution is said to be illiquid. A key justification for the formation of the Federal Reserve System was that the Fed would stand ready to prevent temporarily illiquid banks from failing by serving as the financial system's **lender of last resort.** In this capacity, the Fed stands ready to lend to any temporarily illiquid but otherwise financially healthy banking institution. In this way, the Fed seeks to prevent illiquidity at a few banks from leading to a general loss of depositors' confidence in the overall soundness of the banking system.

7. **The Fed regulates the money supply.** Perhaps the Fed's most important task is to regulate the nation's money supply. To understand how the Fed manages the money supply, we must examine more closely its reserve-holding function and the way in which depository institutions aid in expansion and contraction of the money supply. We will do this in Chapter 16.

8. **The Fed intervenes in foreign currency markets.** Sometimes the Fed attempts to keep the value of the dollar from changing. It does this by buying and selling U.S. dollars in foreign exchange markets. You will read more about this important topic in Chapter 34.

Lender of last resort
The Federal Reserve's role as an institution that is willing and able to lend to a temporarily illiquid bank that is otherwise in good financial condition to prevent the bank's illiquid position from leading to a general loss of confidence in that bank or in others.

QUICK QUIZ See page 393 for the answers. Review concepts from this section in MyEconLab.

A central bank is a banker's bank that typically acts as the _____ _____ for its nation's government as well. The central bank in the United States is the _____ _____ _____, which was established on December 13, 1913.

There are 12 Federal Reserve district banks, with 25 branches. The Federal Reserve System is managed by the _____ of _____ in Washington, D.C. The Fed interacts with virtually all depository institutions in the United States, most of which must keep a certain

percentage of their transactions deposits on reserve with the Fed. The Fed serves as the chief regulatory agency for all depository institutions that have Federal Reserve System membership.

The functions of the Federal Reserve System are to supply fiduciary _____, provide payment-clearing services, hold depository institution _____, act as the government's fiscal agent, supervise depository institutions, act as the _____ of _____ _____, regulate the supply of money, and intervene in foreign currency markets.

You Are There ▶ Would You Like Your Change in Fives, Tens, Melvilles, or Rockwells?

Susan Witt of Berkshire County, Massachusetts, has realized her dream of introducing a new currency to her community. A total of 835,000 "BerkShares," currency notes bearing photos of likenesses of famous historical figures such as author Herman Melville and artist Norman Rockwell, now circulate alongside official U.S. dollars.

Getting the currency into circulation was not an easy task. Witt incurred significant initial expenses to hire a Massachusetts currency printer to create the BerkShare notes, complete with serial numbers and anticounterfeiting features. But her scheme for introducing the new currency helped cover this cost by establishing a rate of exchange of 11 BerkShares per 10

U.S. dollars whenever BerkShares are traded for dollars at local banks. Thus, people who accept BerkShares in exchange must incur a cost of 10 percent each time they cash BerkShares in for dollars. This conversion cost discourages holders of BerkShares from exchanging them for dollars.

Another central aspect of Witt's plan for circulating the BerkShares has been peer pressure. When some local merchants were initially hesitant to accept the currency notes at a one-for-one rate of exchange for U.S. dollars, they began losing customers. In contrast, other businesses that readily accepted the BerkShares in lieu of dollars found that they gained business. Eventually, most merchants chose to accept the currency, although several limit acceptance to "slow days" to reduce the cost they incur when they convert BerkShares to dollars at the close of business.

CRITICAL ANALYSIS QUESTIONS

1. Why do you suppose that promoting widespread acceptability of BerkShares was a linchpin in Witt's successful effort to establish the currency in her community?

2. How might Witt's recent efforts to install an automated teller machine containing only BerkShares assist in widening the currency's acceptability?

Issues and Applications

The Crash of 2008 and the Decline of Investment Banking

CONCEPTS APPLIED

- Financial Intermediaries
- Financial Intermediation
- Moral Hazard

Since the 1990s, two of the largest financial intermediaries in the world have been the Federal National Mortgage Association (FNMA, or "Fannie Mae") and the Federal Home Loan Mortgage Corporation (FHLMC, or "Freddie Mac"). These institutions have specialized in buying hundreds of billions of dollars of private mortgage loans from banking institutions with funds that they raised by issuing mortgage-backed securities purchased by private investors. These two institutions thereby engaged in financial intermediation between savers—investors who purchased mortgage-backed securities—and ultimate real estate borrowers—home buyers who obtained mortgage loans from banking institutions.

Fannie Mae and Freddie Mac have shared a common characteristic that distinguished them from other financial intermediaries: Both have been *government-sponsored enterprises*. The U.S. government created them, and it has provided full or partial guarantees for the mortgage-backed securities that they have issued. This meant that if either institution became unable to honor its obligations, most investors anticipated that the federal government would step in to bail them out. For years, this caused many observers to worry that someday the U.S. government might have to bail out these institutions in the event that U.S. house prices declined, bringing about a nationwide drop in the values of mortgages. For instance, an article published on September 30, 1999, in the *New York Times* stated, "Fannie Mae and Freddie Mac are taking on significantly more risk, which may not pose any difficulties during flush economic times. But the government-subsidized corporations may run into trouble in an economic downturn, prompting a government rescue." In the summer and fall of 2008, this is exactly what happened, and as a consequence in 2008 one type of U.S. financial intermediary that had been on the scene since the 1930s suddenly ceased to exist.

The Financial Crash of 2008

Between 2007 and 2008, average U.S. housing prices declined by more than 15 percent. In some areas, home prices dropped by as much as 30 percent. Market values of a number of houses fell below the amounts people owed on their mortgages. Many people who lost jobs or otherwise experienced earnings declines responded by halting payments on their mortgage loans. Some moved out of their mortgaged houses. Others lost their houses in foreclosure actions. When people stopped paying on their mortgages, receipts by Fannie Mae and Freddie Mac plummeted. Both government-sponsored intermediaries began experiencing billions of dollars of losses. Their stocks became worthless, and the values of their mortgage-backed securities plummeted. Ultimately, the federal government took control of both institutions.

Economists could easily explain why Fannie Mae and Freddie Mac collapsed: *moral hazard*. Because investors had known that the government stood behind the institutions' mortgage-backed securities, they were willing to regard them as nearly free of risk. This had given Fannie Mae and Freddie Mac an incentive to issue too many of these securities and to purchase too many low-quality, risky mortgages from banking institutions. Banking institutions had realized that Fannie Mae and Freddie Mac would buy virtually any mortgage they created, so the banks granted mortgage loans to people who were unable to keep making payments when they experienced tougher economic conditions. Thus, government backing of Fannie and Freddie created a huge moral hazard problem that led to these institutions' failures in the autumn of 2008.

The End of "Investment Banking"

Another type of financial intermediary, known as "investment banks," had existed in the United States since the Great Depression. These institutions specialized in assisting companies that desired to issue new stocks, bonds, and other securities.

At the beginning of 2008, there were five investment banks: Bear Stearns, Goldman Sachs, Lehman Brothers, Merrill Lynch, and Morgan Stanley. Many securities held by these investment banks were related to real estate debts such as those intermediated by Fannie Mae and Freddie Mac. The sudden drop in housing prices and consequent collapse in the market value of these debts bankrupted Bear Stearns, which ultimately was purchased by J.P. Morgan Chase, a commercial bank. Shortly thereafter, Bank of America, another commercial bank, purchased Merrill Lynch. After Lehman Brothers also went bankrupt, Goldman Sachs and Morgan Stanley opted to become commercial banks. Thus, within a matter of weeks during 2008, the U.S. investment banking industry suddenly ceased to exist.

Test your understanding of this chapter by going online to **MyEconLab**.
In the Study Plan for this chapter, select Section N: News.

For Critical Analysis

1. Why do you suppose that many economists suggest that a major U.S. government push for Fannie Mae and Freddie Mac to encourage more lending to lower-income households in the 2000s helped to enlarge the moral hazard problem?

2. A financial institution becomes insolvent and must close when the total value of its assets falls below the total value of its liabilities. Why do you suppose that rapidly declining values of real estate assets thereby created significant problems for investment banks holding so many of these assets?

Web Resources

1. Read an analysis of the history of Fannie Mae and Freddie Mac and the moral hazard problems these government-sponsored enterprises created for the U.S. financial system at www.econtoday.com/chapter15.

2. For an overview of the 2008 demise of the U.S. investment banking industry, go to www.econtoday.com/chapter15.

Research Project

Following the government takeovers of Fannie Mae and Freddie Mac and the elimination of the investment banking industry, the U.S. government helped bail out other institutions, such as a large insurance company, banks, and even U.S. automakers. A number of economists have criticized these bailouts, which they claim expand moral hazard problems faced by U.S. taxpayers. Is this a reasonable argument? Take a stand, and explain your position.

Here is what you should know after reading this chapter. **MyEconLab** will help you identify what you know, and where to go when you need to practice.

WHAT YOU SHOULD KNOW		WHERE TO GO TO PRACTICE
The Key Functions of Money Money is a medium of exchange that people use to make payments for goods, services, and financial assets. It is also a unit of accounting for quoting prices in terms of money values. In addition, money is a store of value, so people can hold money for future use in exchange. Finally, money is a standard of deferred payment, enabling lenders to make loans and buyers to repay those loans with money.	money, 366 medium of exchange, 367 barter, 367 unit of accounting, 368 store of value, 368 standard of deferred payment, 368	• **MyEconLab** Study Plan 15.1 • Audio introduction to Chapter 15 • Video: The Functions of Money
Important Properties of Goods That Serve as Money A good will successfully function as money only if people are widely willing to accept the good in exchange for other goods and services. People must have confidence that others will be willing to trade their goods and services for the good used as money. In addition, though people may continue to use money even if inflation erodes its real purchasing power, they will do so only if the value of money is relatively predictable.	liquidity, 369 transactions deposits, 370 fiduciary monetary system, 370 KEY FIGURE Figure 15-1, 369	• **MyEconLab** Study Plan 15.2 • Video: Monetary Standards, or What Backs Money • Animated Figure 15-1
Official Definitions of the Quantity of Money in Circulation The narrow definition of the quantity of money in circulation, called M1, focuses on money's role as a medium of exchange. It includes only currency, transactions deposits, and traveler's checks. A broader definition, called M2, stresses money's role as a temporary store of value. M2 is equal to M1 plus other highly liquid assets such as savings deposits, small-denomination time deposits, money market deposit accounts, and noninstitutional holdings of money market mutual fund balances.	money supply, 371 transactions approach, 371 liquidity approach, 371 M1, 371 thrift institutions, 371 traveler's checks, 371 M2, 372	• **MyEconLab** Study Plan 15.3

(continued)

 *(continued)*

WHAT YOU SHOULD KNOW   **WHERE TO GO TO PRACTICE**

Why Financial Intermediaries Such as Banks Exist Financial intermediaries help reduce problems stemming from the existence of asymmetric information in financial transactions. Asymmetric information can lead to adverse selection, in which uncreditworthy individuals and firms seek loans, and moral hazard problems, in which an individual or business that has been granted credit begins to engage in riskier practices. Financial intermediaries may also permit savers to benefit from economies of scale, which is the ability to reduce the costs and risks of managing funds by pooling funds and spreading costs and risks across many savers.

- **MyEconLab** Study Plan 15.4
- Animated Figures 15-3, 15-4

Features of Federal Deposit Insurance To help prevent runs on banks, the U.S. government in 1933 established the Federal Deposit Insurance Corporation (FDIC). This government agency provides deposit insurance by charging some depository institutions premiums based on the value of their deposits, and it places these funds in accounts for use in reimbursing failed banks' depositors. Providing deposit insurance creates an adverse selection problem because the availability of deposit insurance can potentially attract risk-taking individuals into the banking business. A moral hazard problem also exists when deposit insurance premiums fail to reflect the full extent of the risks taken on by depository institution managers and when depositors who know they are insured have little incentive to monitor the performance of the institutions that hold their deposit funds.

- **MyEconLab** Study Plan 15.5
- Video: Deposit Insurance and Risk Taking

The Basic Structure and Functions of the Federal Reserve System The Federal Reserve System consists of 12 district banks with 25 branches. The governing body of the Fed is the Board of Governors, which is based in Washington, D.C. Decisions about the quantity of money in circulation are made by

- **MyEconLab** Study Plan 15.6
- Animated Figure 15-7
- Video: The Federal Reserve System

 *(continued)*

the Federal Open Market Committee, which is composed of the Board of Governors and five Federal Reserve bank presidents. The Fed's main functions are supplying the economy with fiduciary currency, providing systems for transmitting and clearing payments, holding depository institutions' reserves, acting as the government's fiscal agent, supervising banks, acting as a lender of last resort, regulating the money supply, and intervening in foreign exchange markets.

Log in to MyEconLab, take a chapter test, and get a personalized Study Plan that tells you which concepts you understand and which ones you need to review. From there, MyEconLab will give you further practice, tutorials, animations, videos, and guided solutions.
Log in to www.myeconlab.com

PROBLEMS

All problems are assignable in myeconlab . *Answers to odd-numbered problems appear at the back of the book.*

15-1. Until 1946, residents of the island of Yap used large doughnut-shaped stones as financial assets. Although prices of goods and services were not quoted in terms of the stones, the stones were often used in exchange for particularly large purchases, such as payments for livestock. To make the transaction, several individuals would insert a large stick through a stone's center and carry it to its new owner. A stone was difficult for any one person to steal, so an owner typically would lean it against the side of his or her home as a sign to others of accumulated purchasing power that would hold value for later use in exchange. Loans would often be repaid using the stones. In what ways did these stones function as money?

15-2. During the late 1970s, prices quoted in terms of the Israeli currency, the shekel, rose so fast that grocery stores listed their prices in terms of the U.S. dollar and provided customers with dollar-shekel conversion tables that they updated daily. Although people continued to buy goods and

services and make loans using shekels, many Israeli citizens converted shekels to dollars to avoid a reduction in their wealth due to inflation. In what way did the U.S. dollar function as money in Israel during this period?

15-3. During the 1945–1946 Hungarian hyperinflation, when the rate of inflation reached 41.9 *quadrillion* percent per month, the Hungarian government discovered that the real value of its tax receipts was falling dramatically. To keep real tax revenues more stable, it created a good called a "tax pengö," in which all bank deposits were denominated for purposes of taxation. Nevertheless, payments for goods and services were made only in terms of the regular Hungarian currency, whose value tended to fall rapidly even though the value of a tax pengö remained stable. Prices were also quoted only in terms of the regular currency. Lenders, however, began denominating loan payments in terms of tax pengös. In what ways did the tax pengö function as money in Hungary in 1945 and 1946?

15-4. Considering the following data (expressed in billions of U.S. dollars), calculate M1 and M2.

Currency	850
Savings deposits and money market deposit accounts	3,500
Small-denomination time deposits	2,000
Traveler's checks outside banks and thrifts	10
Total money market mutual funds	1,300
Institution-only money market mutual funds	200
Transactions deposits	940

15-5. Considering the following data (expressed in billions of U.S. dollars), calculate M1 and M2.

Transactions deposits	825
Savings deposits	2,300
Small-denomination time deposits	1,450
Money market deposit accounts	1,950
Noninstitution money market mutual funds	1,900
Traveler's checks outside banks and thrifts	25
Currency	850
Institution-only money market mutual funds	250

15-6. Identify whether each of the following items is counted in M1 only, M2 only, both M1 and M2, or neither:

a. A $1,000 balance in a transactions deposit at a mutual savings bank

b. A $100,000 certificate of deposit issued by a New York bank

c. A $10,000 time deposit an elderly widow holds at her credit union

d. A $50 traveler's check not issued by a bank

e. A $50,000 money market deposit account balance

15-7. Identify whether each of the following amounts is counted in M1 only, M2 only, both M1 and M2, or neither:

a. $50 billion in U.S. Treasury bills

b. $15 billion in small-denomination time deposits

c. $5 billion in traveler's checks not issued by a bank

d. $20 billion in money market deposit accounts

15-8. Indicate which of the following items are counted in M2 but not in M1.

a. A $20 Federal Reserve note

b. A $500 time deposit

c. A $50 traveler's check not issued by a bank

d. A $25,000 money market deposit account

15-9. Match each of the rationales for financial intermediation listed below with at least one of the following financial intermediaries: insurance company, pension fund, savings bank. Explain your choices.

a. Adverse selection

b. Moral hazard

c. Lower management costs generated by larger scale

15-10. Match each of the rationales for financial intermediation listed below with at least one of the following financial intermediaries: commercial bank, money market mutual fund, stockbroker. Explain your choices.

a. Adverse selection

b. Moral hazard

c. Lower management costs generated by larger scale

15-11. Identify whether each of the following events poses an adverse selection problem or a moral hazard problem in financial markets.

a. A manager of a savings and loan association responds to reports of a likely increase in federal deposit insurance coverage. She directs loan officers to extend mortgage loans to less creditworthy borrowers.

b. A loan applicant does not mention that a legal judgment in his divorce case will require him to make alimony payments to his ex-wife.

c. An individual who was recently approved for a loan to start a new business decides to use some of the funds to take a Hawaiian vacation.

15-12. Identify whether each of the following events poses an adverse selection problem or a moral hazard problem in financial markets.

a. An individual with several children who has just learned that she has lung cancer applies for life insurance but fails to report this recent medical diagnosis.

b. A corporation that recently obtained a loan from several banks to finance installation of a new computer network instead directs some of the funds to executive bonuses.

c. A state-chartered financial institution exempt from laws requiring it to have federal deposit insurance decides to apply for deposit insurance after experiencing severe financial problems that may bankrupt the institution.

15-13. In what sense is currency a liability of the Federal Reserve System?

15-14. In what respects is the Fed like a private banking institution? In what respects is it more like a government agency?

15-15. Take a look at the map of the locations of the Federal Reserve districts and their headquarters in Figure 15-7 on page 384. Today, the U.S. population is centered just west of the Mississippi River—that is, about half of the population is either to the west or the east of a line running roughly just west of this river. Can you reconcile the current locations of Fed districts and banks with this fact? Why do you suppose the Fed has its current geographic structure?

ECONOMICS ON THE NET

What's Happened to the Money Supply? Deposits at banks and other financial institutions make up a portion of the U.S. money supply. This exercise gives you the chance to see how changes in these deposits influence the Fed's measures of money.

Title: FRED (Federal Reserve Economic Data)

Navigation: Go to **www.econtoday.com/chapter15** to visit the Web page of the Federal Reserve Bank of St. Louis.

Application

1. Select the data series for Demand Deposits at Commercial Banks (Bil. of $; M), either seasonally adjusted or not. Scan through the data. Do you notice any recent trend? (Hint: Compare the growth in the figures before 1993 with their growth after 1993.) In addition, take a look at the data series for currency and for other transactions deposits. Do you observe similar recent trends in these series?

2. Back up, and click on *M1 Money Stock (Bil. of $; M)*, again, either seasonally adjusted or not. Does it show any change in pattern beginning around 1993?

For Group Study and Analysis FRED contains considerable financial data series. Assign individual members or groups of the class the task of examining data on assets included in M1, M2, and MZM. Have each student or group look for big swings in the data. Then ask the groups to report to the class as a whole. When did clear changes occur in various categories of the monetary aggregates? Were there times when people appeared to shift funds from one aggregate to another? Are there any other noticeable patterns that may have had something to do with economic events during various periods?

ANSWERS TO QUICK QUIZZES

p. 371: (i) medium of exchange . . . unit of accounting . . . store of value . . . standard of deferred payment; (ii) liquid; (iii) fiduciary; (iv) predictable

p. 373: (i) transactions . . . M1; (ii) Transactions; (iii) M1 . . . M2

p. 378: (i) Financial . . . payment; (ii) asymmetric . . . adverse selection . . . moral hazard

p. 381: (i) Federal Deposit Insurance Corporation; (ii) less . . . riskier . . . higher; (iii) moral . . . premiums . . . moral

p. 386: (i) fiscal agent . . . Federal Reserve System; (ii) Board . . . Governors; (iii) currency . . . reserves . . . lender of last resort

16

Money Creation, the Demand for Money, and Monetary Policy

Commercial banks constitute more than 85 percent of all depository institutions, which also include savings banks, savings and loan associations, and credit unions. Commercial banks also issue more than 90 percent of all transactions deposits and time deposits issued by depository institutions. Nevertheless, in recent years, deposits as a percentage of total funds raised by commercial banks to finance their own lending and other activities have fallen to their lowest level since 1935. Bankers are scrambling to reverse this downward trend. Why have deposit funds traditionally been the pillar of the banking business? How do Federal Reserve policies influence the aggregate quantity of deposits in the banking system? These are key questions addressed in this chapter.

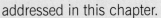

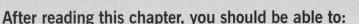

LEARNING OBJECTIVES

myeconlab

MyEconLab helps you master each objective and study more efficiently. See end of chapter for details.

After reading this chapter, you should be able to:

- Describe how the Federal Reserve assesses reserve requirements on banks and other depository institutions
- Understand why the money supply is unaffected when someone deposits in a depository institution funds transferred from a transactions account at another depository institution
- Explain why the money supply changes when someone deposits in a depository institution funds transferred from the Federal Reserve System
- Determine the maximum potential extent to which the money supply will change following a Federal Reserve monetary policy action
- Identify the key factors that influence the quantity of money that people desire to hold
- Describe how Federal Reserve monetary policy actions influence market interest rates

? DID YOU KNOW THAT between Friday, August 10, and Sunday, August 12, 2007, the Federal Reserve purchased *$38 billion* worth of U.S. government bonds, or almost $10 billion more than the Fed's net bond purchases during *all* of 2006? The Fed's bond purchases coincided with action by the European Central Bank (ECB) to extend nearly *$200 billion* of short-term loans to European banks between Thursday, August 9, and Friday, August 10. What was the point of the massive bond purchases by the Fed and the even larger amount of lending by the ECB? The answer is that if the two central banks had not conducted their policy actions, U.S. and European interest rates would have increased considerably. By purchasing bonds and lending to private banks in large volumes, the Fed and the ECB prevented interest rates from rising.

In taking these policy actions, the Fed and the ECB worked through U.S. and European banking systems to generate an increase in the quantity of money in circulation. As any banker will tell you, *by itself* no individual bank can create money. But through actions initiated by a central bank such as the Federal Reserve, depository institutions *together* do create money by adding to the quantity of checkable and debitable deposits. In this chapter, you will learn how policy actions such as Fed purchases of U.S. government bonds and lending to private banks influence the money supply. You will also learn about the money multiplier process, which explains how a Fed injection of funds into the banking system leads to an eventual multiple expansion of the total money supply. Finally, you will learn how the policy actions of central banks influence interest rates.

Banks and Money

As early as 1000 B.C., uncoined gold and silver were being used as money in Mesopotamia. Goldsmiths weighed and assessed the purity of those metals; later they started issuing paper notes indicating that the bearers held gold or silver of given weights and purity on deposit with the goldsmith. These notes could be transferred in exchange for goods and became the first paper currency. The gold and silver on deposit with the goldsmiths were the first bank deposits. Eventually, goldsmiths realized that inflows of gold and silver for deposit always exceeded the average amount of gold and silver withdrawn at any given time—often by a predictable ratio. These goldsmiths started making loans by issuing to borrowers paper notes that exceeded in value the amount of gold and silver the goldsmiths actually kept on hand. They charged interest on these loans. This constituted the earliest form of what is now called **fractional reserve banking.** We know that goldsmiths operated this way in Delphi, Didyma, and Olympia in Greece as early as the seventh century B.C. In Athens, fractional reserve banking was well developed by the sixth century B.C.

Fractional reserve banking
A system in which depository institutions hold reserves that are less than the amount of total deposits.

Depository Institution Reserves

In a fractional reserve banking system, banks do not keep sufficient reserves on hand to cover 100 percent of their depositors' accounts. And the reserves that are held by depository institutions in the United States are not kept in gold and silver, as they were with the early goldsmiths, but rather in the form of deposits on reserve with Federal Reserve district banks and in vault cash. Depository institutions are required by the Fed to maintain a specified percentage of certain customer deposits as **reserves** either in the form of deposits at Federal Reserve banks or as vault cash. There are two types of reserves: required reserves and excess reserves.

Reserves
In the U.S. Federal Reserve System, deposits held by Federal Reserve district banks for depository institutions, plus depository institutions' vault cash.

Required reserves
The value of reserves that a depository institution must hold in the form of vault cash or deposits with the Fed.

Required reserve ratio
The percentage of total transactions deposits that the Fed requires depository institutions to hold in the form of vault cash or deposits with the Fed.

Required Reserves

Required reserves are the minimum amount of reserves that a depository institution (which, for simplicity, we shall assume to be a commercial bank) must have to "back" transactions deposits. They are calculated as a ratio of required reserves to total transactions deposits (banks need hold no reserves on nontransactions deposits such as savings accounts). The **required reserve ratio** for almost all transactions deposits is 10 percent (except for about the first $50 million in deposits at any depository institution, which is subject to only a 3 percent requirement). The general formula is

$$\text{Required reserves} = \text{transactions deposits} \times \text{required reserve ratio}$$

Take a hypothetical example. If the required reserve ratio is 10 percent and the bank has $1 billion in customer transactions deposits, it must hold at least $100 million as reserves. As we shall discuss later in this chapter, during the 1990s, banks discovered a novel way to reduce the amounts of reserves that they are required to hold.

Excess Reserves

Excess reserves
The difference between actual reserves and required reserves.

Go to www.econtoday.com/chapter16 to see Federal Reserve reports on the current amounts of required and excess reserves at U.S. depository institutions.

Depository institutions often hold reserves in excess of what is required by the Fed. This difference between actual reserves and required reserves is called **excess reserves.** (Excess reserves can be negative, but they rarely are. Negative excess reserves indicate that depository institutions do not have sufficient reserves to meet their required reserves. When this happens, they borrow from other depository institutions or from a Federal Reserve district bank, sell assets such as securities including Treasury bills, or call in loans.) Excess reserves are an important potential determinant of the money supply, for as we shall see, it is only to the extent that depository institutions have excess reserves that they can make new loans. Because reserves produce little income, profit-seeking financial institutions have an incentive to minimize excess reserves, disposing of them either to purchase income-producing securities or to make loans with which they earn income through interest payments received.

In the analysis that follows, we examine the relationship between the total level of reserves and the size of the money supply. This analysis implies that factors influencing the level of the reserves of the banking system as a whole will ultimately affect the size of the money supply, other things held constant. We show first that when someone deposits in one depository institution funds transmitted by debit card or check from an account at another depository institution, the two depository institutions involved are individually affected, but the overall money supply does not change. Then we show that when someone deposits in a depository institution funds transmitted from the Fed, a multiple expansion in the money supply results.

How has a Federal Reserve policy change likely significantly altered banks' incentive to minimize their holdings of excess reserves?

POLICY EXAMPLE
Interest on Reserves at Federal Reserve Banks

Ever since the 1970s, the Federal Reserve has sought congressional permission to pay banks interest on the reserves they hold on deposit at Federal Reserve banks. In the past, Congress always balked at this idea,

POLICY EXAMPLE (cont.)

because paying interest on reserves held at Federal Reserve banks would cut into the Federal Reserve System's aggregate net income by at least $2 billion per year. The Fed turns over its net income to Congress, so payment of interest on depository institutions' reserves would leave Congress with $2 billion or so less to spend each year.

Congress recently relented, however, and authorized the Fed to start paying banks interest on reserve deposits in October 2008. Since then, Federal Reserve banks have paid quarterly interest on all bank reserve deposits at a rate below the general level of short-term interest rates. Of course, since

depository institutions began to receive interest payments on reserves, their incentive to minimize excess reserve holdings has been reduced. Consequently, levels of excess reserves in the U.S. banking system have increased.

FOR CRITICAL ANALYSIS
Why will the Fed's current plan to set the interest rate on reserve deposits below prevailing market interest rates mean that banks will still have some incentive to hold down their excess reserves?

QUICK QUIZ   *See page 421 for the answers. Review concepts from this section in MyEconLab.*

Ours is a **fractional reserve banking** system in which depository institutions must hold only a _____ of their deposits as reserves, either on deposit with a Federal Reserve district bank or as _____ cash.

Required reserves are usually expressed as a _____, in percentage terms, of required reserves to total transactions deposits.

The Relationship Between Total Reserves and Total Deposits

To show the relationship between reserves and bank deposits, we first analyze a single bank (existing alongside many others). A single bank is able to make new loans to its customers only to the extent that it has reserves above the level legally required to cover the new deposits. When an individual bank has no excess reserves, it cannot make loans.

How a Single Bank Reacts to an Increase in Reserves

To examine the **balance sheet** of a single bank after its reserves are increased, let's make the following assumptions:

1. The required reserve ratio is 10 percent for all transactions deposits.
2. Transactions deposits are the bank's only liabilities; reserves at a Federal Reserve district bank and loans are the bank's only assets. Loans are promises made by customers to repay some amount in the future; that is, they are customer IOUs and as such are assets to the bank.
3. An individual bank can lend as much as it is legally allowed.

Balance sheet
A statement of the assets and liabilities of any business entity, including financial institutions and the Federal Reserve System. Assets are what is owned; liabilities are what is owed.

4. Every time a loan is made to an individual (consumer or business), all the proceeds from the loan are put into a transactions deposit account; no cash (currency or coins) is withdrawn.

5. Depository institutions seek to keep zero excess reserves because reserves do not earn interest. (Depository institutions are operated to earn profits; we assume that all depository institutions wish to convert excess reserves that do not pay interest into interest-bearing loans.)

Net worth
The difference between assets and liabilities.

6. Depository institutions have zero **net worth.** (In reality, all depository institutions are required to have some positive owners' equity, or capital, which is another name for net worth. It is usually a small percentage of the institutions' total assets.)

Look at the simplified initial position of Typical Bank in Balance Sheet 16-1. Liabilities consist of $1 million in transactions deposits. Assets consist of $100,000 in reserves and $900,000 in loans to customers. Total assets of $1 million equal total liabilities of $1 million. With a 10 percent reserve requirement and $1 million in transactions deposits, the bank has required reserves of $100,000 and therefore no excess reserves.

BALANCE SHEET 16-1

Typical Bank

Assets			Liabilities	
Total reserves		$100,000	Transactions deposits	$1,000,000
Required reserves	$100,000			
Excess reserves	0			
Loans		900,000		
Total		$1,000,000	Total	$1,000,000

Assume that a depositor deposits in Typical Bank a $100,000 debit-card payment drawn on a transactions account at another depository institution. Transactions deposits in Typical Bank immediately increase by $100,000, bringing the total to $1.1 million. After the debit-card transaction is finalized, total reserves of Typical Bank increase to $200,000. A $1.1 million total in transactions deposits means that required reserves will have to be 10 percent of $1.1 million, or $110,000. Typical Bank now has excess reserves equal to $200,000 minus $110,000, or $90,000. This is shown in Balance Sheet 16-2.

BALANCE SHEET 16-2

Typical Bank

Assets			Liabilities	
Total reserves		$200,000	Transactions deposits	$1,100,000
Required reserves	$110,000			
Excess reserves	90,000			
Loans		900,000		
Total		$1,100,000	Total	$1,100,000

Effect on Typical Bank's Balance Sheet

Look at excess reserves in Balance Sheet 16-2 on the facing page. Excess reserves were zero before the $100,000 deposit, and now they are $90,000—that's $90,000 worth of assets not earning any income. By assumption, Typical Bank will now lend out this entire $90,000 in excess reserves in order to obtain interest income. Loans will increase to $990,000. The borrowers who receive the new loans will not leave them on deposit in Typical Bank. After all, they borrow funds to spend them. As they spend them by making debit-card and check transfers that are deposited in other banks, actual reserves will fall to $110,000 (as required), and excess reserves will again become zero, as indicated in Balance Sheet 16-3.

BALANCE SHEET 16-3	Assets		Liabilities	
Typical Bank	Total reserves	$110,000	Transactions deposits	$1,100,000
	Required reserves $110,000			
	Excess reserves 0			
	Loans	990,000		
	Total	$1,100,000	Total	$1,100,000

In this example, a person transmitted a $100,000 debit-card payment from an account at another bank. That $100,000 became part of the reserves of Typical Bank. Because that deposit immediately created excess reserves in Typical Bank, further loans were possible for Typical Bank. The excess reserves were lent out to earn interest. A bank will not lend more than its excess reserves because, by law, it must hold a certain amount of required reserves.

Effect on the Money Supply

A look at the balance sheets for Typical Bank might give the impression that the money supply increased because of the new customer's $100,000 deposit. Remember, though, that the deposit resulted from a debit-card transfer from *another* bank. Therefore, the other bank suffered a *decline* in its transactions deposits and its reserves. While total assets and liabilities in Typical Bank have increased by $100,000, they have *decreased* in the other bank by $100,000. The total amount of money and credit in the economy is unaffected by the transfer of funds from one depository institution to another.

The thing to remember is that new reserves for the banking system as a whole are not created when debit-card or check payments transferred from one bank are deposited in another bank. The Federal Reserve System can, however, create new reserves; that is the subject of the next section.

Why do some airplane pilots stand to lose from rapid decreases in the physical clearing of paper checks by the Federal Reserve and private banks?

EXAMPLE
Why the Decline in Clearing of Paper Checks Is Bad News for Airplane Pilots

The number of transactions deposit payments initiated via debit cards surpassed the number of check transfers a few years back. Within just a few more years, checks likely will account for no more than one-third of all such transfers. Furthermore, the share of checks cleared physically has fallen as banks have opted to transmit digital images of checks electronically rather than clearing physical checks.

The rapid reduction in the rate at which paper checks are physically cleared has affected all those who have traditionally been involved in this process. Among these are airplane pilots. Until recently, the Federal Reserve had a fleet of 47 Lear jets and small cargo planes that it utilized to transport checks cleared by Federal Reserve banks. In addition, clearinghouses operated by private banks used to contract with AirNet Systems and other private air couriers to ship checks. Today, the Fed has sold off the bulk of its air fleet, and large banks have drastically cut back on contracted air freight services. Of course, pilots continue to fly planes transporting other forms of air freight. Nevertheless, there has been a decline in the demand for their services.

FOR CRITICAL ANALYSIS
What types of jobs do you suppose will experience increases in demand as a result of the expansion of electronic payment networks? (Hint: What types of jobs relate to electronic networks?)

QUICK QUIZ See page 421 for the answers. Review concepts from this section in MyEconLab.

If funds are transferred from a transactions deposit account at one depository institution and deposited in another, there is _____ _____ in total deposits or in the total money supply.

_____ additional reserves in the banking system are created following a transfer of funds between transactions deposit accounts at two depository institutions.

Money Expansion by the Banking System

Now let's shift our focus from a single bank and consider the entire banking system. For practical purposes, we can look at all depository institutions taken as a whole. To understand how money is created, we must understand how depository institutions respond to Fed actions that increase reserves in the entire system.

Federal Open Market Committee

The decisions that essentially determine the level of reserves in the monetary system are made by the Fed's Federal Open Market Committee (FOMC). The mechanism through which it works is open market operations. **Open market operations** are FOMC-directed Fed purchases and sales of existing U.S. government securities in the open market, which is the private secondary U.S. securities market in which people exchange government securities that have not yet matured. If the FOMC decides that the Fed should buy or sell bonds, it instructs the New York Federal Reserve Bank's Trading Desk to do so.

Open market operations
The purchase and sale of existing U.S. government securities (such as bonds) in the open private market by the Federal Reserve System.

Fed Purchases of U.S. Government Securities

Assume that the Fed's Trading Desk purchases a $100,000 U.S. government security from a bond dealer. The Trading Desk electronically transfers $100,000 to the bond dealer's transactions deposit account at Bank 1, which prior to this transaction is in the position depicted in Balance Sheet 16-4.

BALANCE SHEET 16-4

Bank 1

This shows Bank 1's original position before the Federal Reserve's purchase of a $100,000 U.S. government security.

Assets			Liabilities	
Total reserves		$100,000	Transactions deposits	$1,000,000
Required reserves	$100,000			
Excess reserves	0			
Loans		900,000		
Total		$1,000,000	Total	$1,000,000

Now look at the balance sheet for Bank 1 shown in Balance Sheet 16-5. Transactions deposits have been increased by $100,000, and total reserves have also increased by $100,000, to $200,000.

Thus, the Fed has created $100,000 of reserves. The Fed can create reserves because it has the ability to add to the reserve accounts of depository institutions whenever it buys U.S. securities. When the Fed buys a U.S. government security in the open market, it initially expands total reserves by the amount of the purchase.

BALANCE SHEET 16-5

Bank 1

Assets			Liabilities	
Total reserves		$200,000	Transactions deposits	$1,100,000
Required reserves	$110,000			
Excess reserves	90,000			
Loans		900,000		
Total		$1,100,000	Total	$1,100,000

EFFECT ON THE MONEY SUPPLY   The purchase of a $100,000 U.S. government security by the Federal Reserve from the public (a bond dealer, for example) increases the money supply immediately by $100,000 because transactions deposits held by the public—the bond dealers are members of the public—are part of the money supply, and no other bank has lost deposits.

The process of money creation does not stop here. Look again at Balance Sheet 16-5. Because required reserves on $1.1 million of transactions deposits are only $110,000, Bank 1 has excess reserves of $90,000. No other depository institution (or combination of depository institutions) has negative excess reserves of $90,000 as a result of the Fed's bond purchase. (Remember, the Fed simply *created* the reserves to pay for the bond purchase.)

Bank 1 will not wish to hold non-interest-bearing excess reserves. Assume that it will expand its loans by $90,000. This is shown in Balance Sheet 16-6 on page 402.

BALANCE SHEET 16-6	Assets			Liabilities	
Bank 1	Total reserves		$110,000	Transactions deposits	$1,100,000
	Required reserves	$110,000			
	Excess reserves	0			
	Loans		990,000		
	Total		$1,100,000	Total	$1,100,000

The individual or business that has received the $90,000 loan will spend these funds, which will then be deposited in other banks. For the sake of simplicity, concentrate only on the balance sheet *changes* resulting from this new deposit, as shown in Balance Sheet 16-7.

BALANCE SHEET 16-7	Assets			Liabilities	
Bank 2 (Changes Only)	Total reserves		+$90,000	New transactions deposits	+$90,000
	Required reserves	+$9,000			
	Excess reserves	+$81,000			
	Total		+$90,000	Total	+$90,000

For Bank 2, the $90,000 deposit becomes an increase in reserves as well as an increase in transactions deposits and hence the money supply. Because the reserve requirement is 10 percent, required reserves increase by $9,000, so Bank 2 will have excess reserves of $81,000. But, of course, excess reserves are not income producing, so by assumption Bank 2 will reduce them to zero by making a loan of $81,000 (which will earn interest income). This is shown in Balance Sheet 16-8.

BALANCE SHEET 16-8	Assets			Liabilities	
Bank 2 (Changes Only)	Total reserves		+$9,000	Transactions deposits	+$90,000
	Required reserves	+$9,000			
	Excess reserves	0			
	Loans		+$81,000		
	Total		+$90,000	Total	+$90,000

Remember that in this example, the original $100,000 deposit was transmitted electronically by a Federal Reserve bank to the bond dealer's transactions deposit account. That $100,000 constituted an immediate increase in the money supply of $100,000. The deposit creation process (in addition to the original $100,000) occurs because of the fractional reserve banking system, coupled with the desire of depository institutions to maintain a minimum level of excess reserves. Under fractional reserve banking, banks must hold only a portion of new deposits as required reserves, and in their quest to earn profits, they seek to transform excess reserves into holdings of loans and securities.

CONTINUATION OF THE DEPOSIT CREATION PROCESS Look at Bank 3's simplified account in Balance Sheet 16-9, where again only *changes* in the assets and liabilities are shown. Assume that the firm borrowing $81,000 from Bank 2 spends these funds, which are deposited in Bank 3; transactions deposits and the money supply increase by $81,000. Total reserves of Bank 3 rise by that amount when the payment transfer occurs.

You Are There

To contemplate how changes in bank procedures for accepting deposits of checks are yielding significant benefits to small businesses, read **Scanning Checks Benefits a Bank's Small-Business Customer,** on page 415.

BALANCE SHEET 16-9

Bank 3 (Changes Only)

Assets			Liabilities	
Total reserves		+$81,000	New transactions deposits	+$81,000
Required reserves	+$8,100			
Excess reserves	+$72,900			
Total		+$81,000	Total	+$81,000

Because the reserve requirement is 10 percent, required reserves rise by $8,100, and excess reserves therefore increase by $72,900. We assume that Bank 3 will want to lend all of those non-interest-earning assets (excess reserves). When it does, loans (and newly created transactions deposits) will increase by $72,900. This bank's total reserves will fall to $8,100, and excess reserves become zero as debit-card or check payments are transferred from the new deposit. This is shown in Balance Sheet 16-10.

BALANCE SHEET 16-10

Bank 3 (Changes Only)

Assets			Liabilities	
Total reserves		+$8,100	New transactions deposits	+$81,000
Required reserves	+$8,100			
Excess reserves	0			
Loans		+$72,900		
Total		+$81,000	Total	+$81,000

How are a growing number of banks speeding the process of clearing checks that you deposit into your account via automated teller machines?

E-COMMERCE EXAMPLE

What Goes on Inside Envelope-Free Automated Teller Machines

The latest in bank automated teller machines (ATMs) is the envelope-free machine. These ATMs allow customers to insert a check for deposit directly into a slot in the machine. Thus, customers no longer have to go to the trouble of putting the check and a deposit slip into an envelope for insertion into the ATM. For the bank, there is another advantage: The new ATMs are equipped with digital cameras that record a digital image of the deposited check, which the bank can transmit immediately to an electronic check-clearing network. This hastens the process of finalizing the customer's deposit, thereby enabling the bank to get faster access to the depositor's funds for purposes of making loans or buying securities.

FOR CRITICAL ANALYSIS
What does a bank gain from speeding its access to funds that its customers deposit at ATMs?

404 | **PART 4** Money, Stabilization, and Growth

TABLE 16-1

Maximum Money Creation with 10 Percent Required Reserves

This table shows the maximum new loans plus investments that banks can make, given the Fed's electronic transfer of $100,000 to a transactions deposit account at Bank 1. The required reserve ratio is 10 percent. We assume that all excess reserves in each bank are used for new loans or investments.

Bank	New Deposits	New Required Reserves	Maximum New Loans
1	$100,000 (from Fed)	$10,000	$90,000
2	90,000	9,000	81,000
3	81,000	8,100	72,900
4	72,900	7,290	65,610
.	.	.	.
.	.	.	.
.	.	.	.
All other banks	656,100	65,610	590,490
Totals	$1,000,000	$100,000	$900,000

What is one of the latest improvements to making check deposits into ATMs and why is this important?

PROGRESSION TO OTHER BANKS This process continues to Banks 4, 5, 6, and so forth. Each bank obtains smaller and smaller increases in deposits because 10 percent of each deposit must be held in required reserves; therefore, each succeeding depository institution makes correspondingly smaller loans. Table 16-1 shows the new deposits, required reserves, and possible loans for the remaining depository institutions in the system.

EFFECT ON TOTAL DEPOSITS In this example, deposits (and the money supply) increased initially by the $100,000 that the Fed paid the bond dealer in exchange for a bond. Deposits (and the money supply) were further increased by a $90,000 deposit in Bank 2, and they were again increased by an $81,000 deposit in Bank 3. Eventually, total deposits and the money supply will increase by $1 million, as shown in Table 16-1. The $1 million consists of the original $100,000 created by the Fed, plus an extra $900,000 generated by deposit-creating bank loans. The deposit creation process is portrayed graphically in Figure 16-1.

Increase in Total Banking System Reserves

Even with fractional reserve banking, if there are zero excess reserves, deposits cannot expand unless total banking system reserves are increased. In our example, the original new deposit in Bank 1 was created by an electronic transfer from a Federal Reserve district bank. It therefore represented new reserves to the banking system. Had that transfer been from an existing account at Bank 3, in contrast, nothing would have happened to the total amount of transactions deposits; there would have been no change in the total money supply. To repeat: Funds transferred electronically or by check from accounts at banks within the system, without any expansion of overall reserves within the banking system, represent transfers of reserves and deposits among depository institutions that do not affect the money supply. *The fundamental way in which the money supply can increase is when additional new reserves and deposits are created by the Federal Reserve System.*

FIGURE 16-1

The Multiple Expansion in the Money Supply Due to $100,000 in New Reserves When the Required Reserve Ratio Is 10 Percent

The banks are all aligned in decreasing order of new deposits created. Bank 1 receives the $100,000 in new reserves and lends out $90,000. Bank 2 receives the $90,000 and lends out $81,000. The process continues through Banks 3 to 19 and then the rest of the banking system. Ultimately, assuming no leakages into currency, the $100,000 of new reserves results in an increase in the money supply of $1 million, or 10 times the new reserves, because the required reserve ratio is 10 percent.

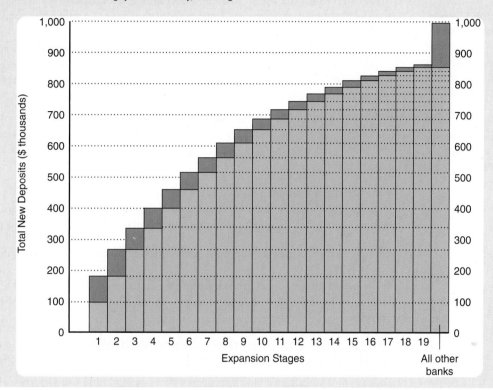

You should be able to work through the foregoing example to show the reverse process when there is a *decrease* in reserves because the Fed sells a $100,000 U.S. government security. The result is a multiple contraction of deposits and, therefore, of the total money supply in circulation.

QUICK QUIZ

See page 421 for the answers. Review concepts from this section in MyEconLab.

When the Fed _____ reserves through a purchase of U.S. government securities, the result is a multiple _____ of deposits and therefore of the supply of money.

When the Fed _____ the banking system's reserves by selling U.S. government securities, the result is a multiple _____ of deposits and therefore of the money supply.

The Money Multiplier

In the example just given, a $100,000 increase in excess reserves generated by the Fed's purchase of a security yielded a $1 million increase in total deposits; deposits increased by a multiple of 10 times the initial $100,000 increase in overall reserves. Conversely, a $100,000 decrease in excess reserves generated by the Fed's sale of a security will yield a $1 million decrease in total deposits; they will decrease by a multiple of 10 times the initial $100,000 decrease in overall reserves.

We can now make a generalization about the extent to which the total money supply will change when the banking system's reserves are increased or decreased. The **money multiplier** gives the change in the money supply due to a change in reserves.

If we assume that no excess reserves are kept and that all loan proceeds are deposited in depository institutions in the system, we obtain the **potential money multiplier**— the *maximum* possible value of the money multiplier when there is a reserve requirement. The following equation applies:

$$\text{Potential money multiplier} = \frac{1}{\text{required reserve ratio}}$$

That is, the maximum possible value of the money multiplier is equal to 1 divided by the required reserve ratio for transactions deposits. The *actual* change in the money supply—currency plus transactions account balances—will be equal to the following:

Actual change in money supply = actual money multiplier × change in total reserves

Now we examine why there is a difference between the potential money multiplier—1 divided by the required reserve ratio—and the actual money multiplier.

Going from the Potential Money Multiplier to the Actual Money Multiplier

We made a number of simplifying assumptions to come up with the potential money multiplier. In the real world, the actual money multiplier is considerably smaller. Two key factors account for this.

LEAKAGES The entire loan from one bank is not always deposited in another bank. At least two leakages can occur:

- *Currency drains.* When deposits increase, the public will want to hold more currency. Currency that is kept in a person's wallet remains outside the banking system and cannot be held by banks as reserves from which to make loans. The greater the amount of cash leakage, the smaller the actual money multiplier.

- *Excess reserves.* Depository institutions may wish to maintain excess reserves greater than zero. For example, a bank may wish to keep excess reserves so that it can make speedy loans when creditworthy borrowers seek funds. To the extent that banks want to keep positive excess reserves, the money multiplier will be smaller. The greater the excess reserves that banks maintain, the smaller the actual money multiplier.

Empirically, the currency drain is more significant than the effect of desired positive excess reserves.

Money multiplier
A number that, when multiplied by a change in reserves in the banking system, yields the resulting change in the money supply.

Potential money multiplier
The reciprocal of the required reserve ratio, assuming no leakages into currency and no excess reserves. It is equal to 1 divided by the required reserve ratio.

REAL-WORLD MONEY MULTIPLIERS   The potential money multiplier is the reciprocal of the required reserve ratio. This potential is never attained for the system as a whole because of currency drains and excess reserves.

Each definition of the money supply, M1 or M2, will yield a different actual money multiplier. In recent years, the actual M1 multiplier has been in a range between 1.5 and 2.0. The actual M2 multiplier, however, has shown an upward trend, rising from 6.5 at the beginning of the 1960s to over 12 in the 2000s.

Other Ways That the Federal Reserve Can Change the Money Supply

As we have just seen, the Fed can change the money supply by directly changing reserves available to the banking system. It does this by engaging in open market operations. To repeat: The purchase of a U.S. government security by the Fed results in an increase in reserves and leads to a multiple expansion in the money supply. A sale of a U.S. government security by the Fed results in a decrease in reserves and leads to a multiple contraction in the money supply.

In principle, the Fed can change the money supply in two other ways, both of which will have multiplier effects similar to those outlined earlier.

BORROWED RESERVES, THE DISCOUNT RATE, AND THE FEDERAL FUNDS RATE   If a depository institution wants to increase its loans but has no excess reserves, it can borrow reserves. One place it can borrow reserves is from the Fed itself. The depository institution goes to the Federal Reserve and asks for a loan of a certain amount of reserves. The Fed charges these institutions for any reserves that it lends them. The interest rate that the Fed charges is the **discount rate,** and the borrowing is said to be done through the Fed's "discount window." Borrowing from the Fed increases reserves and thereby enhances the ability of the depository institution to engage in deposit creation, thus increasing the money supply.

Depository institutions rarely go to the Fed to borrow reserves. In years past, this was because the Fed would not lend them all they wanted to borrow. The Fed encouraged banks to tap an alternative source when they wanted to expand their reserves or when they needed reserves to meet a requirement. The primary source for banks to obtain funds is the **federal funds market.** The federal funds market is an interbank market in reserves, with one bank borrowing the excess reserves of another. The generic term *federal funds market* refers to the borrowing or lending of reserve funds that are usually repaid within the same 24-hour period.

Depository institutions that borrow in the federal funds market pay an interest rate called the **federal funds rate.** Because the federal funds rate is a ready measure of the cost that banks must incur to raise funds, the Federal Reserve often uses it as a yardstick by which to measure the effects of its policies. Consequently, the federal funds rate is a closely watched indicator of the Fed's anticipated intentions.

For almost 80 years, the Fed tended to keep the discount rate unchanged for weeks at a time. From the late 1960s through the early 2000s, the Fed typically set the discount rate slightly below the federal funds rate. Because this gave depository institutions an incentive to borrow from the Fed instead of from other banks in the federal funds market, the Fed established tough lending conditions. Often, when the Fed changed the discount rate, its objective was not necessarily to encourage or discourage depository institutions from borrowing from the Fed. Instead, altering the discount rate would signal to the banking system and financial markets that there had been a change in the Fed's monetary policy.

Discount rate
The interest rate that the Federal Reserve charges for reserves that it lends to depository institutions. It is sometimes referred to as the *rediscount rate* or, in Canada and England, as the *bank rate*.

Federal funds market
A private market (made up mostly of banks) in which banks can borrow reserves from other banks that want to lend them. Federal funds are usually lent for overnight use.

Federal funds rate
The interest rate that depository institutions pay to borrow reserves in the interbank federal funds market.

TODAY'S DISCOUNT RATE POLICY In 2003, the Fed altered the way it lends to depository institutions. It now sets the discount rate *above* the federal funds rate. This discourages depository institutions from seeking loans unless they face significant liquidity problems. Currently, the Fed typically keeps the discount rate between 0.5 and 1.0 percentage point higher than the market-determined federal funds rate. Thus, if the market federal funds rate is 5 percent, the discount rate may be set 0.5 percentage point higher, at 5.5 percent. Then, if the federal funds rate increases to 5.5 percent, the Fed automatically raises the discount rate to 6 percent.

In principle, the Fed can continue to use the discount rate as an instrument of monetary policy by changing the amount by which the discount rate exceeds the federal funds rate. For instance, if the Fed reduced the differential from 0.5 percentage point to 0.25 percentage point, this would reduce depository institutions' disincentive from borrowing from the Fed. As Fed lending increased in response, borrowed reserves would rise, and total reserves in the banking system would increase. The Fed has indicated that it does not plan to conduct monetary policy in this way, however.

RESERVE REQUIREMENT CHANGES The Fed can also potentially alter the money supply by changing the reserve requirements it imposes on all depository institutions. Earlier we assumed that reserve requirements were fixed. Actually, these requirements are set by the Fed within limits established by Congress. The Fed can vary reserve requirements within these broad limits.

What would a change in reserve requirements from 10 to 20 percent do (if there were no excess reserves and if we ignore currency leakages)? We have already seen that the potential money multiplier is the reciprocal of the required reserve ratio. If the required reserve ratio is 10 percent, then the potential money multiplier is the reciprocal of $\frac{1}{10}$, or 10 (assuming no leakages). If, for some reason, the Fed decided to increase reserve requirements to 20 percent, the potential money multiplier would equal the reciprocal of $\frac{1}{5}$, or 5. The potential money multiplier is therefore inversely related to the required reserve ratio. So is the actual money multiplier. If the Fed decides to increase reserve requirements, the actual money multiplier will decrease. Therefore, with any given level of reserves already in existence, the money supply will contract.

In practice, open market operations allow the Federal Reserve to control the money supply much more precisely than changes in reserve requirements do, and they also allow the Fed to reverse itself quickly. In contrast, a small change in reserve requirements could, at least initially, result in a very large change in the money supply. Reserve requirement increases also impose costs on banks by restricting the portion of funds that they can lend, thereby inducing them to find legal ways to evade reserve requirements. That is why the Federal Reserve does not change reserve requirements very often.

Sweep Accounts and the Decreased Relevance of Reserve Requirements

To many economists, reserve requirements are an outdated relic. They argue that reserve requirements might prove useful as a stabilizing tool if central banks really sought to achieve targets for the quantity of money in circulation, but they note that most central banks today pay little attention to variations in money growth. Hence, they contend, reserve requirements around the world should be reduced or even eliminated. In the United States, banks have already taken matters into their own hands through a mechanism called *sweep accounts*.

THE GREAT RESERVE REQUIREMENT LOOPHOLE: SWEEP ACCOUNTS A key simplifying assumption in our example of the money creation process was that transactions deposits were the only bank liability that changes when total reserves change. Of course, banks also issue savings and time deposits. In addition, they offer *automatic transfer accounts*. In these accounts, which banks have offered since the 1970s, funds are automatically transferred from savings deposits to transactions deposits whenever the account holder makes a debit-card transaction or writes a check that would otherwise cause the balance of transactions deposits to become negative. Automatic transfer accounts thereby protect individuals and businesses from overdrawing their transactions deposit accounts.

Beginning in 1993, several U.S. banks discovered a way to use automatic transfer accounts to reduce their required reserves. The banks shift funds *out of* their customers' transactions deposit accounts, which are subject to reserve requirements, and *into* the customers' savings deposits—mainly money market deposit accounts—which are *not* subject to reserve requirements. Automatic transfer accounts with provisions permitting banks to shift funds from transactions deposits to savings deposits to avoid reserve requirements are called **sweep accounts.** Banks gave the accounts this name because they effectively use them to "sweep" funds from one deposit to another.

As panel (a) of Figure 16-2 shows, total funds in U.S. sweep accounts exempt from the 10 percent required reserve ratio have increased dramatically since 1995. Panel (b) indicates that the immediate result was a decline in the reserves that U.S. banks hold at Federal Reserve banks. Reserves have since risen but remain below previous levels.

Sweep account
A depository institution account that entails regular shifts of funds from transactions deposits that are subject to reserve requirements to savings deposits that are exempt from reserve requirements.

FIGURE 16-2

Sweep Accounts and Reserves of U.S. Depository Institutions at Federal Reserve Banks

Panel (a) depicts the growth of sweep accounts, which shift funds from transactions deposits subject to reserve requirements to savings deposits with no legally required reserve ratios. Panel (b) shows that sweep accounts induced an abrupt decline in reserve balances that depository institutions hold at Federal Reserve banks. Reserves have risen slightly and fallen again since (with a brief jump when the Fed made an emergency reserve injection after the 2001 terrorist attacks).

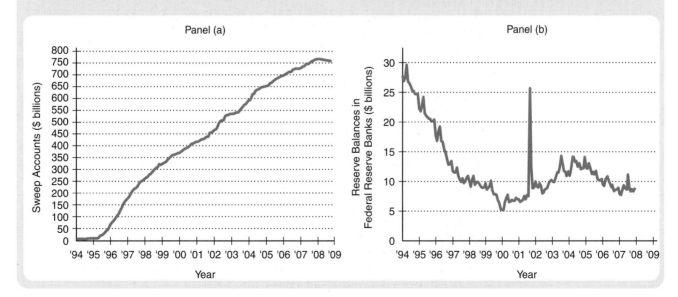

To learn more from the Federal Reserve Bank of St. Louis about the growth of sweep accounts, go to www.econtoday.com/chapter16, and scan down the page to "Retail and Deposit Sweep Program."

IMPLICATIONS OF SWEEP ACCOUNTS FOR MEASURES OF THE MONEY SUPPLY Recall from Chapter 15 that there are two key measures of the U.S. money supply. One is M1, which consists of currency, transactions deposits, and traveler's checks. The other is M2, which is composed of M1 plus various other liquid assets, such as savings accounts, money market deposit accounts, and small-denomination time deposits.

Between 1984 and 1993, M2 grew at an annual rate of just under 5 percent, and M1 grew at an annual rate of just over 8 percent. Since 1993, the annual rate of growth in M2 has varied considerably but on average has been close to 6 percent, but the average annual rate of growth of M1 has been close to 1 percent. The reason is the widespread use of sweep accounts since 1993. When depository institutions began using sweep accounts to shift funds from transactions deposits into savings accounts, the growth of the funds in transactions deposits abruptly halted. Since 1993, M1 has increased by only a few billion dollars. Growth in M2 has continued, however, because funds that depository institutions shift from transactions deposits to savings accounts are already included in M2.

Sweep accounts have therefore artificially changed the behavior of the M1 measure of the money supply. From the Fed's perspective, this has made M1 a less useful way to track total liquidity in the United States. It now relies on M2 as its key measure of the money supply.

QUICK QUIZ   See page 421 for the answers. Review concepts from this section in MyEconLab.

The _____ money multiplier is equal to the reciprocal of the required reserve ratio. The _____ money multiplier is smaller than the _____ money multiplier because of currency drains and excess reserves held by banks.

The Fed can change the money supply through _____ _____ _____, in which it buys and sells existing U.S. government securities. This is the key way in which the Fed conducts monetary policy.

In principle, the Fed can also conduct monetary policy by varying the _____ _____ to encourage changes in depository institutions' borrowings of reserves from the Fed. Starting in 2003, the Fed has kept the _____ _____ above the federal funds rate.

Finally, the Fed can change the amount of deposits created from reserves by changing reserve requirements, but it has rarely done so. Furthermore, since the mid-1990s, U.S. depository institutions have used _____ _____ to shift funds from transactions deposits to savings deposits that are exempt from reserve requirements, thereby reducing the relevance of reserve requirements for monetary policy.

The Demand for Money

So far in this chapter, we have seen how the Fed's open market operations can increase or decrease the money supply. Our focus has been on the effects of the Fed's actions on the banking system. Now we widen our discussion to see how Fed monetary policy actions have an impact on the broader economy by influencing market interest rates. First, though, you must understand the factors that determine how much money people desire to hold—in other words, you must understand the demand for money.

All of us engage in a flow of transactions. We buy and sell things all of our lives. But because we use money—dollars—as our medium of exchange, all *flows* of non-barter transactions involve a *stock* of money. We can restate this as follows:

To use money, one must hold money.

Given that everybody must hold money, we can now talk about the *demand* to hold it. People do not demand to hold money just to look at pictures of past leaders. They hold it to be able to use it to buy goods and services.

The Demand for Money: What People Wish to Hold

People have a certain motivation that causes them to want to hold **money balances**. Individuals and firms could try to do without non-interest-bearing money balances. But life is inconvenient without a ready supply of money balances. There is a demand for money by the public, motivated by several factors.

Money balances
Synonymous with money, money stock, money holdings.

THE TRANSACTIONS DEMAND The main reason people hold money is that money can be used to purchase goods and services. People are paid at specific intervals (once a week, once a month, and so on), but they wish to make purchases more or less continuously. To free themselves from having to make expenditures on goods and services only on payday, people find it beneficial to hold money. The benefit they receive is convenience: They willingly forgo interest earnings in order to avoid the inconvenience and expense of cashing in nonmoney assets such as bonds every time they wish to make a purchase. Thus, people hold money to make regular, *expected* expenditures under the **transactions demand.** As nominal GDP rises, people will want to hold more money because they will be making more transactions.

Transactions demand
Holding money as a medium of exchange to make payments. The level varies directly with nominal GDP.

THE PRECAUTIONARY DEMAND The transactions demand involves money held to make *expected* expenditures. People also hold money for the **precautionary demand** to make *unexpected* purchases or to meet emergencies. When people hold money for the precautionary demand, they incur a cost in forgone interest earnings that they balance against the benefit that having cash on hand provides. The higher the rate of interest, the lower the money balances people wish to hold for the precautionary demand.

Precautionary demand
Holding money to meet unplanned expenditures and emergencies.

THE ASSET DEMAND Remember that one of the functions of money is to serve as a store of value. People can hold money balances as a store of value, or they can hold bonds or stocks or other interest-earning assets. The desire to hold money as a store of value leads to the **asset demand** for money. People choose to hold money rather than other assets for two reasons: its liquidity and the lack of risk.

The disadvantage of holding money balances as an asset, of course, is the interest earnings forgone. Each individual or business decides how much money to hold as an asset by looking at the opportunity cost of holding money. The higher the interest rate—which is the opportunity cost of holding money—the lower the money balances people will want to hold as assets. Conversely, the lower the interest rate offered on alternative assets, the higher the money balances people will want to hold as assets.

Asset demand
Holding money as a store of value instead of other assets such as certificates of deposit, corporate bonds, and stocks.

The Demand for Money Curve

Assume for simplicity's sake that the amount of money demanded for transactions purposes is proportionate to income. That leaves the precautionary and asset demands for money, both determined by the opportunity cost of holding money. If we assume that the interest rate represents the cost of holding money balances, we can graph the relationship between the interest rate and the quantity of money demanded. In Figure 16-3 on page 412, the demand for money curve shows a familiar downward slope. The horizontal axis measures the quantity of money demanded, and

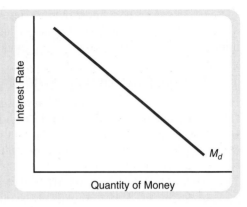

FIGURE 16-3

The Demand for Money Curve

If we use the interest rate as a proxy for the opportunity cost of holding money balances, the demand for money curve, M_d, is downward sloping, similar to other demand curves.

the vertical axis is the interest rate. The rate of interest is the cost of holding money. At a higher interest rate, a lower quantity of money is demanded, and vice versa.

To see this, imagine two scenarios. In the first one, you can earn 20 percent a year if you put your cash into purchases of U.S. government securities. In the other scenario, you can earn 1 percent if you put your cash into purchases of U.S. government securities. If you have $1,000 average cash balances in a non-interest-bearing checking account, in the second scenario over a one-year period, your opportunity cost would be 1 percent of $1,000, or $10. In the first scenario, your opportunity cost would be 20 percent of $1,000, or $200. Under which scenario would you hold more cash instead of securities?

QUICK QUIZ See page 421 for the answers. Review concepts from this section in MyEconLab.

To use money, people must hold money. Therefore, they have a _____ for money balances.

The determinants of the demand for money balances are the _____ demand, the _____ demand, and the _____ demand.

Because holding money carries an _____ cost—the interest income forgone—the demand for money curve showing the relationship between the quantity of money balances demanded and the interest rate slopes _____.

How the Fed Influences Interest Rates

When the Fed takes actions that alter the rate of growth of the money supply, it is seeking to influence investment, consumption, and total aggregate expenditures. As we discussed earlier in the chapter, in taking these monetary policy actions, the Fed in principle has three tools at its disposal: open market operations, discount rate changes, and changes in the required reserve ratio. Let's consider the effects of open market operations, the tool that the Fed regularly employs on a day-to-day basis.

Open Market Operations

As we saw earlier in this chapter, the Fed changes the amount of reserves in the banking system by its purchases and sales of government bonds issued by the U.S. Treasury. To understand how these actions by the Fed influence the market interest rate, you must first start out in an equilibrium in which all individuals, including the holders of bonds, are satisfied with the current situation. There is some equilibrium level of interest rate (and bond prices). Now, if the Fed wants to conduct open market operations, it must somehow induce individuals, businesses, and foreign residents to hold more or fewer U.S. Treasury bonds. The inducement must be in the form of making people better off. So, if the Fed wants to buy bonds, it is going to have to offer to buy them at a higher price than exists in the private marketplace. If the Fed wants to sell bonds, it is going to have to offer them at a lower price than exists in the private marketplace. Thus, an open market operation must cause a change in the price of bonds.

Go to www.econtoday.com/chapter16 to learn about the Federal Reserve's current policy regarding open market operations. Scan down the page, and select the "Minutes" for the most recent date.

GRAPHING THE SALE OF BONDS The Fed sells some of the bonds in its portfolio. This is shown in panel (a) of Figure 16-4 on the following page. Notice that the supply of bonds is shown here as a vertical line with respect to price. The demand for bonds is downward sloping. If the Fed offers more bonds it owns for sale, the supply curve shifts from S_1 to S_2. People will not be willing to buy the extra bonds at the initial equilibrium bond price, P_1. They will be satisfied holding the additional bonds at the new equilibrium price, P_2.

THE FED'S PURCHASE OF BONDS The opposite occurs when the Fed purchases bonds. You can view this purchase of bonds as a reduction in the stock of bonds available for private investors to hold. In panel (b) of Figure 16-4 on the next page, the original supply curve is S_1. The new supply curve of outstanding bonds will end up being S_3 because of the Fed's purchases of bonds. To get people to give up these bonds, the Fed must offer them a more attractive price. The price will rise from to P_1 to P_3.

Relationship Between the Price of Existing Bonds and the Rate of Interest

There is an inverse relationship between the price of existing bonds and the rate of interest. Assume that the average yield on bonds is 5 percent. You decide to purchase a bond. A local corporation agrees to sell you a bond that will pay you $50 a year forever. What is the price you are willing to pay for the bond? It is $1,000. Why? Because $50 divided by $1,000 equals 5 percent, which is as good as the best return you can earn elsewhere. You purchase the bond. The next year something happens in the economy, and you can now obtain bonds that have effective yields of 10 percent. (In other words, the prevailing interest rate in the economy is now 10 percent.) What will happen to the market price of the existing bond that you own, the one you purchased the year before? It will fall. If you try to sell the bond for $1,000, you will discover that no investors will buy it from you. Why should they when they can obtain the same $50-a-year yield from someone else by paying only $500? Indeed, unless you offer your bond for sale at a price of $500, no buyers will be forthcoming. Hence, an increase in the prevailing interest rate in the economy has caused the market value of your existing bond to fall.

FIGURE 16-4

Determining the Price of Bonds

In panel (a), the Fed offers more bonds for sale. The price drops from P_1 to P_2. In panel (b), the Fed purchases bonds. This is the equivalent of a reduction in the supply of bonds available for private investors to hold. The price of bonds must rise from P_1 to P_3 to clear the market.

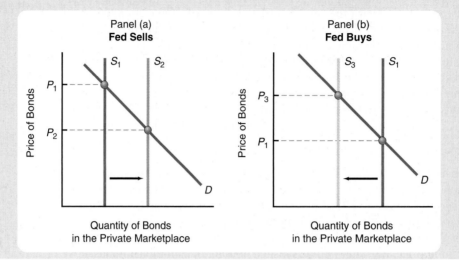

The important point to be understood is this:

The market price of existing bonds (and all fixed-income assets) is inversely related to the rate of interest prevailing in the economy.

As a consequence of the inverse relationship between the price of existing bonds and the interest rate, engaging in open market operations allows the Fed to influence the prevailing interest rate. A Fed open market sale that reduces the equilibrium price of bonds brings about an increase in the rate of interest. A Fed open market purchase that boosts the equilibrium price of bonds generates a decrease in the rate of interest.

QUICK QUIZ   *See page 421 for the answers. Review concepts from this section in MyEconLab.*

When the Fed sells bonds, it must offer them at a _____ price. When the Fed buys bonds, it must pay a _____ price.

There is an _____ relationship between the prevailing rate of interest in the economy and the market price of existing bonds (and all fixed-income assets).

A Federal Reserve open market sale generates a _____ in the price of existing bonds and an _____ in the market interest rate. An open market purchase brings about an _____ in the price of existing bonds and a _____ in the market rate of interest.

You Are There

Scanning Checks Benefits a Bank's Small-Business Customer

Jack Longo, a co-owner of The Stone Age, a business that sells decorative stones, bricks, and statues to landscapers in Totowa, New Jersey, used to spend five hours per week driving from his office to the nearest bank branch of PNC Financial Services. At the end of every weekday, he had to transport check payments from customers to the bank and deposit them in the firm's deposit account.

Now Longo rarely makes the 10-mile trip more than a couple of times per month. Instead, his employees utilize a single-feed check-scanning device to make digital images of each check received in the regular course of business. After both sides of the check are scanned, the device reads the routing number and dollar value of the check and creates an electronic deposit slip. Accompanying software updates the company's income statement, transmits the virtual deposit slip to the firm's bank via the Internet, and credits the company's account balance with the bank.

Now The Stone Age no longer has to pay an outside bookkeeper to perform these accounting tasks. Of course,

cutting down on trips to the bank has reduced the firm's gasoline costs and expenses related to wear and tear on its vehicles. Additionally, there is an implicit cost reduction: Longo now can devote about five additional hours per week to other aspects of his business, which previously were the opportunity cost of the time allocated to those daily bank visits. In these ways, a small check-scanning device and an inexpensive software program have generated significant cost reductions for his small business.

CRITICAL ANALYSIS QUESTIONS

1. How do The Stone Age's check-scanning activities help to speed the clearing of the checks it electronically deposits with PNC Financial Services?

2. How do you suppose that digital scanning of checks has helped to hasten the deposit creation process?

Issues and Applications

Together, Bankers Cry, "Please Deposit Your Cash!"

U.S. commercial banks are depository institutions. Nevertheless, as shown in Figure 16-5 on page 416, deposits have trended downward in relation to banks' other liabilities and net worth. Of course, across all bank balance sheets, total liabilities and net worth equal total assets, so Figure 16-5 also shows that the share of commercial bank asset holdings financed by deposits has generally declined. Four and a half decades ago, about 90 percent of the funds that commercial banks used to

CONCEPTS APPLIED

➤ Balance Sheet

➤ Net Worth

➤ Fractional Reserve Banking

extend loans, purchase securities, or allocate to reserves came from customer deposits. Today, less than 65 percent of bank assets are funded from deposits. Why did this decline in the relative importance of deposits occur? Does the downward trend in deposits as a share of bank liabilities and net worth matter to the owners and managers of commercial banks?

FIGURE 16-5

Commercial Bank Deposits, Other Liabilities, and Net Worth Since 1960

Since the 1960s, there has been a continuing decline in deposits' overall share of total liabilities and net worth at U.S. commercial banks. Starting in the early 1990s, banks came to rely more heavily on other liabilities, such as funds borrowed from private investors, to finance their loans and other assets.

Source: Federal Deposit Insurance Corporation.

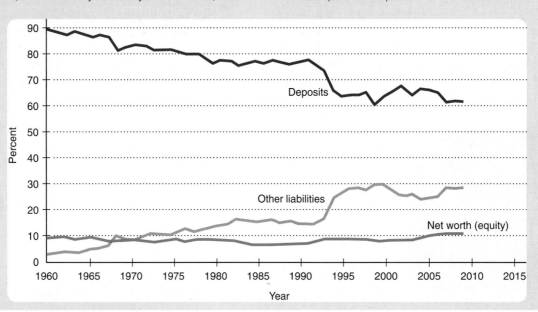

Why Deposits' Share of U.S. Bank Liabilities and Net Worth Has Fallen

Two factors explain the downward trend in deposits as a percentage of total bank liabilities and net worth. One is that many banks decided long ago to rely less on deposits than they had in prior years. During the 1960s and 1970s, theories of bank management began to stress the benefits of active "asset-liability management." These theories suggested that banks could boost profits by adjusting the mixes of assets and liabilities with an aim to maximizing the difference between interest revenues on assets and interest costs of liabilities as a percentage of total assets. Thus, banks focused on pushing up this difference, called the *net interest margin*. Pursuing this strategy called for issuing bonds and other liabilities to obtain funds from private investors, which allowed banks to respond more speedily to opportunities to lend at higher rates of interest. Naturally, this

$?$DID YOU KNOW THAT at various times during the mid-2000s, the Bank of Japan—the central bank of Japan charged with regulating the quantity of money in circulation—sought to keep an interest rate equal to 0 percent? The interest rate targeted at 0 percent by the Bank of Japan applied to "overnight call-money loans" that private banks in Japan extend to the nation's bond dealers. Officials at the Bank of Japan stated that they felt that varying the rate of money supply growth as necessary to keep this interest rate at 0 percent was consistent with broader objectives for "economic and price conditions."

What does varying the supply of money or the rate at which it grows have to do with interest rates such as the Japanese overnight call-money loan rate? Answering this question is one objective of this chapter. Let's begin, however, by considering how changes in the quantity of money in circulation affect real GDP and the price level.

Effects of an Increase in the Money Supply

How does monetary policy influence real GDP and the price level? To understand how monetary policy works in its simplest form, we are going to run an experiment in which you increase the money supply in a very direct way. Assume that the government has given you hundreds of millions of dollars in just-printed bills that you load into a helicopter. You then fly around the country, dropping the money out of the window. People pick it up and put it in their pockets. Some deposit the money in their transactions deposit accounts. The first thing that happens is that they have too much money—not in the sense that they want to throw it away but rather in relation to other assets that they own. There are a variety of ways to dispose of this "new" money.

What types of decisions do these directors of the Bank of Japan make?

Direct Effect

The simplest thing that people can do when they have excess money balances is to go out and spend them on goods and services. Here they have a direct impact on aggregate demand. Aggregate demand rises because with an increase in the money supply, at any given price level people now want to purchase more output of real goods and services.

Indirect Effect

Not everybody will necessarily spend the newfound money on goods and services. Some people may wish to deposit a portion or all of those excess money balances in banks. The recipient banks now discover that they have higher reserves than they wish to hold. As you learned in Chapter 16, one thing that banks can do to get interest-earning assets is to lend out the excess reserves. But banks cannot induce people to borrow more funds than they were borrowing before unless the banks lower the interest rate that they charge on loans. This lower interest rate encourages people to take out those loans. Businesses will therefore engage in new investment with the funds loaned. Individuals will engage in more consumption of durable goods such as housing, autos, and home entertainment centers. Either way, the increased loans generate a rise in aggregate demand. More people will be involved in more spending—even those who did not pick up any of the money that was originally dropped out of your helicopter.

Graphing the Effects of an Expansionary Monetary Policy

Look at Figure 17-1 on the following page. We start out in a situation in which the economy is operating at less than full employment. You see a recessionary gap in the

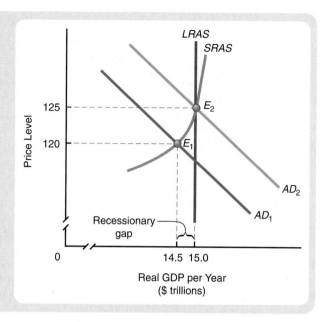

FIGURE 17-1

Expansionary Monetary Policy with Underutilized Resources

If we start out with equilibrium at E_1, expansionary monetary policy will shift AD_1 to AD_2. The new equilibrium will be at E_2.

figure, which is measured as the horizontal difference between the long-run aggregate supply curve, *LRAS*, and the current equilibrium. Short-run equilibrium is at E_1, with a price level of 120 and real GDP of $14.5 trillion. The *LRAS* curve is at $15 trillion. Assume now that the Fed increases the money supply. Because of the direct and indirect effects of this increase in the money supply, aggregate demand shifts outward to the right to AD_2. The new equilibrium is at an output rate of $15 trillion of real GDP per year and a price level of 125. Here expansionary monetary policy can move the economy toward its *LRAS* curve sooner than otherwise.

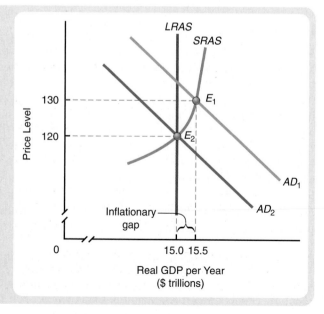

FIGURE 17-2

Contractionary Monetary Policy with Overutilized Resources

If we begin at short-run equilibrium at point E_1, contractionary monetary policy will shift the aggregate demand curve from AD_1 to AD_2. The new equilibrium will be at point E_2.

Graphing the Effects of Contractionary Monetary Policy

Assume that there is an inflationary gap as shown in Figure 17-2 on the facing page. There you see that the short-run aggregate supply curve, *SRAS*, intersects aggregate demand, AD_1, at E_1. This is to the right of the *LRAS* of real GDP per year of $15 trillion. Contractionary monetary policy can eliminate this inflationary gap. Because of both the direct and indirect effects of monetary policy, the aggregate demand curve shifts inward from AD_1 to AD_2. Equilibrium is now at E_2, which is at a lower price level, 120. Equilibrium real GDP has now fallen from $15.5 trillion to $15 trillion.

Note that contractionary monetary policy involves a reduction in the money supply, with a consequent decline in the price level (deflation). In the real world, contractionary monetary policy more commonly involves reducing the *rate of growth* of the money supply, thereby reducing the rate of increase in the price level (inflation). Similarly, real-world expansionary monetary policy typically involves increasing the rate of growth of the money supply.

QUICK QUIZ   *See page 444 for the answers. Review concepts from this section in MyEconLab.*

The _____ effect of an increase in the money supply arises because people desire to spend more on real goods and services when they have excess money balances.

The _____ effect of an increase in the money supply works through a _____ in the interest rate, which encourages businesses to make new investments with the funds loaned to them. Individuals will also engage in more consumption (on consumer durables) because of _____ interest rates.

Open Economy Transmission of Monetary Policy

So far we have discussed monetary policy in a closed economy. When we move to an open economy, with international trade and the international purchase and sale of all assets including dollars and other currencies, monetary policy becomes more complex. Consider first the effect of monetary policy on exports.

Go to www.econtoday.com/chapter17 for links to central banks around the globe, provided by the Bank for International Settlements.

The Net Export Effect of Contractionary Monetary Policy

To see how a change in monetary policy can affect net exports, suppose that the Federal Reserve implements a contractionary policy that boosts the market interest rate. The higher U.S. interest rate, in turn, tends to attract foreign investment in U.S. financial assets, such as U.S. government securities.

If more residents of foreign countries decide that they want to purchase U.S. government securities or other U.S. assets, they first have to obtain U.S. dollars. As a consequence, the demand for dollars goes up in foreign exchange markets. The international price of the dollar therefore rises. This is called an *appreciation* of the dollar, and it tends to reduce net exports because it makes our exports more expensive in terms of foreign currency and imports cheaper in terms of dollars. Foreign residents demand fewer of our goods and services, and we demand more of theirs.

This reasoning implies that when contractionary monetary policy increases the after-tax U.S. interest rate at the current price level, there will be a negative net export effect because foreign residents will want more U.S. financial instruments. Hence, they will demand additional dollars, thereby causing the international price of the dollar to rise. This makes our exports more expensive for the rest of the world, which then demands a smaller quantity of our exports. It also means that foreign goods and services are less expensive in the United States, so we therefore demand more imports. We come up with this conclusion:

> *Contractionary monetary policy causes interest rates to rise. Such a **rise** will induce international inflows of financial capital, thereby raising the international value of the dollar and making U.S. goods less attractive abroad. The net export effect of contractionary monetary policy will be in the same direction as the monetary policy effect, thereby amplifying the effect of such policy.*

The Net Export Effect of Expansionary Monetary Policy

Now assume that the economy is experiencing a recession and the Federal Reserve wants to pursue an expansionary monetary policy. In so doing, it will cause interest rates to fall in the short run, as discussed earlier. Declining interest rates will cause financial capital to flow out of the United States. The demand for dollars will decrease, and their international price will go down. Foreign goods will now look more expensive to U.S. residents, and imports will fall. Foreign residents will desire more of our exports, and exports will rise. The result will be an increase in net exports. Again, the international consequences reinforce the domestic consequences of monetary policy.

Globalization of International Money Markets

On a broader level, the Fed's ability to control the rate of growth of the money supply may be hampered as U.S. money markets become less isolated. With the push of a computer button, billions of dollars can change hands halfway around the world. If the Fed reduces the growth of the money supply, individuals and firms in the United States can obtain dollars from other sources. People in the United States who want more liquidity can obtain their dollars from foreign residents. Indeed, as world markets become increasingly integrated, U.S. residents, who can already hold U.S. bank accounts denominated in foreign currencies, more regularly conduct transactions using other nations' currencies.

When the international price of the dollar goes up, how do residents of foreign nations react?

QUICK QUIZ   See page 444 for the answers. Review concepts from this section in MyEconLab.

Monetary policy in an open economy has repercussions for net _____.

If contractionary monetary policy raises U.S. interest rates, there is a _____ net export effect because foreign residents will demand _____ U.S. financial instruments, thereby demanding _____ dollars and hence causing the international price of the dollar to rise. This makes our exports more expensive for the rest of the world.

When expansionary monetary policy causes interest rates to fall, foreign residents will want _____ U.S. financial instruments. The resulting _____ in the demand for dollars will reduce the dollar's value in foreign exchange markets, leading to an _____ in net exports.

Monetary Policy and Inflation

Most media discussions of inflation focus on the short run. The price index can fluctuate in the short run because of events such as oil price shocks, labor union strikes, or discoveries of large amounts of new natural resources. In the long run, however, empirical studies show that excessive growth in the money supply results in inflation.

If the supply of money rises relative to the demand for money, people have more money balances than desired. They adjust their mix of assets to reduce money balances in favor of other items. This ultimately causes their spending on goods and services to increase. The result is a rise in the price level, or inflation.

The Equation of Exchange and the Quantity Theory

A simple way to show the relationship between changes in the quantity of money in circulation and the price level is through the **equation of exchange,** developed by Irving Fisher (note that $\equiv$ refers to an identity or truism):

$$M_sV \equiv PY$$

where M_s = actual money balances held by the nonbanking public
V = **income velocity of money,** which is the number of times, on average per year, each monetary unit is spent on final goods and services
P = price level or price index
Y = real GDP per year

Equation of exchange
The formula indicating that the number of monetary units (M_s) times the number of times each unit is spent on final goods and services (V) is identical to the price level (P) times real GDP (Y).

Income velocity of money (V)
The number of times per year a dollar is spent on final goods and services; identically equal to nominal GDP divided by the money supply.

Consider a numerical example involving a one-commodity economy. Assume that in this economy, the total money supply, M_s, is \$8.25 trillion; real GDP, Y, is \$15 trillion (in base-year dollars); and the price level, P, is 1.1 (110 in index number terms). Using the equation of exchange,

$$M_sV \equiv PY$$

$$\$8.25 \text{ trillion} \times V \equiv 1.1 \times \$15 \text{ trillion}$$

$$\$8.25 \text{ trillion} \times V \equiv \$16.5 \text{ trillion}$$

$$V \equiv 2$$

Thus, each dollar is spent an average of two times a year.

THE EQUATION OF EXCHANGE AS AN IDENTITY The equation of exchange must always be true—it is an *accounting identity*. The equation of exchange states that the total amount of funds spent on final output, M_sV, is equal to the total amount of funds *received* for final output, PY. Thus, a given flow of funds can be viewed from either the buyers' side or the producers' side. The value of goods purchased is equal to the value of goods sold.

If Y represents real GDP and P is the price level, PY equals the dollar value of national output of goods and services or *nominal* GDP. Thus,

$$M_sV \equiv PY \equiv \text{nominal GDP}$$

THE QUANTITY THEORY OF MONEY AND PRICES If we now make some assumptions about different variables in the equation of exchange, we come up with the simplified theory of why the price level changes, called the **quantity theory of money and prices.** If we assume that the velocity of money, V, is constant and that real GDP, Y, is also constant, the simple equation of exchange tells us that a change in the money supply can lead only to an equiproportional change in the price level. Continue with

Quantity theory of money and prices
The hypothesis that changes in the money supply lead to equiproportional changes in the price level.

FIGURE 17-3

The Relationship Between Money Supply Growth Rates and Rates of Inflation

If we plot rates of inflation and rates of monetary growth for different countries, we come up with a scatter diagram that reveals an obvious direct relationship. If you were to draw a line through the "average" of the points in this figure, it would be upward sloping, showing that an increase in the rate of growth of the money supply leads to an increase in the rate of inflation.

Sources: International Monetary Fund and national central banks. Data are for latest available periods.

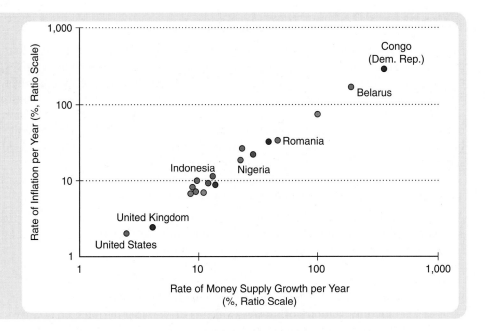

our numerical example. Y is $15 trillion. V equals 2. If the money supply increases by 20 percent, to $9.9 trillion, the only thing that can happen is that the price level, P, has to go up from 1.1 to 1.32. In other words, the price level must also increase by 20 percent. Otherwise the equation is no longer in balance. Money supply growth at a rate of 20 percent results in an inflation rate of 20 percent.

EMPIRICAL VERIFICATION There is considerable evidence of the empirical validity of the relationship between monetary growth and high rates of inflation. Figure 17-3 tracks the correspondence between money supply growth and the rates of inflation in various countries around the world.

Why do you suppose that several of Europe's central banks are devoting more attention to recent money supply growth rates when determining their monetary policy strategies?

INTERNATIONAL POLICY EXAMPLE
Paying Attention to Money Supply Growth Rates in Europe

Ben Bernanke, chair of the Federal Reserve's Board of Governors, has argued that a "heavy reliance" on money supply growth as an indicator of U.S. inflation is "unwise" in light of unpredictable short-term effects of money growth on inflation. Central bank officials in Europe have come to the opposite conclusion. Officials of the European System of Central Banks and at the Bank of England agree with Bernanke that there are variable lags in the effects of money supply growth on inflation. Nevertheless, their judgment is that growth in the money supply ultimately foreshadows *future* growth in the level of prices. Throughout the 2000s, these European central banks factored observed changes in the rate of growth of the money supply into formulations of their policy strategies. They credit this approach with keeping the average annual European inflation rates lower than the average annual U.S. inflation rate.

FOR CRITICAL ANALYSIS
If the annual money growth rate is higher in the United States than in Europe but velocity and real GDP growth rates are the same in both regions, what will be true of the U.S. inflation rate as compared with the European inflation rate?

QUICK QUIZ   *See page 444 for the answers. Review concepts from this section in MyEconLab.*

The _____ of _____ states that the expenditures by some people will equal income receipts by others, or $M_sV \equiv PY$ (money supply times velocity equals nominal GDP).

Viewed as an accounting identity, the equation of exchange is always _____, because the amount of funds _____ on final output of goods and services must equal the total amount of funds _____ for final output.

The quantity theory of money and prices states that a change in the _____ _____ will bring about an equiproportional change in the _____ _____.

Monetary Policy in Action: The Transmission Mechanism

At the start of this chapter, we talked about the direct and indirect effects of monetary policy. The direct effect is simply that an increase in the money supply causes people to have excess money balances. To get rid of these excess money balances, people increase their expenditures. The indirect effect, depicted in Figure 17-4 as the interest-rate-based money transmission mechanism, occurs because some people have decided to purchase interest-bearing assets with their excess money balances. This causes the price of such assets—bonds—to go up. Because of the inverse relationship between the price of existing bonds and the interest rate, the interest rate in the economy falls. This lower interest rate induces people and businesses to spend more than they otherwise would have spent.

An Interest-Rate-Based Transmission Mechanism

The indirect, interest-rate-based transmission mechanism can be seen explicitly in Figure 17-5 on the following page. In panel (a), you see that an increase in the money supply reduces the interest rate. The economywide demand curve for money is labeled M_d in panel (a). At first, the money supply is at M_s, a vertical line determined by our central bank, the Federal Reserve System. The equilibrium interest rate is r_1. This occurs where the money supply curve intersects the money demand curve. Now assume that the Fed increases the money supply, say, via open market operations. This will shift the money supply curve outward to the right to M'_s. People find themselves with too much cash (liquidity). They buy bonds. When they buy bonds, they bid up the prices of bonds, thereby lowering the interest rate. The interest rate falls to r_2, where the new money supply curve M'_s intersects the money demand curve M_d. This

FIGURE 17-4

The Interest-Rate-Based Money Transmission Mechanism

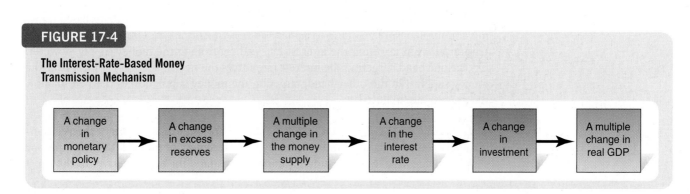

FIGURE 17-5

Adding Monetary Policy to the Aggregate Demand–Aggregate Supply Model

In panel (a), we show a demand for money function, M_d. It slopes downward to show that at lower rates of interest, a larger quantity of money will be demanded. The money supply is given initially as M_s, so the equilibrium rate of interest will be r_1. At this rate of interest, we see from the planned investment schedule given in panel (b) that the quantity of planned investment demanded

per year will be I_1. After the shift in the money supply to M_s', the resulting increase in investment from I_1 to I_2 shifts the aggregate demand curve in panel (c) outward from AD_1 to AD_2. Equilibrium moves from E_1 to E_2, at real GDP of $15 trillion per year.

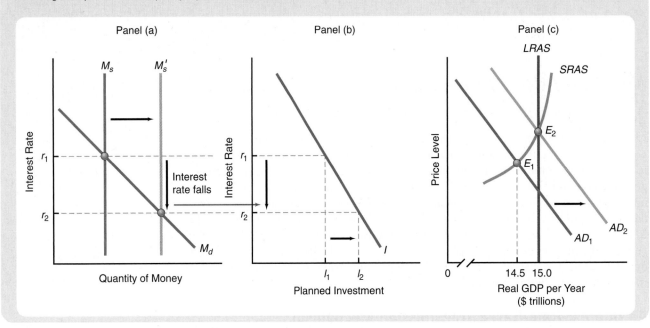

reduction in the interest rate from r_1 to r_2 has an effect on planned investment, as can be seen in panel (b). Planned investment per year increases from I_1 to I_2. An increase in investment will increase aggregate demand, as shown in panel (c). Aggregate demand increases from AD_1 to AD_2. Equilibrium in the economy increases from real GDP per year of $14.5 trillion, which is not on the *LRAS*, to equilibrium real GDP per year of $15 trillion, which is on the *LRAS*.

The Fed's Target Choice:
The Interest Rate or the Money Supply?

The Federal Reserve has often sought to take advantage of the interest-rate-based transmission mechanism by aiming to achieve an *interest rate target*. There is a fundamental tension between targeting the interest rate and controlling the money supply, however. On the one hand, targeting the interest rate forces the Fed to abandon control over the money supply. On the other hand, targeting the money supply forces the Fed to allow the interest rate to fluctuate.

THE INTEREST RATE OR THE MONEY SUPPLY? Figure 17-6 shows the relationship between the total demand for money and the supply of money. Note that money supply changes generate movements along the demand for money curve. In the short

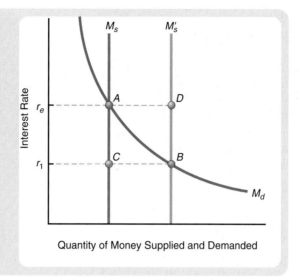

FIGURE 17-6

Choosing a Monetary Policy Target

The Fed, in the short run, can select an interest rate or a money supply target, but not both. It cannot, for example, choose r_e and M_s'. If it selects r_e, it must accept M_s. If it selects M_s', it must allow the interest rate to fall to r_1. The Fed can obtain point A or B. It cannot get to point C or D. It must therefore choose one target or the other.

run, the Fed can choose either a particular interest rate (r_e or r_1) or a particular money supply (M_s or M_s').

If the Fed wants interest rate r_e, it must select money supply M_s. If it desires a lower interest rate in the short run, it must increase the money supply. Thus, by targeting an interest rate, the Fed must relinquish control of the money supply. Conversely, if the Fed wants to target the money supply at, say, M_s', it must allow the interest rate to fall to r_1.

CHOOSING A POLICY TARGET But which target should the Fed choose—the interest rate or the money supply? It is generally agreed that the answer depends on whether variations in autonomous spending on goods and services, such as changes in autonomous consumption, are larger or smaller than variations in the demand for money. If variations in autonomous spending are relatively large and commonplace, a money supply target should be set and pursued because if the interest rate were targeted, spending variations would cause maximum volatility of real GDP. To see this, suppose that changed profit expectations induce firms to decrease their flow of autonomous investment spending. The resulting decline in real GDP causes the demand for money curve to shift leftward and pushes down the equilibrium interest rate. To keep the interest rate from falling, the Fed would have to cut the money supply, which would reduce aggregate demand and cause real GDP to fall even farther, thereby destabilizing the economy. Thus, keeping the money supply unchanged at a target level would be preferable to targeting the interest rate.

If the demand for money is highly variable, however, an interest rate target automatically offsets the effect of changes in money demand. For example, suppose that people anticipate significant drops in stock and bond prices. They react to these altered expectations by shifting more of their wealth from holdings of stocks and bonds to holdings of money. This causes the demand for money curve to shift rightward. If the Fed were to keep the money supply unchanged at a target level, the equilibrium interest rate would rise, which would cause total planned expenditures to drop. Real GDP would decline. In this situation, when the demand for money increases, it would be better for the Fed to increase the money supply and keep the interest rate from changing, thereby preventing real GDP from falling.

Go to **www.econtoday.com/chapter17** for Federal Reserve news events announcing its latest monetary policy actions.

QUICK QUIZ *See page 444 for the answers. Review concepts from this section in MyEconLab.*

According to the interest-rate-based monetary policy transmission mechanism, monetary policy operates through a change in _____ _____, which changes _____, causing a multiple change in the equilibrium level of real GDP per year.

If the Federal Reserve targets the money supply, then the _____ _____ must adjust to an equilibrium at which the quantity of _____ demanded is equal to the quantity of _____ supplied.

The Federal Reserve can attempt to stabilize the _____ _____ or the _____ _____, but not both.

The Way Fed Policy Is Currently Implemented

No matter what the Fed is actually targeting, at present it announces an interest rate target. You should not be fooled, however. When the chair of the Fed states that the Fed is raising "the" interest rate from, say, 5.25 percent to 5.50 percent, he is really referring to the federal funds rate, or the rate at which banks can borrow excess reserves from other banks. Furthermore, even if the Fed talks about changing interest rates, it can do so only by actively entering the market for federal government securities (usually Treasury bills). So, if the Fed wants to raise "the" interest rate, it essentially must engage in contractionary open market operations. That is to say, it must sell more Treasury securities than it buys, thereby reducing total reserves in the banking system and, hence, the money supply. This tends to boost the rate of interest. Conversely, when the Fed wants to decrease "the" rate of interest, it engages in expansionary open market operations, thereby increasing reserves and the money supply.

The Market for Bank Reserves and the Federal Funds Rate

To see how the Federal Reserve can use open market operations to influence the federal funds rate, consider Figure 17-7. This figure depicts the market for bank reserves. The Fed supplies these reserves. Banks demand reserves to hold on reserve as vault cash or reserve deposits at Federal Reserve district banks.

THE EQUILIBRIUM FEDERAL FUNDS RATE Panel (a) depicts the determination of the equilibrium federal funds rate in the market for bank reserves. The quantity of reserves supplied is equal to the accumulated amount of reserves that the Fed has created through past open market operations—$44 billion in panel (a). Fed actions determine this amount of reserves, so the quantity of reserves supplied is unrelated to the federal funds rate. Thus, the supply curve is vertical at $44 billion.

Because banks must satisfy their reserve requirements, the minimum quantity of reserves that they must hold is required reserves—the required reserve ratio times transactions deposits. This is $RR = \$43$ billion in panel (a) of Figure 17-7. In addition, many banks also desire to hold some excess reserves. By holding excess reserves, banks forgo the opportunity to lend the reserves to other banks in the federal funds market and thereby earn interest at the federal funds rate, which exceeds the interest rate paid on reserves held with the Fed. Thus, as the opportunity cost of excess reserves, the federal funds rate less the Fed's interest rate on reserves, declines, banks are more willing to hold additional excess reserves. At lower values of the federal funds

FIGURE 17-7

The Market for Bank Reserves and the Federal Funds Rate

In panel (a), the minimum quantity of reserves demanded by banks is their required reserves, which equal $43 billion. As the federal funds rate declines, the opportunity cost of holding excess reserves falls, and banks are willing to hold more excess reserves. Hence, the demand for reserves is a downward-sloping curve, D. At the equilibrium federal funds rate of 6 percent, the total quantity of reserves demanded by banks equals the quantity of reserves supplied by the Fed, which is $44 billion. Panel (b) shows how the Fed can bring about a reduction in the equilibrium federal funds rate. An open market purchase of $0.2 billion increases the supply of reserves from S to S′, which reduces the equilibrium federal funds rate to 5.5 percent.

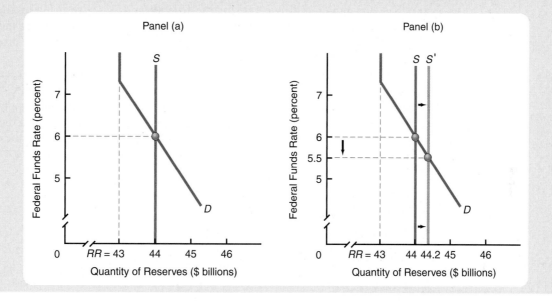

rate, banks hold more excess reserves. Thus, the demand for reserves is a downward-sloping curve, as shown in panel (a). At the equilibrium federal funds rate, which is 6 percent, the quantity of reserves demanded by banks is equal to the quantity of reserves supplied by the Fed.

USING OPEN MARKET OPERATIONS TO INFLUENCE THE EQUILIBRIUM FEDERAL FUNDS RATE Panel (b) of Figure 17-7 shows how the Fed can use open market operations to influence the equilibrium federal funds rate. In panel (b), the initial equilibrium federal funds rate is 6 percent, as in panel (a). Suppose that the Fed desires for the federal funds rate to be 5.5 percent instead of 6 percent. By conducting an open market purchase—a purchase of $0.2 billion in the example depicted in panel (b)—the Fed can increase the supply of reserves. Consequently, the supply schedule shifts rightward by $0.2 billion.

Immediately following the open market purchase, at the initial federal funds rate of 6 percent, the quantity of reserves supplied increases to $44.2 billion in panel (b). The quantity of reserves demanded at the 6 percent rate, however, is still $44 billion. Hence, after the Fed's open market purchase, there is an excess quantity of reserves supplied equal to $0.2 billion, the amount of its purchase. Banks desire to hold fewer reserves than the quantity supplied at the original 6 percent rate. They will offer to lend more reserves to other banks in the federal funds market, and as they do so, the federal funds rate declines to a new equilibrium value of 5.5 percent. At this new equilibrium federal funds rate, the quantity of reserves demanded by banks is again equal to the quantity of reserves supplied by the Fed. In this way, the open market operation enables the Fed to push the federal funds rate to the desired value, which in this example is the Fed's *target* for the federal funds rate.

Laying Out the Fed Policy Strategy

The policy decisions that determine the open market operations by which the Fed pursues its announced objective for the federal funds rate are made by the Federal Open Market Committee (FOMC). Every six to eight weeks, the voting members of the FOMC—the seven Fed board governors and five regional bank presidents—determine the Fed's general strategy of open market operations.

FOMC Directive

A document that summarizes the Federal Open Market Committee's general policy strategy, establishes near-term objectives for the federal funds rate, and specifies target ranges for money supply growth.

The FOMC outlines its strategy in a document called the **FOMC Directive.** This document lays out the FOMC's general economic objectives, establishes short-term federal funds rate objectives, and specifies target ranges for money supply growth. After each meeting, the FOMC issues a brief statement to the media, which then publish stories about the Fed's action or inaction and what it is likely to mean for the economy. Typically, these stories have headlines such as "Fed Cuts Key Interest Rate," "Fed Acts to Push Up Interest Rates," or "Fed Decides to Leave Interest Rates Alone."

The Trading Desk

Trading Desk

An office at the Federal Reserve Bank of New York charged with implementing monetary policy strategies developed by the Federal Open Market Committee.

The FOMC leaves the task of implementing the Directive to officials who manage an office at the Federal Reserve Bank of New York known as the **Trading Desk.** The media spend little time considering how the Fed's Trading Desk conducts its activities, taking it for granted that the Fed can implement the policy action that it has announced to the public.

The Trading Desk's open market operations typically are confined within a one-hour interval each weekday morning. If the Trading Desk purchases government securities during this interval, it increases the quantity of reserves available to banks, thereby increasing the supply of reserves as depicted in panel (b) of Figure 17-7 on page 433.

How do legions of economists, investors, and financial analysts pore over the Fed's policy statements in search of tiny hints about the Fed's future policy stance?

POLICY EXAMPLE
Reading the Tea Leaves of Fed Policy Statements

Just as special expertise is necessary for translating symbols and pictures used in ancient languages such as Egyptian hieroglyphics, considerable skill is required to interpret Fed policy statements. After each meeting, the Federal Open Market Committee issues a statement explaining the rationale for its Directive to the Trading Desk. Even if the FOMC leaves the federal funds rate target unchanged, economists, investors, and financial analysts watch for subtle changes in wording that may provide hints about possible *future* changes in interest rate policy.

For instance, early in the summer of 2007, the FOMC left its federal funds rate target unchanged, but it dropped from its public

statement a phrase indicating that a future increase in the federal funds rate "may yet be needed" to contain inflation. That omission, along with a brief observation that economic growth might be slowing, signaled to experts on "Fed-speak" that the FOMC was likely to reduce its federal funds rate target within a few weeks' time. Sure enough, at the end of the summer the Fed cut its federal funds rate target by half a percentage point.

FOR CRITICAL ANALYSIS

Why do you suppose that members of the FOMC devote a considerable portion of their time at meetings to carefully crafting changes in the FOMC's policy statement to the public?

Selecting the Federal Funds Rate Target

Now that you have seen how the Federal Reserve adjusts the supply of reserves to achieve the Federal Open Market Committee's target for the federal funds rate, we can address another question: How does the FOMC select the target value of this interest rate?

The Neutral Federal Funds Rate

The FOMC aims to set the target value of the federal funds rate equal to the **neutral federal funds rate.** At the neutral federal funds rate, the growth rate of real GDP tends neither to speed up nor to slow down in relation to the long-run, or potential, rate of real GDP growth, given the expected rate of inflation.

IDENTIFYING THE NEUTRAL FEDERAL FUNDS RATE Suppose, for instance, that the actual equilibrium federal funds rate is 6 percent, but the neutral federal funds rate is 5.5 percent. The higher actual federal funds rate of 6 percent would inhibit growth in interest-sensitive consumption and investment spending. The depressed short-run growth in aggregate demand would, in the short run, cause real GDP to grow at a slower pace than the potential real GDP growth rate.

To boost aggregate demand and increase real GDP growth to the long-run rate of real GDP growth, the Fed would seek to push the equilibrium federal funds rate down to the target level—the neutral federal funds rate of 5.5 percent. The Trading Desk would conduct open market purchases to raise the supply of reserves sufficiently to attain the 5.5 percent target, as depicted in Figure 17-7 on page 433.

TRYING TO TARGET THE NEUTRAL FEDERAL FUNDS RATE Policymakers on the FOMC face a fundamental problem: The value of the neutral federal funds rate varies over time. The potential rate of growth of real GDP is not constant. It depends on the speed at which the economy's long-run aggregate supply increases over time, which varies with factors such as productivity growth and the pace of technological improvements. Naturally, aggregate supply shocks can suddenly add to or subtract from the natural pace at which aggregate supply rises, thereby causing the potential real GDP growth rate to speed up or slow down unexpectedly.

Whenever the rate of growth of potential real GDP rises or falls, so does the value of the neutral federal funds rate. The FOMC, in turn, must respond by *changing* the target for the federal funds rate that it includes in the FOMC Directive transmitted to the Trading Desk. This explains why you so often see media reports speculating about whether the "Fed has decided to push interest rates up" or to "push interest rates down." The FOMC is always trying to aim at a moving interest rate target—a neutral federal funds rate that varies as economic conditions change.

The Taylor Rule

In light of the difficulties the Fed faces in determining the neutral federal funds rate at any given point in time, could an easier procedure exist for selecting a federal funds rate target? In 1990, John Taylor suggested a relatively simple equation that the Fed might use for this purpose. This equation would direct the Fed to set the federal funds rate target based on an estimated long-run real interest rate, the current deviation of the actual inflation rate from the Fed's inflation objective, and the proportionate gap between actual real GDP and a measure of potential real GDP. Taylor and other economists have applied his equation, which has become known as the **Taylor rule,** to actual Fed policy choices. They have concluded that the Taylor rule's

Neutral federal funds rate
A value of the interest rate on interbank loans at which the growth rate of real GDP tends neither to rise nor to fall relative to the rate of growth of potential, long-run, real GDP, given the expected rate of inflation.

> ### You Are There
>
> To contemplate why choosing the target for the federal funds rate can sometimes be a challenging task for the Federal Open Market Committee, read **It's Time for the FOMC to Make a Tough Call,** on pages 437 and 438.

Taylor rule
An equation that specifies a federal funds rate target based on an estimated long-run real interest rate, the current deviation of the actual inflation rate from the Federal Reserve's inflation objective, and the gap between actual real GDP and a measure of potential real GDP.

recommendations for federal funds rate target values come close to the actual targets the Fed has selected over time.

PLOTTING THE TAYLOR RULE ON A GRAPH The Federal Reserve Bank of St. Louis now regularly tracks target levels for the federal funds rate predicted by a basic Taylor-rule equation. Figure 17-8 displays paths of both the actual federal funds rate (the red line) and alternative Taylor-rule recommendations under different assumptions about the Fed's inflation objective (represented by green lines consistent with goals of 0, 1, 2, 3, or 4 percent inflation).

When the actual federal funds rate is at a level consistent with a particular inflation rate goal, then the Taylor rule indicates that Fed policymaking will tend to produce that inflation rate. For instance, at the middle of 2002 the actual federal funds rate was at a level that the Taylor rule specified to be consistent with a 3 percent inflation target.

ASSESSING THE STANCE OF FED POLICY WITH THE TAYLOR RULE Suppose that the actual federal funds rate is *below* the rate implied by a particular inflation goal. In this situation, the Taylor rule implies that the Fed's policymaking is expansionary. As a consequence, the actual inflation rate will rise above the Fed's goal for the inflation rate. Thus, during most of the 2003–2005 interval, the actual federal funds rate was below the level consistent with a 4 percent inflation rate. This implies that Fed policymaking was very expansionary during this period, sufficiently so as to be expected to yield a long-run inflation rate in excess of 4 percent per year. The Taylor-rule graph implies that in the first half of 2007, the Fed's policy stance became much more contractionary, with the actual federal funds rate above the level consistent with 0 percent inflation. Then, the graph suggests, Fed policymaking became expansionary once more during 2008.

Until recently, the actual federal funds rate remained relatively close to the Taylor-rule predictions over time. Since 2003, the Fed has deviated from setting its federal funds rate target in a manner consistent with the Taylor rule.

FIGURE 17-8

Actual Federal Funds Rates and Values Predicted by a Taylor Rule

This figure displays both the actual path of the federal funds rate since 1999 and the target paths specified by a Taylor-rule equation for alternative annual inflation objectives of 0, 1, 2, 3, and 4 percent.

Source: Federal Reserve Bank of St. Louis; *Monetary Trends,* various issues.

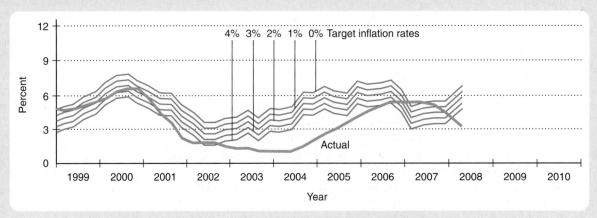

Why do some economists promote the "Taylor principle" as a supplement to the Taylor rule?

POLICY EXAMPLE
Supplementing the Taylor Rule with the Taylor Principle

The Taylor rule yields a proposed target for the federal funds rate that is based on both the Fed's inflation goal and the gap between actual and potential real GDP. The rule's designer, John Taylor, has also suggested adding another element to the proposed rule, now known as the *Taylor principle*: The Fed should adjust its federal funds rate target more than one-for-one with movements in inflation. That is, if the inflation rate rises by 0.25 percentage point, the Taylor principle calls for the Fed to boost the federal funds rate by more than 0.25 percentage point.

A key presumption of the Taylor principle is that the public's expectations of inflation adjust rapidly to changes in actual inflation. Thus, the principle is based on the assumption that if the actual inflation rate rises by 0.25 percentage point, inflation expectations will reflect this change. Thus, if the Fed fails to push the federal funds rate up by at least 0.25 percentage point, the *real* federal funds rate—the difference between the nominal federal funds rate that the Fed targets and the expected inflation rate—will actually decline. A fall in the real interest rate would give businesses an incentive to raise their planned investment spending, thereby causing aggregate demand to rise and pushing up the price level and actual inflation. In contrast, raising the federal funds rate more than one-for-one with an increase in the inflation rate ensures that the real federal funds rate will rise, which automatically tends to dampen inflation.

FOR CRITICAL ANALYSIS
Why is it impossible for the Fed to precisely target the real federal funds rate? (Hint: Can the Fed "control" inflation expectations?)

QUICK QUIZ   *See page 444 for the answers. Review concepts from this section in MyEconLab.*

At present, the policy strategy of the Federal Open Market Committee (FOMC) focuses on aiming for a target value of the _____ _____ rate, which the FOMC seeks to achieve via _____ _____ _____ that alter the supply of reserves to the banking system.

The FOMC outlines the Fed's general monetary policy strategy in the FOMC _____, which it transmits to the Trading Desk of the Federal Reserve Bank of _____ _____ for implementation.

In principle, the appropriate target for the federal funds rate is the _____ federal funds rate. Given the difficulties in determining this rate, some economists have promoted the _____ _____, which is based on an equation involving an estimated long-run real interest rate, the deviation of inflation from the Fed's inflation goal, and the gap between actual real GDP and potential real GDP.

You Are There   ▶ It's Time for the FOMC to Make a Tough Call

Janet Yellen, president and chief executive officer of the Federal Reserve Bank of San Francisco, steps to the podium. She is about to address members of the National Association of Business Economists in San Francisco. The topic of her speech is "Recent Financial Developments and the U.S. Economic Outlook." All ears in the room are attuned to her remarks. Even though Yellen is not currently among the voting members of the Federal Open Market Committee, many in the audience believe that her views reflect the FOMC's policy perspective.

You Are There (cont.)

The economists listening to Yellen's speech know that the FOMC faces a difficult decision. U.S. financial markets have been in turmoil following a sharp rise in mortgage loan delinquencies and foreclosures. A number of observers, including several prominent economists in the audience, have argued that the FOMC should not reduce its target for the federal funds rate. Pushing down interest rates, they worry, would be tantamount to "bailing out" investors who had taken on considerable financial risks during the preceding several years. If the Fed pushes down interest rates, these observers fear, it may create a moral hazard problem by leading investors to believe that the Fed will protect them from such risks in the future. In contrast, others in the audience have argued that the mortgage loan disruptions have contributed to falling housing prices and hence lower household wealth. These economists are concerned that consumers are responding by reducing spending, which is causing firms to cut back on production and employment. In their view, a significant cut in the FOMC's target for the federal funds rate is already overdue.

Yellen begins to speak. As she gets farther into her prepared remarks, those in the audience opposed to a cut in interest rates begin to frown. Many in the audience, however, break into open smiles. It is clear that the strong emphasis of her speech is on the downside risks faced by the U.S. economy. There are hints, she suggests, that real GDP is falling below potential real GDP and that inflation is subdued. To all the economists in the room, her statements provide a clear signal that the FOMC is leaning toward reducing its target for the federal funds rate.

A few days later, both groups learn that their reactions to Yellen's speech were appropriate. The FOMC cuts the federal funds rate by 0.5 percentage point.

CRITICAL ANALYSIS QUESTIONS

1. Based on Yellen's summary of the conditions prevailing at the time of her speech, do you think that a Taylor rule might have prescribed a reduction in the Fed's target for the federal funds rate? (Hint: Also take a look back at the early 2007 period in Figure 17-8 on page 436.)

2. What type of open market operations would the Trading Desk have implemented in order to generate the 0.5-percentage-point reduction in the federal funds rate specified in the FOMC Directive issued a few days after Yellen's speech?

The Fed Tackles a Credit Crisis

Issues and Applications

CONCEPTS APPLIED

- ➤ Neutral Federal Funds Rate
- ➤ Trading Desk
- ➤ FOMC Directive

The late 2000s were a tough period for many U.S. financial institutions. They were also trying times for the Federal Reserve, which implemented a number of policy actions intended to maintain financial stability.

The Housing Crisis Changes the Equation

Throughout the 2000s, as in preceding years, various financial institutions, such as savings banks, extended mortgage loans to finance most households' home purchases. Among these were loans to lower-income households, known among bankers as *subprime loans* because lending to such households involved greater risks than lending to higher-income, more creditworthy households. The depository institutions then sold most of these mortgage loans to agencies such as the Federal National Mortgage Loan Association, which in turn sold shares in the mortgages—called *mortgage-backed securities*—to individual investors.

In 2007 and 2008, market clearing prices of houses dropped throughout much of the United States. In a number of locales, house prices dropped so low that the market values of homes fell below the amounts that depository institutions had loaned to households when they purchased their homes. For many low-income households, it made little sense to continue paying off loans that exceeded the values of the properties they had purchased. Others simply exhausted their household resources attempting to pay off their loans. Either way, the result was a steady wave of *foreclosures*, in which numerous houses became the properties of mortgage lenders. These houses were worth less than the original loans, however, so lenders and investors who had bought shares in those loans experienced large losses.

These significant mortgage loan losses had several consequences. One consequence was that savings banks and other financial institutions began cutting back on lending in an effort to avoid ending up with any more bad loans. Another was that many private investors stopped purchasing mortgage-backed securities. Furthermore, financial institutions began to lose trust in each other. In the absence of information about just how exposed other institutions might be to loan losses that could result in bank failures, some financial institution managers were hesitant to lend even in the federal funds market. Thus,

sources of funds to all financial institutions began to dry up, resulting in a protracted credit crisis.

Fed Crisis Management Shifts into High Gear

The Federal Reserve sought to combat the credit crisis along several dimensions. First, once it had determined that the neutral federal funds rate had been pushed down by the credit crisis, the Fed adjusted two of its monetary policy tools: (1) The Federal Open Market Committee issued a series of FOMC Directives instructing the Trading Desk to implement significant reductions in the target federal funds rate. (2) The Fed's Board of Governors reduced the differential between the discount rate and the federal funds rate in an effort to make direct borrowing from Federal Reserve banks more attractive.

Second, the Fed created a temporary supplemental mechanism for dispersing reserves directly to depository institutions. It established a *Term Auction Facility*, a mechanism through which it periodically sold reserves to the highest bidders for their use during fixed intervals, under an agreement that the winning bidders would return the funds plus interest.

Third, the Fed used emergency powers granted by the Banking Act of 1935 to broaden the scope of its lending activities. Among the institutions hardest hit by the credit crisis were Wall Street investment and brokerage firms. After consulting with Congress, the Fed began allowing these firms to borrow funds from Federal Reserve banks. There was a precondition to this access to the discount window, however: The Wall Street firms had to agree to permit Fed supervisors to examine these firms' income statements and balance sheets on a regular basis. Thus, investment and brokerage firms that utilized the discount window essentially had to submit themselves to regulatory oversight similar to the Fed supervision faced by depository institutions.

Test your understanding of this chapter by going online to **MyEconLab.**
In the Study Plan for this chapter, select Section N: News.

For Critical Analysis

1. How was the Fed's Term Auction Facility similar in function to the discount window? How did the Term Auction Facility operate differently than the discount window?

2. When the Fed grants access to discount window loans to financial institutions, why do you suppose it requires them to submit to regular supervisory examinations?

Web Resources

1. For background on how losses on subprime mortgage loans triggered the credit crisis of the late 2000s, go to www.econtoday.com/chapter17.

2. To read a summary of some of the Fed's key crisis-management policies, go to www.econtoday.com/chapter17.

Research Project

During a financial crisis, the demand for money often rises, because people desire to have greater liquidity. In such a situation, how must the Fed adjust the money supply if it wishes to push the market interest rate even lower instead of permitting it to increase? In light of your answer, what can you predict happened to the rate of money supply growth and the inflation rate in the late 2000s, other things being equal? Use a money supply–money demand diagram, an aggregate demand–aggregate supply diagram, and the equation of exchange to help explain your answer.

 Here is what you should know after reading this chapter. **MyEconLab** will help you identify what you know, and where to go when you need to practice.

WHAT YOU SHOULD KNOW		WHERE TO GO TO PRACTICE
How Expansionary and Contractionary Monetary Policies Affect Equilibrium Real GDP and the Price Level in the Short Run By pushing up the money supply and inducing a fall in market interest rates, an expansionary monetary policy action causes total planned expenditures to rise at any given price level. Hence, the aggregate demand curve shifts rightward, which can eliminate a short-run recessionary gap in real GDP. In contrast, a contractionary monetary policy action reduces the money supply and causes an increase in market interest rates, thereby generating a fall in total planned expenditures at any given price level. This results in a leftward shift in the aggregate demand curve, which can eliminate a short-run inflationary gap.	KEY FIGURES Figure 17-1, 424 Figure 17-2, 424	• **MyEconLab** Study Plans 17.1, 17.2 • Audio introduction to Chapter 17 • Animated Figures 17-1, 17-2
The Equation of Exchange and the Quantity Theory of Money and Prices The equation of exchange is a truism that states that the quantity of money in circulation times the average number of times a unit of money is used in exchange—the income velocity of money—must equal nominal GDP, or the price level times real GDP. The quantity theory of money and prices assumes that the income velocity of money is constant and real GDP is relatively stable. Thus, a rise in the quantity of money leads to an equiproportional increase in the price level.	equation of exchange, 427 income velocity of money (V), 427 quantity theory of money and prices, 427	• **MyEconLab** Study Plan 17.3 • Video: The Quantity Theory of Money

(continued)

 *(continued)*

WHAT YOU SHOULD KNOW

WHERE TO GO TO PRACTICE

The Interest-Rate-Based Transmission Mechanism of Monetary Policy The interest-rate-based approach to the monetary policy transmission mechanism operates through effects of monetary policy actions on market interest rates, which bring about changes in desired investment and thereby affect equilibrium real GDP via the multiplier effect.

KEY FIGURES
Figure 17-4, 429
Figure 17-5, 430

- **MyEconLab** Study Plan 17.4
- Animated Figures 17-4, 17-5
- Video: The Monetary Rule

Why the Federal Reserve Cannot Stabilize the Money Supply and the Interest Rate Simultaneously To target the money supply, the Fed must let the market interest rate vary whenever the demand for money rises or falls. Thus, stabilizing the money supply entails some interest rate volatility. To target the interest rate, however, the Federal Reserve must be willing to adjust the money supply when there are variations in the demand for money. Hence, stabilizing the interest rate requires variations in the money supply.

KEY FIGURE
Figure 17-6, 431

- **MyEconLab** Study Plans 17.5, 17.6
- Animated Figure 17-6

How the Federal Reserve Achieves a Target Value of the Federal Funds Rate At present, the Fed uses an interest rate target, which is the federal funds rate, or the interest rate at which banks can borrow excess reserves from other banks. This interest rate is at an equilibrium level when the quantity of reserves demanded by banks—the sum of required reserves and excess reserves—equals the quantity of reserves supplied by the Fed. The Trading Desk at the Federal Reserve Bank of New York is responsible for achieving the target for the federal funds rate specified by the policy Directive of the Federal Open Market Committee (FOMC). The Trading Desk conducts open market purchases or sales to alter the supply of reserves as necessary to keep the equilibrium federal funds rate at the FOMC's target.

FOMC Directive, 434
Trading Desk, 434

- **MyEconLab** Study Plans 17.5, 17.6

Issues the Federal Reserve Confronts in Selecting Its Target for the Federal Funds Rate In principle, the Federal Open Market Committee's target is the neutral federal funds rate, at which the growth rate of real GDP tends neither to rise above nor fall below the rate of growth of long-run potential real GDP. It is difficult, however, for Fed policymakers to identify the neutral federal funds rate, particularly because it varies over time with changes in factors such as productivity growth and technological change. For this reason, some economists favor using a Taylor rule to determine the federal funds rate target. A Taylor rule specifies an equation for the federal funds rate target based on an estimated long-run real interest rate, the current deviation of actual inflation from the Fed's inflation goal, and the gap between actual real GDP and a measure of potential real GDP.

neutral federal funds rate, 435
Taylor rule, 435

- **MyEconLab** Study Plans 17.5, 17.6

Log in to MyEconLab, take a chapter test, and get a personalized Study Plan that tells you which concepts you understand and which ones you need to review. From there, MyEconLab will give you further practice, tutorials, animations, videos, and guided solutions.
Log in to www.myeconlab.com

PROBLEMS

All problems are assignable in 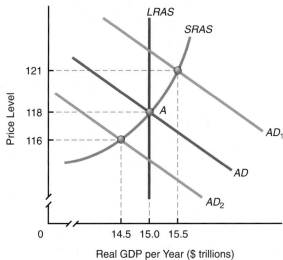 *myeconlab. Answers to odd-numbered problems appear at the back of the book.*

17-1. You learned in Chapter 11 that if there is an inflationary gap in the short run, then in the long run a new equilibrium arises when input prices and expectations adjust upward, causing the aggregate supply curve to shift upward and to the left and pushing equilibrium real GDP back to its long-run potential value. In this chapter, however, you learned that the Federal Reserve can eliminate an inflationary gap in the short run by undertaking a policy action that reduces aggregate demand.

   a. Propose one monetary policy action that could eliminate an inflationary gap in the short run.

   b. In what way might society gain if the Fed implements the policy you have proposed instead of simply permitting long-run adjustments to take place?

17-2. In addition, you learned in Chapter 11 that if there is a recessionary gap in the short run, then in the long run a new equilibrium arises when input prices and expectations adjust downward, causing the aggregate supply curve to shift downward and to the right and pushing equilibrium real GDP back to its long-run potential value. In this chapter, however, you learned that the Federal Reserve can eliminate a recessionary gap in the short run by undertaking a policy action that raises aggregate demand.

   a. Propose a monetary policy action that could eliminate a recessionary gap in the short run but uses a different tool of monetary policy than the one you considered in Problem 17-1.

   b. In what way might society gain if the Fed implements the policy you have proposed instead of simply permitting long-run adjustments to take place?

17-3. Explain why the net export effect of a contractionary monetary policy reinforces the usual impact that monetary policy has on equilibrium real GDP in the short run.

17-4. Suppose that, initially, the U.S. economy was in an aggregate demand–aggregate supply equilibrium at point *A* along the aggregate demand curve *AD* in the diagram in the next column. Now, however, the value of the U.S. dollar has suddenly appreciated relative to foreign currencies. This appreciation

happens to have no measurable effects on either the short-run or the long-run aggregate supply curve in the United States. It does, however, influence U.S. aggregate demand.

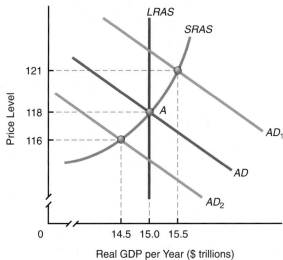

   a. Explain in your own words how the dollar appreciation will affect U.S. net export expenditures.

   b. Of the alternative aggregate demand curves depicted in the figure—AD_1 versus AD_2—which could represent the aggregate demand effect of the U.S. dollar's appreciation? What effects does the appreciation have on real GDP and the price level?

   c. What policy action might the Federal Reserve take to prevent the dollar's appreciation from affecting equilibrium real GDP in the short run?

17-5. Use a diagram to illustrate how the Fed can reduce inflationary pressures by conducting open market sales of U.S. government securities.

17-6. Suppose that the quantity of money in circulation is fixed but the income velocity of money doubles. If real GDP remains at its long-run potential level, what happens to the equilibrium price level?

17-7. Suppose that following the events in Problem 17-6, the Fed cuts the money supply in half. How does the price level now compare with its value before the income velocity and the money supply changed?

17-8. Consider the following data: The money supply is $1 trillion, the price level equals 2, and real GDP is $5 trillion in base-year dollars. What is the income velocity of money?

17-9. Consider the data in Problem 17-8. Suppose that the money supply increases by $100 billion and real GDP and the income velocity remain unchanged.

    a. According to the quantity theory of money and prices, what is the new price level after the increase in the money supply?

    b. What is the percentage increase in the money supply?

    c. What is the percentage change in the price level?

    d. How do the percentage changes in the money supply and price level compare?

17-10. Assuming that the Fed judges inflation to be the most significant problem in the economy and that it wishes to employ all three of its policy instruments, what should the Fed do with its three policy tools?

17-11. Suppose that the Fed implements each of the policy changes you discussed in Problem 17-10. Now explain how the net export effect resulting from these monetary policy actions will reinforce their effects that operate through interest rate changes.

17-12. Suppose that the Federal Reserve wishes to keep the nominal interest rate at a target level of 4 percent. Draw a money supply and demand diagram in which the current equilibrium interest rate is 4 percent. Explain a specific policy action that the Fed, using one of its three tools of monetary policy, could take to keep the interest rate at its target level if the demand for money suddenly declines.

17-13. Imagine working at the Trading Desk at the New York Fed. Explain whether you would conduct open market purchases or sales in response to each of the following events. Justify your recommendation.

    a. The latest FOMC Directive calls for an increase in the target value of the federal funds rate.

    b. For a reason unrelated to monetary policy, the Fed's Board of Governors has decided to raise the differential between the discount rate and the federal funds rate. Nevertheless, the FOMC

Directive calls for maintaining the present federal funds rate target.

17-14. Consider the following diagram of the market for bank reserves, in which the current equilibrium value of the federal funds rate, 5.50 percent, also corresponds to the Federal Open Market Committee's target for this interest rate.

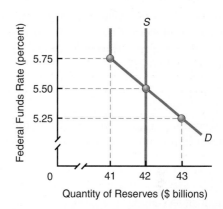

    a. Suppose that the FOMC issues a new Directive to the Trading Desk at the Federal Reserve Bank of New York specifying a new federal funds rate target of 5.25 percent. What policy action should the Trading Desk implement to comply with the new FOMC Directive?

    b. Explain the adjustments that will take place in the above diagram following the policy action you identified in part (a).

17-15. Explain the concept of the neutral federal funds rate in your own words, and then answer the following questions.

    a. Suppose that the Federal Open Market Committee's current target for the federal funds rate is lower than the neutral federal funds rate that Fed staff economists are confident they have correctly identified. If the FOMC is convinced that the Fed staff economists are correct, what new policy strategy should the FOMC implement with its next Directive to the Trading Desk?

    b. What action should the Trading Desk undertake to carry out the new FOMC policy strategy you identified in part (a)?

ECONOMICS ON THE NET

The Fed's Policy Report to Congress Congress requires the Fed to make periodic reports on its recent activities. In this application, you will study recent reports to learn about what factors affect Fed decisions.

Title: Monetary Policy Report to the Congress

Navigation: Go to **www.econtoday.com/chapter17** to view the Federal Reserve's Monetary Policy Report to the Congress (formerly called the Humphrey-Hawkins Report).

Application Read the report; then answer the following questions.

1. According to the report, what economic events were most important in shaping recent monetary policy?

2. Based on the report, what are the Fed's current monetary policy goals?

For Group Study and Analysis Divide the class into "domestic" and "foreign" groups. Have each group read the past four monetary policy reports and then explain to the class how domestic and foreign factors, respectively, appear to have influenced recent Fed monetary policy decisions. Which of the two types of factors seems to have mattered most during the past year?

ANSWERS TO QUICK QUIZZES

p. 425: (i) direct; (ii) indirect . . . reduction . . . lower
p. 426: (i) exports; (ii) negative . . . more . . . more; (iii) fewer . . . decrease . . . increase
p. 429: (i) equation . . . exchange; (ii) true . . . spent . . . received; (iii) money supply . . . price level
p. 432: (i) interest rates . . . investment; (ii) interest rate . . . money . . . money; (iii) interest rate . . . money supply
p. 437: (i) federal funds . . . open market operations; (ii) Directive . . . New York; (iii) neutral . . . Taylor rule

Monetary Policy: A Keynesian Perspective

According to the traditional Keynesian approach to monetary policy, changes in the money supply can affect the level of aggregate demand only through their effect on interest rates. Moreover, interest rate changes act on aggregate demand solely by changing the level of real planned investment spending. Finally, the traditional Keynesian approach argues that there are plausible circumstances under which monetary policy may have little or no effect on interest rates and thus on aggregate demand.

Figure D-1 measures real GDP along the horizontal axis and total planned expenditures (aggregate demand) along the vertical axis. The components of aggregate demand are real consumption (C), investment (I), government spending (G), and net exports (X). The height of the schedule labeled $C + I + G + X$ shows total real planned expenditures (aggregate demand) as a function of real GDP. This schedule slopes upward because consumption depends positively on real GDP. All along the line labeled $Y = C + I + G + X$, real planned spending equals real GDP. At point Y^*, where the $C + I + G + X$ line intersects this 45-degree reference line, real planned spending is consistent with real GDP. At any real GDP level less than Y^*, spending exceeds real GDP, so real GDP and thus spending will tend to rise. At any level of real GDP greater than Y^*, real planned spending is less than real GDP, so real GDP and thus spending will tend to decline. Given the determinants of C, I, G, and X, total spending (aggregate demand) will be Y^*.

Increasing the Money Supply

According to the Keynesian approach, an increase in the money supply pushes interest rates down. This induces firms to increase the level of investment spending from I to I'. As a result, the $C + I + G + X$ line shifts upward in Figure D-1 by the full

---

FIGURE D-1

An Increase in the Money Supply

An increase in the money supply increases real GDP by lowering interest rates and thus increasing investment from I to I'.

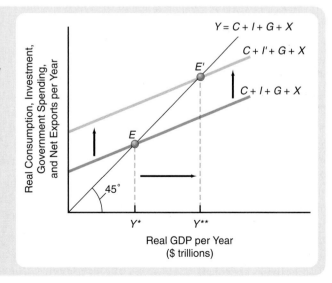

amount of the rise in investment spending, thus yielding the line $C + I' + G + X$. The rise in investment spending causes real GDP to rise, which in turn causes real consumption spending to rise, which further increases real GDP. Ultimately, aggregate demand rises to Y^{**}, where spending again equals real GDP. A key conclusion of the Keynesian analysis is that total spending rises by *more* than the original rise in investment spending because consumption spending depends positively on real GDP.

Decreasing the Money Supply

Not surprisingly, contractionary monetary policy works in exactly the reverse manner. A reduction in the money supply pushes interest rates up. Firms respond by reducing their investment spending, and this pushes real GDP downward. Consumers react to the lower real GDP by scaling back on their real consumption spending, which further depresses real GDP. Thus, the ultimate decline in real GDP is larger than the initial drop in investment spending. Indeed, because the change in real GDP is a multiple of the change in investment, Keynesians note that changes in investment spending (similar to changes in government spending) have a *multiplier* effect on the economy.

Arguments Against Monetary Policy

It might be thought that this multiplier effect would make monetary policy a potent tool in the Keynesian arsenal, particularly when it comes to getting the economy out of a recession. In fact, however, many traditional Keynesians argue that monetary policy is likely to be relatively ineffective as a recession fighter. According to their line of reasoning, although monetary policy has the potential to reduce interest rates, changes in the money supply have little *actual* impact on interest rates. Instead, during recessions, people try to build up as much as they can in liquid assets to protect themselves from risks of unemployment and other losses of income. When the monetary authorities increase the money supply, individuals are willing to allow most of it to accumulate in their bank accounts. This desire for increased liquidity thus prevents interest rates from falling very much, which in turn means that there will be virtually no change in investment spending and thus little change in aggregate demand.

PROBLEMS

All problems are assignable in myeconlab. *Answers to odd-numbered problems appear at the back of the book.*

D-1. Suppose that each 0.1-percentage-point decrease in the equilibrium interest rate induces a $10 billion increase in real planned investment spending by businesses. In addition, the investment multiplier is equal to 5, and the money multiplier is equal to 4. Furthermore, every $20 billion increase in the money supply brings about a 0.1-percentage-point reduction in the equilibrium interest rate. Use this information to answer the following questions under the assumption that all other things are equal.

a. How much must real planned investment increase if the Federal Reserve desires to bring about a $100 billion increase in equilibrium real GDP?

b. How much must the money supply change for the Fed to induce the change in real planned investment calculated in part (a)?

c. What dollar amount of open market operations must the Fed undertake to bring about the money supply change calculated in part (b)?

D-2. Suppose that each 0.1-percentage-point increase in the equilibrium interest rate induces a $5 billion decrease in real planned investment spending by businesses. In addition, the investment multiplier is equal to 4, and the money multiplier is equal to 3. Furthermore, every $9 billion decrease in the money supply brings about a 0.1-percentage-point increase in the equilibrium interest rate. Use this information to answer the following questions under the assumption that all other things are equal.

a. How much must real planned investment decrease if the Federal Reserve desires to bring about an $80 billion decrease in equilibrium real GDP?

b. How much must the money supply change for the Fed to induce the change in real planned investment calculated in part (a)?

c. What dollar amount of open market operations must the Fed undertake to bring about the money supply change calculated in part (b)?

D-3. Assume that the following conditions exist:

a. All banks are fully loaned up—there are no excess reserves, and desired excess reserves are always zero.

b. The money multiplier is 3.

c. The planned investment schedule is such that at a 6 percent rate of interest, investment is $1,200 billion; at 5 percent, investment is $1,225 billion.

d. The investment multiplier is 3.

e. The initial equilibrium level of real GDP is $12 trillion.

f. The equilibrium rate of interest is 6 percent.

Now the Fed engages in expansionary monetary policy. It buys $1 billion worth of bonds, which increases the money supply, which in turn lowers the market rate of interest by 1 percentage point. Determine how much the money supply must have increased, and then trace out the numerical consequences of the associated reduction in interest rates on all the other variables mentioned.

D-4. Assume that the following conditions exist:

a. All banks are fully loaned up—there are no excess reserves, and desired excess reserves are always zero.

b. The money multiplier is 4.

c. The planned investment schedule is such that at a 4 percent rate of interest, investment is $1,400 billion. At 5 percent, investment is $1,380 billion.

d. The investment multiplier is 5.

e. The initial equilibrium level of real GDP is $13 trillion.

f. The equilibrium rate of interest is 4 percent.

Now the Fed engages in contractionary monetary policy. It sells $2 billion worth of bonds, which reduces the money supply, which in turn raises the market rate of interest by 1 percentage point. Determine how much the money supply must have decreased, and then trace out the numerical consequences of the associated increase in interest rates on all the other variables mentioned.

18

Stabilization in an Integrated World Economy

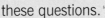

ate in the spring of 2003, Federal Reserve officials openly worried that the annual inflation rate might be dropping too low, and they responded by implementing expansionary monetary policy actions. Actual inflation rose. So too did expectations of future inflation. By 2007, some in the Fed were publicly suggesting that because inflation expectations had increased, reducing inflation would be difficult and time-consuming. Hence, the Fed officials concluded, society might be better off accepting slightly higher inflation. How do changes in actual inflation influence the public's inflation expectations? How do changes in expectations of future inflation affect actual inflation? Do the answers to these questions have anything to do with variations in real GDP and the unemployment rate? This chapter addresses these questions.

LEARNING OBJECTIVES

myeconlab

MyEconLab helps you master each objective and study more efficiently. See end of chapter for details.

After reading this chapter, you should be able to:

➤ Explain why the actual unemployment rate might depart from the natural rate of unemployment

➤ Describe why there may be an inverse relationship between the inflation rate and the unemployment rate, reflected by the Phillips curve

➤ Evaluate how expectations affect the actual relationship between the inflation rate and the unemployment rate

➤ Understand the rational expectations hypothesis and its implications for economic policymaking

➤ Distinguish among alternative modern approaches to strengthening the case for active policymaking

? **DID YOU KNOW THAT** the average length of the 21 U.S. recessions that have occurred since the beginning of the twentieth century is about 15 months? In recent decades, the average recession has shortened. Between 1900 and 1945, an average recession lasted 19 months. Since 1945, the average duration of a recession has fallen to approximately 9 months.

At the same time, business expansions have lengthened. Not including the most recent expansion, the 20 expansions since the start of the twentieth century have had an average length of 39 months. Splitting the twentieth century into two periods, the average expansion between 1900 and 1945 lasted about 31 months. The average duration of an expansion since 1945 has been 50 months.

To some observers, shorter recessions and longer expansions have obviously resulted from improved monetary and fiscal policymaking. Others, however, are not so sure that policymakers really deserve much of the credit.

Active versus Passive Policymaking

Central to determining if policymakers deserve a collective pat on the back is whether the credit for a generally more stable U.S. economy should be given to **active (discretionary) policymaking.** This is the term for actions that monetary and fiscal policymakers undertake in reaction to or in anticipation of a change in economic performance. On the other side of the debate is the view that the best way to achieve economic stability is through **passive (nondiscretionary) policymaking,** in which there is no deliberate stabilization policy at all. Policymakers follow a rule and do not attempt to respond in a discretionary manner to actual or potential changes in economic activity. Recall from Chapter 13 that there are lags between the time when the national economy enters a recession or a boom and the time when that fact becomes known and acted on by policymakers. Proponents of passive policy argue that such time lags often render short-term stabilization policy ineffective or, worse, procyclical.

To take a stand on this debate concerning active versus passive policymaking, you first need to know the potential trade-offs that policymakers believe they face. Then you need to see what the data actually show. The most important policy trade-off appears to be between price stability and unemployment. Before exploring that, however, we need to look at the economy's natural, or long-run, rate of unemployment.

Active (discretionary) policymaking
All actions on the part of monetary and fiscal policymakers that are undertaken in response to or in anticipation of some change in the overall economy.

Passive (nondiscretionary) policymaking
Policymaking that is carried out in response to a rule. It is therefore not in response to an actual or potential change in overall economic activity.

You Are There

To consider how the Fed might passively target the inflation rate, read **Inflation Targeting Catches On—Except at the Fed,** on page 470.

The Natural Rate of Unemployment

Recall from Chapter 7 that there are different types of unemployment: frictional, cyclical, structural, and seasonal. *Frictional unemployment* arises because individuals take the time to search for the best job opportunities. Much unemployment is of this type, except when the economy is in a recession or a depression, when cyclical unemployment rises.

Note that we did not say that frictional unemployment was the *sole* form of unemployment during normal times. *Structural unemployment* is caused by a variety of "rigidities" throughout the economy. Structural unemployment results from factors such as these:

1. Government-imposed minimum wage laws, laws restricting entry into occupations, and welfare and unemployment insurance benefits that reduce incentives to work

2. Union activity that sets wages above the equilibrium level and also restricts the mobility of labor

All of these factors reduce individuals' abilities or incentives to choose employment rather than unemployment.

Consider the effect of unemployment insurance benefits on the probability of an unemployed person's finding a job. When unemployment benefits run out, according to economists Lawrence Katz and Bruce Meyer, the probability of an unemployed person's finding a job doubles. The conclusion is that unemployed workers are more serious about finding a job when they are no longer receiving such benefits.

Frictional unemployment and structural unemployment both exist even when the economy is in long-run equilibrium—they are a natural consequence of costly information (the need to conduct a job search) and the existence of rigidities such as those noted above. Because these two types of unemployment are a natural consequence of imperfect and costly information and rigidities, they are components of what economists call the **natural rate of unemployment.** As we discussed in Chapter 7, this is defined as the rate of unemployment that would exist in the long run after everyone in the economy fully adjusted to any changes that have occurred. Recall that real GDP tends to return to the level implied by the long-run aggregate supply curve (*LRAS*). Thus, whatever rate of unemployment the economy tends to return to in long-run equilibrium can be called the natural rate of unemployment.

How has the natural rate of unemployment changed over the years?

Natural rate of unemployment
The rate of unemployment that is estimated to prevail in long-run macroeconomic equilibrium, when all workers and employers have fully adjusted to any changes in the economy.

EXAMPLE
The U.S. Natural Rate of Unemployment

In 1950, the unemployment rate was about 5 percent. By the late 2000s, it was at this level once again. These two nearly matching endpoints of unemployment rates prove nothing by themselves. But look at Figure 18-1. There you see not only what has happened to the unemployment rate over that same time period but an estimate of the natural rate of unemployment. The line labeled "Natural rate of unemployment" is produced by averaging unemployment rates from five years earlier to

five years later at each point in time (except for the end period, which is estimated). This computation reveals that until the late 1980s, the natural rate of unemployment was rising. But since then, a generally downward trend has taken hold.

FOR CRITICAL ANALYSIS
Why does the natural rate of unemployment differ from the actual rate of unemployment?

EXAMPLE   (cont.)

FIGURE 18-1

Estimated Natural Rate of Unemployment in the United States

As you can see in this figure, the actual rate of unemployment has varied widely in the United States in recent decades. If we generate the natural rate of unemployment by averaging unemployment rates from five years earlier to five years later at each point in time, we get the line so labeled. It rose from the 1950s until the late 1980s and then gradually declined.

Sources: Economic Report of the President; Economic Indicators, various issues; author's estimates.

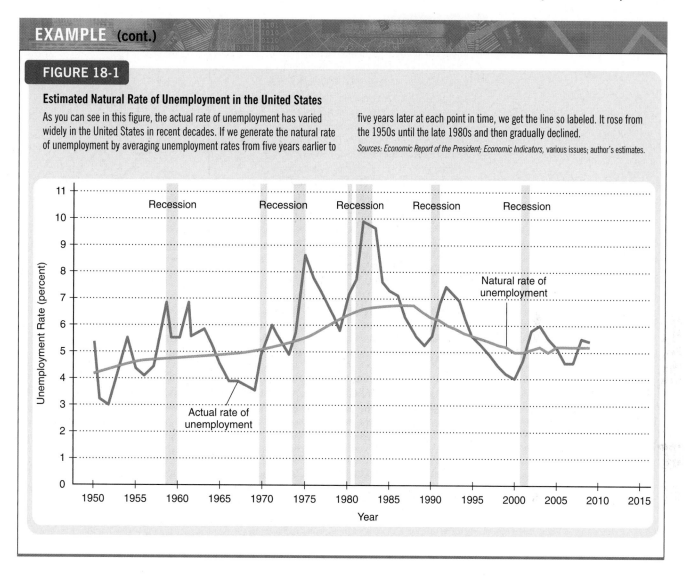

Departures from the Natural Rate of Unemployment

Even though the unemployment rate has a strong tendency to stay at and return to the natural rate, it is possible for other factors, such as changes in private spending or fiscal and monetary policy actions, to move the actual unemployment rate away from the natural rate, at least in the short run. Deviations of the actual unemployment rate from the natural rate are called *cyclical unemployment* because they are observed over the course of nationwide business fluctuations. During recessions, the overall unemployment rate exceeds the natural rate; cyclical unemployment is positive. During periods of economic booms, the overall unemployment rate can go below the natural rate; at such times, cyclical unemployment is negative.

To see how departures from the natural rate of unemployment can occur, let's consider two examples. In Figure 18-2 on the next page, we begin in equilibrium at point E_1 with the associated price level 117 and real GDP per year of $15 trillion.

FIGURE 18-2

Impact of an Increase in Aggregate Demand on Real GDP and Unemployment

If the economy is operating at E_1, it is in both short-run and long-run equilibrium. Here the actual rate of unemployment is equal to the natural rate of unemployment. Subsequent to expansionary monetary or fiscal policy, the aggregate demand curve shifts outward to AD_2. The price level rises from 117 to 120 at point E_2, and real GDP per year increases to $15.4 trillion in base-year dollars. The unemployment rate is now below its natural rate. We are at a short-run equilibrium at E_2. In the long run, expectations of input owners are revised. The short-run aggregate supply curve shifts from $SRAS_1$ to $SRAS_2$ because of higher prices and higher resource costs. Real GDP returns to the *LRAS* level of $15 trillion per year, at point E_3. The price level increases to 122. The unemployment rate returns to the natural rate.

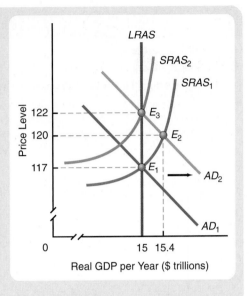

THE IMPACT OF EXPANSIONARY POLICY Now imagine that the government decides to use fiscal or monetary policy to stimulate the economy. Further suppose, for reasons that will soon become clear, that this policy surprises decision makers throughout the economy in the sense that they did not anticipate that the policy would occur.

As shown in Figure 18-2, the expansionary policy action causes the aggregate demand curve to shift from AD_1 to AD_2. The price level rises from 117 to 120. Real GDP, measured in base-year dollars, increases from $15 trillion to $15.4 trillion.

In the labor market, individuals find that conditions have improved markedly relative to what they expected. Firms seeking to expand output want to hire more workers. To accomplish this, they recruit more actively and possibly ask workers to work overtime, so individuals in the labor market find more job openings and more possible hours they can work. Consequently, as you learned in Chapter 7, the average duration of unemployment falls, and so does the unemployment rate.

The *SRAS* curve does not stay at $SRAS_1$ indefinitely, however. Input owners, such as workers and owners of capital and raw materials, revise their expectations. The short-run aggregate supply curve shifts to $SRAS_2$ as input prices rise. We find ourselves at a new equilibrium at E_3, which is on the *LRAS*. Long-run real GDP per year is $15 trillion again, but at a higher price level, 122. The unemployment rate returns to its original, natural level.

THE CONSEQUENCES OF CONTRACTIONARY POLICY Instead of expansionary policy, the government could have decided to engage in contractionary (or deflationary) policy. As shown in Figure 18-3, the sequence of events would have been in the opposite direction of those in Figure 18-2.

Beginning from an initial equilibrium E_1, an unanticipated reduction in aggregate demand puts downward pressure on both prices and real GDP; the price level falls from 120 to 118, and real GDP declines from $15 trillion to $14.7 trillion. Fewer firms are hiring, and those that are hiring offer fewer overtime possibilities. Individuals looking for jobs find that it takes longer than predicted. As a result, unemployed individuals remain unemployed longer. The average duration of unemployment rises, and so does the rate of unemployment.

FIGURE 18-3

Impact of a Decline in Aggregate Demand on Real GDP and Unemployment

Starting from equilibrium at E_1, a decline in aggregate demand to AD_2 leads to a lower price level, 118, and real GDP declines to $14.7 trillion. The unemployment rate will rise above the natural rate of unemployment. Equilibrium at E_2 is temporary, however. At the lower price level, the expectations of input owners are revised. $SRAS_1$ shifts to $SRAS_2$. The new long-run equilibrium is at E_3, with real GDP equal to $15 trillion and a price level of 116. The actual unemployment rate is once again equal to the natural rate of unemployment.

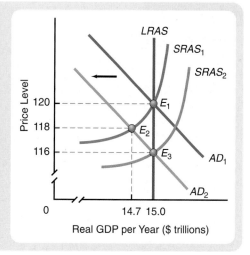

The equilibrium at E_2 is only a short-run situation, however. As input owners change their expectations about future prices, $SRAS_1$ shifts to $SRAS_2$, and input prices fall. The new long-run equilibrium is at E_3, which is on the long-run aggregate supply curve, *LRAS*. In the long run, the price level declines farther, to 116, as real GDP returns to $15 trillion. Thus, in the long run the unemployment rate returns to its natural level.

The Phillips Curve: A Rationale for Active Policymaking?

Let's recap what we have just observed. In the short run, an *unexpected increase* in aggregate demand causes the price level to rise and the unemployment rate to fall. Conversely, in the short run, an *unexpected decrease* in aggregate demand causes the price level to fall and the unemployment rate to rise. Moreover, although not shown explicitly in either diagram, two additional points are true:

1. The greater the unexpected increase in aggregate demand, the greater the amount of inflation that results in the short run, and the lower the unemployment rate.

2. The greater the unexpected decrease in aggregate demand, the greater the deflation that results in the short run, and the higher the unemployment rate.

THE NEGATIVE SHORT-RUN RELATIONSHIP BETWEEN INFLATION AND UNEMPLOYMENT Figure 18-4 on the following page summarizes these findings. The inflation rate (*not* the price level) is measured along the vertical axis, and the unemployment rate is measured along the horizontal axis. Point *A* shows an initial starting point, with the unemployment rate at the natural rate, *U**.

Note that as a matter of convenience, we are starting from an equilibrium in which the price level is stable (the inflation rate is zero). In the short run, unexpected increases in aggregate demand cause the price level to rise—the inflation rate becomes positive—and cause the unemployment rate to fall. Thus, the economy moves upward to the left from *A* to *B*.

Conversely, in the short run, unexpected decreases in aggregate demand cause the price level to fall and the unemployment rate to rise above the natural rate—the economy moves from point *A* to point *C*. If we look at both increases and decreases in aggregate demand, we see that high inflation rates tend to be associated with low unemployment rates (as at *B*) and that low (or negative) inflation rates tend to be accompanied by high unemployment rates (as at *C*).

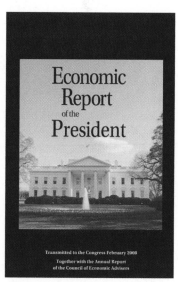

Do you think the economists who work for the president and who write the Economic Report of the President *are in favor of active or passive policymaking?*

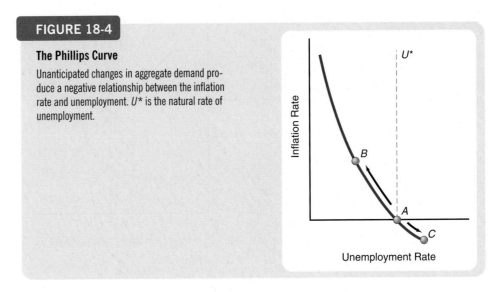

FIGURE 18-4

The Phillips Curve

Unanticipated changes in aggregate demand produce a negative relationship between the inflation rate and unemployment. U^* is the natural rate of unemployment.

Phillips curve

A curve showing the relationship between unemployment and changes in wages or prices. It was long thought to reflect a trade-off between unemployment and inflation.

IS THERE A TRADE-OFF? The apparent negative relationship between the inflation rate and the unemployment rate shown in Figure 18-4 has come to be called the **Phillips curve,** after A. W. Phillips, who discovered that a similar relationship existed historically in Great Britain. Although Phillips presented his findings only as an empirical regularity, economists quickly came to view the relationship as representing a *trade-off* between inflation and unemployment. In particular, policymakers who favored active policymaking believed that they could *choose* alternative combinations of unemployment and inflation. Thus, it seemed that a government that disliked unemployment could select a point like *B* in Figure 18-4, with a positive inflation rate but a relatively low unemployment rate. Conversely, a government that feared inflation could choose a stable price level at *A*, but only at the expense of a higher associated unemployment rate. Indeed, the Phillips curve seemed to suggest that it was possible for discretionary policymakers to fine-tune the economy by selecting the policies that would produce the exact mix of unemployment and inflation that suited current government objectives. As it turned out, matters are not so simple.

Nonaccelerating inflation rate of unemployment (NAIRU)

The rate of unemployment below which the rate of inflation tends to rise and above which the rate of inflation tends to fall.

THE NAIRU If one accepts that a trade-off exists between the rate of inflation and the rate of unemployment, then the notion of "noninflationary" rates of unemployment seems appropriate. In fact, some economists have proposed what they call the **nonaccelerating inflation rate of unemployment (NAIRU).** The NAIRU is the rate of unemployment that corresponds to a stable rate of inflation. When the unemployment rate is less than the NAIRU, the rate of inflation tends to increase. When the unemployment rate is more than the NAIRU, the rate of inflation tends to decrease. When the rate of unemployment is equal to the NAIRU, inflation continues at an unchanged rate. If the Phillips curve trade-off exists and if the NAIRU can be estimated, that estimate will define the potential short-run trade-off between the rate of unemployment and the rate of inflation.

DISTINGUISHING BETWEEN THE NATURAL UNEMPLOYMENT RATE AND THE NAIRU The NAIRU is not always the same as the natural rate of unemployment. Recall that the natural rate of unemployment is the unemployment rate that is observed whenever all cyclical factors have played themselves out. Thus, the natural unemployment rate applies to a long-run equilibrium in which any short-run adjustments have concluded. It depends on structural factors in the labor market and typically changes gradually over relatively lengthy intervals.

In contrast, the NAIRU is simply the rate of unemployment that is consistent at present with a steady rate of inflation. The unemployment rate consistent with a steady inflation rate can potentially change during the course of cyclical adjustments in the economy. Thus, the NAIRU typically varies by a relatively greater amount and relatively more frequently than the natural rate of unemployment.

The Importance of Expectations

The reduction in unemployment that takes place as the economy moves from A to B in Figure 18-4 occurs because the wage offers encountered by unemployed workers are unexpectedly high. As far as the workers are concerned, these higher *nominal* wages appear, at least initially, to be increases in *real* wages; it is this perception that induces them to reduce the duration of their job search. This is a sensible way for the workers to view the world if aggregate demand fluctuates up and down at random, with no systematic or predictable variation one way or another. But if activist policymakers attempt to exploit the apparent trade-off in the Phillips curve, according to economists who support passive policymaking, aggregate demand will no longer move up and down in an *unpredictable* way.

THE EFFECTS OF AN UNANTICIPATED POLICY Consider Figure 18-5, for example. If the Federal Reserve attempts to reduce the unemployment rate to U_1, it must increase the rate of growth of the money supply enough to produce an inflation rate (IR) of IR_1. If this is an unexpected one-shot action in which the rate of growth of the money supply is first increased and then returned to its previous level, the inflation rate will temporarily rise to IR_1, and the unemployment rate will temporarily fall to U_1. Proponents of passive policymaking contend that past experience with active

FIGURE 18-5

A Shift in the Phillips Curve

When there is a change in the expected inflation rate, the Phillips curve (PC) shifts to incorporate the new expectations. PC_0 shows expectations of zero inflation. PC_5 reflects a higher expected inflation rate, such as 5 percent.

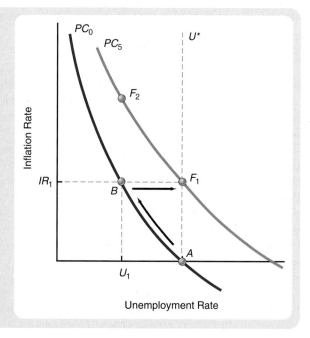

policies indicates that after the money supply stops growing, the inflation rate will soon return to zero and unemployment will return to U^*, its natural rate. Thus, an unexpected temporary increase in money supply growth will cause a movement from point A to point B, and the economy will move on its own back to A.

Did you know that the inflation rate that the Fed regards as most relevant is not the inflation rate that most of the rest of us consider to be most important?

POLICY EXAMPLE
When It Comes to Inflation, the Fed Keeps Its Eyes Off the Headlines

Even though media headlines focus on overall inflation as measured by the rate of change in the Consumer Price Index (CPI), during the 2000s Federal Reserve policymakers have paid most attention to *core PCE inflation*. This is the rate of change in the personal consumption expenditure (PCE) index after food and energy prices have been removed from calculation of the index. Recall from Chapter 7 that the PCE index tracks the average price level using weights developed from continuously updated surveys of consumer expenditures. Fed officials prefer this approach to the method used to compute the CPI, which experiences measurement biases because CPI weights rarely change over time. They also prefer subtracting out food and energy prices because prices of these items tend to be more volatile than prices of other goods and services. Removing the more variable food and energy price inflation seemed to make the current core PCE inflation rate more useful in Fed efforts to forecast future inflation rates.

At least, this was true until the mid-2000s. Since then, the previously observed forecasting improvements from using current core PCE inflation to forecast future inflation rates have evaporated. Furthermore, annual *overall* inflation rates including food and energy price inflation—whether measured by the CPI or the PCE index—have persistently exceeded annual core PCE inflation rates by at least 0.7 percentage point. Indeed, the differential between overall inflation rates reported in media headlines and the core PCE inflation rate has been widening over time. Thus, Fed officials have found themselves in the awkward position of patting themselves on the back for keeping core PCE inflation low even as measures of overall inflation actually experienced by the public have increased.

FOR CRITICAL ANALYSIS
If the public pays more attention to overall inflation rates reported in headlines than to the core PCE inflation rate that is the focus of Fed policy, which actual inflation rate will influence people's expectations of future inflation?

To try out the "biz/ed" Web site's virtual economy and use the Phillips curve as a guide for policymaking in the United Kingdom, go to www.econtoday.com/chapter18.

ADJUSTING EXPECTATIONS AND A SHIFTING PHILLIPS CURVE Why do those advocating passive policymaking argue that variations in the unemployment rate from its natural rate typically are temporary? If activist authorities wish to prevent the unemployment rate from returning to U^* in Figure 18-5 on the previous page, they will conclude that the money supply must grow fast enough to keep the inflation rate up at IR_1. But if the Fed does this, argue those who favor passive policymaking, all of the economic participants in the economy—workers and job seekers included—will come to *expect* that inflation rate to continue. This, in turn, will change their expectations about wages. For example, suppose that IR_1 equals 5 percent per year. When the expected inflation rate was zero, a 5 percent rise in nominal wages meant a 5 percent expected rise in real wages, and this was sufficient to induce some individuals to take jobs rather than remain unemployed. It was this expectation of a rise in real wages that reduced search duration and caused the unemployment rate to drop from U^* to U_1. But if the expected inflation rate becomes 5 percent, a 5 percent rise in nominal wages means *no* rise in *real* wages. Once workers come to expect the higher inflation rate, rising nominal wages will no longer be sufficient to entice them out of unemployment. As a result, as the *expected* inflation rate moves up from 0 percent to 5 percent, the unemployment rate will move up also.

In terms of Figure 18-5 on page 455, as authorities initially increase aggregate demand, the economy moves from point A to point B. If the authorities continue the stimulus in an effort to keep the unemployment rate down, workers' expectations will adjust, causing the unemployment rate to rise. In this second stage, the economy moves from B to point F_1. The unemployment rate returns to the natural rate, U^*, but the inflation rate is now IR_1 instead of zero. Once the adjustment of expectations has taken place, any further changes in policy will have to take place along a curve such as PC_5, say, a movement from F_1 to F_2. This new schedule is also a Phillips curve, differing from the first, PC_0, in that the actual inflation rate consistent with any given unemployment rate is higher because the expected inflation rate is higher.

QUICK QUIZ   *See page 476 for the answers. Review concepts from this section in MyEconLab.*

The **natural rate of unemployment** is the rate that exists in _____-run equilibrium, when workers' _____ are consistent with actual conditions.

Departures from the natural rate of unemployment can occur when individuals encounter unanticipated changes in fiscal or monetary policy. An unexpected _____ in aggregate demand will reduce unemployment below the natural rate, whereas an unanticipated _____ in aggregate demand will push unemployment above the natural rate.

The _____ curve exhibits a negative short-run relationship between the inflation rate and the unemployment rate that can be observed when there are *unanticipated* changes in aggregate _____.

_____ policymakers seek to take advantage of a proposed Phillips curve trade-off between inflation and unemployment.

Rational Expectations, the Policy Irrelevance Proposition, and Real Business Cycles

You already know that economists assume that economic participants act *as though* they were rational and calculating. We assume that firms rationally maximize profits when they choose today's rate of output and that consumers rationally maximize satisfaction when they choose how much of what goods to consume today. One of the pivotal features of current macro policy research is the assumption that economic participants think rationally about the future as well as the present. This relationship was developed by Robert Lucas, who won the Nobel Prize in 1995 for his work. In particular, there is widespread agreement among many macroeconomics researchers that the **rational expectations hypothesis** extends our understanding of the behavior of the macroeconomy. This hypothesis has two key elements:

1. Individuals base their forecasts (expectations) about the future values of economic variables on all readily available past and current information.

2. These expectations incorporate individuals' understanding about how the economy operates, including the operation of monetary and fiscal policy.

Rational expectations hypothesis
A theory stating that people combine the effects of past policy changes on important economic variables with their own judgment about the future effects of current and future policy changes.

In essence, the rational expectations hypothesis holds that Abraham Lincoln was correct when he said, "You may fool all the people some of the time; you can even fool some of the people all of the time; but you can't fool *all* of the people *all* the time."

If we further assume that there is pure competition in all markets and that all prices and wages are flexible, we obtain what many call the *new classical* approach to evaluating the effects of macroeconomic policies. To see how rational expectations operate in the new classical perspective, let's take a simple example of the economy's response to a change in monetary policy.

Flexible Wages and Prices, Rational Expectations, and Policy Irrelevance

Consider Figure 18-6, which shows the long-run aggregate supply curve (*LRAS*) for the economy, as well as the initial aggregate demand curve (*AD*$_1$) and the short-run aggregate supply curve (*SRAS*$_1$). The money supply is initially given by $M = M_1$, and the price level and real GDP are shown by P_1 and Y_1, respectively. Thus, point A represents the initial long-run equilibrium.

Suppose now that the money supply is unexpectedly increased to M_2, thereby causing the aggregate demand curve to shift outward to *AD*$_2$. Given the location of the short-run aggregate supply curve, this increase in aggregate demand will cause real GDP and the price level to rise to Y_2 and P_2, respectively. The new short-run equilibrium is at B. Because real GDP is *above* the long-run equilibrium level of Y_1, unemployment must be below long-run levels (the natural rate), and so workers will soon respond to the higher price level by demanding higher nominal wages. This will cause the short-run aggregate supply curve to shift upward vertically. As indicated by the black arrow, the economy moves from point B to a new long-run equilibrium at C. The price level thus continues its rise to P_3, even as real GDP declines back down to Y_1 (and unemployment returns to the natural rate). So, as we have seen before, even though an increase in the money supply can raise real GDP and lower unemployment in the short run, it has no effect on either variable in the long run.

FIGURE 18-6

Responses to Anticipated and Unanticipated Increases in Aggregate Demand

An increase in the money supply, from M_1 to M_2, causes the aggregate demand curve to shift rightward. If people anticipate the increase in the money supply, then workers will insist on higher nominal wages, which causes the short-run aggregate supply curve to shift leftward immediately, from *SRAS*$_1$ to *SRAS*$_2$. Hence, there is a direct movement, indicated by the green arrow, from point A to point C. In contrast, an unanticipated increase in the money supply causes an initial upward movement along *SRAS*$_1$ from point A to point B, indicated by the black arrow. Thus, in the short run, real GDP rises from Y_1 to Y_2. In the long run, workers then recognize that the price level has increased and demand higher wages, causing the *SRAS* curve to shift leftward, resulting in a movement from point B to point C.

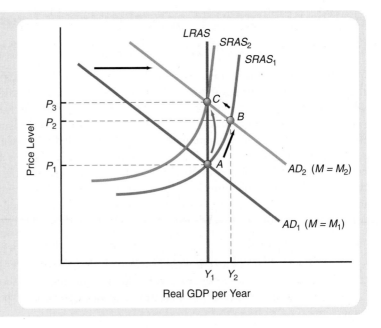

THE RESPONSE TO ANTICIPATED POLICY   Now let's look at this disturbance with the perspective given by the rational expectations hypothesis when wages and prices are flexible in a purely competitive environment. Suppose that workers (and other input owners) know ahead of time that this increase in the money supply is about to take place. Assume also that they know when it is going to occur and understand that its ultimate effect will be to push the price level from P_1 to P_3. Will workers wait until after the price level has increased to insist that their nominal wages go up? The rational expectations hypothesis says that they will not. Instead, they will go to employers and insist that their nominal wages move upward in step with the higher prices. From the workers' perspective, this is the only way to protect their real wages from declining due to the anticipated increase in the money supply.

THE POLICY IRRELEVANCE PROPOSITION   As long as economic participants behave in this manner, we must take their expectations into account when we consider the *SRAS* curve. Let's look again at Figure 18-6 to do this. In the initial equilibrium at point *A* of the figure, the short-run aggregate supply curve $SRAS_1$ corresponds to a situation in which the expected money supply and the actual money supply are equal. When the money supply changes in a way that is anticipated by economic participants, the aggregate supply curve will shift to reflect this expected change in the money supply. The new short-run aggregate supply curve $SRAS_2$ reflects this. According to the rational expectations hypothesis, the short-run aggregate supply curve will shift upward *simultaneously* with the rise in aggregate demand. As a result, the economy will move directly from point *A* to point *C*, without passing through *B*, as depicted by the green arrow in Figure 18-6. The *only* response to the rise in the money supply is a rise in the price level from P_1 to P_3. Neither output nor unemployment changes at all. This conclusion—that fully anticipated monetary policy is irrelevant in determining the levels of real variables—is called the **policy irrelevance proposition:**

> *Under the assumption of rational expectations on the part of decision makers in the economy,* anticipated *monetary policy cannot alter either the rate of unemployment or the level of real GDP. Regardless of the nature of the anticipated policy, the unemployment rate will equal the natural rate, and real GDP will be determined solely by the economy's long-run aggregate supply curve.*

Policy irrelevance proposition
The conclusion that policy actions have no real effects in the short run if the policy actions are anticipated and none in the long run even if the policy actions are unanticipated.

WHAT MUST PEOPLE KNOW?   There are two important matters to keep in mind when considering this proposition. First, our discussion has assumed that economic participants know in advance exactly what the change in monetary policy is going to be and precisely when it is going to occur. In fact, the Federal Reserve does not announce exactly what the future course of monetary policy is going to be. Instead, the Fed tries to keep most of its plans secret, announcing only in general terms what policy actions are intended for the future.

It is tempting to conclude that because the Fed's intended policies are not fully known, they are not available at all. But such a conclusion would be wrong. Economic participants have great incentives to learn how to predict the future behavior of the monetary authorities, just as businesses try to forecast consumer behavior and college students do their best to forecast what their next economics exam will look like. Even if the economic participants are not perfect at forecasting the course of policy, they are likely to come a lot closer than they would in total ignorance. The policy irrelevance proposition really assumes only that *people don't persistently make the same mistakes in forecasting the future.*

If you believe that the Federal Reserve's monetary policy cannot alter the level of real GDP or the rate of unemployment, then you subscribe to what proposition?

WHAT HAPPENS IF PEOPLE DON'T KNOW EVERYTHING? This brings us to our second point. Once we accept the fact that people's ability to predict the future is not perfect, the possibility emerges that some policy actions will have systematic effects that look much like the movements, depicted by black arrows, from A to B to C in Figure 18-6 on page 458. For example, just as other economic participants sometimes make mistakes, it is likely that the Federal Reserve sometimes makes mistakes—meaning that the money supply may change in ways that even the Fed does not predict. And even if the Fed always accomplished every policy action it intended, there is no guarantee that other economic participants would fully forecast those actions.

What happens if the Fed makes a mistake or if firms and workers misjudge the future course of policy? Matters will look much as they do in panel (a) of Figure 18-7, which shows the effects of an *unanticipated* increase in the money supply. Economic participants' expectation of the money supply, M_e, is equal to a quantity of money M_1, but the actual money supply turns out to be M_2. Because $M_2 > M_1$, aggregate demand shifts relative to aggregate supply. The result is a rise in real GDP in the short run from Y_1 to Y_2. Corresponding to this rise in real GDP will be an increase in employment and hence a fall in the unemployment rate. So, even under the rational expectations hypothesis, monetary policy *can* have an effect on real variables in the short run, but only if the policy is unsystematic and therefore unanticipated.

FIGURE 18-7

Effects of an Unanticipated Rise in Aggregate Demand

In panel (a), an unanticipated increase in the money supply shifts the *AD* curve rightward, generating an upward movement along the *SRAS* curve, which remains in position because the rise in the money supply is unexpected. Thus, there is a movement from point E_1 to point E_2. The equilibrium price level increases, from P_1 to P_2, and equilibrium real GDP increases, from Y_1 to Y_2.

In contrast, in panel (b), a rise in the money supply, which again shifts the *AD* curve rightward, is fully anticipated, and as a result the *SRAS* curve shifts leftward. The final equilibrium is at point E_3. The equilibrium price level increases, from P_1 to P_3, and equilibrium real GDP remains at its initial level.

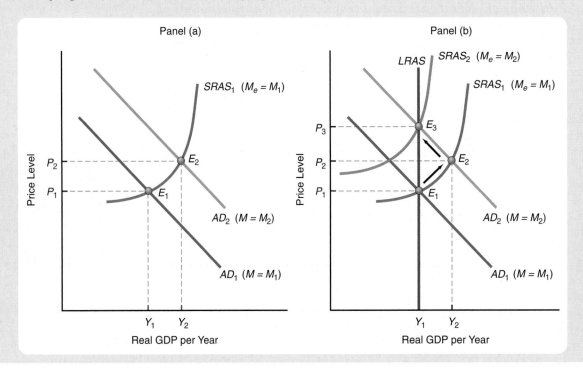

In the long run, this effect on real variables will disappear because people will figure out that the Fed either accidentally increased the money supply or intentionally increased it in a way that somehow fooled individuals. Either way, people will soon revise their money supply expectation to match the actual money supply ($M_e = M_2$), and as a result the short-run aggregate supply curve will shift upward. As shown in panel (b) of Figure 18-7, real GDP will return to long-run levels, meaning that so will the employment and unemployment rates.

Another Challenge to Policy Activism: Real Business Cycles

When confronted with the policy irrelevance proposition, many economists began to reexamine the first principles of macroeconomics with fully flexible wages and prices.

THE DISTINCTION BETWEEN REAL AND MONETARY SHOCKS Some economists argue that real, as opposed to purely monetary, forces might help explain aggregate economic fluctuations. Consider Figure 18-8, which illustrates the concept of *real business cycles*. We begin at point E_1 with the economy in both short- and long-run equilibrium, with the associated supply curves, $SRAS_1$ and $LRAS_1$. Initially, the level of real GDP is $15 trillion, and the price level is 108. Because the economy is in long-run equilibrium, the unemployment rate must be at the natural rate.

A reduction in the supply of a key productive resource, such as oil, causes the $SRAS$ curve to shift to the left to $SRAS_2$ because fewer goods will be available for sale due to the reduced supplies. If the reduction in, for example, oil supplies is (or is believed to be) permanent, the $LRAS$ shifts to the left also. This assumption is reflected in Figure 18-8, where $LRAS_2$ shows the new long-run aggregate supply curve associated with the lowered output of oil.

FIGURE 18-8

Effects of a Reduction in the Supply of Resources

The position of the *LRAS* depends on our endowments of all types of resources. Hence, a permanent reduction in the supply of one of those resources, such as oil, causes a reduction—an inward shift—in the aggregate supply curve from $LRAS_1$ to $LRAS_2$. In addition, there is a rise in the equilibrium price level and a fall in the equilibrium rate of real GDP per year.

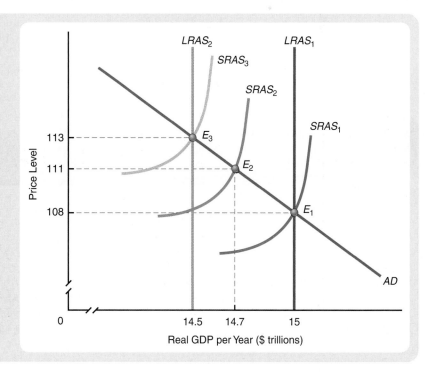

In the short run, two adjustments begin to occur simultaneously. First, the prices of oil and petroleum-based products begin to rise, so the overall price level rises to 111. Second, the higher costs of production occasioned by the rise in oil prices induce firms to cut back production, so real GDP falls to $14.7 trillion in the short run. The new temporary short-run equilibrium occurs at E_2, with a higher price level (111) and a lower level of real GDP ($14.7 trillion).

This is not the full story, however. Owners of nonoil inputs, such as labor, are also affected by the reduction in oil supplies. For instance, individuals who are employed experience real wage reductions as the price level increases following the movement from point E_1 to point E_2. Even though most individuals may be willing to put up with reduced real payments in the short run, not every worker will tolerate them in the long run. Thus, some workers who were willing to continue on the job at lower real wages in the short run will eventually decide to switch from full-time to part-time employment or to drop out of the labor force altogether. In effect, there is a fall in the supply of nonoil inputs, reflected in an upward shift in the *SRAS* curve from $SRAS_2$ to $SRAS_3$. This puts additional upward pressure on the price level and exerts a downward force on real GDP. Thus, the final long-run equilibrium occurs at point E_3, with the price level at 113 and real GDP at $14.5 trillion.

STAGFLATION Notice that in the example depicted in Figure 18-8 on the previous page, real GDP declines over the same interval that the price level increases. Hence, there is real economic stagnation, which is associated with lower employment and a higher unemployment rate, combined with higher inflation, often called **stagflation.**

The most recent prolonged periods of stagflation in the United States occurred during the 1970s and early 1980s. One factor contributing to stagflation episodes during those years was sharp reductions in the supply of oil, as in the example illustrated in Figure 18-8. In addition, Congress enacted steep increases in marginal tax rates and implemented a host of new federal regulations on firms in the early 1970s. All these factors together acted to reduce long-run aggregate supply and hence contributed to stagflation. Increases in oil supplies, cuts in marginal tax rates, and deregulation during the 1980s and 1990s helped to prevent stagflation episodes from occurring after the early 1980s.

Is the United States currently experiencing a new stagflation episode?

Stagflation

A situation characterized by lower real GDP, lower employment, and a higher unemployment rate during the same period that the rate of inflation increases.

EXAMPLE
Does the United States Face a Stagflation Threat?

Between 2006 and 2009, the annual inflation rate in the United States steadily increased from 2.5 percent to about 4.5 percent. During the same interval, the U.S. unemployment rate increased from 4.6 percent to about 5.5 percent. Does this mean that the United States is experiencing a renewed threat of persistent stagflation? There is some reason to worry that the answer to this question could be yes. World oil prices have increased considerably since 2006. Furthermore, the U.S. Congress is boosting marginal

tax rates and significantly increasing regulatory burdens on U.S. industries. Taken together, these developments are contributing to stagnation in the growth of the nation's long-run aggregate supply. Other things being equal, the result could be a new period of stagflation for the U.S. economy.

FOR CRITICAL ANALYSIS
Could U.S. stagflation be averted if labor productivity and capital investment were to increase independently?

QUICK QUIZ See page 476 for the answers. Review concepts from this section in MyEconLab.

The _____ _____ hypothesis assumes that individuals' forecasts incorporate all readily available information, including an understanding of government policy and its effects on the economy.

If the **rational expectations hypothesis** is valid, there is pure competition, and all prices and wages are flexible, then the _____ _____ proposition follows: Fully anticipated monetary policy actions cannot alter

either the rate of unemployment or the level of real GDP.

Even if all prices and wages are perfectly flexible, aggregate _____ shocks such as sudden changes in technology or in the supplies of factors of production can cause national economic fluctuations. To the extent that these _____ _____ cycles predominate as sources of economic fluctuations, the case for active policymaking is weakened.

Modern Approaches to Justifying Active Policymaking

The policy irrelevance proposition and the idea that real shocks are important causes of business cycles are major attacks on the desirability of trying to stabilize economic activity with activist policies. Both anti-activism suggestions arise from combining the rational expectations hypothesis with the assumptions of pure competition and flexible wages and prices. It should not be surprising, therefore, to learn that economists who see a role for activist policymaking do not believe that market clearing models of the economy can explain business cycles. They contend that the "sticky" wages and prices assumed by Keynes in his major work (see Chapter 11) remain important in today's economy. To explain how aggregate demand shocks and policies can influence a nation's real GDP and unemployment rate, these economists, who are sometimes called *new Keynesians*, have tried to refine the theory of aggregate supply.

Small Menu Costs and Sticky Prices

If prices do not respond to demand changes, two conditions must be true: someone must be consciously deciding not to change prices, and that decision must be in the decision maker's self-interest. One approach to explaining why many prices might be sticky in the short run supposes that much of the economy is characterized by imperfect competition and that it is costly for firms to change their prices in response to changes in demand. The costs associated with changing prices are called *menu costs*, and they include the costs of renegotiating contracts, printing price lists (such as menus), and informing customers of price changes.

Many such costs may not be very large, so economists call them **small menu costs.** Some of the costs of changing prices, however, such as those incurred in bringing together business managers from points around the nation or the world for meetings on price changes or renegotiating deals with customers, may be significant.

Firms in different industries have different cost structures. Such differences explain diverse small menu costs. Therefore, the extent to which firms hold their prices constant in the face of changes in demand for their products will vary across industries. Not all prices will be rigid. Nonetheless, some economists who promote policy activism argue that many—even most—firms' prices are sticky for relatively long time intervals. As a result, in the short run the aggregate level of prices could be very nearly rigid because of small menu costs. In recent years, these economists have produced a

Small menu costs
Costs that deter firms from changing prices in response to demand changes—for example, the costs of renegotiating contracts or printing new price lists.

theory in which temporary rigidities in firms' price adjustments cause the short-run aggregate supply curve to be horizontal, as in the traditional Keynesian model.

Real GDP and the Price Level in a Sticky-Price Economy

According to the new Keynesians, sticky prices strengthen the argument favoring active policymaking as a means of preventing substantial short-run swings in real GDP and, as a consequence, employment.

NEW KEYNESIAN INFLATION DYNAMICS To see why the idea of price stickiness strengthens the case for active policymaking, consider panel (a) of Figure 18-9. If a significant portion of all prices do not adjust rapidly, then in the short run the aggregate supply curve effectively is horizontal, as assumed in the traditional Keynesian theory discussed in Chapter 11. This means that a decline in aggregate demand, such as the shift from AD_1 to AD_2 shown in panel (a), will induce the largest possible decline in equilibrium real GDP, from $15 trillion to $14.7 trillion. When prices are sticky, economic contractions induced by aggregate demand shocks are as severe as they can be.

As panel (a) shows, in contrast to the traditional Keynesian theory, the new Keynesian sticky-price theory indicates that the economy will find its own way back to a long-run equilibrium. The theory presumes that small menu costs induce firms not to

---

FIGURE 18-9

Short- and Long-Run Adjustments in the New Keynesian Sticky-Price Theory

Panel (a) shows that when prices are sticky, the short-run aggregate supply curve is horizontal, here at a price level of 118. As a consequence, the short-run effect of a fall in aggregate demand from AD_1 to AD_2 generates the largest possible decline in real GDP, from $15 trillion at point E_1 to $14.7 trillion at point E_2. In the long run, producers perceive that they can increase their profits sufficiently by cutting prices and incurring the menu costs of doing so. The resulting decline in the price level implies a downward shift of the *SRAS* curve, so that the price level falls to 116 and real GDP returns to $15 trillion at point E_3. Panel (b) illustrates the argument for active policymaking based on the new Keynesian theory. Instead of waiting for long-run adjustments to occur, policymakers can engage in expansionary policies that shift the aggregate demand curve back to its original position, thereby shortening or even eliminating a recession.

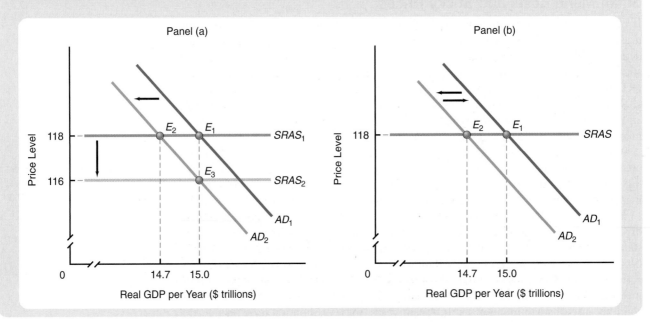

change their prices in the short run. In the long run, however, the profit gains to firms from reducing their prices to induce purchases of more goods and services cause them to cut their prices. Thus, in the long run, the price level declines in response to the decrease in aggregate demand. As firms reduce their prices, the horizontal aggregate supply curve shifts downward, from $SRAS_1$ to $SRAS_2$, and equilibrium real GDP returns to its former level, other things being equal.

Of course, an increase in aggregate demand would have effects opposite to those depicted in panel (a) of Figure 18-9. A rise in aggregate demand would cause real GDP to rise in the short run. In the long run, firms would gain sufficient profits from raising their prices to compensate for incurring menu costs, and the short-run aggregate supply curve would shift upward. Consequently, an economy with growing aggregate demand should exhibit so-called **new Keynesian inflation dynamics:** initial sluggish adjustment of the price level in response to aggregate demand increases followed by higher inflation later on.

New Keynesian inflation dynamics
In new Keynesian theory, the pattern of inflation exhibited by an economy with growing aggregate demand—initial sluggish adjustment of the price level in response to increased aggregate demand followed by higher inflation later.

WHY ACTIVE POLICYMAKING CAN PAY OFF WHEN PRICES ARE STICKY To think about why the new Keynesian sticky-price theory supports the argument for active policymaking, let's return to the case of a decline in aggregate demand illustrated in panel (a) of Figure 18-9. Panel (b) shows the same decline in aggregate demand as in panel (a) and the resulting maximum contractionary effect on real GDP.

Monetary and fiscal policy actions that influence aggregate demand are as potent as possible when prices are sticky and short-run aggregate supply is horizontal. In principle, therefore, all that a policymaker confronted by the leftward shift in aggregate demand depicted in panel (b) must do is to conduct the appropriate policy to induce a rightward shift in the *AD* curve back to its previous position. Indeed, if the policymaker acts rapidly enough, the period of contraction experienced by the economy may be very brief. Active policymaking can thereby moderate or even eliminate recessions.

Is There a New Keynesian Phillips Curve?

A fundamental thrust of the new Keynesian theory is that activist policymaking can promote economic stability. Assessing this implication requires evaluating whether policymakers face an *exploitable* relationship between the inflation rate and the unemployment rate and between inflation and real GDP. By "exploitable," economists mean a relationship that is sufficiently predictable and long-lived to allow enough time for policymakers to reduce unemployment or to push up real GDP when economic activity falls below its long-run level.

The U.S. Experience with the Phillips Curve

For more than 40 years, economists have debated the existence of a policy-exploitable Phillips curve relationship between the inflation rate and the rate of unemployment. In separate articles in 1968, the late Milton Friedman and Edmond Phelps published pioneering studies suggesting that the apparent trade-off suggested by the Phillips curve could *not* be exploited by activist policymakers. Friedman and Phelps both argued that any attempt to reduce unemployment by boosting inflation would soon be thwarted by the incorporation of the new higher inflation rate into the public's expectations. The Friedman-Phelps research thus implies that for any given unemployment rate, *any* inflation rate is possible, depending on the actions of policymakers.

Figure 18-10 appears to provide support for the propositions of Friedman and Phelps. It clearly shows that in the past, a number of inflation rates have proved feasible at the same rates of unemployment.

The New Keynesian Phillips Curve

Today's new Keynesian theorists are not concerned about the lack of an apparent long-lived relationship between inflation and unemployment revealed by Figure 18-10. From their point of view, the issue is not whether a relationship between inflation and unemployment or between inflation and real GDP breaks down over a period of years. All that matters for policymakers, the new Keynesians suggest, is whether such a relationship is exploitable in the near term. If so, policymakers can intervene in the economy as soon as actual unemployment and real GDP vary from their long-run levels. Appropriate activist policies, new Keynesians conclude, can dampen cyclical fluctuations and make them shorter-lived.

EVALUATING NEW KEYNESIAN INFLATION DYNAMICS To assess the predictions of new Keynesian inflation dynamics, economists seek to evaluate whether inflation is closely related to two key factors that theory indicates should determine the inflation rate. The first of these factors is anticipated future inflation. The new Keynesian theory implies that menu costs reduce firms' incentive to adjust their prices. When some

FIGURE 18-10

The Phillips Curve: Theory versus Data

If we plot points representing the rate of inflation and the rate of unemployment for the United States from 1953 to the present, there does not appear to be any trade-off between the two variables.

Sources: Economic Report of the President; Economic Indicators, various issues.

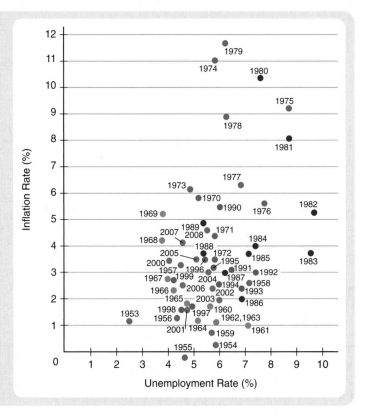

firms *do* adjust their prices, however, they will seek to set prices at levels based on expected future positions of demand curves for their products. The expected future inflation rate signals to firms how much equilibrium prices are likely to increase during future months, so firms will take into account the expected future inflation rate when setting prices at the present time.

The second key factor that new Keynesian theory indicates should affect current inflation is the average inflation-adjusted (real) per-unit costs that firms incur in producing goods and services. Thus, new Keynesians propose a positive relationship between inflation and an aggregate measure of real per-unit costs faced by firms throughout the economy. If firms' average inflation-adjusted per-unit costs increase, the prediction is that there will be higher prices at the portion of firms that do adjust their prices in the current period and, hence, greater current inflation.

Empirical evidence does indicate that increases in expected future inflation and greater real per-unit production costs are indeed associated with higher observed rates of inflation. In light of this support for these key predictions of the new Keynesian theory, the theory is exerting increasing influence on U.S. policymakers. For instance, media reports commonly refer to Fed officials' careful attention to changes in inflation expectations and firms' production costs that they interpret as signals of altered inflationary pressures.

JUST HOW EXPLOITABLE IS THE NEW KEYNESIAN PHILLIPS CURVE? Not all economists are persuaded that the new Keynesian theory is correct. They point out that new classical theory already indicates that when prices are *flexible*, higher inflation expectations should reduce short-run aggregate supply and contribute to increased inflation. In addition, all macroeconomic theories suggest that various factors that push up firms' production costs should have the same effect on short-run aggregate supply and inflation in a flexible-price economy.

Even if one were convinced that new Keynesian theory is correct, a fundamental issue is whether the new Keynesian theory has truly identified *exploitable* relationships. At the heart of this issue is just how often firms adjust their prices. If the average interval between firms' price adjustments is relatively long, then the horizontal new Keynesian aggregate supply curve will remain in position for a longer interval. As a result, a decline in aggregate demand will have a longer-lasting negative effect on real GDP. Then there will be a greater potential scope for activist policymaking to be able to boost aggregate demand and stabilize real GDP and unemployment. In contrast, if the average interval between changes in prices is short, then prices will adjust relatively quickly to a change in aggregate demand. There will be less scope for activist policies to stabilize the economy, because speedier adjustments of prices will automatically tend to dampen movements in real GDP and the unemployment rate.

Naturally, economists are hard at work trying to determine the average interval between price changes in national economies. So far, conclusions are mixed. Initially, studies of new Keynesian inflation dynamics yielded estimates of average price-adjustment intervals for the United States as long as two years. More recent studies, however, have produced estimated price-adjustment intervals no longer than one year. Some suggest that average periods between price adjustments are even shorter. At present, therefore, little agreement exists about just how much scope activist policymakers might have to stabilize real GDP and the unemployment rate under the new Keynesian theory.

Why are there such wide differences in estimated average periods between price changes by U.S. firms?

EXAMPLE

Measurement Issues Complicate Assessing the Speed of U.S. Price Adjustment

A by-product of the methods that new Keynesian economists use to assess how expectations of future inflation and per-unit real production costs influence actual inflation is an estimate of the average interval between price changes. Most studies measure the inflation rate as the percentage change in the GDP deflator. They also measure changes in average per-unit real production costs as deviations of aggregate real labor costs from their average level, and they assume no cyclical variation in real labor costs. Evaluating U.S. data from the mid-1960s through the mid-2000s using the percentage change in the GDP deflator yields an estimated average interval between price changes at U.S. firms of almost 19 months, or just over 1.5 years.

New Keynesian sticky-price theories focus on how menu costs affect the prices firms charge to consumers. The Producer Price Index (PPI) measures the actual prices charged by firms, so it is arguable that the percentage change in the PPI is a better inflation measure for evaluating the new Keynesian theory. Carl Gwin of Pepperdine University and David

VanHoose of Baylor University have found that using this measure of inflation cuts the estimated average price-adjustment interval by about 50 percent, to just over 9 months.

There is another complication. Even though most studies of new Keynesian inflation dynamics assume that real labor costs are constant, these costs vary considerably over time. Gwin and VanHoose find that taking into account variations in real labor costs over time slashes the estimate of the average price-adjustment interval to just over 5 months. Clearly, how economists decide to measure inflation and real per-unit production costs influences their estimates of how often firms change prices.

FOR CRITICAL ANALYSIS

Why do you suppose that some economists worry that measuring inflation as the percentage change in the GDP deflator, which varies more smoothly over time than other price indexes, biases the estimate toward the conclusion that prices are "sticky"?

Summing Up: Economic Factors Favoring Active versus Passive Policymaking

To many people who have never taken a principles of economics course, it seems apparent that the world's governments should engage in active policymaking aimed at achieving high and stable real GDP growth and a low and stable unemployment rate. As you have learned in this chapter, the advisability of policy activism is not so obvious.

Several factors are involved in assessing whether policy activism is really preferable to passive policymaking. Table 18-1 summarizes the issues involved in evaluating the case for active policymaking versus the case for passive policymaking.

The current state of thinking on the relative desirability of active or passive policymaking may leave you somewhat frustrated. On the one hand, most economists agree that active policymaking is unlikely to exert sizable long-run effects on any nation's economy. Most also agree that aggregate supply shocks contribute to business cycles. Consequently, there is general agreement that there are limits on the effectiveness of monetary and fiscal policies. On the other hand, a number of economists continue to argue that there is evidence indicating stickiness of prices and wages. They argue, therefore, that monetary and fiscal policy actions can offset, at least in the short run and perhaps even in the long run, the effects that aggregate demand shocks would otherwise have on real GDP and unemployment.

What might be some of the topics for discussion at this meeting of leaders from the eight largest industrialized nations?

TABLE 18-1

Issues That Must Be Assessed in Determining the Desirability of Active versus Passive Policymaking

Economists who contend that active policymaking is justified argue that for each issue listed in the first column, there is evidence supporting the conclusions listed in the second column. In contrast, economists who suggest that passive policymaking is appropriate argue that for each issue in the first column, there is evidence leading to the conclusions in the third column.

Issue	Support for Active Policymaking	Support for Passive Policymaking
Phillips curve inflation–unemployment trade-off	Stable in the short run; perhaps predictable in the long run	Varies with inflation expectations; at best fleeting in the short run and nonexistent in the long run
Aggregate demand shocks	Induce short-run and perhaps long-run effects on real GDP and unemployment	Have little or no short-run effects and certainly no long-run effects on real GDP and unemployment
Aggregate supply shocks	Can, along with aggregate demand shocks, influence real GDP and unemployment	Cause movements in real GDP and unemployment and hence explain most business cycles
Pure competition	Is not typical in most markets, where imperfect competition predominates	Is widespread in markets throughout the economy
Price flexibility	Is uncommon because factors such as small menu costs induce firms to change prices infrequently	Is common because firms adjust prices immediately when demand changes
Wage flexibility	Is uncommon because labor market adjustments occur relatively slowly	Is common because nominal wages adjust speedily to price changes, making real wages flexible

These diverging perspectives help explain why economists reach differing conclusions about the advisability of pursuing active or passive approaches to macroeconomic policymaking. Different interpretations of evidence on the issues summarized in Table 18-1 will likely continue to divide economists for years to come.

QUICK QUIZ See page 476 for the answers. Review concepts from this section in MyEconLab.

Some new Keynesian economists suggest that _____ _____ costs inhibit many firms from making speedy changes in their prices and that this price stickiness can make the short-run aggregate supply curve _____. Variations in aggregate demand have the largest possible effects on real GDP in the short run, so policies that influence aggregate demand also have the greatest capability to stabilize real GDP in the face of aggregate demand shocks.

Even though there is little evidence supporting a long-run trade-off between inflation and unemployment, new Keynesian theory suggests that activist policymaking may be able to stabilize real GDP and employment in the _____ run. This is possible, according to the theory, if stickiness of _____ adjustment is sufficiently great that policymakers can exploit a _____-run trade-off between inflation and real GDP.

You Are There Inflation Targeting Catches On—Except at the Fed

The special conference of officials from the Fed's Board of Governors and its 12 Federal Reserve district banks is under way. The central issue of the conference is *inflation targeting*. Since the late 1990s, central banks in a number of countries, including Canada, New Zealand, and the United Kingdom, have aimed to achieve target rates of inflation. To understand how they try to target inflation, recall from Chapter 17 on page 427 that the equation of exchange is $M_s V \equiv PY$. If the income velocity of money (V) and real GDP (Y) are predictable, then a central bank can seek to attain a specific percentage change in the price level (P)—that is, an inflation target—by ensuring that the money supply (M_s) grows at the appropriate rate. Under this policy, the central bank adjusts the money supply as appropriate to attain a single objective: a target rate of inflation. It would not engage in short-run money supply changes aimed at influencing real GDP growth or the unemployment rate.

As soon as Congress confirmed Ben Bernanke as Fed chair, many inside and outside the Fed had anticipated a conference such as this one, because Bernanke was a proponent of inflation targeting prior to assuming his duties. Indeed, before the special conference, some observers had anticipated that Bernanke might actively push for the Fed to join the growing list of inflation-targeting central banks.

By the conclusion of the conference, however, it is clear that Bernanke has opted to sit on the fence on the issue instead of pressing his pro-inflation-targeting viewpoint. Indeed, media reporters adept at vote counting in the political arena have concluded that fewer than half of the members of the Federal Open Market Committee have expressed even lukewarm support for the idea of adopting an explicit inflation target. Among FOMC members opposed to the idea, several have echoed Fed Vice Chair Don Kohn's view that inflation targeting would inhibit the Fed's capability to respond actively to short-term real GDP downturns. Others have expressed doubts that the Fed could settle on a single measure of inflation deemed appropriate for such a targeting policy. As the conference breaks up, one thing is certain: The Fed will not be using an explicit inflation-targeting strategy any time soon.

CRITICAL ANALYSIS QUESTIONS

1. Does inflation targeting represent active or passive policy-making?

2. Why do you suppose that some new Keynesian theorists have suggested that the Fed should try to target a measure of the expected rate of inflation?

Are U.S. Inflation Expectations Rising?

Issues and Applications

CONCEPTS APPLIED

- New Keynesian Inflation Dynamics
- Rational Expectations Hypothesis
- Phillips Curve

New Keynesian inflation dynamics indicate that the public's expectations of future inflation are a fundamental determinant of the current inflation rate. Hence, expectations of low inflation become self-fulfilling: Low inflation expectations precede low actual inflation. This new Keynesian perspective helps to explain why former Fed Board Governor Frederic Mishkin suggested that inflation expectations appear to be "anchored" above 2 percent per year. Mishkin concluded that bringing about a decrease in inflation "would require a shift in expectations, and generating such a shift could be difficult and time-consuming."

Some economists are concerned that the Fed may be overrelying on the new Keynesian theory in developing its strategy for monetary policy and that, as a result, the Fed's strategy may be self-fulfilling in a manner that it does not intend. Specifically, the Fed may be tempted to exploit expectations of low future inflation, engage in inflationary policies, and thereby boost inflation expectations, which, as Mishkin argued, may then prove difficult to bring back down.

Evidence of Gradually Rising U.S. Inflation Expectations

In May 2003, the U.S. inflation rate appeared to be dropping toward 1 percent. The Fed issued a press release indicating that it perceived that "the probability of an unwelcome substantial fall in inflation, though minor, exceeds that of a pickup in inflation from its already low level." Most observers interpreted this statement as suggesting that an inflation rate of about 1 percent per year was near the lower limit of the Fed's long-run inflation objective. The Fed then proceeded to engage in a series of policy actions that many observers viewed as likely to boost inflation slightly. Nevertheless, a few months later, the Fed issued a statement expressing the judgment that "on balance, the risk of inflation becoming undesirably low is likely to be the predominant concern for the foreseeable future." This statement was followed by additional rounds of expansive monetary policy actions.

Figure 18-11 on page 472 provides evidence about how the Fed's policy strategy after May 2003 affected the public's inflation expectations. The figure shows the differential between the interest rate on a regular U.S. Treasury security and an inflation-indexed Treasury security. The regular U.S. Treasury security pays a nominal rate of return that is not adjusted for inflation.

In contrast, holders of an inflation-indexed Treasury security are compensated for inflation, so this security pays a rate of return that should approximately equal the real rate of interest. Hence, the differential between the interest rates on the two securities should equal the nominal interest rate minus the real interest rate, or the expected inflation rate. As you can see, until the summer of 2003 this differential averaged just over 1.7 percent. Following the Fed's pronouncements expressing concern about low inflation and its expansionary monetary policy actions, the differential rose to an average of about 2.4 percent. That is, expectations of future annual rates of inflation rose from 1.7 percent to 2.4 percent. Actual inflation also drifted upward, from about 1.9 percent in 2003 to a range between 2 and 4.5 percent in the mid and later 2000s.

Do Inflation Expectations Precede or Lag Behind Actual Inflation?

Since the advent of the rational expectations hypothesis, there has been little disagreement among economists that inflation expectations play a fundamental role in influencing the actual rate of inflation. Nevertheless, there is less agreement about whether inflation expectations are a leading indicator of inflation or, in fact, tend to lag behind actual movements in inflation. The new

FIGURE 18-11

The Differential Between Interest Rates on Non-Inflation-Indexed and Inflation-Indexed 10-Year Treasury Securities Since 2001

Holders of inflation-indexed Treasury securities are compensated for inflation, so the interest rate on these securities indicates the real rate of interest. Thus, subtracting this interest rate from the nominal interest rate on regular, non-inflation-adjusted Treasury securities provides a measure of the expected inflation rate. This measure of expected inflation increased after 2003.

Source: Federal Reserve Bank of St. Louis.

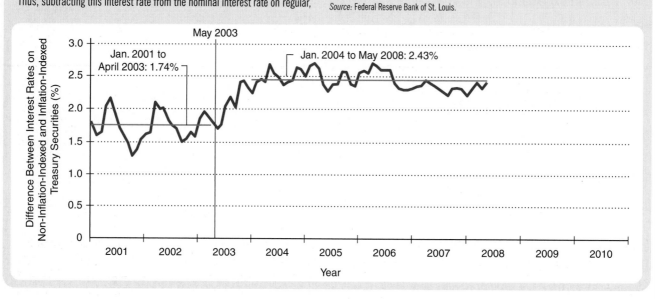

Keynesian inflation dynamics theory suggests that inflation expectations precede inflation, but other theories indicate that shifts in inflation expectations lag behind actual changes in the inflation rate. The evidence on this issue is mixed and hence subject to either interpretation.

Critics of the Fed's policy strategy are convinced that in the long run, inflation expectations ultimately must adjust to reflect actual inflation. Furthermore, they contend that ultimately the money supply growth that the Fed's policies determine is the fundamental factor influencing the inflation rate. In their view, the Fed's belief that inflation expectations exclusively precede actual inflation provides a dangerous temptation. The Fed may attempt to exploit a perceived new Keynesian Phillips curve trade-off by pushing up inflation in an effort to boost real GDP and employment. The result, they suggest, is depicted in Figure 18-11: higher inflation expectations *accompanying* higher actual rates of inflation, which in turn the Fed ultimately generates by conducting overly expansionary monetary policies.

---

myeconlab

Test your understanding of this chapter by going online to **MyEconLab**.
In the Study Plan for this chapter, select Section N: News.

For Critical Analysis

1. Why do you suppose that some economists doubt the new Keynesian view that variations in inflation expectations and per-unit real production costs, rather than changes in money supply growth, are the main determinants of inflation? (Hint: Recall the quantity equation discussed in Chapter 17.)

2. Why might it be possible for inflation expectations to both precede and lag behind actual inflation?

Web Resources

1. Read a speech by former Fed Board Governor Frederic Mishkin outlining his view on the role of inflation expectations in influencing the dynamics of inflation at www.econtoday.com/chapter18.

2. For an evaluation of the evidence on whether inflation expectations precede or lag behind actual inflation, go to www.econtoday.com/chapter18.

Research Project

Some economists have suggested that the Fed should conduct monetary policy with an aim to targeting the interest rate differential displayed in Figure 18-11. What rationale(s) might be offered for pursuing such a policy goal? Explain.

 **myeconlab** Here is what you should know after reading this chapter. MyEconLab will help you identify what you know, and where to go when you need to practice.

WHAT YOU SHOULD KNOW

WHERE TO GO TO PRACTICE

Why the Actual Unemployment Rate Might Depart from the Natural Rate of Unemployment An unexpected increase in aggregate demand can cause real GDP to rise in the short run, which results in a reduction in the unemployment rate. Hence, for a time the actual unemployment rate can fall below the natural rate of unemployment. Likewise, an unanticipated reduction in aggregate demand can push down real GDP in the short run, thereby causing the actual unemployment rate to rise above the natural unemployment rate.

active (discretionary) policymaking, 449
passive (nondiscretionary) policymaking, 449
natural rate of unemployment, 450
KEY FIGURES
Figure 18-1, 451
Figure 18-2, 452
Figure 18-3, 453

- **MyEconLab** Study Plans 18.1, 18.2
- Audio introduction to Chapter 18
- Animated Figures 18-1, 18-2, 18-3
- Video: The Natural Rate of Unemployment

The Phillips Curve An unexpected increase in aggregate demand that causes a drop in the unemployment rate also induces a rise in the equilibrium price level and, consequently, inflation. Thus, other things being equal, there should be an inverse relationship between the inflation rate and the unemployment rate. This downward-sloping relationship is called the Phillips curve, and it implies that there may be a short-run trade-off between inflation and unemployment.

Phillips curve, 454
nonaccelerating inflation rate of unemployment (NAIRU), 454
KEY FIGURES
Figure 18-4, 454
Figure 18-5, 455

- **MyEconLab** Study Plan 18.2
- Animated Figures 18-4, 18-5

How Expectations Affect the Actual Relationship Between the Inflation Rate and the Unemployment Rate Theory predicts that there will be a Phillips curve relationship only when expectations are unchanged. If people anticipate policymakers' efforts to exploit the Phillips curve trade-off via inflationary policies aimed at pushing down the unemployment rate, then input prices such as nominal wages will adjust more rapidly to an increase in the price level. As a result, the Phillips curve will shift outward, and the economy will adjust more speedily toward the natural rate of unemployment. When plotted on a chart, therefore, the actual relationship between the inflation rate and the unemployment rate will not be a downward-sloping Phillips curve.

- **MyEconLab** Study Plan 18.2

(continued)

 *(continued)*

WHAT YOU SHOULD KNOW

WHERE TO GO TO PRACTICE

Rational Expectations, Policy Ineffectiveness, and Real-Business-Cycle Theory According to the rational expectations hypothesis, people form expectations of future economic variables such as inflation using all available past and current information and based on their understanding of how the economy functions. If pure competition also prevails and wages and prices are flexible, then only unanticipated policy actions can induce even short-run changes in real GDP. If people completely anticipate the actions of policymakers, wages and other input prices adjust immediately, so real GDP remains unaffected. A key implication is the policy irrelevance proposition, which states that the unemployment rate is unaffected by fully anticipated policy actions. Technological changes and labor market shocks such as variations in the composition of the labor force can induce business fluctuations, called real business cycles, which weaken the case for active policymaking.

rational expectations hypothesis, 457
policy irrelevance proposition, 459
stagflation, 462

KEY FIGURES
Figure 18-6, 458
Figure 18-8, 461

- **MyEconLab** Study Plan 18.3
- Animated Figures 18-6, 18-8

Modern Approaches to Bolstering the Case for Active Policymaking New Keynesian approaches suggest that firms facing costs of adjusting their prices may be slow to change prices in the face of variations in demand. Thus, the short-run aggregate supply curve is horizontal, and changes in aggregate demand have the largest possible effects on real GDP in the short run, which gives discretionary policies scope to offset aggregate demand shocks. Hence, prices and wages are sufficiently inflexible in the short run that there is an exploitable trade-off between inflation and real GDP. According to new Keynesian theory, therefore, discretionary policy actions can stabilize real GDP.

small menu costs, 463
new Keynesian inflation dynamics, 465

- **MyEconLab** Study Plans 18.4, 18.5, 18.6
- Video: The New Keynesian Economics

Log in to MyEconLab, take a chapter test, and get a personalized Study Plan that tells you which concepts you understand and which ones you need to review. From there, MyEconLab will give you further practice, tutorials, animations, videos, and guided solutions.
Log in to www.myeconlab.com

PROBLEMS

All problems are assignable in myeconlab. *Answers to odd-numbered problems appear at the back of the book.*

18-1. Suppose that the government altered the computation of the unemployment rate by including people in the military as part of the labor force.

   a. How would this affect the actual unemployment rate?

   b. How would such a change affect estimates of the natural rate of unemployment?

   c. If this computational change were made, would it in any way affect the logic of the short-run and long-run Phillips curve analysis and its implications for policymaking? Why might the government wish to make such a change?

18-2. When Alan Greenspan was nominated for his third term as chair of the Federal Reserve's Board of Governors, a few senators held up his confirmation. One of them explained their joint action to hinder his confirmation by saying, "Every time growth starts to go up, they [the Federal Reserve] push on the brakes, robbing working families and businesses of the benefits of faster growth." Evaluate this statement in the context of short-run and long-run perspectives on the Phillips curve.

18-3. Economists have not reached agreement on how lengthy the time horizon for "the long run" is in the context of Phillips curve analysis. Would you anticipate that this period is likely to have been shortened or extended by the advent of more sophisticated computer and communications technology? Explain your reasoning.

18-4. The natural rate of unemployment depends on factors that affect the behavior of both workers and firms. Make lists of possible factors affecting workers and firms that you believe are likely to influence the natural rate of unemployment.

18-5. What distinguishes the nonaccelerating inflation rate of unemployment (NAIRU) from the natural rate of unemployment? (Hint: Which is easier to quantify?)

18-6. When will the natural rate of unemployment and the NAIRU differ? When will they be the same?

18-7. Suppose that more unemployed people who are classified as part of frictional unemployment decide to stop looking for work and start their own businesses instead. What is likely to happen to each of the following, other things being equal?

   a. The natural unemployment rate

   b. The NAIRU

   c. The economy's Phillips curve

18-8. People called "Fed watchers" earn their living by trying to forecast what policies the Federal Reserve will implement within the next few weeks and months. Suppose that Fed watchers discover that the current group of Fed officials is following very systematic and predictable policies intended to reduce the unemployment rate. The Fed watchers then sell this information to firms, unions, and others in the private sector. If pure competition prevails, prices and wages are flexible, and people form rational expectations, are the Fed's policies enacted after the information sale likely to have their intended effects on the unemployment rate?

18-9. Suppose that economists were able to use U.S. economic data to demonstrate that the rational expectations hypothesis is true. Would this be sufficient to demonstrate the validity of the policy irrelevance proposition?

18-10. Evaluate the following statement: "In an important sense, the term *policy irrelevance proposition* is misleading because even if the rational expectations hypothesis is valid, economic policy actions can have significant effects on real GDP and the unemployment rate."

18-11. Consider the diagram below, which is drawn under the assumption that the new Keynesian sticky-price theory of aggregate supply applies. Assume that at present, the economy is in long-run equilibrium at point *A*. Answer the following questions.

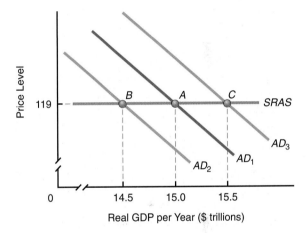

   a. Suppose that there is a sudden increase in desired investment expenditures. Which of the alternative aggregate demand curves—AD_2 or AD_3—will apply after this event occurs? Other things being equal, what will happen to the equilibrium price level and to equilibrium real GDP in the *short run*? Explain.

   b. Other things being equal, after the event and adjustments discussed in part (a) have taken place, what will happen to the equilibrium price level and to equilibrium real GDP in the *long run*? Explain.

18-12. Both the traditional Keynesian theory discussed in Chapter 11 and the new Keynesian theory considered in this chapter indicate that the short-run aggregate supply curve is horizontal.

   a. In terms of their *short-run* implications for the price level and real GDP, is there any difference between the two approaches?

b. In terms of their *long-run* implications for the price level and real GDP, is there any difference between the two approaches?

18-13. The real-business-cycle approach attributes even short-run increases in real GDP largely to aggregate supply shocks. Rightward shifts in aggregate supply tend to push down the equilibrium price level. How could the real-business-cycle perspective explain the low but persistent inflation that the United States experienced until 2007?

18-14. Normally, when aggregate demand increases, firms find it more profitable to raise prices than to leave prices unchanged. The idea behind the small-menu-cost explanation for price stickiness is that firms will leave their prices unchanged if their profit gain from adjusting prices is less than the menu costs they would incur if they change prices. If firms anticipate that a rise in demand is likely to last for a long time, does this make them more or less likely to adjust their prices when they face small menu costs? (Hint: Profits are a flow that firms earn from week to week and month to month, but small menu costs are a one-time expense.)

18-15. The policy relevance of new Keynesian inflation dynamics based on the theory of small menu costs and sticky prices depends on the exploitability of the implied relationship between inflation and real GDP. Explain in your own words why the average time between price adjustments by firms is a crucial determinant of whether policymakers can actively exploit this relationship to try to stabilize real GDP.

ECONOMICS ON THE NET

The Inflation–Unemployment Relationship According to the basic aggregate demand and aggregate supply model, the unemployment rate should be inversely related to changes in the inflation rate, other things being equal. This application allows you to take a direct look at unemployment and inflation data to judge for yourself whether the two variables appear to be related.

Title: Bureau of Labor Statistics: Economy at a Glance

Navigation: Go to **www.econtoday.com/chapter18** to visit the Bureau of Labor Statistics Economy at a Glance home page.

Application Perform the indicated operations, and then answer the following questions.

1. Click on the graph box next to *Consumer Price Index*. Take a look at the solid line showing inflation. How much has inflation varied in recent years? Compare this with previous years, especially the mid-1970s to mid-1980s.

2. Back up to *Economy at a Glance*, and now click on the graph box next to *Unemployment Rate*. During what recent years was the unemployment rate approaching and at its peak value? Do you note any appearance of an inverse relationship between the unemployment rate and the inflation rate?

For Group Study and Analysis Divide the class into groups, and have each group search through the *Economy at a Glance* site to develop an explanation for the key factors accounting for the recent behavior of the unemployment rate. Have each group report on its explanation. Is there any one factor that best explains the recent behavior of the unemployment rate?

ANSWERS TO QUICK QUIZZES

p. 457: (i) long . . . expectations; (ii) increase . . . decrease; (iii) Phillips . . . demand; (iv) Activist

p. 463: (i) rational expectations; (ii) policy irrelevance; (iii) supply . . . real business

p. 469: (i) small menu . . . horizontal; (ii) short . . . price . . . short

Policies and Prospects for Global Economic Growth

19

In 2008, a contagion swept around the globe. It began in the United States and then spread to the United Kingdom, Germany, and Iceland. Eventually, the contagion spread to Russia and other developing nations. The source of the contagion was a sharp decline in U.S. housing prices that generated a collapse in the values of numerous housing-related financial assets. Many investors responded by removing their funds from U.S. and European banks. Global investment and real GDP growth dropped markedly. Does this event send a signal to developing nations that they should not copy industrialized nations by relying on private financing? Answering this question ultimately depends on whether potentially volatile private international investment flows to developing nations generate long-run economic growth. Assessing how international flows of private investment funds influence economic growth is a key topic addressed in this chapter.

LEARNING OBJECTIVES

MyEconLab helps you master each objective and study more efficiently. See end of chapter for details.

After reading this chapter, you should be able to:

➤ Explain why population growth can have uncertain effects on economic growth

➤ Understand why the existence of dead capital retards investment and economic growth in much of the developing world

➤ Describe how government inefficiencies have contributed to the creation of relatively large quantities of dead capital in the world's developing nations

➤ Discuss the sources of international investment funds for developing nations and identify obstacles to international investment in these nations

➤ Identify the key functions of the World Bank and the International Monetary Fund

➤ Explain the basis for recent criticisms of policymaking at the World Bank and the International Monetary Fund

? DID YOU KNOW THAT when the president of the Republic of the Congo (also known as Congo-Brazzaville) recently visited New York City for a few days, his office paid for 44 rooms at the Waldorf-Astoria Hotel and ran up a bill of $252,000? This expense came within a few weeks of another $150,000 visit at the same hotel. The government of the Republic of the Congo paid these expenses just a few months after receiving aid packages from the International Monetary Fund (IMF) and the World Bank totaling $2.9 billion. These multinational institutions had provided the aid even though the country already had more than $9 billion in existing debts. The IMF and World Bank determined that the nation was too poor to meet its outstanding obligations, despite the fact that the nation typically receives more than $2.5 billion per year in revenues from the sale of oil. More than 3 million people in the Republic of the Congo—in excess of 70 percent of its citizens—earn incomes equivalent to less than $3 per day.

Some observers question whether the IMF and World Bank were wise to provide financial assistance to a nation whose leaders allocate at least part of the funds to expensive stays in high-priced New York hotels. Evaluating the activities of these multinational institutions is one topic of this chapter. First, however, we focus on how some of the world's nations are able to grow much faster on their own than others, such as the Republic of the Congo, which regularly turn to the IMF and the World Bank for assistance.

Labor Resources and Economic Growth

You learned in Chapter 9 that the main determinants of economic growth are the growth of labor and capital resources and the rate of increase of labor and capital productivity. Human resources are abundant around the globe. Currently, the world's population increases by more than 75 million people each year. This population growth is not spread evenly over the earth's surface. Among the relatively wealthy nations of Europe, women bear an average of just over one child during their lifetimes. In the United States, a typical woman bears about 1.5 children. But in the generally poorer nations of Africa, women bear an average of six children.

Population growth does not necessarily translate into an increase in labor resources in the poorest regions of the world. Many people in poor nations do not join the labor force. Many who do so have trouble obtaining employment.

A common assumption is that high population growth in a less developed nation hinders the growth of its per capita GDP. Certainly, this is the presumption in China, where the government has imposed an absolute limit of one child per female resident. In fact, however, the relationship between population growth and economic growth is not really so clear-cut.

Basic Arithmetic of Population Growth and Economic Growth

Does a larger population raise or lower per capita real GDP? If a country has fixed borders and an unchanged level of aggregate real GDP, a higher population directly reduces per capita real GDP. After all, if there are more people, then dividing a constant amount of real GDP by a larger number of people reduces real GDP per capita.

This basic arithmetic works for growth rates too. We can express the growth rate of per capita real GDP in a nation as

$$\text{Rate of growth of per capita real GDP} = \text{rate of growth in real GDP} - \text{rate of growth of population}$$

Hence, if real GDP grows at a constant rate of 4 percent per year and the annual rate of population growth increases from 2 percent to 3 percent, the annual rate of growth of per capita real GDP will decline, from 2 percent to 1 percent.

Why has the Chinese government imposed a limit of one child per female resident?

HOW POPULATION GROWTH CAN CONTRIBUTE TO ECONOMIC GROWTH The arithmetic of the relationship between economic growth and population growth can be misleading. Certainly, it is a mathematical fact that the rate of growth of per capita real GDP equals the difference between the rate of growth in real GDP and the rate of growth of the population. Economic analysis, however, indicates that population growth can affect the rate of growth of real GDP. Thus, these two growth rates generally are not independent.

Recall from Chapter 9 that a higher rate of labor force participation by a nation's population contributes to increased growth of real GDP. If population growth is also accompanied by growth in the rate of labor force participation, then population growth can contribute to *per capita* real GDP growth. Even though population growth by itself tends to reduce the growth of per capita real GDP, greater labor force participation by an enlarged population can boost real GDP growth sufficiently to more than compensate for the increase in population. On balance, the rate of growth of per capita real GDP can thereby increase.

WHETHER POPULATION GROWTH HINDERS OR CONTRIBUTES TO ECONOMIC GROWTH DEPENDS ON WHERE YOU LIVE On net, does an increased rate of population growth detract from or add to the rate of economic growth? Table 19-1 indicates that the answer depends on which nation one considers. In some nations that have experienced relatively high average rates of population growth, such as China, Singapore, and, to a lesser extent, India and Pakistan, economic growth has accompanied population growth. In contrast, in nations such as Saudi Arabia, Niger, and Zambia, there has been a negative relationship between population growth and per capita real GDP growth. Other factors apparently must affect how population growth and economic growth ultimately interrelate.

The Role of Economic Freedom

A crucial factor influencing economic growth is the relative freedom of a nation's residents. Particularly important is the degree of **economic freedom**—the rights to own private property and to exchange goods, services, and financial assets with minimal government interference—available to the residents of a nation.

Economic freedom
The rights to own private property and to exchange goods, services, and financial assets with minimal government interference.

TABLE 19-1			
Population Growth and Growth in Per Capita Real GDP in Selected Nations Since 1970	Country	Average Annual Population Growth Rate (%)	Average Annual Rate of Growth of Per Capita Real GDP (%)
	China	1.3	7.0
	Ghana	2.9	−1.3
	India	2.0	2.9
	Jordan	4.2	−0.5
	Niger	3.5	−3.1
	Pakistan	2.8	2.6
	Saudi Arabia	4.2	−2.7
	Sierra Leone	2.2	−1.8
	Singapore	2.0	6.1
	South Korea	1.3	7.0
	United States	1.1	1.7
	Zambia	3.2	−2.4

Source: World Bank.

Go to www.econtoday.com/chapter19 to review the Heritage Foundation's evaluations of the degree of economic freedom in different nations.

Approximately two-thirds of the world's people reside in about three dozen nations with governments unwilling to grant residents significant economic freedom. The economies of these nations, even though they have the majority of the world's population, produce only 13 percent of the world's total output. Several of these countries have experienced rates of economic growth at or above the 1.2 percent annual average for the world's nations during the past 30 years, but many are growing much more slowly. More than 30 of these countries have experienced negative rates of per capita income growth.

Only 17 nations, with 17 percent of the world's people, grant their residents high degrees of economic freedom. These nations, some of which have very high population densities, together account for 81 percent of total world output. All of the countries that grant considerable economic freedom have experienced positive rates of economic growth, and most are close to or above the world's average rate of economic growth.

U.S. residents usually regard local police and state and national militaries as protectors of economic freedom, which in turn promotes economic growth. Is it possible that in Indonesia, *fewer* police and *lower* troop levels might *stimulate* economic growth?

INTERNATIONAL EXAMPLE
In Indonesia, Cutting Back on Policing Might Enhance Growth

The Indonesian province of Aceh has two main roads. Along these roads, police officers and troops regularly establish checkpoints through which all traffic, including trucks bearing items being shipped to markets in the province's main towns and cities, must pass. Recently, two economists accompanied trucks on 304 trips along one of these roads, a nearly 400-mile route between the cities of Medan and Meulaboh, which included 27 police and military checkpoints. At most of these checkpoints, police officers and military officials would not allow the trucks to pass unless the drivers handed over bribes. The economists saw the drivers pay more than 6,000 bribes, ranging from packs of cigarettes to several dollars. They calculated that, on aver-

age, the bribes increased the total cost of each truck trip by about 13 percent—or more than the wages earned by a truck driver to make the trip. The economists concluded that reducing police and military "protection" along key Indonesian transportation arteries could significantly cut the costs of cross-country trade. In Indonesia, less policing ostensibly aimed at protecting economic freedom might actually promote freer markets and greater economic growth.

FOR CRITICAL ANALYSIS
Why is there likely to be a "best" size of police and military forces that is consistent with the highest possible rate of economic growth in Indonesia?

The Role of Political Freedom

Interestingly, *political freedom*—the right to openly support and democratically select national leaders—appears to be less important than economic freedom in determining economic growth. Some countries that grant considerable economic freedom to their citizens have relatively strong restrictions on their residents' freedoms of speech and the press.

When nondemocratic countries have achieved high standards of living through consistent economic growth, they tend to become more democratic over time. This suggests that economic freedom tends to stimulate economic growth, which then leads to more political freedom.

QUICK QUIZ   *See page 499 for the answers. Review concepts from this section in MyEconLab.*

For a given rate of growth of aggregate real GDP, higher population growth tends to _____ the growth of per capita real GDP.

To the extent that increased population growth leads to greater _____ _____ participation that raises the growth of total real GDP, a higher population growth rate can potentially _____ the rate of growth in per capita real GDP.

In general, the extent of _____ freedom does not necessarily increase the rate of economic growth. A greater degree of _____ freedom, however, does have a positive effect on a nation's growth prospects.

Capital Goods and Economic Growth

A fundamental problem developing countries face is that a significant portion of their capital goods, or manufactured resources that may be used to produce other items in the future, is what economists call **dead capital**, a term coined by economist Hernando de Soto. This term describes a capital resource lacking clear title of ownership. Dead capital may actually be put to some productive purpose, but individuals and firms face difficulties in exchanging, insuring, and legally protecting their rights to this resource. Thus, dead capital is a resource that people cannot readily allocate to its *most efficient* use. As economists have dug deeper into the difficulties confronting residents of the world's poorest nations, they have found that dead capital is among the most significant impediments to growth of per capita incomes in these countries.

Dead capital
Any capital resource that lacks clear title of ownership.

Dead Capital and Inefficient Production

Physical structures used to house both business operations and labor resources are forms of capital goods. Current estimates indicate that unofficial, nontransferrable physical structures valued at more than $9 trillion are found in developing nations around the world. Because people in developing countries do not officially own this huge volume of capital goods, they cannot easily trade these resources. Thus, it is hard for many of the world's people to use capital goods in ways that will yield the largest feasible output of goods and services.

Consider, for instance, a hypothetical situation faced by an individual in Cairo, Egypt, a city in which an estimated 90 percent of all physical structures are unofficially owned. Suppose this person unofficially owns a run-down apartment building but has no official title of ownership for this structure. Also suppose that the building is better suited for use as a distribution center for a new import-export firm. The individual would like to sell or lease the structure to the new firm, but because he does not formally own the building, he is unable to do so. If the costs of obtaining formal title to the property are sufficiently high relative to the potential benefit—as they apparently are at present for about 9 out of every 10 Cairo businesses and households—this individual's capital resource will likely not be allocated to its highest-valued use.

This example illustrates a basic problem of dead capital. People who unofficially own capital goods are commonly constrained in their ability to use them efficiently. As a result, large quantities of capital goods throughout the developing world are inefficiently employed.

Dead Capital and Economic Growth

Recall from Chapter 2 that when we take into account production choices over time, any society faces a trade-off between consumption goods and capital goods. Whenever we make a choice to produce more consumption goods today, we incur an opportunity cost of fewer goods in the future. This means that when we make a choice to aim for more future economic growth to permit consumption of more goods in the future, we must allocate more resources to producing capital goods today. This entails incurring an opportunity cost today because society must allocate fewer resources to the current production of consumption goods.

This growth trade-off applies to any society, whether in a highly industrialized nation or a developing country. In a developing country, however, the inefficiencies of dead capital greatly reduce the rate of return on investment by individuals and firms. The resulting disincentives to invest in new capital goods can greatly hinder economic growth.

GOVERNMENT INEFFICIENCIES, INVESTMENT, AND GROWTH A major factor contributing to the problem of dead capital in many developing nations is significant and often highly inefficient government regulation. Governments in many of the world's poorest nations place tremendous obstacles in the way of entrepreneurs interested in owning capital goods and directing them to profitable opportunities.

In addition to creating a problem with dead capital, overzealously administered government regulations that impede private resource allocation tend to reduce investment in new capital goods. If newly produced capital goods cannot be easily devoted to their most efficient uses, there is less incentive to invest. In a nation with a stifling government bureaucracy regulating the uses of capital goods, newly created capital will all too likely become dead capital.

Thus, government inefficiency can be a major barrier to economic growth. Figure 19-1 depicts the relationship between average growth of per capita incomes and index measures of governmental inefficiency for various nations. As you can see, the

FIGURE 19-1

Bureaucratic Inefficiency and Economic Growth

Inefficiencies in government bureaucracies reduce the incentive to invest and thereby detract from economic growth.

Sources: International Monetary Fund; World Bank.

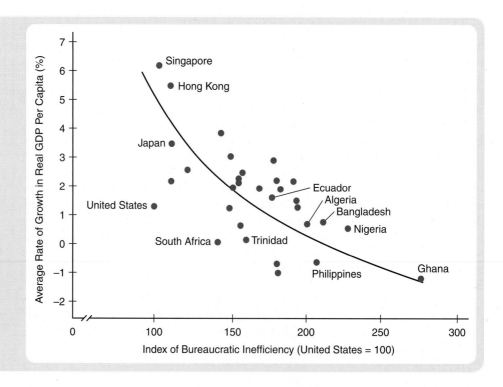

economies of countries with less efficient governments tend to grow at relatively slower rates. The reason is that bureaucratic inefficiencies in these nations complicate efforts to direct capital goods to their most efficient uses.

ACCESS TO CREDIT MATTERS The 2006 Nobel Peace Prize went to Muhammad Yunus of Bangladesh. Yunus contends that access to private credit is vital for promoting economic growth in poverty-stricken countries, where, in his view, present credit arrangements are inadequate.

Private lenders, Yunus suggests, are more likely to grant loans if borrowers can provide marketable collateral in the form of capital assets that lenders can obtain if a borrower defaults. Loan applicants cannot offer as collateral capital assets that they do not officially own, however. Even if an applicant has legal title to capital assets, a lender is unlikely to accept them as collateral if government rules and inefficiencies inhibit the marketability of those assets in the event that the borrower defaults.

Figure 19-2 on the following page displays both the top five and the bottom five nations of the world ranked by their ratios of private credit to GDP. Common features of the bottom five nations are significant stocks of informally used but officially unowned capital goods and very inefficient government bureaucracies. Access to credit in these nations is very limited, so ratios of private credit to GDP are low.

Yunus received his Nobel Peace Prize for his efforts to operate a *microlender*, a banking institution that specializes in making very small loans to entrepreneurs seeking to lift themselves up from the lowest rungs of poverty. In some of the poorest nations in which microlending activities are beginning to flourish, tens of millions of people are obtaining access to credit for the first time in their lives. As a consequence, ratios of private credit to GDP are climbing.

How have governments sometimes emerged as major obstacles to successful operations of private microlenders?

> ## You Are There
>
> To learn about the real-world experience of a company that specializes in offering small amounts of private credit in rural India, read **A Microlender Succeeds in India—In Part by Avoiding Overexposure to Water Buffalo,** on pages 491 and 492.

INTERNATIONAL EXAMPLE
Small Lenders Meet with Big Successes—If Governments Do Not Put Them Out of Business

The list of countries in which microlending has emerged as a thriving business is growing. These countries include Argentina, Bolivia, Bosnia, India, Mexico, Peru, and Venezuela. By carefully screening borrowers and finding ways to operate in locales lacking basic infrastructure such as telephone and electricity services, microlenders specialize in loans ranging from as low as $1 to typically no more than $200. Economists have found evidence that rates of economic growth are higher in areas served by microlenders.

Some government officials, however, contend that microlenders who profit from their activities are exploiting the poor. In particular, the officials object to the high annual interest rates that microlenders charge, which can exceed 50 percent per year in some areas. Microlenders argue that the high interest rates are necessary to compensate for the significant expenses they face in operating in remote areas and for the high loan default rates they experience.

Nevertheless, governments in nations such as Venezuela have placed caps on microlenders' interest rates. Government supervisors in some nations, such as India, have begun subjecting microlenders to banking regulations that drive up their costs. In other countries, such as Argentina, governments have set up publicly funded microlending operations that charge lower, taxpayer-subsidized interest rates. Because these government-sponsored microlenders operate less efficiently than private firms, they typically are not as successful in promoting growth.

FOR CRITICAL ANALYSIS
Why might the fact that governments collect taxes and levy fines for failing to follow legal rules make many prospective borrowers less willing to apply for microloans from government agencies than from private microlenders?

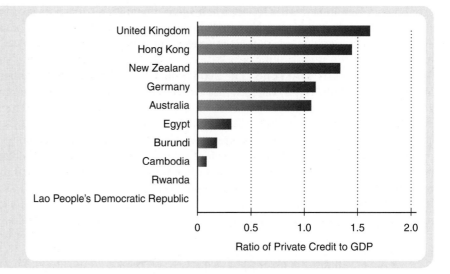

FIGURE 19-2

The Ratio of Private Credit to GDP in Selected Nations

This figure displays the top five and bottom five nations of the world ranked according to ratios of private credit to GDP.

Source: Federal Reserve Bank of St. Louis.

QUICK QUIZ   *See page 499 for the answers. Review concepts from this section in MyEconLab.*

Dead capital is a capital resource without clear title of _____. It is difficult for a buyer to trade, insure, or maintain a right to use dead capital.

The inability to put dead capital to its most efficient use contributes to _____ economic growth, particularly

in _____ nations, where dead capital can be a relatively large portion of total capital goods.

Inefficient government _____ contribute to the dead capital problem, which reduces the incentive to invest in additional capital goods.

Private International Financial Flows as a Source of Global Growth

Given the large volume of inefficiently employed capital goods in developing nations, what can be done to promote greater global growth? One approach is to rely on private markets to find ways to direct capital goods toward their best uses in most nations. Another is to entrust the world's governments with the task of developing and implementing policies that enhance economic growth in developing nations. Let's begin by considering the market-based approach to promoting global growth.

Private Investment in Developing Nations

Since 1995, at least $150 billion per year in private funds have flowed to developing nations in the form of loans or purchases of bonds or stock. Of course, from year to year, international investors fail to renew loans to many developing nations and sell off quantities of government-issued bonds and private-company stocks issued by these countries. When these international outflows of funds are taken into account, the *net* flows of funds to developing countries have averaged just over $100 billion per year since 1995. This is equivalent to more than one-tenth of the annual net investment that takes place within the United States.

Nearly all the funds that flow into developing countries do so to finance investment projects in those nations. Economists group these international flows of investment funds into three categories. One is loans from banks and other sources. The second is **portfolio investment,** or purchases of less than 10 percent of the shares of ownership in a company. The third is **foreign direct investment,** or the acquisition of sufficient stocks to obtain more than a 10 percent share of a firm's ownership.

Figure 19-3 displays percentages of each type of international investment financing provided to developing nations since 1980. As you can see, three decades ago, bank loans accounted for the bulk of international funding of investment in the world's less developed nations. Today, direct ownership shares in the form of portfolio investment and foreign direct investment account for most international investment financing.

Obstacles to International Investment

There is an important difficulty with depending on international flows of funds to finance capital investment in developing nations. The markets for loans, bonds, and stocks in developing countries are particularly susceptible to problems relating to *asymmetric information* (see Chapter 15). International investors are well aware of the informational problems to which they are exposed in developing nations, so many stand ready to withdraw their financial support at a moment's notice.

ASYMMETRIC INFORMATION AS A BARRIER TO FINANCING GLOBAL GROWTH

Recall from Chapter 15 that asymmetric information in financial markets exists when institutions that make loans or investors who hold bonds or stocks have less information than those who seek to use the funds. *Adverse selection* problems arise when those who wish to obtain funds for the least worthy projects are among those who attempt to borrow or issue bonds or stocks. If banks and investors have trouble identifying these higher-risk individuals and firms, they may be less willing to channel funds to even creditworthy borrowers. Another asymmetric information problem is *moral hazard*. This is the potential for recipients of funds to engage in riskier behavior after receiving financing.

Portfolio investment

The purchase of less than 10 percent of the shares of ownership in a company in another nation.

Foreign direct investment

The acquisition of more than 10 percent of the shares of ownership in a company in another nation.

For a link to an Asian Development Bank analysis of the effects of foreign direct investment on developing nations, go to www.econtoday.com/chapter19.

FIGURE 19-3

Sources of International Investment Funds

Since 1980, international funding of capital investment in developing nations has shifted from lending by banks to ownership shares via portfolio investment and foreign direct investment.

Source: International Monetary Fund (including estimates).

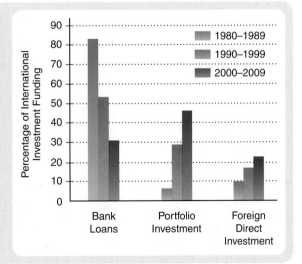

In light of the adverse selection problem, anyone thinking about funding a business endeavor in any locale must study the firm carefully before extending financial support. The potential for moral hazard requires a lender to a firm or someone who has purchased the firm's bonds or stock to continue to monitor the company's performance after providing financial support.

By definition, financial intermediation is still relatively undeveloped in less advanced regions of the world. Consequently, individuals interested in financing potentially profitable investments in developing nations typically cannot rely on financial intermediaries based in these countries. Asymmetric information problems may be so great in some developing nations that very few private lenders or investors will wish to direct their funds to worthy capital investment projects. In some countries, therefore, concerns about adverse selection and moral hazard can be a significant obstacle to economic growth.

INCOMPLETE INFORMATION AND INTERNATIONAL FINANCIAL CRISES Those who are willing to contemplate making loans or buying bonds or stocks issued in developing nations must either do their own careful homework or follow the example of other lenders or investors whom they regard as better informed. Many relatively unsophisticated lenders and investors, such as relatively small banks and individual savers, rely on larger lenders and investors to evaluate risks in developing nations.

International financial crisis
The rapid withdrawal of foreign investments and loans from a nation.

This has led some economists to suggest that a follow-the-leader mentality can influence international flows of funds. In extreme cases, they contend, the result can be an **international financial crisis.** This is a situation in which lenders rapidly withdraw loans made to residents of developing nations and investors sell off bonds and stocks issued by firms and governments in those countries. An international financial crisis occurred during the 1980s, for instance, following a severe drop in bank lending that affected many South American nations. The growth rates of a number of developing nations also were reduced in the wake of international financial crises that took place in Southeast Asia, Central Asia, and Latin America in the late 1990s and early 2000s. This undoubtedly helps explain why there was a decline in flows of private funds to developing countries during the early and middle 2000s.

QUICK QUIZ See page 499 for the answers. Review concepts from this section in MyEconLab.

The three main categories of international flows of investment funds are loans by _____, _____ investment that involves purchasing less than 10 percent of the shares of ownership in a company, and _____ _____ investment that involves purchasing more than 10 percent of a company's ownership shares.

On net, an average of about $_____ billion in international investment funds flows to developing nations each year. In years past, bank loans were the source of most foreign funding of investment in developing countries, but recently _____ investment and _____ _____ investment have predominated.

Obstacles to private financing of capital accumulation and growth in developing nations include _____ _____ and _____ _____ problems caused by asymmetric information, which can restrain and sometimes destabilize private flows of funds.

International Institutions and Policies for Global Growth

There has long been a recognition that adverse selection and moral hazard problems can both reduce international flows of private funds to developing nations and make these flows relatively variable. Since 1945, the world's governments have taken an active role in supplementing private markets. Two international institutions, the World Bank and the International Monetary Fund, have been at the center of government-directed efforts to attain higher rates of global economic growth.

The World Bank

The **World Bank** specializes in extending relatively long-term loans for capital investment projects that otherwise might not receive private financial support. When the World Bank was first formed in 1945, it provided assistance in the post–World War II rebuilding period. In the 1960s, the World Bank broadened its mission by widening its scope to encompass global antipoverty efforts.

Today, the World Bank makes loans solely to about 100 developing nations containing roughly half the world's population. Governments and firms in these countries typically seek loans from the World Bank to finance specific projects, such as improved irrigation systems, road improvements, and better hospitals.

The World Bank is actually composed of five separate institutions: the International Development Association, the International Bank for Reconstruction and Development, the International Finance Corporation, the Multinational Investment Guarantee Agency, and the International Center for Settlement of Investment Disputes. These World Bank organizations each have between 137 and 182 member nations, and on their behalf, the approximately 10,000 people employed by World Bank institutions coordinate the funding of investment activities undertaken by various governments and private firms in developing nations. Figure 19-4 displays the current regional distribution of nearly $20 billion in World Bank lending. Governments of the world's wealthiest countries provide most of the funds that the World Bank lends each year, although the World Bank also raises some of its funds in private financial markets.

World Bank
A multinational agency that specializes in making loans to about 100 developing nations in an effort to promote their long-term development and growth.

FIGURE 19-4

Distribution of World Bank Lending Since 1990

Currently, about 40 percent of the World Bank's loans go to developing nations in the East Asia/Pacific and South Asia regions.

Source: World Bank.

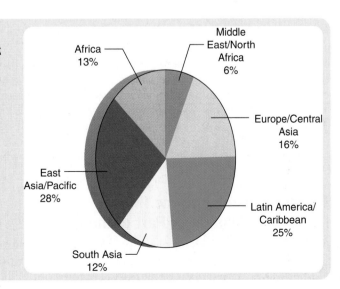

Africa 13%
Middle East/North Africa 6%
Europe/Central Asia 16%
Latin America/Caribbean 25%
South Asia 12%
East Asia/Pacific 28%

The International Monetary Fund

International Monetary Fund (IMF)
A multinational organization that aims to promote world economic growth through more financial stability.

Quota subscription
A nation's account with the International Monetary Fund, denominated in special drawing rights.

The **International Monetary Fund (IMF)** is an international organization that aims to promote global economic growth by fostering financial stability. At present, the IMF has more than 180 member nations.

When a country joins the IMF, it deposits funds to an account called its **quota subscription.** These funds are measured in terms of an international unit of accounting called *special drawing rights* (*SDRs*), which have a value based on a weighted average of a basket of four key currencies: the euro, the pound sterling, the yen, and the dollar. At present, one SDR is equivalent to just over $1.50.

The IMF assists developing nations primarily by making loans to their governments. Originally, the IMF's primary function was to provide short-term loans, and it continues to offer these forms of assistance.

After the 1970s, however, nations' demands for short-term credit declined, and the IMF adapted by expanding its other lending programs. It now provides certain types of credit directly to poor and heavily indebted countries, either as long-term loans intended to support growth-promoting projects or as short- or long-term assistance aimed at helping countries experiencing problems in repaying existing debts. Under these funding programs, the IMF seeks to assist any qualifying member experiencing an unusual fluctuation in exports or imports, a loss of confidence in its own financial system, or spillover effects from financial problems originating elsewhere.

Why is the IMF revamping the relative clout of member nations within its organizational structure?

INTERNATIONAL EXAMPLE
The IMF Rethinks Nations' Voting Shares

A nation's IMF quota subscription determines how much the country can borrow from the IMF under the organization's standard credit arrangements. It also determines the nation's voting power within the IMF. Nevertheless, many nations' shares of quota subscriptions do not correspond to their relative importance in the world economy. The quota subscriptions of China, Indonesia, Malaysia, Mexico, South Korea, and Turkey, for instance, are much smaller than their economies' shares of world GDP.

The IMF is in the process of developing a plan to reconfigure nations' voting power within the organization. One factor complicating this endeavor is that countries with relative voting power exceeding their economies' shares of world GDP do not wish to give up any of their voting rights. Ultimately, the IMF may address the issue simply by creating additional voting rights and granting these "extra" voting rights to underrepresented countries.

FOR CRITICAL ANALYSIS
Would handing "extra" voting rights to currently underrepresented IMF nations actually leave the relative clout of the currently overrepresented *countries undiminished? (Hint: If some nations are granted more votes within the IMF while other nations' votes remain the same, what happens to the percentage of voting shares held by nations whose voting rights remain unchanged?)*

The World Bank and the IMF:
Part of the Solution or Part of the Problem?

Among the World Bank's client nations, meager economic growth in recent decades shows up in numerous ways. The average resident in a nation receiving World Bank assistance lives on less than $2 per day. Hundreds of millions of people in nations receiving its financial support will never attend school, and about 40,000 people in these countries die of preventable diseases every day. Thus, there is an enormous range of areas where World Bank funds might be put to use.

The International Monetary Fund also continues to deal with an ongoing string of major international financial crisis situations. Countries most notably involved in such crises have included Mexico in 1995; Thailand, Indonesia, Malaysia, and South Korea in 1997; Russia in 1998; Brazil in 1999 and 2000; Turkey in 2001; and Argentina in 2001 and 2002.

Naturally, officials of both organizations conclude that world economic growth would have been even lower and financial instability even greater if the institutions did not exist. In recent years, however, economists have increasingly questioned World Bank and IMF policymaking.

DOES THE WORLD BANK REALLY HAVE A MISSION ANYMORE? In some nations, particularly in Africa, attracting private investment has proved difficult. Consequently, the World Bank has been a key source of credit for these nations. Nevertheless, as Figure 19-4 on page 487 indicates, only about 13 percent of lending by the World Bank since 1990 has been directed to African countries.

The World Bank's official mission is to make loans to developing nations that fund projects incapable of attracting private financing from investors at home or abroad. Nevertheless, the World Bank makes many of its loans to nations that have little trouble attracting private funds, such as rapidly growing Asian countries. Critics of such loans argue that they often interfere with the private market for financing capital goods and encourage the kind of inefficient investment that contributed to Asia's economic woes in the late 1990s and to Argentina's financial collapse in the early 2000s.

Some observers also contend that a number of countries that receive World Bank funds are inappropriate recipients of development assistance. For instance, China has reserves of currencies of other nations exceeding $1 trillion, and its residents are net *lenders* of funds to other nations of the world. Nevertheless, the Chinese government and Chinese companies annually borrow between $2 billion and $3 billion from the World Bank.

ASYMMETRIC INFORMATION AND THE WORLD BANK AND IMF Like any other lenders, the World Bank and IMF encounter adverse selection and moral hazard problems. In an effort to address these problems, both institutions impose conditions that borrowers must meet to receive funds.

Officials of these organizations do not publicly announce all terms of lending agreements, however, so it is largely up to the organizations to monitor whether borrower nations are wisely using funds donated by other countries. In addition, the World Bank and IMF tend to place very imprecise initial conditions on the loans they extend. They typically toughen conditions only after a borrowing nation has violated the original arrangement. By giving nations that are most likely to try to take advantage of vague conditions a greater incentive to seek funding, this policy worsens the adverse selection problem the World Bank and IMF face.

Some policymakers, economists, and other observers contend that the policies of the World Bank and the IMF have contributed to international financial crises. They argue that when the World Bank and the IMF provide subsidized credit for industries and governments, private lenders and investors anticipate that these two institutions will back up nations' debts. Thus, private lenders and investors may lower their standards and make loans to, and buy bonds and stocks from, less creditworthy borrowers. Furthermore, if governments know that they can apply for World Bank and IMF assistance in the event of widespread financial failures, they have little incentive to rein in risky business practices.

RETHINKING LONG-TERM DEVELOPMENT LENDING Since the early 1990s, one of the main themes of development economics has been the reform of market processes in developing nations. Markets work better at promoting growth when a developing nation has more effective institutions, such as basic property rights, well-run legal systems, and uncorrupt government agencies.

Hence, there is considerable agreement that a top priority of the World Bank and the IMF should be to identify ways to put basic market foundations into place by guaranteeing property and contract rights. This requires constructing legal systems that can credibly enforce laws protecting these rights. Another key requirement is simplifying the processes for putting capital goods to work in developing countries.

A fundamental issue is what, if anything, international organizations such as the World Bank and the IMF can do to promote pro-growth institutional improvements in developing nations. From one standpoint, there may be little that the World Bank and the IMF can accomplish. After all, the forms of national legal institutions are largely political matters for the nations' leaders to decide. Nevertheless, a number of economists have suggested that the World Bank and the IMF should adopt strict policies against countries with institutional structures that fail to promote individual property rights, law enforcement, and anticorruption efforts. This would, they argue, give countries an incentive to shape up their institutional structures.

Other economists, in contrast, advocate direct financial assistance to governments attempting to implement such institutional reforms. Funds put to such use, they argue, could compensate those who lose power as a result of reform efforts, when shifting to a more capitalist system takes away a ruling group's dictatorial powers to control national resources. Such financial assistance could also help fund investments required to make reforms work. Those proposing this more active role for international lenders contend that the result could be much larger long-term returns for borrowing and lending nations alike. They argue that the overall return would be much greater than the sum of piecemeal payoffs from such projects as dams, power plants, and bridges.

ALTERNATIVE INSTITUTIONAL STRUCTURES FOR LIMITING FINANCIAL CRISES
There are also different views on the appropriate role for the International Monetary Fund in anticipating and reacting to international financial crises. In recent years, economists have advanced a wide variety of proposals. Many of these proposals share common features, such as more frequent and in-depth releases of information both by the IMF and by countries that borrow from this institution. Nearly all economists also recommend improved financial and accounting standards for those receiving funds from multinational lenders, as well as other changes that might help reduce moral hazard problems in IMF lending.

Nevertheless, many of the proposals for change diverge sharply. The IMF and its supporters have proposed maintaining its current structure but working harder to develop so-called early warning systems of financial crises so that aid can be provided to head off crises before they develop. Some economists have proposed establishing an international system of rules restricting capital outflows that might threaten international financial stability.

Other economists call for more dramatic changes. For instance, one proposal suggests creating a board composed of finance ministers of member nations to be directly in charge of day-to-day management of the IMF. Another suggests providing government incentives, in the form of tax breaks and subsidies, for increased private-sector lending that would supplement or even replace loans now made by the IMF.

To learn about the International Monetary Fund's view on its role in international financial crises, go to **www.econtoday.com/ chapter19.**

TIME TO REPLACE THE WORLD BANK AND THE IMF? A few economists have called for completely eliminating both the World Bank and the IMF. Even economists who think these institutions should disappear, however, disagree on what should replace them. On the one hand, a proposal calls for reducing the current scope of government involvement in multinational lending by replacing the World Bank and the IMF with a single institution that would make only short-term loans to countries experiencing temporary financial difficulties. On the other hand, another proposal suggests broadening the roles of governments by developing a "global central bank" that would engage in open market operations using funds raised from new international taxes and other government funds.

So far, few proposals for altering the international financial architecture have led to actual change. The IMF has adopted some minor changes in its procedures for collecting and releasing information, and it has stiffened some of the financial and accounting standards that borrowers must follow to obtain credit. Naturally, the member nations of the IMF would have to agree to the adoption of more dramatic proposals for change. To date there has been little movement in this direction. Undoubtedly, consideration of proposals for an altered international financial structure will continue to generate global debate in the years to come.

QUICK QUIZ   *See page 499 for the answers. Review concepts from this section in MyEconLab.*

The **World Bank** is an umbrella institution for _____ international organizations, each of which has more than 130 member nations, which coordinate _____-term loans to governments and private firms in developing nations.

The **International Monetary Fund** is an organization with more than 180 member nations. It coordinates mainly _____-term and some longer-term financial assistance to developing nations in an effort to _____ international flows of funds.

In principle, the World Bank's role is to provide loans to developing countries where _____ _____ problems deter private investment. But in recent years, the World Bank has provided funds to countries and companies that could have obtained financing from private investors.

Like other lenders, the World Bank and the IMF confront _____ _____ and _____ _____ problems. Some observers worry that failure to deal with these problems has actually contributed to a string of international financial crises. Recently, there have been suggestions that both institutions should impose tougher preconditions on borrowers, such as requiring internal reforms that promote domestic investment.

You Are There ▶ A Microlender Succeeds in India—In Part by Avoiding Overexposure to Water Buffalo

In the poorest regions of India, access to credit traditionally has been virtually nonexistent. Now, however, it is possible to obtain loans of $350 or less to purchase items such as water buffalo or bicycles. Residents are acquiring the loans from microlenders, which are spreading throughout the countryside.

Vikram Akula operates a typical Indian microlender, SKS Microfinance, which he founded about four years ago. After waiting six months for government approval to start SKS Microfinance, Akula and his company's first employee extended their first loans. Initially, to collect the loan payments, they had to traipse through muddy fields to find individual

borrowers. To make their microlending operation more efficient, Akula began requiring groups of borrowers to meet at
designated times. When the profits from the company's
microlending operations increased, Akula obtained loan-
management software that helps his firm avoid overexposing
itself to certain risks. For instance, at one point Akula realized
that customers were using 80 percent of his loans to buy
water buffalo. This meant that SKS Microfinance could have
faced huge defaults if an epidemic killed off water buffalo or if
the price of buffalo milk dropped. The company adjusted by
gradually redirecting more of its loans to brick makers, owners of tea shops, tire re-treaders, and tractor mechanics.

To date, SKS Microfinance has extended in excess of
$60 million in loans to more than 200,000 people, many

of whom are repeat borrowers. The company is expanding
its operations following investments by several foreign
banks, which now see that there are profits to be earned by
making small loans to some of the world's poorest people.
Now that these people have access to credit, they likely will
not be so poor in the future.

CRITICAL ANALYSIS QUESTIONS

1. Why is microlending in developing nations likely to be
   both a labor-intensive business and a risky business?

2. In light of your answer to Question 1, why do you suppose that annual interest rates on Indian microloans
   typically range between 24 percent and 36 percent?

Private International Investment: Source of Instability or Engine of Economic Growth?

Issues and Applications

CONCEPTS APPLIED

- International Financial Crisis
- Foreign Direct Investment
- Portfolio Investment

The financial contagion of 2008 was the most serious international financial crunch since the Asian crisis of 1997-
1998. To some observers, the lesson taught by these
episodes was that developing nations should turn to the International
Monetary Fund and the World Bank for development assistance
rather than soliciting private international investment. Others, however, viewed the 1997-1998 and 2008 episodes as just bumps on
an escalator ride to economic growth that is increasingly powered by
foreign direct investment.

The Changing Mix of Private International Investment

As shown in Figure 19-3 on page 485, in recent years bank loans have gradually decreased as a source of private funding in developing nations. As this source of funds has declined, private international investment has increased. Portfolio investment, the purchase of up to 10 percent of stocks and bonds issued by private companies, has increased most noticeably. Today, portfolio investment accounts for more than 40 percent of all international investment funds.

In addition, the share of funds provided by foreign direct investment, the purchase of more than 10 percent of ownership in private companies, has steadily increased since the late 1970s. Foreign direct investment now accounts for close to 25 percent of all international funds inflows around the globe.

Which Form of International Investment Is Riskiest for Developing Nations?

Figure 19-5 displays index measures of worldwide portfolio stock investment, portfolio bond investment, and foreign direct investment flows into other nations since 1990. Both forms of international portfolio investment dropped during the 1990s. Indeed, the portfolio bond index exhibited *negative* values during the Asian crisis and into the early 2000s, indicating net *outflows* of funds held in bonds during this interval. Clearly, Figure 19-5

FIGURE 19-5

Worldwide Flows of Portfolio Stock Investment, Portfolio Bond Investment, and Foreign Direct Investment Since 1990

In recent years, index measures of portfolio stock investment and, especially, portfolio bond investment have exhibited much greater variability than an index measure of foreign direct investment.

Source: World Bank.

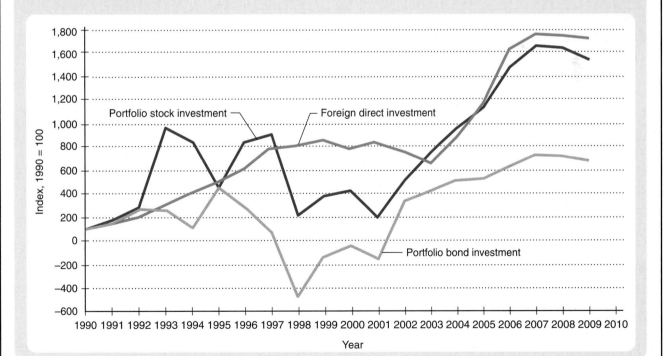

indicates that portfolio investment, especially in bonds, has been considerably more volatile than foreign direct investment, which grew steadily until the early 2000s, dipped slightly for a few years, and then increased again during the mid-2000s.

Economists have found that greater volatility of private international investment tends to be associated with lower economic growth. For instance, since 1970, the variability of private investment flows to Argentina, South Africa, and Venezuela has been two to three times greater than the worldwide average, and the pace of economic growth in these nations has been less than 2 percent per year. In contrast—and in spite of the Asian crisis of 1997–1998—private investment flows to China, Indonesia, and Pakistan, since 1970 have been less than half as volatile as the global average. Indonesia and Pakistan have experienced annual growth rates of 5 percent. China's average annual rate of growth of real income per capita has been about 9 percent.

Benefiting from Low Barriers to Foreign Direct Investment

Why have Argentina, South Africa, and Venezuela experienced more volatile flows of international investment? The answer is that these low-growth nations have typically received much more portfolio investment, particularly in the form of foreign purchases of bonds, than foreign direct investment.

In contrast, China, Indonesia, and Pakistan are recipients of larger shares of global foreign direct investment. In general, these and other Asian nations have fewer legal restraints on foreign direct investment than countries in South America and Africa. Thus, most of the world's foreign direct investment flowing to developing nations is making its way to countries in Asia, which continue to experience much faster rates of economic growth than South American and African countries.

Test your understanding of this chapter by going online to **MyEconLab.**
In the Study Plan for this chapter, select Section N: News.

For Critical Analysis

1. Why do you think that greater volatility in private international investment inflows tends be associated with lower economic growth? (Hint: Instability in ownership of capital goods complicates managing the production of goods and services.)

2. Why do you suppose that companies based in Argentina, South Africa, and Venezuela lobby their governments to enact policies that inhibit inflows of foreign direct investment? (Hint: Typically, common sources of private foreign direct investment in a country are foreign companies seeking to establish facilities for manufacturing and selling their products in that nation.)

Web Resources

1. For a good review of the pros and cons of foreign direct investment for economic growth of developing nations, go to www.econtoday.com/chapter19.

2. For access to detailed World Bank data on foreign direct investment, go to www.econtoday.com/chapter19.

Research Project

Read the first of the Web resources. Why does the author conclude that from the perspective of developing nations, foreign direct investment "should be the preferred form of foreign investment"? Why does the author suggest that the risks associated with foreign direct investment are more likely to fall on the investors themselves, rather than on the residents of developing countries?

 Here is what you should know after reading this chapter. **MyEconLab** will help you identify what you know, and where to go when you need to practice.

WHAT YOU SHOULD KNOW		WHERE TO GO TO PRACTICE
Effects of Population Growth on Economic Growth Increased population growth has contradictory effects on economic growth. On the one hand, for a given growth rate of real GDP, increased population growth tends to reduce growth of per capita real GDP. On the other hand, if increased population growth is accompanied by higher labor productivity, the growth rate of real GDP can increase. The net effect can be an increase in the growth rate of per capita GDP.	economic freedom, 479	• **MyEconLab** Study Plan 19.1 • Audio introduction to Chapter 19
Why Dead Capital Deters Investment and Slows Economic Growth Relatively few people in less developed countries establish legal ownership of capital goods. These unofficially owned resources are known as dead capital. Inability to trade, insure, and enforce rights to dead capital make it difficult for unofficial owners to use these resources most efficiently. As a result, in many developing nations, there is a disincentive to accumulate capital, which tends to limit economic growth.	dead capital, 481	• **MyEconLab** Study Plan 19.2
Government Inefficiencies and Dead Capital in Developing Nations In many developing nations, government regulations and red tape impose very high costs on those who officially register capital ownership. The dead capital problem that these government inefficiencies create reduces investment and growth. Thus, there is a negative relationship between measures of government inefficiency and economic growth.	KEY FIGURE Figure 19-1, 482	• **MyEconLab** Study Plan 19.2 • Animated Figure 19-1
Sources of International Investment Funds and Obstacles to Investing in Developing Nations International flows of funds to developing nations can potentially do much to promote global economic growth. There are three basic categories of these flows of funds: (1) bank loans; (2) portfolio investment, or purchases of less than 10 percent of the shares of ownership in a company; and (3) foreign direct investment, or purchases of more than 10 percent of the shares of ownership in a company. Problems relating to asymmetric information, such as adverse selection and moral hazard problems, are likely to be particularly acute in developing nations. Thus, asymmetric information problems present obstacles to international flows of funds.	portfolio investment, 485 foreign direct investment, 485 international financial crisis, 486 KEY FIGURE Figure 19-3, 485	• **MyEconLab** Study Plan 19.3 • Animated Figure 19-3

(continued)

 *(continued)*

WHAT YOU SHOULD KNOW		WHERE TO GO TO PRACTICE
The Functions of the World Bank and the International Monetary Fund Adverse selection and moral hazard problems faced by private investors can both limit and destabilize international flows of funds to developing countries. The World Bank's function is to finance capital investment in countries that have trouble attracting funds from private individuals and firms. A fundamental duty of the International Monetary Fund is to stabilize international financial flows by extending loans to countries caught up in international financial crises.	World Bank, 487 International Monetary Fund (IMF), 488 quota subscription, 488	• **MyEconLab** Study Plan 19.4
The Basis for Recent Criticisms of World Bank and IMF Policymaking Critics of the World Bank contend that it has recently extended credit to companies and governments that could have obtained funds in private loan markets. Critics also contend that the World Bank and the IMF have failed to deal effectively with the adverse selection and moral hazard problems they face. These critics suggest that the World Bank and the IMF should place more stringent conditions on access to credit, including requiring government borrowers to implement reforms that give domestic residents more incentive to invest.		• **MyEconLab** Study Plan 19.4

Log in to MyEconLab, take a chapter test, and get a personalized Study Plan that tells you which concepts you understand and which ones you need to review. From there, MyEconLab will give you further practice, tutorials, animations, videos, and guided solutions.
Log in to www.myeconlab.com

PROBLEMS

All problems are assignable in myeconlab. *Answers to odd-numbered problems appear at the back of the book.*

19-1. A country's real GDP is growing at an annual rate of 3.1 percent, and the current rate of growth of per capita real GDP is 0.3 percent. What is the population growth rate in this nation?

19-2. The annual rate of growth of real GDP in a developing nation is 0.3 percent. Initially, the country's population was stable from year to year. Recently, however, a significant increase in the nation's birthrate has raised the annual rate of population growth to 0.5 percent.

a. What was the rate of growth of per capita real GDP before the increase in population growth?

b. If the rate of growth of real GDP remains unchanged, what is the new rate of growth of per capita real GDP following the increase in the birthrate?

19-3. A developing country has determined that each additional $1 billion of investment in capital goods adds 0.01 percentage point to its long-run average annual rate of growth of per capita real GDP.

a. Domestic entrepreneurs recently began to seek official approval to open a range of businesses employing capital resources valued at $20 billion. If the entrepreneurs undertake these investments, by what fraction of a percentage point will the nation's long-run average annual rate of growth of per capita real GDP increase, other things being equal?

b. After weeks of effort trying to complete the first of 15 stages of bureaucratic red tape necessary to obtain authorization to start their businesses, a number of entrepreneurs decide to drop their investment plans completely, and the amount of official investment that actually takes place turns out to be $10 billion. Other things being equal, by what fraction of a percentage point will this decision reduce the nation's long-run average annual rate of growth of per capita real GDP from what it would have been if investment had been $20 billion?

19-4. Consider the estimates that the World Bank has assembled for the following nations:

Country	Legal Steps Required to Start a Business	Days Required to Start a Business	Cost of Starting a Business as a Percentage of Per Capita GDP
Angola	14	146	838%
Bosnia-Herzegovina	12	59	52%
Morocco	11	36	19%
Togo	14	63	281%
Uruguay	10	27	47%

Rank the nations in order starting with the one you would expect to have the highest rate of economic growth, other things being equal. Explain your reasoning.

19-5. Suppose that every $500 billion of dead capital reduces the average rate of growth in worldwide per capita real GDP by 0.1 percentage point. If there is $10 trillion in dead capital in the world, by how many percentage points does the existence of dead capital reduce average worldwide growth of per capita real GDP?

19-6. Assume that each $1 billion in investment in capital goods generates 0.3 percentage point of the average percentage rate of growth of per capita real GDP, given the nation's labor resources. Firms have been investing exactly $6 billion in capital goods each year, so the annual average rate of growth of per capita real GDP has been 1.8 percent. Now a government that fails to consistently adhere to the rule of law has come to power, and firms must make $100

million in bribe payments to gain official approval for every $1 billion in investment in capital goods. In response, companies cut back their total investment spending to $4 billion per year. If other things are equal and companies maintain this rate of investment, what will be the nation's new average annual rate of growth of per capita real GDP?

19-7. During the past year, several large banks extended $200 million in loans to the government and several firms in a developing nation. International investors also purchased $150 million in bonds and $350 million in stocks issued by domestic firms. Of the stocks that foreign investors purchased, $100 million were shares that amounted to less than a 10 percent interest in domestic firms. This was the first year this nation had ever permitted inflows of funds from abroad.

a. Based on the investment category definitions discussed in this chapter, what was the amount of portfolio investment in this nation during the past year?

b. What was the amount of foreign direct investment in this nation during the past year?

19-8. Last year, $100 million in outstanding bank loans to a developing nation's government were not renewed, and the developing nation's government paid off $50 million in maturing government bonds that had been held by foreign residents. During that year, however, a new group of banks participated in a $125 million loan to help finance a major government construction project in the capital city. Domestic firms also issued $50 million in bonds and $75 million in stocks to foreign investors. All of the stocks issued gave the foreign investors more than 10 percent shares of the domestic firms.

a. What was gross foreign investment in this nation last year?

b. What was net foreign investment in this nation last year?

19-9. Identify which of the following situations currently faced by international investors are examples of adverse selection and which are examples of moral hazard.

a. Among the governments of several developing countries that are attempting to issue new bonds this year, it is certain that a few will fail to collect taxes to repay the bonds when they mature. It is difficult, however, for investors considering buying government bonds to predict which governments will experience this problem.

b. Foreign investors are contemplating purchasing stock in a company that, unknown to them, may have failed to properly establish legal ownership over a crucial capital resource.

c. Companies in a less developed nation have already issued bonds to finance the purchase of new capital goods. After receiving the funds from the bond issue, however, the company's managers pay themselves large bonuses instead.

d. When the government of a developing nation received a bank loan three years ago, it ultimately repaid the loan but had to reschedule its payments after officials misused the funds for unworthy projects. Now the government, which still has many of the same officials, is trying to raise funds by issuing bonds to foreign investors, who must decide whether or not to purchase them.

19-10. Identify which of the following situations currently faced by the World Bank or the International Monetary Fund are examples of adverse selection and which are examples of moral hazard.

a. The World Bank has extended loans to the government of a developing country to finance construction of a canal with a certain future flow of earnings. Now, however, the government has decided to redirect those funds to build a casino that may or may not generate sufficient profits to allow the government to repay the loan.

b. The IMF is considering extending loans to several nations that failed to fully repay loans they received from the IMF during the past decade but now claim to be better credit risks. Now the IMF is not sure in advance which of these nations are unlikely to fully repay new loans.

c. The IMF recently extended a loan to a government directed by democratically elected officials that would permit the nation to adjust to an abrupt reduction in private flows of funds from abroad. A coup has just occurred, however, in response to newly discovered corruption within the government's elected leadership. The new military dictator has announced tentative plans to disburse some of the funds in equal shares to all citizens.

19-11. For each of the following situations, explain which of the policy issues discussed in this chapter is associated with the stance the institution has taken.

a. The World Bank offers to make a loan to a company in an impoverished nation at a lower interest rate than the company had been about to agree to pay to borrow the same amount from a group of private banks.

b. The World Bank makes a loan to a company in a developing nation that has not yet received formal approval to operate there, even though the government approval process typically takes 15 months.

c. The IMF extends a loan to a developing nation's government, with no preconditions, to enable the government to make already overdue payments on a loan it had previously received from the World Bank.

19-12. For each of the following situations, explain which of the policy issues discussed in this chapter is associated with the stance the institution has taken.

a. The IMF extends a long-term loan to a nation's government to help it maintain publicly supported production of goods and services that the government otherwise would have turned over to private companies.

b. The World Bank makes a loan to companies in an impoverished nation in which government officials typically demand bribes equal to 50 percent of companies' profits before allowing them to engage in any new investment projects.

c. The IMF offers to make a loan to banks in a country in which the government's rulers commonly require banks to extend credit to finance high-risk investment projects headed by the rulers' friends and relatives.

19-13. Answer the following questions concerning proposals to reform long-term development lending programs currently offered by the IMF and World Bank.

a. Why might the World Bank face moral hazard problems if it were to offer to provide funds to governments that promise to allocate the funds to major institutional reforms aimed at enhancing economic growth?

b. How does the IMF face an adverse selection problem if it is considering making loans to governments in which the ruling parties have already shown predispositions to try to "buy" votes by creating expensive public programs in advance of elections? How might following an announced rule in which the IMF cuts off future loans to governments that engage in such activities reduce this problem and promote increased economic growth in nations that do receive IMF loans?

ECONOMICS ON THE NET

The International Monetary Fund The purpose of this exercise is to evaluate the IMF's role in promoting global economic growth.

Title: International Monetary Fund

Navigation: Go to the home page of the IMF on the Web at **www.econtoday.com/chapter19**, and click on *About the IMF* in the left-hand column.

Application Read each entry, and then answer the question.

1. Click on the link at the top-middle of the Web page titled *What the IMF Does*. Which of the IMF's purposes are most directly related to promoting a higher rate of global economic growth? Are any related more indirectly to this goal?

2. Back up to *About the IMF*, and click on *Surveillance*. Based on this discussion, what type of asymmetric information problem does IMF surveillance attempt to address?

3. Back up to *About the IMF*, and click on *Financial Assistance*. Which IMF lending "facilities" appear to be aimed at maintaining stability of international flows of funds? Which appear to be longer-term loans similar to those extended by the World Bank?

For Group Study and Analysis The section titled *How Does the IMF Lend?* discusses interest rate terms applied to different groups of nations. What are the likely rationales for charging some nations lower interest rates than others? Are there any potential problems with this policy? (Hint: Consider the adverse selection and moral hazard problems faced by the IMF.)

ANSWERS TO QUICK QUIZZES

p. 481: (i) reduce; (ii) labor force . . . increase; (iii) political . . . economic

p. 484: (i) ownership; (ii) lower . . . developing; (iii) bureaucracies

p. 486: (i) banks . . . portfolio . . . foreign direct; (ii) 100 . . . portfolio . . . foreign direct; (iii) adverse selection . . . moral hazard

p. 491: (i) five . . . long; (ii) short . . . stabilize; (iii) asymmetric information; (iv) adverse selection . . . moral hazard

33

Comparative Advantage and the Open Economy

The costs of shipping, trucking, or flying physical goods exported from one nation to another have increased dramatically during the past few years. Indeed, since 2006 the per-unit cost of transporting internationally traded items has nearly tripled. A number of policymakers have expressed concern that this upswing in transport costs will eventually bring about a reduction in international trade. Why is international trade important to the world's people? Is it likely that rising costs of moving goods from exporting nations to importing countries really will slow or even halt the growth of international trade? By the time you have finished reading this chapter, you will be able to evaluate these questions.

LEARNING OBJECTIVES

myeconlab

MyEconLab helps you master each objective and study more efficiently. See end of chapter for details.

After reading this chapter, you should be able to:

- Discuss the worldwide importance of international trade

- Explain why nations can gain from specializing in production and engaging in international trade

- Understand common arguments against free trade

- Describe ways that nations restrict foreign trade

- Identify key international agreements and organizations that adjudicate trade disputes among nations

DID YOU KNOW THAT each year, U.S. residents spend more than $5 million on U.S. flags manufactured outside the United States? This figure may fall somewhat in future years, however, if some state governments have their way. Arizona requires public schools and colleges to buy only U.S. flags manufactured in the United States. Tennessee requires all publicly funded purchases of the U.S. flag to be limited to U.S.-manufactured versions. In Minnesota, it is illegal for anyone to sell any U.S. flag that was not manufactured within the United States. The Minnesota restriction is the toughest in the land, with violations punishable by a maximum fine of $1,000 and a jail sentence of up to 90 days.

What effects do restrictions on imports have on quantities and prices of domestically produced goods and services? You will learn the answer to this question in this chapter. First, however, you must learn more about international trade.

The Worldwide Importance of International Trade

Look at panel (a) of Figure 33-1 on the following page. Since the end of World War II, world output of goods and services (world real gross domestic product, or world real GDP) has increased almost every year; it is now almost nine times what it was then. Look at the top line in panel (a). World trade has increased to more than 28 times what it was in 1950.

The United States figured prominently in this expansion of world trade. In panel (b) of Figure 33-1, you see imports and exports expressed as a percentage of total annual yearly income (GDP). Whereas imports added up to barely 4 percent of annual U.S. GDP in 1950, today they account for more than 17 percent. International trade has definitely become more important to the economy of the United States, and it may become even more so as other countries loosen their trade restrictions.

How do you and others take advantage of international trade when you order certain types of seafood at restaurants?

Go to www.econtoday.com/chapter33 for the World Trade Organization's most recent data on world trade.

INTERNATIONAL EXAMPLE
Have Seafood, Will Travel

Increasingly, U.S. restaurants strive to offer fresh seafood, which often requires some kinds of seafood to be shipped long distances. For instance, a number of the live lobsters caught each day in Nova Scotia take a 30-hour truck ride to Louisville, Kentucky. There, they are placed in 25,000-gallon saltwater pools. When restaurant orders arrive, United Parcel Service, which operates a major shipping center in Louisville, transports lobsters directly to restaurants.

Some types of seafood travel even farther to reach your plate. Every day, in Uganda, Nile perch from Africa's Lake Victoria are processed and chilled to near-freezing tempera-

tures. The fish are added to cargo freight transported by British Airways passenger planes to San Francisco. From there, the fish make their way to restaurants across the land, in some cases as much as 8,000 miles distant from their original location in Africa.

FOR CRITICAL ANALYSIS
Some critics claim that international trade causes nations to "lose jobs." Why do you suppose that hundreds of workers in Uganda's Nile perch industry might disagree with this statement?

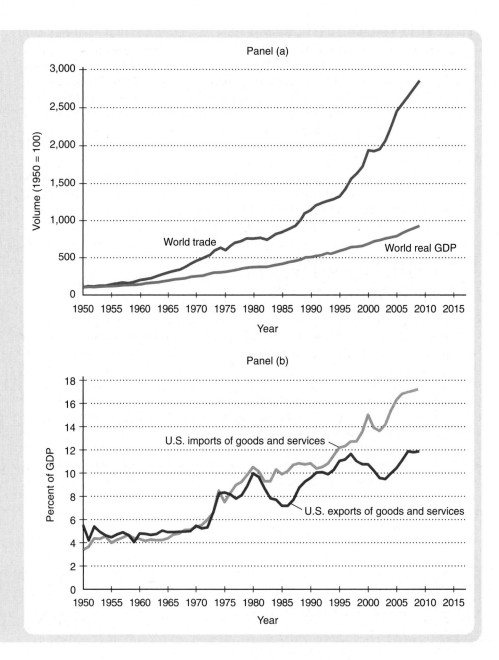

FIGURE 33-1

The Growth of World Trade

In panel (a), you can see the growth in world trade in relative terms because we use an index of 100 to represent real world trade in 1950. By the late 2000s, that index had increased to over 2,800. At the same time, the index of world real GDP (annual world real income) had gone up to only around 900. World trade is clearly on the rise: In the United States, both imports and exports, expressed as a percentage of annual national income (GDP) in panel (b), have generally been rising since 1950.

Sources: Steven Husted and Michael Melvin, *International Economics*, 3d ed. (New York: HarperCollins, 1995), p. 11, used with permission; World Trade Organization; Federal Reserve System; U.S. Department of Commerce.

Why We Trade: Comparative Advantage and Mutual Gains from Exchange

You have already been introduced to the concept of specialization and mutual gains from trade in Chapter 2. These concepts are worth repeating because they are essential to understanding why the world is better off because of more international trade. The best way to understand the gains from trade among nations is first to understand the output gains from specialization between individuals.

The Output Gains from Specialization

Suppose that a creative advertising specialist can come up with two pages of ad copy (written words) an hour or generate one computerized art rendering per hour. At the same time, a computer artist can write one page of ad copy per hour or complete one computerized art rendering per hour. Here the ad specialist can come up with more pages of ad copy per hour than the computer specialist and seemingly is just as good as the computer specialist at doing computerized art renderings. Is there any reason for the creative specialist and the computer specialist to "trade"? The answer is yes because such trading will lead to higher output.

Consider the scenario of no trading. Assume that during each eight-hour day, the ad specialist and the computer whiz devote half of their day to writing ad copy and half to computerized art rendering. The ad specialist would create eight pages of ad copy (4 hours × 2) and four computerized art renderings (4 × 1). During that same period, the computer specialist would create four pages of ad copy (4 hours × 1) and four computerized art renderings (4 × 1). Each day, the combined output for the ad specialist and the computer specialist would be 12 pages of ad copy and eight computerized art renderings.

If the ad specialist specialized only in writing ad copy and the computer whiz specialized only in creating computerized art renderings, their combined output would rise to 16 pages of ad copy (8 × 2) and eight computerized art renderings (8 × 1). Overall, production would increase by four pages of ad copy per day with no decline in art renderings.

Note that this example implies that to create one additional computerized art rendering during a day, the ad specialist has to sacrifice creating two pages of ad copy. The computer specialist, however, only has to give up creating one page of ad copy to create one more computerized art rendering. Thus, the creative advertising employee has a comparative advantage in writing ad copy, and the computer specialist has a comparative advantage in doing computerized art renderings. **Comparative advantage** is simply the ability to produce something at a lower opportunity cost than other producers, as we pointed out in Chapter 2.

Why do you suppose that countries in Africa and the Middle East have a comparative advantage in producing a specific type of milk?

Go to www.econtoday.com/chapter33 for data on U.S. trade with all other nations of the world.

Comparative advantage
The ability to produce a good or service at a lower opportunity cost than other producers.

INTERNATIONAL EXAMPLE
The Comparative Advantage of Desert Dairies

Research has found that camel's milk contains 10 times more iron per unit than cow's milk. Camel's milk also has antibodies that could help fight cancer and potentially even forestall Alzheimer's disease. There are more than 20 million camels in the world. The bulk of these camels are located in the desert lands of Africa and the Middle East, which enables residents of nations in those regions to produce camel's milk at a lower opportunity cost than residents of other nations. In addition to cartons of camel's milk, companies in nations such as Kenya are now producing ice cream and chocolate candies made from camel's milk, which they recently have begun exporting to other parts of the world.

FOR CRITICAL ANALYSIS
If residents of nations in regions other than Africa and the Middle East were to develop methods of raising camels and producing camel's milk, would African and Middle Eastern residents necessarily lose their comparative advantage?

Specialization Among Nations

To demonstrate the concept of comparative advantage for nations, let's consider a simple two-country, two-good world. As a hypothetical example, let's suppose that the nations in this world are India and the United States.

PRODUCTION AND CONSUMPTION CAPABILITIES IN A TWO-COUNTRY, TWO-GOOD WORLD In Table 33-1, we show maximum feasible quantities of computer software and personal computers (PCs) that may be produced during an hour using all resources—labor, capital, land, and entrepreneurship—available in the United States and in India. As you can see from the table, U.S. residents can utilize all their resources to produce either 90 units of software per hour or 225 PCs per hour. Residents of India are able to utilize all their resources to produce either 100 units of software per hour or 50 PCs per hour.

COMPARATIVE ADVANTAGE Suppose that in each country, there are constant opportunity costs of producing software and PCs. Table 33-1 implies that allocating all available resources to production of 50 PCs would require residents of India to sacrifice the production of 100 units of software. Thus, the opportunity cost in India of producing 1 PC is equal to 2 units of software. At the same time, the opportunity cost of producing 1 unit of software in India is 0.5 PC.

In the United States, allocating all available resources to production of 225 PCs would require U.S. residents to give up producing 90 units of software. This means that the opportunity cost in the United States of producing 1 PC is equal to 0.4 unit of software. Alternatively, we can say that the opportunity cost to U.S. residents of producing 1 unit of software is 2.5 PCs.

The opportunity cost of producing a PC is lower in the United States than in India. At the same time, the opportunity cost of producing software is lower in India than in the United States. Thus, the United States has a comparative advantage in manufacturing PCs, and India has a comparative advantage in producing software.

PRODUCTION WITHOUT TRADE Table 33-2 tabulates two possible production choices in a situation in which U.S. and Indian residents choose not to engage in international trade. Let's suppose that in the United States, residents choose to produce and

---

TABLE 33-1

Maximum Feasible Hourly Production Rates of Either Commercial Software or Personal Computers Using All Available Resources

This table indicates maximum feasible rates of production of software and personal computers if all available resources are allocated to producing either one item or the other. If U.S. residents allocate all resources to producing a single good, they can produce either 90 units of software per hour or 225 PCs per hour. If residents of India allocate all resources to manufacturing one good, they can produce either 100 units of software per hour or 50 PCs per hour.

Product	United States	India
Units of software	90	100
Personal computers	225	50

TABLE 33-2

U.S. and Indian Production and Consumption Without Trade

This table indicates two possible hourly combinations of production and consumption of software and personal computers in the absence of trade in a "world" encompassing the United States and India. U.S. residents produce 30 units of software, and residents of India produce 25 units of software, so the total amount of software that can be consumed worldwide is 55 units. In addition, U.S. residents produce 150 PCs, and Indian residents produce 37.5 PCs, so worldwide production and consumption of PCs amount to 187.5 PCs per hour.

Product	United States	India	Actual World Output
Units of software (per hour)	30	25	55
Personal computers (per hour)	150	37.5	187.5

consume 30 units of software. To produce this amount of software requires producing 75 fewer PCs (30 units of software times 2.5 PCs per unit of software) than the maximum feasible PC production of 225 PCs, or 150 PCs. Thus, in the absence of trade, 30 units of software and 150 PCs are produced and consumed in the United States.

Table 33-2 indicates that during an hour's time in India, residents choose to produce and consume 37.5 PCs. Obtaining this amount of PCs entails producing 75 fewer units of software (37.5 PCs times 2 units of software per PC) than the maximum of 100 units, or 25 units of software. Thus, in the absence of trade, 37.5 PCs and 25 units of software are produced and consumed in India.

Finally, Table 33-2 displays production of software and PCs for this two-country world given the nations' production (and, implicitly, consumption) choices in the absence of trade. In an hour's time, U.S. software production is 30 units, and Indian software production is 25 units, so total world software production is 55 units. Thus, the total amount of software available for world consumption is also 55 units. Hourly U.S. PC production is 150 PCs, and Indian PC production is 37.5 PCs, so total world production is 187.5 PCs per hour. Consequently, the total number of PCs available for consumption in this two-country world is 187.5 PCs per hour.

SPECIALIZATION IN PRODUCTION More realistically, residents of the United States will choose to specialize in the activity for which they experience a lower opportunity cost. In other words, U.S. residents will specialize in the activity in which they have a comparative advantage, which is the production of personal computers, which they can offer in trade to residents of India. Likewise, residents of India will specialize in the area of manufacturing in which they have a comparative advantage, which is the production of commercial software, which they can offer in trade to residents of the United States.

By specializing, the two countries can gain from engaging in international trade. To see why, suppose that U.S. residents allocate all available resources to producing 225 PCs, the good in which they have a comparative advantage. In addition, residents of India utilize all resources they have on hand to produce 100 units of commercial software, the good in which they have a comparative advantage.

CONSUMPTION WITH SPECIALIZATION AND TRADE U.S. residents will be willing to buy a unit of Indian commercial software as long as they must provide in exchange no more than 2.5 PCs, which is the opportunity cost of producing 1 unit of software at home. At the same time, residents of India will be willing to buy a U.S. PC as long as they must provide in exchange no more than 2 units of software, which is their opportunity cost of producing a PC.

For instance, suppose that residents of both countries agree to trade at a rate of exchange of 1 PC for 1 unit of software and that U.S. residents agree with Indian residents to trade 75 PCs for 75 units of software. Table 33-3 displays the outcomes that result in both countries. By specializing in PC production and engaging in trade, U.S. residents can continue consuming 150 PCs. In addition, U.S. residents are also able to import and consume 75 units of software produced in India. At the same time, specialization and exchange allow residents of India to continue to consume 25 units of software. Producing 75 more units of software for export to the United States allows India to import 75 PCs.

GAINS FROM TRADE Table 33-4 summarizes the rates of consumption of U.S. and Indian residents with and without trade. Column 1 displays U.S. and Indian software and PC consumption rates with specialization and trade from Table 33-3, and it sums these to determine total consumption rates in this two-country world. Column 2 shows U.S., Indian, and worldwide consumption rates without international trade from Table 33-2. Column 3 gives the differences between the two columns.

Table 33-4 indicates that by producing 75 additional PCs for export to India in exchange for 75 units of software, U.S. residents are able to expand their software consumption from 30 units to 75 units. Thus, the U.S. gain from specialization and trade is 45 units of software. This is a net gain in software consumption for the two-country world as a whole, because neither country had to give up consuming any PCs for U.S. residents to realize this gain from trade.

TABLE 33-3

U.S. and Indian Production and Consumption with Specialization and Trade

In this table, U.S. residents produce 225 personal computers and no software, and Indian residents produce 100 units of software and no PCs. Residents of the two nations then agree to a rate of exchange of 1 PC for 1 unit of software and proceed to trade 75 U.S. PCs for 75 units of Indian software. Specialization and trade allow U.S. residents to consume 75 units of software imported from India and to consume 150 PCs produced at home. By specializing and engaging in trade, Indian residents consume 25 units of software produced at home and import 75 PCs from the United States.

Product	U.S. Production and Consumption with Trade		Indian Production and Consumption with Trade	
Units of software (per hour)	U.S. production	0	Indian production	100
	+Imports from India	75	−Exports to U.S.	75
	Total U.S. consumption	75	Total Indian consumption	25
Personal computers (per hour)	U.S. production	225	Indian production	0
	−Exports to India	75	+Imports from U.S.	75
	Total U.S. consumption	150	Total Indian consumption	75

TABLE 33-4

National and Worldwide Gains from Specialization and Trade

This table summarizes the consumption gains experienced by the United States, India, and the two-country world. U.S. and Indian software and PC consumption rates with specialization and trade from Table 33-3 are listed in column 1, which sums the national consumption rates to determine total worldwide consumption with trade. Column 2 shows U.S., Indian, and worldwide consumption rates without international trade, as reported in Table 33-2. Column 3 gives the differences between the two columns, which are the resulting national and worldwide gains from international trade.

Product	(1) National and World Consumption with Trade		(2) National and World Consumption without Trade		(3) Worldwide Consumption Gains from Trade	
Units of	U.S. consumption	75	U.S. consumption	30	Change in U.S. consumption	+45
software	+Indian consumption	25	+Indian consumption	25	Change in Indian consumption	+0
(per hour)	World consumption	100	World consumption	55	**Change in world consumption**	**+45**
Personal	U.S. consumption	150	U.S. consumption	150	Change in U.S. consumption	+0
computers	+Indian consumption	75	+Indian consumption	37.5	Change in Indian consumption	+37.5
(per hour)	World consumption	225	World consumption	187.5	**Change in world consumption**	**+37.5**

In addition, without trade residents of India could have used all resources to produce and consume only 37.5 PCs and 25 units of software. By using all resources to specialize in producing 100 units of software and engaging in trade, residents of India can consume 37.5 *more* PCs than they could have produced and consumed alone without reducing their software consumption. Thus, the Indian gain from trade is 37.5 PCs. This represents a worldwide gain in PC consumption, because neither country had to give up consuming any PCs for Indian residents to realize this gain from trade.

SPECIALIZATION IS THE KEY This example shows that when nations specialize in producing goods for which they have a comparative advantage and engage in international trade, considerable consumption gains are possible for those nations and hence for the world. Why is this so? The answer is that specialization and trade enable Indian residents to obtain each PC at an opportunity cost of 1 unit of software instead of 2 units of software and permit U.S. residents to obtain each unit of software at an opportunity cost of 1 PC instead of 2.5 PCs. Indian residents effectively experience a gain from trade of 1 unit of software for each PC purchased from the United States, and U.S. residents experience a gain from trade of 1.5 PCs for each unit of software purchased from India. Thus, specializing in producing goods for which the two nations have a comparative advantage allows both nations to produce more efficiently. As a consequence, worldwide production capabilities increase. This makes greater worldwide consumption possible through international trade.

Of course, not everybody in our example is better off when free trade occurs. In our example, the U.S. software industry and Indian computer industry have disappeared. Thus, U.S. software makers and Indian computer manufacturers are worse off.

Some people are worried that the United States (or any country, for that matter) might someday "run out of exports" because of overaggressive foreign competition. The analysis of comparative advantage tells us the contrary. No matter how much

FIGURE 33-2

World Trade Flows

International merchandise trade amounts to more than $15.6 trillion worldwide. The percentage figures show the proportion of trade flowing in the various directions throughout the globe.

Sources: World Trade Organization and author's estimates (data are for 2009).

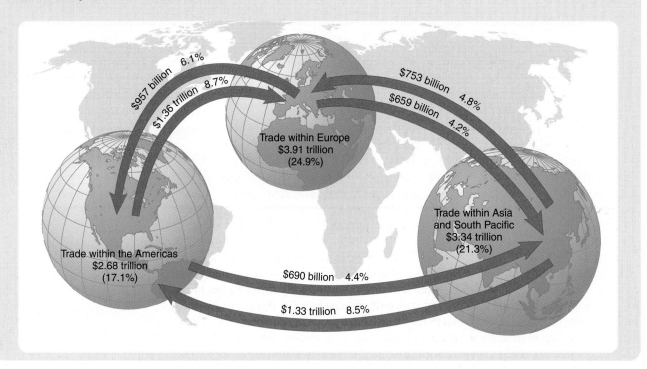

other countries compete for our business, the United States (or any other country) will always have a comparative advantage in something that it can export. In 10 or 20 years, that something may not be what we export today, but it will be exportable nonetheless because we will have a comparative advantage in producing it. Consequently, the significant flows of world trade shown in Figure 33-2 will continue because the United States and other nations will retain comparative advantages in producing various goods and services.

Can nations ever lose their comparative advantages in producing certain types of items to trade with other countries?

INTERNATIONAL EXAMPLE
China Discovers a New Comparative Advantage

From the 1950s until the 1990s, companies based in Japan made that nation a major exporter of electronic devices, including radios, stereo equipment, and televisions. In the 1990s, U.S. companies elbowed out Japanese firms by developing music players, videogame consoles, handheld devices, and digital cameras. Then, in the 2000s, Chinese firms developed comparative advantages in many of those same products. During the decade, China's trade in

INTERNATIONAL EXAMPLE (cont.)

information-technology (IT) products grew at an annual rate exceeding 30 percent. In 2003, China's IT exports passed those of both the European Union and Japan. By the late 2000s, China had also passed the United States and had become the world's top exporter of IT products. Today, the United States is the destination for 30 percent of China's IT exports.

FOR CRITICAL ANALYSIS

If firms in China have a comparative advantage in producing certain types of IT products, what must be true of the opportunity cost of producing these items in China compared with the opportunity cost elsewhere?

Other Benefits from International Trade: The Transmission of Ideas

Beyond the fact that comparative advantage results in an overall increase in the output of goods produced and consumed, there is another benefit to international trade. International trade bestows benefits on countries through the international transmission of ideas. According to economic historians, international trade has been the principal means by which new goods, services, and processes have spread around the world. For example, coffee was initially grown in Arabia near the Red Sea. Around AD 675, it began to be roasted and consumed as a beverage. Eventually, it was exported to other parts of the world, and the Dutch started cultivating it in their colonies during the seventeenth century and the French in the eighteenth century. The lowly potato is native to the Peruvian Andes. In the sixteenth century, it was brought to Europe by Spanish explorers. Thereafter, its cultivation and consumption spread rapidly. It became part of the North American agricultural scene in the early eighteenth century.

New processes have also been transmitted through international trade. An example is the Japanese manufacturing innovation that emphasized redesigning the system rather than running the existing system in the best possible way. Inventories were reduced to just-in-time levels by reengineering machine setup methods.

In addition, international trade has enabled *intellectual property* to spread throughout the world. New music, such as rock and roll in the 1950s and 1960s and hip-hop in the 1990s and 2000s, has been transmitted in this way, as have the software applications and computer communications tools that are common for computer users everywhere.

To what extent has international trade been responsible for the world-wide spread of spices and coffee?

The Relationship Between Imports and Exports

The basic proposition in understanding all of international trade is this:

In the long run, imports are paid for by exports.

The reason that imports are ultimately paid for by exports is that foreign residents want something in exchange for the goods that are shipped to the United States. For the most part, they want U.S.-made goods. From this truism comes a remarkable corollary:

Any restriction of imports ultimately reduces exports.

How has international trade bene-fited the music industry?

This is a shocking revelation to many people who want to restrict foreign competition to protect domestic jobs. Although it is possible to "protect" certain U.S. jobs by restricting foreign competition, it is impossible to make *everyone* better off by imposing import restrictions. Why? The reason is that ultimately such restrictions lead to a reduction in employment and output—and hence incomes—in the export industries of the nation.

International Competitiveness

"The United States is falling behind." "We need to stay competitive internationally." Statements such as these are often heard in government circles when the subject of international trade comes up. There are two problems with such talk. The first has to do with a simple definition. What does "global competitiveness" really mean? When one company competes against another, it is in competition. Is the United States like one big corporation, in competition with other countries? Certainly not. The standard of living in each country is almost solely a function of how well the economy functions *within that country*, not relative to other countries.

Another point relates to real-world observations. According to the Institute for Management Development in Lausanne, Switzerland, the United States continues to lead the pack in overall productive efficiency, ahead of Japan, Germany, and the rest of the European Union. According to the report, the top ranking of the United States has been due to widespread entrepreneurship, more than a decade of economic restructuring, and information-technology investments. Other factors include the open U.S. financial system and large investments in scientific research.

How have new efficiencies in transporting imported goods and domestic goods intended for export helped the United States maintain its international competitiveness?

EXAMPLE
How "Transfer Points" Contribute to U.S. Competitiveness

During the early 2000s, U.S. railroads suffered significant bottlenecks in moving imported goods and domestic goods to be exported between ports and distribution centers. In response to increasing congestion on the tracks, trucking firms and railroad companies, including Union Pacific and Burlington Northern Santa Fe, created "transfer points." These are inland rail yards located on the outer fringes of metropolitan rail networks near cities such as Chicago and San Francisco. Instead of sending freight cars carrying shipping containers directly to cities and adding to rail congestion, railroad companies route trains to transfer points near Rochelle, Illinois, Meridian, Mississippi, and other small communities.

There, the containers are transferred to trucks for transport. Containers filled with imported goods go to distribution centers serving the metropolitan centers, and those with items for export are trucked to ports for shipment abroad. In this way, a cost-efficient flow of internationally traded goods proceeds unabated, day and night, throughout the United States.

FOR CRITICAL ANALYSIS
Why do you suppose that it is often more efficient to offload items from trains at transfer points and truck them to final destination cities than it would be to leave all the goods on trains bound for those cities?

QUICK QUIZ   *See page 862 for the answers. Review concepts from this section in MyEconLab.*

A nation has a **comparative advantage** when its residents are able to produce a good or service at a _____ opportunity cost than residents of another nation.

Specializing in production of goods and services for which residents of a nation have a _____ _____ allows the nation's residents to _____ more of all goods and services.

_____ from trade arise for all nations in the world that engage in international trade because specialization and trade allow countries' residents to _____ more goods and services without necessarily giving up consumption of other goods and services.

Arguments Against Free Trade

Numerous arguments are raised against free trade. They mainly focus on the costs of trade; they do not consider the benefits or the possible alternatives for reducing the costs of free trade while still reaping benefits.

The Infant Industry Argument

A nation may feel that if a particular industry is allowed to develop domestically, it will eventually become efficient enough to compete effectively in the world market. Therefore, the nation may impose some restrictions on imports in order to give domestic producers the time they need to develop their efficiency to the point where they can compete in the domestic market without any restrictions on imports. In graphic terminology, we would expect that if the protected industry truly does experience improvements in production techniques or technological breakthroughs toward greater efficiency in the future, the supply curve will shift outward to the right so that the domestic industry can produce larger quantities at each and every price. National policymakers often assert that this **infant industry argument** has some merit in the short run. They have used it to protect a number of industries in their infancy around the world.

Such a policy can be abused, however. Often the protective import-restricting arrangements remain even after the infant has matured. If other countries can still produce more cheaply, the people who benefit from this type of situation are obviously the stockholders (and specialized factors of production that will earn economic rents) in the industry that is still being protected from world competition. The people who lose out are the consumers, who must pay a price higher than the world price for the product in question. In any event, it is very difficult to know beforehand which industries will eventually survive making it possible, perhaps even likely, that policymakers will choose to protect industries that have no reasonable chance of competing on their own in world markets. Note that when we speculate about which industries "should" be protected, we are in the realm of *normative economics*. We are making a value judgment, a subjective statement of what *ought to be*.

After years of operations, what industry is still regarded as an infant industry in Canada? See the following page.

Infant industry argument
The contention that tariffs should be imposed to protect from import competition an industry that is trying to get started. Presumably, after the industry becomes technologically efficient, the tariff can be lifted.

E-COMMERCE EXAMPLE
Canadian Consumers Cheat to Watch U.S. TV Programming

In Canada, TV viewers cannot watch ESPN, HBO, MTV, Nickelodeon, Showtime, and a number of other popular U.S. channels. Very little of this U.S. programming is available via Canadian cable systems. To view U.S. TV programming, perhaps as many as 1 million residents of Canada pay monthly bills for satellite TV services using U.S. addresses or convince U.S. satellite-TV companies that they reside in the United States. Alternatively, they intercept U.S. satellite signals without paying for the right to do so.

Why do Canadians have to go to such lengths to see U.S. TV programs? The Canadian government still regards Canada's decades-old TV industry as an infant industry. Thus, there are laws prohibiting Canadian residents from receiving signals transmitting U.S. TV programming. The Canadian government actively enforces the laws, as evidenced by recent high-profile prosecutions of individuals who allegedly broke the law by selling satellite systems capable of capturing U.S. TV programs.

FOR CRITICAL ANALYSIS
What is the likely effect of laws excluding U.S. TV programming on the prices Canadians must pay to watch programming produced by Canadian firms?

Countering Foreign Subsidies and Dumping

Go to www.econtoday.com/chapter33 for a Congressional Budget Office review of antidumping actions in the United States and around the world.

Another common argument against unrestricted foreign trade has to do with countering other nations' subsidies to their own producers. When a foreign government subsidizes its producers, our producers claim that they cannot compete fairly with these subsidized foreign producers. To the extent that such subsidies fluctuate, it can be argued that unrestricted free trade will seriously disrupt domestic producers. They will not know when foreign governments are going to subsidize their producers and when they are not. Our competing industries will be expanding and contracting too frequently.

The phenomenon called *dumping* is also used as an argument against unrestricted trade. **Dumping** is said to occur when a producer sells its products abroad below the price that is charged in the home market or at a price below its cost of production. Often, when a foreign producer is accused of dumping, further investigation reveals that the foreign nation is in the throes of a recession. The foreign producer does not want to slow down its production at home. Because it anticipates an end to the recession and doesn't want to hold large inventories, it dumps its products abroad at prices below home prices. U.S. competitors may also allege that it sells its output at prices below its full costs in an effort to cover variable costs of production.

Dumping
Selling a good or a service abroad below the price charged in the home market or at a price below its cost of production.

Protecting Domestic Jobs

Perhaps the argument used most often against free trade is that unrestrained competition from other countries will eliminate jobs in the United States because other countries have lower-cost labor than we do. (Less restrictive environmental standards in other countries might also lower their private costs relative to ours.) This is a compelling argument, particularly for politicians from areas that might be threatened by foreign competition. For example, a representative from an area with shoe factories would certainly be upset about the possibility of constituents' losing their jobs because of competition from lower-priced shoe manufacturers in Brazil and Italy. But, of course, this argument against free trade is equally applicable to trade between the states within the United States.

Economists David Gould, G. L. Woodbridge, and Roy Ruffin examined the data on the relationship between increases in imports and the rate of unemployment. Their conclusion was that there is no causal link between the two. Indeed, in half the cases they studied, when imports increased, unemployment fell.

Another issue has to do with the cost of protecting U.S. jobs by restricting international trade. The Institute for International Economics examined just the restrictions on foreign textiles and apparel goods. U.S. consumers pay $9 billion a year more than they would otherwise pay for those goods to protect jobs in those industries. That comes out to $50,000 *a year* for each job saved in an industry in which the average job pays only $20,000 a year. Similar studies have yielded similar results: Restrictions on imports of Japanese cars have cost $160,000 *per year* for every job saved in the auto industry. Every job preserved in the glass industry has cost $200,000 each and every year. Every job preserved in the U.S. steel industry has cost an astounding $750,000 per year.

How does a charitable U.S. government program aimed at saving millions of people from hunger also seek to protect domestic jobs from foreign competition?

POLICY EXAMPLE
Paying More for U.S.-Grown Charitable Food Donations

Since 1954, the U.S. government's Food for Peace program has worked with about 50 charities and foreign government organizations to donate food to other countries. In recent years, this program has coordinated the annual delivery of more than 3 million metric tons of food aid to about 80 nations at a cost of $1.2 billion in taxpayer funds per year. If the government could use these funds to buy less expensive foods grown in countries located close to recipient nations, assistance could be provided to hundreds of thousands more people. Nevertheless, the law governing the Food for Peace program requires virtually all food items to be produced in the United States. Thus, instead of paying Ugandan farmers $180 per ton of corn used for African food donations, the U.S. government spends nearly $450 per ton purchasing corn from U.S. farmers and shipping the U.S.-grown corn to Africa.

FOR CRITICAL ANALYSIS
Who benefits from rules requiring the Food for Peace program to purchase only U.S.-grown corn?

Emerging Arguments Against Free Trade

In recent years, two new antitrade arguments have been advanced. One of these focuses on environmental and safety concerns. For instance, many critics of free trade have suggested that genetic engineering of plants and animals could lead to accidental production of new diseases and that people, livestock, and pets could be harmed by tainted foods imported for human and animal consumption. These worries have induced the European Union to restrain trade in such products.

Another argument against free trade arises from national defense concerns. Major espionage successes by China in the late 1990s and early 2000s led some U.S. strategic experts to propose sweeping restrictions on exports of new technology.

Free trade proponents counter that at best these are arguments for the judicious regulation of trade. They continue to argue that, by and large, broad trade restrictions mainly harm the interests of the nations that impose them.

QUICK QUIZ   See page 862 for the answers. Review concepts from this section in MyEconLab.

The _____ industry argument against free trade contends that new industries should be _____ against world competition so that they can become technologically efficient in the long run.

Unrestricted foreign trade may allow foreign governments to subsidize exports or foreign producers to engage in

_____, or selling products in other countries below their cost of production. Critics claim that to the extent that foreign export subsidies and _____ create more instability in domestic production, they may impair our well-being.

Ways to Restrict Foreign Trade

International trade can be stopped or at least stifled in many ways. These include quotas and taxes (the latter are usually called *tariffs* when applied to internationally traded items). Let's talk first about quotas.

Quotas

Quota system

A government-imposed restriction on the quantity of a specific good that another country is allowed to sell in the United States. In other words, quotas are restrictions on imports. These restrictions are usually applied to one or several specific countries.

Under a **quota system,** individual countries or groups of foreign producers are restricted to a certain amount of trade. An import quota specifies the maximum amount of a commodity that may be imported during a specified period of time. For example, the government might allow no more than 200 million barrels of foreign crude oil to enter the United States in a particular month.

Consider the example of quotas on textiles. Figure 33-3 presents the demand and supply curves for imported textiles. In an unrestricted import market, the equilibrium quantity imported is 900 million yards at a price of $1 per yard (expressed in

FIGURE 33-3

The Effect of Quotas on Textile Imports

Without restrictions, at point E_1, 900 million yards of textiles would be imported each year into the United States at the world price of $1.00 per yard. If the federal government imposes a quota of only 800 million yards, the effective supply curve becomes vertical at that quantity. It intersects the demand curve at point E_2, so the new equilibrium price is $1.50 per yard.

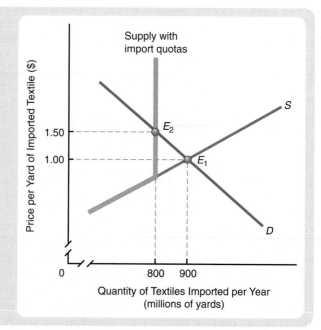

constant-quality units). When an import quota is imposed, the supply curve is no longer S. Instead, the supply curve becomes vertical at some amount less than the equilibrium quantity—here, 800 million yards per year. The price to the U.S. consumer increases from $1.00 to $1.50.

Clearly, the output restriction generated by a quota on foreign imports of a particular item has the effect of raising the domestic price of the imported item. Two groups benefit. One group is importers that are able to obtain the rights to sell imported items domestically at the higher price, which raises their revenues and boosts their profits. The other group is domestic producers. Naturally, a rise in the price of an imported item induces an increase in the demand for domestic substitutes. Thus, the domestic prices of close substitutes for the item subject to the import restriction also increase, which generates higher revenues and profits for domestic producers.

VOLUNTARY QUOTAS Quotas do not have to be explicit and defined by law. They can be "voluntary." Such a quota is called a **voluntary restraint agreement (VRA)**. In the early 1980s, Japanese automakers voluntarily restrained exports to the United States. These restraints stayed in place into the 1990s. Today, there are VRAs on machine tools and textiles.

The opposite of a VRA is a **voluntary import expansion (VIE)**. Under a VIE, a foreign government agrees to have its companies import more foreign goods from another country. The United States almost started a major international trade war with Japan in 1995 over just such an issue. The U.S. government wanted Japanese automobile manufacturers to voluntarily increase their imports of U.S.-made automobile parts. Ultimately, Japanese companies did make a token increase in their imports of U.S. auto parts.

Tariffs

We can analyze tariffs by using standard supply and demand diagrams. Let's use as our commodity laptop computers, some of which are made in Japan and some of which are made domestically. In panel (a) of Figure 33-4 on the following page, you see the demand for and supply of Japanese laptops. The equilibrium price is $1,000 per constant-quality unit, and the equilibrium quantity is 10 million per year. In panel (b), you see the same equilibrium price of $1,000, and the *domestic* equilibrium quantity is 5 million units per year.

Now a tariff of $500 is imposed on all imported Japanese laptops. The supply curve shifts upward by $500 to S_2. For purchasers of Japanese laptops, the price increases to $1,250. The quantity demanded falls to 8 million per year. In panel (b), you see that at the higher price of imported Japanese laptops, the demand curve for U.S.-made laptops shifts outward to the right to D_2. The equilibrium price increases to $1,250, and the equilibrium quantity increases to 6.5 million units per year. So the tariff benefits domestic laptop producers because it increases the demand for their products due to the higher price of a close substitute, Japanese laptops. This causes a redistribution of income from Japanese producers and U.S. consumers of laptops to U.S. producers of laptops.

TARIFFS IN THE UNITED STATES In Figure 33-5 on page 855, we see that tariffs on all imported goods have varied widely. The highest rates in the twentieth century occurred with the passage of the Smoot-Hawley Tariff in 1930.

CURRENT TARIFF LAWS The Trade Expansion Act of 1962 gave the president the authority to reduce tariffs by up to 50 percent. Subsequently, tariffs were reduced by

You Are There

To consider how laws affecting the ability of people to move internationally can protect certain domestic industries from foreign competition, read **How Visa Rules Protect U.S. Pop Stars from a British Invasion,** on page 857.

Voluntary restraint agreement (VRA)
An official agreement with another country that "voluntarily" restricts the quantity of its exports to the United States.

Voluntary import expansion (VIE)
An official agreement with another country in which it agrees to import more from the United States.

Go to www.econtoday.com/chapter33 to take a look at the U.S. State Department's reports on economic policy and trade practices.

FIGURE 33-4

The Effect of a Tariff on Japanese-Made Laptop Computers

Without a tariff, the United States buys 10 million Japanese laptops per year at an average price of $1,000, at point E_1 in panel (a). U.S. producers sell 5 million domestically made laptops, also at $1,000 each, at point E_1 in panel (b). A $500-per-laptop tariff will shift the Japanese import supply curve to S_2 in

panel (a), so that the new equilibrium is at E_2 with price increased to $1,250 and quantity sold reduced to 8 million per year. The demand curve for U.S.-made laptops (for which there is no tariff) shifts to D_2, in panel (b). Domestic sales increase to 6.5 million per year, at point E_2.

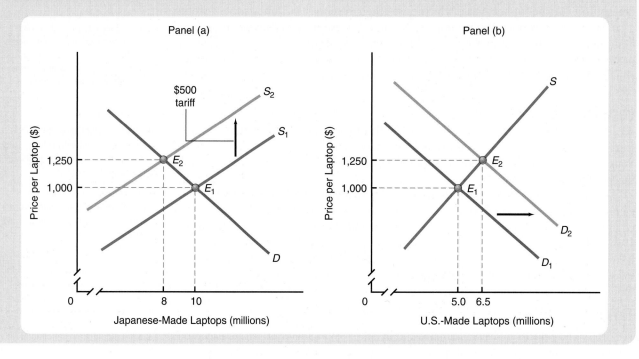

about 35 percent. In 1974, the Trade Reform Act allowed the president to reduce tariffs further. In 1984, the Trade and Tariff Act resulted in the lowest tariff rates ever. All such trade agreement obligations of the United States were carried out under the auspices of the **General Agreement on Tariffs and Trade (GATT),** which was signed in 1947. Member nations of the GATT account for more than 85 percent of world trade. As you can see in Figure 33-5, U.S. tariff rates have declined since the early 1960s, when several rounds of negotiations under the GATT were initiated. In 2002, the U.S. government proposed eliminating all tariffs on manufactured goods by 2015.

General Agreement on Tariffs and Trade (GATT)

An international agreement established in 1947 to further world trade by reducing barriers and tariffs. The GATT was replaced by the World Trade Organization in 1995.

International Trade Organizations

The widespread effort to reduce tariffs around the world has generated interest among nations in joining various international trade organizations. These organizations promote trade by granting preferences in the form of reduced or eliminated tariffs, duties, or quotas.

The World Trade Organization (WTO)

World Trade Organization (WTO)

The successor organization to the GATT that handles trade disputes among its member nations.

The most important international trade organization with the largest membership is the **World Trade Organization (WTO),** which was ratified by the final round of negotiations of the General Agreement on Tariffs and Trade at the end of 1993. The

FIGURE 33-5

Tariff Rates in the United States Since 1820

Tariff rates in the United States have bounced around like a football; indeed, in Congress, tariffs are a political football. Import-competing industries prefer high tariffs. In the twentieth century, the highest tariff was the Smoot-Hawley Tariff of 1930, which was about as high as the "tariff of abominations" in 1828.

Source: U.S. Department of Commerce.

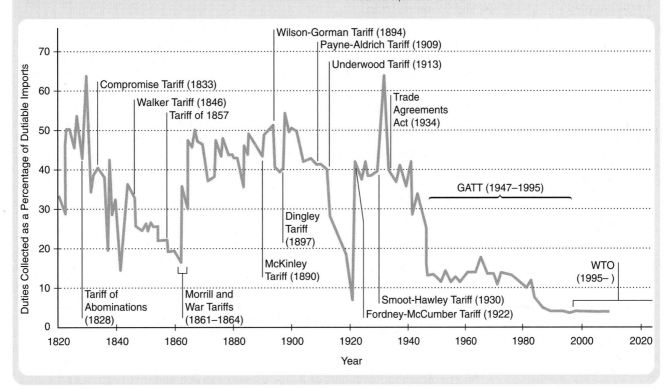

WTO, which as of 2009 had 153 member nations and included 30 observer governments, began operations on January 1, 1995. WTO decisions have concerned such topics as special U.S. steel tariffs imposed in the early 2000s, which the U.S. government removed after the WTO determined that they violated its rules. The WTO also adjudicated the European Union's "banana wars" and determined that the EU's policies unfairly favored many former European colonies in Africa, the Caribbean, and the Pacific at the expense of banana-exporting countries in Latin America. Now those former colonies no longer have a privileged position in European markets.

On a larger scale, the WTO fostered the most important and far-reaching global trade agreement ever covering financial institutions, including banks, insurers, and investment companies. The more than 100 signatories to this new treaty have legally committed themselves to giving foreign residents more freedom to own and operate companies in virtually all segments of the financial services industry.

Regional Trade Agreements

Numerous other international trade organizations exist alongside the WTO. Sometimes known as **regional trade blocs,** these organizations are created by special deals among groups of countries that grant trade preferences only to countries within their groups. Currently, more than 230 bilateral or regional trade agreements are in effect

Regional trade bloc
A group of nations that grants members special trade privileges.

around the globe. Examples include groups of industrial powerhouses, such as the European Union, the North American Free Trade Agreement, and the Association of Southeast Asian Nations. Nations in South America with per capita real GDP nearer the world average have also formed regional trade blocs called Mercosur and the Andean Community. Less developed nations have also formed regional trade blocs, such as the Economic Community of West African States and the Community of East and Southern Africa.

DO REGIONAL TRADE BLOCS SIMPLY DIVERT TRADE? Figure 33-6 shows that the formation of regional trade blocs, in which the European Union and the United States are often key participants, is on an upswing. An average African nation participates in four separate regional trading agreements. A typical Latin American country belongs to eight different regional trade blocs.

In the past, economists worried that the formation of regional trade blocs could mainly result in **trade diversion,** or the shifting of trade from countries outside a regional trade bloc to nations within a bloc. Indeed, a study by Jeffrey Frankel of the University of California at Berkeley found evidence that some trade diversion does take place. Nevertheless, Frankel and other economists have concluded that the net effect of regional trade agreements has been to boost overall international trade, in some cases considerably.

THE TRADE DEFLECTION ISSUE Today, the primary issue associated with regional trade blocs is **trade deflection.** This occurs when a company located in a nation outside a regional trade bloc moves goods that are not quite fully assembled into a member country, completes assembly of the goods there, and then exports them to other nations in the bloc. To try to reduce incentives for trade deflection, regional trade agreements often include **rules of origin,** which are regulations carefully defining categories of products that are eligible for trading preferences under the agreements. Some rules of origin, for instance, require any products trading freely among members of a bloc to be composed mainly of materials produced within a member nation.

Trade diversion
Shifting existing international trade from countries outside a regional trade bloc to nations within the bloc.

Trade deflection
Moving partially assembled products into a member nation of a regional trade bloc, completing assembly, and then exporting them to other nations within the bloc, so as to benefit from preferences granted by the trade bloc.

Rules of origin
Regulations that nations in regional trade blocs establish to delineate product categories eligible for trading preferences.

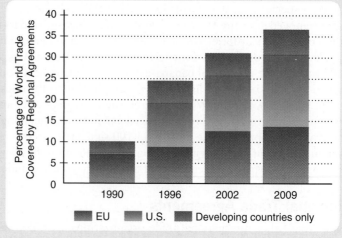

FIGURE 33-6

The Percentage of World Trade Within Regional Trade Blocs

As the number of regional trade agreements has increased since 1990, the share of world trade undertaken among nations that are members of regional trade blocs—involving the European Union (EU), United States, and developing nations—has also increased.

Source: World Bank.

Proponents of free trade worry, however, about the potential for parties to regional trade agreements to use rules of origin to create barriers to trade. Sufficiently complex rules of origin, they suggest, can provide disincentives for countries to utilize the trade-promoting preferences that regional trade agreements ought to provide. Indeed, some free trade proponents applaud successful trade deflection. They contend that it helps to circumvent trade restrictions and thus allows nations within regional trade blocs to experience additional gains from trade.

QUICK QUIZ   *See page 862 for the answers. Review concepts from this section in MyEconLab.*

One means of restricting foreign trade is an import quota, which specifies a _____ amount of a good that may be imported during a certain period. The resulting increase in import prices benefits those who gain the right to sell the imported item and domestic _____ that receive higher prices resulting from substitution to domestic goods.

Another means of restricting imports is a **tariff,** which is a _____ on imports only. An import tariff _____ import-competing industries and harms consumers by raising prices.

The main international institution created to improve trade among nations was the General Agreement on Tariffs and Trade (GATT). The last round of trade talks under the GATT led to the creation of the _____ _____ _____.

_____ _____ agreements among numerous nations of the world have established more than 230 _____ _____ blocs, which grant special trade privileges such as reduced tariff barriers and quota exemptions to member nations.

You Are There ▸ How Visa Rules Protect U.S. Pop Stars from a British Invasion

For weeks, rising British pop singer Lily Allen has been set to perform at the MTV Video Music Awards in Las Vegas. Her itinerary included a trip to the West Coast to perform at sold-out concerts. Instead, she now finds herself at home in London.

Like many recent musical splashes from the United Kingdom, including singers such as James Blunt and Holly Golightly and bands such as Coldplay and Klaxons, Allen is unable to meet U.S. visa rules for foreign music acts. To obtain a P-1 class visitor's visa required for foreign musicians seeking to perform in the United States, Allen had to prove that she has been "internationally recognized" for a "sustained and substantial" period of time. Last week, her manager offered considerable proof that her rapid rise in the popular music world is evidence of international recognition. Nevertheless, a U.S. visa adjudications supervisor

ruled that her recognition has been too short lived to qualify for U.S. entry.

Allen watches on TV as a U.S. performer fills her time slot at the MTV Video Music Awards. As she watches, she finds herself wondering what U.S. musical act will be booked in her place for the West Coast concert tour.

CRITICAL ANALYSIS QUESTIONS

1. How do visa requirements shutting out the musical performers mentioned here, plus numerous other British performers, such as M.I.A., Mysterious Jets, and New Model Army, affect the demand for performances by U.S. musicians?

2. How do restrictions on the entry of British musical performers affect the price that U.S. musicians receive for concert performances?

Higher Shipping Costs: A Barrier to Trade or a By-Product of Its Growth?

CONCEPTS APPLIED

- Tariffs and Quotas
- Gains from Trade
- Comparative Advantage

Recently, some observers have suggested that the most significant barrier to international trade today may not be protectionism. In their view, tariffs and quotas are becoming a minor hindrance to global trade growth. Instead, these observers argue, increased costs of transporting exported items and delivering the items to the nations that import them may be the chief obstacle to the growth of international trade.

Sharp Rises in Global Freight Costs

The costs of physically moving exported goods have jumped significantly. Since 2006, the Baltic Dry Index, which tracks the cost of shipping "dry" goods such as iron ore, coal, and grains around the world, has increased by about 170 percent.

One reason for the rise in shipping costs faced by exporting and importing firms has been that the world has too few cargo ships to handle all the traded goods. New flotillas of cargo ships, some of which can carry as many as 9,000 shipping containers, are either under construction or being launched. Nevertheless, the world's current fleet of cargo ships already has difficulty finding sufficient space to dock at existing ports. Thus, the cost of transporting goods via the sea-lanes promises to remain relatively high for years to come.

Another factor pushing up global trade costs has been the expansion of trade across Asia. Although ships handle much of the trade along Asia's southern and eastern tier, there has been a significant increase in the flow of exports across overland routes in Europe, the Americas, Africa, and Asia. Trucks transporting items across Asia's vast expanse struggle to maintain average speeds as high as 25 miles per hour. As global oil and gasoline prices have continued to climb, so have the costs of this overland trading. Many companies have opted to cut transport times by using cargo jets to fly export goods, but higher oil prices have also pushed up jet fuel expenses considerably.

Trade Barrier or a Symptom of Trade's Popularity?

Undoubtedly, increases in transportation costs discourage some businesses and individuals from opting to export goods to other nations or to import goods from other countries. Higher transportation costs cut into realized gains from trade. In some countries, the resulting reductions in net gains from trade can translate into a reduced incentive to specialize in production and to engage in international trade.

Nevertheless, a key factor underlying the increase in global costs of using ships, overland trucking, and air transit to transport exported goods is a rise in the demand for such services as nations have pursued gains from trade. Nations around the globe have discovered new sources of comparative advantage throughout the past two decades, and efforts to exploit these advantages are a key source of the rising demand for sea, land, and air transportation services. For most businesses throughout much of the world, the higher prices of these services arguably are a symptom of the quest for gains from trade, not a fundamental hindrance to trade.

Test your understanding of this chapter by going online to **MyEconLab**.
In the Study Plan for this chapter, select Section N: News.

For Critical Analysis

1. How do you suppose that higher shipping and air freight costs might be contributing to the increased use of overland transportation in Asia and the resulting increase in overland transport prices? (Hint: Overland transport is a substitute for services provided by cargo ships and air freight businesses.)

2. Why are net gains from trade—gains from trade minus costs of transporting traded goods—what really matter for determining how much international trade actually takes place?

Web Resources

1. To view trends in the Baltic Dry Index and the latest variations in global freight transport rates, go to www.econtoday.com/chapter33.

2. To see how importing and exporting firms calculate shipping rates, go to www.econtoday.com/chapter33.

Research Project

Draw a diagram of an initial equilibrium in the market for export transportation services, in which the demand and supply curves have their normal slopes. When increased growth in trade fuels a rise in demand for these services, does the equilibrium quantity of services provided change by the amount of the rise in demand? Why or why not? Does the equilibrium quantity of transportation services rise on net, however? How does your answer help support the argument that higher transportation costs generated by greater trade undoubtedly discourage some international exchange yet may be a symptom of trade rather than a threat? Explain.

Here is what you should know after reading this chapter. **MyEconLab** will help you identify what you know, and where to go when you need to practice.

WHAT YOU SHOULD KNOW		WHERE TO GO TO PRACTICE
The Worldwide Importance of International Trade Total trade among nations has been growing faster than total world GDP. The growth of U.S. exports and imports relative to U.S. GDP parallels this global trend. Today, exports constitute 12 percent of total national production. In some countries, trade accounts for a much higher share of total economic activity.	KEY FIGURE Figure 33-1, 840	• **MyEconLab** Study Plan 33.1 • Audio introduction to Chapter 33 • Animated Figure 33-1 • ABC News Video: How Outsourcing Affects Our Lives
Why Nations Can Gain from Specializing in Production and Engaging in Trade A country has a comparative advantage in producing a good if it can produce that good at a lower opportunity cost, in terms of forgone production of a second good, than another nation. Because the other nation has a comparative	comparative advantage, 841 KEY FIGURE Figure 33-2, 846	• **MyEconLab** Study Plan 33.2 • Animated Figure 33-2 • Video: The Gains from Trade

(continued)

 (continued)

WHAT YOU SHOULD KNOW		WHERE TO GO TO PRACTICE

advantage in producing the second good, both nations can gain by specializing in producing the goods in which they have a comparative advantage and engaging in international trade. Together, they can then produce and consume more than they would have produced and consumed in the absence of specialization and trade.

Arguments Against Free Trade One argument against free trade is that temporary import restrictions might permit an "infant industry" to develop to the point at which it could compete without such restrictions. Another argument concerns dumping, in which foreign companies allegedly sell some of their output in domestic markets at prices below the prices in the companies' home markets or even below the companies' costs of production. In addition, some environmentalists contend that nations should restrain foreign trade to prevent exposing their countries to environmental hazards to plants, animals, or even humans. Finally, some contend that countries should limit exports of technologies that could pose a threat to their national defense.

infant industry
  argument, 849
dumping, 850

- **MyEconLab** Study
  Plans 33.3, 33.4, 33.5
- Video: Arguments
  Against Free Trade

Ways That Nations Restrict Foreign Trade One way to restrain trade is to impose a quota, or a limit on imports of a good. This action restricts the supply of the good in the domestic market, thereby pushing up the equilibrium price of the good. Another way to reduce trade is to place a tariff on imported goods. This reduces the supply of foreign-made goods and increases the demand for domestically produced goods, thereby bringing about a rise in the price of the good.

quota system, 852
voluntary restraint
  agreement (VRA), 853
voluntary import
  expansion (VIE), 853
General Agreement
  on Tariffs and Trade
  (GATT), 854

KEY FIGURES
Figure 33-3, 852
Figure 33-4, 854

- **MyEconLab** Study
  Plan 33.6
- Animated Figures 33-3,
  33-4

Key International Trade Agreements and Organizations From 1947 to 1995, nations agreed to abide by the General Agreement on Tariffs and Trade (GATT), which laid an international legal foundation for relaxing quotas and reducing tariffs. Since 1995, the World Trade Organization (WTO) has adjudicated trade disputes that arise between or among nations. Now there are also more than 230 regional trade blocs, including the North American Free Trade Agreement and the European Union, that provide special trade preferences to member nations.

World Trade
  Organization, 854
regional trade bloc, 855
trade diversion, 856
trade deflection, 856
rules of origin, 856

KEY FIGURE
Figure 33-5, 855

- **MyEconLab** Study
  Plan 33.7
- Animated Figure 33-5

Log in to MyEconLab, take a chapter test, and get a personalized Study Plan that tells you which concepts you understand and which ones you need to review. From there, MyEconLab will give you further practice, tutorials, animations, videos, and guided solutions.
Log in to www.myeconlab.com

PROBLEMS

All problems are assignable in **myeconlab** *. Answers to the odd-numbered problems appear at the back of the book.*

33-1. To answer the questions that follow, consider the following table for the neighboring nations of Northland and West Coast. The table lists maximum feasible hourly rates of production of pastries if no sandwiches are produced and maximum feasible hourly rates of production of sandwiches if no pastries are produced. Assume that the opportunity costs of producing these goods are constant in both nations.

Product	Northland	West Coast
Pastries (per hour)	50,000	100,000
Sandwiches (per hour)	25,000	200,000

   a. What is the opportunity cost of producing pastries in Northland? Of producing sandwiches in Northland?

   b. What is the opportunity cost of producing pastries in West Coast? Of producing sandwiches in West Coast?

33-2. Based on your answers to Problem 33-1, which nation has a comparative advantage in producing pastries? Which nation has a comparative advantage in producing sandwiches?

33-3. Suppose that the two nations in Problems 33-1 and 33-2 choose to specialize in producing the goods for which they have a comparative advantage. They agree to trade at a rate of exchange of 1 pastry for 1 sandwich. At this rate of exchange, what are the maximum possible numbers of pastries and sandwiches that they could agree to trade?

33-4. Residents of the nation of Border Kingdom can forgo production of digital televisions and utilize all available resources to produce 300 bottles of high-quality wine per hour. Alternatively, they can forgo producing wine and instead produce 60 digital TVs per hour. In the neighboring country of Coastal Realm, residents can forgo production of digital TVs and use all resources to produce 150 bottles of high-quality wine per hour, or they can forgo wine production and produce 50 digital TVs per hour. In both nations, the opportunity costs of producing the two goods are constant.

   a. What is the opportunity cost of producing digital TVs in Border Kingdom? Of producing bottles of wine in Border Kingdom?

   b. What is the opportunity cost of producing digital TVs in Coastal Realm? Of producing bottles of wine in Coastal Realm?

33-5. Based on your answers to Problem 33-4, which nation has a comparative advantage in producing digital TVs? Which nation has a comparative advantage in producing bottles of wine?

33-6. Suppose that the two nations in Problem 33-4 decide to specialize in producing the good for which they have a comparative advantage and to engage in trade. Will residents of both nations agree to trade wine for digital TVs at a rate of exchange of 4 bottles of wine for 1 digital TV? Why or why not?

To answer Problems 33-7 and 33-8, refer to the following table, which shows possible combinations of hourly outputs of modems and flash memory drives in South Shore and neighboring East Isle, in which opportunity costs of producing both products are constant.

South Shore		East Isle	
Modems	Flash Drives	Modems	Flash Drives
75	0	100	0
60	30	80	10
45	60	60	20
30	90	40	30
15	120	20	40
0	150	0	50

33-7. Consider the above table and answer the questions that follow.

   a. What is the opportunity cost of producing modems in South Shore? Of producing flash memory drives in South Shore?

   b. What is the opportunity cost of producing modems in East Isle? Of producing flash memory drives in East Isle?

   c. Which nation has a comparative advantage in producing modems? Which nation has a comparative advantage in producing flash memory drives?

33-8. Refer to your answers to Problem 33-7 when answering the following questions.

　　a. Which *one* of the following rates of exchange of modems for flash memory drives will be acceptable to *both* nations: (i) 3 modems for 1 flash drive; (ii) 1 modem for 1 flash drive; or (iii) 1 flash drive for 2.5 modems? Explain.

　　b. Suppose that each nation decides to use all available resources to produce only the good for which it has a comparative advantage and to engage in trade at the single feasible rate of exchange you identified in part (a). Prior to specialization and trade, residents of South Shore chose to produce and consume 30 modems per hour and 90 flash drives per hour, and residents of East Isle chose to produce and consume 40 modems per hour and 30 flash drives per hour. Now, residents of South Shore agree to export to East Isle the same quantity of South Shore's specialty good that East Isle residents were consuming prior to engaging in international trade.

How many units of East Isle's specialty good does South Shore import from East Isle?

　　c. What is South Shore's hourly consumption of modems and flash drives after the nation specializes and trades with East Isle? What is East Isle's hourly consumption of modems and flash drives after the nation specializes and trades with South Shore?

　　d. What consumption gains from trade are experienced by South Shore and East Isle?

33-9. Critics of the North American Free Trade Agreement (NAFTA) suggest that much of the increase in exports from Mexico to the United States now involves goods that Mexico otherwise would have exported to other nations. Mexican firms choose to export the goods to the United States, the critics argue, solely because the items receive preferential treatment under NAFTA tariff rules. What term describes what these critics are claiming is occurring with regard to U.S.-Mexican trade as a result of NAFTA? Explain your reasoning.

ECONOMICS ON THE NET

How the World Trade Organization Settles Trade Disputes A key function of the WTO is to adjudicate trade disagreements that arise among nations. This application helps you learn about the process that the WTO follows when considering international trade disputes.

Title: The World Trade Organization: Settling Trade Disputes

Navigation: Go to **www.econtoday.com/chapter33** to access the WTO's Web page titled *Dispute Settlement*. Under "Introduction to dispute settlement in the WTO," click on *How does the WTO settle disputes?*

Application Read the article; then answer the following questions.

1. As the article discusses, settling trade disputes often takes at least a year. What aspects of the WTO's dispute settlement process take the longest time?

2. Does the WTO actually "punish" a country it finds has broken international trading agreements? If not, who does impose sanctions?

For Group Study and Analysis Go to the WTO's main site at **www.econtoday.com/chapter33**, and click on *About the WTO*. Divide the class into groups, and have the groups explore this information on areas of WTO involvement. Have a class discussion of the pros and cons of WTO involvement in these areas. Which are most important for promoting world trade? Which are least important?

ANSWERS TO QUICK QUIZZES

p. 849: (i) lower; (ii) comparative advantage . . . consume; (iii) Gains . . . consume

p. 852: (i) infant . . . protected; (ii) dumping . . . dumping

p. 857: (i) maximum . . . producers; (ii) tax . . . benefits; (iii) World Trade Organization; (iv) Regional trade . . . regional trade

Exchange Rates and the Balance of Payments

34

In the mid-1990s, the world's developed nations together exported more goods and services to other countries than they imported. Since then, however, they have become net importers of goods and services. During the same period, so-called emerging countries—primarily a number of previously less developed nations in Asia—experiencing rapid rates of economic growth have observed the opposite trend. They began as net importers of goods and services in the mid-1990s, but today they export significantly more than they import. In this chapter, you will learn how economists keep track of nations' exports and imports of goods and services. By the time you have finished reading the chapter, you will also understand why emerging countries have become net exporters at the same time that developed nations have switched to being net importers.

LEARNING OBJECTIVES

myeconlab

MyEconLab helps you master each objective and study more efficiently. See end of chapter for details.

After reading this chapter, you should be able to:

- ➡ Distinguish between the balance of trade and the balance of payments
- ➡ Identify the key accounts within the balance of payments
- ➡ Outline how exchange rates are determined in the markets for foreign exchange
- ➡ Discuss factors that can induce changes in equilibrium exchange rates
- ➡ Understand how policymakers can go about attempting to fix exchange rates
- ➡ Explain alternative approaches to limiting exchange rate variability

? DID YOU KNOW THAT since 1980, in years when the U.S. *trade deficit*—the excess of imports of physical goods over exports of such goods—decreased, U.S. real GDP growth was much lower than in years when the trade deficit increased? Over this time interval, in years of a decrease, the trade deficit has declined an average of about 1.4 percent, and during those years average annual U.S. real GDP growth has been just under 1.9 percent. In contrast, in years of a trade deficit increase, the average increase has been approximately 2.7 percent, and in those years average annual real GDP growth has been about 3.5 percent. Trade deficits also are not necessarily associated with lower job growth. The United States has experienced a trade deficit in every year since 2001, while the European Union has experienced a *trade surplus*—more exports of goods than imports. U.S. job growth, however, has been more than twice as high as European Union job growth.

Clearly, experiencing a trade deficit is not necessarily "bad news" for a nation. In this chapter, you will learn how the U.S. trade deficit is measured, and you will also learn that the trade deficit is just a part of an international accounting system called the *balance of payments*.

The Balance of Payments and International Capital Movements

Governments typically keep track of each year's economic activities by calculating the gross domestic product—the total of expenditures on all newly produced final domestic goods and services—and its components. A summary information system has also been developed for international trade. It covers the balance of trade and the balance of payments. The **balance of trade** refers specifically to exports and imports of physical goods, or merchandise, as discussed in Chapter 33. When international trade is in balance, the value of exports equals the value of imports. When the value of imports exceeds the value of exports, we are running a deficit in the balance of trade. When the value of exports exceeds the value of imports, we are running a surplus.

The **balance of payments** is a more general concept that expresses the total of all economic transactions between a nation and the rest of the world, usually for a period of one year. Each country's balance of payments summarizes information about that country's exports and imports of services as well as physical goods, earnings by domestic residents on assets located abroad, earnings on domestic assets owned by foreign residents, international capital movements, and official transactions by central banks and governments. In essence, then, the balance of payments is a record of all the transactions between households, firms, and the government of one country and the rest of the world. Any transaction that leads to a *payment* by a country's residents (or government) is a deficit item, identified by a negative sign (−) when the actual numbers are given for the items listed in the second column of Table 34-1. Any transaction that leads to a *receipt* by a country's residents (or government) is a surplus item and is identified by a plus sign (+) when actual numbers are considered. Table 34-1 gives a listing of the surplus and deficit items on international accounts.

Accounting Identities

Accounting identities—definitions of equivalent values—exist for financial institutions and other businesses. We begin with simple accounting identities that must hold for families and then go on to describe international accounting identities.

Balance of trade
The difference between exports and imports of physical goods.

Balance of payments
A system of accounts that measures transactions of goods, services, income, and financial assets between domestic households, businesses, and governments and residents of the rest of the world during a specific time period.

Accounting identities
Values that are equivalent by definition.

TABLE 34-1

Surplus (+) and Deficit (−) Items on the International Accounts

Surplus Items (+)	Deficit Items (−)
Exports of merchandise	Imports of merchandise
Private and governmental gifts from foreign residents	Private and governmental gifts to foreign residents
Foreign use of domestically operated travel and transportation services	Use of foreign-operated travel and transportation services
Foreign tourists' expenditures in this country	U.S. tourists' expenditures abroad
Foreign military spending in this country	Military spending abroad
Interest and dividend receipts from foreign entities	Interest and dividends paid to foreign residents
Sales of domestic assets to foreign residents	Purchases of foreign assets
Funds deposited in this country by foreign residents	Funds placed in foreign depository institutions
Sales of gold to foreign residents	Purchases of gold from foreign residents
Sales of domestic currency to foreign residents	Purchases of foreign currency

If a family unit is spending more than its current income, such a situation necessarily implies that the family unit must be doing one of the following:

1. Reducing its money holdings or selling stocks, bonds, or other assets
2. Borrowing
3. Receiving gifts from friends or relatives
4. Receiving public transfers from a government, which obtained the funds by taxing others (a transfer is a payment, in money or in goods or services, made without receiving goods or services in return)

We can use this information to derive an identity: If a family unit is currently spending more than it is earning, it must draw on previously acquired wealth, borrow, or receive either private or public aid. Similarly, an identity exists for a family unit that is currently spending less than it is earning: It must be increasing its money holdings or be lending and acquiring other financial assets, or it must pay taxes or bestow gifts on others. When we consider businesses and governments, each unit in each group faces its own identities or constraints. Ultimately, net lending by households must equal net borrowing by businesses and governments.

DISEQUILIBRIUM Even though our individual family unit's accounts must balance, in the sense that the identity discussed previously must hold, sometimes the item that brings about the balance cannot continue indefinitely. *If family expenditures exceed family income and this situation is financed by borrowing, the household may be considered to be in disequilibrium because such a situation cannot continue indefinitely.* If such a deficit is financed by drawing on previously accumulated assets, the family may also be in disequilibrium because it cannot continue indefinitely to draw on its wealth. Eventually, it will become impossible for that family to continue such a lifestyle. (Of course, if the family members are retired, they may well be in equilibrium by drawing on previously acquired assets to finance current deficits. This example illustrates that it is necessary to understand circumstances fully before pronouncing an economic unit in disequilibrium.)

EQUILIBRIUM Individual households, businesses, and governments, as well as the entire group of households, businesses, and governments, must eventually reach equilibrium. Certain economic adjustment mechanisms have evolved to ensure equilibrium. Deficit households must eventually increase their income or decrease their expenditures. They will find that they have to pay higher interest rates if they wish to borrow to finance their deficits. Eventually, their credit sources will dry up, and they will be forced into equilibrium. Businesses, on occasion, must lower costs or prices—or go bankrupt—to reach equilibrium.

AN ACCOUNTING IDENTITY AMONG NATIONS When people from different nations trade or interact, certain identities or constraints must also hold. People buy goods from people in other nations; they also lend to and present gifts to people in other nations. If residents of a nation interact with residents of other nations, an accounting identity ensures a balance (but not necessarily an equilibrium, as will soon become clear). Let's look at the three categories of balance of payments transactions: current account transactions, capital account transactions, and official reserve account transactions.

Current Account Transactions

During any designated period, all payments and gifts that are related to the purchase or sale of both goods and services constitute the **current account** in international trade. Major types of current account transactions include the exchange of merchandise, the exchange of services, and unilateral transfers.

Current account

A category of balance of payments transactions that measures the exchange of merchandise, the exchange of services, and unilateral transfers.

MERCHANDISE TRADE EXPORTS AND IMPORTS The largest portion of any nation's balance of payments current account is typically the importing and exporting of merchandise. During 2009, for example, as can be seen in lines 1 and 2 of Table 34-2, the United States exported an estimated $1,334.8 billion of merchandise and imported $2,221.4 billion. The balance of merchandise trade is defined as the difference between the value of merchandise exports and the value of merchandise imports. For 2009, the United States had a balance of merchandise trade deficit because the value of its merchandise imports exceeded the value of its merchandise exports. This deficit was about $886.6 billion (line 3).

SERVICE EXPORTS AND IMPORTS The balance of (merchandise) trade has to do with tangible items—things you can feel, touch, and see. Service exports and imports have to do with invisible or intangible items that are bought and sold, such as shipping, insurance, tourist expenditures, and banking services. Also, income earned by foreign residents on U.S. investments and income earned by U.S. residents on foreign investments are part of service imports and exports. As can be seen in lines 4 and 5 of Table 34-2, in 2009, estimated service exports were $457.3 billion, and service imports were $332.2 billion. Thus, the balance of services was about $125.1 billion in 2009 (line 6). Exports constitute receipts or inflows into the United States and are positive; imports constitute payments abroad or outflows of money and are negative.

When we combine the balance of merchandise trade with the balance of services, we obtain a balance on goods and services equal to –$761.5 billion in 2009 (line 7).

UNILATERAL TRANSFERS U.S. residents give gifts to relatives and others abroad, the federal government makes grants to foreign nations, foreign residents give gifts to U.S. residents, and in the past some foreign governments have granted funds to the U.S. government. In the current account, we see that net unilateral transfers—the total amount of gifts given by U.S. residents and the government minus the total

TABLE 34-2

U.S. Balance of Payments Account, 2009 (in billions of dollars)

Current Account

(1) Exports of merchandise goods	+1,334.8	
(2) Imports of merchandise goods	−2,221.4	
(3) Balance of merchandise trade		−886.6
(4) Exports of services	+457.3	
(5) Imports of services	−332.2	
(6) Balance of services		+125.1
(7) Balance on goods and services [(3) + (6)]		−761.5
(8) Net unilateral transfers	−132.1	
(9) Balance on current account		−893.6

Capital Account

(10) U.S. private capital going abroad	−1,361.9	
(11) Foreign private capital coming into the United States	+1,815.4*	
(12) Balance on capital account [(10) + (11)]		+453.5
(13) Balance on current account plus balance on capital account [(9) + (12)]		−440.1

Official Reserve Transactions Account

(14) Official transactions balance		+440.1
(15) Total (balance)		0

Sources: U.S. Department of Commerce, Bureau of Economic Analysis; author's estimates.
*Includes an approximately $28 billion statistical discrepancy, probably uncounted capital inflows, many of which relate to the illegal drug trade.

amount received from abroad by U.S. residents and the government—came to an estimated −$132.1 billion in 2009 (line 8). The fact that there is a minus sign before the number for unilateral transfers means that U.S. residents gave more to foreign residents than foreign residents gave to U.S. residents.

BALANCING THE CURRENT ACCOUNT The balance on current account tracks the value of a country's exports of goods and services (including military receipts plus income on investments abroad) and transfer payments (private and government) relative to the value of that country's imports of goods and services and transfer payments (private and government). In 2009, it was estimated to be −$893.6 billion (line 9).

If the sum of net exports of goods and services plus net unilateral transfers plus net investment income exceeds zero, a **current account surplus** *is said to exist; if this sum is negative, a current account deficit is said to exist. A* **current account deficit** *means that we are importing more goods and services than we are exporting. Such a deficit must be paid for by the export of financial assets.*

Go to **www.econtoday.com/chapter34** for the latest U.S. balance of payments data from the Bureau of Economic Analysis.

Capital Account Transactions

In world markets, it is possible to buy and sell not only goods and services but also real (e.g., real estate) and financial assets. These are the international transactions measured in the **capital account.** Capital account transactions occur because of foreign investments—either by foreign residents investing in the United States or by

Capital account
A category of balance of payments transactions that measures flows of real and financial assets.

U.S. residents investing in other countries. The purchase of shares of stock in British firms on the London stock market by a U.S. resident causes an outflow of funds from the United States to Britain. The construction of a Japanese automobile factory in the United States causes an inflow of funds from Japan to the United States. Any time foreign residents buy U.S. government securities, there is an inflow of funds from other countries to the United States. Any time U.S. residents buy foreign government securities, there is an outflow of funds from the United States to other countries. Loans to and from foreign residents cause outflows and inflows.

Line 10 of Table 34-2 on the preceding page indicates that in 2009, the value of private capital going out of the United States was an estimated −$1,361.9 billion, and line 11 shows that the value of private capital coming into the United States (including a statistical discrepancy) was $1,815.4 billion. U.S. capital going abroad constitutes payments or outflows and is therefore negative. Foreign capital coming into the United States constitutes receipts or inflows and is therefore positive. Thus, there was a positive net capital movement of $453.5 billion into the United States (line 12). This net private flow of capital is also called the balance on capital account.

There is a relationship between the current account balance and the capital account balance, assuming no interventions by the finance ministries or central banks of nations.

In the absence of interventions by finance ministries or central banks, the current account balance and the capital account balance must sum to zero. Stated differently, the current account deficit must equal the capital account surplus when governments or central banks do not engage in foreign exchange interventions. In this situation, any nation experiencing a current account deficit, such as the United States, must also be running a capital account surplus.

This basic relationship is apparent in the United States, as you can see in Figure 34-1. As the figure shows, U.S. current account deficits experienced since the early 1980s have largely been balanced by private capital inflows, but there are exceptions, for reasons that we explain in the next section.

Official Reserve Account Transactions

The third type of balance of payments transaction concerns official reserve assets, which consist of the following:

1. Foreign currencies
2. Gold
3. **Special drawing rights (SDRs),** which are reserve assets that the **International Monetary Fund** created to be used by countries to settle international payment obligations
4. The reserve position in the International Monetary Fund
5. Financial assets held by an official agency, such as the U.S. Treasury Department

Special drawing rights (SDRs)
Reserve assets created by the International Monetary Fund for countries to use in settling international payment obligations.

International Monetary Fund
An agency founded to administer an international foreign exchange system and to lend to member countries that had balance of payments problems. The IMF now functions as a lender of last resort for national governments.

To consider how official reserve account transactions occur, look again at Table 34-2 on the previous page. The surplus in the U.S. capital account was $453.5 billion. But the deficit in the U.S. current account was −$893.6 billion, so the United States had a net deficit on the combined accounts (line 13) of −$440.1 billion. In other words, the United States obtained less in foreign funds in all its international transactions than it used. How is this deficiency made up? By foreign central banks and governments adding to their U.S. funds, shown by the +$440.1 billion in official transactions on line 14 in Table 34-2. There is a plus sign on line 14 because this represents an *inflow* of foreign exchange in our international transactions.

FIGURE 34-1

The Relationship Between the Current Account and the Capital Account

To a large extent, the capital account is the mirror image of the current account. We can see this in most years since 1970. Typically, when the current account was in surplus, the capital account was in deficit. When the current account was in deficit, the capital account was in surplus. There are exceptions, such as the 1996–1998 and 2005–2007 intervals, during which the current account balance and capital account balance declined at the same time. During these periods, the official reserve transactions balance increased significantly as a result of particularly large purchases of U.S. financial assets by foreign governments and central banks.

Sources: International Monetary Fund; *Economic Indicators.*

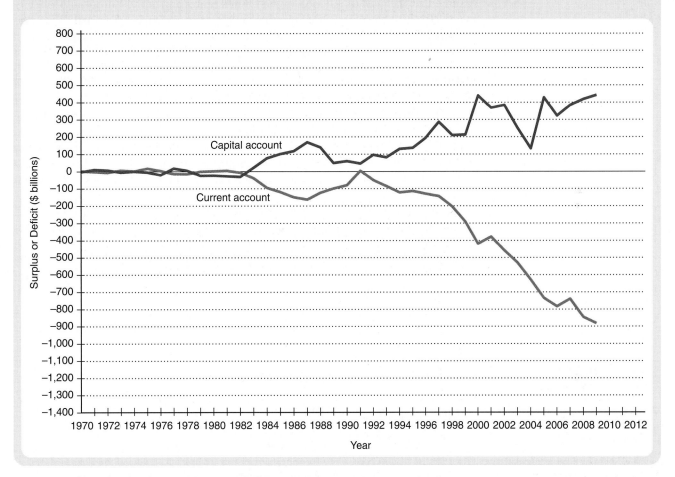

The balance (line 15) in Table 34-2 is zero, as it must be with double-entry bookkeeping. The U.S. balance of payments deficit is measured by the official transactions figure on line 14.

The official reserve account transactions also explain why the movements in the current account balance and the capital account balance in Figure 34-1 are not exact mirror images. This is because the official reserve transactions balance has also varied over time. In recent years, there have been significant surpluses in the official reserve transactions balance. Foreign governments and central banks have purchased large volumes of U.S. financial assets, and these official capital inflows have also offset U.S. current account deficits within the overall balance of payments account.

For instance, between 1996 and 1998 and again between 2005 and 2007, the current account balance and the capital account balance declined simultaneously. During these periods, foreign governments and central banks purchased particularly large quantities of U.S. financial assets. Thus, the official reserve transactions balance increased significantly during these intervals.

What Affects the Distribution of Account Balances Within the Balance of Payments?

A major factor affecting the distribution of account balances within any nation's balance of payments is its rate of inflation relative to that of its trading partners. Assume that the rates of inflation in the United States and in the European Monetary Union (EMU)—the nations that use the euro as their currency—are equal. Now suppose that all of a sudden, the U.S. inflation rate increases. EMU residents will find that U.S. products are becoming more expensive, and U.S. firms will export fewer of them to EMU nations. At the current dollar-euro exchange rate, U.S. residents will find EMU products relatively cheaper, and they will import more. The reverse will occur if the U.S. inflation rate suddenly falls relative to that of the EMU. All other things held constant, whenever the U.S. rate of inflation exceeds that of its trading partners, we expect to see a larger deficit in the U.S. balance of merchandise trade and in the U.S. current account balance. Conversely, when the U.S. rate of inflation is less than that of its trading partners, other things being constant, we expect to see a smaller deficit in the U.S. balance of merchandise trade and in the U.S. current account balance.

Another important factor that sometimes influences account balances within a nation's balance of payments is its relative political stability. Political instability causes *capital flight*. Owners of capital in countries anticipating or experiencing political instability will often move assets to countries that are politically stable, such as the United States. Hence, the U.S. capital account balance is likely to increase whenever political instability looms in other nations in the world.

QUICK QUIZ   *See page 890 for the answers. Review concepts from this section in MyEconLab.*

The _____ of _____ reflects the value of all transactions in international trade, including goods, services, financial assets, and gifts.

The merchandise trade balance gives us the difference between exports and imports of _____ items.

Included in the _____ account along with merchandise trade are service exports and imports relating to commerce in intangible items, such as shipping, insurance, and tourist expenditures. The _____ account also includes income earned by foreign residents on U.S. investments and income earned by U.S. residents on foreign investments.

_____ _____ involve international private gifts and federal government grants or gifts to foreign nations.

When we add the balance of merchandise trade and the balance of services and take account of net unilateral transfers

and net investment income, we come up with the balance on the _____ account, a summary statistic.

There are also _____ account transactions that relate to the buying and selling of financial and real assets. Foreign capital is always entering the United States, and U.S. capital is always flowing abroad. The difference is called the balance on the _____ account.

Another type of balance of payments transaction concerns the _____ _____ assets of individual countries, or what is often simply called official transactions. By standard accounting convention, official transactions are exactly equal to but opposite in sign from the sum of the current account balance and the capital account balance.

Account balances within a nation's balance of payments can be affected by its relative rate of _____ and by its _____ stability relative to other nations.

Determining Foreign Exchange Rates

When you buy foreign products, such as European pharmaceuticals, you have dollars with which to pay the European manufacturer. The European manufacturer, however, cannot pay workers in dollars. The workers are European, they live in Europe, and they must have euros to buy goods and services in nations that are members of the European Monetary Union (EMU) and use the euro as their currency. There must therefore be some way of exchanging dollars for euros that the pharmaceuticals manufacturer will accept. That exchange occurs in a **foreign exchange market,** which in this case involves the exchange of euros and dollars.

The particular **exchange rate** between euros and dollars that prevails—the dollar price of the euro—depends on the current demand for and supply of euros and dollars. In a sense, then, our analysis of the exchange rate between dollars and euros will be familiar, for we have used supply and demand throughout this book. If it costs you $1.50 to buy 1 euro, that is the foreign exchange rate determined by the current demand for and supply of euros in the foreign exchange market. The European person going to the foreign exchange market would need 0.67 euro to buy 1 dollar.

Now let's consider what determines the demand for and supply of foreign currency in the foreign exchange market. We will continue to assume that the only two regions in the world are the EMU and the United States.

Demand for and Supply of Foreign Currency

You wish to purchase European-produced pharmaceuticals directly from a manufacturer located in an EMU nation. To do so, you must have euros. You go to the foreign exchange market (or your U.S. bank). Your desire to buy the pharmaceuticals therefore causes you to offer (supply) dollars to the foreign exchange market. Your demand for EMU euros is equivalent to your supply of U.S. dollars to the foreign exchange market.

> *Every U.S. transaction involving the importation of foreign goods constitutes a supply of dollars and a demand for some foreign currency, and the opposite is true for export transactions.*

In this case, the import transaction constitutes a demand for EMU euros.

In our example, we will assume that only two goods are being traded, European pharmaceuticals and U.S. computer printers. The U.S. demand for European pharmaceuticals creates a supply of dollars and a demand for euros in the foreign exchange market. Similarly, the European demand for U.S. computer printers creates a supply of euros and a demand for dollars in the foreign exchange market. Under a system of **flexible exchange rates,** the supply of and demand for dollars and euros in the foreign exchange market will determine the equilibrium foreign exchange rate. The equilibrium exchange rate will tell us how many euros a dollar can be exchanged for—that is, the euro price of dollars—or how many dollars a euro can be exchanged for—the dollar price of euros.

The Equilibrium Foreign Exchange Rate

To determine the equilibrium foreign exchange rate, we have to find out what determines the demand for and supply of foreign exchange. We will ignore for the moment any speculative aspect of buying foreign exchange. That is, we assume that there are no individuals who wish to buy euros simply because they think that their price will go up in the future.

The idea of an exchange rate is no different from the idea of paying a certain price for something you want to buy. If you like coffee, you know you have to pay about $1.50 a cup. If the price went up to $2.50, you would probably buy fewer cups. If the price went

Foreign exchange market
A market in which households, firms, and governments buy and sell national currencies.

Exchange rate
The price of one nation's currency in terms of the currency of another country.

Flexible exchange rates
Exchange rates that are allowed to fluctuate in the open market in response to changes in supply and demand. Sometimes called *floating exchange rates*.

Go to **www.econtoday.com/chapter34** for recent data from the Federal Reserve Bank of St. Louis on the exchange value of the U.S. dollar relative to the major currencies of the world.

down to 50 cents, you would likely buy more. In other words, the demand curve for cups of coffee, expressed in terms of dollars, slopes downward following the law of demand. The demand curve for euros slopes downward also, and we will see why.

Let's think more closely about the demand schedule for euros. Let's say that it costs you $1.35 to purchase 1 euro; that is the exchange rate between dollars and euros. If tomorrow you had to pay $1.50 for the same euro, the exchange rate would have changed. Looking at such a change, we would say that there has been an **appreciation** in the value of the euro in the foreign exchange market. But another way to view this increase in the value of the euro is to say that there has been a **depreciation** in the value of the dollar in the foreign exchange market. The dollar used to buy 0.74 euro; tomorrow, the dollar will be able to buy only 0.67 euro at a price of $1.50 per euro. If the dollar price of euros rises, you will probably demand fewer euros. Why? The answer lies in the reason you and others demand euros in the first place.

Why is an appreciating currency good news for some residents of a country but bad news for other residents?

Appreciation
An increase in the exchange value of one nation's currency in terms of the currency of another nation.

Depreciation
A decrease in the exchange value of one nation's currency in terms of the currency of another nation.

INTERNATIONAL EXAMPLE
Going Loony over an Appreciating Loonie

One face of a Canadian dollar coin displays an image of a bird called the loon, so the Canadian dollar is informally known as the "loonie." In the mid-2000s, the loonie was worth only about 75 U.S. cents. In the late 2000s, however, its value soared to over 1 U.S. dollar. For Canadians who enjoy making sightseeing-shopping trips to the United States, the loonie's significant appreciation was a bonanza. These Canadians could use their loonies to obtain about a third more U.S. dollars than before, so U.S. travel expenses and goods were more than 30 percent cheaper.

Nevertheless, for Canadian export firms and their employees, the loonie's considerable appreciation rapidly made their products more expensive to U.S. residents. Hence, U.S. purchases of Canadian products plummeted, and Canadian profits and job opportunities declined. In addition, U.S. residents cut back on visits to Canada, because prices of touring Canada and buying its goods and services increased. This only intensified the bad news for Canadian retailers who had already lost considerable business when Canadian shoppers headed south to grab U.S. bargains.

FOR CRITICAL ANALYSIS
Which groups in the United States gained and which lost when the loonie appreciated?

Which Canadians have been hurt by the rise in the U.S. dollar value of the Canadian "loonie."

APPRECIATION AND DEPRECIATION OF EUROS Recall that in our example, you and others demand euros to buy European pharmaceuticals. The demand curve for European pharmaceuticals follows the law of demand and therefore slopes downward. If it costs more U.S. dollars to buy the same quantity of European pharmaceuticals, presumably you and other U.S. residents will not buy the same quantity; your quantity demanded will be less. We say that your demand for euros is *derived from* your demand for European pharmaceuticals. In panel (a) of Figure 34-2 we present the hypothetical demand schedule for packages of European pharmaceuticals by a representative set of U.S. consumers during a typical week. In panel (b), we show graphically the U.S. demand curve for European pharmaceuticals in terms of U.S. dollars taken from panel (a).

AN EXAMPLE OF DERIVED DEMAND Let us assume that the price of a package of European pharmaceuticals in Europe is 100 euros. Given that price, we can find the

Panel (a)
Demand Schedule for Packages of European Pharmaceuticals in the United States per Week

Price per Package	Quantity Demanded
$155	100
150	300
145	500
140	700

Panel (b)
U.S. Demand Curve for European Pharmaceuticals

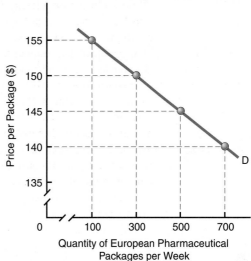

Panel (c)
Euros Required to Purchase Quantity Demanded
(at P = 100 euros per package of pharmaceuticals)

Quantity Demanded	Euros Required
100	10,000
300	30,000
500	50,000
700	70,000

Panel (d)
Derived Demand Schedule for Euros in the United States with Which to Pay for Imports of Pharmaceuticals

Dollar Price of One Euro	Dollar Price of Pharmaceuticals	Quantity of Pharmaceuticals Demanded	Quantity of Euros Demanded per Week
$1.55	$155	100	10,000
1.50	150	300	30,000
1.45	145	500	50,000
1.40	140	700	70,000

FIGURE 34-2

Deriving the Demand for Euros

In panel (a), we show the demand schedule for European pharmaceuticals in the United States, expressed in terms of dollars per package of pharmaceuticals. In panel (b), we show the demand curve, D, which slopes downward. In panel (c), we show the number of euros required to purchase up to 700 packages of pharmaceuticals. If the price per package of pharmaceuticals is 100 euros, we can now find the quantity of euros needed to pay for the various quantities demanded. In panel (d), we see the derived demand for euros in the United States in order to purchase the various quantities of pharmaceuticals given in panel (a). The resultant demand curve, D_1, is shown in panel (e). This is the U.S. derived demand for euros.

Panel (e)
U.S. Derived Demand for Euros

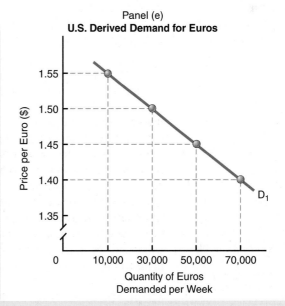

number of euros required to purchase 500 packages of European pharmaceuticals. That information is given in panel (c) of Figure 34-2. If purchasing one package of European pharmaceuticals requires 100 euros, 500 packages require 50,000 euros. Now we have enough information to determine the derived demand curve for euros. If 1 euro costs $1.45, a package of pharmaceuticals would cost $145 (100 euros per package × $1.45 per euro = $145 per package). At $145 per package, the representative group of U.S. consumers would, we see from panel (a) of Figure 34-2, demand 500 packages of pharmaceuticals.

From panel (c), we see that 50,000 euros would be demanded to buy the 500 packages of pharmaceuticals. We show this quantity demanded in panel (d). In panel (e), we draw the derived demand curve for euros. Now consider what happens if the price of euros goes up to $1.50. A package of European pharmaceuticals priced at 100 euros in Europe would now cost $150. From panel (a), we see that at $150 per package, 300 packages of pharmaceuticals will be imported from Europe into the United States by our representative group of U.S. consumers. From panel (c), we see that 300 packages of pharmaceuticals would require 30,000 euros to be purchased; thus, in panels (d) and (e), we see that at a price of $1.50 per euro, the quantity demanded will be 30,000 euros.

We continue similar calculations all the way up to a price of $1.55 per euro. At that price, a package of European pharmaceuticals costing 100 euros in Europe would cost $155, and our representative U.S. consumers would import only 100 packages of pharmaceuticals.

DOWNWARD-SLOPING DERIVED DEMAND As can be expected, as the price of the euro rises, the quantity demanded will fall. The only difference here from the standard demand analysis developed in Chapter 3 and used throughout this text is that the demand for euros is derived from the demand for a final product—European pharmaceuticals in our example.

SUPPLY OF EUROS Assume that European pharmaceutical manufacturers buy U.S. computer printers. The supply of euros is a derived supply in that it is derived from the European demand for U.S. computer printers. We could go through an example similar to the one for pharmaceuticals to come up with a supply schedule of euros in Europe. It slopes upward. Obviously, Europeans want dollars to purchase U.S. goods. European residents will be willing to supply more euros when the dollar price of euros goes up, because they can then buy more U.S. goods with the same quantity of euros. That is, the euro would be worth more in exchange for U.S. goods than when the dollar price for euros was lower.

AN EXAMPLE Let's take an example. Suppose a U.S.-produced computer printer costs $200. If the exchange rate is $1.45 per euro, a European resident will have to come up with 137.93 euros (= $200 at $1.45 per euro) to buy one computer printer. If, however, the exchange rate goes up to $1.50 per euro, a European resident must come up with only 133.33 euros (= $200 at $1.50 per euro) to buy a U.S. computer printer. At this lower price (in euros) of U.S. computer printers, Europeans will demand a larger quantity. In other words, as the price of euros goes up in terms of dollars, the quantity of U.S. computer printers demanded will go up, and hence the quantity of euros supplied will go up. Therefore, the supply schedule of euros, which is derived from the European demand for U.S. goods, will slope upward, as seen in Figure 34-3 on the following page.

TOTAL DEMAND FOR AND SUPPLY OF EUROS Let us now look at the total demand for and supply of euros. We take all U.S. consumers of European pharma-

FIGURE 34-3

The Supply of Euros

If the market price of a U.S.-produced computer printer is $200, then at an exchange rate of $1.45 per euro, the price of the printer to a European consumer is 137.93 euros. If the exchange rate rises to $1.50 per euro, the European price of the printer falls to 133.33 euros. This induces an increase in the quantity of printers demanded by European consumers and consequently an increase in the quantity of euros supplied in exchange for dollars in the foreign exchange market. In contrast, if the exchange rate falls to $1.40 per euro, the European price of the printer rises to 142.86 euros. This causes a decrease in the quantity of printers demanded by European consumers. As a result, there is a decline in the quantity of euros supplied in exchange for dollars in the foreign exchange market.

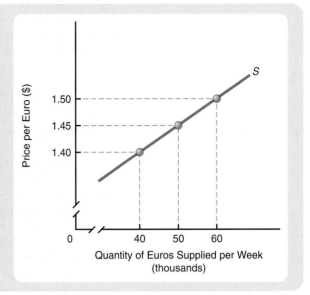

ceuticals and all European consumers of U.S. computer printers and put their demands for and supplies of euros together into one diagram. Thus, we are showing the total demand for and total supply of euros. The horizontal axis in Figure 34-4 represents the quantity of foreign exchange—the number of euros per year. The vertical axis represents the exchange rate—the price of foreign currency (euros) expressed in dollars (per euro). The foreign currency price of $1.50 per euro means it will cost you $1.50 to buy 1 euro. At the foreign currency price of $1.45 per euro, you know that it will cost you $1.45 to buy 1 euro. The equilibrium, E, is again established at $1.45 for 1 euro.

In our hypothetical example, assuming that there are only representative groups of pharmaceutical consumers in the United States and computer printer consumers in Europe, the equilibrium exchange rate will be set at $1.45 per euro.

FIGURE 34-4

Total Demand for and Supply of Euros

The market supply curve for euros results from the total European demand for U.S. computer printers. The demand curve, D, slopes downward like most demand curves, and the supply curve, S, slopes upward. The foreign exchange price, or the U.S. dollar price of euros, is given on the vertical axis. The number of euros is repre-sented on the horizontal axis. If the foreign exchange rate is $1.50—that is, if it takes $1.50 to buy 1 euro—U.S. residents will demand 20 billion euros. The equilib-rium exchange rate is at the intersection of D and S, or point E. The equilibrium exchange rate is $1.45 per euro. At this point, 30 billion euros are both demanded and supplied each year.

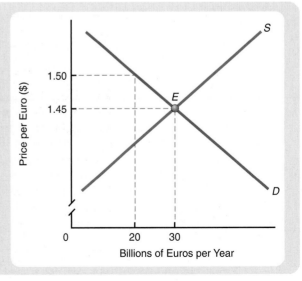

This equilibrium is not established because U.S. residents like to buy euros or because Europeans like to buy dollars. Rather, the equilibrium exchange rate depends on how many computer printers Europeans want and how many European pharmaceuticals U.S. residents want (given their respective incomes, their tastes, and, in our example, the relative prices of pharmaceuticals and computer printers).

A SHIFT IN DEMAND Assume that a successful advertising campaign by U.S. pharmaceutical importers has caused U.S. demand for European pharmaceuticals to rise. U.S. residents demand more pharmaceuticals at all prices. Their demand curve for European pharmaceuticals has shifted outward to the right.

The increased demand for European pharmaceuticals can be translated into an increased demand for euros. All U.S. residents clamoring for European pharmaceuticals will supply more dollars to the foreign exchange market while demanding more euros to pay for the pharmaceuticals. Figure 34-5 presents a new demand schedule, D_2, for euros; this demand schedule is to the right of the original demand schedule. If Europeans do not change their desire for U.S. computer printers, the supply schedule for euros will remain stable.

A new equilibrium will be established at a higher exchange rate. In our particular example, the new equilibrium is established at an exchange rate of $1.50 per euro. It now takes $1.50 to buy 1 euro, whereas formerly it took $1.45. This will be translated into an increase in the price of European pharmaceuticals to U.S. residents and into a decrease in the price of U.S. computer printers to Europeans. For example, a package of European pharmaceuticals priced at 100 euros that sold for $145 in the United States will now be priced at $150. Conversely, a U.S. printer priced at $200 that previously sold for 137.93 euros will now sell for 133.33 euros.

A SHIFT IN SUPPLY We just assumed that the U.S. demand for European pharmaceuticals had shifted due to a successful ad campaign. Because the demand for euros is derived from the demand by U.S. residents for pharmaceuticals, this is translated into a shift in the demand curve for euros. As an alternative exercise, we might assume that the supply curve of euros shifts outward to the right. Such a supply shift could occur

---

FIGURE 34-5

A Shift in the Demand Schedule

The demand schedule for European pharmaceuticals shifts to the right, causing the derived demand schedule for euros to shift to the right also. We have shown this as a shift from D_1 to D_2. We have assumed that the supply schedule for euros has remained stable—that is, European demand for U.S. computer printers has remained constant. The old equilibrium foreign exchange rate was $1.45 per euro. The new equilibrium exchange rate will be E_2. It will now cost $1.50 to buy 1 euro. The higher price of euros will be translated into a higher U.S. dollar price for European pharmaceuticals and a lower euro price for U.S. computer printers.

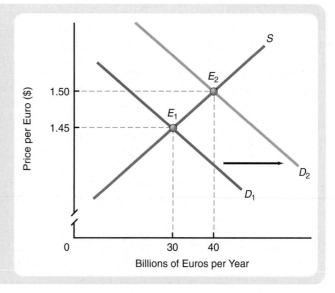

FIGURE 34-6

A Shift in the Supply of Euros

There has been a shift in the supply curve for euros. The new equilibrium will occur at E_1, meaning that $1.40, rather than $1.45, will now buy 1 euro. After the exchange rate adjustment, the annual amount of euros demanded and supplied will increase from 30 billion to 60 billion.

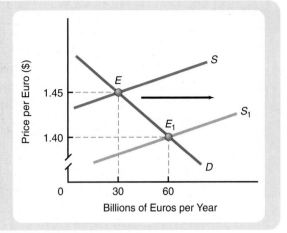

for many reasons, one of which is a relative rise in the European price level. For example, if the prices of all European-manufactured computer peripherals went up 20 percent in euros, U.S. computer printers would become relatively cheaper. That would mean that European residents would want to buy more U.S. computer printers. But remember that when they want to buy more U.S. printers, they supply more euros to the foreign exchange market.

Thus, we see in Figure 34-6 that the supply curve of euros moves from S to S_1. In the absence of restrictions—that is, in a system of flexible exchange rates—the new equilibrium exchange rate will be $1.40 equals 1 euro. The quantity of euros demanded and supplied will increase from 30 billion per year to 60 billion per year. We say, then, that in a flexible international exchange rate system, shifts in the demand for and supply of foreign currencies will cause changes in the equilibrium foreign exchange rates. Those rates will remain in effect until world supply or demand shifts.

Market Determinants of Exchange Rates

The foreign exchange market is affected by many other variables in addition to changes in relative price levels, including the following:

- *Changes in real interest rates.* Suppose that the U.S. interest rate, corrected for people's expectations of inflation, increases relative to the rest of the world. Then international investors elsewhere seeking the higher returns now available in the United States will increase their demand for dollar-denominated assets, thereby increasing the demand for dollars in foreign exchange markets. An increased demand for dollars in foreign exchange markets, other things held constant, will cause the dollar to appreciate and other currencies to depreciate.
- *Changes in consumer preferences.* If Germany's citizens suddenly develop a taste for U.S.-made automobiles, this will increase the derived demand for U.S. dollars in foreign exchange markets.
- *Perceptions of economic stability.* As already mentioned, if the United States looks economically and politically more stable relative to other countries, more foreign residents will want to put their savings into U.S. assets than in their own domestic assets. This will increase the demand for dollars.

QUICK QUIZ *See page 890 for the answers. Review concepts from this section in MyEconLab.*

The foreign _____ _____ is the rate at which one country's currency can be exchanged for another's.

The _____ for foreign exchange is a derived _____; it is derived from the demand for foreign goods and services (and financial assets). The _____ of foreign exchange is derived from foreign residents' demands for U.S. goods and services.

The demand curve of foreign exchange slopes _____, and the supply curve of foreign exchange slopes

_____. The equilibrium foreign exchange rate occurs at the intersection of the demand and supply curves for a currency.

A _____ in the demand for foreign goods will result in a shift in the _____ for foreign exchange, thereby changing the equilibrium foreign exchange rate. A shift in the supply of foreign currency will also cause a change in the equilibrium exchange rate.

The Gold Standard and the International Monetary Fund

The current system of more or less freely floating exchange rates is a relatively recent development. In the past, we have had periods of a gold standard, fixed exchange rates under the International Monetary Fund, and variants of the two.

The Gold Standard

Until the 1930s, many nations were on a gold standard. The value of their domestic currency was fixed, or *pegged*, in units of gold. Nations operating under this gold standard agreed to redeem their currencies for a fixed amount of gold at the request of any holder of that currency. Although gold was not necessarily the means of exchange for world trade, it was the unit to which all currencies under the gold standard were pegged. And because all currencies in the system were pegged to gold, exchange rates between those currencies were fixed. Indeed, the gold standard has been offered as the prototype of a fixed exchange rate system. The heyday of the gold standard was from about 1870 to 1914.

There was (and always is) a relationship between the balance of payments and changes in domestic money supplies throughout the world. Under a gold standard, the international financial market reached equilibrium through the effect of gold flows on each country's money supply. When the sum of a nation's current account balance and its capital account balance was negative, more gold would flow out than in. Because the domestic money supply was based on gold, an outflow of gold to foreign residents caused an automatic reduction in the domestic money supply. This caused several things to happen. Interest rates rose, thereby attracting foreign capital and pushing the sum of the current account balance and the capital account balance back toward zero. At the same time, the reduction in the money supply was equivalent to a restrictive monetary policy, which caused national output and prices to fall. Imports were discouraged and exports were encouraged, thereby again increasing net exports.

Two problems plagued the gold standard. One was that by fixing the value of its currency in relation to the amount of gold, a nation gave up control of its domestic monetary policy. Another was that the world's commerce was at the mercy of gold discoveries. Throughout history, each time new veins of gold were found, desired domestic expenditures on goods and services increased. If production of goods and services failed to increase proportionately, inflation resulted.

Bretton Woods and the International Monetary Fund

In 1944, as World War II was ending, representatives from the world's capitalist countries met in Bretton Woods, New Hampshire, to create a new international payment system to replace the gold standard, which had collapsed during the 1930s. The Bretton Woods Agreement Act was signed on July 31, 1945, by President Harry Truman. It created a new permanent institution, the International Monetary Fund (IMF). The IMF's task was to administer the agreement and to lend to member countries for which the sum of the current account balance and the capital account balance was negative, thereby helping them maintain an offsetting surplus in their official reserve transactions accounts. The arrangements thus provided are now called the old IMF system or the Bretton Woods system.

Member governments agreed to maintain the value of their currencies within 1 percent of the declared **par value**—the officially determined value. The United States, which owned most of the world's gold stock, was similarly obligated to maintain gold prices within a 1 percent margin of the official rate of $35 an ounce. Except for a transitional arrangement permitting a onetime adjustment of up to 10 percent in par value, members could alter exchange rates thereafter only with the approval of the IMF.

On August 15, 1971, President Richard Nixon suspended the convertibility of the dollar into gold. On December 18, 1971, the United States officially devalued the dollar—that is, lowered its official value—relative to the currencies of 14 major industrial nations. Finally, on March 16, 1973, the finance ministers of the European Economic Community (now the European Union) announced that they would let their currencies float against the dollar, something Japan had already begun doing with its yen. Since 1973, the United States and most other trading countries have had either freely floating exchange rates or managed ("dirty") floating exchange rates, in which their governments or central banks intervene from time to time to try to influence world market exchange rates.

Par value
The officially determined value of a currency.

Fixed versus Floating Exchange Rates

The United States went off the Bretton Woods system of fixed exchange rates in 1973. As Figure 34-7 indicates, many other nations of the world have been less willing to permit the values of their currencies to vary in the foreign exchange markets.

FIGURE 34-7

Current Foreign Exchange Rate Arrangements

Today, 22 percent of the member nations of the International Monetary Fund have an independent float, and just over 22 percent have a managed float exchange rate arrangement. Slightly over 21 percent of all nations use the currencies of other nations instead of issuing their own currencies.

Source: International Monetary Fund.

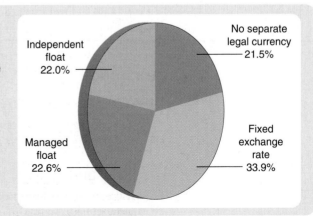

FIGURE 34-8

A Fixed Exchange Rate

This figure illustrates how the Central Bank of Bahrain could fix the dollar-dinar exchange rate in the face of an increase in the supply of dinars caused by a rise in the demand for U.S. goods by Bahraini residents. In the absence of any action by the Central Bank of Bahrain, the result would be a movement from point E_1 to point E_2. The dollar value of the dinar would fall from $2.66 to $2.00. The Central Bank of Bahrain can prevent this exchange rate change by purchasing dinars with dollars in the foreign exchange market, thereby raising the demand for dinars. At the new equilibrium point, E_3, the dinar's value remains at $2.66.

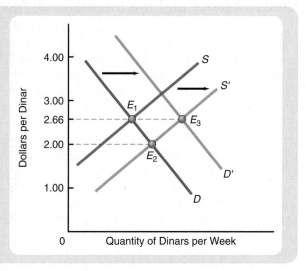

Fixing the Exchange Rate

How did nations fix their exchange rates in years past? How do many countries accomplish this today? Figure 34-8 shows the market for dinars, the currency of Bahrain. At the initial equilibrium point E_1, U.S. residents had to give up $2.66 to obtain 1 dinar. Suppose now that there is an increase in the supply of dinars for dollars, perhaps because Bahraini residents wish to buy more U.S. goods. Other things being equal, the result would be a movement to point E_2 in Figure 34-8. The dollar value of the dinar would fall to $2.00.

To prevent a dinar depreciation from occurring, however, the Central Bank of Bahrain could increase the demand for dinars in the foreign exchange market by purchasing dinars with dollars. The Central Bank of Bahrain can do this using dollars that it has on hand as part of its *foreign exchange reserves*. All central banks hold reserves of foreign currencies. Because the U.S. dollar is a key international currency, the Central Bank of Bahrain and other central banks typically hold billions of dollars in reserve so that they can make transactions such as the one in this example. Note that a sufficiently large purchase of dinars could, as shown in Figure 34-8, cause the demand curve to shift rightward to achieve the new equilibrium point E_3, at which the dinar's value remains at $2.66. Provided that it has enough dollar reserves on hand, the Central Bank of Bahrain could maintain—effectively fix—the exchange rate in the face of the rise in the supply of dinars.

The Central Bank of Bahrain has maintained the dollar-dinar exchange rate in this manner since 2001. This basic approach—varying the amount of the national currency demanded at any given exchange rate in foreign exchange markets when necessary—is also the way that *any* central bank seeks to keep its nation's currency value unchanged in light of changing market forces.

> *Central banks can keep exchange rates fixed as long as they have enough foreign exchange reserves to deal with potentially long-lasting changes in the demand for or supply of their nation's currency.*

Pros and Cons of a Fixed Exchange Rate

Why might a nation such as Bahrain wish to keep the value of its currency from fluctuating? One reason is that changes in the exchange rate can affect the market values of assets that are denominated in foreign currencies. This can increase the financial risks that a nation's residents face, thereby forcing them to incur costs to avoid these risks.

FOREIGN EXCHANGE RISK   The possibility that variations in the market value of assets can take place due to changes in the value of a nation's currency is the **foreign exchange risk** that residents of a country face because their nation's currency value can vary. For instance, if companies in Bahrain had many loans denominated in dollars but earned nearly all their revenues in dinars from sales within Bahrain, a decline in the dollar value of the dinar would mean that Bahraini companies would have to allocate a larger portion of their earnings to make the same *dollar* loan payments as before. Thus, a fall in the dinar's value would increase the operating costs of these companies, thereby reducing their profitability and raising the likelihood of eventual bankruptcy.

Limiting foreign exchange risk is a classic rationale for adopting a fixed exchange rate. Nevertheless, a country's residents are not defenseless against foreign exchange risk. In what is known as a **hedge,** they can adopt strategies intended to offset the risk arising from exchange rate variations. For example, a company in Bahrain that has significant euro earnings from sales in Germany but sizable loans from U.S. investors could arrange to convert its euro earnings into dollars via special types of foreign exchange contracts called *currency swaps*. The Bahraini company could likewise avoid holdings of dinars and shield itself—*hedge*—against variations in the dinar's value.

What do currency traders do when a nation's currency value is so volatile that it is difficult to determine the current market exchange rate?

Foreign exchange risk
The possibility that changes in the value of a nation's currency will result in variations in the market value of assets.

Hedge
A financial strategy that reduces the chance of suffering losses arising from foreign exchange risk.

INTERNATIONAL EXAMPLE
Measuring the Value of Zimbabwe's Dollar

For years, Zimbabwe's government has stated that the "official" value of its currency has been a few hundred Zimbabwe dollars per U.S. dollar. Nevertheless, for some time the actual market rates of exchange have been in *millions* of Zimbabwe dollars per U.S. dollar. Recently, the value of the Zimbabwe dollar went through numerous gyrations, mostly in a downward direction. Foreign exchange market trades in Zimbabwe dollars are relatively infrequent, so currency traders experienced difficulties in assessing a true market rate of exchange.

Then traders found out that prices of shares of an insurance company called Old Mutual are traded in both Zimbabwe and the United Kingdom. Each share in the company

is worth the same after adjusting for valuation in the different currencies. Thus, dividing the Zimbabwe dollar price of a share in Old Mutual by the British pound price in London markets yields a market measure of the exchange rate in Zimbabwe dollars per British pound. Multiplying this exchange rate by the market exchange rate of British pounds per U.S. dollar then yields the market rate of exchange of Zimbabwe dollars per U.S. dollar.

FOR CRITICAL ANALYSIS
Why might the fact that Zimbabwe's annual inflation rate has exceeded 2.5 million percent help to explain why the nation's currency has experienced sudden depreciations?

THE EXCHANGE RATE AS A SHOCK ABSORBER   If fixing the exchange rate limits foreign exchange risk, why do so many nations allow the exchange rates to float? The answer must be that there are potential drawbacks associated with fixing exchange rates. One is that exchange rate variations can actually perform a valuable service for a

You Are There

To think about how even individual households in some nations can face foreign exchange risks, consider **Literally Betting the House on an Exchange Rate,** on page 884.

Is this resident of Zimbabwe rich because he has local currency that shows 10,000,000 on each bill?

Dirty float

Active management of a floating exchange rate on the part of a country's government, often in cooperation with other nations.

nation's economy. Consider a situation in which residents of a nation speak only their own nation's language. As a result, the country's residents are very *immobile*: They cannot trade their labor skills outside their own nation's borders.

Now think about what happens if this nation chooses to fix its exchange rate. Imagine a situation in which other countries begin to sell products that are close substitutes for the products its people specialize in producing, causing a sizable drop in worldwide demand for the nation's goods. If wages and prices do not instantly and completely adjust downward, the result will be a sharp decline in production of goods and services, a falloff in national income, and higher unemployment. Contrast this situation with one in which the exchange rate floats. In this case, a sizable decline in outside demand for the nation's products will cause it to experience a trade deficit, which will lead to a significant drop in the demand for that nation's currency. As a result, the nation's currency will experience a sizable depreciation, making the goods that the nation offers to sell abroad much less expensive in other countries. People abroad who continue to consume the nation's products will increase their purchases, and the nation's exports will increase. Its production will begin to recover somewhat, as will its residents' incomes. Unemployment will begin to fall.

This example illustrates how exchange rate variations can be beneficial, especially if a nation's residents are relatively immobile. It can be difficult, for example, for a Polish resident who has never studied Portuguese to move to Lisbon, even if she is highly qualified for available jobs there. If many residents of Poland face similar linguistic or cultural barriers, Poland could be better off with a floating exchange rate even if its residents must incur significant costs hedging against foreign exchange risk as a result.

Splitting the Difference: Dirty Floats and Target Zones

In recent years, national policymakers have tried to soften the choice between adopting a fixed exchange rate and allowing exchange rates full flexibility in the foreign exchange markets by "splitting the difference" between the two extremes.

A DIRTY FLOAT One way to split the difference is to let exchange rates float most of the time but "manage" exchange rate movements part of the time. U.S. policymakers have occasionally engaged in what is called a **dirty float,** the active management of flexible exchange rates. The management of flexible exchange rates has usually come about through international policy cooperation.

Is it possible for nations to "manage" foreign exchange rates? Some economists do not think so. For example, economists Michael Bordo and Anna Schwartz studied the foreign exchange intervention actions coordinated by the Federal Reserve and the U.S. Treasury during the second half of the 1980s. Besides showing that such interventions were sporadic and variable, Bordo and Schwartz came to an even more compelling conclusion: Exchange rate interventions were trivial relative to the total trading of foreign exchange on a daily basis. For example, in April 1989, total foreign exchange trading amounted to $129 billion per day, yet the U.S. central bank purchased only $100 million in deutsche marks and yen during that entire month (and did so on a single day). For all of 1989, Fed purchases of marks and yen were only $17.7 billion, or the equivalent of less than 13 percent of the amount of an average *day's* trading in April of that year. Their conclusion is that foreign exchange market interventions by the U.S. central bank or the central banks of other nations do not influence exchange rates in the long run.

CRAWLING PEGS Another approach to splitting the difference between fixed and floating exchange rates is called a **crawling peg.** This is an automatically adjusting target for the value of a nation's currency. For instance, a central bank might announce that it wants the value of its currency relative to the U.S. dollar to decline at an annual rate of 5 percent, a rate of depreciation that it feels is consistent with long-run market forces. The central bank would then try to buy or sell foreign exchange reserves in sufficient quantities to be sure that the currency depreciation takes place gradually, thereby reducing the foreign exchange risk faced by the nation's residents. In this way, a crawling peg functions like a floating exchange rate in the sense that the exchange rate can change over time. But it is like a fixed exchange rate in the sense that the central bank always tries to keep the exchange rate close to a target value. In this way, a crawling peg has elements of both kinds of exchange rate systems.

Crawling peg
An exchange rate arrangement in which a country pegs the value of its currency to the exchange value of another nation's currency but allows the par value to change at regular intervals.

TARGET ZONES A third way to try to split the difference between fixed and floating exchange rates is to adopt an exchange rate **target zone.** Under this policy, a central bank announces that there are specific upper and lower *bands*, or limits, for permissible values for the exchange rate. Within those limits, which define the exchange rate target zone, the central bank permits the exchange rate to move flexibly. The central bank commits itself, however, to intervene in the foreign exchange markets to ensure that its nation's currency value will not rise above the upper band or fall below the lower band. For instance, if the exchange rate measured in units of foreign currency per unit of domestic currency approaches the upper band, the central bank must sell foreign exchange reserves in sufficient quantities to prevent additional depreciation of its nation's currency. If the exchange rate approaches the lower band, the central bank must purchase sufficient amounts of foreign exchange reserves to halt any further currency appreciation.

In 1999, officials from the European Union attempted to get the U.S. and Japanese governments to agree to target zones for the exchange rate between the newly created euro, the dollar, and the yen. So far, however, no target zones have been created, and the euro has floated freely.

Target zone
A range of permitted exchange rate variations between upper and lower exchange rate bands that a central bank defends by selling or buying foreign exchange reserves.

QUICK QUIZ See page 890 for the answers. Review concepts from this section in MyEconLab.

The International Monetary Fund was developed after World War II as an institution to maintain _____ exchange rates in the world. Since 1973, however, _____ exchange rates have disappeared in most major trading countries. For these nations, exchange rates are largely determined by the forces of demand and supply in foreign exchange markets.

Many other nations, however, have tried to fix their exchange rates, with varying degrees of success. Although fixing the exchange rate helps protect a nation's residents from foreign exchange _____, this policy makes less mobile residents susceptible to greater volatility in income and employment.

Countries have experimented with exchange rate systems between the extremes of fixed and floating exchange rates. Under a _____ float, a central bank permits the value of its nation's currency to float in foreign exchange markets but intervenes from time to time to influence the exchange rate. Under a _____ peg, a central bank tries to push the value of its nation's currency in a desired direction. Pursuing a _____ _____ policy, a central bank aims to keep the exchange rate between upper and lower bands, intervening only when the exchange rate approaches either limit.

You Are There Literally Betting the House on an Exchange Rate

When Tamas Bencze, a resident of Budapest, Hungary, opened a recent statement from his bank regarding his mortgage loan, he received an unpleasant surprise: His monthly payment had gone up 10 percent. The interest rate and other terms of the loan had not been altered, but the exchange rate had changed. Bencze, like about half of all homeowners in Hungary, has a mortgage denominated in a currency other than the Hungarian currency, called the *forint*. Bencze's mortgage is valued in Swiss francs, but he makes his mortgage payments in Hungarian forint. Thus, every time the forint depreciates in relation to the Swiss franc, he has to pay more forint.

Why do Bencze and so many other residents of Hungary arrange to borrow Swiss francs instead of Hungarian forint when they finance purchases of their homes? The answer is that market interest rates on loans denominated in the Hungarian forint are more than twice as high as rates on Swiss franc loans. Of course, one reason Hungarian rates are higher than Swiss rates is that most individuals anticipate that the Hungarian currency will tend to depreciate in relation to the Swiss franc. Consequently, they require a higher interest return on Hungarian assets—such as mortgage loans—to induce them to hold the assets alongside Swiss assets.

Bencze and other Hungarian residents who have their mortgages denominated in Swiss francs have made a choice. They have opted for the certainty of a lower loan interest rate, but in doing so they have taken on a foreign exchange risk: the potential for sudden exchange rate changes such as the one that has just occurred. Now that this risk has been realized and pushed up his mortgage payments, while his annual forint-denominated income has barely changed, Bencze can only hope that the forint will not lose even more value in relation to the Swiss franc. After all, he has literally bet his house on the hope that the value of the forint will not experience a significant decline.

CRITICAL ANALYSIS QUESTIONS

1. Do you suppose that Bencze and others with foreign-currency-denominated loans would prefer for Hungary's central bank to opt for a floating exchange rate or a fixed exchange rate?

2. How might Bencze shield himself from the foreign exchange risk exposure he faces through his mortgage loan arrangement?

The Current Account Deficit for One Group of Nations Is the Current Account Surplus for Another

Issues and Applications

CONCEPTS APPLIED

➤ Current Account

➤ Balance of Payments

➤ Capital Account

As you have learned in this chapter, the United States has been experiencing a significant current account deficit in recent years. It is not the only developed nation with a deficit in the current account of its balance of payments. All told, the United States and other highly developed nations are experiencing a combined current account deficit of close to $1 trillion per year. Who is financing these current account deficits? The answer must be the so-called *emerging countries*—nations with previously less developed economies, such as China and India, that are now experiencing significant growth. Let's see why this is so and contemplate the implications.

Mirror Image Current Account Balances for Developed and Developing Countries

Figure 34-9 displays the combined current account balances of the world's most developed nations since 1996. Until 1997, developed nations were operating with a combined current account surplus, but then they fell into a deficit position that has widened dramatically in recent years.

The figure also shows the combined current account balances of emerging countries. Until 1997, emerging countries experienced a combined current account deficit. Since then, they have operated with current account surpluses that have steadily increased in magnitude. The fact that emerging countries' combined current account surpluses have been nearly the mirror image of the deficits of developed nations is no accident. After all, in the long run net imports of goods, services, and gifts from abroad by developed nations must correspond to net exports of goods, services, and gifts by the rest of the world—which means primarily emerging countries.

Implications for Capital Account Balances

Recall that because surplus and deficit items cancel out in the balance of payments, any nation's current account deficit will be associated with a capital account surplus. Hence, the recent combined current account deficit experienced by the world's developed nations closely

FIGURE 34-9

Combined Current Account Balances of Developed Nations and of Emerging Countries

Since 1997, developed nations have experienced higher combined current account deficits. During the same time, emerging nations have had increasing combined current account surpluses that have been nearly a mirror image of the developed nations' current account deficits.

Sources: International Monetary Fund; author's estimates.

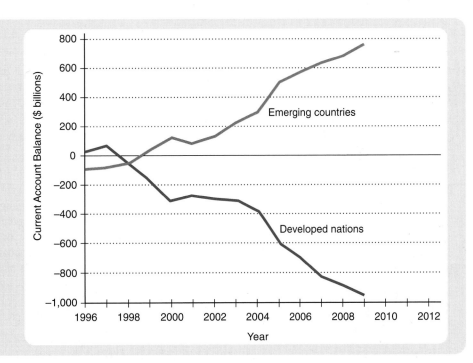

corresponds to a combined capital account surplus. Conversely, the combined current account surpluses recently experienced by emerging countries imply a combined capital account deficit for these countries.

This means that residents of developed nations have been financing their imports and thus their current account deficits by obtaining funds from emerging countries. As funds have flowed out of emerging countries, their capital accounts have experienced deficits. As the funds have flowed into developed nations, their capital accounts have experienced surpluses. Effectively, emerging countries have provided developed nations with the funds required to buy the emerging countries' exports.

Two Contrasting Scenarios for the Future

Some observers look at Figure 34-9 and see the potential for major balance of payments readjustments in the future. In their view, residents of emerging countries are likely to tire of financing the current account deficits of developed nations by purchasing the latter's stocks and bonds. Once this occurs, according to this view, residents of developed nations will no longer be able to finance their spending on goods and services imported from emerging countries. If this happens all at once, these observers worry, the world may experience significant difficulties: Residents of emerging countries will be unable to find buyers for their exports, and residents of developed nations will be unable to pay their debts.

Others examine Figure 34-9 and see only evidence of the gains from trade discussed in Chapter 33. In their view, emerging countries are willing to invest in developed nations because the latter offer high rates of return on investments. The emerging countries gain because residents of developed nations buy their exports. Residents of developed nations, in turn, expand their consumption of items imported from emerging countries and thereby gain from trade. From this perspective, the relationship shown in Figure 34-9 is a "win-win situation" for both sets of nations—and hence is likely to continue for years to come.

Test your understanding of this chapter by going online to **MyEconLab**.
In the Study Plan for this chapter, select Section N: News.

For Critical Analysis

1. If the current account balances of the world's least developed nations—those outside the sets of developed nations and emerging countries—were added to the combined current account surplus of emerging countries, would the result exactly mirror the current account deficit of the world's developed nations? Why or why not?

2. If combined capital account, current account, and official reserve transactions balances were computed for all the nations of the world, what should the sum of all three turn out to be? Explain.

Web Resources

1. To see a typical example of the view that the current account deficits of the United States and other developed nations pose a threat to the world economy, go to www.econtoday.com/chapter34.

2. For a discussion of the size of the U.S. current account deficit in relation to the current account deficits of other developed nations, go to www.econtoday.com/chapter34.

Research Project

If the capital account balances of the world's least developed nations—those outside the sets of developed nations and emerging countries—were added to the combined capital account deficit of emerging countries, would the result exactly mirror the capital account surplus of the world's developed nations? Why or why not? Explain your reasoning. (Hint: Recall that another financial account in every country's balance of payments is its official reserve transactions account.)

 Here is what you should know after reading this chapter. **MyEconLab** will help you identify what you know, and where to go when you need to practice.

WHAT YOU SHOULD KNOW		WHERE TO GO TO PRACTICE
The Balance of Trade versus the Balance of Payments The balance of trade is the difference between exports and imports of physical goods, or merchandise, during a given period. The balance of payments is a system of accounts for all transactions between a nation's residents and the residents of other countries of the world. In addition to exports and imports, therefore, the balance of payments includes cross-border exchanges of services and financial assets within a given time interval.	balance of trade, 864 balance of payments, 864 accounting identities, 864	• **MyEconLab** Study Plan 34.1 • Audio introduction to Chapter 34
The Key Accounts Within the Balance of Payments There are three important accounts within the balance of payments. The current account measures net exchanges of goods and services, transfers, and income flows across a nation's borders. The capital account measures net flows of financial assets. The official reserve transactions account tabulates cross-border exchanges of financial assets involving the home nation's government and central bank as well as foreign governments and central banks. Because each international exchange generates both an inflow and an outflow, the sum of the balances on all three accounts must equal zero.	current account, 866 capital account, 867 special drawing rights (SDRs), 868 International Monetary Fund, 868 KEY FIGURE Figure 34-1, 869	• **MyEconLab** Study Plan 34.1 • Animated Figure 34-1
Exchange Rate Determination in the Market for Foreign Exchange From the perspective of the United States, the demand for a nation's currency by U.S. residents is derived largely from the demand for imports from that nation. Likewise, the supply of a nation's currency is derived mainly from the supply of U.S. exports to that country. The equilibrium exchange rate is the rate of exchange between the dollar and the other nation's currency at which the quantity of the currency demanded is equal to the quantity supplied.	foreign exchange market, 871 exchange rate, 871 flexible exchange rates, 871 appreciation, 872 depreciation, 872 KEY FIGURES Figure 34-2, 873 Figure 34-3, 875 Figure 34-4, 875 Figure 34-5, 876	• **MyEconLab** Study Plan 34.2 • Animated Figures 34-2, 34-3, 34-4, 34-5 • Video: Market Determinants of Foreign Exchange Rates
Factors That Can Induce Changes in Equilibrium Exchange Rates The equilibrium exchange rate changes in response to changes in the demand for or supply of another nation's currency. Changes in desired flows of exports or imports, real interest rates, tastes and preferences of consumers, and perceptions of economic stability are key factors that can affect the positions of the demand and supply curves in foreign exchange markets. Thus, changes in these factors can induce variations in equilibrium exchange rates.	KEY FIGURES Figure 34-6, 877	• **MyEconLab** Study Plan 34.2 • Animated Figures 34-6 • Video: Market Determinants of Foreign Exchange Rates

(continued)

 *(continued)*

WHAT YOU SHOULD KNOW		WHERE TO GO TO PRACTICE

How Policymakers Can Attempt to Keep Exchange Rates Fixed If the current price of the home currency in terms of another nation's currency starts to fall below the level where the home country wants it to remain, the home country's central bank can use reserves of the other nation's currency to purchase the home currency in foreign exchange markets. This raises the demand for the home currency and thereby pushes up the currency's value in terms of the other nation's currency. In this way, the home country can keep the exchange rate fixed at a desired value, as long as it has sufficient reserves of the other currency to use for this purpose.

par value, 879
foreign exchange risk, 881
hedge, 881

KEY FIGURE
Figure 34-8, 880

- **MyEconLab** Study Plans 34.3, 34.4
- Animated Figure 34-8
- Video: Pros and Cons of a Fixed Exchange Rate

Alternative Approaches to Limiting Exchange Rate Variability Today, many nations permit their exchange rates to vary in foreign exchange markets. Others pursue policies that limit the variability of exchange rates. Some engage in a dirty float, in which they manage exchange rates, often in cooperation with other nations. Some establish crawling pegs, in which the target value of the exchange rate is adjusted automatically over time. And some establish target zones, with upper and lower limits on the extent to which exchange rates are allowed to vary.

dirty float, 882
crawling peg, 883
target zone, 883

- **MyEconLab** Study Plan 34.4

Log in to MyEconLab, take a chapter test, and get a personalized Study Plan that tells you which concepts you understand and which ones you need to review. From there, MyEconLab will give you further practice, tutorials, animations, videos, and guided solutions.
Log in to www.myeconlab.com

PROBLEMS

All problems are assignable in **myeconlab**. *Answers to the odd-numbered problems appear at the back of the book.*

34-1. Over the course of a year, a nation tracked its foreign transactions and arrived at the following amounts:

Merchandise exports	500
Service exports	75
Net unilateral transfers	10
Domestic assets abroad (capital outflows)	−200
Foreign assets at home (capital inflows)	300
Changes in official reserves	−35
Merchandise imports	600
Service imports	50

What are this nation's balance of trade, current account balance, and capital account balance?

34-2. Identify whether each of the following items creates a surplus item or a deficit item in the current account of the U.S. balance of payments.

a. A Central European company sells products to a U.S. hobby-store chain.

b. Japanese residents pay a U.S. travel company to arrange hotel stays, ground transportation, and tours of various U.S. cities, including New York, Chicago, and Orlando.

c. A Mexican company pays a U.S. accounting firm to audit its income statements.

d. U.S. churches and mosques send relief aid to Pakistan following a major earthquake in that nation.

e. A U.S. microprocessor manufacturer purchases raw materials from a Canadian firm.

34-3. Explain how the following events would affect the market for the Mexican peso, assuming a floating exchange rate.

a. Improvements in Mexican production technology yield superior guitars, and many musicians around the world buy these guitars.

b. Perceptions of political instability surrounding regular elections in Mexico make international investors nervous about future business prospects in Mexico.

34-4. Explain how the following events would affect the market for South Africa's currency, the rand, assuming a floating exchange rate.

a. A rise in U.S. inflation causes many U.S. residents to seek to buy gold, which is a major South African export good, as a hedge against inflation.

b. Major discoveries of the highest-quality diamonds ever found occur in Russia and Central Asia, causing a significant decline in purchases of South African diamonds.

34-5. Suppose that the following two events take place in the market for China's currency, the yuan: U.S. parents are more willing than before to buy action figures and other Chinese toy exports, and China's government tightens restrictions on the amount of U.S. dollar–denominated financial assets that Chinese residents may legally purchase. What happens to the dollar price of the yuan? Does the yuan appreciate or depreciate relative to the dollar?

34-6. On Wednesday, the exchange rate between the Japanese yen and the U.S. dollar was $0.0125 per yen. On Thursday, it was $0.0110. Did the dollar appreciate or depreciate against the yen? By how much, expressed as a percentage change?

34-7. On Wednesday, the exchange rate between the euro and the U.S. dollar was $1.45 per euro, and the exchange rate between the Canadian dollar

and the U.S. dollar was U.S. $0.94 per Canadian dollar. What is the exchange rate between the Canadian dollar and the euro?

34-8. Suppose that signs of an improvement in the Japanese economy lead international investors to resume lending to the Japanese government and businesses. Policymakers, however, are worried about how this will influence the yen. How would this event affect the market for the yen? How should the central bank, the Bank of Japan, respond to this event if it wants to keep the value of the yen unchanged?

34-9. Briefly explain the differences between a flexible exchange rate system, a fixed exchange rate system, a dirty float, and the use of target zones.

34-10. Suppose that under a gold standard, the U.S. dollar is pegged to gold at a rate of $35 per ounce and the pound sterling is pegged to gold at a rate of £17.50 per ounce. Explain how the gold standard constitutes an exchange rate arrangement between the dollar and the pound. What is the exchange rate between the U.S. dollar and the pound sterling?

34-11. Suppose that under the Bretton Woods system, the dollar is pegged to gold at a rate of $35 per ounce and the pound sterling is pegged to the dollar at a rate of $2 = £1. If the dollar is devalued against gold and the pegged rate is changed to $40 per ounce, what does this imply for the exchange value of the pound in terms of dollars?

34-12. Suppose that the People's Bank of China wishes to peg the rate of exchange of its currency, the yuan, in terms of the U.S. dollar. In each of the following situations, should it add to or subtract from its dollar foreign exchange reserves? Why?

a. U.S. parents worrying about safety begin buying fewer Chinese-made toys for their children.

b. U.S. interest rates rise relative to interest rates in China, so Chinese residents seek to purchase additional U.S. financial assets.

c. Chinese furniture manufacturers produce high-quality early American furniture and successfully export large quantities of the furniture to the United States.

ECONOMICS ON THE NET

Daily Exchange Rates It is an easy matter to keep up with changes in exchange rates every day using the Web site of the Federal Reserve Bank of New York. In this application, you will learn how hard it is to predict exchange rate movements, and you will get some practice thinking about what factors can cause exchange rates to change.

Title: The Federal Reserve Bank of New York: Foreign Exchange 12 PM Rates

Navigation: Go to **www.econtoday.com/chapter34** to visit the Federal Reserve Bank of New York's Statistics home page. Click on *Foreign Exchange 12 PM Rates*.

Application Answer the following questions.

1. For each currency listed, how many dollars does it take to purchase a unit of the currency in the spot foreign exchange market?

2. For each day during a given week (or month), choose a currency from those listed and keep track of its

value relative to the dollar. Based on your tabulations, try to predict the value of the currency at the end of the week *following* your data collections. Use any information you may have, or just do your best without any additional information. How far off did your prediction turn out to be?

For Group Study and Analysis Each day, you can also click on a report titled "Foreign Exchange 10 AM Rates," which shows exchange rates for a subset of countries listed in the noon report. Assign each country in the 10 AM report to a group. Ask the group to determine whether the currency's value appreciated or depreciated relative to the dollar between 10 AM and noon. In addition, ask each group to discuss what kinds of demand or supply shifts could have caused the change that occurred during this interval.

ANSWERS TO QUICK QUIZZES

p. 870: (i) balance . . . payments; (ii) physical; (iii) current . . . current; (iv) Unilateral transfers; (v) current; (vi) capital . . . capital; (vii) official reserve; (viii) inflation . . . political

p. 878: (i) exchange rate; (ii) demand . . . demand . . . supply; (iii) downward . . . upward; (iv) shift . . . demand

p. 883: (i) fixed . . . fixed; (ii) risk; (iii) dirty . . . crawling . . . target zone

Answers to Odd-Numbered Problems

Chapter 1

1-1. Economics is the study of how individuals allocate limited resources to satisfy unlimited wants.

  a. Among the factors that a rational, self-interested student will take into account are her income, the price of the textbook, her anticipation of how much she is likely to study the textbook, and how much studying the book is likely to affect her grade.

  b. A rational, self-interested government official will, for example, recognize that higher taxes will raise more funds for mass transit while making more voters, who have limited resources, willing to elect other officials.

  c. A municipality's rational, self-interested government will, for instance, take into account that higher hotel taxes will produce more funds if as many visitors continue staying at hotels, but that the higher taxes will also discourage some visitors from spending nights at hotels.

1-3. Because wants are unlimited, the phrase applies to very high-income households as well as low- and middle-income households. Consider, for instance, a household with a low income and unlimited wants at the beginning of the year. The household's wants will still remain unlimited if it becomes a high-income household later in the year.

1-5. Sally is displaying rational behavior if all of these activities are in her self-interest. For example, Sally likely derives intrinsic benefit from volunteer and extracurricular activities and may believe that these activities, along with good grades, improve her prospects of finding a job after she completes her studies. Hence, these activities are in her self-interest even though they reduce some available study time.

1-7. The rationality assumption states that people do not intentionally make choices that leave them worse off. The bounded rationality hypothesis suggests that people are *almost*, but not completely, rational.

1-9. Suppose that there is a change in the environment that a person faces, and the person adjusts to this change as predicted by the rationality assumption.

If the new environment becomes predictable, then the individual who actually behaves as predicted by the traditional rationality assumption may settle into behavior that *appears* to involve repetitive applications of a rule of thumb.

1-11. a. The model using prices from the Iowa Electronic Market is more firmly based on the rationality assumption, because people who trade assets on this exchange based on poor forecasts actually experience losses. This gives them a strong incentive to make the best possible forecasts. Unpaid respondents to opinion polls have less incentive to give truthful answers about whether and how they will vote.

  b. An economist would develop a means of evaluating whether prices in the Iowa Electronic Market or results of opinion polls did a better job of matching actual electoral outcomes.

1-13. a. Positive
  b. Normative
  c. Normative
  d. Positive

APPENDIX A

A-1. a. Independent: price of a notebook; Dependent: quantity of notebooks
  b. Independent: work-study hours; Dependent: credit hours
  c. Independent: hours of study; Dependent: economics grade

A-3. a. above x axis; left of y axis
  b. below x axis, right of y axis
  c. on x axis; to right of y axis

A-5.

y	x
−20	−4
−10	−2
0	0
10	2
20	4

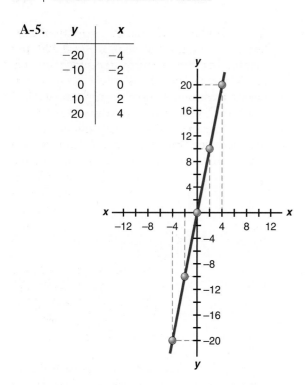

A-7. Each one-unit increase in x yields a 5-unit increase in y, so the slope given by the change in y corresponding to the change in x is equal to 5.

Chapter 2

2-1. The opportunity cost of attending a class at 11:00 A.M. is the next-best use of that hour of the day. Likewise, the opportunity cost of attending an 8:00 A.M. class is the next-best use of that particular hour of the day. If you are an early riser, it is arguable that the opportunity cost of the 8:00 A.M. hour is lower, because you will already be up at that time but have fewer choices compared with the 11:00 A.M. hour when shops, recreation centers, and the like are open. If you are a late riser, it may be that the opportunity cost of the 8:00 A.M. hour is higher, because you place a relatively high value on an additional hour of sleep in the morning.

2-3. The bank apparently determined that the net gain that it anticipated receiving from trying to sell the house to someone else, taking into account the opportunity cost of resources that the bank would have had to devote to renovating the house, was less than $10.

2-5. If the student allocates additional study time to economics in order to increase her score from 90 to 100, her biology score declines from 50 to 40, so the opportunity cost of earning 10 additional points in economics is 10 fewer points in biology.

2-7.

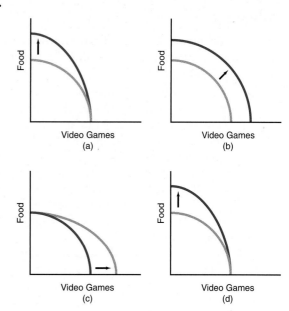

2-9. D

2-11. a. If the nation's residents increase production of consumption goods from 0 units to 10 units, the opportunity cost is 3 units of human capital forgone. If the nation's residents increase production of consumption goods from 0 units to 60 units, the opportunity cost is 100 units of human capital.
  b. Yes, because successive 10-unit increases in production of consumption goods generate larger sacrifices of human capital, equal to 3, 7, 15, 20, 25, and 30.

2-13. Because it takes you less time to do laundry, you have an absolute advantage in laundry. Neither you nor your roommate has an absolute advantage in meal preparation. You require 2 hours to fold a basket of laundry, so your opportunity cost of folding a basket of laundry is 2 meals. Your roommate's opportunity cost of folding a basket of laundry is 3 meals. Hence, you have a comparative advantage in laundry, and your roommate has a comparative advantage in meal preparation.

2-15. It may be that the professor is very proficient at doing yard work relative to teaching and research activities, so in fact the professor may have a comparative advantage in doing yard work.

Chapter 3

3-1. The equilibrium price is $21 per DVD, and the equilibrium quantity is 80 million DVDs. At a price of $20 per DVD, the quantity of DVDs demanded is 90 million, and the quantity of DVDs supplied is 60 million. Hence, there is a shortage of 30 million DVDs at a price of $20 per DVD.

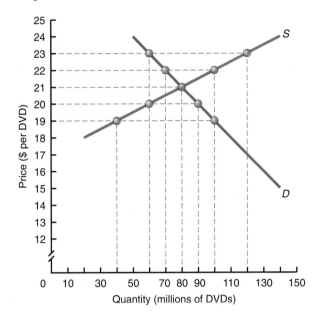

3-3. a. DSL and cable Internet access services are substitutes, so a reduction in the price of cable Internet access services causes a decrease in the demand for DSL high-speed Internet access services.

b. A decrease in the price of DSL Internet access services generates an increase in the quantity of these services demanded.

c. DSL high-speed Internet access services are a normal good, so a fall in the incomes of consumers reduces the demand for these services.

d. If consumers expect that the price of DSL high-speed Internet services will fall in the future, then the demand for these services will tend to decrease today.

3-5. a. Complement: eggs; Substitute: sausage

b. Complement: tennis balls; Substitute: racquet-ball racquets

c. Complement: cream; Substitute: tea

d. Complement: gasoline; Substitute: city bus

3-7. a. At the $1,000 rental rate, the quantity of one-bedroom apartments supplied is 8,500 per month, but the quantity demanded is only 7,000 per month. Thus, there is an excess quantity of one-bedroom apartments supplied equal to 1,500 apartments per month.

b. To induce consumers to lease unrented one-bedroom apartments, some landlords will reduce their rental rates. As they do so, the quantity demanded will increase. In addition, some landlords will choose not to offer apartments for rent at lower rates, and the quantity supplied will decrease. At the equilibrium rental rate of $800 per month, there will be no excess quantity supplied.

c. At the $600 rental rate, the quantity of one-bedroom apartments demanded is 8,000 per month, but the quantity supplied is only 6,500 per month. Thus, there is an excess quantity of one-bedroom apartments demanded equal to 1,500 apartments per month.

d. To induce landlords to make more one-bedroom apartments available for rent, some consumers will offer to pay higher rental rates. As they do so, the quantity supplied will increase. In addition, some consumers will choose not to try to rent apartments at higher rates, and the quantity demanded will decrease. At the equilibrium rental rate of $800 per month, there will be no excess quantity demanded.

3-9. a. Because memory chips are an input in the production of laptop computers, a decrease in the price of memory chips causes an increase in the supply of laptop computers. The market supply curve shifts to the right, which causes the market price of laptop computers to fall and the equilibrium quantity of laptop computers to increase.

b. Machinery used to produce laptop computers is an input in the production of these devices, so an increase in the price of machinery generates a decrease in the supply of laptop computers. The market supply curve shifts to the left, which causes the market price of laptop computers to rise and the equilibrium quantity of laptop computers to decrease.

c. An increase in the number of manufacturers of laptop computers causes an increase in the supply of laptop computers. The market supply curve shifts rightward. The market price of laptop computers declines, and the equilibrium quantity of laptop computers increases.

 d. The demand curve for laptop computers shifts to the left along the supply curve, so there is a decrease in the quantity supplied. The market price falls, and the equilibrium quantity declines.

3-11. The decline in the price of palladium, a substitute for platinum, will cause a decrease in the demand for platinum, so the platinum demand curve will shift leftward. Both the market clearing price and the equilibrium quantity of platinum will decrease.

3-13. Because processor chips are an input in the production of personal computers, a decrease in the price of processor chips generates an increase in the supply of personal computers. The market price of personal computers will decrease, and the equilibrium quantity will increase.

Chapter 4

4-1. The ability to produce music CDs at lower cost and the entry of additional producers shift the supply curve rightward, from S_1 to S_2. At the same time, reduced prices of substitute goods result in a leftward shift in the demand for music CDs, from D_1 to D_2. Consequently, the equilibrium price of music CDs declines, from P_1 to P_2. The equilibrium quantity may rise, fall, or, as shown in the diagram, remain unchanged.

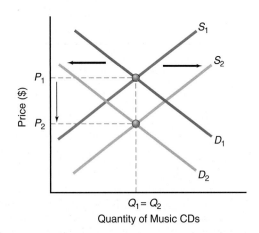

4-3. The market rental rate is $700 per apartment, and the equilibrium quantity of apartments rented to tenants is 2,000. At a ceiling price of $650 per month, the number of apartments students desire

to rent increases to 2,500 apartments. At the ceiling price, the number of apartments that owners are willing to supply decreases to 1,800 apartments. Thus, there is a shortage of 700 apartments at the ceiling price, and only 1,800 are rented at the ceiling price.

4-5. At the above-market price of sugar in the U.S. sugar market, U.S. chocolate manufacturers that use sugar as an input face higher costs. Thus, they supply less chocolate at any given price of chocolate, and the market supply curve shifts leftward. This pushes up the market price of chocolate products and reduces the equilibrium quantity of chocolate. U.S. sugar producers also sell surplus sugar in foreign sugar markets, which causes the supply curve for sugar in foreign markets to shift rightward. This reduces the market price of foreign sugar and raises the equilibrium quantity in the foreign market.

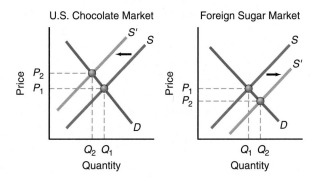

4-7. The market price is $400, and the equilibrium quantity of seats is 1,600. If airlines cannot sell tickets to more than 1,200 passengers, then passengers are willing to pay $600 per seat. Normally, airlines would be willing to sell each ticket for $200, but they will be able to charge a price as high as $600 for each of the 1,200 tickets they sell. Hence, the quantity of tickets sold declines from 1,600, and the price of a ticket rises from $400 to as high as $600.

4-9. a. Consumers buy 10 billion kilograms at the support price of $0.20 per kilogram and hence spend $2 billion on wheat.

 b. The amount of surplus wheat at the support price is 8 billion kilograms, so at the $0.20-per-kilogram support price, the government must spend $1.6 billion to purchase this surplus wheat.

 c. Pakistani wheat farmers receive a total of $3.6 billion for the wheat they produce at the support price.

4-11. a. At the present minimum wage of $9 per hour, the quantity of labor supplied is 102,000 workers, and the quantity of labor demanded by firms is 98,000. There is an excess quantity supplied of 4,000 workers, which is the number of people who are unemployed.

b. At a minimum wage of $6 per hour, there would be nothing to prevent market forces from pushing the wage rate to the market clearing level of $8 per hour. This $8-per-hour wage rate would exceed the legal minimum and hence would prevail. There would be no unemployed workers.

c. At a $10-per-hour minimum wage, the quantity of labor supplied would increase to 106,000 workers, and the quantity of labor demanded would decline to 96,000. There would be an excess quantity of labor supplied equal to 10,000 workers, which would then be the number of people unemployed.

4-13. a. The rise in the number of wheat producers causes the market supply curve to shift rightward, so more wheat is supplied at the support price.

b. The quantity of wheat demanded at the same support price is unchanged.

c. Because quantity demanded is unchanged while quantity supplied has increased, the amount of surplus wheat that the government must purchase has risen.

Chapter 5

5-1. In the absence of laws forbidding cigar smoking in public places, people who are bothered by the odor of cigar smoke will experience costs not borne by cigar producers. Because the supply of cigars will not reflect these costs, from society's perspective the market cigar supply curve will be in a position too far to the right. The market price of cigars will be too low, and too many cigars will be produced and consumed.

5-3. Imposing the tax on pesticides causes an increase in the price of pesticides, which are an input in the production of oranges. Hence, the supply curve in the orange market shifts leftward. The market price of oranges increases, and the equilibrium quantity of oranges declines. Hence, orange consumers indirectly help to pay for dealing with the spillover costs of pesticide production by paying more for oranges.

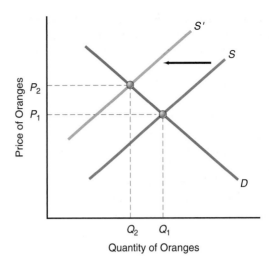

5-5. a. As shown in the figure below, if the social benefits associated with bus ridership were taken into account, the demand schedule would be D' instead of D, and the market price would be higher. The equilibrium quantity of bus rides would be higher.

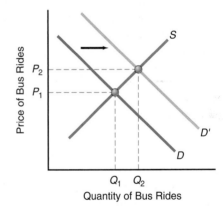

b. The government could pay commuters a subsidy to ride the bus, thereby shifting the demand curve outward and to the right. This would increase the market price and equilibrium number of bus rides.

5-7. At present, the equilibrium quantity of residences with Internet access is 2 million. To take into account the external benefit of Internet access and boost the quantity of residences with access to 3 million, the demand curve would have to shift upward by $20 per month at any given quantity, to D_2 from the current position D_1. Thus, the government would have to offer a $20-per-month subsidy to raise the quantity of residences with Internet access to 3 million.

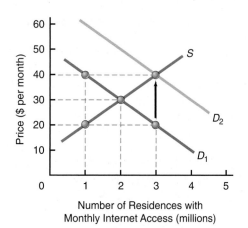

Price ($ per month)

Number of Residences with Monthly Internet Access (millions)

5-9. The problem is that although most people around the lighthouse will benefit from its presence, there is no incentive for people to voluntarily contribute if they believe that others ultimately will pay for it. That is, the city is likely to face a free-rider problem in its efforts to raise its share of the funds required for the lighthouse.

5-11. No, the outcome will be different. If the government had simply provided grants to attend private schools at the current market tuition rate, parents and students receiving the grants would have paid a price equal to the market valuation of the last unit of educational services provided. Granting a subsidy to private schools allows the private schools to charge parents and students a price less than the market price. Private schools thereby will receive a higher-than-market price for the last unit of educational services they provide. Consequently, they will provide a quantity of educational services in excess of the market equilibrium quantity. At this quantity, parents and students place a lower value on the services than the price received by the private schools.

5-13. a. $40 million
b. The effective price of a DVD drive to consumers will be lower after the government pays the subsidy, so people will purchase a larger quantity.
c. $60 million
d. $90 million

5-15. a. $60 − $50 = $10
b. Expenditures after the program expansion are $2.4 million. Before the program expansion, expenditures were $1 million. Hence, the increase in expenditures is $1.4 million.
c. At a per-unit subsidy of $50, the share of the per-unit $60 price paid by the government is 5/6, or 83.3 percent. Hence, this is the government's share of total expenditures on the 40,000 devices that consumers purchase.

Chapter 6

6-1. a. The average tax rate is the total tax of $40 divided by the $200 in income: $40/$200 = 0.2, or 20 percent.
b. The marginal tax rate for the last hour of work is the change in taxes, $3, divided by the change in income, $8: $3/$8 = 0.375, or 37.5 percent.

6-3. 2001: $300 million; 2003: $350 million; 2005: $400 million; 2007: $400 million; 2009: $420 million

6-5. During 2008, the income tax base was an amount of income equal to $20 million/0.05 = $400 million. During 2009, the income tax base was equal to $19.2 million/0.06 = $320 million. Although various factors could have contributed to the fall in taxable income, dynamic tax analysis suggests that the higher income tax rate induced people to reduce their reported income. For instance, some people might have earned less income subject to city income taxes, and others might have even moved outside the city to avoid paying the higher income tax rate.

6-7. a. The supply of tickets for flights into and out of London shifts upward by $154. The equilibrium quantity of flights in and out of London declines. The market clearing price of London airline tickets rises by an amount less than the tax.

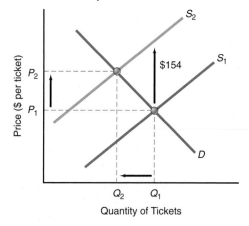

Price ($ per ticket)

Quantity of Tickets

b. Tickets for flights into and out of London are substitutes for tickets for flights into and out of nearby cities. Thus, the demand for tickets for flights into and out of these cities will increase. This will cause an increase in the equilibrium quantities of these tickets and an increase in the market clearing prices.

6-9. As shown in the diagram, if the supply and demand curves have their normal shapes, then the $2-per-month tax on DSL Internet access services shifts the market supply curve upward by $2. The equilibrium quantity of DSL access services produced and consumed declines. In addition, the monthly market price of DSL access increases by an amount less than $2 per month. Consequently, consumers and producers share in paying the tax on each unit.

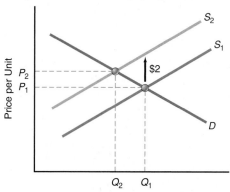

Quantity of DSL Access Services

6-11. If the market price of DSL access for businesses does not change, then as shown in the diagram, over the relevant range the demand for Internet access services by businesses is horizontal. The quantity of services demanded by businesses is very highly responsive to the tax, so DSL access providers must bear the tax in the form of higher costs. Providers of DSL access services pay all of the tax.

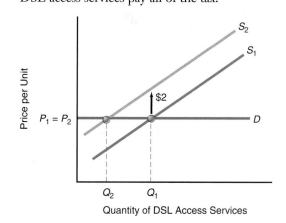

Quantity of DSL Access Services

6-13. a. 50 percent
b. −20 percent

Chapter 7

7-1. a. Multiplying the fraction of people who participate in the labor force, 0.7, times the adult, noninstitutionalized, nonmilitary population of 200.0 million yields a labor force of 140.0 million.
b. Subtracting the 7.5 million unemployed from the labor force of 140.0 million yields 132.5 million people who are employed.
c. Dividing the 7.5 million unemployed by the 140.0 million in the labor force and multiplying by 100 yields an unemployment rate of about 5.36 percent.

7-3. a. The labor force equals the number employed plus the number unemployed, or 156 million + 8 million = 164 million. In percentage terms, therefore, the unemployment rate is 100 times 8 million/164 million, or 4.9 percent.
b. These 60 million people are not in the labor force. The labor force participation rate is, in percentage terms, 100 times 164 million/224 million, or 73.2 percent.

7-5. a. Four of the 100 people are always continuously unemployed because they are between jobs, so the frictional unemployment rate is (4/100) × 100 = 4 percent.
b. Three of the 100 people are always unemployed as a result of government regulations, so the structural unemployment rate is (3/100) × 100 = 3 percent.
c. The unemployment rate is the sum of the frictional and structural rates of unemployment, or 7 percent.

7-7. The overall unemployment rate is 8 percent, and the natural rate of unemployment is 5 percent.

7-9. a. 2010
b. 10 percent
c. 10 percent
d. $1,800 in 2009; $3,000 in 2013

7-11. The expected rate of inflation is equal to 100 × [(99 − 90)/90] = 10 percent. Hence, the real interest rate equals the difference between the 12 percent nominal interest rate and the 10 percent anticipated inflation rate, or 2 percent.

7-13. a. The homeowner gains; the savings bank loses.
  b. The tenants gain; the landlord loses.
  c. The auto buyer gains; the bank loses.
  d. The employer gains; the pensioner loses.

Chapter 8

8-1. a. When Juanita does all the work herself, only purchases of the materials in markets (magazines, texturing materials, paint brushes, and paints), which total to $280 per year, count in GDP.
  b. She must pay the market price of $200 for the texturing, so her contribution to annual GDP from this project, including the materials, is $480.
  c. Because Juanita now pays for the entire project via market transactions, her total contribution to GDP equals the sum of the $280 for material purchases from part (a), $200 for the texturing from part (b), and $350 for the painting, or $830 per year.

8-3. a. GDP = $16.6 trillion; NDP = $15.3 trillion; NI = $14.5 trillion.
  b. GDP in 2013 will equal $15.5 trillion.

8-5. a. Gross domestic income = $14.6 trillion; GDP = $14.6 trillion.
  b. Gross private domestic investment = $2.0 trillion.
  c. Personal income = $12.0 trillion; personal disposable income = $10.3 trillion.

8-7. a. Measured GDP declines.
  b. Measured GDP increases.
  c. Measured GDP does not change (the firearms are not newly produced).

8-9. a. The chip is an intermediate good, so its purchase in June is not included in GDP; only the final sale in November is included.
  b. This is a final sale of a good that is included in GDP for the year.
  c. This is a final sale of a service that is included in GDP for the year.

8-11. a. Nominal GDP for 2009 is $2,300; for 2013, nominal GDP is $2,832.
  b. Real GDP for 2009 is $2,300; for 2013, real GDP is $2,229.

8-13. The price index is (2012 nominal GDP/2012 real GDP) × 100 = ($88,000/$136,000) × 100 = 64.7.

8-15. The $1 billion expended to pay for employees and equipment and the additional $1 billion paid to clean up the oil spill would be included in GDP, for a total of $2 billion added to GDP in 2013. The rise in oil reserves increases the stock of wealth but is not included in the current flow of newly produced goods and services. In addition, the welfare loss relating to the deaths of wildlife is also not measured in the marketplace and therefore is not included in GDP.

Chapter 9

9-1. a. Y
  b. X

9-3. The nation will maintain its stock of capital goods at its current level, so its rate of economic growth will be zero.

9-5. A: $8,250 per capita; B: $4,500 per capita; C: $21,000 per capita

9-7. 1.77 times higher after 20 years; 3.16 times higher after 40 years

9-9. 5 years

9-11. 4 percent

9-13. Per capita real GDP in 2010 was 10 percent higher than in 2009, or $2,200. The level of real GDP is $2,200 per person × 5 million people = $11 billion.

Chapter 10

10-1. The amount of unemployment would be the sum of frictional, structural, and seasonal unemployment.

10-3. The real value of the new full-employment level of nominal GDP is ($17.7 trillion/1.15) = $15.39 trillion, so the long-run aggregate supply curve has shifted rightward by $2.35 trillion, in base-year dollars.

10-5. This change implies a rightward shift of the long-run aggregate supply curve along the unchanged aggregate demand curve, so the long-run equilibrium price level will decline.

10-7. There are three effects. First, there is a real-balance effect, because the rise in the price level reduces real money balances, inducing people to cut back on their spending. In addition, there is an interest rate effect as a higher price level pushes up interest rates, thereby reducing the attractiveness of purchases of autos, houses, and plants and equipment. Finally, there is an open-economy effect as home residents respond to the higher price level by reducing purchases of domestically produced goods in favor of foreign-produced goods, while foreign residents cut back on their purchases of home-produced goods. All three effects entail a reduction in purchases of goods and services, so the aggregate demand curve slopes downward.

10-9. **a.** At the price level P_2 above the equilibrium price level P_1, the total quantity of real goods and services that people plan to consume is less than the total quantity that is consistent with firms' production plans. One reason is that at the higher-than-equilibrium price level, real money balances are lower, which reduces real wealth and induces lower planned consumption. Another is that interest rates are higher at the higher-than-equilibrium price level, which generates a cutback in consumption spending. Finally, at the higher-than-equilibrium price level P_2, people tend to cut back on purchasing domestic goods in favor of foreign-produced goods, and foreign residents reduce purchases of domestic goods. As unsold inventories of output accumulate, the price level drops toward the equilibrium price level P_1, which ultimately causes planned consumption to rise toward equality with total production.

b. At the price level P_3 below the equilibrium price level P_1, the total quantity of real goods and services that people plan to consume exceeds the total quantity that is consistent with firms' production plans. One reason is that at the lower-than-equilibrium price level, real money balances are higher, which raises real wealth and induces higher planned consumption. Another is that interest rates are lower at the lower-than-equilibrium price level, which generates an increase in consumption spending. Finally, at the lower-than-equilibrium price level P_3, people tend to raise their purchases of domestic goods and cut back on buying foreign-produced goods, and foreign residents increase purchases of domestic goods. As inventories of output are depleted, the price level begins to rise toward the equilibrium price level P_1, which ultimately causes planned consumption to fall toward equality with total production.

10-11. **a.** When the price level falls with deflation, there is a movement downward along the *AD* curve.

b. The decline in foreign real GDP levels reduces incomes of foreign residents, who cut back on their spending on domestic exports. Thus, the domestic *AD* curve shifts leftward.

c. The fall in the foreign exchange value of the nation's currency makes domestic-produced goods and services less expensive to foreign residents, who increase their spending on domestic exports. Thus, the domestic *AD* curve shifts rightward.

d. An increase in the price level causes a movement upward along the *AD* curve.

10-13. **a.** The aggregate demand curve shifts leftward along the long-run aggregate supply curve; the equilibrium price level falls, and equilibrium real GDP remains unchanged.

b. The aggregate demand curve shifts rightward along the long-run aggregate supply curve; the equilibrium price level rises, and equilibrium real GDP remains unchanged.

c. The long-run aggregate supply curve shifts rightward along the aggregate demand curve; the equilibrium price level falls, and equilibrium real GDP increases.

d. The aggregate demand curve shifts rightward along the long-run aggregate supply curve; the equilibrium price level rises, and equilibrium real GDP remains unchanged.

10-15. **a.** The income flows are mainly influencing relatives' consumption, so the main effect is on the aggregate demand curve.

b. A rise in aggregate demand will lead to an increase in the equilibrium price level.

Chapter 11

11-1. **a.** Because saving increases at any given interest rate, the desired saving curve shifts rightward. This causes the equilibrium interest rate to decline.

b. There is no effect on current equilibrium real GDP, because in the classical model the vertical long-run aggregate supply curve always applies.

c. A change in the saving rate does not directly affect the demand for labor or the supply of labor in the classical model, so equilibrium employment does not change.

d. The decrease in the equilibrium interest rate generates a rightward and downward movement along the demand curve for investment. Consequently, desired investment increases.

e. The rise in current investment implies greater capital accumulation. Other things being equal, this will imply increased future production and higher equilibrium real GDP in the future.

11-3. False. In fact, there is an important distinction. The classical model of short-run real GDP determination applies to an interval short enough that some factors of production, such as capital, are fixed. Nevertheless, the classical model implies that even in the short run the economy's aggregate supply curve is the same as its long-run aggregate supply curve.

11-5. a. The labor supply curve shifts rightward, and equilibrium employment increases.

b. The rise in employment causes the aggregate supply curve to shift rightward, and real GDP rises.

c. Because the immigrants have higher saving rates, the nation's saving supply curve shifts to the right along its investment curve, and the equilibrium interest rate declines.

d. The fall in the equilibrium interest rate induces a rise in investment, and equilibrium saving also rises.

e. Capital accumulation rises, and more real GDP will be forthcoming in future years.

11-7. In the long run, the aggregate supply curve is vertical because all input prices adjust fully and people are fully informed in the long run. Thus, the short-run aggregate supply curve is more steeply sloped if input prices adjust more rapidly and people become more fully informed within a short-run interval.

11-9. This event would cause the aggregate demand curve to shift leftward. In the short run, the equilibrium price level would decline, and equilibrium real GDP would fall.

11-11. To prevent a short-run decrease in real GDP from taking place after the temporary rise in oil prices shifts the SRAS curve leftward, policymakers should increase the quantity of money in circulation. This will shift the AD curve rightward and prevent equilibrium real GDP from declining in the short run.

11-13. a. *E:* The union wage boost causes the SRAS curve to shift leftward, from $SRAS_1$ to $SRAS_3$. The reduction in incomes abroad causes import spending in this nation to fall, which induces a leftward shift in the AD curve, from AD_1 to AD_3.

b. *B:* The short-term reduction in production capabilities causes the SRAS curve to shift leftward, from $SRAS_1$ to $SRAS_3$, and the increase in money supply growth generates a rightward shift in the AD curve, from AD_1 to AD_2.

c. *C:* The strengthening of the value of this nation's currency reduces the prices of imported inputs that domestic firms utilize to produce goods and services, which causes the SRAS curve to shift rightward, from $SRAS_1$ to $SRAS_2$. At the same time, the currency's strengthening raises the prices of exports and reduces the prices of imports, so net export spending declines, thereby inducing a leftward shift in the AD curve, from AD_1 to AD_3.

Chapter 12

12-1. a. Flow
b. Flow
c. Stock
d. Flow
e. Stock
f. Flow
g. Stock

12-3. a. The completed table follows (all amounts in dollars):

Real GDP	Consumption	Saving	Investment
2,000	2,000	0	1,200
4,000	3,600	400	1,200
6,000	5,200	800	1,200
8,000	6,800	1,200	1,200
10,000	8,400	1,600	1,200
12,000	10,000	2,000	1,200

MPC = 1,600/2000 = 0.8; MPS = 400/2,000 = 0.2.

b. The graph appears below.

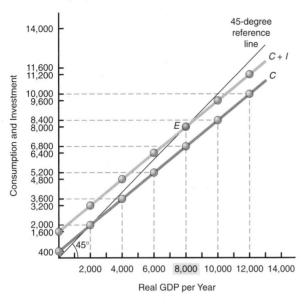

c. The graph appears below. Equilibrium real GDP on both graphs equals $8,000.

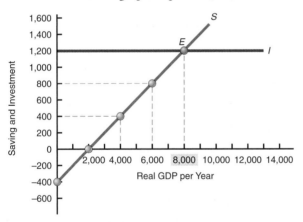

d. APS = $1,200/$8,000 = 0.15.

e. The multiplier is $1/(1 - MPC) = 1/(1 - 0.8) = 1/0.2 = 5$. Thus, if autonomous consumption were to rise by $100, then equilibrium real GDP would increase by $100 times 5, or $500.

12-5. The multiplier is $1/(1 - MPC) = 4$, so $1 - MPC = 0.25$, which implies that MPC = 0.75. Thus, when real GDP equals $15 trillion, consumption is $1 trillion + (0.75 × $15 trillion) = $12.25 trillion.

12-7. The multiplier is $1/(1 - MPC) = 1/(1 - 0.75) = 4$, so the increase in equilibrium real GDP is $250 billion × 4 = $1 trillion, and the level of real GDP at the new point on the aggregate demand curve is $16 trillion.

12-9. a. The MPS is equal to 1/3.
   b. $0.1 trillion

Chapter 13

13-1. a. A key factor that could help explain why the actual effect may have turned out to be lower is the crowding-out effect. Some government spending may have entailed direct expenditure offsets that reduced private expenditures on a dollar-for-dollar basis. In addition, indirect crowding out may have occurred. Because the government did not change taxes, it probably sold bonds to finance its increased expenditures, and this action likely pushed up interest rates, thereby discouraging private investment. Furthermore, the increase in government spending likely pushed up aggregate demand, which may have caused a short-run increase in the price level. This, in turn, may have induced foreign residents to reduce their expenditures on U.S. goods. It also could have reduced real money holdings sufficiently to discourage consumers from spending as much as before. On net, therefore, real GDP rose in the short run but not by the full amount predicted by the basic multiplier effect.

   b. In the long run, as the increased spending raised aggregate demand, wages and other input prices likely increased in proportion to the resulting increase in the price level. Thus, in the long run the aggregate supply schedule was vertical, and the increase in government spending induced only a rise in the price level.

13-3. Because of the recognition time lag entailed in gathering information about the economy, policymakers may be slow to respond to a downturn in real GDP. Congressional approval of policy actions to address the downturn may be delayed; hence, an action time lag may also arise. Finally, there is an effect time lag, because policy actions take time to exert their full effects on the economy. If these lags are sufficiently long, it is possible that by the time a policy to address a downturn has begun to have its effects, real GDP may already be rising. If so, the policy action may push real GDP up faster than intended, thereby making real GDP less stable.

13-5. Situation *b* is an example of indirect crowding out because the reduction in private expenditures takes place indirectly in response to a change in the interest rate. In contrast, situations *a* and *c* are examples of direct expenditure offsets.

13-7. Situation *b* is an example of a discretionary fiscal policy action because this is a discretionary action by Congress. So is situation *d* because the president uses discretionary authority. Situation *c* is an example of monetary policy, not fiscal policy, and situation *a* is an example of an automatic stabilizer.

13-9. There is a recessionary gap, because at point *A* equilibrium real GDP of $15.5 trillion is below the long-run level of $16.0 trillion. To eliminate the recessionary gap of $0.5 trillion, government spending must increase sufficiently to shift the *AD* curve rightward to a long-run equilibrium, which will entail a price level increase from 115 to 120. Hence, the spending increase must shift the *AD* curve rightward by $1 trillion, or by the multiplier, which is 1/0.20 = 5, times the increase in spending. Government spending must rise by $200 billion, or $0.2 trillion.

13-11. Because the MPC is 0.80, the multiplier equals 1/(1 − MPC) = 1/0.2 = 5. Net of indirect crowding out, therefore, total autonomous expenditures must rise by $40 billion in order to shift the aggregate demand curve rightward by $200 billion. If the government raises its spending by $50 billion, the market interest rate rises by 0.5 percentage point and thereby causes planned investment spending to fall by $10 billion, which results in a net rise in total autonomous expenditures equal to $40 billion. Consequently, to accomplish its objective the government should increase its spending by $50 billion.

13-13. A cut in the tax rate should induce a rise in consumption and, consequently, a multiple short-run increase in equilibrium real GDP. In addition, however, a tax-rate reduction reduces the automatic-stabilizer properties of the tax system, so equilibrium real GDP would be less stable in the face of changes in autonomous spending.

APPENDIX C

C-1. a. The marginal propensity to consume is equal to 1 − MPS, or 6/7.

b. The required increase in equilibrium real GDP is $0.35 trillion, or $350 billion. The multiplier equals 1/(1 − MPC) = 1/MPS = 1/(1/7) = 7. Hence, investment or government spending must increase by $50 billion to bring about a $350 billion increase in equilibrium real GDP.

c. The multiplier relevant for a tax change equals −MPC/(1−MPC)=−MPC/MPS= −(6/7)/(1/7) = −6. Thus, the government would have to cut taxes by $58.33 billion to induce a rise in equilibrium real GDP equal to $350 billion.

C-3. a. The aggregate expenditures curve shifts up by $1 billion; equilibrium real GDP increases by $5 billion.

b. The aggregate expenditures curve shifts down by the MPC times the tax increase, or by 0.8 × $1 billion = 0.8 billion; equilibrium real income falls by $4 billion.

c. The aggregate expenditures curve shifts upward by (1 − MPC) times $1 billion = $0.2 billion. Equilibrium real income rises by $1 billion.

d. No change; no change.

Chapter 14

14-1. $0.4 trillion

14-3. A higher deficit creates a higher public debt.

14-5. The net public debt is obtained by subtracting government interagency borrowing from the gross public debt.

14-7. When foreign dollar holders hold more domestic government bonds issued to finance higher domestic government budget deficits, they purchase fewer domestic exports, so the domestic trade deficit rises, other things being equal.

14-9. In the diagram on the next page, the increase in government spending and/or tax reduction that creates the budget deficit also causes the aggregate demand curve to shift rightward, from *AD* to AD_2. Real GDP rises to its long-run equilibrium level of $15 trillion at point *B*. The equilibrium price level increases to a value of 130 at this point. As real GDP rises, the government's tax collections increase and benefit payouts fall, both of which will help ultimately reduce the deficit.

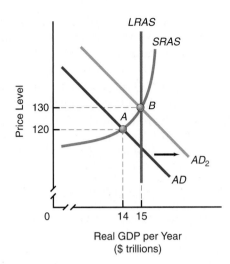

14-11. "The rich" are likely to respond to higher tax rates by reducing their activities that generate taxable income, so actual tax collections from "the rich" will not turn out to be as high as the politician suggests.

Chapter 15

15-1. medium of exchange; store of value; standard of deferred payment

15-3. store of value; standard of deferred payment

15-5. M1 equals transactions deposits plus currency plus traveler's checks, or $825 billion + $850 billion + $25 billion = $1,700 billion; M2 equals M1 + savings deposits plus small-denomination time deposits plus money market deposit accounts plus retail (noninstitution) money market mutual funds, or $1,700 billion + $2,300 billion + $1,450 billion + $1,950 billion + $1,900 billion = $9,300 billion.

15-7. **a.** neither
   b. M2 only
   c. M1 and M2
   d. M2 only

15-9. In principle, each institution can match with each rationale; your explanations are the most important aspects of your answers.
   a. Insurance companies limit adverse selection by screening applicants for policies.
   b. Savings banks limit moral hazard by monitoring borrowers after loans have been made.
   c. Pension funds reduce management costs by pooling the funds of many future pensioners.

15-11. **a.** moral hazard problem
   b. adverse selection problem
   c. moral hazard problem

15-13. In an extreme case in which the U.S. government were to close down the Federal Reserve System, it would have to compensate holders of Federal Reserve notes for the market value of those notes.

15-15. Back in 1913, the population was centered farther to the east. Thus, congressional representation was centered farther to the east, so political concerns together with a view that the Fed districts should be designed to best serve the existing population helped determine the geographic boundaries. These have not been redrawn since.

Chapter 16

16-1. **a.** asset
   b. liability
   c. liability
   d. asset

16-3. The bank's reserves are its required reserves, which equal $0.10 \times \$15$ million = $1.5 million. Total assets equal total liabilities, or $15 million. Hence, its remaining loans and securities must amount to its total assets of $15 million minus its reserves of $1.5 million, or $13.5 million.

16-5. Yes, the bank holds $50 million in excess reserves. The bank's current total assets equal its $2 billion in total liabilities. It must hold 15 percent of its $2 billion in transactions deposits, or $0.30 billion, as required reserves. Its total reserves equal $2 billion in total assets minus $1.65 billion in loans and securities, or $0.35 billion. Hence, the bank has $0.05 billion, or $50 million, in excess reserves.

16-7. The dealer's bank must hold 15 percent of the $1 million, or $150,000, as required reserves. Thus, the bank can lend out the excess reserves of $850,000.

16-9. **a.** Total liabilities and net worth = total assets = $0.26 billion in total reserves + $3.6 billion in loans + $1 billion in securities + $0.14 billion in other assets = $5 billion.

   b. The bank could lend its $10 million in excess reserves.

   c. Transactions deposits equal required reserves of $0.25 billion/0.1 = $2.5 billion.

16-11. When you purchase a U.S. government security, you draw on existing funds in a deposit account and thereby redistribute funds already within the banking system; in contrast, the Federal Reserve creates funds that had not previously existed in the banking system.

16-13. The maximum potential money multiplier is $1/0.01 = 100$, so total deposits in the banking system will increase by $5 million $\times 100 = 500 million.

16-15. **a.** You expect that the value of your bond holdings will decline by one-half.

b. You would reduce your bond holdings, which implies a reallocation of wealth to money holdings. Consequently, the quantity of money that you desire to hold would increase.

Chapter 17

17-1. **a.** One possible policy action would be an open market sale of securities, which would reduce the money supply and shift the aggregate demand curve leftward. Others would be to increase the discount rate relative to the federal funds rate or to raise the required reserve ratio.

b. In principle, the Fed's action would reduce inflation more quickly.

17-3. Because a contractionary monetary policy causes interest rates to increase, financial capital begins to flow into the United States. This causes the demand for dollars to rise, which pushes up the international value of the dollar and makes U.S. exports more expensive to foreign residents. They cut back on their purchases of U.S. products, which tends to reduce U.S. real GDP.

17-5.

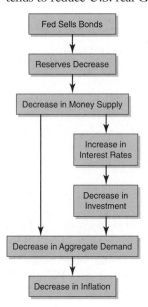

17-7. The price level remains at its original value. Because $M_sV = PY$, V has doubled, and Y is unchanged, cutting M_s in half leaves P unchanged.

17-9. **a.** $M_sV = PY$, so $P = M_sV/Y = (\$1.1$ trillion $\times 10)/\$5$ trillion $= 2.2$.

b. 100 billion/1 trillion $= 0.1$, or 10 percent

c. $0.2/2 = 0.1$, or 10 percent

d. Both the money supply and the price level increased by 10 percent.

17-11. Any one of these contractionary actions will tend to raise interest rates, which in turn will induce international inflows of financial capital. This pushes up the value of the dollar and makes U.S. goods less attractive abroad. As a consequence, real planned total expenditures on U.S. goods decline even further.

17-13. **a.** To push the equilibrium federal funds rate up to the new target value, the Trading Desk will have to reduce the money supply by selling U.S. government securities.

b. The increase in the differential between the discount rate and the federal funds rate will induce more depository institutions to borrow reserves from Federal Reserve banks. In the absence of a Trading Desk action, this would cause the equilibrium interest rate to increase. To prevent this from occurring, the Trading Desk will have to boost the money supply by purchasing U.S. government securities.

17-15. The neutral federal funds rate is the level of the interest rate on interbank loans at which, given current inflation expectations, the growth rate of real GDP tends neither to rise nor to fall relative to the rate of growth of potential, long-run, real GDP.

a. The FOMC should instruct the Trading Desk to aim to achieve a higher target for the federal funds rate.

b. The Trading Desk should engage in open market sales and thereby reduce the quantity of reserves supplied, which will bring about an increase in the equilibrium federal funds rate.

APPENDIX D

D-1. **a.** $20 billion increase

b. $40 billion increase

c. $10 billion open market purchase

D-3. Through its purchase of $1 billion in bonds, the Fed increased reserves by $1 billion. This ultimately caused a $3 billion increase in the money supply after full multiple expansion. The 1 percentage-point drop in the interest rate, from 6 percent to 5 percent, caused investment to rise by $25 billion, from $1,200 billion to $1,225 billion. An investment multiplier of 3 indicates that equilibrium real GDP rose by $75 billion, to $12,075 billion, or $12.075 trillion.

Chapter 18

18-1. a. The actual unemployment rate, which equals the number of people unemployed divided by the labor force, would decline, because the labor force would rise while the number of people unemployed would remain unchanged.
b. Natural unemployment rate estimates also would be lower.
c. The logic of the short- and long-run Phillips curves would not be altered. The government might wish to make this change if it feels that those in the military "hold jobs" and therefore should be counted as employed within the U.S. economy.

18-3. The "long run" is an interval sufficiently long that input prices fully adjust and people have full information. Adoption of more sophisticated computer and communications technology provides people with more immediate access to information, which can reduce this interval.

18-5. The natural rate of unemployment is the rate of unemployment that would exist after full adjustment has taken place in response to any changes that have occurred. In contrast, the nonaccelerating inflation rate of unemployment is the rate of unemployment that corresponds to a stable rate of inflation, which is easier to quantify.

18-7. a. The measured unemployment rate when all adjustments have occurred will now always be lower than before, so the natural unemployment rate will be smaller.
b. The unemployment rate consistent with stable inflation will now be reduced, so the NAIRU will be smaller.
c. The Phillips curve will shift inward.

18-9. No. It could still be true that wages and other prices of factors of production adjust sluggishly to changes in the price level. Then a rise in aggregate demand that boosts the price level brings about an upward movement along the short-run aggregate supply curve, causing equilibrium real GDP to rise.

18-11. a. An increase in desired investment spending induces an increase in aggregate demand, so AD_3 applies. The price level is unchanged in the short run, and equilibrium real GDP rises from $15 trillion at point A to $15.5 trillion at point C.
b. Over time, firms perceive that they can increase their profits by adjusting prices upward in response to the increase in aggregate demand. Thus, firms eventually will incur the menu costs required to make these price adjustments. As they do so, the aggregate supply curve will shift upward, from $SRAS_1$ to $SRAS_2$, as shown in the diagram below. Real GDP will return to its original level of $15 trillion, in base-year dollars. The price level will increase to a level above 119, such as 124.

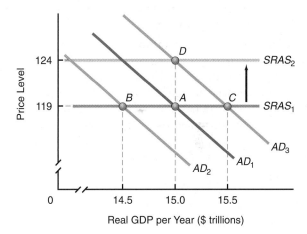

18-13. The explanation would be that aggregate demand increased at a faster pace than the rise in aggregate supply caused by economic growth. On net, therefore, the price level rose during those years.

18-15. If the average time between price adjustments by firms is significant, then the short-run aggregate supply curve could be regarded as horizontal, as hypothesized by the New Keynesian theorists. As a consequence, there would be a short-run trade-off between inflation and real GDP that policymakers potentially could exploit.

Chapter 19

19-1. Population growth rate = real GDP growth rate − rate of growth of per capita real GDP = 3.1 percent − 0.3 percent = 2.8 percent.

19-3. **a.** 20 × 0.01 percent = 0.2 percent.
b. 10 × 0.01 percent = 0.1 percent.

19-5. $10 trillion/$0.5 trillion × 0.1 = 2 percentage points.

19-7. **a.** Portfolio investment is equal to $150 million in bonds plus $100 million in stocks representing ownership of less than 10 percent, or $250 million. (Bank loans are neither portfolio investment nor foreign direct investment.)
b. Foreign direct investment is equal to $250 million in stocks representing an ownership share of at least 10 percent. (Bank loans are neither portfolio investment nor foreign direct investment.)

19-9. **a.** adverse selection
b. adverse selection
c. moral hazard
d. adverse selection

19-11. **a.** The company had already qualified for funding at a market interest rate, so the World Bank is interfering with functioning private markets for credit. In addition, by extending credit to the company at a below-market rate, the World Bank provides an incentive for the company to borrow additional funds for less efficient investment.
b. In this situation, the World Bank effectively is tying up funds in dead capital. There is an associated opportunity cost, because the funds could instead be allocated to another investment that would yield more immediate returns.
c. In this case, the IMF contributes to a moral hazard problem, because the government has every incentive not to make reforms that will enable it to repay this and future loans it may receive.

19-13. **a.** There is an incentive for at least some governments to fail to follow through with reforms, even if those governments might have had good intentions when they applied for World Bank loans.

b. National governments most interested in obtaining funds to "buy" votes will be among those most interested in obtaining IMF loans. The proposed IMF rule could help reduce the number of nations whose governments seek to obtain funds to try to "buy" votes.

Chapter 33

33-1. **a.** The opportunity cost of pastries in Northland is 0.5 sandwich per pastry. The opportunity cost of sandwiches in Northland is 2 pastries per sandwich.
b. The opportunity cost of pastries in West Coast is 2 sandwiches per pastry. The opportunity cost of sandwiches in West Coast is 0.5 pastries per sandwich.

33-3. If Northland specializes in producing pastries, the maximum number of pastries it can produce and trade to West Coast is 50,000 pastries. Hence, the maximum number of units of each good that the two countries can trade at a rate of exchange of 1 pastry for 1 sandwich is 50,000.

33-5. Coastal Realm has a comparative advantage in producing digital TVs, and Border Kingdom has a comparative advantage in wine production.

33-7. **a.** The opportunity cost of modems in South Shore is 2 flash drives per modem. The opportunity cost of flash drives in South Shore is 0.5 modem per flash drive.
b. The opportunity cost of modems in East Isle is 0.5 flash drive per modem. The opportunity cost of flash drives in East Isle is 2 modems per flash drive.
c. Residents of South Shore have a comparative advantage in producing flash drives, and residents of East Isle have a comparative advantage in producing modems.

33-9. The critics are suggesting that Mexican exporters are shifting exports that would have gone to other nations to the United States, a nation within NAFTA, which would constitute trade diversion.

Chapter 34

34-1. The trade balance is merchandise exports minus merchandise imports, which equals 500 − 600 = −100, or a deficit of 100. Adding service exports of 75 and subtracting net unilateral transfers of 10 and service imports of 50 yields $-100 + 75 - 10 - 50 = -85$, or a current account balance of -85. The capital account balance equals the difference between capital inflows and capital outflows, or $300 - 200 = +100$, or a capital account surplus of 100.

34-3. a. The increase in demand for Mexican-made guitars increases the demand for Mexican pesos, and the peso appreciates.

b. International investors will remove some of their financial capital from Mexico. The increase in the supply of pesos in the foreign exchange market will cause the peso to depreciate.

34-5. The demand for Chinese yuan increases, and the supply of yuan decreases. The dollar-yuan exchange rate rises, so the yuan appreciates.

34-7. The Canadian dollar–euro exchange rate is found by dividing the U.S. dollar–euro exchange rate by the U.S. dollar–Canadian dollar exchange rate, or (1.45 \$US/euro)/(0.94 \$US/\$C) = 1.54 \$C/euro, or 1.54 Canadian dollars per euro.

34-9. A flexible exchange rate system allows the exchange value of a currency to be determined freely in the foreign exchange market with no intervention by the government. A fixed exchange rate pegs the value of the currency, and the authorities responsible for the value of the currency intervene in foreign exchange markets to maintain this value. A dirty float involves occasional intervention by the exchange authorities. A target zone allows the exchange rate to fluctuate, but only within a given range of values.

34-11. When the dollar is pegged to gold at a rate of \$35 and the pound is pegged to the dollar at \$2 = £1, an implicit value between gold and the pound is established at £17.50 = 1 ounce of gold. If the dollar falls in value relative to gold, yet the pound is still valued to the dollar at \$2 = £1, the pound become undervalued relative to gold. The exchange rate between the dollar and the pound will have to be adjusted to 2.29 \$/£.

Glossary

A

Absolute advantage The ability to produce more units of a good or service using a given quantity of labor or resource inputs. Equivalently, the ability to produce the same quantity of a good or service using fewer units of labor or resource inputs.

Accounting identities Values that are equivalent by definition.

Accounting profit Total revenues minus total explicit costs.

Action time lag The time between recognizing an economic problem and implementing policy to solve it. The action time lag is quite long for fiscal policy, which requires congressional approval.

Active (discretionary) policymaking All actions on the part of monetary and fiscal policymakers that are undertaken in response to or in anticipation of some change in the overall economy.

Ad valorem taxation Assessing taxes by charging a tax rate equal to a fraction of the market price of each unit purchased.

Adverse selection The likelihood that individuals who seek to borrow may use the funds that they receive for high-risk projects.

Age-earnings cycle The regular earnings profile of an individual throughout his or her lifetime. The age-earnings cycle usually starts with a low income, builds gradually to a peak at around age 50, and then gradually curves down until it approaches zero at retirement.

Aggregate demand The total of all planned expenditures in the entire economy.

Aggregate demand curve A curve showing planned purchase rates for all final goods and services in the economy at various price levels, all other things held constant.

Aggregate demand shock Any event that causes the aggregate demand curve to shift inward or outward.

Aggregate supply The total of all planned production for the economy.

Aggregate supply shock Any event that causes the aggregate supply curve to shift inward or outward.

Aggregates Total amounts or quantities; aggregate demand, for example, is total planned expenditures throughout a nation.

Anticipated inflation The inflation rate that we believe will occur; when it does, we are in a situation of fully anticipated inflation.

Antitrust legislation Laws that restrict the formation of monopolies and regulate certain anticompetitive business practices.

Appreciation An increase in the exchange value of one nation's currency in terms of the currency of another nation.

Asset demand Holding money as a store of value instead of other assets such as certificates of deposit, corporate bonds, and stocks.

Assets Amounts owned; all items to which a business or household holds legal claim.

Asymmetric information Information possessed by one party in a financial transaction but not by the other party.

Automatic, or built-in, stabilizers Special provisions of certain federal programs that cause changes in desired aggregate expenditures without the action of Congress and the president. Examples are the federal progressive tax system and unemployment compensation.

Autonomous consumption The part of consumption that is independent of (does not depend on) the level of disposable income. Changes in autonomous consumption shift the consumption function.

Average fixed costs Total fixed costs divided by the number of units produced.

Average physical product Total product divided by the variable input.

Average propensity to consume (APC) Real consumption divided by real disposable income; for any given level of real income, the proportion of total real disposable income that is consumed.

Average propensity to save (APS) Real saving divided by real disposable income; for any given level of real income, the proportion of total real disposable income that is saved.

Average tax rate The total tax payment divided by total income. It is the proportion of total income paid in taxes.

Average total costs Total costs divided by the number of units produced; sometimes called *average per-unit total costs*.

Average variable costs Total variable costs divided by the number of units produced.

B

Balance of payments A system of accounts that measures transactions of goods, services, income, and financial assets between domestic households, businesses, and governments and residents of the rest of the world during a specific time period.

Balance of trade The difference between exports and imports of physical goods.

Balance sheet A statement of the assets and liabilities of any business entity, including financial institutions and the Federal Reserve System. Assets are what is owned; liabilities are what is owed.

Balanced budget A situation in which the government's spending is exactly equal to the total taxes and other revenues it collects during a given period of time.

Bank runs Attempts by many of a bank's depositors to convert transactions and time deposits into currency out of fear that the bank's liabilities may exceed its assets.

Barter The direct exchange of goods and services for other goods and services without the use of money.

Base year The year that is chosen as the point of reference for comparison of prices in other years.

Base-year dollars The value of a current sum expressed in terms of prices in a base year.

Behavioral economics An approach to the study of consumer behavior that emphasizes psychological limitations and complications that potentially interfere with rational decision making.

Bilateral monopoly A market structure consisting of a monopolist and a monopsonist.

Black market A market in which goods are traded at prices above their legal maximum prices or in which illegal goods are sold.

Bond A legal claim against a firm, usually entitling the owner of the bond to receive a fixed annual coupon payment, plus a lump-sum payment at the bond's maturity date. Bonds are issued in return for funds lent to the firm.

Bounded rationality The hypothesis that people are *nearly*, but not fully, rational, so that they cannot examine every possible choice available to them but instead use simple rules of thumb to sort among the alternatives that happen to occur to them.

Budget constraint All of the possible combinations of goods that can be purchased (at fixed prices) with a specific budget.

Bundling Offering two or more products for sale as a set.

Business fluctuations The ups and downs in business activity throughout the economy.

C

Capital account A category of balance of payments transactions that measures flows of real and financial assets.

Capital consumption allowance Another name for depreciation, the amount that businesses would have to save in order to take care of deteriorating machines and other equipment.

Capital gain A positive difference between the purchase price and the sale price of an asset. If a share of stock is bought for $5 and then sold for $15, the capital gain is $10.

Capital goods Producer durables; nonconsumable goods that firms use to make other goods.

Capital loss A negative difference between the purchase price and the sale price of an asset.

Capture hypothesis A theory of regulatory behavior that predicts that regulators will eventually be captured by special interests of the industry being regulated.

Cartel An association of producers in an industry that agree to set common prices and output quotas to prevent competition.

Central bank A banker's bank, usually an official institution that also serves as a country's treasury's bank. Central banks normally regulate commercial banks.

Certificate of deposit (CD) A time deposit with a fixed maturity date offered by banks and other financial institutions.

Ceteris paribus **[KAY-ter-us PEAR-uh-bus] assumption** The assumption that nothing changes except the factor or factors being studied.

Ceteris paribus **conditions** Determinants of the relationship between price and quantity that are unchanged along a curve; changes in these factors cause the curve to shift.

Closed shop A business enterprise in which employees must belong to the union before they can be hired and must remain in the union after they are hired.

Collective bargaining Negotiation between the management of a company or of a group of companies and the management of a union or a group of unions for the purpose of reaching a mutually agreeable contract that sets wages, fringe benefits, and working conditions for all employees in all the unions involved.

Collective decision making How voters, politicians, and other interested parties act and how these actions influence nonmarket decisions.

Common property Property that is owned by everyone and therefore by no one. Air and water are examples of common property resources.

Comparative advantage The ability to produce a good or service at a lower opportunity cost than other producers.

Complements Two goods are complements when a change in the price of one causes an opposite shift in the demand for the other.

Concentration ratio The percentage of all sales contributed by the leading four or leading eight firms in an industry; sometimes called the *industry concentration ratio*.

Constant dollars Dollars expressed in terms of real purchasing power using a particular year as the base or standard of comparison, in contrast to current dollars.

Constant returns to scale No change in long-run average costs when output increases.

Constant-cost industry An industry whose total output can be increased without an increase in long-run per-unit costs; its long-run supply curve is horizontal.

Consumer optimum A choice of a set of goods and services that maximizes the level of satisfaction for each consumer, subject to limited income.

Consumer Price Index (CPI) A statistical measure of a weighted average of prices of a specified set of goods and services purchased by typical consumers in urban areas.

Consumer surplus The total difference between the total amount that consumers would have been willing to pay for a good or service and the total amount that they actually pay.

Consumption Spending on new goods and services to be used up out of a household's current income. Whatever is not consumed is saved. Consumption includes such things as buying food and going to a concert.

Consumption function The relationship between amount consumed and disposable income. A consumption function tells us how much people plan to consume at various levels of disposable income.

Consumption goods Goods bought by households to use up, such as food and movies.

Contraction A business fluctuation during which the pace of national economic activity is slowing down.

Cooperative game A game in which the players explicitly cooperate to make themselves better off. As applied to firms, it involves companies colluding in order to make higher than perfectly competitive rates of return.

Corporation A legal entity that may conduct business in its own name just as an individual does; the owners of a corporation, called shareholders, own shares of the firm's profits and enjoy the protection of limited liability.

Cost-of-living adjustments (COLAs) Clauses in contracts that allow for increases in specified nominal values to take account of changes in the cost of living.

Cost-of-service regulation Regulation that allows prices to reflect only the actual average cost of production and no monopoly profits.

Cost-push inflation Inflation caused by decreases in short-run aggregate supply.

Craft unions Labor unions composed of workers who engage in a particular trade or skill, such as baking, carpentry, or plumbing.

Crawling peg An exchange rate arrangement in which a country pegs the value of its currency to the exchange value of another nation's currency but allows the par value to change at regular intervals.

Creative response Behavior on the part of a firm that allows it to comply with the letter of the law but violate the spirit, significantly lessening the law's effects.

Credence good A product with qualities that consumers lack the expertise to assess without assistance.

Cross price elasticity of demand (E_{xy}) The percentage change in the demand for one good (holding its price constant) divided by the percentage change in the price of a related good.

Crowding-out effect The tendency of expansionary fiscal policy to cause a decrease in planned investment or planned consumption in the private sector; this decrease normally results from the rise in interest rates.

Current account A category of balance of payments transactions that measures the exchange of merchandise, the exchange of services, and unilateral transfers.

Cyclical unemployment Unemployment resulting from business recessions that occur when aggregate (total) demand is insufficient to create full employment.

D

Dead capital Any capital resource that lacks clear title of ownership.

Deadweight loss The portion of consumer surplus that no one in society is able to obtain in a situation of monopoly.

Decreasing-cost industry An industry in which an increase in output leads to a reduction in long-run per-unit costs, such that the long-run industry supply curve slopes downward.

Deflation A sustained decrease in the average of all prices of goods and services in an economy.

Demand A schedule showing how much of a good or service people will purchase at any price during a specified time period, other things being constant.

Demand curve A graphical representation of the demand schedule; a negatively sloped line showing the inverse relationship between the price and the quantity demanded (other things being equal).

Demand-pull inflation Inflation caused by increases in aggregate demand not matched by increases in aggregate supply.

Dependent variable A variable whose value changes according to changes in the value of one or more independent variables.

Depository institutions Financial institutions that accept deposits from savers and lend funds from those deposits out at interest.

Depreciation A decrease in the exchange value of one nation's currency in terms of the currency of another nation.

Depression An extremely severe recession.

Derived demand Input factor demand derived from demand for the final product being produced.

Development economics The study of factors that contribute to the economic growth of a country.

Diminishing marginal utility The principle that as more of any good or service is consumed, its extra benefit declines. Otherwise stated, increases in total utility from the consumption of a good or service become smaller and smaller as more is consumed during a given time period.

Direct expenditure offsets Actions on the part of the private sector in spending income that offset government fiscal policy actions. Any increase in government spending in an area that competes with the private sector will have some direct expenditure offset.

Direct marketing Advertising targeted at specific consumers, typically in the form of postal mailings, telephone calls, or e-mail messages.

Direct relationship A relationship between two variables that is positive, meaning that an increase in one variable is associated with an increase in the other and a decrease in one variable is associated with a decrease in the other.

Dirty float Active management of a floating exchange rate on the part of a country's government, often in cooperation with other nations.

Discount rate The interest rate that the Federal Reserve charges for reserves that it lends to depository institutions. It is sometimes referred to as the *rediscount rate* or, in Canada and England, as the *bank rate*.

Discounting The method by which the present value of a future sum or a future stream of sums is obtained.

Discouraged workers Individuals who have stopped looking for a job because they are convinced that they will not find a suitable one.

Diseconomies of scale Increases in long-run average costs that occur as output increases.

Disposable personal income (DPI) Personal income after personal income taxes have been paid.

Dissaving Negative saving; a situation in which spending exceeds income. Dissaving can occur when a household is able to borrow or use up existing assets.

Distribution of income The way income is allocated among the population.

Dividends Portion of a corporation's profits paid to its owners (shareholders).

Division of labor The segregation of resources into different specific tasks; for example, one automobile worker puts on bumpers, another doors, and so on.

Dominant strategies Strategies that always yield the highest benefit. Regardless of what other players do, a dominant strategy will yield the most benefit for the player using it.

Dumping Selling a good or a service abroad below the price charged in the home market or at a price below its cost of production.

Durable consumer goods Consumer goods that have a life span of more than three years.

Dynamic tax analysis Economic evaluation of tax rate changes that recognizes that the tax base eventually declines with ever-higher tax rates, so that tax revenues may eventually decline if the tax rate is raised sufficiently.

E

Economic freedom The rights to own private property and to exchange goods, services, and financial assets with minimal government interference.

Economic goods Goods that are scarce, for which the quantity demanded exceeds the quantity supplied at a zero price.

Economic growth Increases in per capita real GDP measured by its rate of change per year.

Economic profits Total revenues minus total opportunity costs of all inputs used, or the total of all implicit and explicit costs.

Economic rent A payment for the use of any resource over and above its opportunity cost.

Economics The study of how people allocate their limited resources to satisfy their unlimited wants.

Economies of scale Decreases in long-run average costs resulting from increases in output.

Effect time lag The time that elapses between the implementation of a policy and the results of that policy.

Efficiency The case in which a given level of inputs is used to produce the maximum output possible. Alternatively, the situation in which a given output is produced at minimum cost.

Effluent fee A charge to a polluter that gives the right to discharge into the air or water a certain amount of pollution; also called a *pollution tax*

Elastic demand A demand relationship in which a given percentage change in price will result in a larger percentage change in quantity demanded.

Empirical Relying on real-world data in evaluating the usefulness of a model.

Endowments The various resources in an economy, including both physical resources and such human resources as ingenuity and management skills.

Entitlements Guaranteed benefits under a government program such as Social Security, Medicare, or Medicaid.

Entrepreneurship The component of human resources that performs the functions of raising capital, organizing, managing, and assembling other factors of production, making basic business policy decisions, and taking risks.

Equation of exchange The formula indicating that the number of monetary units (M_s) times the number of times each unit is spent on final goods and services (V) is identical to the price level (P) times real GDP (Y).

Equilibrium The situation when quantity supplied equals quantity demanded at a particular price.

Excess reserves The difference between actual reserves and required reserves.

Exchange rate The price of one nation's currency in terms of the currency of another country.

Excise tax A tax levied on purchases of a particular good or service.

Expansion A business fluctuation in which the pace of national economic activity is speeding up.

Expenditure approach Computing GDP by adding up the dollar value at current market prices of all final goods and services.

Experience good A product that an individual must consume before the product's quality can be established.

Explicit costs Costs that business managers must take account of because they must be paid; examples are wages, taxes, and rent.

Externality A consequence of an economic activity that spills over to affect third parties. Pollution is an externality.

F

Featherbedding Any practice that forces employers to use more labor than they would otherwise or to use existing labor in an inefficient manner.

Federal Deposit Insurance Corporation (FDIC) A government agency that insures the deposits held in banks and most other depository institutions; all U.S. banks are insured this way.

Federal funds market A private market (made up mostly of banks) in which banks can borrow reserves from other banks that want to lend them. Federal funds are usually lent for overnight use.

Federal funds rate The interest rate that depository institutions pay to borrow reserves in the interbank federal funds market.

Fiduciary monetary system A system in which money is issued by the government and its value is based uniquely on the public's faith that the currency represents command over goods and services.

Final goods and services Goods and services that are at their final stage of production and will not be transformed into yet other goods or services. For example, wheat ordinarily is not considered a final good because it is usually used to make a final good, bread.

Financial capital Funds used to purchase physical capital goods, such as buildings and equipment, and patents and trademarks.

Financial intermediaries Institutions that transfer funds between ultimate lenders (savers) and ultimate borrowers.

Financial intermediation The process by which financial institutions accept savings from businesses, households, and governments and lend the savings to other businesses, households, and governments.

Firm A business organization that employs resources to produce goods or services for profit. A firm normally owns and operates at least one "plant" or facility in order to produce.

Fiscal policy The discretionary changing of government expenditures or taxes to achieve national economic goals, such as high employment with price stability.

Fixed costs Costs that do not vary with output. Fixed costs typically include such expenses as rent on a building. These costs are fixed for a certain period of time (in the long run, though, they are variable).

Fixed investment Purchases by businesses of newly produced producer durables, or capital goods, such as production machinery and office equipment.

Flexible exchange rates Exchange rates that are allowed to fluctuate in the open market in response to changes in supply and demand. Sometimes called *floating exchange rates.*

Flow A quantity measured per unit of time; something that occurs over time, such as the income you make per week or per year or the number of individuals who are fired every month.

FOMC Directive A document that summarizes the Federal Open Market Committee's general policy strategy, establishes near-term objectives for the federal funds rate, and specifies target ranges for money supply growth.

Foreign direct investment The acquisition of more than 10 percent of the shares of ownership in a company in another nation.

Foreign exchange market A market in which households, firms, and governments buy and sell national currencies.

Foreign exchange rate The price of one currency in terms of another.

Foreign exchange risk The possibility that changes in the value of a nation's currency will result in variations in the market value of assets.

45-degree reference line The line along which planned real expenditures equal real GDP per year.

Fractional reserve banking A system in which depository institutions hold reserves that are less than the amount of total deposits.

Free-rider problem A problem that arises when individuals presume that others will pay for public goods so that, individually, they can escape paying for their portion without causing a reduction in production.

Frictional unemployment Unemployment due to the fact that workers must search for appropriate job offers. This takes time, and so they remain temporarily unemployed.

Full employment An arbitrary level of unemployment that corresponds to "normal" friction in the labor market. In 1986, a 6.5 percent rate of unemployment was considered full employment. Today, it is assumed to be around 5 percent.

G

Game theory A way of describing the various possible outcomes in any situation involving two or more interacting individuals when those individuals are aware of the interactive nature of their situation and plan accordingly. The plans made by these individuals are known as *game strategies.*

GDP deflator A price index measuring the changes in prices of all new goods and services produced in the economy.

General Agreement on Tariffs and Trade (GATT) An international agreement established in 1947 to further world trade by reducing barriers and tariffs. The GATT was replaced by the World Trade Organization in 1995.

Goods All things from which individuals derive satisfaction or happiness.

Government budget constraint The limit on government spending and transfers imposed by the fact that every dollar the government spends, transfers, or uses to repay borrowed funds must ultimately be provided by the user charges and taxes it collects.

Government budget deficit An excess of government spending over government revenues during a given period of time.

Government budget surplus An excess of government revenues over government spending during a given period of time.

Government, or political, goods Goods (and services) provided by the public sector; they can be either private or public goods.

Government-inhibited good A good that has been deemed socially undesirable through the political process. Heroin is an example.

Government-sponsored good A good that has been deemed socially desirable through the political process. Museums are an example.

Gross domestic income (GDI) The sum of all income—wages, interest, rent, and profits—paid to the four factors of production.

Gross domestic product (GDP) The total market value of all final goods and services produced during a year by factors of production located within a nation's borders.

Gross private domestic investment The creation of capital goods, such as factories and machines, that can yield production and hence consumption in the future. Also included in this definition are changes in business inventories and repairs made to machines or buildings.

Gross public debt All federal government debt irrespective of who owns it.

H

Health savings account (HSA) A tax-exempt health care account into which individuals can pay on a regular basis and out of which medical expenses can be paid.

Hedge A financial strategy that reduces the chance of suffering losses arising from foreign exchange risk.

Horizontal merger The joining of firms that are producing or selling a similar product.

Human capital The accumulated training and education of workers.

I

Implicit costs Expenses that managers do not have to pay out of pocket and hence normally do not explicitly calculate, such as the opportunity cost of factors of production that are owned; examples are owner-provided capital and owner-provided labor.

Import quota A physical supply restriction on imports of a particular good, such as sugar. Foreign exporters are unable to sell in the United States more than the quantity specified in the import quota.

Incentive structure The system of rewards and punishments individuals face with respect to their own actions.

Incentives Rewards for engaging in a particular activity.

Income approach Measuring GDP by adding up all components of national income, including wages, interest, rent, and profits.

Income elasticity of demand (E_i) The percentage change in demand for any good, holding its price constant, divided by the percentage change in income; the responsiveness of demand to changes in income, holding the good's relative price constant.

Income in kind Income received in the form of goods and services, such as housing or medical care; to be contrasted with money income, which is simply income in dollars, or general purchasing power, that can be used to buy any goods and services.

Income velocity of money (V) The number of times per year a dollar is spent on final goods and services; identically equal to nominal GDP divided by the money supply.

Income-consumption curve The set of optimal consumption points that would occur if income were increased, relative prices remaining constant.

Increasing-cost industry An industry in which an increase in industry output is accompanied by an increase in long-run per-unit costs, such that the long-run industry supply curve slopes upward.

Independent variable A variable whose value is determined independently of, or outside, the equation under study.

Indifference curve A curve composed of a set of consumption alternatives, each of which yields the same total amount of satisfaction.

Indirect business taxes All business taxes except the tax on corporate profits. Indirect business taxes include sales and business property taxes.

Industrial unions Labor unions that consist of workers from a particular industry, such as automobile manufacturing or steel manufacturing.

Industry supply curve The locus of points showing the minimum prices at which given quantities will be forthcoming; also called the *market supply curve.*

Inefficient point Any point below the production possibilities curve, at which the use of resources is not generating the maximum possible output.

Inelastic demand A demand relationship in which a given percentage change in price will result in a less than propor-

tionate percentage change in the quantity demanded.

Infant industry argument The contention that tariffs should be imposed to protect from import competition an industry that is trying to get started. Presumably, after the industry becomes technologically efficient, the tariff can be lifted.

Inferior goods Goods for which demand falls as income rises.

Inflation A sustained increase in the average of all prices of goods and services in an economy.

Inflation-adjusted return A rate of return that is measured in terms of real goods and services; that is, after the effects of inflation have been factored out.

Inflationary gap The gap that exists whenever equilibrium real GDP per year is greater than full-employment real GDP as shown by the position of the long-run aggregate supply curve.

Information product An item that is produced using information-intensive inputs at a relatively high fixed cost but distributed for sale at a relatively low marginal cost.

Informational advertising Advertising that emphasizes transmitting knowledge about the features of a product.

Innovation Transforming an invention into something that is useful to humans.

Inside information Information that is not available to the general public about what is happening in a corporation.

Interactive marketing Advertising that permits a consumer to follow up directly by searching for more information and placing direct product orders.

Interest The payment for current rather than future command over resources; the cost of obtaining credit.

Interest rate effect One of the reasons that the aggregate demand curve slopes downward: Higher price levels increase the interest rate, which in turn causes businesses and consumers to reduce desired spending due to the higher cost of borrowing.

Intermediate goods Goods used up entirely in the production of final goods.

International financial crisis The rapid withdrawal of foreign investments and loans from a nation.

International Monetary Fund An agency founded to administer an international foreign exchange system and to lend to member countries that had balance of payments problems. The IMF now functions as a lender of last resort for national governments.

Inventory investment Changes in the stocks of finished goods and goods in process, as well as changes in the raw materials that businesses keep on hand. Whenever inventories are decreasing, inventory investment is negative; whenever they are increasing, inventory investment is positive.

Inverse relationship A relationship between two variables that is negative, meaning that an increase in one variable is associated with a decrease in the other and a decrease in one variable is associated with an increase in the other.

Investment Any use of today's resources to expand tomorrow's production or consumption.

J

Job leaver An individual in the labor force who quits voluntarily.

Job loser An individual in the labor force whose employment was involuntarily terminated.

Jurisdictional dispute A disagreement involving two or more unions over which should have control of a particular jurisdiction, such as a particular craft or skill or a particular firm or industry.

K

Keynesian short-run aggregate supply curve The horizontal portion of the aggregate supply curve in which there is excessive unemployment and unused capacity in the economy.

L

Labor Productive contributions of humans who work.

Labor force Individuals aged 16 years or older who either have jobs or who are looking and available for jobs; the number of employed plus the number of unemployed.

Labor force participation rate The percentage of noninstitutionalized working-age individuals who are employed or seeking employment.

Labor productivity Total real domestic output (real GDP) divided by the number of workers (output per worker).

Labor unions Worker organizations that seek to secure economic improvements for their members; they also seek to improve the safety, health, and other benefits (such as job security) of their members.

Land The natural resources that are available from nature. Land as a resource includes location, original fertility and mineral deposits, topography, climate, water, and vegetation.

Law of demand The observation that there is a negative, or inverse, relationship between the price of any good or service and the quantity demanded, holding other factors constant.

Law of diminishing marginal product The observation that after some point, successive equal-sized increases in a variable factor of production, such as labor, added to fixed factors of production, will result in smaller increases in output.

Law of increasing relative cost The fact that the opportunity cost of additional units of a good generally increases as society attempts to produce more of that good. This accounts for the bowed-out shape of the production possibilities curve.

Law of supply The observation that the higher the price of a good, the more of that good sellers will make available over a specified time period, other things being equal.

Leading indicators Events that have been found to occur before changes in business activity.

Lemons problem The potential for asymmetric information to bring about a general decline in product quality in an industry.

Lender of last resort The Federal Reserve's role as an institution that is willing and able to lend to a temporarily illiquid bank that is otherwise in good financial condition to prevent the bank's illiquid position from leading to a general loss of confidence in that bank or in others.

Liabilities Amounts owed; the legal claims against a business or household by nonowners.

Limited liability A legal concept in which the responsibility, or liability, of the owners of a corporation is limited to the value of the shares in the firm that they own.

Liquidity The degree to which an asset can be acquired or disposed of without much danger of any intervening loss in *nominal* value and with small transaction costs. Money is the most liquid asset.

Liquidity approach A method of measuring the money supply by looking at money as a temporary store of value.

Long run The time period during which all factors of production can be varied.

Long-run aggregate supply curve A vertical line representing the real output of goods and services after full adjustment has occurred. It can also be viewed as representing the real GDP of the economy under conditions of full employment—the full-employment level of real GDP.

Long-run average cost curve The locus of points representing the minimum unit cost of producing any given rate of output, given current technology and resource prices.

Long-run industry supply curve A market supply curve showing the relationship between prices and quantities after firms have been allowed the time to enter into or exit from an industry, depending on whether there have been positive or negative economic profits.

Lorenz curve A geometric representation of the distribution of income. A Lorenz curve that is perfectly straight represents complete income equality. The more bowed a Lorenz curve, the more unequally income is distributed.

Lump-sum tax A tax that does not depend on income. An example is a $1,000 tax that every household must pay, irrespective of its economic situation.

M

M1 The money supply, measured as the total value of currency plus transactions deposits plus traveler's checks not issued by banks.

M2 M1 plus (1) savings and small-denomination time deposits at all depository institutions, (2) balances in retail money market mutual funds, and (3) money market deposit accounts (MMDAs).

Macroeconomics The study of the behavior of the economy as a whole, including such economywide phenomena as changes in unemployment, the general price level, and national income.

Majority rule A collective decision-making system in which group decisions are made on the basis of more than 50 percent of the vote. In other words, whatever more than half of the electorate votes for, the entire electorate has to accept.

Marginal cost pricing A system of pricing in which the price charged is equal to the opportunity cost to society of producing one more unit of the good or service in question. The opportunity cost is the marginal cost to society.

Marginal costs The change in total costs due to a one-unit change in production rate.

Marginal factor cost (MFC) The cost of using an additional unit of an input. For example, if a firm can hire all the workers it wants at the going wage rate, the marginal factor cost of labor is the wage rate.

Marginal physical product The physical output that is due to the addition of one more unit of a variable factor of production; the change in total product occurring when a variable input is increased and all other inputs are held constant; also called *marginal product.*

Marginal physical product (MPP) of labor The change in output resulting from the addition of one more worker. The MPP of the worker equals the change in total output accounted for by hiring the worker, holding all other factors of production constant.

Marginal propensity to consume (MPC) The ratio of the change in consumption to the change in disposable income. A marginal propensity to consume of 0.8 tells us that an additional $100 in take-home pay will lead to an additional $80 consumed.

Marginal propensity to save (MPS) The ratio of the change in saving to the change in disposable income. A marginal propensity to save of 0.2 indicates that out of an additional $100 in take-home pay, $20 will be saved. Whatever is not saved is consumed. The marginal propensity to save plus the marginal propensity to consume must always equal 1, by definition.

Marginal revenue The change in total revenues resulting from a one-unit change in output (and sale) of the product in question.

Marginal revenue product (MRP) The marginal physical product (MPP) times marginal revenue (MR). The MRP gives the additional revenue obtained from a one-unit change in labor input.

Marginal tax rate The change in the tax payment divided by the change in income, or the percentage of additional dollars that must be paid in taxes. The marginal tax rate is applied to the highest tax bracket of taxable income reached.

Marginal utility The change in total utility due to a one-unit change in the quantity of a good or service consumed.

Market All of the arrangements that individuals have for exchanging with one another. Thus, for example, we can speak of the labor market, the automobile market, and the credit market.

Market clearing, or equilibrium, price The price that clears the market, at which quantity demanded equals quantity supplied; the price where the demand curve intersects the supply curve.

Market demand The demand of all consumers in the marketplace for a particular good or service. The summation at each price of the quantity demanded by each individual.

Market failure A situation in which an unrestrained market operation leads to either too few or too many resources going to a specific economic activity.

Market share test The percentage of a market that a particular firm supplies; used as the primary measure of monopoly power.

Mass marketing Advertising intended to reach as many consumers as possible, typically through television, newspaper, radio, or magazine ads.

Medium of exchange Any item that sellers will accept as payment.

Microeconomics The study of decision making undertaken by individuals (or households) and by firms.

Minimum efficient scale (MES) The lowest rate of output per unit time at which long-run average costs for a particular firm are at a minimum.

Minimum wage A wage floor, legislated by government, setting the lowest hourly rate that firms may legally pay workers.

Models, or theories Simplified representations of the real world used as the basis for predictions or explanations.

Money Any medium that is universally accepted in an economy both by sellers of goods and services as payment for those goods and services and by creditors as payment for debts.

Money balances Synonymous with money, money stock, money holdings.

Money illusion Reacting to changes in money prices rather than relative prices. If a worker whose wages double when the price level also doubles thinks he or she is better off, that worker is suffering from money illusion.

Money market deposit accounts (MMDAs) Accounts issued by banks yielding a market rate of interest with a minimum balance requirement and a limit on transactions. They have no minimum maturity.

Money market mutual funds Funds obtained from the public that investment companies hold in common and use to acquire short-maturity credit instruments, such as certificates of deposit and securities sold by the U.S. government.

Money multiplier A number that, when multiplied by a change in reserves in the banking system, yields the resulting change in the money supply.

Money price The price that we observe today, expressed in today's dollars; also called the *absolute* or *nominal price.*

Money supply The amount of money in circulation.

Monopolist The single supplier of a good or service for which there is no close substitute. The monopolist therefore constitutes its entire industry.

Monopolistic competition A market situation in which a large number of firms produce similar but not identical products. Entry into the industry is relatively easy.

Monopolization The possession of monopoly power in the relevant market and the willful acquisition or maintenance of that power, as distinguished from growth or development as a consequence of a superior product, business acumen, or historical accident.

Monopoly A firm that can determine the market price of a good. In the extreme case, a monopoly is the only seller of a good or service.

Monopsonist The only buyer in a market.

Monopsonistic exploitation Paying a price for the variable input that is less than its marginal revenue product; the difference between marginal revenue product and the wage rate.

Moral hazard The possibility that a borrower might engage in riskier behavior after a loan has been obtained.

Multiplier The ratio of the change in the equilibrium level of real GDP to the change in autonomous real expenditures; the number by which a change in autonomous real investment or autonomous real consumption, for example, is multiplied to get the change in equilibrium real GDP.

Multiproduct firm A firm that produces and sells two or more different items.

N

National income (NI) The total of all factor payments to resource owners. It can be obtained from net domestic product (NDP) by subtracting indirect business taxes and transfers and adding net U.S. income earned abroad and other business income adjustments.

National income accounting A measurement system used to estimate national income and its components; one approach to measuring an economy's aggregate performance.

Natural monopoly A monopoly that arises from the peculiar production characteristics in an industry. It usually arises when there are large economies of scale relative to the industry's demand such that one firm can produce at a lower average cost than can be achieved by multiple firms.

Natural rate of unemployment The rate of unemployment that is estimated to prevail in long-run macroeconomic equilibrium, when all workers and employers have fully adjusted to any changes in the economy.

Negative market feedback A tendency for a good or service to fall out of favor with more consumers because other consumers have stopped purchasing the item.

Negative-sum game A game in which players as a group lose during the process of the game.

Net domestic product (NDP) GDP minus depreciation.

Net investment Gross private domestic investment minus an estimate of the wear and tear on the existing capital stock. Net investment therefore measures the change in the capital stock over a one-year period.

Net public debt Gross public debt minus all government interagency borrowing.

Net worth The difference between assets and liabilities.

Network effect A situation in which a consumer's willingness to purchase a good or service is influenced by how many others also buy or have bought the item.

Neutral federal funds rate A value of the interest rate on interbank loans at which the growth rate of real GDP tends neither to rise nor to fall relative to the rate of growth of potential, long-run, real GDP, given the expected rate of inflation.

New entrant An individual who has never held a full-time job lasting two weeks or longer but is now seeking employment.

New growth theory A theory of economic growth that examines the factors that determine why technology, research, innovation, and the like are undertaken and how they interact.

New Keynesian inflation dynamics In new Keynesian theory, the pattern of inflation exhibited by an economy with growing aggregate demand—initial sluggish adjustment of the price level in response to increased aggregate demand followed by higher inflation later.

Nominal rate of interest The market rate of interest expressed in today's dollars.

Nominal values The values of variables such as GDP and investment expressed in current dollars, also called *money values*; measurement in terms of the actual market prices at which goods and services are sold.

Nonaccelerating inflation rate of unemployment (NAIRU) The rate of unemployment below which the rate of inflation tends to rise and above which the rate of inflation tends to fall.

Noncontrollable expenditures Government spending that changes automatically without action by Congress.

Noncooperative game A game in which the players neither negotiate nor cooperate in any way. As applied to firms in an industry, this is the common situation in which there are relatively few firms and each has some ability to change price.

Nondurable consumer goods Consumer goods that are used up within three years.

Nonincome expense items The total of indirect business taxes and depreciation.

Nonprice rationing devices All methods used to ration scarce goods that are price-controlled. Whenever the price system is not allowed to work, nonprice rationing devices will evolve to ration the affected goods and services.

Normal goods Goods for which demand rises as income rises. Most goods are normal goods.

Normal rate of return The amount that must be paid to an investor to induce investment in a business; also known as the *opportunity cost of capital*.

Normative economics Analysis involving value judgments about economic policies; relates to whether things are good or bad. A statement of *what ought to be*.

Number line A line that can be divided into segments of equal length, each associated with a number.

O

Oligopoly A market structure in which there are very few sellers. Each seller knows that the other sellers will react to its changes in prices, quantities, and qualities.

Open economy effect One of the reasons that the aggregate demand curve slopes downward: Higher price levels result in foreign residents desiring to buy fewer U.S.-made goods, while U.S. residents now desire more foreign-made goods, thereby reducing net exports. This is equivalent to a reduction in the amount of real goods and services purchased in the United States.

Open market operations The purchase and sale of existing U.S. government securities (such as bonds) in the open private market by the Federal Reserve System.

Opportunistic behavior Actions that focus solely on short-run gains because long-run benefits of cooperation are perceived to be smaller.

Opportunity cost The highest-valued, next-best alternative that must be sacrificed to obtain something or to satisfy a want.

Opportunity cost of capital The normal rate of return, or the available return on the next-best alternative investment. Economists consider this a cost of production, and it is included in our cost examples.

Optimal quantity of pollution The level of pollution for which the marginal benefit of one additional unit of pollution abatement just equals the marginal cost of that additional unit of pollution abatement.

Origin The intersection of the y axis and the x axis in a graph.

Outsourcing A firm's employment of labor outside the country in which the firm is located.

P

Par value The officially determined value of a currency.

Partnership A business owned by two or more joint owners, or partners, who share the responsibilities and the profits of the firm and are individually liable for all the debts of the partnership.

Passive (nondiscretionary) policymaking Policymaking that is carried out in response to a rule. It is therefore not in response to an actual or potential change in overall economic activity.

Patent A government protection that gives an inventor the exclusive right to make, use, or sell an invention for a limited period of time (currently, 20 years).

Payment intermediaries Institutions that facilitate transfers of funds between depositors who hold transactions deposits with those institutions.

Payoff matrix A matrix of outcomes, or consequences, of the strategies available to the players in a game.

Perfect competition A market structure in which the decisions of *individual* buyers and sellers have no effect on market price.

Perfectly competitive firm A firm that is such a small part of the total *industry* that it cannot affect the price of the product it sells.

Perfectly elastic demand A demand that has the characteristic that even the slightest increase in price will lead to zero quantity demanded.

Perfectly elastic supply A supply characterized by a reduction in quantity supplied to zero when there is the slightest decrease in price.

Perfectly inelastic demand A demand that exhibits zero responsiveness to price changes; no matter what the price is, the quantity demanded remains the same.

Perfectly inelastic supply A supply for which quantity supplied remains constant, no matter what happens to price.

Personal Consumption Expenditure (PCE) Index A statistical measure of average prices that uses annually updated weights based on surveys of consumer spending.

Personal income (PI) The amount of income that households actually receive before they pay personal income taxes.

Persuasive advertising Advertising that is intended to induce a consumer to purchase a particular product and discover a previously unknown taste for the item.

Phillips curve A curve showing the relationship between unemployment and changes in wages or prices. It was long thought to reflect a trade-off between unemployment and inflation.

Physical capital All manufactured resources, including buildings, equipment, machines, and improvements to land that are used for production.

Planning curve The long-run average cost curve.

Planning horizon The long run, during which all inputs are variable.

Plant size The physical size of the factories that a firm owns and operates to produce its output. Plant size can be defined by square footage, maximum physical capacity, and other physical measures.

Policy irrelevance proposition The conclusion that policy actions have no real effects in the short run if the policy actions are anticipated and none in the long run even if the policy actions are unanticipated.

Portfolio investment The purchase of less than 10 percent of the shares of ownership in a company in another nation.

Positive economics Analysis that is *strictly* limited to making either purely descriptive statements or scientific predictions; for example, "If A, then B." A statement of *what is*.

Positive market feedback A tendency for a good or service to come into favor with additional consumers because other consumers have chosen to buy the item.

Positive-sum game A game in which players as a group are better off at the end of the game.

Potential money multiplier The reciprocal of the required reserve ratio, assuming no leakages into currency and no excess reserves. It is equal to 1 divided by the required reserve ratio.

Precautionary demand Holding money to meet unplanned expenditures and emergencies.

Present value The value of a future amount expressed in today's dollars; the most that someone would pay today to receive a certain sum at some point in the future.

Price ceiling A legal maximum price that may be charged for a particular good or service.

Price controls Government-mandated minimum or maximum prices that may be charged for goods and services.

Price differentiation Establishing different prices for similar products to reflect differences in marginal cost in providing those commodities to different groups of buyers.

Price discrimination Selling a given product at more than one price, with the price difference being unrelated to differences in marginal cost.

Price elasticity of demand (E_p) The responsiveness of the quantity demanded of a commodity to changes in its price; defined as the percentage change in quantity demanded divided by the percentage change in price.

Price elasticity of supply (E_s) The responsiveness of the quantity supplied of a commodity to a change in its price; the percentage change in quantity supplied divided by the percentage change in price.

Price floor A legal minimum price below which a good or service may not be sold. Legal minimum wages are an example.

Price index The cost of today's market basket of goods expressed as a percentage of the cost of the same market basket during a base year.

Price searcher A firm that must determine the price-output combination that maximizes profit because it faces a downward-sloping demand curve.

Price system An economic system in which relative prices are constantly changing to reflect changes in supply and demand for different commodities. The prices of those commodities are signals to everyone within the system as to what is relatively scarce and what is relatively abundant.

Price taker A perfectly competitive firm that must take the price of its product as given because the firm cannot influence its price.

Price-consumption curve The set of consumer-optimum combinations of two goods that the consumer would choose as the price of one good changes, while money income and the price of the other good remain constant.

Principle of rival consumption The recognition that individuals are rivals in consuming private goods because one person's consumption reduces the amount available for others to consume.

Principle of substitution The principle that consumers shift away from goods and services that become priced relatively higher in favor of goods and services that are now priced relatively lower.

Prisoners' dilemma A famous strategic game in which two prisoners have a choice between confessing and not confessing to a crime. If neither confesses, they serve a minimum sentence. If both confess, they serve a longer sentence. If one confesses and the other doesn't, the one who confesses goes free. The dominant strategy is always to confess.

Private costs Costs borne solely by the individuals who incur them. Also called *internal costs.*

Private goods Goods that can be consumed by only one individual at a time.

Private goods are subject to the principle of rival consumption.

Private property rights Exclusive rights of ownership that allow the use, transfer, and exchange of property.

Producer durables, or capital goods Durable goods having an expected service life of more than three years that are used by businesses to produce other goods and services.

Producer Price Index (PPI) A statistical measure of a weighted average of prices of goods and services that firms produce and sell.

Product compatibility The capability of a product sold by one firm to function together with another firm's complementary product.

Product differentiation The distinguishing of products by brand name, color, and other minor attributes. Product differentiation occurs in other than perfectly competitive markets in which products are, in theory, homogeneous, such as wheat or corn.

Production function The relationship between inputs and maximum physical output. A production function is a technological, not an economic, relationship.

Production possibilities curve (PPC) A curve representing all possible combinations of maximum outputs that could be produced assuming a fixed amount of productive resources of a given quality.

Production Any activity that results in the conversion of resources into products that can be used in consumption.

Profit-maximizing rate of production The rate of production that maximizes total profits, or the difference between total revenues and total costs; also, the rate of production at which marginal revenue equals marginal cost.

Progressive taxation A tax system in which, as income increases, a higher percentage of the additional income is paid as taxes. The marginal tax rate exceeds the average tax rate as income rises.

Property rights The rights of an owner to use and to exchange property.

Proportional rule A decision-making system in which actions are based on the proportion of the "votes" cast and are in proportion to them. In a market system, if 10 percent of the "dollar votes" are cast for blue cars, 10 percent of automobile output will be blue

Proportional taxation A tax system in which, regardless of an individual's income, the tax bill comprises exactly the same proportion.

Proprietorship A business owned by one individual who makes the business decisions, receives all the profits, and is legally responsible for the debts of the firm.

Public debt The total value of all outstanding federal government securities.

Public goods Goods for which the principle of rival consumption does not apply; they can be jointly consumed by many individuals simultaneously at no additional cost and with no reduction in quality or quantity. Also no one who fails to help pay for the good can be denied the benefit of the good.

Purchasing power The value of money for buying goods and services. If your money income stays the same but the price of one good that you are buying goes up, your effective purchasing power falls, and vice versa.

Purchasing power parity Adjustment in exchange rate conversions that takes into account differences in the true cost of living across countries.

Q

Quantity theory of money and prices The hypothesis that changes in the money supply lead to equiproportional changes in the price level.

Quota subscription A nation's account with the International Monetary Fund, denominated in special drawing rights.

Quota system A government-imposed restriction on the quantity of a specific good that another country is allowed to sell in the United States. In other words, quotas are restrictions on imports. These restrictions are usually applied to one or several specific countries.

R

Random walk theory The theory that there are no predictable trends in securities prices that can be used to "get rich quick."

Rate of discount The rate of interest used to discount future sums back to present value.

Rate of return The proportional annual benefit that results from making an investment.

Rate-of-return regulation Regulation that seeks to keep the rate of return in an industry at a competitive level by not allowing prices that would produce economic profits.

Rational expectations hypothesis A theory stating that people combine the effects of past policy changes on important economic variables with their own judgment about the future effects of current and future policy changes.

Rationality assumption The assumption that people do not intentionally make decisions that would leave them worse off.

Reaction function The manner in which one oligopolist reacts to a change in price, output, or quality made by another oligopolist in the industry.

Real disposable income Real GDP minus net taxes, or after-tax real income.

Real rate of interest The nominal rate of interest minus the anticipated rate of inflation.

Real values Measurement of economic values after adjustments have been made for changes in the average of prices between years.

Real-balance effect The change in expenditures resulting from a change in the real value of money balances when the price level changes, all other things held constant; also called the wealth effect.

Real-income effect The change in people's purchasing power that occurs when, other things being constant, the price of one good that they purchase changes. When that price goes up, real income, or purchasing power, falls, and when that price goes down, real income increases.

Recession A period of time during which the rate of growth of business activity is consistently less than its long-term trend or is negative.

Recessionary gap The gap that exists whenever equilibrium real GDP per year is less than full-employment real GDP as shown by the position of the long-run aggregate supply curve.

Recognition time lag The time required to gather information about the current state of the economy.

Reentrant An individual who used to work full-time but left the labor force and has now reentered it looking for a job.

Regional trade bloc A group of nations that grants members special trade privileges.

Regressive taxation A tax system in which as more dollars are earned, the percentage of tax paid on them falls. The marginal tax rate is less than the average tax rate as income rises.

Reinvestment Profits (or depreciation reserves) used to purchase new capital equipment.

Relative price The money price of one commodity divided by the money price of another commodity; the number of units of one commodity that must be sacrificed to purchase one unit of another commodity.

Rent control Price ceilings on rents.

Repricing, or menu, cost of inflation The cost associated with recalculating prices and printing new price lists when there is inflation.

Required reserve ratio The percentage of total transactions deposits that the Fed requires depository institutions to hold in the form of vault cash or deposits with the Fed.

Required reserves The value of reserves that a depository institution must hold in the form of vault cash or deposits with the Fed.

Reserves In the U.S. Federal Reserve System, deposits held by Federal Reserve district banks for depository institutions, plus depository institutions' vault cash.

Resources Things used to produce goods and services to satisfy people's wants.

Retained earnings Earnings that a corporation saves, or retains, for investment in other productive activities; earnings that are not distributed to stockholders.

Ricardian equivalence theorem The proposition that an increase in the government budget deficit has no effect on aggregate demand.

Right-to-work laws Laws that make it illegal to require union membership as a condition of continuing employment in a particular firm.

Rule of 70 A rule stating that the approximate number of years required for per capita real GDP to double is equal to 70 divided by the average rate of economic growth.

Rules of origin Regulations that nations in regional trade blocs establish to delineate product categories eligible for trading preferences.

S

Sales taxes Taxes assessed on the prices paid on most goods and services.

Saving The act of not consuming all of one's current income. Whatever is not consumed out of spendable income is, by definition, saved. *Saving* is an action measured over time (a flow), whereas *savings* are a stock, an accumulation resulting from the act of saving in the past.

Savings deposits Interest-earning funds that can be withdrawn at any time without payment of a penalty.

Say's law A dictum of economist J. B. Say that supply creates its own demand; producing goods and services generates the means and the willingness to purchase other goods and services.

Scarcity A situation in which the ingredients for producing the things that people desire are insufficient to satisfy all wants at a zero price.

Search good A product with characteristics that enable an individual to evaluate the product's quality in advance of a purchase.

Seasonal unemployment Unemployment resulting from the seasonal pattern of work in specific industries. It is usually due to seasonal fluctuations in demand or to changing weather conditions that render work difficult, if not impossible, as in the agriculture, construction, and tourist industries.

Secondary boycott A refusal to deal with companies or purchase products sold by companies that are dealing with a company being struck.

Secular deflation A persistent decline in prices resulting from economic growth in the presence of stable aggregate demand.

Securities Stocks and bonds.

Services Mental or physical labor or help purchased by consumers. Examples are the assistance of physicians, lawyers, dentists, repair personnel, housecleaners, educators, retailers, and wholesalers; items purchased or used by consumers that do not have physical characteristics.

Share of stock A legal claim to a share of a corporation's future profits. If it is *common stock*, it incorporates certain voting rights regarding major policy decisions of the corporation. If it is *preferred stock*, its owners are accorded preferential treatment in the payment of dividends but do not have any voting rights.

Share-the-gains, share-the-pains theory A theory of regulatory behavior that holds that regulators must take account of the demands of three groups: legislators, who established and oversee the regulatory agency; firms in the regulated industry; and consumers of the regulated industry's products.

Short run The time period during which at least one input, such as plant size, cannot be changed.

Shortage A situation in which quantity demanded is greater than quantity supplied at a price below the market clearing price.

Short-run aggregate supply curve The relationship between total planned economywide production and the price level in the short run, all other things held constant. If prices adjust incompletely in the short run, the curve is positively sloped.

Short-run break-even price The price at which a firm's total revenues equal its total costs. At the break-even price, the firm is just making a normal rate of return on its capital investment. (It is covering its explicit and implicit costs.)

Short-run economies of operation A distinguishing characteristic of an information product arising from declining short-run average total cost as more units of the product are sold.

Short-run shutdown price The price that covers average variable costs. It occurs just below the intersection of the marginal cost curve and the average variable cost curve.

Signals Compact ways of conveying to economic decision makers information needed to make decisions. An effective signal not only conveys information but also provides the incentive to react appropriately. Economic profits and economic losses are such signals.

Slope The change in the *y* value divided by the corresponding change in the *x* value of a curve; the "incline" of the curve.

Small menu costs Costs that deter firms from changing prices in response to demand changes—for example, the costs of renegotiating contracts or printing new price lists.

Social costs The full costs borne by society whenever a resource use occurs. Social costs can be measured by adding external costs to private, or internal, costs.

Social Security contributions The mandatory taxes paid out of workers' wages and salaries.

Special drawing rights (SDRs) Reserve assets created by the International Monetary Fund for countries to use in settling international payment obligations.

Specialization The organization of economic activity so that what each person (or region) consumes is not identical to what that person (or region) produces. An individual may specialize, for example, in law or medicine. A nation may specialize in the production of coffee, computers, or digital cameras.

Stagflation A situation characterized by lower real GDP, lower employment, and a higher unemployment rate during the same period that the rate of inflation increases.

Standard of deferred payment A property of an item that makes it desirable for use as a means of settling debts maturing in the future; an essential property of money.

Static tax analysis Economic evaluation of the effects of tax rate changes under the assumption that there is no effect on the tax base, meaning that there is an unambiguous positive relationship between tax rates and tax revenues.

Stock The quantity of something, measured at a given point in time—for example, an inventory of goods or a bank account. Stocks are defined

independently of time, although they are assessed at a point in time.

Store of value The ability to hold value over time; a necessary property of money.

Strategic dependence A situation in which one firm's actions with respect to price, quality, advertising, and related changes may be strategically countered by the reactions of one or more other firms in the industry. Such dependence can exist only when there are a limited number of major firms in an industry.

Strategy Any rule that is used to make a choice, such as "Always pick heads."

Strikebreakers Temporary or permanent workers hired by a company to replace union members who are striking.

Structural unemployment Unemployment resulting from a poor match of workers' abilities and skills with current requirements of employers.

Subsidy A negative tax; a payment to a producer from the government, usually in the form of a cash grant per unit.

Substitutes Two goods are substitutes when a change in the price of one causes a shift in demand for the other in the same direction as the price change.

Substitution effects The tendency of people to substitute cheaper commodities for more expensive commodities.

Supply A schedule showing the relationship between price and quantity supplied for a specified period of time, other things being equal.

Supply curve The graphical representation of the supply schedule; a line (curve) showing the supply schedule, which generally slopes upward (has a positive slope), other things being equal.

Supply-side economics The suggestion that creating incentives for individuals and firms to increase productivity will cause the aggregate supply curve to shift outward.

Surplus A situation in which quantity supplied is greater than quantity demanded at a price above the market clearing price.

Sweep account A depository institution account that entails regular shifts of funds from transactions deposits that are subject to reserve requirements to savings deposits that are exempt from reserve requirements.

Sympathy strike A work stoppage by a union in sympathy with another union's strike or cause.

T

Target zone A range of permitted exchange rate variations between upper and lower exchange rate bands that a central bank defends by selling or buying foreign exchange reserves.

Tariffs Taxes on imported goods.

Tax base The value of goods, services, wealth, or incomes subject to taxation.

Tax bracket A specified interval of income to which a specific and unique marginal tax rate is applied.

Tax incidence The distribution of tax burdens among various groups in society.

Tax rate The proportion of a tax base that must be paid to a government as taxes.

Taylor rule An equation that specifies a federal funds rate target based on an estimated long-run real interest rate, the current deviation of the actual inflation rate from the Federal Reserve's inflation objective, and the gap between actual real GDP and a measure of potential real GDP.

Technology Society's pool of applied knowledge concerning how goods and services can be produced.

Terms of exchange The conditions under which trading takes place. Usually, the terms of exchange are equal to the price at which a good is traded.

The Fed The Federal Reserve System; the central bank of the United States.

Theory of public choice The study of collective decision making.

Third parties Parties who are not directly involved in a given activity or transaction. For example, in the relationship between caregivers and patients, fees may be paid by third parties (insurance companies, government).

Thrift institutions Financial institutions that receive most of their funds from the savings of the public; they include savings banks, savings and loan associations, and credit unions.

Tie-in sales Purchases of one product that are permitted by the seller only if the consumer buys another good or service from the same firm.

Time deposit A deposit in a financial institution that requires notice of intent to withdraw or must be left for an agreed period. Withdrawal of funds prior to the end of the agreed period may result in a penalty.

Tit-for-tat strategic behavior In game theory, cooperation that continues as long as the other players continue to cooperate.

Total costs The sum of total fixed costs and total variable costs.

Total income The yearly amount earned by the nation's resources (factors of production). Total income therefore includes wages, rent, interest payments, and profits that are received by workers, landowners, capital owners, and entrepreneurs, respectively.

Total revenues The price per unit times the total quantity sold.

Trade deflection Moving partially assembled products into a member nation of a regional trade bloc, completing assembly, and then exporting them to other nations within the bloc, so as to benefit from preferences granted by the trade bloc.

Trade diversion Shifting existing international trade from countries outside a regional trade bloc to nations within the bloc.

Trading Desk An office at the Federal Reserve Bank of New York charged with implementing monetary policy strategies developed by the Federal Open Market Committee.

Transaction costs All costs associated with making, reaching, and enforcing agreements.

Transactions approach A method of measuring the money supply by looking at money as a medium of exchange.

Transactions demand Holding money as a medium of exchange to make payments. The level varies directly with nominal GDP.

Transactions deposits Checkable and debitable account balances in commercial banks and other types of financial institutions, such as credit unions and savings banks; any accounts in financial institutions from which you can easily transmit debit-card and check payments.

Transfer payments Money payments made by governments to individuals for which no services or goods are rendered in return. Examples are Social Security old-age and disability benefits and unemployment insurance benefits.

Transfers in kind Payments that are in the form of actual goods and services, such as food stamps, subsidized public housing, and medical care, and for which no goods or services are rendered in return.

Traveler's checks Financial instruments obtained from a bank or a nonbanking organization and signed during purchase that can be used as cash upon a second signature by the purchaser.

U

Unanticipated inflation Inflation at a rate that comes as a surprise, either higher or lower than the rate anticipated.

Unemployment The total number of adults (aged 16 years or older) who are willing and able to work and who are actively looking for work but have not found a job.

Union shop A business enterprise that may hire nonunion members, conditional on their joining the union by some specified date after employment begins.

Unit elasticity of demand A demand relationship in which the quantity demanded changes exactly in proportion to the change in price.

Unit of accounting A measure by which prices are expressed; the common denominator of the price system; a central property of money.

Unit tax A constant tax assessed on each unit of a good that consumers purchase.

Unlimited liability A legal concept whereby the personal assets of the owner of a firm can be seized to pay off the firm's debts.

Util A representative unit by which utility is measured.

Utility The want-satisfying power of a good or service.

Utility analysis The analysis of consumer decision making based on utility maximization.

V

Value added The dollar value of an industry's sales minus the value of intermediate goods (for example, raw materials and parts) used in production.

Variable costs Costs that vary with the rate of production. They include wages paid to workers and purchases of materials.

Versioning Selling a product in slightly altered forms to different groups of consumers.

Vertical merger The joining of a firm with another to which it sells an output or from which it buys an input.

Voluntary exchange An act of trading, done on an elective basis, in which both parties to the trade expect to be better off after the exchange.

Voluntary import expansion (VIE) An official agreement with another country in which it agrees to import more from the United States.

Voluntary restraint agreement (VRA) An official agreement with another country that "voluntarily" restricts the quantity of its exports to the United States.

W

Wants What people would buy if their incomes were unlimited.

Wealth The stock of assets owned by a person, household, firm, or nation. For a household, wealth can consist of a house, cars, personal belongings, stocks, bonds, bank accounts, and cash.

World Bank A multinational agency that specializes in making loans to about 100 developing nations in an effort to promote their long-term development and growth.

World Trade Organization (WTO) The successor organization to the GATT that handles trade disputes among its member nations.

X

x axis The horizontal axis in a graph.

Y

y axis The vertical axis in a graph.

Z

Zero-sum game A game in which any gains within the group are exactly offset by equal losses by the end of the game.

Index

Consumption goods: defined, 288–289; tradeoff between capital goods and, 39–40
Consumption plus investment line, 300
Consumption spending: in Germany, 310; in U.S., interest rate changes and, 311–312
Contraction, 174
Cook's, 371
Core PCE inflation, 456
Corporation(s): dividends of, 140–141; double taxation and, 140–141; retained earnings and, 140–141, 296
Cost(s): external, 109–110; forgone opportunity as, 31, 33; of inputs used to produce product, as determinant of supply, 67; management, 375; menu. *See* Menu cost(s); opportunity. *See* Opportunity cost; relative, increasing, law of, 36–37; small menu, 463–464; transaction. *See* Transaction cost(s); transportation, 838, 858
Costco, 160, 203
Cost-of-living adjustments (COLAs), 173
Cost-push inflation, 276–277
Cotton, government subsidies and, 96
Cotton, Robert, 233
Council of Economic Advisers (CEA), 166
Coupons, rationing by, 89
CPI. *See* Consumer Price Index
Crash of 2008, 365, 380, 387–388, 477, 492
Crawling pegs, 883
"Creative destruction," 232
Credit, access to, economic growth and, 483–484, 492
Credit crisis, 422, 438–439
Credit market, equilibrium in, 264
Creditors, unanticipated inflation and, 173
Crowding-out effect(s): defined, 323; of government health care spending, 332; indirect, 322–324; public debt and, 349; step by step, 323
Cuba, private property nationalized in, 232
Currency, in U.S., 371
Currency drains, 406
Currency swaps, 881
Current account: balancing of, 867; defined, 866; of developed nations and of emerging nations, 885; relationship between capital account and, 869; transactions in, 866–867
Curve(s): demand. *See* Demand curve(s); Laffer, 326–327, 331; linear (slope of a line), 21–25; nonlinear, slopes of, 24–25; Phillips. *See* Phillips curve; production possibilities. *See* Production possibilities curve; supply. *See* Supply curve(s)
Cyclical unemployment, 165, 449, 451

D

Dalum Papir, 279–280
Dating: online, health insurance as incentive in, 5; transaction costs of, 84

de Soto, Hernando, 481
Dead capital, 481–483
Death, regulation of, 35–36
Debit card, transaction using, clearance of, 376–377, 400
Debtors, unanticipated inflation and, 173
Deferred payment, standard of, 367, 368–369
Deflation: defined, 167; inflation and, 167–172; secular, 248–249; in U.S. history, 171
Dell, Inc., 379
Demand, 52–54; aggregate. *See* Aggregate demand; asset, 411; changes in. *See* Demand shifts; defined, 52; derived. *See* Derived demand; determinants of, 58–61; for diamonds, 60; for foreign currency, 871; for helium, increase in, and simultaneous decrease of supply, 87; law of, 52–53; for money, 410–412; precautionary, 411; shifts in. *See* Demand shifts; supply and, 70–74; total, for EMU euros, 874–877; for toy helicopters, 59; transactions, 411; for weed-eating bugs, 75
Demand curve(s), 55–56; aggregate. *See* Aggregate demand curve; defined, 56; horizontal summation of, 56; market, individual demand curve versus, 56–57; market demand curve versus, 56–57; movement along, 62; shift in, 58, 76–77
Demand for money curve, 411–412
Demand schedule(s), 55–57; individual, 55; market, 57; supply schedule combined with, 70–72
Demand shifts, 58–62; versus changes in quantity demanded, 61–62; effects of, 85–86; with shift in supply, 86–87
Demand-pull inflation, 276–277
Demand-side inflation, 251–252
Denmark: GDP of, 215; government oil consumption program in, 279–280; government unemployment program in, 176–177; real GDP growth in, 280
Dentistry, digital imaging and, 67
Dependent variable, 18
Deposit(s): certificates of (CDs), 373; increase in, sought by banks, 415–417; savings, 372; time, 372–373; total, relationship between total reserves and, 397–399; transactions, 371
Deposit insurance, 378–381. *See also* Federal Deposit Insurance Corporation; adverse selection in, 380; moral hazard in, 380–381; rationale for, 378–379; reform and, 381; risk taking by bank managers caused by, 379–380
Deposit Insurance Fund (DIF), 381
Depository institutions: defined, 372; the Fed and, 383, 385–386; reserves held by, 395. *See also* Reserve(s)
Depreciation: calculating GDP and, 196; defined, 193, 872; of EMU

euros, 872; net domestic product (NDP) and, 193–195
Depression: defined, 174; Great. *See* Great Depression
Derived demand: downward-sloping, 874; for EMU euros, 872–874; example of, 872–874
Development economics, 229. *See also* Economic development
Diamonds, real versus synthetic, demand for, 60
DIF (Deposit Insurance Fund), 381
Digital billboards, as negative externality, 109
Digital imaging, 67
Direct expenditure offsets, 325–326
Direct financing, indirect financing versus, 374
Direct relationship, 18–19
Directions, getting, 8
Dirty float, 882–883
Discount rate: borrowed reserves, federal funds rate and, 407; defined, 407; today's policy regarding, 408
Discouraged workers, 163
Diseases, tobacco-related, in China, 117
Disequilibrium, 865
Disposable personal income (DPI), 199
Dissaving: autonomous consumption and, 291–292; defined, 291
Dividends, 140–141
Division of labor, 42–43; defined, 42; at motor speedway, 27, 45–46
Dollar(s): base-year, 241; constant, 200; weaker. *See* Dollar, weaker
Dollar, weaker: aggregate demand affected by, 278–279; aggregate supply affected by, 277–278; inflation and real GDP affected by, 279
Domestic output, 193
Double coincidence of wants, 367
Double taxation, 140–141
Doxey, Graham, 126
DPI (disposable personal income), 199
Dumping, 850
Durable consumer goods, 191
Dynamic tax analysis, 143, 144–145

E

Earnings, retained, 140–141, 296
Eberstadt, Nicholas, 231
ECB (European Central Bank), 395, 428
Economic analysis, power of, 2
Economic Community of West African States, 856
Economic development, 229–232; keys to, 231–232; population growth and, 229–231; stages of, 231
Economic freedom, 479–480
Economic goods, 29–30
Economic growth: access to credit and, 483–484, 492; capital goods

Photo Credits

Cover photo credits: Euro banknotes money, Shutterstock Images; Rows of green and red lettuces, Laurent Renault/Shutterstock Images; Woman boarding a train, Mikael Damkier/Shutterstock Images; Doctor with stethoscope, Bill Blakey/Shutterstock Images; Man shopping in produce, Monkey Business Images/Shutterstock; Windmills, Gencay M. Emin/Shutterstock

Chapter 1: 2 Getty Royalty Free; **4** AFP/Getty Images; **11** Shutterstock. **Chapter 2: 28** Morton Beebe/Corbis; **30** Corbis Royalty Free; **31** Shutterstock; **43** Shutterstock. **Chapter 3: 52** Getty Royalty Free; **61** AP Wideworld Photos; **69** AP Wideworld Photos. **Chapter 4: 84** Getty Images News; **89** Getty Royalty Free; **95** Shutterstock. **Chapter 5: 108** AFP/Getty Images; **111** Getty Image News; **116** AP Wideworld Photos; **119** Shutterstock. **Chapter 6: 138** Shutterstock; **143** Shutterstock; **147** Shutterstock. **Chapter 7: 160** Shutterstock; **166** DAG/Getty Royalty Free; **168** Shutterstock.

Chapter 8: 189 Shutterstock; **192** Getty Editorial; **203** Shutterstock. **Chapter 9: 214** Corbis Rights Managed; **217** Getty Editorial; **226** Shutterstock. **Chapter 10: 243** Sabine Lubenow/Getty Images; **251** Corbis Rights Managed. **Chapter 11: 264** Getty Royalty Free; **279** ArabianEye/Getty Images. **Chapter 12: 289** Photodisc; **294** Blend Images/Getty Royalty Free; **296** Getty Royalty Free. **Chapter 13: 319** Rubberball/Getty Royalty Free; **329** Corbis Rights Managed; **330** National Archives and Records Administration (PAL AAAC-SKJ0). **Chapter 14: 346** National Geographic/Getty Royalty Free; **349** Digital Vision; **353** Purestock Getty Royalty Free. **Chapter 15: 366** Shutterstock; **382** Shutterstock. **Chapter 16: 404** Getty Royalty Free. **Chapter 17: 423** Getty Editorial; **426** Getty Royalty Free. **Chapter 18: 453** The Council of Economic Advisors; **459** U.S. Federal Reserve Board; **468** AP Wideworld Photos. **Chapter 19: 478** Blend Images/Getty Royalty Free. **Chapter 33: 847** Shutterstock; **848** AP Photo/Matt Sayle. **Chapter 34: 872** Beth Anderson; **882** AP Photo/Tsvangirayi Mukwazhi.

MACROECONOMIC PRINCIPLES

Nominal versus Real Interest Rate

$$i_n = i_r + \text{expected rate of inflation}$$

where i_n = nominal rate of interest
i_r = real rate of interest

Marginal versus Average Tax Rates

$$\text{Marginal tax rate} = \frac{\text{change in taxes due}}{\text{change in taxable income}}$$

$$\text{Average tax rate} = \frac{\text{total taxes due}}{\text{total taxable income}}$$

GDP—The Expenditure and Income Approaches

$$GDP = C + I + G + X$$

where C = consumption expenditures
I = investment expenditures
G = government expenditures
X = net exports

$$GDP = \text{wages} + \text{rent} + \text{interest} + \text{profits}$$

Say's Law

Supply creates its own demand, or *desired* aggregate expenditures will equal *actual* aggregate expenditures.

Saving, Consumption, and Investment

$$\text{Consumption} + \text{saving} = \text{disposable income}$$

$$\text{Saving} = \text{disposable income} - \text{consumption}$$

Average and Marginal Propensities

$$APC = \frac{\text{real consumption}}{\text{real disposable income}}$$

$$APS = \frac{\text{real saving}}{\text{real disposable income}}$$

$$MPC = \frac{\text{change in real consumption}}{\text{change in real disposable income}}$$

$$MPS = \frac{\text{change in real saving}}{\text{change in real disposable income}}$$

The Multiplier Formula

$$\text{Multiplier} = \frac{1}{MPS} = \frac{1}{1 - MPC}$$

$$\text{Multiplier} \times \begin{matrix}\text{change in}\\ \text{autonomous}\\ \text{spending}\end{matrix} = \begin{matrix}\text{change in}\\ \text{equilibrium level}\\ \text{of national income}\end{matrix}$$

Relationship Between Bond Prices and Interest Rates

The market price of existing (old) bonds is inversely related to "the" rate of interest prevailing in the economy.

Government Spending and Taxation Multipliers

$$M_g = \frac{1}{MPS}$$

$$M_t = -MPC \times \frac{1}{MPS}$$